FUNDAMENTALS OF HELICOPTER MAINTENANCE

by
Joseph Schafer

For sale by: Aviation Maintenance Publishers, Inc.
P.O. Box 890, Basin, Wyoming 82410
Tel: (307) 568-2413

International Standard Book Number 0-89100-118-2

Aviation Maintenance Publishers, Inc.
211 South Fourth Street, Basin, Wyoming 82410

TABLE OF CONTENTS

Introduction

The concept of the helicopter has been dreamed of for hundreds of years. The first recorded drawings of such a machine were made by Leonardo da Vinci in 1483.

This machine was an aerial screw which he envisioned as being able to move vertically into the air with a rotor built with a 96-foot helix. It was from this drawing that the helicopter derived its name — from the two Greek words *heliko* and *pleron* meaning helical wing.

It was not until the latter part of the 18th century that any further developments were achieved with helicopters. At that time interest developed in both France and England. Jean Pierre Blanchad flew a model helicopter for the French Acadamie de Sciences and Sir George Caley drew several helicopter designs while making contributions to the basic knowledge of the principles of flight.

Throughout the 19th century, with the invention of the internal combustion engine, men from all nations pursued the problem of flight. In spite of the efforts of these inventors, no real significant advances were made in flight. By the latter part of the 19th century and the beginning of the 20th century, all emphasis was placed on powering gliders.

Thomas Edison summed up the situation for rotary wing aircraft by stating that an inherent limitation in helicopter development at that time was the lack of a lightweight engine — a handicap which was somewhat less restrictive to the fixed wing concept.

By 1903 the Wright Brothers had made the first manned powered flight. With this success, the emphasis shifted from rotary to fixed wing for all but a few inventors. These few realized the drawbacks of the fixed wing, such as the necessity for long runways and forward speed to prevent stalling.

In 1907 Louis Breguet and Professor Richet of France constructed a machine of 45 horsepower with four rotors. This rose to a height of five feet. It did not, however, receive the distinction of the first free flight because it had to be steadied by four assistants. Instead, this distinction fell to another Frenchman Paul Cornu, just a few weeks later, who attained a height of five feet with a passenger hanging underneath.

In 1910 a young Russian designer by the name of Igor Sikorsky built a coaxial helicopter powered by a 25 horsepower engine. This helicopter was only capable of lifting its own weight. At that time the young designer directed his talents to fixed wing aircraft and it was many years before he redirected his talents to helicopters.

During the first quarter of a century, after the first flight, designers from all parts of the world became involved in building rotary wing aircraft. None of these passed the experimental stage of development. Although much was learned that would result in the future development of a successful helicopter, there were still problems to be encountered by these would-be designers. These fell into three main categories:

1. The engine torque tended to rotate the fuselage in the opposite direction of the rotor.

2. The rotating mass of the rotor was affected by gyroscopic precision. (Meaning that a tilt of the rotor would result in a movement 90° from the applied force.)

3. The lift forces produced by the advancing blade were greater than the lifting force of the retreating blade in horizontal flight, resulting in disymmetry of lift which would overturn the helicopter.

In spite of these overwhelming problems, experimentation continued through the 1920's. One of the experimenters was Juan de la Cierva, who had designed the first Spanish-built fixed wing aircraft. After the crash of one of his designs due to a stall, he devoted the rest of his life to building a safer, slow-moving aircraft that was not dependent on its forward speed to make safe landings. To insure these goals he designed an aircraft which had the wings free to rotate about a vertical axis, giving the wings their own velocity.

Cierva's invention employed a conventional aircraft to produce forward thrust with freely rotating wings to produce lift. This wind-milling is known as *autorotation*. Thus the *autogyro* received its name.

The first model built by Cierva had two counter rotating rotors. He had hoped that the gyroscopic effects would be cancelled and the differential of lift would be neutralized. However, the unequal flow conditions of the two rotors made this arrangement inefficient.

Cierva next decided to build a single rotor system in spite of the known problems. His first two attempts with the single rotor system ended in failure. However, the next attempt was an entirely new design which solved the problem of the autogyro and paved the way for the helicopter.

The blades of this new rotor system were hinged so that they could rise and fall freely during flight. The flapping hinge allowed the blades to compensate for any variations of velocity and lift. In addition to the *flapping* hinge, Cierva also introduced the *lead-lag* hinge. This enabled it to land without power (autorotate) and added pitch change to the rotor.

In 1936, at the time of Cierva's death, the autogyro was well established and was being built in several countries including England, France, Italy, and the U.S. However, the helicopter still seemed to be far from successful.

In 1937, the Focke-Achgelis FW-61 was demonstrated by Hanna Reitsch, the first woman helicopter pilot, inside the *Deutschland Halle* in Berlin in front of a large audience. In an area, 100 by 250 feet, she hovered, moved forward and backward, and made 360° turns. This helicopter later broke all existing records, and helped to remove any doubts regarding the future of the helicopter.

Anto Flettner, another German helicopter designer invented the syncro-rotor blade system which had two contra-rotating two-bladed rotors mounted side-by-side, so they intermeshed. By 1941 a later model of Flettner's helicopter was put into production to protect German convoys from enemy submarines. If it had not been for WWII this helicoper would have undoubtedly set new world records.

In 1940, thirty years after his first unsuccessful attempt, Igor Sikorsky reentered the field of helicopter development with the VS-300 which in May 1941 broke the world's helicopter endurance record held by the FW-61. In 1942, Sikorsky started the production of the 4B of which more than 400 were produced for the U.S. Army, Navy, Coast Guard, and for Great Britain.

Subsequent to this production, other names appeared in the helicopter field including Bell, Hiller, and Piasecki. A whole new generation of rotary wing aircraft evolved and a market for such an aircraft had appeared. These aircraft formed the first generation of helicopters. Most of these helicopters were built with one main rotor system and one anti-torque rotor, which was the result of Sikorsky's experimentation. Although these helicopters were lacking such desirable characteristics as reliability and maintainability, the demand for them continued. For the next decade constant improvement to basic designs was pursured until the helicopter gained respectability.

One weakness that continued was the lack of a powerplant designed for the helicopter. Since so few helicopters were built, it was uneconomical to construct an engine specifically for them. The powerplants chosen for helicopters were modified versions of the existing aircraft engine inventory.

During this time the military developed a major interest in the helicopter. This lead to the development of a specially designed turbine powerplant for helicopters.

This advancement brought about a new generation of helicopters to accommodate these engines. The second generation had increased capabilities, better reliablity, and was better to maintain. They also opened the way for a corporate transportation market.

Today with the third generation of helicopters, we observe a civil fleet over three times the size of the U.S. air carrier fleet. It is comprised of two generations of helicopters being joined with the third to perform work in all phases of industry, easier, faster, and more economical than many other methods. This facet of the aviation industry is presently growing at an unprecedented rate with no end to its growth potential in the foreseeable future.

SECTION I

Helicopters In Use Today

The helicopters in use today cover a period of time from 1947 to the present. During this time they have gone from being a novelty to being the work horse of the aviation industry, performing tasks of every imaginable description. In this period the industry has developed a large commercial fleet which has exceeded the air carrier fleet several times and has also exceeded the corporate aviation fleet. This unprecedented growth did not occur by accident but because of the versatility of the machine and the ingenuity of the operators seeking new possibilities for their use as a fast and efficient method of completing various tasks, including construction, agriculture, forestry, and business. At this time there is probably no area of the economy that is not touched by the helicopter in some manner.

To meet the ever-increasing demand to fulfill the needs of the helicopter operators, the helicopter manufacturers have increased the reliability, decreased the maintenance requirements and built new helicopters to meet these needs. These include three generations of machines from reciprocating two-place helicopters to those that are turbine powered and carry many passengers. Because of the many different types, it is important to know about those in use today and their capabilities as described in this section.

Bell Helicopter Textron's Model 222 mid-size twin turbine helicopter is representative of todays generation of helicopter.

1

A. Bell Helicopters

1. Bell 47

The Bell 47 was the first helicopter to receive civilian certification in 1946. This helicopter enjoyed a long production life until 1974 when it became too expensive to manufacture. During this period it was manufactured in a great number of models and its components have been used to build special purpose helicopters as well as presently being converted to turbine powerplants. This helicopter once enjoyed such popularity that more Bell 47's were in use than any other helicopter in the world. Although this is no longer true, they are still in wide use today performing numerous tasks such as flight training, agricultural work, traffic control, etc. It will undoubtedly lose its popularity as new and more modern equipment is introduced, but at this time it could certainly be considered the DC-3 of the helicopter industry. Fig. 1-1 shows two models of the Bell 47.

Because of the great number of models manufactured each individual model cannot be shown. The following is a list of the various models and their major differences. Of course this list cannot point out all the differences of the various models of this helicopter. Because of the great numbers of this helicopter built for civilian and military use, and the continual updating of the older models, no attempt will be made to give the number of them in existance.

Model	Date Approved	Engine	H.P.	Fuel Cap.	Oil Cap.	Max. Weight	Rotor Limits	Airspeed MPH	No. of Seats
47B	11-4-47/Type Cert. H-1	Franklin 6V4-178-B3	178	24	3	2200	350 Max. 285 Min.	92	2

Remarks: 40 pounds maximum baggage — pressure fuel system.

Model	Date Approved	Engine	H.P.	Fuel Cap.	Oil Cap.	Max. Weight	Rotor Limits	Airspeed MPH	No. of Seats
47B3	7-2-48	Franklin 6V4-178-B32	178	24	3	2200	350 Max. 285 Min.	92	2

Remarks: 40 pound maximum baggage — revised cockpit enclosure, furnishing and cowling.

Model	Date Approved	Engine	H.P.	Fuel Cap.	Oil Cap.	Max. Weight	Rotor Limits	Airspeed MPH	No. of Seats
47D	2-25-48	Franklin 6V4-178-B32	178	24	3	2200	350 Max. 285 Min.	92	2

Remarks: Similar to B3 except cockpit enclosure, wheel with brakes, 24V electrical.

Model	Date Approved	Engine	H.P.	Fuel Cap.	Oil Cap.	Max. Weight	Rotor Limits	Airspeed MPH	No. of Seats
47D1	3-29-49	Franklin 6V4-178-B32 or 6V4-200-C32	178	29	3	2200	350 Max. 285 Min.	95	3

Remarks: No baggage allowance — cockpit enclosure ventral fin-fixed tab combination, main rotor counterweights, movable battery, gravity fuel system, roller bearing type transmission, elimination of cowling and tailboom covering.

Model	Date Approved	Engine	H.P.	Fuel Cap.	Oil Cap.	Max. Weight	Rotor Limits	Airspeed MPH	No. of Seats
47E	4-18-50	Franklin 6V4-200-C32	200	24	3	2350	360 Max. 294 Min.	98	2

Remarks: 40 pounds baggage

Model	Date Approved	Engine	H.P.	Fuel Cap.	Oil Cap.	Max. Weight	Rotor Limits	Airspeed MPH	No. of Seats
47G	6-19-53	Franklin 6V4-200-C32	200	43	3	2350	360 Max. 294 Min.	100	3

Remarks: No baggage allowance — similar to D1 except saddle tanks, battery location, synchronized elevator, ventral fin and tail rotor gear box.

Model	Date Approved	Engine	H.P.	Fuel Cap.	Oil Cap.	Max. Weight	Rotor Limits	Airspeed MPH	No. of Seats
47G-2	1-20-55	Lycoming VO-435-A1A or A1B, A1D	200	43	3.5	2450	360 Max. 294 Min.	100	3

Remarks: No baggage allowance — similar to G except for engine and the relocation of the fore, aft, and lateral cyclinder hydraulic boost controls and the installation of lock and load valves.

| 47H-1 | 3-21-55 | Franklin 6V4-200-C32 | 200 | 35 | 2.7 | 2350 | 360 Max. 294 Min. | 100 | 3 |

Remarks: Maximum baggage 200 pounds — similar to 47G except for semi-monocoque tailboom, increased cabin width, contour fuel tanks, revised skid type landing gear, addition to baggage compartment.

| 47J | 8-23-56/Type Cert. 2H1 | Lycoming VO-435-A1B | 220 | 35 | 2.9 | 2565 | 370 Max. 333 Min. | 105 | 4 |

Remarks: Maximum baggage 250 pounds

| 47G-2A-1 | 12-28-62 | Lycoming VO-435-A1E or A1F | 240 | 61.6 | 3 | 2850 | 370 Max. 333 Min. | 105 | 3 |

| 47G-3B-1 | 1-25-63 | Lycoming TVO-435-B1A or B1B | 270 | 61.6 | 4-1/4 | 2950 | 370 Max. 322 Min. | 105 | 3 |

Remarks: External supercharger.

| 47G-4 | 1-3-64 | Lycoming VO-540-B1B | 260 | 61.6 | 3 | 2950 | 370 Max. 333 Min. | 105 | 3 |

Remarks: Similar to 47G-2A-1 except larger engine, and addition of collective boost system.

| 47G-4A | 1-3-66 | Lycoming VO-540-B1B-3 | 280 | 61-6 | 5 | 2950 | 370 Max. 333 Min. | 105 | 3 |

| 47G-5 | 1-21-66 | Lycoming VO-435-B1A | 260 | 28 | 3 | 2850 | 370 Max. 333 Min. | 105 | 3 |

Remarks: Only one saddle tank on right, low instrument panel. Approved: dual saddle tanks, 3 seat capacity.

| 47K | 3-30-59 | Lycoming VO-435-6A or VO-435-A1D | 240 | 35 | 2.7 | 2565 | 370 Max. 333 Min. | 105 | 2 |

Remarks: Similar to 47J except for cabin, open engine compartment, oil system, and lights.

| 47J-2 | 1-14-60 | Lycoming VO-540-B1B or B1B3 | 240 | 48 | 4.3 | 2850 | 370 Max. 333 Min. | 105 | 4 |

Remarks: Similar to 47J except metal main rotor blades, fixed stabilizer, engine, and blue tinted bubble.

Model	Date Approved	Engine	H.P.	Fuel Cap.	Oil Cap.	Max. Weight	Rotor Limits	Airspeed MPH	No. of Seats
47J-2A	3-4-64	Lycoming VO-540-B1B3	260	48	4.3		370 Max. 333 Min.	105	4

Remarks: Similar to 47J except increased weight, addition of collective boost system and main rotor tip weights, change in C.G. limits.

Model	Date Approved	Engine	H.P.	Fuel Cap.	Oil Cap.	Max. Weight	Rotor Limits	Airspeed MPH	No. of Seats
47G-3	3-17-60/Type Cert. 2H3	Franklin 6VS-335-A	225	43	2	2650	370 Max. 322 Min.	105	3
47G-2A	12-10-60	Lycoming VO-435-A1E	240	43	2	2850	370 Max. 333 Min.	105	3
47G-3B2	5-24-61	Lycoming TVO-435-A1A	260	43	2	2850	370 Max. 322 Min.	105	3

Remarks: External supercharger.

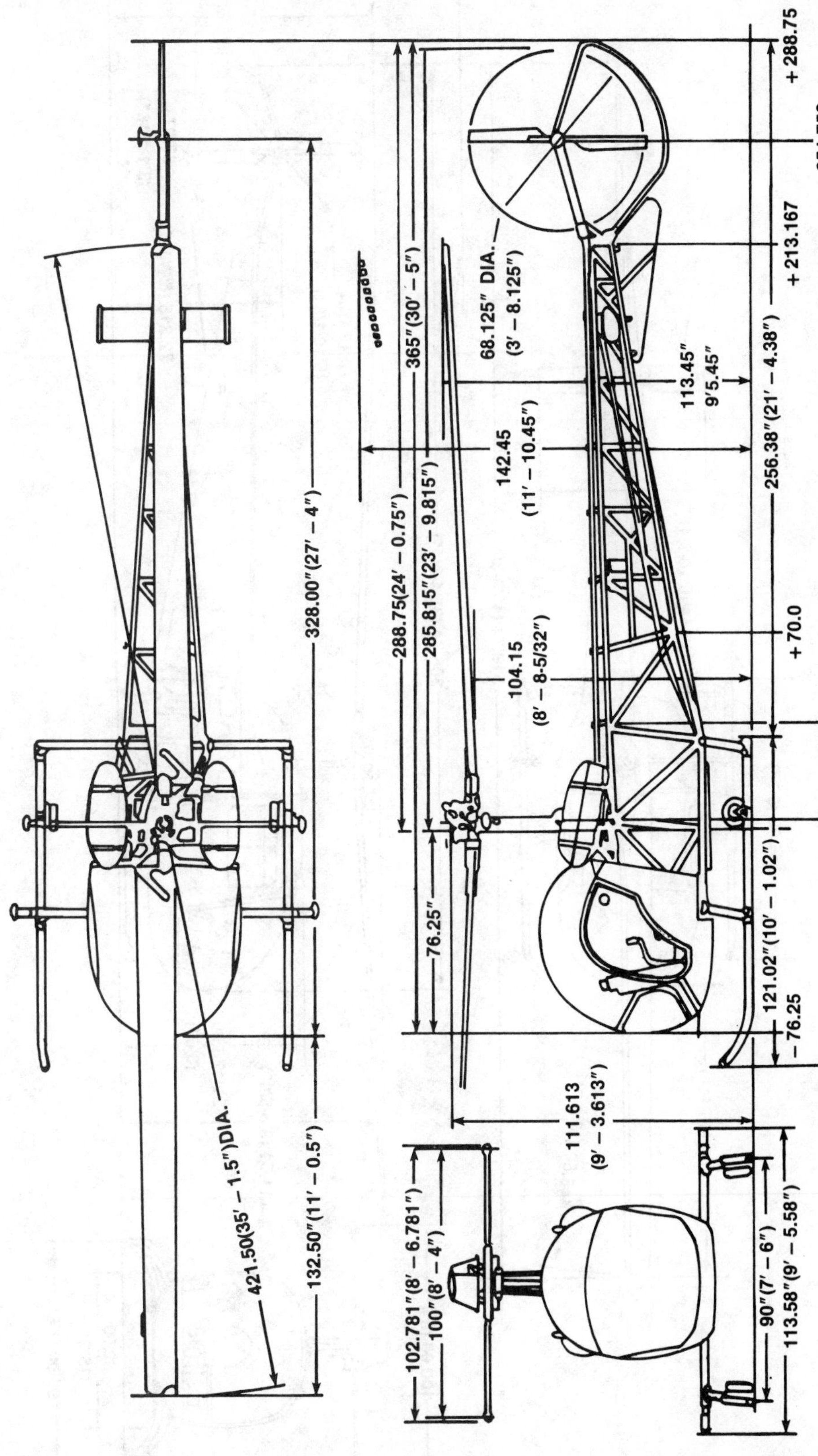

Fig. 1-1A   Bell 47G

421.50(35' – 1.5")DIA.

328.00"(27' – 4")

132.50"(11' – 0.5")

288.75(24' – 0.75")

365"(30' – 5")

285.815"(23' – 9.815")

142.45
(11' – 10.45")

68.125" DIA.
(3' – 8.125")

104.15
(8' – 8-5/32")

113.45"
9'5.45"

256.38"(21' – 4.38")

76.25"

+ 288.75

+ 251.753

+ 213.167

+ 70.0

+ 36.99

+ 2

121.02"(10' – 1.02")

– 76.25

– 88.65

111.613
(9' – 3.613")

102.781"(8' – 6.781")

100"(8' – 4")

90"(7' – 6")

113.58"(9' – 5.58")

5

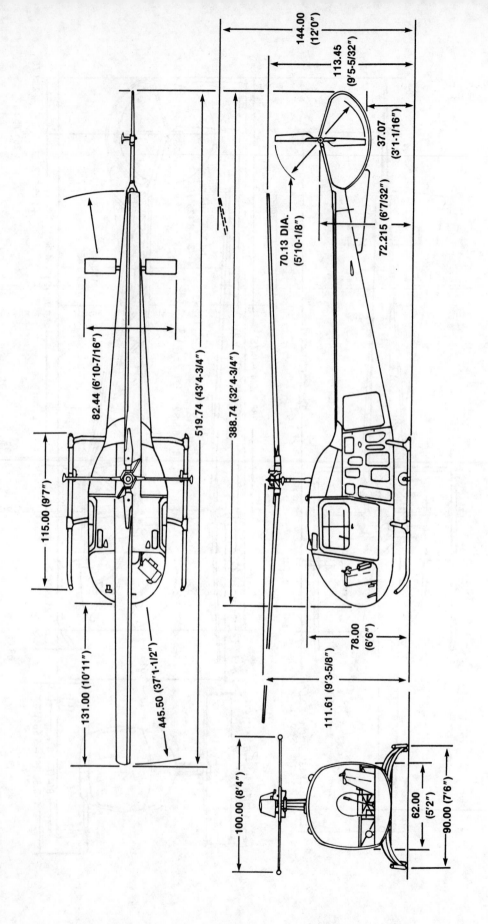

Fig. 1-1B Bell 47J

6

2. Bell 204

From its beginning with the Bell 47, the company grew, building several additional models for civilian and military use. Many of the military models were modified in design and later became civilian models.

The 204B model was one of these helicopters which was a derivative of the U-H1 series of helicopters built for the military. Although the two helicopters appear very similar in appearance, many changes were made between the civilian and the military aircraft including the length of the tailboom, baggage area, and rotor blades.

The 204B is an 11-place helicopter with turbine power (Fig. 1-2). Although a large number of this model was not built, it paved the way for the turbine-powered helicopter and the use of such helicopters by the petroleum support industry

A brief summary of the Bell 204B specifications follows:

Model	Date Approved	Engine	H.P.	Fuel Cap.	Oil Cap.	Max. Weight	Rotor Limits	Airspeed (KIAS)	No. of Seats
204B	4-4-63/Type Cert. H1SW	Lycoming T5309A, B, C, or T5311A	1100	160	4	8500	324 Max. 310 Min.	120	11

Remarks: Transport helicopter — 400 pounds maximum baggage.

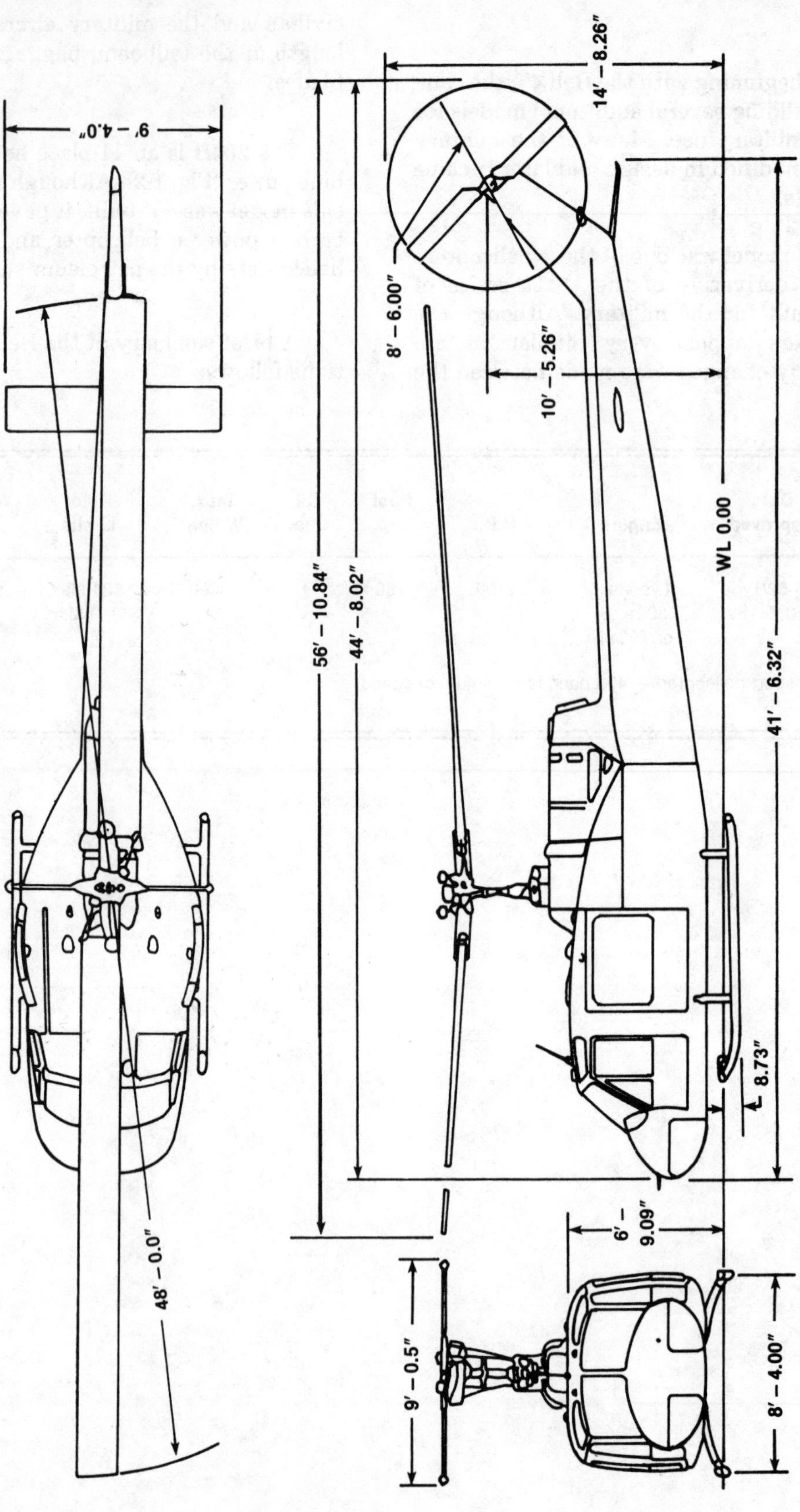

Fig. 1-2 Bell 204B

Dimensions shown: 14' – 8.26", 8' – 6.00", 10' – 5.26", WL 0.00, 41' – 6.32", 8.73", 6' – 9.09", 8' – 4.00", 9' – 0.5", 56' – 10.84", 44' – 8.02", 48' – 0.0", 9' – 4.0"

3. Bell 205

Following the development of the 204B were two improved versions of this aircraft. These are the Bell 205A and the Bell 205-A1 (Fig. 1-3).

The 205-A1 has experienced a long production run since its inception in 1968 with new aircraft being built in 1978 of this configuration. The major use of this series has been in the petroleum support industry.

Some general information on the two 205 models follows:

Model	Date Approved	Engine	H.P.	Fuel Cap.	Oil Cap.	Max. Weight	Rotor Limits	Airspeed (KIAS)	No. of Seats
205A	6-13-68/Type Cert. H1SW	Lycoming T5311A or B	1100	215	3.5	8500	324 Max. 314 Min.	120	15

Remarks: Transport helicopter — 400 pounds maximum baggage.

Model	Date Approved	Engine	H.P.	Fuel Cap.	Oil Cap.	Max. Weight	Rotor Limits	Airspeed (KIAS)	No. of Seats
205-A1	10-25-68	Lycoming T5313A or B	1250	220	3.15	9500	324 Max. 314 Min.	120	15

Remarks: Transport helicopter category B — 400 pounds maximum baggage.

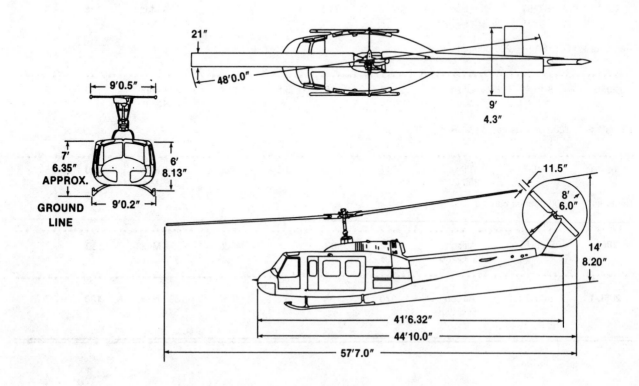

Fig. 1-3 Bell 205

4. Bell 206

During the time in which the 204 and 205 series of helicopters were being built to meet the market of a turbine-powered 10 to 15 passenger helicopter, a smaller turbine-powered helicopter was placed on the market — the Model 206, better known as the Jet Ranger.

The 206 was first certified in 1964. Because of its size and versatility it immediately found a substantial outlet in the civilian market. At the present time it enjoys an unprecedented popularity in many areas which include corporate, agriculture, construction, petroleum support, and ambulance service. This helicopter may be found in almost all areas of the world performing various missions. A profile of a Jet Ranger is shown in Fig. 1-4A and B.

A list of the various models and abbreviated information about the helicopter follows:

Model	Date Approved	Engine	H.P.	Fuel Cap.	Oil Cap.	Max. Weight	Rotor Limits	Airspeed (KIAS)	No. of Seats
206	4-28-64/Type Cert. H2SW	Allison 250-C10	250	76	5.5	2750	394 Max. 374 Min.	115	4
Remarks:	Same as military model — OH-4A 1200 pounds cargo								
206A	10-20-66	Allison 250-C18, C18B, or 250-C20	317	76	5.5	3000	394 Max. 374 Min.	130	5
Remarks:	1200 pounds cargo.								
206A1	5-6-69	Allison 250-C10D	317	71.5	5.5	3000	354 Max. 347 Min.	115	4
Remarks:	OH-58A — 1200 pounds cargo.								
206B	8-19-71	Allison 250-C20	317	76	5.5	3200	394 Max. 374 Min.	130	5
Remarks:	1200 pounds cargo (Jet Ranger II).								
206B-1	11-10-71	Allison 250-C20	317	70.3	5.5	3200	354 Max. 347 Min.	120	5
Remarks:	1200 pounds cargo								
206L	9-22-75	Allison 230C-20B	370	98	5.5	4000	394 Max. 374 Min.	130	7
206L-1	5-17-78	Allison 250C-28B	370	98	5.5	4050	394 Max. 374 Min.	130	7

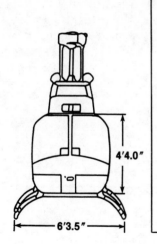

LENGTH	FEET/INCHES	METERS	HEIGHT	FEET/INCHES	METERS
Overall (Main Rotor Fore and Aft) to Aft End of Tail Skid	38 ft. 9.5 in.	11.824	Forward Tip of Main Rotor (Static Position) to Ground with Droop	9 ft. 6.5 in.	2.908
Nose of Cabin to Aft End of Tail Skid	31 ft. 2.0 in.	9.500	Forward Tip of Main Rotor to Ground (Tie-Down)	11 ft. 7.5 in.	3.543
Nose of Cabin to Center Line of Main Rotor	8 ft. 10.1 in.	2.695	Forward Tip of Main Rotor to Ground (Forward Down)	5 ft. 11.5 in.	1.816
Skid Gear	7 ft. 6.8 in.	2.306	Ground to Top of Main Rotor Reservoirs	9 ft. 6.5 in.	2.908
Nose of Cabin to Center Line of Forward Cross Tube	6 ft. 0.0 in.	1.829	Bottom of Cabin*	12.0 in.	0.305
Nose of Cabin to Center Line of Aft Cross Tube	10 ft. 6.5 in.	3.213	Top of Vertical Stabilizer	8 ft. 4.0 in.	2.540
Pilot Tube	6.8 in.	0.173	Tail Skid to Ground	1 ft. 7.5 in.	0.495
WIDTH			**DIAMETERS**		
Skid Gear	6 ft. 3.5 in.	1.918	Main Rotor	33 ft. 4.0 in.	10.160
Horizontal Stabilizer	6 ft. 5.7 in.	1.974	Tail Rotor	5 ft. 2.0 in.	1.575

*Check antennas that may protrude lower

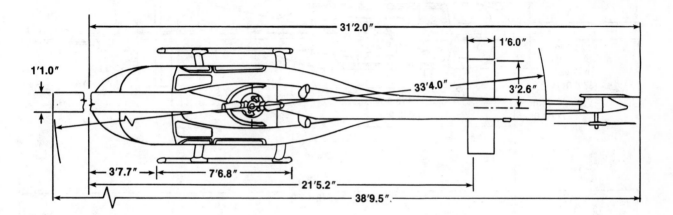

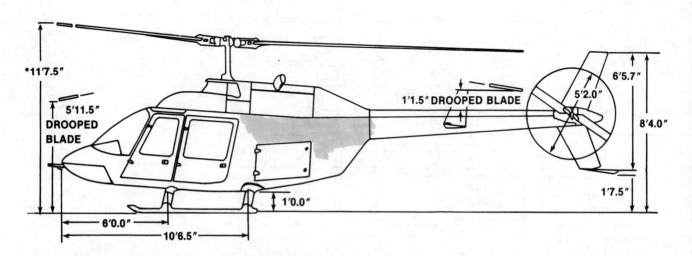

*Measurement is taken with main rotor blade raised against the dynamic flap restraint.

Fig. 1-4A   Bell 206

11

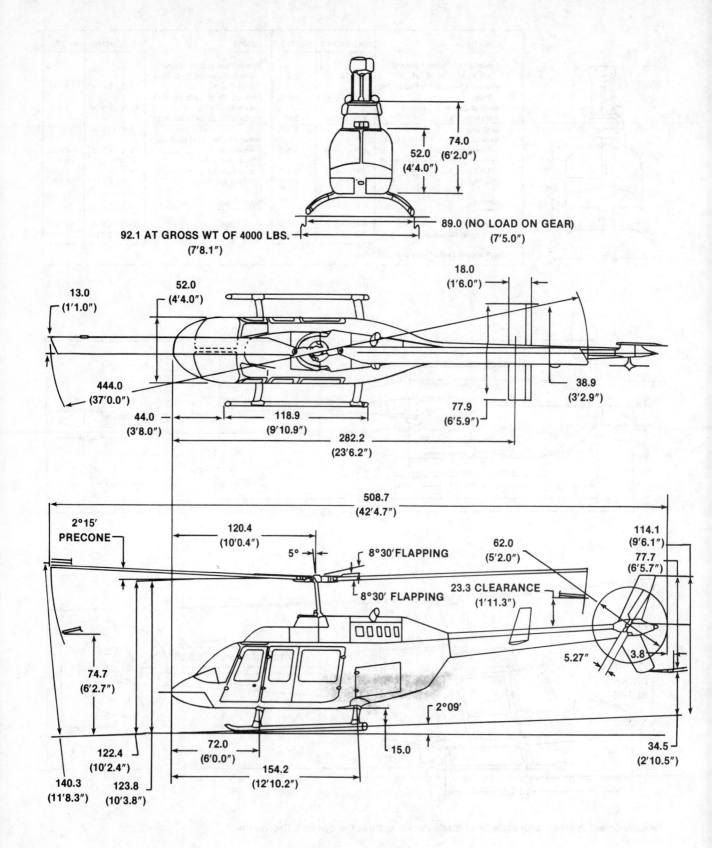

74.0
(6'2.0")

52.0
(4'4.0")

89.0 (NO LOAD ON GEAR)
(7'5.0")

92.1 AT GROSS WT OF 4000 LBS.
(7'8.1")

13.0
(1'1.0")

52.0
(4'4.0")

18.0
(1'6.0")

444.0
(37'0.0")

44.0
(3'8.0")

118.9
(9'10.9")

282.2
(23'6.2")

77.9
(6'5.9")

38.9
(3'2.9")

508.7
(42'4.7")

2°15'
PRECONE

120.4
(10'0.4")

5°

8°30' FLAPPING

8°30' FLAPPING

62.0
(5'2.0")

23.3 CLEARANCE
(1'11.3")

114.1
(9'6.1")

77.7
(6'5.7")

74.7
(6'2.7")

5.27"

3.8

122.4
(10'2.4")

72.0
(6'0.0")

2°09'

15.0

34.5
(2'10.5")

140.3
(11'8.3")

123.8
(10'3.8")

154.2
(12'10.2")

Fig. 1-4B   Bell 206L

12

5. Bell 212

In addition to the large single turbine helicopters built by Bell, an additional twin engine was added to the Bell fleet — the Model 212. The 212 added twin engine reliability and IFR capability to the helicopters used for petroleum support and construction. A new version of this helicopter will be on the market in the near future. Known as the 412, it will be equipped with a four-blade rotor system. It will also be possible to update the present fleet to the latest configuration. Model 212 is shown in Fig. 1-5. A brief summary of its specifications follows:

Model	Date Approved	Engine	H.P.	Fuel Cap.	Oil Cap.	Max. Weight	Rotor Limits	Airspeed (KIAS)	No. of Seats
212	10-30-70 Category B 6-30-70	United A/C of Canada PT6T-3	645 per engine	220	3.76	10,000 or 11,200	324 Max. 314 Min.	115	15
	Category A Type Cert. H4SW	Twin Pac Turboshaft							

Remarks: Transport helicopter category A or B — 400 pounds maximum baggage. One engine inoperative (emergency) 30 minute rating 928 SHP.

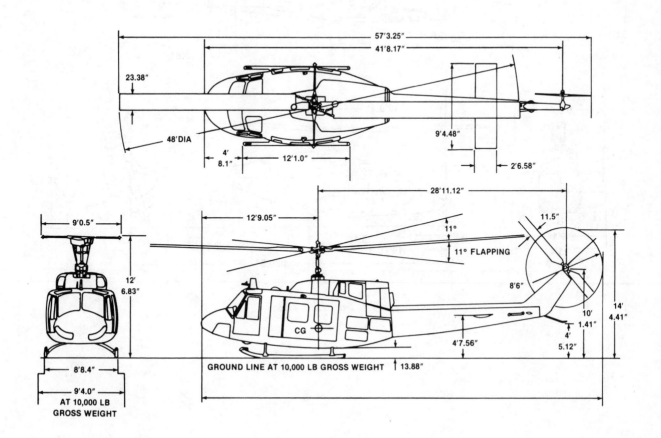

Fig. 1-5   Bell 212

13

6. Bell 222

The latest of the Bell models to go into production is the Model 222. This helicopter is primarily aimed at the corporate market because of the twin turbine reliability and IFR capability (Fig. 1-6). A brief summary of its specifications follows:

Model	Date Approved	Engine	H.P.	Fuel Cap.	Oil Cap.	Max. Weight	Rotor Limits	Airspeed (KIAS)	No. of Seats
222	10-1-79 Type Cert. H9SW	2LTS101	615 each	189	3.7	7200	362 Max. 338 Min.	150 knots	10

Remarks: 370 NMI with 20 minute reserve at 8000 feet. Flexible seating of 6-, 8-, and 10-place configurations.

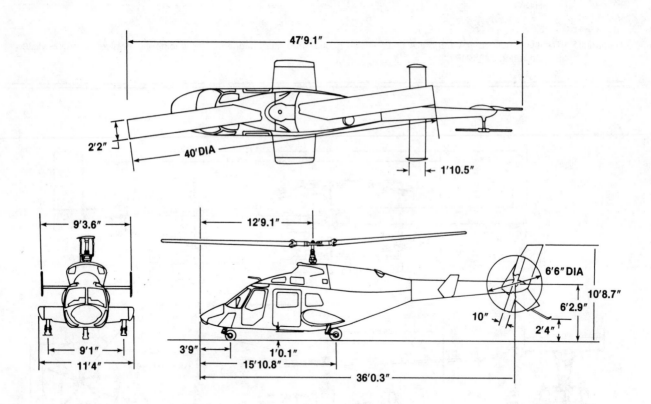

Fig. 1-6   Bell 222

14

B. Hiller Helicopters

1. Hiller UH-12

Shortly after the certification of the Bell 47, another light helicopter went into production, the Hiller 12. The Hiller, like the Bell 47, was manufactured in a number of different models and enjoyed popularity as both a civilian and a military helicopter. Although it may not have enjoyed the same popularity as the Bell a great number of various models of the Hiller 12 are still in use today. In fact, the Hiller 12E (Fig. 1-7) is still being produced in small numbers as both a reciprocating-powered and as a turbine-powered helicopter. Like the Bell 47, the Hiller has been employed in numerous tasks which include training, agriculture, construction, and forestry. They are found throughout the world with one of the highest concentrations in the northwestern United States. Many operators prefer the Hiller for sling load operations because of its load carrying capabilities.

The following is a brief summary of the specifications of the various models of the Hiller 12 and some of the major differences:

Model	Date Approved	Engine	H.P.	Fuel Cap.	Oil Cap.	Max. Weight	Rotor Limits	Airspeed (KIAS)	No. of Seats
UH-12	10-14-48 Type Cert. 6H	Franklin 6V4-178-B33	178	27	2-1/2	2247	350 Max. 294 Min.	73	3
Remarks:	No baggage allowance.								
UH-12A	5-8-50	Franklin 6V4-178-B33	178	27	2-1/2	2400	350 Max. 294 Min.	73	3
UH-12B	11-2-51/Type Cert. 6H2	Franklin 6V4-200-C33	200	28	2-1/2	2500	360 Max. 300 Min.	73	3
Remarks:	No baggage allowance.								
UH-12C	12-12-44	Franklin 6V4-200-C33	200	28	2-1/2	2500	360 Max. 300 Min.	73	3
Remarks:	No baggage allowance.								
UH-12D	12-23-57 Type Cert. 4H10	Lycoming VO-435-A1C	250	46	2.3	2750	395 Max. 314 Min.	83	3
Remarks:	No baggage allowance.								
UH-12E	1-6-59/Type Cert. 4H11	Lycoming VO-540-A1A, B1A-B1E, C1A-C1B	305	46	2.3	2750	395 Max. 314 Min.	83	3
Remarks:	Modification available to 4 seats. Baggage per flight manual. 12.3 quarts oil with auxiliary fuel tanks.								
UH-12E-L	9-18-63/Type Cert. 4H11	Lycoming VO-540-C2A	305	46	2	2750	370 Max. 285 Min.	92	3
Remarks:	Baggage per flight manual. Engine and transmission oil systems are separate. Maximum weight 3100 pounds only with cargo sling used.								
UH-12L	2-28-64/Type Cert. H1WE	Lycoming VO-540-C2A	305	46	2	3100	370 Max. 285 Min.	93	3
UH-12L4	52-28-64/Type Cert. H1WE	Lycoming VO-540-C2A	315	46	2 trans 1.12	3100	370 Max. 285 Min.	93	4
Remarks:	3 seats in UH-12L and 4 seats in UH-12L4. Maximum weight 3500 pounds, only with cargo sling used.								

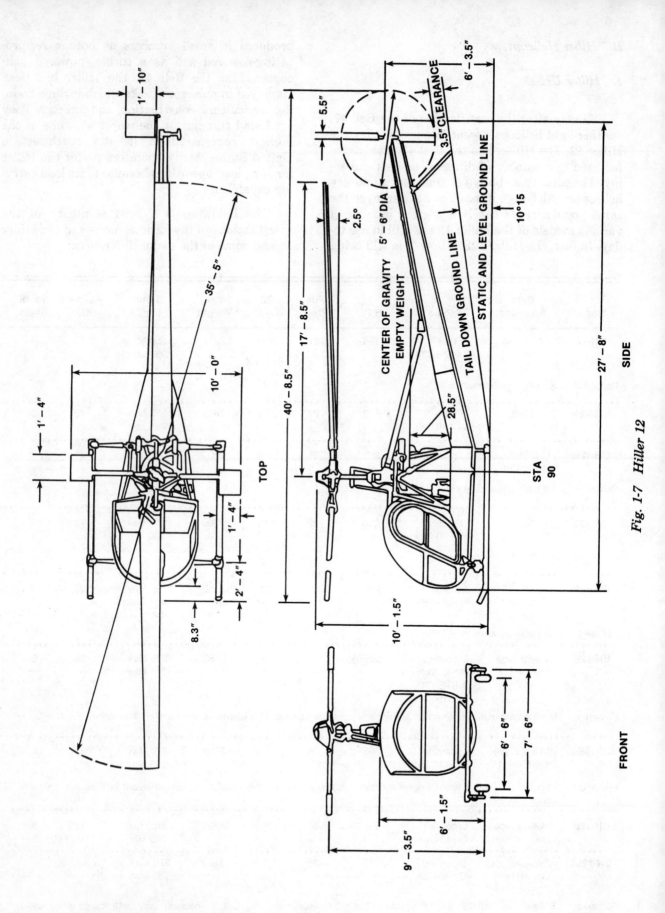

Fig. 1-7 Hiller 12

FRONT

TOP

SIDE

1' – 10"

10' – 0"

1' – 4"

1' – 4"

2' – 4"

8.3"

35' – 5"

5.5"

6' – 3.5"

3.5" CLEARANCE

CENTER OF GRAVITY
EMPTY WEIGHT

5' – 6" DIA

2.5°

TAIL DOWN GROUND LINE

STATIC AND LEVEL GROUND LINE

10°15

17' – 8.5"

40' – 8.5"

28.5"

STA
90

10' – 1.5"

27' – 8"

6' – 6"

7' – 6"

6' – 1.5"

9' – 3.5"

2. Hiller FH-1100

In addition to the Hiller 12, another model of the Hiller was built and marketed. This model, known as the FH-1100 (Fig. 1-8), was a 5-place turbine helicopter and was marketed by the new-ly mergered Fairchild Hiller Corporation. This model did not obtain the popularity of the Hiller 12 and production was dropped after a few years. However, the 1100 is now going back into production. Today there are still a limited number of the older 1100's operating. Listed is a summary of its specifications:

Model	Date Approved	Engine	H.P.	Fuel Cap.	Oil Cap.	Max. Weight	Rotor Limits	Airspeed (KIAS)	No. of Seats
FH-1100	11-10-66 Type Cert. H2WE	Allison 250-C18	274	68.5	Eng. 2.76 Trans. 2.6	2750	390 Max. 295 Min.	110	5

Remarks: 1100 pounds maximum.

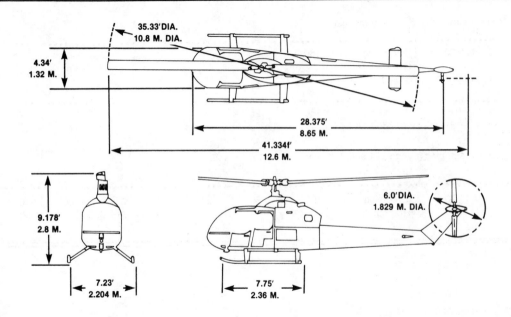

CABIN ENCLOSURE
The FH-1100's cabin overhead enclosure is constructed of aluminum alloy sheet, and the transparent windscreen and inside panels of vacuum-formed plastic. The basic structure of the rear cabin wall is a stainless steel firewall. The cabin doors open forward for ease of entrance, and the cabin itself is so designed to serve either for cargo or passenger flights. The area behind the two pilot stations has the capacity for 1,100 pounds of cargo at a maximum density of 100 pounds per square foot.

BASIC BODY STRUCTURE
The basic body is constructed of aluminum in a semi-monocoque structure, with a compartment behind the cabin and beneath the engine deck housing oil tanks, radio, electrical and other equipment. This compartment's hatches, at both sides of the aircraft, open to provide rigid platforms capable of supporting two mechanics during procedures. The basic body lower section also contains a controls tunnel and the fuel cell.

ENGINE SECTION
The entire engine section is faired and the cowling slides aft for ready access. The 136-pound engine is positioned by six steel members with integral end fittings to the engine deck/firewall. A heat shield separates the engine from cooling fan units and all other components within the engine compartment. The transmission and main rotor structure are suspended independently from the engine. Complete engine changes can be made with the drive system remaining in place. In addition, all of the individual engine components can be changed without removing the basic engine.

TAIL BOOM
The low aspect tail boom affords minimum drag and high stability in flight. The aircraft's overall low-drag configuration is maintained by the boom's uninterrupted underside fuselage. The tail boom is of aluminum alloy, semi-monocoque construction.

LANDING GEAR
Tubular aluminum skid runners take-offs and landings. The skid runners are supported by four aerodynamically faired struts to impact-absorbing torsion tubes. The two longitudinal torsion tube structures themselves provide a secondary, impact-absorbing, emergency land gear. Landing gear clearance allows landings on slopes to 10 degrees.

BLADE CONSTRUCTION
The all-metal rotor blades have a stainless steel leading edge spar and shear web. The trailing section is of aluminum and aluminum honeycomb sandwich construction. The blades contain reinforcement doublers at the root section to transfer load to points of attachment. Permanent mass balance is provided, and each blade has an aerodynamic tracking tab. Blades are individually interchangeable without field balancing. The main rotor blades may also be folded for shipping or storage without retracking.

HUB CONSTRUCTION AND BLADE RETENTION
The main rotor head or hub is of 4335 V Steel AMS 6429. Blades are secured to the hub by a main pin (and a secondary attachment for the drag strut) through a retention cuff which is secured to the hub by bearings. A sight gauge facilitates oil level inspection at each cuff bearing reservoir. The rotor head is attached to the drive shaft by an assembly which allows teetering to a 10° axis. Teeter bearing lubrication reservoirs also have sight guages.

Fig. 1-8   Hiller FH-1100

C. Hughes Helicopters

1. Hughes HU-269

Hughes began to build helicopters in the 1950's. Their first production helicopter was the Model 269, a simple two-place reciprocating powered helicopter. A great number of these aircraft were manufactured for the military. Large numbers have also been manufactured for civilian use and are being used for such tasks as training, agricultural, and police work.

Like most of the smaller helicopters, the Hughes 269 has been built in several different models. One of these is shown in Fig. 1-9. A brief summary of their specifications follows:

Model	Date Approved	Engine	H.P.	Fuel Cap.	Oil Cap.	Max. Weight	Rotor Limits	Airspeed (KIAS)	No. of Seats
269A	4-9-59/Type Cert. 4H12	Lycoming HO-360-B1A HO-360-B2B	180 165	25	2	1550	530 Max. 400 Min.	75	2
Remarks:	Maximum cargo. See flight manual.								
269A-1	8-23-63	Lycoming H10-360-B1A or B1B	180	25	2	1670	530 Max. 400 Min.	75	2
269B	12-30-63	Lycoming H10-360-A1A	180	25	2	1670	530 Max. 400 Min.	76	3
Remarks:	269B restricted category. 1 seat left side.								
269C	4-15-70	Lycoming H10-360D1A	190	30	2	1900	540 Max. 390 Min.	109? MPH	3

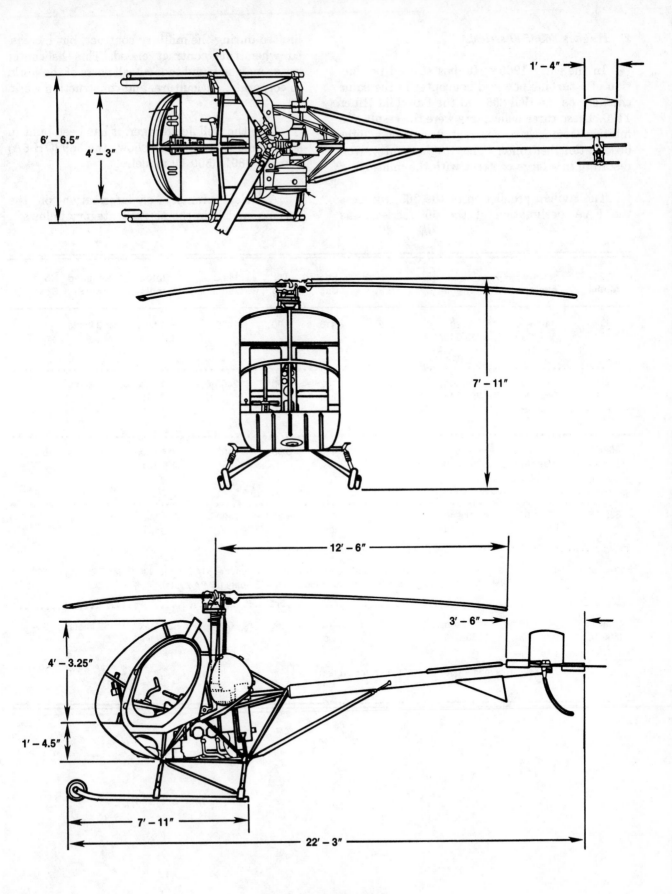

Fig. 1-9 Hughes 269

19

2. *Hughes 369 (500 series)*

In the early 1960's Hughes started production of a turbine powered helicopter in the same category as the Bell 206 and the Fairchild Hiller 1100. These three helicopters were the result of a military competitive contract design of a light observation helicopter. The Hughes entry won resulting in a large contract with the military.

The civilian production of the 369, which is the FAA designation of the 500 series, was limited during the military contract, but increased when this contract ended. This helicopter series may be found today in all parts of the world in corporate, agriculture, and construction work.

Like the Bell Jet Ranger, it has been built in several models. Fig. 1-10 shows the 369 (OH-6A) and the 369D (500 D) models.

A brief summary of information on the various models in the normal category follows:

Model	Date Approved	Engine	H.P.	Fuel Cap.	Oil Cap.	Max. Weight	Rotor Limits	Airspeed (KIAS)	No. of Seats
369H	11-15-66 Type Cert. H3WE	Allison 250-C18A	243	416 lbs.	5.90	2400	514 Max. 400 Min.	130 knots	5
369HM	4-8-68 Type Cert. H3WE	Allison 250-C18A	243	402 lbs.	5.90	2400	514 Max. 400 Min.	130 knots	4
369HS	1-3-69 Type Cert. H3WE	Allison 250-C18A	243	416 lbs.	5.90	2400	514 Max. 400 Min.	130 knots	5
369HE	5-21-69 Type Cert. H3WE	Allison 250-C18A	243	416 lbs.	5.90	2400	514 Max. 400 Min.	130 knots	5

Remarks: Many engines are modified for the Allison 250-C20 - rotor limits: C-18 engine 514 RPM to 400 RPM; C-20 engine 523 RPM to 400 RPM. Maximum weight SN 101 and up: 2550 pounds. 5 seats (HM 4 seats).

Model	Date Approved	Engine	H.P.	Fuel Cap.	Oil Cap.	Max. Weight	Rotor Limits	Airspeed (KIAS)	No. of Seats
369D (500 D)	12-8-76 Type Cert. H3WE	Allison 250-C20B	350	402 lbs.	11.60	3000	523 Max. 410 Min.	152 knots	5

Remarks: This model uses a five blade rotor system.

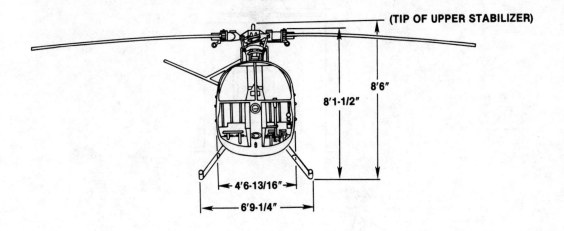

(TIP OF UPPER STABILIZER)

8'6"

8'1-1/2"

4'6-13/16"

6'9-1/4"

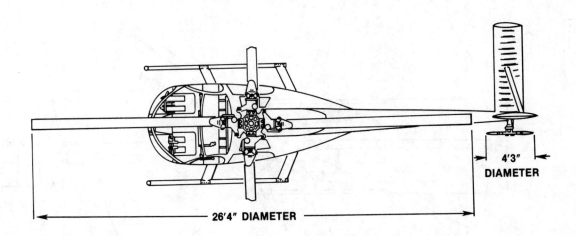

26'4" DIAMETER

4'3"
DIAMETER

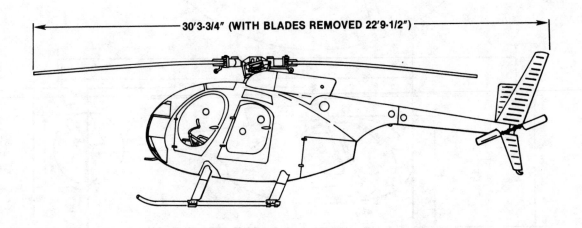

30'3-3/4" (WITH BLADES REMOVED 22'9-1/2")

Fig. 1-10a   369 (OH-6A)

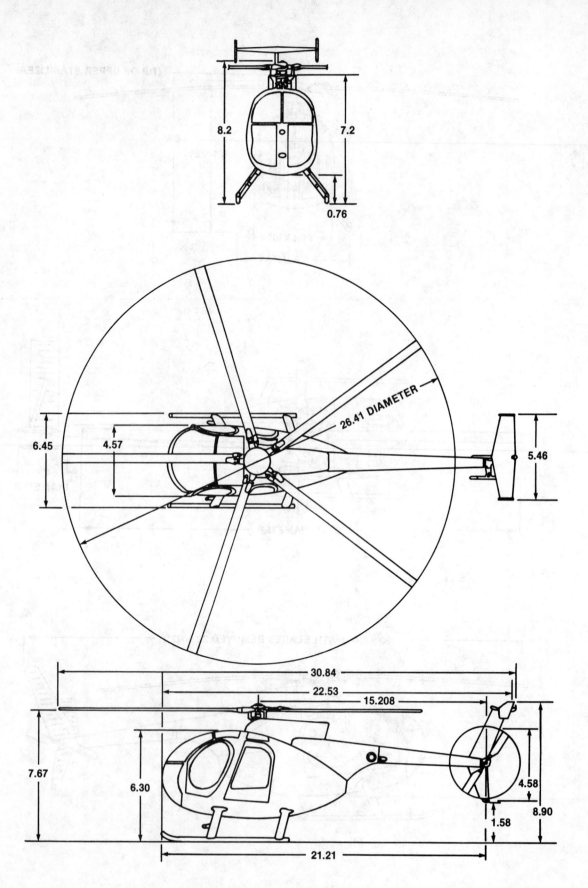

Fig. 1-10B   Hughes 500D

22

D. Sikorsky Helicopters

1. Sikorsky S55

Production of Sikorsky helicopters began in 1942 with the R4 helicopter for the military. This helicopter was built prior to the Bell 47, but early Sikorskies were not certified because they were built for the military. The first civilian certified Sikorsky was the S51 model. It was certified in April 1947 shortly after the Bell 47. Both the S51 and the S52 were manufactured in small numbers and it is quite doubtful if any of these exist today.

The S55 series, however, established Sikorsky as the manufacturer of large helicopters, even if they would not be considered large by today's standards (Fig. 1-11).

At present some of these helicopters are still in use, mainly in lift work and large agricultural operations. A brief summary of the S55 specifications follows:

Model	Date Approved	Engine	H.P.	Fuel Cap.	Oil Cap.	Max. Weight	Rotor Limits	Airspeed (KIAS)	No. of Seats
S55	3-25-52 Type Cert. 1H4	Pratt & Whitney SIH2	Max. Cont. 550	104	9.4	7200	245 Max. 170 Min.	95 knots	9

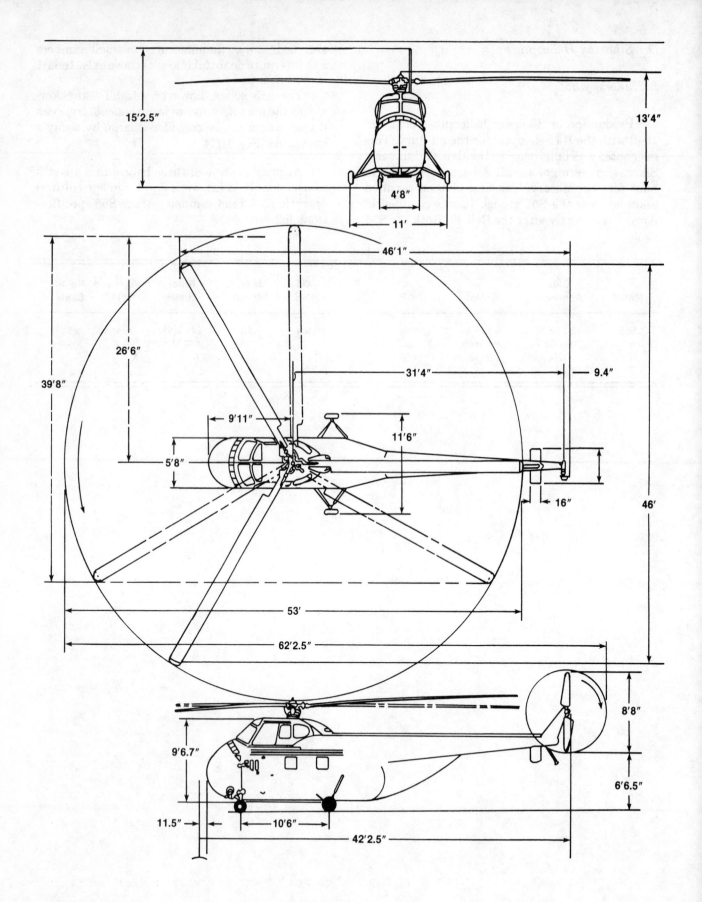

Fig. 1-11   Sikorsky S 55

2. Sikorsky S58

The S55 soon led the way for the production of the S58 (Fig. 1-12) which was larger and more powerful than the S55. This model enjoyed a long production with the civilian and military counterpart, the H34. This popularity led the helicopter to all parts of the world. It was used in the early helicopter airline concept and became a standard. A brief summary of the S58's specifications follows:

Model	Date Approved	Engine	H.P.	Fuel Cap.	Oil Cap.	Max. Weight	Rotor Limits	Airspeed (KIAS)	No. of Seats
S58A	8-2-56 Type Cert. 1H11	Wright Cyclone 989C9HE-2	Max. 1275	285	10.5	12700	258 Max. 170 Min.	117	14
S58B	8-2-56 Type Cert. 1HII	Wright Cyclone 989C9HE-2	Max. 1275	285	10.5	12700	258 Max. 170 Min.	117	14
S58C	8-2-56 Type Cert. 1H11	Wright Cyclone 989C9HE-2	Max. 1275	285	10.5	12700	258 Max. 107 Min.	117	14
S58D	12-15-61 Type Cert. 1H11	Wright Cyclone 989C9HE-2	Max. 1275	254	10.5	13000	258 Max. 170 Min.	117	14
S58E	5-27-71	Wright Cyclone 989C9HE-2	Max. 1275	254	10.5	13000	258 Max. 170 Min.	117	14
S58F	3-15-72	Wright Cyclone 989C9HE-2	Max. 1275	254	10.5	12500	258 Max. 170 Min.	117	14
S58G	3-15-72	Wright Cyclone 989C9HE-2	Max. 1275	254	10.5	12500	258 Max. 170 Min.	117	14
S58H	3-15-72	Wright Cyclone 989C9HE-2	Max. 1275	254	10.5	12500	258 Max. 170 Min.	117	14
S58I	3-15-72	Wright Cyclone 989C9HE-2	Max. 1275	254	10.5	12500	258 Max. 170 Min.	117	14
S58J	3-15-72	Wright Cyclone 989C9HE-2	Max. 1275	254	10.5	12500	258 Max. 170 Min.	117	14

Today the S58 is used in lift operations and has been converted to a turbine powerplant. This will extend the S58's life even more. A brief summary of the S58 turbine conversions specifications follows:

Model	Date Approved	Engine	H.P.	Fuel Cap.	Oil Cap.	Max. Weight	Rotor Limits	Airspeed (KIAS)	No. of Seats
S58BT	2-18-72 Type Cert. 1H11	United A/C of Canada PT6-3 Twin Pack	Max. Cont. 1262	279	1.6	13000	258 Max. 170 Min.	117	14
S58DT	2-18-72	United A/C of Canada PT6-3 Twin Pack	Max. Cont. 1262	244	1.6	13000	258 Max. 107 Min.	117	14
S58ET	2-18-72	United A/C of Canada PT6-3 Twin Pack	Max. Cont. 1262	279	1.6	13000	258 Max. 107 Min.	117	14
S58FT	3-27-72	United A/C of Canada PT6-3 Twin Pack	Max. Cont. 1262	279	1.6	12500	258 Max. 107 Min.	117	14
S58HT	3-27-72	United A/C of Canada PT6-3 Twin Pack	Max. Cont. 1262	244	1.6	12500	258 Max. 107 Min.	117	14
S58JT	3-27-72	United A/C of Canada PT6-3 Twin Pack	Max. Cont. 1262	279	1.6	12500	258 Max. 107 Min.	117	14

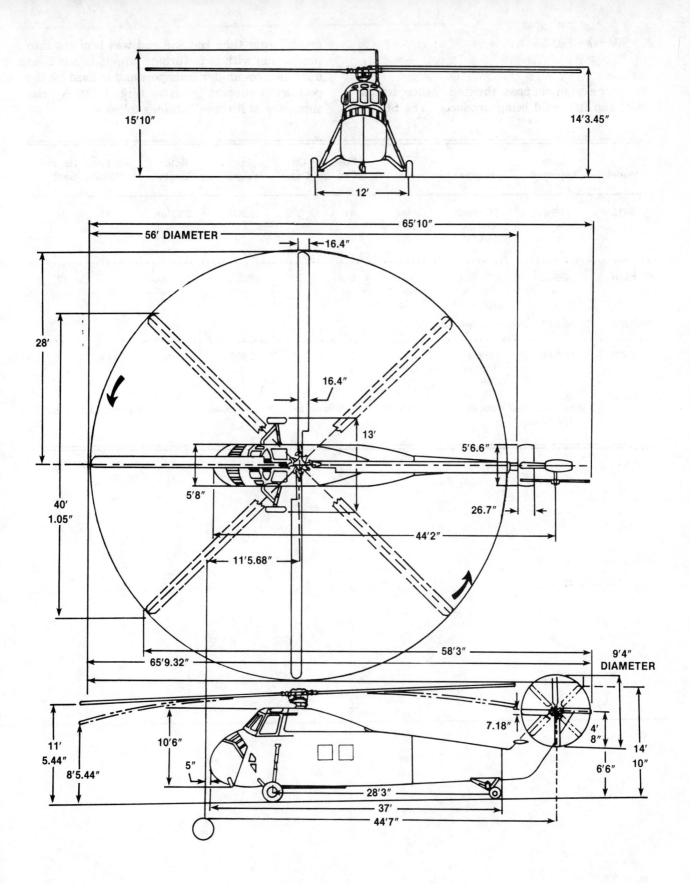

Fig. 1-12 Sikorsky S 58

27

3. Sikorsky S61

Sikorsky introduced the S61 helicopter in 1961, and it is still being produced. The S61 is much larger than the S58 and was brought into production with twin turbine power. It has been used as a commuter transport and is used by the petroleum support industry (Fig. 1-13). A brief summary of its specifications follows:

Model	Date Approved	Engine	H.P.	Fuel Cap.	Oil Cap.	Max. Weight	Rotor Limits	Airspeed (KIAS)	No. of Seats
S61L	11-2-61 Type Cert. 1h15	2 General Electric CT58-110-1	Max. Cont. 1050	410	5	19,000	225 Max. 184 Min.	127	39
S61N	9-9-63	2 General Electric CT58-110-1	Max. Cont. 1050	654	5	19,000	225 Max.	130	39

Remarks: Same as L except hull fuselage.

Model	Date Approved	Engine	H.P.	Fuel Cap.	Oil Cap.	Max. Weight	Rotor Limits	Airspeed (KIAS)	No. of Seats
S61R	12-30-63	2 General Electric CT58-110-1	Max. Cont. 1050	683	5.9	19,500	225 Max.	143	39

Remarks: Same as L except modified complete hull, rear loading ramp, airfoil shaped sponsons, retractable gear, and modified tail rotor pylon.

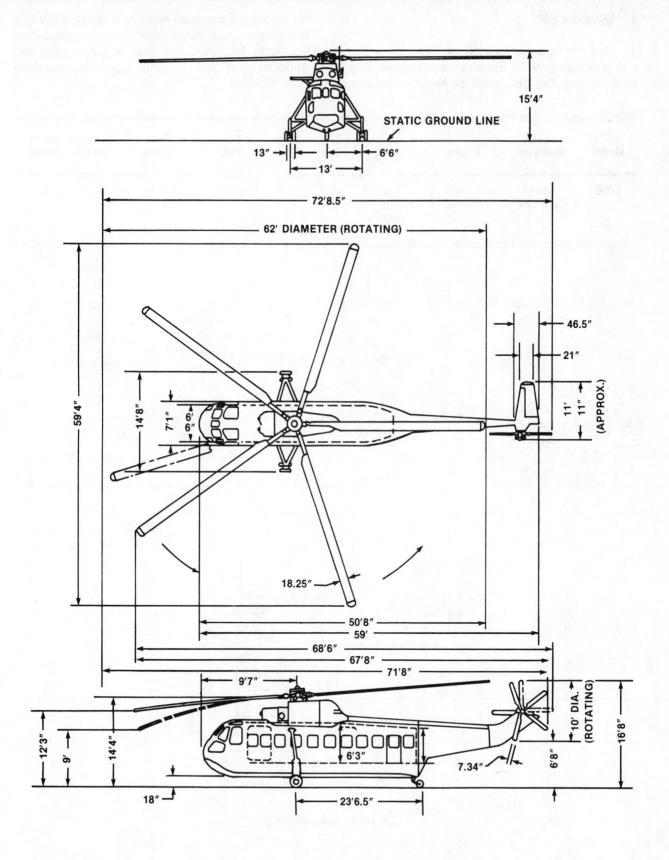

Fig. 1-13 Sikorsky S 61

29

4. Sikorsky S64

One of the most interesting helicopters that was manufactured by Sikorsky was the S64 (Fig. 1-14). It was the first attempt by any manufacturer to build a special purpose helicopter. Only a few of these machines were ever manufactured, but it is felt that this was a noteworthy accomplishment. A brief summary of its specifications follows:

Model	Date Approved	Engine	H.P.	Fuel Cap.	Oil Cap.	Max. Weight	Rotor Limits	Airspeed (KIAS)	No. of Seats
S64E	7-30-65 Type Cert. H1EA	2 Pratt & Whitney JFTD12A-1	Max. Cont. 4000	1356	2.8	42,000	204 Max. 671 Min.	115	5

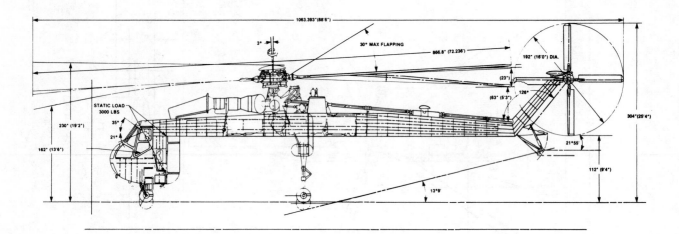

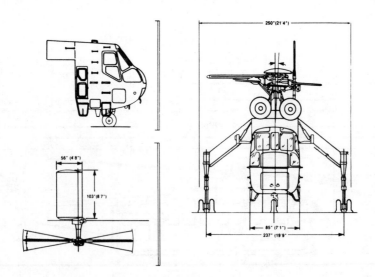

Fig. 1-14   Sikorsky S-64

5. Sikorsky S76

The latest of the Sikorsky helicopter models is the S76. It is primarily aimed at the corporate industry, but will also be used in the petroleum support industry (Fig. 1-15).

Model	Date Approved	Engine	H.P.	Fuel Cap.	Oil Cap.	Max. Weight	Rotor Limits	Airspeed (KIAS)	No. of Seats
S76A	7-26-79 Type Cert. H1NE	2 Allison 250-C30	650 each	286.4	1.27 per eng.	10,000	336 Max. 255 Min.	156	up to 14

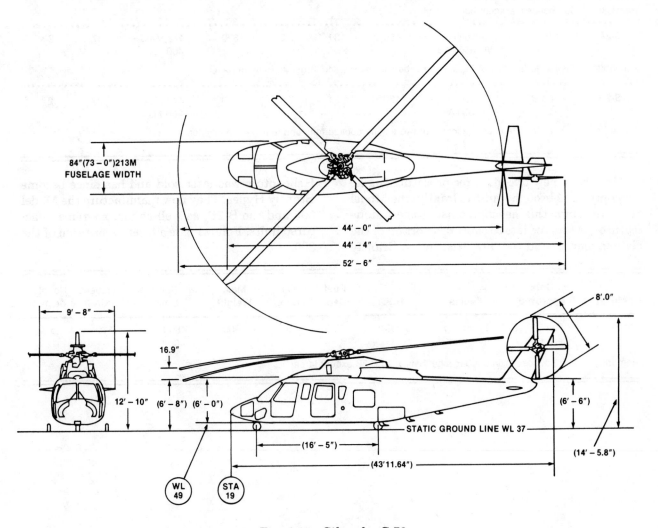

Fig. 1-15   Sikorsky S-76

31

E. Brantly Helicopters

1. Brantly B-2 and 305

In the late 1950's another helicopter made its appearance on the market. This was the Brantly B-2 (Fig. 1-16). It was a two-place helicopter with a unique three-bladed rotor system having lag hinges built into the blade. After the original model was produced two other models followed. Most of these were bought for private use and training. A brief summary of the B-2 models with their specifications follows:

Model	Date Approved	Engine	H.P.	Fuel Cap.	Oil Cap.	Max. Weight	Rotor Limits	Airspeed (KIAS)	No. of Seats
B-2	4-27-59/Type Cert. 2H2	Lycoming VO-360-A1B or B1A	180	31	7.3	1600	500 Max. 400 Min.	87	2
Remarks:	50 pounds maximum baggage.								
B-2A	12-21-62	Lycoming VO-360-A1B	180	31	7.3	1600	472 Max. 400 Min.	87	2
Remarks:	Similar to B-2 except bucket seats, bubble, doors, and larger instrument panel.								
B-2B	7-1-63	Lycoming IVO-360-A1A	180	31	7.3	1670	472 Max. 400 Min.	87	2
Remarks:	Similar to B-2A except addition of two engine cooling fans and fuel injection system.								

In 1965 a new five-place reciprocating engine helicopter was brought out by Brantly, the Model 305. Although this helicopter had some unique features, it was too late to capture a portion of the civilian market and very few exist today. Brantly Helicopters was later sold and has since become Brantly Hynes. They now manufacture the Model 305 and the B-2B, as well as factory remanufactured units. Following is a brief description of the 305:

Model	Date Approved	Engine	H.P.	Fuel Cap.	Oil Cap.	Max. Weight	Rotor Limits	Airspeed (KIAS)	No. of Seats
305	7-29-65/Type Cert. H3SW	Lycoming IVO-540-A1A	305	43.5	9	2900	480 Max. 400 Min.	104	5
Remarks:	200 pounds maximum baggage. Similar to B-2B except larger.								

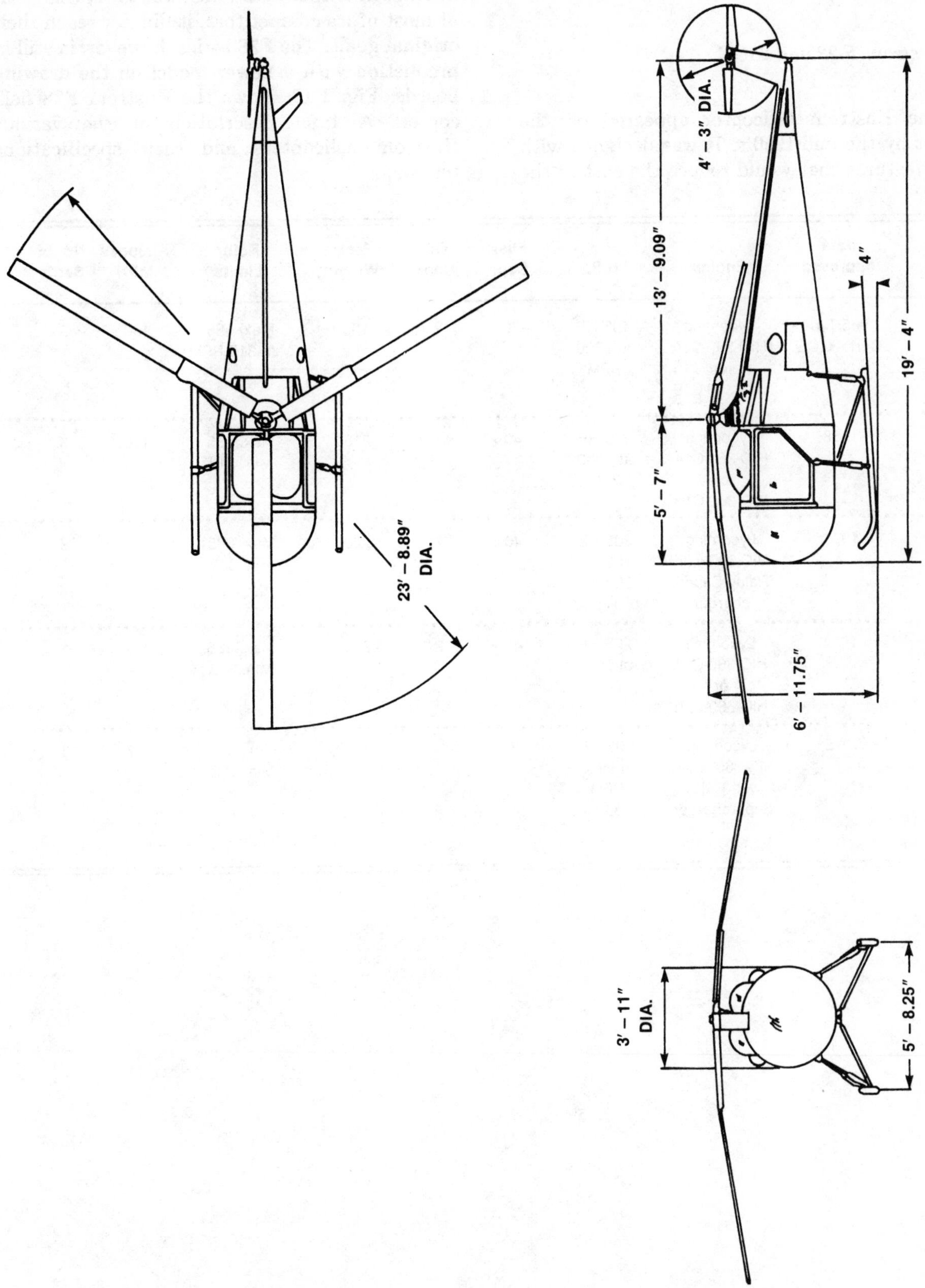

Fig. 1-16 Brantly B-2B

23' – 8.89" DIA.

4' – 3" DIA.

13' – 9.09"

5' – 7"

19' – 4"

4"

6' – 11.75"

3' – 11" DIA.

5' – 8.25"

F. Enstrom Helicopters

1. Enstrom F-28 and 280C

The Enstrom helicopter appeared on the market by the mid-1960's. It was designed with many features that would reduce the cost of the helicopter. Although the cost was lower than that of most of its competitors, it did not reach their original goals. The F28 series, however, is still in production with a newer model on the drawing boards. Fig. 1-17 shows the Enstrom F28 helicopter. A brief description of the various Enstrom helicopters and their specifications follows:

Model	Date Approved	Engine	H.P.	Fuel Cap.	Oil Cap.	Max. Weight	Rotor Limits	Airspeed MPH	No. of Seats
F-28	1965/Type Cert. H1CE	Lycoming HIO-360-C1A or HIO-360-C1B	195 HP at 2700 RPM	30	2	1950	Max. 385 Min. 315 RPM	100	3
F-28A	1968	Lycoming HIO-360-C1A or HIO-360-C1B	205 HP at 2900 RPM	40	2	2150	Max. 385 Min. 313	100	3
F-28C	1975	Lycoming HIO-360 with Rajay Super-charger	205 HP at 2900 36.5 in. Hg.	40	2	2200	Max. 385 Min. 332	112	3
280	1974	Lycoming HIO-360-C1A or HIO-360-C1B	205 HP at 2900 RPM	40	2	2150	Max. 385 Min. 313	112	3
280C	1975	Lycoming HIO-360-E1AD with Rajay Supercharger	205 HP at 2900 RPM 36.5 in. Hg.	40	2	2200	Max. 385 Min. 332	117	3

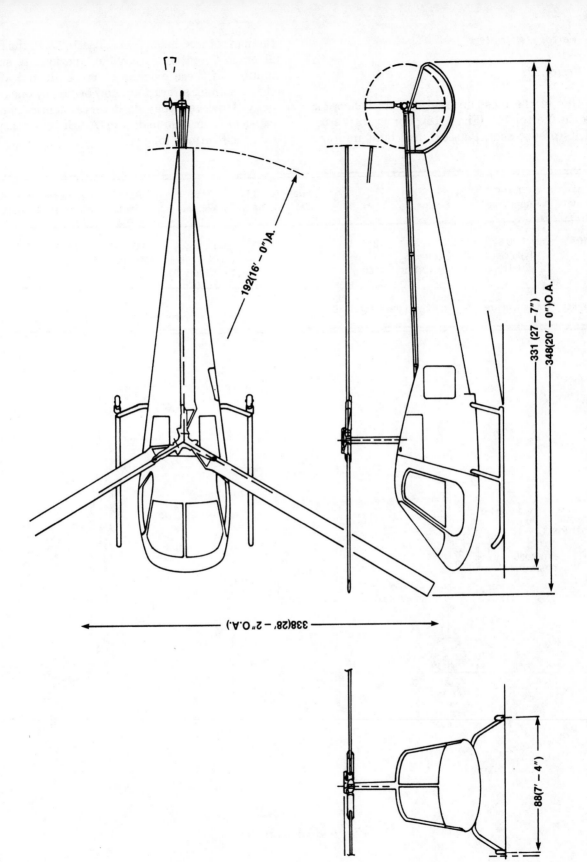

192(16' – 0")A.

331 (27 – 7")

348(20' – 0")O.A.

338(28' – 2" O.A.)

88(7' – 4")

Fig. 1-17 Enstrom F-28A

G. Vertol Helicopters

1. Vertol 107

One of the most unusual civilian helicopter was the Vertol 107 (Fig. 1-18). For years Vertol and its predecessor, Piasecki, had built military tandem-rotored helicopters. The 107 was the first attempt to enter the civilian market. A small number of these machines were built and all of the remaining aircraft are now owned by one company. However, they do deserve mentioning because of their unique design. A brief summary of its specifications follows:

Model	Date Approved	Engine	H.P.	Fuel Cap.	Oil Cap.	Max. Weight	Rotor Limits	Airspeed MPH	No. of Seats
107	7-26-62 Type Cert. 1H16	2 General Electric CT58-110-1 or -2	1250 Max. Takeoff 1050 Max. Continuous	350	4.2	Category A 17,900 lbs. Category B 19,000 lbs.	Max. 299 Min. 233	168	41

Remarks: Minimum crew 2 — maximum passengers 39

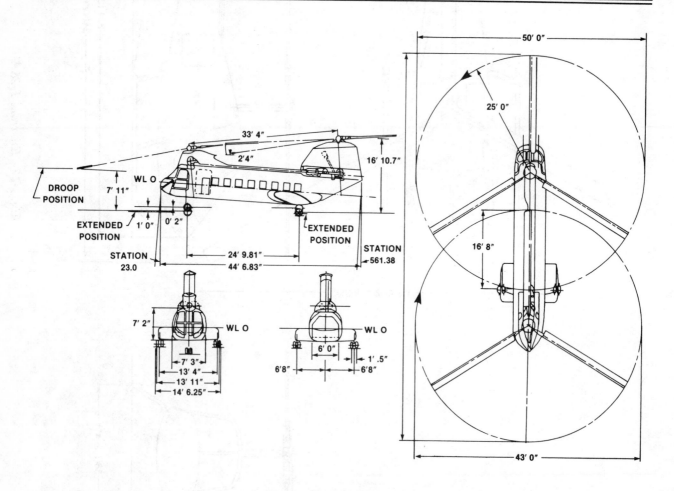

Fig. 1-18   Vertol 107

H. Imported Helicopters

Some emphasis has been placed in recent years on the importation of helicopters to this country from Germany and France.

1. Messerschmitt-Bolkow BO-105A

The German helicopter, the B0-105, is imported and marketed in the U.S. by Boeing Vertol. The B0-105A is built by Messerschmitt-Bolkow and Blohm in Germany (Fig. 1-19). It is a twin engine, rigid rotor helicopter, and is mainly being used by the petroleum support industry. A brief description follows:

Model	Date Approved	Engine	H.P.	Fuel Cap.	Oil Cap.	Max. Weight	Rotor Limits	Airspeed (KIAS)	No. of Seats
B0105A	4-19-71/Type Cert. H3EU	2 Allison 250-C18	317 Max. Takeoff 270 Max. Continuous	153	2.4	4,629	Max. 433 Min. 403	135 knots	5

Remarks: Minimum crew 1 — passengers 4.

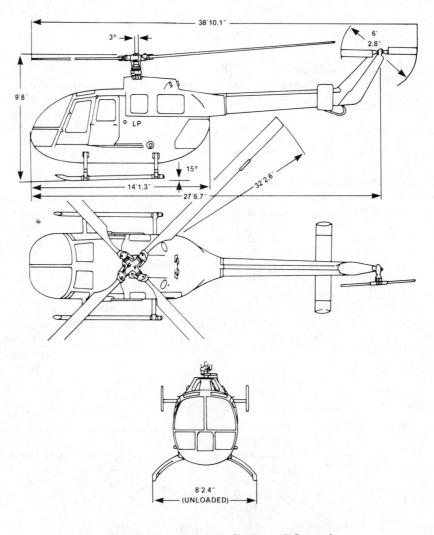

Fig. 1-19   Messerschmitt-Bolkow BO-105A

2. Aerospatiale Helicopters

a. Aerospatiale Alouette and Lama

The French helicopters are manufactured by Aerospatiale and were originally marketed by L.T.V. Corportion. They are now marketed by Aerospatiale in the United States.

Aerospatiale Helicopters has been one of the leading helicopter manufacturers in Europe for many years. They have exported several models to this country in recent years. These include the Alouette series, the Lama, Gazelle, Dauphin, Puma, and the AStar. These helicopters cover a wide range of capabilities from 4 to 17 passengers, and all are turbine powered.

The Alouette is the oldest of these models with several configurations. The original design of this helicopter dates back to the late 1950's and a U.S. Type Certificate was first issued in 1962. Two Alouette models are shown in Fig. 1-20. A brief summary of the different models and their specifications follows:

Model	Date Approved	Engine	H.P.	Fuel Cap.	Oil Cap.	Max. Weight	Rotor Limits	Airspeed (KIAS)	No. of Seats
SE160 Alouette III	3-27-62/Type Cert. H1IN	Turbomeca Artouste IIIB	Max. Takeoff 5 minutes 33500 RPM 562HP Max. Cont. 33500 RPM 444 HP	149	2.6	4630	Max. 420 RPM Min. 270 RPM	113 knots	7
Remarks:	Pilot and 2 front — 4 passengers rear.								
SA319B Alouette III	11-20-72	Turbomeca Astazou XIVB	Max. Takeoff 43000 RPM 592 HP Max. Cont. 43000 RPM 494 HP	149	2.6	4960	Max. 420 RPM Min. 270 RPM Cont. 358 RPM	118 knots	7
Remarks:	Pilot and 2 front — 4 passengers rear.								
SA316C Alouette III	11-20-72	Turbomeca Artouste IIID	Max. Takeoff 33500 RPM 592 HP Max. Cont. 33500 RPM 494 HP	149	2.6	4960	Max. 420 RPM Min. 270 RPM Cont. 358 RPM	118 knots	7
Remarks:	Pilot and 2 front — 4 passengers rear.								
SA316B Alouette III	3-25-71 Type Cert. H1IN	Turbomeca Artouste IIIB	Max. Takeoff 33500 RPM 542 HP Max. Cont. 33500 RPM 444 HP	149	2.6	4850	Max. 420 RPM Min. 270 RPM Cont. 353.2 RPM	113	7
Remarks:	Pilot and 2 front — 4 passengers rear. SA316B may be obtained by conversion of SA160.								
315B Lama	2-25-72	Turbomeca Artouste IIIB	Max. Takeoff 33500 RPM 592 HP Max. Cont. 33500 RPM 494 HP	149	2.6	4300 lbs Internal 5070 lbs External	Max. 420 RPM Min. 270 RPM Cont. 353 RPM	113 knots	5
Remarks:	Pilot and 1 front — 3 passengers rear.								

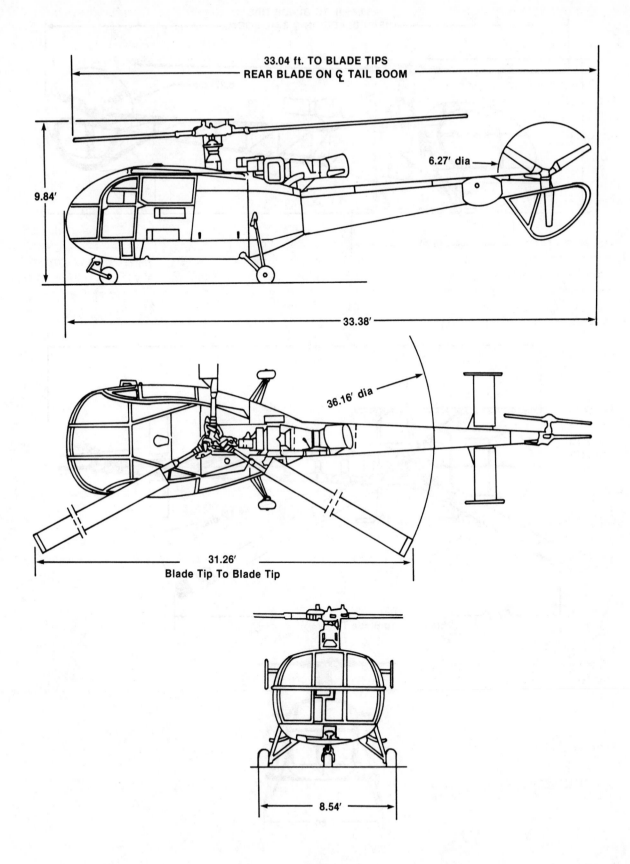

Fig. 1-20A   Aerospatiale Alouette III

39

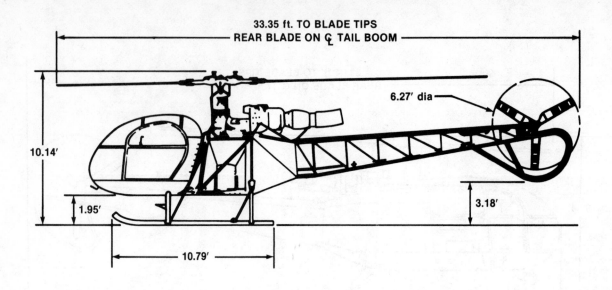

33.35 ft. TO BLADE TIPS
REAR BLADE ON ℄ TAIL BOOM

6.27' dia

10.14'

1.95'

3.18'

10.79'

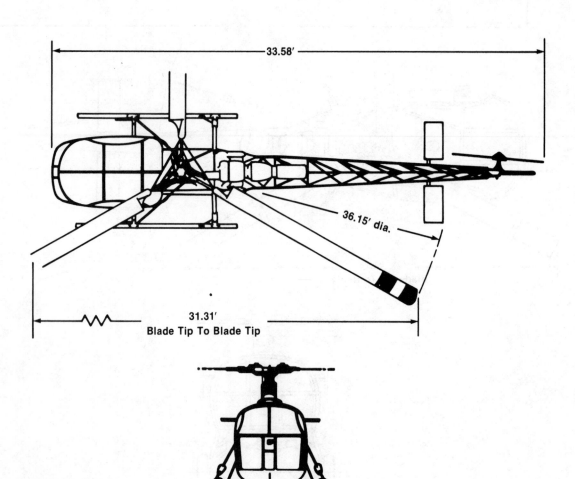

33.58'

6.27' dia

36.15' dia.

31.31'
Blade Tip To Blade Tip

7.80'

Fig. 1-20B   Aerospatiale Lama

40

b. Aerospatiale Gazelle

In 1972 Aerospatiale introduced the Gazelle. This helicopter was aimed at the corporate market as a 4-place helicopter (Fig. 1-21). A brief summary its specifications follows:

Model	Date Approved	Engine	H.P.	Fuel Cap.	Oil Cap.	Max. Weight	Rotor Limits	Airspeed (KIAS)	No. of Seats
SA341G Gazelle	9-18-72/Type Cert. H6EU	Tubomeca Astazou IIIA	Max. Takeoff 43500 RPM 494 HP Max. Cont. 43500 RPM 494 HP	120.7	2.4	3970	Max. 430 RPM Min. 310 RPM Power in flight 378 ± 12 RPM	168 knots	4
Remarks:	Pilot and 1 front — 2 passengers rear.								
SA342J Gazelle	1977	Turbomeca Astazou XIVH	Max. Takeoff 43500 RPM 570 HP Max. Cont. 43500 RPM 570 HP	120.7	2.4	4190	Max 393 RPM Min. 320 RPM Power in flight 349 ± 12 RPM	170 knots VNE	4
Remarks:	Pilot and 1 front — 2 passengers rear.								

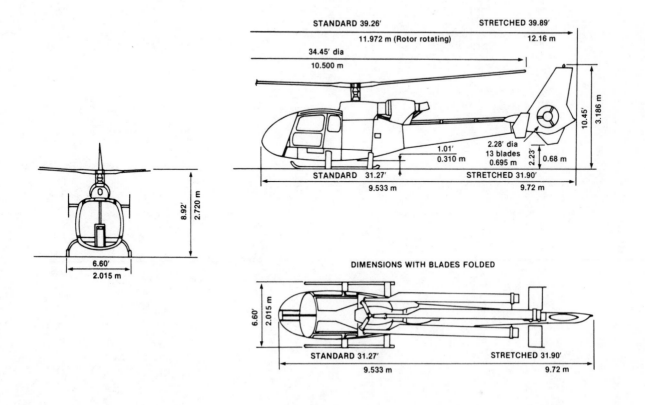

Fig. 1-21   Aerospatiale Gazelle

41

c. Aerospatiale Dauphin

Aerospatiale introduced the Dauphin in 1976. This model was soon followed by the Dauphin 2 giving twin engine reliability to the helicopter (Fig. 1-22). It is used mainly for transport by the petroleum support operators. A brief summary of the Dauphin models and their specifications follows:

Model	Date Approved	Engine	H.P.	Fuel Cap.	Oil Cap.	Max. Weight	Rotor Limits	Airspeed (KIAS)	No. of Seats
SA360C Dauphin	1976/Type Cert. H8EU	Turbomeca Astazou XVIII A	Max. Takeoff 43000 RPM 871 HP Max. Cont. 43000 RPM 804 HP	169	2.3	6400	Max. 393 RPM Min. 320 RPM Power in flight 349 ± 12 RPM	170 knots	14
Remarks:	Minimum crew 1 — maximum passengers 13								
SA365 Twin Dauphin	10-11-78	2 Turbomeca Arriel	Max. Takeoff 642 HP Max. Cont. 592 HP	169	2.8	7495	420 Max. Min. 320	170 knots	14
Remarks:	Maximum passengers — 1 pilot and 13 passengers.								

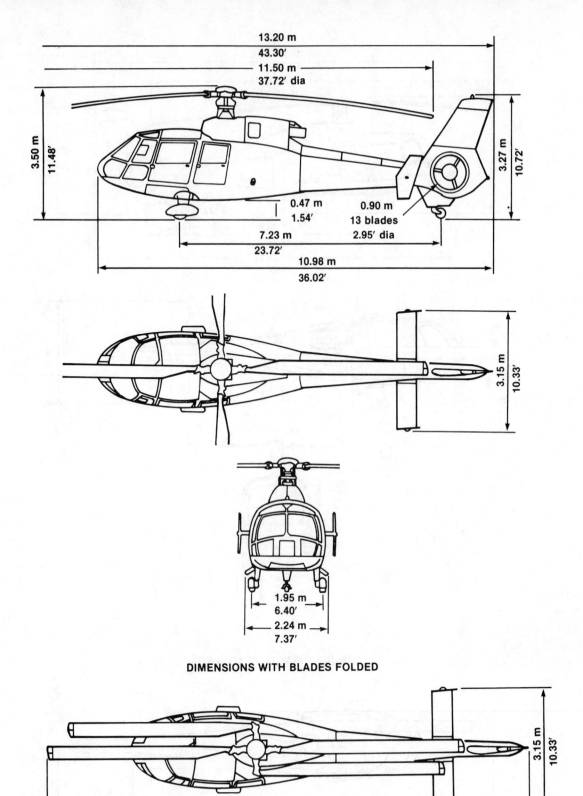

DIMENSIONS WITH BLADES FOLDED

Fig. 1-22A   Aerospatiale Dauphin

43

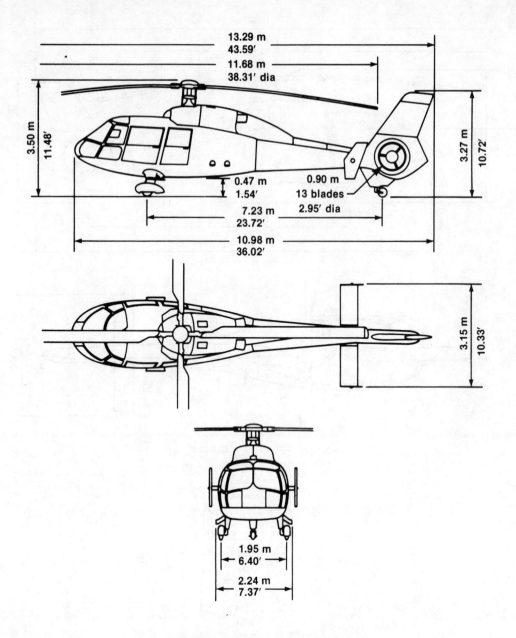

DIMENSIONS WITH BLADES FOLDED

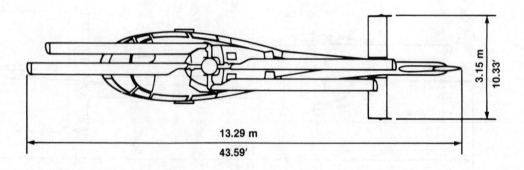

Fig. 1-22B   Aerospatiale Dauphin II

44

d. Aerospatiale Puma

A few of the Puma helicopters have been exported to this country. These are being used in the petroleum support industry (Fig. 1-23). A brief summary of its specifications follows:

Model	Date Approved	Engine	H.P.	Fuel Cap.	Oil Cap.	Max. Weight	Rotor Limits	Airspeed (KIAS)	No. of Seats
SA330J Puma	6-9-76 Type Cert. H4EU	2 Turbomeca Turmo IV C	Max. Takeoff 1494 HP Max. Cont. 1262 HP	414	6.34	7055	Max. 310 Min. 220	167 knots	20

Remarks: Crew — 2 pilots — maximum passengers 18

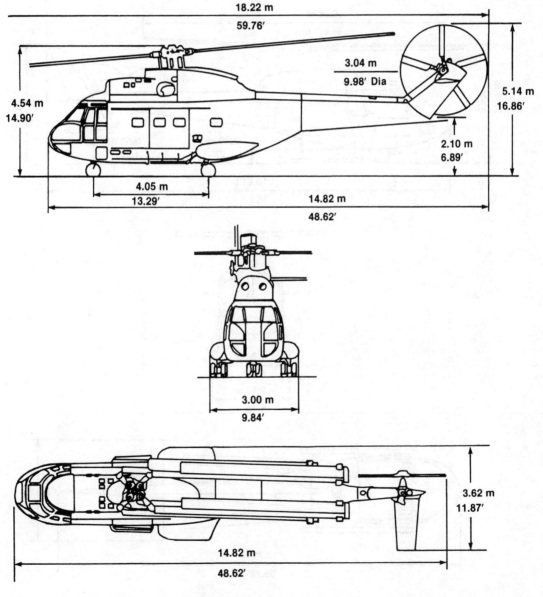

Fig. 1-23 Aerospatiale Puma

45

e. Aerospatiale AStar-350

The helicopter which appears to have the most sales is the Aerospatiale AStar 350. A great number of these were sold before production began. Although the helicopter is new, the technology and desirable characteristics have made a great number of sales in this country (Fig. 1-24). A brief summary of the AStar-350 and its specifications follows:

Model	Date Approved	Engine	H.P.	Fuel Cap.	Oil Cap.	Max. Weight	Rotor Limits	Airspeed (KIAS)	No. of Seats
AStar 350C	12-21-77/Type Cert. H9EU	LTS 101-66A2	Max. Takeoff 615 HP	140	1	4190	Max. 424 Min. 320	147 knots	6

Remarks: 1 pilot and 5 passengers.

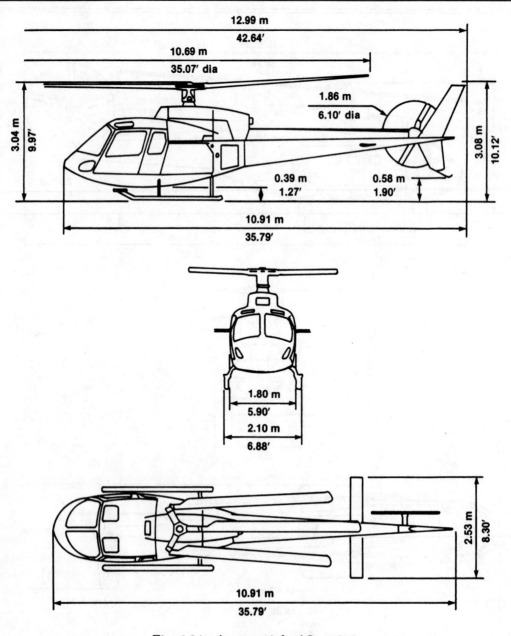

Fig. 1-24   Aerospatiale AStar 350

46

The helicopter has gone from its infancy to a multi-billion dollar business. The helicopter industry has approached thirty-seven billion dollars in sales in 1978 and employs 25,000 people in the production of helicopters. This figure does not include the number of people employed in the operation of these helicopters nor does it reflect their salaries.

It is predicted that in the time period of 1979-1987 the civilian helicopter fleet will grow to 25,815 units, of which most will be single engine turbine helicopters. This will represent a 154% growth rate.

The new helicopter which will be built during this period is predicted to be as follows:

a. 10,543 single engine turbine helicopters,

b. 3,464 twin turbine engine helicopters, and

c. 1,786 single engine piston powered helicopters.

In this time period additional money will be spent for research and development. New helicopters will appear on the market. This facet of aviation appears to have one of the largest growth rates in the aviation industry.

QUESTIONS:

1. The first type certificated helicopter was the:

    A. S55

    B. Bell 47

    C. Hiller

2. All Bell 47's were three-place helicopters.

    A. True

    B. False

3. The Bell 204B was quite similar to the Bell 206 model.

    A. True

    B. False

4. The Bell 206 is powered by an Allison engine.

    A. True

    B. False

5. The Hiller 12 was built in three different models only.

    A. True

    B. False

6. The largest Hiller built was the five-place FH-1100.

    A. True

    B. False

7. The FH-1100, Bell 206, and Hughes 369 (500 series) all use the same basic engine.

    A. True

    B. False

8. The Hughes 369 (500 series) has been built in only one model.

    A. True

    B. False

9. The S58 is powered by a:

    A. Pratt and Whitney engine.

    B. Wright engine.

    C. Lycoming engine.

10. No reciprocating powered helicopter has ever been converted to a turbine engine.

    A. True

    B. False

11. The largest special purpose helicopter is the:

    A. S58

    B. S64

    C. S76

12. Boeing Vertol markets the _____ in this country.

    A. AStar

    B. BO-105

    C. Alouette

13. The only tandem-rotored helicopter to be certificated in the U.S. at this time is:

    A. 107

    B. 222

    C. S61

14. Aerospatiale only manufacturers single engine helicopters.

    A. True

    B. False

15. The Enstrom helicopter has the engine mounted vertically.

    A. True

    B. False

Principles of Flight

A. Introduction

The helicopter as we know it today is a complex aircraft capable of flight maneuvers of hover, vertical, forward, backward, and sideward flight. In spite of the fact that the helicopter is capable of maneuvers that are not possible to the fixed wing aircraft, it still operates because of the same basic principles.

The need for maintenance personnel to study these principles may not be apparent at first. However, upon careful examination, it is very necessary because a thorough knowledge will be required to understand the maintenance and troubleshooting practices of the various systems.

Like the fixed wing aircraft, the helicopter flies because of its airfoils. The airfoils of the fixed wing are primarily its wings. However, the tail surfaces and sometimes the fuselage, as well as the propeller may also be airfoils. The primary airfoil of the helicopter is the main rotor. For this reason the helicopter is often referred to as a rotary wing aircraft. An *airfoil*, by definition, is any surface which gets a useful dynamic reaction from the air.

For our purposes, this reaction will be lift and thrust which will be necessary for flight and maneuvering the helicopter.

B. Aerodynamic Principles

The blades of the main rotor are the airfoils. With these airfoils certain nomenclature is used.

The span of the blade is the distance from the root of the blade to the tip of the blade measured along the center line (Fig. 2-1).

If a cross section of the blade is shown, it may have an imaginary line drawn from the leading edge to the trailing edge. This line is referred to as the chord of the blade as shown in Fig. 2-2.

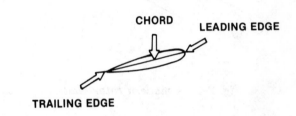

Fig. 2-2   Nomenclature of the cross section of an airfoil.

The shape of the airfoil section may take many different forms. This shape actually affects the flight characteristics of the aircraft. Certain airfoils are noted for high speed while others are known for low speed, high lift, and supersonic characteristics. See Fig. 2-3 for the general characteristics of various airfoils.

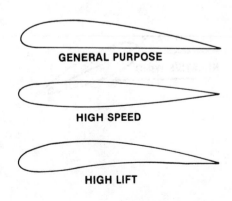

Fig. 2-3   Various airfoil cross sections.

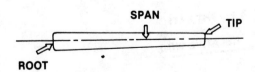

Fig. 2-1   Nomenclature of the blade.

The airfoils which are used for helicopters are usually referred to as symetrical airfoils, meaning that the airfoil section has the same shape on the top and bottom of the chord line. This curvature of the airfoil is referred to as the camber. However, some successful designs have been built with an unsymmetrical airfoil, meaning that the top and bottom camber are not the same shape.

Some efforts are being made to change the airfoil shape along the span to achieve better flight characteristics in the blade (Fig. 2-4).

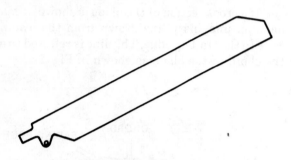

Fig. 2-4 A modern rotor blade.

1. Relative wind

As the rotor blade moves, it is subjected to relative wind. The *relative wind* is the direction of the airflow with respect to the blade. This is always opposite the flight path of the blade. For example, if the blade moves forward horizontally, the relative wind moves backward horizontally. If the blade moves backward horizontally, the relative wind moves forward horizontally. If the blade moves forward and upward, the relative wind moves backward and downward. If the blade moves backward and downward, the relative wind moves forward and downward (Fig. 2-5).

At first, one might wonder how the blade can move backwards. It must be remembered that this is in relation to the nose of the helicopter. For this reason the forward moving blade is referred to as the advancing blade while the backward blade is called the retreating blade. The relative wind may be affected by several factors such as movement of the rotor blades, horizontal movement of the helicopter, flapping of the rotor blade, wind speed and direction. The relative wind of the helicopter is the flow of air with respect to the rotor blades. For example: when the rotor is stopped, the wind blowing over the rotor blades creates a relative wind. When the helicopter is hovering in a no-wind condition, the relative wind is created by the motion of the rotor blades. If the helicopter is hovering in a wind, the relative wind is a combination of the wind and the rotor blade movement. When the helicopter is in forward flight, the relative wind is created by the rotor blades, the movement of the helicopter, and possibly a wind factor.

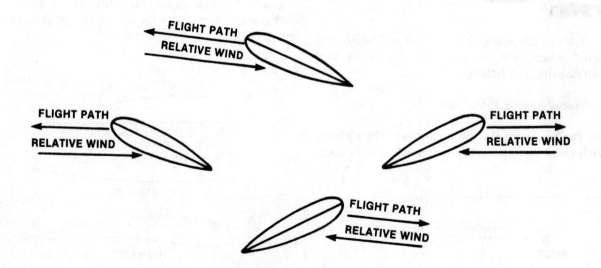

Fig. 2-5 The relationship of the rotor blades and the relative wind.

2. Pitch angle

Pitch angle is the acute angle between the rotor blade chord and a reference plane. The reference plane of the helicopter will be determined by the main rotor hub. The pitch angle is varied by movement of the collective control which will rotate the blade about the hub axis increasing or decreasing the pitch (Fig. 2-6). The pitch angle may also be varied by movement of the cyclic control which will be discussed in detail later in this section. Often the pitch angle is confused with the angle of attack.

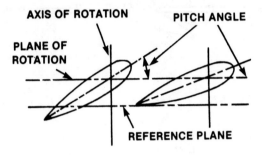

Fig. 2-6 The relationship of the pitch angle to the plane of rotation.

3. Angle of attack

The angle of attack is the acute angle between the chord line of the airfoil and the relative wind. The angle of attack may be equal to the pitch angle. However, it may also be greater or less than the angle of attack (Fig. 2-7). The pilot can increase or decrease the angle of attack by moving the pitch angle of the rotor. When the pitch angle is increased, the angle of attack is increased and when the pitch angle is decreased, the angle of attack is also decreased. Since the angle of attack is dependent upon the relative wind, the

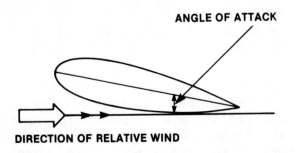

Fig. 2-7 The angle of attack in relation to the relative wind.

same factors that affect the relative wind also affect the angle of attack.

4. Lift

Lift is the force produced by the airfoil that is perpendicular to the relative wind and opposes gravity. The lift is developed by the rotor blade by Bernoulli's Principle which simply states that as velocity is increased, the pressure is decreased. This principle creates a low pressure at the top of the rotor blade while the bottom of the blade has an increased pressure. This applies to both symmetrical and unsymmetrical airfoils (Fig 2-8). Whenever lift is produced, drag is also produced.

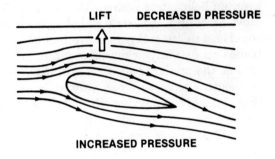

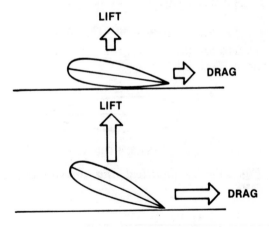

Fig. 2-8 Lift versus drag

5. Drag

Drag is the force which tends to resist the airfoil's passage through the air. Drag is always parallel to the relative wind and perpendicular to lift. It is this force that tends to slow down the rotor when the angle of attack is increased in order to produce more lift. In fact, drag varies as a square of velocity.

51

6. Center of pressure

The center of pressure is an imaginary point where the result of all the aerodynamic forces of the airfoil are considered to be concentrated. This center of pressure can move as forces change.

On some unsymmetrical airfoils, this movement can cover a great distance of the chord of the airfoil because as the angle of attack is increased the center of pressure moves forward along the airfoil surface and as the angle of attack is decreased the center of pressure moves aft along the airfoil surface. This is of little consequence in fixed wing aircraft because longitudinal stability may be achieved in several ways. However, on helicopters because the rotor blades are moved from a fixed axis (the hub), this situation could lead to instability in the rotor with the rotor blades constantly changing pitch. For this reason, the preferred airfoil is symmetrical where the center of pressure has very little movement (Fig. 2-9). Accompanying lift and drag is stall.

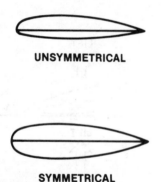

UNSYMMETRICAL

SYMMETRICAL

Fig. 2-9 Symmetrical and unsymmetrical airfoils.

7. Blade stalls

Stall is the condition under which the streamline flow of air separates from the camber of the blade and reverse flow occurs resulting in an almost complete loss of lift. As the angle of attack increases, lift increases until the stall angle is reached provided the velocity remains the same. However, as the angle of attack is increased the lift increases, but so does drag. Because of this increase in drag, the rotor blades have a tendency to slow down. If this should occur the stall angle will be reached prematurely (Fig. 2-10).

This is the reason that power must also be added in order to maintain the velocity of the rotor when the pitch is added to the rotor system. This also means that the lift of the rotor could be controlled by varying the speed of the rotor by increasing or decreasing the relative wind. However, this situation is avoided because of the slow reaction time in favor of keeping the velocity constant and changing the angle of attack.

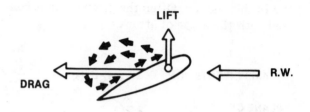

Fig. 2-10 The stall angle of the airfoil.

C. Effects on Lift

Lift will also vary with the density of the air. The air density is affected by temperature, altitude, and humidity. On a hot day the air is less dense than on a cold day. Because of this a higher angle of attack will be required of the rotor system to produce the same lift. This will require more power to maintain the velocity. The same situation is true when changes in altitude occur. Often a helicopter may be able to hover at sea level with a certain load but not at altitude because air is only two-thirds as dense at 10,000 feet of altitude as it is at sea level. The humidity will have the same effect since the humid air is less dense than dry air.

The lift developed by the helicopter has to be sufficient to overcome the weight. The heavier the weight is the greater is the pitch angle and power requirement to overcome the weight vs. lift action.

Also acting on the helicopter will be thrust and drag. Thrust is the force moving the helicopter in the desired direction while drag is the force which tends to resist thrust. Therefore, before any movement may take place thrust must overcome drag (Fig. 2-11).

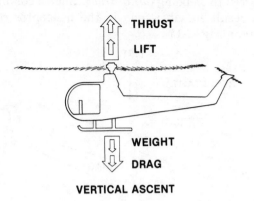

THRUST

LIFT

WEIGHT

DRAG

VERTICAL ASCENT

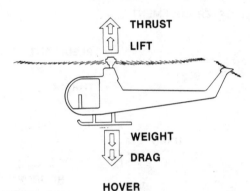

THRUST

LIFT

WEIGHT

DRAG

HOVER

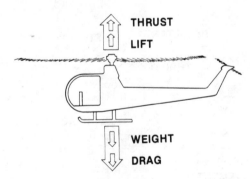

THRUST

LIFT

WEIGHT

DRAG

VERTICAL DESCENT

Fig. 2-11 *Lift, thrust, weight, and drag components in relationship to the helicopter.*

D. Forces on the Rotor

Thus far the principles of flight have been much the same as that of the fixed wing airplane. However, it must be remembered that the actual movements that govern flight will be accomplished by driving the rotor blades in a circle rather than the wings being flown in a straight line. Considering this situation a number of forces are applied to the rotor system that are not present with the fixed wing.

The rotor consists of a hub which is driven by the shaft (mast). Attached to the hub are the blades. The blades are somewhat flexible and when at rest will droop due to the weight and span of the blade. This is referred to as *blade droop* (Fig. 2-12).

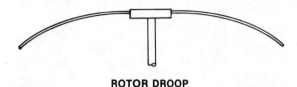

ROTOR DROOP

Fig. 2-12 *Rotor droop occurs when the rotor is at rest.*

When the rotor is turned, this droop is overcome by centrifugal force which will straighten the blade (Fig. 2-13). This centrifugal force will be dependent upon the weight of the blade and its velocity. On small rotor systems this could be approximately 20,000 pounds while larger systems may approach 100,000 pounds of centrifugal force per blade. With forces of this magnitude, the utmost care must be taken in maintenance procedures.

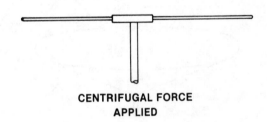

CENTRIFUGAL FORCE
APPLIED

Fig. 2-13 *A rotating rotor system.*

In addition to the centrifugal force, lift will react perpendicular to the rotor as pitch is applied to the rotor. This will result in the blade seeking a new position which will be the result of centrifugal force and lift (Fig. 2-14).

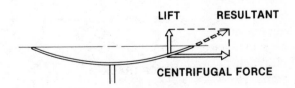

LIFT   RESULTANT

CENTRIFUGAL FORCE

Fig. 2-14 *A loaded rotating rotor system.*

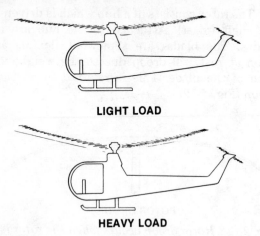

LIGHT LOAD

HEAVY LOAD

Fig. 2-15 Coning is affected by the weight of the helicopter.

This movement of the blades is referred to as *coning* of the rotor. The amount of coning is dependent upon the amount of lift and the weight of the helicopter. Therefore a helicopter with a light load will have less coning than a heavily loaded helicopter (Fig. 2-15). It may be noted that the blade tips will pass through a circular surface formed by the rotor blades. This circular plane is referred to as the rotor disk or the *tip path plane* (Fig. 2-16).

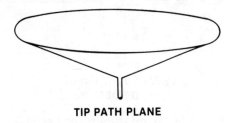

TIP PATH PLANE

Fig. 2-16 The rotor disc or tip path plane.

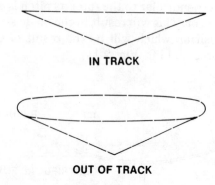

IN TRACK

OUT OF TRACK

Fig. 2-17 In track and out of track condition.

The satisfactory relationship of the rotor blades to each other in flight is referred to as *track*. If this relationship is incorrect, this is referred to as being *out of track*. Such a condition will result in vibrations in the helicopter rotor system (Fig. 2-17).

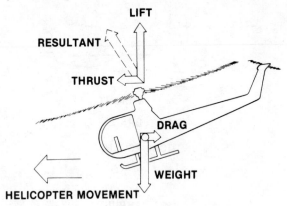

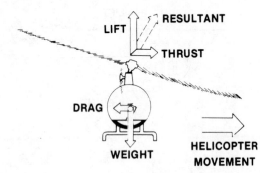

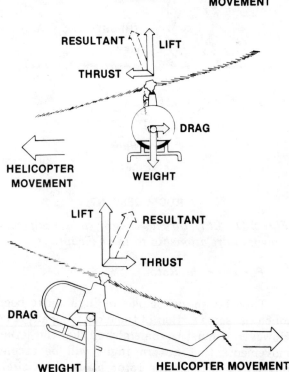

Fig. 2-18 Aerodynamic force vectors applied during modes of flight.

E. Thrust

Thus far we have discussed the flight of the helicopter only in regards to obtaining lift with little mention of thrust. Since the rotor will produce the lift force and at the same time propel the helicopter directionally, thrust is most important because it is thrust that gives this directional movement.

The thrust is obtained by movement of the tip path plane of the rotor or rotor disc. If the helicopter is ascending vertically or at a hover, lift and thrust are both in the same direction, vertical. However, in order to obtain forward, backward, or sideward directional flight, the rotor disc will be tilted in the direction of the movement desired. This will result in lift and thrust being perpendicular to each other with the result being the ability of the helicopter to maintain flight and move directionally (Fig. 2-18).

The movement of the tip path plane to change the direction of the helicopter is done by changing the angle of attack of the individual blades as they pass along the disc. In order to accomplish this the hub must have provisions for a *feathering axis* which simply allows the pitch to be moved as shown in Fig. 2-19.

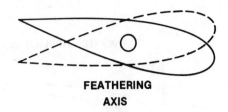

FEATHERING AXIS

Fig. 2-19 The feathering axis or pitch axis of the rotor.

1. Collective pitch

By changing the pitch angle of the blade more or less lift will be created. This pitch change can be accomplished by the use of the *collective* by the pilot to raise or lower the helicopter in the air. This raises or lowers the pitch angle of all the blades the same amount throughout the tip path plane. If this lift is increased at one point and decreased at another point 180° apart the blades will climb and dive, thus moving the disc. This is accomplished as the pilot moves the cyclic control which in turn moves each blade a predetermined and equal amount as shown in Fig. 2-20.

2. Gyroscopic precession

At this time another property of the rotor must be discussed before the total directional

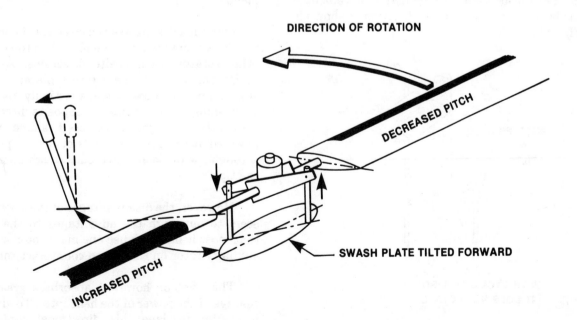

DIRECTION OF ROTATION

DECREASED PITCH

SWASH PLATE TILTED FORWARD

INCREASED PITCH

Fig. 2-20 Cyclic pitch change through the swashplate.

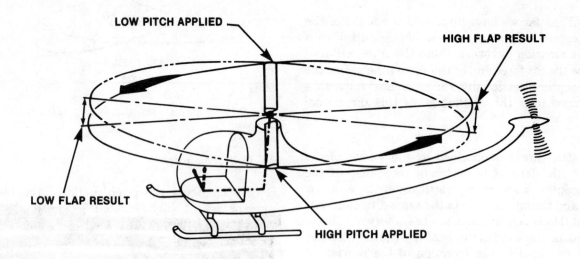

LOW PITCH APPLIED

HIGH FLAP RESULT

LOW FLAP RESULT

HIGH PITCH APPLIED

Fig. 2-22 The results of gyroscopic precession as applied to the main rotor system.

control can be understood. Since the rotor path is considered as a disc, it has the same properties as that of any other rotating mass. The property of most interest is *gyroscopic precession* which means that action occurs 90° from the force applied in the same direction as rotation. This means that the blades do not raise and lower the maximum deflection until a point 90° later than the input (Fig. 2-21). For this reason a device which is called a swashplate or star assembly is used to place the input of the cyclic to the main rotor at the location required for the movement of the helicopter in the desired direction as shown in Fig. 2-22.

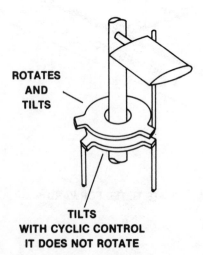

ROTATES
AND
TILTS

TILTS
WITH CYCLIC CONTROL
IT DOES NOT ROTATE

Fig. 2-21 Basic principles of the swashplate operation.

3. Torque

Newton's third law states that for every action there is an opposite and equal reaction. Therefore when power is applied to the rotor system the fuselage of the helicopter will tend to move in the opposite direction of the rotor. This tendency is referred to as torque. The torque problem has plagued designers since the inception of the helicopter. Several designs of the helicopter rotor systems were tried to eliminate this problem.

One such design was the coaxial helicopter in which two main rotors were placed on top of each other rotating in opposite directions. Another design requires two main rotors placed side by side. Some of these designs actually used intermeshing rotors turning in opposite directions. Still other designs have used single rotors powered at the tip by ramjets or hot air passing through the blade and ejected through nozzles at the tip.

However, the disadvantages of these systems seem to outweigh the advantages to the point that most helicopters use one main rotor with an auxiliary rotor on the tail to counteract torque.

This system, however, absorbs a great percentage of the power of the helicopter. To give the helicopter fuselage this directional control, a variable pitch rotor is vertically mounted on the tail. In order to keep the fuselage straight when increasing power the pitch of the tail rotor is increased to counteract the torque. This is accomplished by foot pedals which are moved by the pilot (Fig. 2-23).

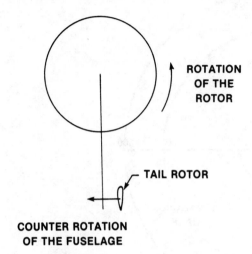

Fig. 2-23 Anti-torque control is applied by the tail rotor.

Many of the conventional helicopters using tail rotors which use power have found methods to help reduce this power requirement in flight. One of these methods is a vertical fin which is offset in order to keep the fuselage straight during forward flight. This in turn unloads the tail rotor.

4. *Blade twist*

In viewing the main rotor from the top in a no-wind hover condition (Fig. 2-24) it is quite evident that different parts of the rotor are moving at different speeds. The fastest portion is at the tip of the rotor and the least amount of speed is at the root portion of the blade. The blade will often have a twist built into the blade in order to improve the lift characteristics of the rotor throughout the blade. This twist will increase from the tip to the root. This twist will increase the angle of attack of the slower portions of the blade, thus increasing the lift of the blade (Fig. 2-25).

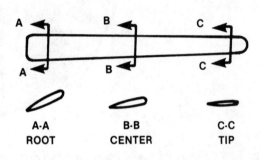

Fig. 2-25 More twist at the root of the blade increases the lift.

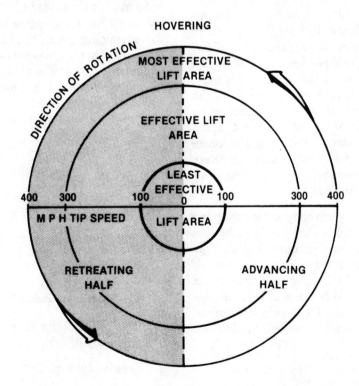

Fig. 2-24 The rotor speed increases from the root of the blade outward.

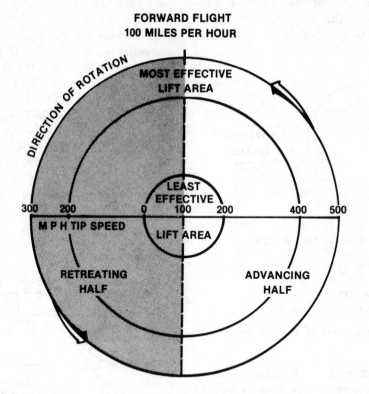

FORWARD FLIGHT
100 MILES PER HOUR

DIRECTION OF ROTATION

MOST EFFECTIVE
LIFT AREA

LEAST
EFFECTIVE
LIFT AREA

300   200   0   100   200   400   500

M P H TIP SPEED

RETREATING
HALF

ADVANCING
HALF

Fig. 2-26   Forward speed increases the difference in speed between the advancing and retreating blades.

F.   Dissymmetry of Lift

The speed of the rotor, however, is also affected by wind and forward flight (Fig. 2-26). In this situation the helicopter is traveling at a forward speed of 100 miles per hour. It should be noted that the right half of the rotor disc is moving at 200 miles per hour faster speed than the left half. This right half of the disc is referred to as the advancing half of the disc while the left half is referred to as the retreating half. Consequently, the rotor blades passing through these disc areas will be referred to as the *advancing blades* and the *retreating blades*.

At this point it is quite easy to see that the lift on the retreating half of the disc will be less than that of the advancing half of the disc. This difference in lift is referred to as *dissymmetry of lift*. Many of the early helicopter inventors could not achieve forward flight because of this dissymmetry of lift. It was Juan De Cierva who incorporated the flapping hinge into each blade eliminating this problem.

1.   Flapping hinge

This system is still used today in most of the multi-bladed systems. This flapping hinge allows

each blade to move freely about its vertical axis or to move up and down. This movement is referred to as *flapping*. Since more lift is created by the advancing blade, the blade has a tendency to move up. This decreases the amount of lift on the advancing side of the disc. At the same time the retreating blade takes a more horizontal position which creates more lift because less lift is being created by the retreating half of the disc (Fig. 2-27).

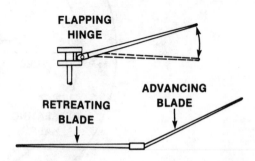

FLAPPING
HINGE

ADVANCING
BLADE

RETREATING
BLADE

Fig. 2-27   The flapping hinge is used to control dissymmetry of lift.

2.   Seesaw system

Another method which is quite widely used for the correction of dissymmetry of lift is the

58

seesaw system. This system utilizes a two-bladed system. With this system one blade is advancing while the other is retreating. Since the advancing blade has the greatest lift, the advancing blade moves up, and because the two blades are connected, the retreating blade moves down a like amount, thus creating the seesaw action (Fig. 2-28).

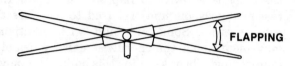

Fig. 2-28 This seesaw action is used on semi-rigid rotors.

3. Corriolis effect

The system that utilizes the individual flapping hinge is also subjected to the *corriolis effect* to a greater degree than the seesaw system. The corriolis effect is the change in blade velocity to compensate for the change in distance of the center from the axis of rotation as the blade flaps. In other words, as each individual blade flaps upward on the advancing side, the center of gravity moves closer to the axis of rotation (the mast). This has a tendency to accelerate the blade in much the same manner as a figure skater accelerates a spin by moving her arms inward. The opposite reaction occurs on the retreating blade with its center of gravity moving outward and the blade tends to slow down. If the corriolis effect is not corrected, it will cause geometric imbalance of the rotor system if the blades are held in their respective positions. This geometric imbalance will cause severe vibration and undue stress on the blade roots due to the bending action in a chordwise direction.

4. Drag or lead-lag hinge

For this reason rotor systems which incorporate individual flapping hinges are also provided with a drag hinge which is sometimes referred to as a lead-lag hinge. This hinge allows the blade to hunt or to move about the chordwise axis, as shown in Fig. 2-29. This allows the advancing blade, which has a tendency to accelerate due to the center of gravity movement closer to the rotation axis, to move forward. The retreating blade will likewise seek an aft position, thus the terms lead and lag. This movement of the blades will

correct the geometric imbalance caused by the corriolis effect by relieving the lead-lag motion placed on the blade roots and hub. Associated with these hinges are dampeners which assist the lead-lag hinge by limiting travel and making smooth movements in the lead-lag position.

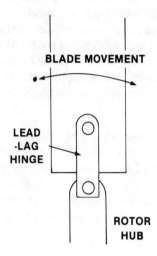

Fig. 2-29 Lead-lag action is required on systems using the flapping hinge.

5. Underslung rotor

The rotor systems utilizing the seesaw system or flap as a unit system are subject to the corriolis effect to a much lesser degree than the individual blade flapping system. This is the result of underslinging the rotor. The *underslung* rotor is mounted below the top of the mast which keeps the distance from the center of gravity of the blades to the axis of rotation small. In addition to this feature, some of the rotors are double gimbaled, which means that additional movement may take place in the chordwise direction or allowing the hub to rock about the mast. The mast is always quite long and mounted with flexibility between the rotor and the airframe to absorb any geometric imbalance that might occur.

Other systems that are not gimbaled for hub rock make corrections in blade pitch throughout the rotation of the rotor.

G. Rotor Heads

There are actually three various types of rotor heads in use today. They are described as rigid, semi-rigid, and fully articulated. The latter two types (semi-rigid and fully articulated) are the most widely used rotor systems.

1. *Rigid rotor*

The rigid rotor system makes use of a feathering axis only. For this reason the possibilities of this system have been neglected over the years due to the inability to correct for dissymmetry in lift. The certified helicopters that make use of the rigid rotors today use fiberglass blades which are designed to flex, giving flapping motion as well as the lead-lag properties to the blade rather than to the hub.

At least one other rigid rotor was built and used experimentally in which the blade angles of each individual blade were changed during rotation. By using this method, corrections in dissymmetry in lift were made (Fig. 2-30). However, experimental work in this area has been discounted at this time.

2. *Semi-rigid rotor*

The semi-rigid rotor is probably the most popular rotor system at present. However, some of the newly designed heads may change this situation within a few years. The semi-rigid rotor, like the rigid rotor, makes use of a feathering axis for pitch change. In addition to this movement, the rotor is allowed to flap as a unit. For this reason it is sometimes referred to as a seesaw rotor system. Some are built with additional movement about the chordwise axis by use of a gimbal ring. The reason for this additional movement is to compensate for the corriolis effect as described earlier in this text. Other semi-rigid systems correct for this problem by a built-in correction factor in the swashplate which changes pitch angles during rotation.

An example of both types of semi-rigid rotors is shown in Fig. 2-31.

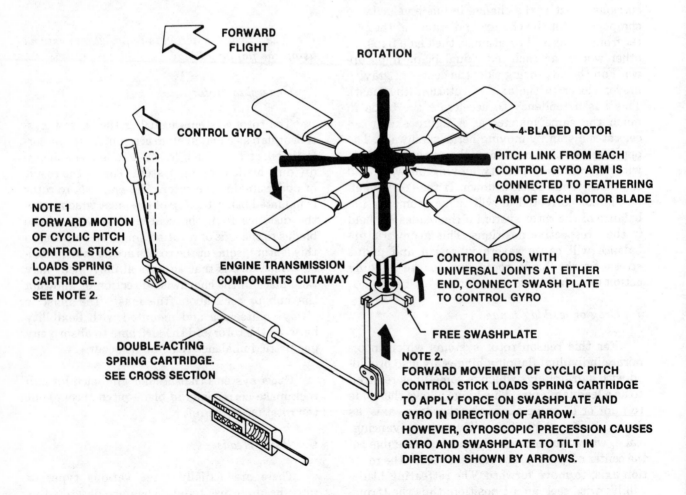

Fig. 2-30   This rigid rotor system was used experimentally by the U.S. Army.

60

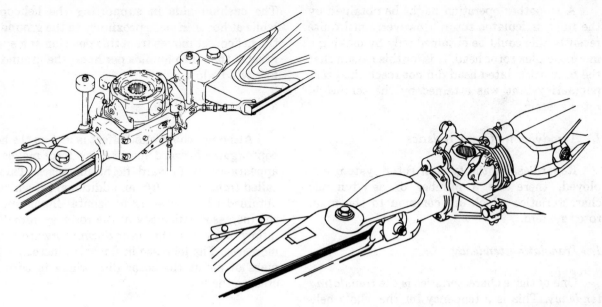

Fig. 2-31 The head shown in the top view has movement on two axis while the bottom head has movement on one axis only.

3. Fully articulated rotor

The fully articulated rotor system is one that utilizes the feathering axis for the blade pitch, an individual flapping hinge for each blade, and a lead-lag hinge for each blade. At the present time there are probably not as many fully articulated heads as semi-rigid heads, but because of the new technological developments in this area this trend may soon be reversed.

H. Relative Merits of Rotor Systems

Both the semi-rigid rotors and the fully articulated rotors have advantages and disadvantages which we will attempt to point out:

Function and Effects of the Semi-Rigid Rotor

1. The elimination of flapping and drag hinges simplifies construction.

2. The blades are fixed to the hub and do not depend on centrifugal force for rigidity.

3. Because of the seesaw flapping it is more subject to wind gusts.

4. More bending forces are applied to the blade roots because of the lack of hinges.

5. Semi-rigid rotors require underslinging of the rotor.

It is quite obvious that the semi-rigid rotors can be built quite simple and can also perform quite well but are not as smooth as the fully articulated head when both are functioning correctly.

Function and Effects of the Fully Articulated Rotor

1. The rotor disc may tilt without tilting the mast because of the flapping hinge.

2. Flapping hinges relieve bending forces at the root of the blade allowing coning of the rotor.

3. The flapping hinge reduces gust sensitivity due to the individual blade flap.

4. Flapping hinge bearing areas are subjected to heavy centrifugal loads.

5. The flapping hinge introduces geometric imbalance.

6. This geometric imbalance requires an additional drag hinge.

7. The drag hinge relieves bending stresses during acceleration of the rotor.

8. Drag hinge bearings are subject to high centrifugal loads.

A smoother operation might be obtained by the fully articulated rotor. However, until quite recently this could be obtained only by making a more complex rotor head. It is for this reason that the fully articulated head did not reach the great popularity that was attained by the semi-rigid rotor system.

I. Aerodynamic Characteristics

Regardless of the type of rotor system employed, there are a number of aerodynamic characteristics which are common to the main rotor system.

1. Translating tendency

One of these characteristics is the *translating tendency*. This is a tendency for the whole helicopter to drift in the direction of the tail rotor thrust. This is the result of the thrust of the tail rotor acting on the whole helicopter. The situation is normally corrected by offsetting the mast of the helicopter, which will change the tip path plane of the rotor. The built-in tilt of the rotor will cancel the translating tendency during hover of the helicopter. In other helicopters the tip path plane is altered by rigging the cyclic system to give the required tilt when the cyclic is level (Fig. 2-32).

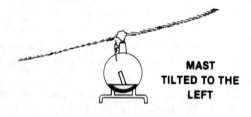

MAST TILTED TO THE LEFT

Fig. 2-32 Mast tilt is sometimes used to cancel translating tendency.

2. Ground effect

Another rotor characteristic is ground effect, and as the name implies, it appears when the helicopter is within one-half of a rotor diameter from the ground. What actually takes place is that the rotor is displacing air downward at a much faster rate than it can escape from beneath the helicopter. This air will become more dense and form an air cushion beneath the helicopter.

The cushion aids in supporting the helicopter while at hover in close proximity to the ground. If the helicopter moves from this position at a speed greater than 3 to 5 miles per hour, the ground effect will be lost.

3. Translational lift

Although the ground effect is lost as the helicopter gains forward speed, a new force makes its appearance as forward flight increases. This is called *translational lift*, an additional lift which is obtained when entering horizontal flight due to the increased efficiency of the rotor system. The inflow of air into the rotor during forward flight increases. The increase in flow also increases the mass of air at the rotor disc which in turn increases the lift.

Although this increase takes place any time the helicopter moves horizontally, it is readily noticed at an airspeed of 15 to 20 miles per hour. The additional lift which is available at this speed is referred to as *effective translational lift*. It might also be noted that since this is an effect of air speed and that it may happen at various points, including hover, if the wind velocity is great enough. It might also be noted that this additional lift will eventually be canceled by the increased drag of the fuselage.

A transverse flow effect takes place in the rotor system as forward flight begins because the air is being induced or pulled into the rotor system when the disc is tilted. The airflow at the rear of the disc is at a higher downwash angle than the air on the forward portion (Fig. 2-33). Because of this situation the lift-drag ratio will change between the rear and front portions of the disc with the greater lift being on the rear portion of the disc. The first noticeable effect on a semi-rigid rotor is a two-per-revolution beat and lateral cyclic feedback. The vibration happens when the rotor blades are in the fore and aft position. This lift-drag imbalance may also result in a roll force to the left as effective translational lift occurs. The roll effect is caused by gyroscopic precession of the rotor due to the imbalance. This tendency is not noticeable in fully articulated heads because of the effect of the hinges of the head. It might also be noted that as the forward speed of the helicopter is increased, the ram effect of the airflow will decrease the transverse flow effect of the rotor system and any results of this tendency

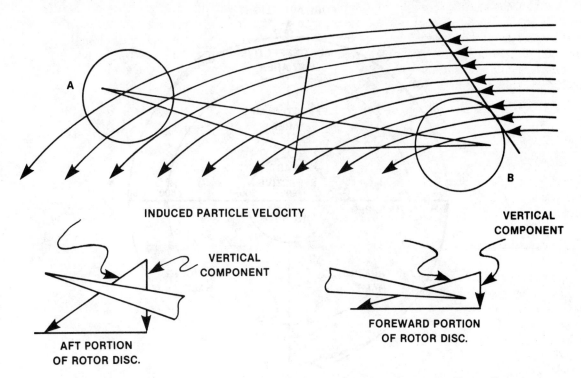

INDUCED PARTICLE VELOCITY

VERTICAL COMPONENT

VERTICAL COMPONENT

AFT PORTION OF ROTOR DISC.

FOREWARD PORTION OF ROTOR DISC.

Fig. 2-33   The variation in downward airflow causing the transverse flow effect.

will be unnoticeable at approximately 20 miles per hour of airspeed.

J. Blade Tip Stall

The helicopter rotor blades, like any airfoil, are subject to stall. However, a stall of the rotor is quite different from that of the fixed wing.

As a brief review, it was learned that in forward speed the advancing blade is moving at a faster speed than the retreating blade. As the speed of the helicopter increases this speed differential becomes greater.

Because of the dissymmetry of lift the retreating blade will be seeking a higher angle of attack than the advancing blade. This coupled with the low airspeed of the retreating blade can lead to *blade tip stall.*

An airfoil may stall due to any of the following reasons:

1. Insufficient airspeed

2. Too great an angle of attack

3. Heavy wing loading

In a helicopter flying at 200 miles per hours the advancing blade will have a tip speed of approximately 600 miles per hour while the retreating blade tip speed is reduced to 200 miles per hour (Fig 2-34). At this point the root areas are producing no lift. The retreating blade must continue to seek a higher angle of attack in order to maintain lift. Even though the blade has a twist built into it, the inflow of air into the rotor will be such that it will increase the angle of atack at the tips. This is due to the tilting of the rotor and its relationship to the inflow of air to the rotor.

It is not possible, however, to predict at what point the rotor will stall each time due to the forward speed because several other factors must also be considered. One of these is wing loading. It is more likely for the blade to stall under heavy loads than under light loads. Heavy loading will only decrease the speed at which the stall will occur. Other factors such as temperature, altitude, and maneuvers must also be considered. For these reasons a stall may occur at rather low operating speeds.

In Fig. 2-35 a view of a rotor system is shown with the stall area marked. It can be seen that as the tip enters the stall condition, only a few

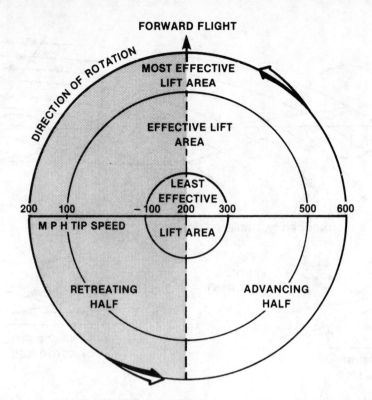

Fig. 2-34 Forward speed is a major factor in retreating blade stall.

inches are involved; but as the blade continues, several feet towards the middle of the blade travel in the stall area, and then it will move out toward the tip.

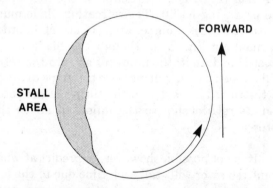

Fig. 2-35 Stall occurs first on the retreating half of the disc.

The indication of a stall condition will first be a vibration as each blade passes through the stall region. The beat could be 2:1, 3:1, or 4:1 depending upon the number of blades in the rotor system. If the stall continues, the helicopter will pitch up. Although the stall will occur on the left side of the helicopter due to the gyroscopic precession, the result will be at the tail of the helicopter, which will pitch the nose up.

When a stall is experienced, the corrective action is to reduce forward speed, reduce pitch, and increase rotor speed if possible; but the important factor is always to unload the rotor system.

K. Autorotation

Autorotation is the process of producing lift with the rotor blades as they freely rotate as a result of the flow of air up through the rotor system. This ability of the helicopter is one of the features which separates it from the fixed wing aircraft from a safety standpoint. With an engine or power train failure the rotor system will be disengaged leaving the rotor system to move freely in its original direction and produce lift allowing the helicopter to glide.

During normal operation of the helicopter the flow of air going through the main rotor is downward. When the engine is no longer producing power or it is disengaged from the rotor, the flow of air is upward. This upward flow of air through the rotor will allow the rotor to continue turning.

The autorotative region of the blade is an area approximately 25 - 75% of the blade which drives the rotor with the upward flow of air. The inner portion of the blade is known as the pro-

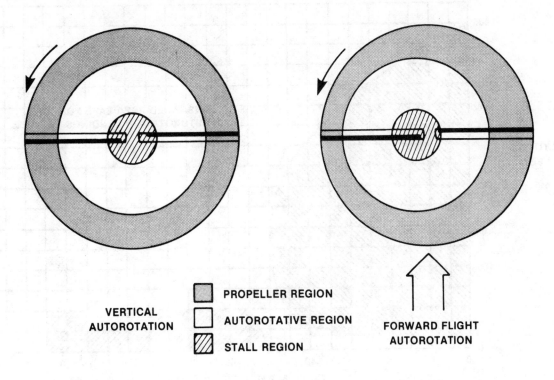

VERTICAL
AUTOROTATION

◼ PROPELLER REGION

☐ AUTOROTATIVE REGION

▨ STALL REGION

FORWARD FLIGHT
AUTOROTATION

Fig. 2-36   The autorotative region changes in forward flight.

peller region of the rotor. This area tends to slow down the tip speed of the rotor due to a small drag force. These regions are shown in Fig. 2-36.

During autorotation it is most important that the RPM of the rotor be controlled. When the aerodynamic forces of thrust and drag equalize on the rotor blades, the RPM of the rotor will stabilize. If the rotor entered an updraft, the RPM would increase and a general lessening of the angle of attack will follow along the entire blade. The change in the angle of attack will change the force vectors which will tend to slow the rotor down. The opposite will happen if the rotor is caught in a downdraft with the autorotative forces tending to accelerate the rotor back to normal speed. If the collective pitch remains constant an overall increase in the angle of attack will increase rotor RPM. For example: placing the helicopter in a flare. If the helicopter is tilted nose down the rotor RPM will decrease.

Once forward speed is established in the autorotative descent, the rotor disc may be inclined rearward. This will cause a flare. When this occurs, the greater lift will cause the forward speed to decrease and will cause the descent rate to

zero. When this occurs on landing the helicopter may be landed with no roll or skid.

Autorotation is most critical to forward speed as well as descent. The actual height in which successful autorotation may occur is directly dependent on the forward speed. Although an autorotation may be successfully completed at a 300-foot hover, it would not be possible at a 100-foot hover due to the inertia of the blade. At the 300-foot hover the blade will carry enough inertia to allow autorotation.

On most helicopters an area from approximately 12 feet to 300 feet would not be a safe area for autorotation without forward speed (Fig 2-37). It should be noted that autorotation characteristics are affected by the same elements that alter flight performance, such as density, altitude, and maximum weight.

It should also be noted that during autoroatation, the tail rotor will be at a negative pitch rather than a positive pitch as in normal flight. This is caused by the change in torque effect of the main rotor.

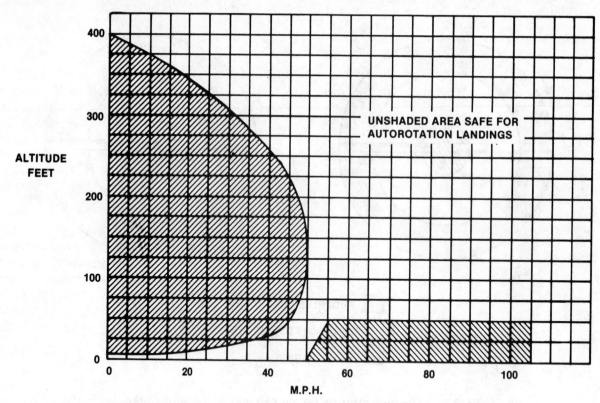

Fig. 2-37 Autorotation is not safe at low altitude and low airspeed.

L. Ground Resonance

Ground resonance is a self-excited vibration which, as the name implies, occurs on the ground. It may manifest slowly with a gradual buildup or it may appear very rapidly. If ground resonance is not corrected immediately, it will often destroy the helicopter. This problem is associated with fully articulated rotor systems and is the result of geometric imbalance of the main rotor system. The fully articulated head is hinged about the lead-lag axis in order to provide corrections for the corriolis effect. It is this correction factor which allows the rotor blades to become out-of-phase and result in ground resonance.

What actually occurs is that the blades take abnormal positions, one blade leads while the adjacent blade lags. This unbalances the rotor which moves the center of gravity of the rotor off center. This imbalance of the rotor causes an oscillation which is transmitted throughout the whole helicopter giving movement from side to side as well as fore and aft. If this action becomes violent enough it may roll the helicopter over or cause structural damage.

This situation may be further aggravated by the reaction of the helicopter and the ground through the gear struts and wheels. During landing a set of blades that are already out-of-phase may be further aggravated by the touchdown, especially on a one-wheel landing such as occurs on a slope landing or with a flat tire or strut.

When this occurs the forces of the vibration cannot be absorbed by the strut or tire and a counterwave is sent back through the helicopter usually resulting in further imbalance of the rotor.

Although ground resonance is associated with landing, it may also occur during ground run-up or during takeoff when the helicopter is partially airborne. It will be further aggravated by incorrect strut pressure and tire inflation.

When this situation occurs, immediate power application and takeoff will stop this condition by changing the natural frequencies of the helicopter. In recent years the manufacturers have reduced these occurrences considerably by redesigning the dampeners, oleo struts, tires, and the gears.

66

M. Stability

Stability is a term used to describe the behavior of an aircraft after it has been disturbed from its trimmed position.

1. Static stability

Statically stable means that after a disturbance the tendency is to return to its original position as shown in Fig. 2-38. If an object is statically unstable, it will continue to move in the direction of the disturbance as seen in Fig. 2-39.

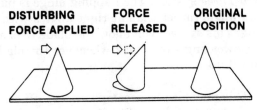

POSITIVE STATIC STABILITY

Fig. 2-38 All aircraft must be able to demonstrate stability.

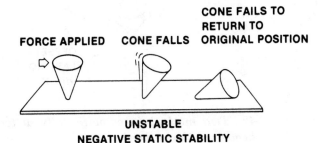

**UNSTABLE
NEGATIVE STATIC STABILITY**

Fig. 2-39 Negative stability will result in problems of controlability.

If the helicopter is statically unstable and a disturbance pitched the nose upward the helicopter would continue upward. If it were statically stable it would try to return to its normal position.

2. Dynamic stability

Dynamic stability is related to all objects that possess static stability. This term is used to describe the behavior of the object after the disturbance. If an object continues to oscillate at the same rate after a disturbance it is said to be of neutral dynamic stability. If the object continues to oscillate at a slower rate after the initial disturbance, it has positive dynamic stability.

The helicopter is usually considered statically stable and dynamically unstable if the pilot keeps the controls in a fixed position after a disturbance (Fig. 2-40). This instability is greater in the longitudinal direction than in the lateral direction which is mainly due to the inertia of the tail. In other words most helicopters are directionally stable.

3. Causes of instability

It must be remembered that the helicopter obtains forward flight by tilting the rotor. If any change to the rotor tilt occurs the helicopter will move in that direction. For this reason there are three basic items that contribute to the dynamic instability of the helicopter. They are as follows:

1. *The rotor disc will follow the fuselage.* Any pitch of the fuselage about its axis will cause a pitch change to the rotor head through the cyclic controls. This in turn will affect the blade flapping which will tilt the rotor disc in the direction of the disturbance. This will cause the pitch to accelerate in the direction of the disturbance.

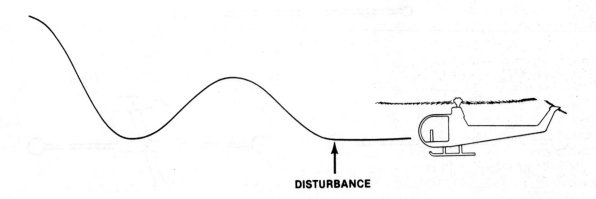

DISTURBANCE

Fig. 2-40 The helicopter is usually considered statically stable and dynamically unstable.

2. *A change in speed will cause the rotor to tilt. As speed in increased, the rotor will tend to tilt backwards. If the speed is decreased, the rotor will tend to tilt forward. This will accelerate the movements of the helicopter.*

3. *A change in the rotor system speed will cause the center of gravity to oscillate the tilt of the fuselage which in turn will aggravate the rotor disc.* This is because the helicopter's center of gravity is below the rotor head.

The helicopter will tend to repeat the motions with increasing magnitude because these conditions cannot be tolerated in helicopters without a correction factor. Some of the methods used to correct this situation are as follows:

4. *The Bell method*

The Bell method makes use of a stabilizer bar which acts as a gyroscope with the property of rigidity. Once the object is in motion, it tends to stay in its same plane of rotation. Control levers from the cyclic are attached to the stabilizer bar with mixing levers attached to the pitch change of the rotor head (Fig. 2-41). By using this method the rotor remains independent of the mast, so any tilt of the rotor head is automatically corrected by the mixing levers of the stabilizer bar and any movement of the fuselage is not transmitted to the rotor. In recent years this stabilizer bar

system has been eliminated on some of the newer models because of new designs.

5. *The offset hinge*

The offset hinge is used on some of the fully articulated helicopters in order to correct for dynamic instability. Placing the flapping hinges of the rotor more outboard of the mast allows the movement to take place further from the center of gravity of the fuselage.

Another method that has been used is the *Delta Three* system. The flapping hinge is placed at an angle rather than at right angles with the blade. This system will allow the blade to change to a lower angle of attack whenever the blade is flapped up.

This may also be accomplished by off setting the pitch-change horn (Fig. 2-42).

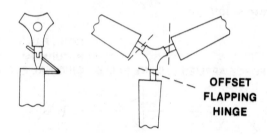

OFFSET
FLAPPING
HINGE

Fig. 2-42 Two methods used with fully articulated heads are shown here.

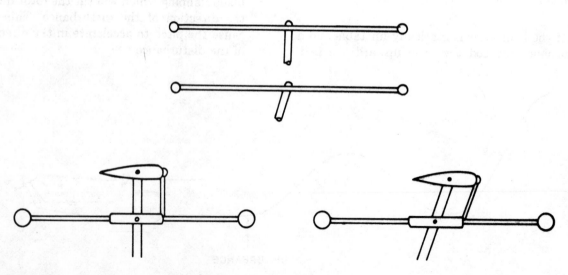

Fig. 2-41 The stabilizer bar is the most common method used to obtain dynamic stability on semi-rigid rotors.

N. Flight Control

This section has dealt mainly with the main rotor system, but there are other factors that affect the flight characteristics of the helicopter.

The helicopter has three basic controls that are used to control its flight. These are the collective, the anti-torque pedals, and the cyclic control (Fig. 2-43).

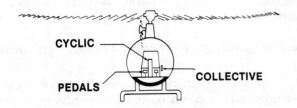

Fig. 2-43 Controls used to maintain flight.

1. Collective

The collective is a lever which is located on the left side of the pilot's seat. The lever pivots from the aft end and moves up and down. When the collective is moved upward, the pitch of all the rotor blades increases simultaneously, causing the helicopter to increase altitude. When the collective is lowered the pitch of the blades decreases, decreasing the altitude of the helicopter. The purpose of the collective is primarily an altitude control.

This movement of the collective increases the pitch of the rotor blades which also increases the amount of power required to maintain the same rotor RPM. For this reason most reciprocating

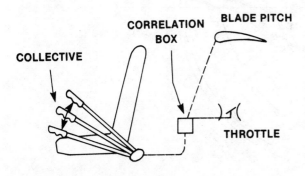

Fig. 2-44 Raising of the collective requires more engine power.

powerplant helicopters have additional linkage attached to the collective in order to increase the throttle linkage as the collective is raised. This addition is referred to as the correlation linkage or correlation box because it provides the correct relationship between the engine power and the rotor pitch (Fig. 2-44).

On turbine-powered helicopters two different systems are used. The free turbine engines make use of a cam, referred to as a compensating cam, which feeds a signal to the fuel control as collective is added to increase the power output. On the direct-drive turbine engines a constant RPM is maintained by a governor on the engine, and no linkage is required between the collective and the engine.

2. Anti-torque pedals

The anti-torque pedals are sometimes referred to as the rudder pedals. They are operated by the pilot's feet and change the pitch of the tail rotor which is used to control the torque of the main rotor. In addition to the anti-torque correction, the pitch of the tail rotor is changed to give the helicopter heading control. During takeoff the power applied to the main rotor is at its maximum. At this time the highest positive pitch will be required by the tail rotor. This is added to the tail rotor by depressing the left pedal on U.S.-made helicopters.

NOTE: Foreign-made helicopters have main rotors that turn in the clockwise direction, which means that the torque will react in the opposite direction requiring right pedal to be added during takeoff. During cruising flight, the pedals are held in the neutral position which applies some positive pitch to the tail rotor in order to correct for the lesser amount of torque applied by the main rotor.

The right pedal is applied when it is desirable to move the nose of the helicopter to the right. This moves the tail rotor pitch to a negative angle. By applying the left pedal the nose of the aircraft may be moved to the left (Fig. 2-45).

In addition to giving directional control to the helicopter under engine power, the tail rotor must be able to supply negative thrust during autorotation.

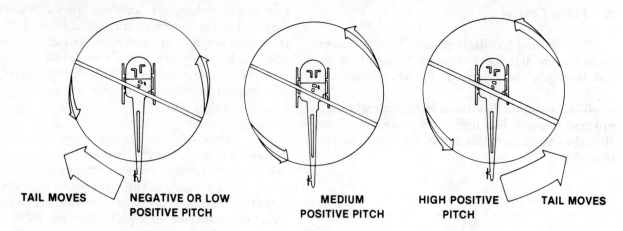

TAIL MOVES — **NEGATIVE OR LOW POSITIVE PITCH**   **MEDIUM POSITIVE PITCH**   **HIGH POSITIVE PITCH** — **TAIL MOVES**

Fig. 2-45   The movement of the anti-torque pedals are directly related to the amount of main rotor pitch.

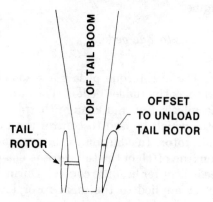

TOP OF TAIL BOOM

OFFSET TO UNLOAD TAIL ROTOR

TAIL ROTOR

Fig. 2-46   The offset fin method is often used to unload the tail rotor.

Since the tail rotor absorbs power from the engine which could be used to produce lift and thrust, it is advantageous to unload the tail rotor as much as possible in forward flight. This is usually accomplished by a vertical fin on the tail of the helicopter. This fin is often offset from the centerline assisting in torque correction during forward flight (Fig. 2-46).

Another system used is the ducted fan tail rotor (Fig. 2-47). With this system the shroud of the tail rotor is an airfoil which assists in creating thrust eliminating some of the power requirement.

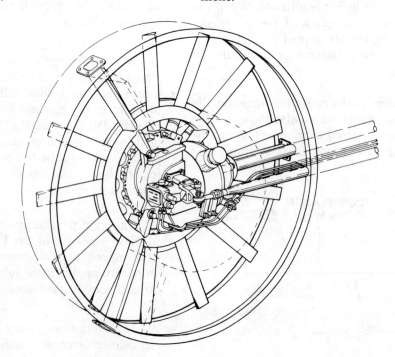

Fig. 2-47   The ducted fan may be used to increase the tail rotor efficiency.

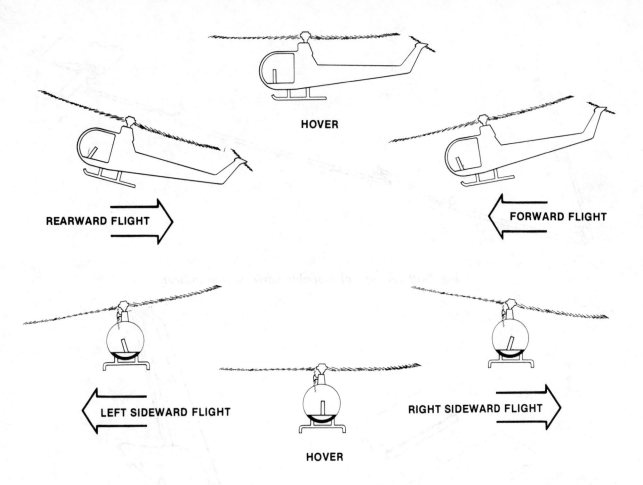

HOVER

REARWARD FLIGHT

FORWARD FLIGHT

LEFT SIDEWARD FLIGHT

RIGHT SIDEWARD FLIGHT

HOVER

Fig. 2-48 The cyclic control is used to obtain directional control of the helicopter.

3. Cyclic control

The cyclic control is used to tilt the tip path plane of the main rotor. This moves the thrust of the rotor and lift of the helicopter, pulling the helicopter in the direction of the tip path plane. As the cyclic is moved forward, the disc tilts forward moving the helicopter forward. Likewise, when the cyclic is moved aft, the disc moves aft moving the helicopter aft. The cyclic may also be moved from side to side moving the helicopter sideways (Fig. 2-48). This tilt of the main rotor is accomplished by changing the pitch of each individual rotor blade 90° prior to the displacement of the cyclic stick because of gyroscopic precession.

Sometimes the cyclic linkage of the main rotor is connected to a horizontal stabilizer placed on the tail of the helicopter. This is sometimes referred to as an elevator. However, its function is different than that of a fixed wing elevator. In cruise flight the normal tendency is for the tail of the helicopter to be high and the nose to be low due to the thrust of the main rotor. This tendency increases the drag ratio, undesirable when speed is important. For this reason, the stabilizer keeps the tail down so that a level flight attitude may be maintained. Under other circumstances, such as takeoffs, it may be desirable to fly in a nose-down attitude in order to build up airspeed by obtaining maximum thrust from the main rotor. At this time the stabilizer may be used to allow the tail to come up, allowing the maximum thrust to be obtained as in a landing configuration. It is important that the nose be allowed to come up and be brought down. This may also be assisted by the movable stabilizer (Fig. 2-49).

On some helicopters the horizontal stabilizer is fixed in one position and may be shaped as an inverted airfoil forcing the tail downward with a spoiler strip for flares (Fig. 2-50). Some of the

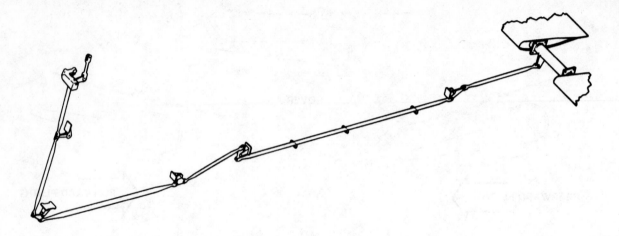

Fig. 2-49   A typical movable horizontal stabilizer.

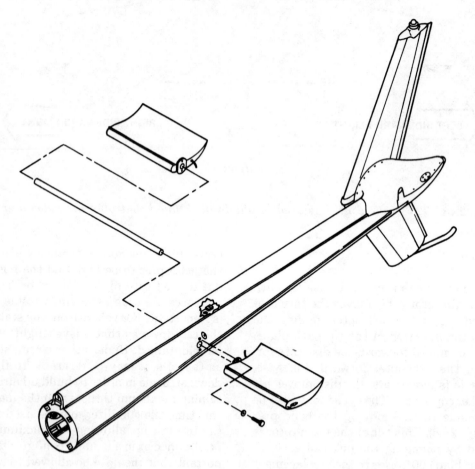

Fig. 2-50   A typical fixed position horizontal stabilizer.

newer helicopters are moving the stabilizer electronically in order to meet the demands of the helicopter's airspeed and attitude.

   This discussion of the principles of helicopter flight is by no means complete, but should be sufficient to help the maintenance technician to understand more thoroughly the principles regarding various maintenance practices that are performed on helicopters.

16. The most widely used airfoil for helicopters is the symmetrical airfoil.

    A. True

    B. False

17. Which blade is traveling faster in relation to the air in forward flight?

    A. Advancing

    B. Retreating

18. In flight, rotor droop is overcome by:

    A. centrifugal force.

    B. centrifugal force and lift.

    C. coning force.

19. The fastest moving point on the blade is at the:

    A. tip.

    B. root.

    C. Both move at the same speed.

20. The amount of coning of the rotor is dependent upon the weight of the helicopter.

    A. True

    B. False

21. The feathering axis is the same as the pitch axis.

    A. True

    B. False

22. Twist is often built into the blade to improve the lift of the whole blade.

    A. True

    B. False

23. In forward flight, more lift is created on the _____ blade.

    A. Advancing

    B. Retreating

24. Blades may flap independently to correct for dissymmetry of lift.

    A. True

    B. False

25. The drag hinge is used to correct for dissymmetry of lift.

    A. True

    B. False

26. The semi-rigid rotor and the fully articulated rotor utilize independent flapping of the blades.

    A. True

    B. False

27. The semi-rigid rotor is smoother than the fully articulated rotor.

    A. True

    B. False

28. Blade stall will occur on the _____ blade first.

    A. Advancing

    B. Retreating

29. Autorotation is possible from all altitudes regardless of the airspeed.

    A. True

    B. False

30. Ground resonance is a self-excited vibration found in fully articulated rotors.

    A. True

    B. False

SECTION III

Documentation, Publications, and Historical Records

The helicopter, like the fixed wing aircraft, has a certain amount of documentation and publications which attest to the airworthiness of the aircraft. This paperwork not only assures the legal but the physical airworthiness of the helicopter. In many instances the same paperwork is utilized by both fixed wing aircraft and helicopters. However, in other instances the helicopter has additional requirements. The common items will be discussed quite briefly and detail will be presented for the additional information that is required.

A. FAA Publications

The FAA material mainly covers the same areas that are covered for the fixed wing aircraft. However, some of the material varies slightly from the fixed wing due to the flight capabilities and the differences in the mechanical operation.

1. Federal Air Regulations

Federal Air Regulations are written for both fixed wing and rotary wing aircraft. Many of these apply to both types while some apply to one or the other.

The first of these to be observed by the maintenance personnel are the FARs regarding the requirements for airworthiness. The rotor wing aircraft are covered by FAR Parts 27 and 29. Part 27 refers to Normal Category Rotorcraft and Part 29 refers to Transport Category Rotorcraft. These regulations refer to the requirements for the certification of helicopters and contain the same type of information that is found in Parts 23 and 25 which apply to fixed wing aircraft.

In addition to those parts that refer to External Load Operations and Scheduled Air Carriers, the other FARs which are familiar to fixed wing aircraft, such as 43, 91, 135, and 137, refer to both fixed wing and rotorcraft. Additional information may be contained regarding rotorcraft.

One of the FARs containing additional information is FAR 43. In this publication rotorcraft are referred to in two specific areas which are of importance to maintenance personnel. These areas read as follows: FAR 43.15(b) states: "Each person performing a 100-hour, annual, or progressive inspection of a rotorcraft shall inspect the following systems in accordance with the maintenance manual of the manufacturer concerning:

1. driveshafts or similar systems,

2. the main rotor transmission gearbox for obvious defects,

3. the main rotor and center section (or equivalent area), and

4. the auxiliary rotor on helicopters."

FAR 43.16 has a paragraph which reads as follows: "For rotorcraft for which a Rotorcraft Maintenance Manual containing an 'Airworthiness Limitations' section has been issued, each person performing an inspection or other work specified in that section of the manual shall perform the inspection or work in accordance with that section of the manual."

These two paragraphs are quite typical of the additional information that may be contained in the FARs applying to both fixed wing and rotary aircraft.

2. Type certificate data sheets

In addition to FARs the rotorcraft have the same type certificate information as do the fixed wing. These are either in the form of Aircraft Specification Sheets or Aircraft Specification Data Sheets as are found in Volume 4 of the

Specifications. They usually follow the same format as the fixed wing specifications. There are, however, variations in these sheets, such as maximum rotor limits, that are peculiar to helicopters. The retirement time of various components is always mentioned either by listing the various components that have finite lives or by referring to the maintenance manual section which contains this information.

Most sheets have a note stating that the helicopter must be maintained in conformance with the instructions given by the manufacturer.

Many of the civilian helicopters are either military derivatives or have military counterparts. Additional information may be given as to where the information or the conversion data are to be obtained.

3. Airworthiness directives and certificates

The airworthiness directives and inspection information are handled in the same manner for rotorcraft as for fixed wing aircraft, and are contained in the same summary and bi-weekly directives.

Other documentation such as the *airworthiness certificate* is issued by the FAA at the time of manufacture or when the helicopter receives its original airworthiness inspection. For example, a military surplus helicopter may have an airworthiness certificate issued long after the manufacture or the aircraft may have been moved to a "restricted" category only, as is often the situation with surplus military aircraft. This document remains in the aircraft and is valid as long as it is maintained in accordance with the FAR.

4. Registration

The second document that is found in the aircraft is the Aircraft Registration. This simply states who the owner of the aircraft is, and his address at the date given.

All aircraft are required to carry a current Weight and Balance Report and Equipment List. This may have been issued by the manufacturer or may have been made up during the life of the helicopter. These documents may vary somewhat from those normally found with fixed wing aircraft with movable ballast and lateral centers of gravity on the Weight and Balance Report. Their explanations will be contained in the operator's manual. The equipment may also be different because many of the older generations of helicopters have been updated several times in an effort to improve them. This is done by the use of kits, service bulletins, and supplemental type certificates. All of these will show up on the Equipment List and the Weight and Balance Report.

B. Maintenance Records

1. Retirement schedule

In addition to these documents found on all aircraft, the helicopter must have a *retirement schedule*. This schedule is a historical record of the critical parts which have a finite life. They indicate that certain parts of the helicopter are to be scrapped after the flight-hour requirement has been reached. The service life of these components depends upon the continual stresses imposed upon them and the service record of the like component. In many instances, these lives have been extended or shortened as information about the part has been obtained. Sometimes a part with no finite life has been given a retirement life while others have gone from having a finite life to being a conditional item.

This record is the responsibility of the owner and operator, but it is usually kept up to date by the maintenance technician. Items which might have finite lives would be rotor hubs, blades, and other rotating parts. If these records are lost or destroyed, it can become very difficult to establish the time on the component. Estimates of time in service are not permitted, and no option is open except for the technician to replace any item with a finite life when the time cannot be established. The loss of these records on one helicopter could amount to thousands of dollars in replaced parts.

The system used in keeping these records varies considerably from one operator to another. The most common systems are of three basic types — the sheet method, the card method, and the computer method. In some situations a combination system is used to insure that no costly errors are made. The system utilized usually depends upon the number of helicopters operated and the components owned in order to support the helicopters.

For example: the single-ship operator who is involved in seasonal work will probably schedule the major inspections and overhauls of components in the off-season. For this reason his spare components will be limited or non-existant. In this situation the same components would always return to the same helicopter making recordkeeping quite simple, and even on a single piece of paper often attached to the logbook. This record would contain the following information: the part number, serial number, aircraft time when installed, the time on the component when installed, the hour-life of the part and the aircraft time when it is to be removed (Fig. 3-1)

a. Sheet and card methods

However, the operator who owns several of the same type of helicopter and operates on a year-round basis will have spare components in his inventory so that a maximum utilization factor might be realized. In this situation the major inspection and overhaul of components will consist of exchange units rather than the buildup of the same components on the same ship. In this situation components may be removed prematurely for repairs and a different component used rather than grounding the helicopter while repairs are made. It is necessary for this type of operator to use a card system in order to keep the records of parts with finite lives. Basically the same information that was kept on the sheet would be kept on the card, but it should also include the helicopter on which it is installed. A number of cards may be placed together to form the retirement schedule of parts on a helicopter. Fig. 3-2 shows a sample parts card.

b. Computer method

When a helicopter operation becomes still larger, the possibility of the same component ever returning to the same ship becomes more remote and several sets of components are kept as spares. The task of the retirement schedule becomes monumental. It may become even more complicated by maintenance crew changes and distances from the maintenance facility, so a computerized system is established. With this type of system maintenance is scheduled, components are shipped, and accuracy is maintained. Such a system often includes other information such as recurring AD notes and overhaul schedules. It may also be used to analyze maintenance trends to include extended life on components. A sample of this type of form is shown in Fig. 3-3.

2. Overhaul or major inspection records

In addition to a retirement schedule an overhaul or major inspection record is kept on the rotating components of the helicopter. These, like the mandatory retirement schedule, may be kept in several systems such as the sheet, card, or computer method. The system which is used is the owner's preference and is usually combined with the retirement schedule — not only because of the convenience but because it gives a better overall view of the maintenance.

The information as to the life of the component or part is obtained from either the Aircraft Specification Sheet or the Manufacturer's Maintenance Manual. The maintenance manual is updated more often. If the operator keeps up with the amendments, the information will be most accurate.

Like the fixed wing operator, the helicopter operator keeps a Service Bulletin and an Airworthiness Directive Record on the aircraft. This is usually kept separate from the aircraft's logbook, but may be incorporated into it in small operations. It must be understood, however, that such a list does not replace an entry. It is used to simplify the search for compliances and items of a recurring nature.

3. Logbooks

The logbooks (or logs as they are called), like the other helicopter records, vary from operator to operator. With the small one ship operation they often appear much the same as those found with any small general aviation aircraft with replacement of parts and inspections written in by hand.

For many of the newer helicopters and larger operations, books in which the material is analyzed in order to determine maintenance trends and life expectancies for the helicopter are available. These include carbon copies of each page to be sent to operation's headquarters and used for logistic support purposes. These include billing, cost analysis, spare parts, and necessary computer information including finite life and overhaul time. In some of these logs an additional page is sent to the manufacturer, who uses this information to analyze the product for product improvement and spare part support as well as to detect maintenance trends that could result in the

Bell Helicopter, Model D-1
Serial #476, N2215
Date of Mfg., June 1952

COMPONENT TIMES and OVERHAUL
or RETIREMENT SCHEDULE
DATE 4-12-78   A/C   TT 3828.5 Hrs.

COMPONENT	ACFT TT WHEN NEW	ACFT TT WHEN LAST OVERHAULED	REPLACE OR OVERHAUL ACFT TT	TACH TIME
M/R Hub yoke 47-120-177-1	2731.5	3739.2	6331.5	3343.3
Inspect	NA	NA	4339.2	1351.0
M/R Grip S.N. SR-01017 47-120-135-5	3828.5	NA	6328.5	3354.6
Inspect	NA	NA	4339.2	1351.0
M/R Grip S.N. SR-00953 47-120-135-5	3828.5	NA	6328.5	3354.6
Inspect	NA	NA	4339.2	1351.0
Gimble Ring S.N. RE-1505 47-120-014-023	3828.5	NA	5028.5	2054.6
Inspect	NA	NA	4339.2	1351.0
Mast 47-130-114-7	1967.8	3739.2	Unlimited	
Inspect	NA	NA	4339.2	1351.0
Mast Controls	2903.3	3739.2	Unlimited	
Inspect	NA	NA	4339.2	1351.0
T/R Blade Grip Retaining Bolts 47-641-194-1	3828.5	NA	4428.5	1454.6
Inspect	NA	NA	4339.5	1351.0
T/R Hub yoke S.N. N29-1395 (34 Hr. since new when installed)	3828.5	NA	4194.5	1220.6
T/R Shafting (R) 47-644-187-17 (F) 47-644-180- 9 (M) 47-644-180-11	3739.2	NA	Unlimited	
Inspect	NA	NA	4339.2	1351.0
T/R Gear box 47-640-044-7	2848.5	3739.2	Unlimited	
Inspect	NA	NA	4039.2	1051.0
T/R Blades 47-642-102-49	3739.2	NA	4339.2	1351.0
Inspect	NA	NA	4039.2	1051.0
Engine YO-355-5 S.N. E-590135 (7 Hr. since new when installed)	3828.5	NA	4421.5	1447.6
Fan Belts 47-661-041-3	3828.5	NA	4728.5	1754.6
Inspect (Check tension every 50 hrs.)				
Transmission 47-620-600-5	------	3739.2	4339.2	1351.0
Inspect (Inspect clutch shoes at 300 hr.)				
Engine Mount 47-612-135-1	2988.2	3739.2	5488.2	2500.0
Inspect	NA	NA	4039.2	1051.0

END OF PAGE ONE

Fig. 3-1   Sheet method used for retirement and overhaul schedule.

NOMENCLATURE ____________________

OWNER ____________________

PAGE __________ OF __________

> NOTICE: WHEN COMPONENT IDENTIFIED BELOW IS RETURNED TO BHC. FOR A REASON IT IS MANDATORY THAT THIS SERVICE RECORD ACCOMPANY THE COMPONENT
>
> P/N __________ SER. NO. __________

HISTORICAL SERVICE RECORD

INSTALLATION DATA						REMOVAL DATA				
DATE	INSTALLED ON A/C#	BY (ACTIVITY)	INSTALLED AT A/C HRS	COMP. HRS.		DATE	REMOVED AT A/C HRS	COMPL HRS		REASON FOR REMOVAL
				SINCE NEW	SINCE O/H			SINCE NEW	SINCE O/H	

TECHNICAL DIRECTIVES AND HISTORY OVERHAUL					
DIRECTIVE NO. IF APPLICABLE	PRIORITY OR STATUS	DESCRIPTION	COMPLIANCE		SIGNATURE
			BY (ACTIVITY)	DATE	

Fig. 3-2 Card method used for keeping records.

COMPONENT ASSY. OR PART	SERIAL NOS.	ITEM TOTAL TIME PRIOR TO INSTL.	HELICOPTER OR COMPONENT T.T.		T.T. ON PART ASSY. OR COMPONENT
			AT INSTL.	AT REMOVAL	
NAME:					
NO:					
NAME:					
NO:					
NAME:					
NO:					
NAME:					
NO:					
NAME:					
NO:					
NAME:					
NO:					
NAME:					
NO:					
NAME:					
NO:					
NAME:					
NO:					
NAME:					
NO:					
NAME:					
NO:					
NAME:					
NO:					
NAME:					
NO:					
NAME:					
NO:					

Fig. 3-2 Card method continued.

DATE PAINTED 01/76	MODEL CODE 30		REPORT DATE 9/20/78	DATE LAST FLIGHT 9/18/78		MODEL NO. 2068		REG. NO. N 7612S
COMPONENT	DESCRIPTION	SERVICE LIFE	COMP S/N	T.T. OR CYCLE	T.S.I. T.S.O.	TIME TO O/H OR INSP.	RETIRE-CYC OR T.T.	REMOVE AT A/C HOURS
100000	A/F IN DUE 8/00/79	UL	5	10339.50				
100900	* TURB TEMP SYS	300 IN		10339.50	194.15	105.45		10445 *
101000	ENGINE C-20	UL	CAE-821029	2992.50				
101900	COMPRESSOR	3000 OH	CAC-30282	5221.50	2011.50	988.10		11328
102100	IMPELLER 6876873	3050 RT	H-29021	2729.05			320.55	10660
102200	IMPELLER CYC	9150 CY	H-29021	5144.			4006	
103000	GEARBOX ASSY	UL	CAG-31041	2992.50				
103009	TURB-AD 77-15-12	500 IN	CAT-38088P	2679.05	121.55	378.05		10717
103900	TURBINE-W/RIM	1500 IN	CAT-38088P	2679.05	1200.35	299.25		10639
103901	TURBINE-W/RIM	3000 OH	CAT-38088P	2679.05	2679.05	320.55		10660
104100	1ST STG WHL	1550 RT	X47087	1200.35			349.25	10689
104200	1ST STG CYC	3000 CY	X47087	2298.			702	
104300	2ND STG WHL	1550 RT	X33893	1200.35			349.25	10689
104400	2ND STG CYC	3000 CY	X33893	2298.			702	
104500	3RD STG WHL	4550 RT	X33530	2679.05			1870.55	12210
104600	3RD STG CYC	6000 CY	X33530	4127.			1873	
104700	4TH STG WHL	4550 RT	X27333	2679.05			1870.55	12210
104800	4TH STG CYC	6000 CY	X27333	4127.			1873	
105000	F/C-A11-A10	3500 OH	4AAC2826	3123.45	3123.45	376.15		10716
105500	FUEL NOZZLE	1500 OH	AG-27939	UNK	1011.15	488.45		10828
107000	GOV-A13	2000 OH	7AAD4100	367.10	367.10	1632.50		11972
108000	*#FUEL PUMP-SE	750 IN	PE-2746	UNK	619.20	130.40		10470#*
109000	FUEL PUMP-SE	2250 OH	PE-2746	UNK	1306.05	943.55		11283
110000	BLEED VALVE	2000 OH	FF-11907	5270.15	994.25	1005.35		11345
110500	#OIL FILTER	1000 RT	1921	546.20			453.40	10793#
110600	FUEL FILTER 6 Mo							
110605	INSP DUE 12/00/78							
110900	STARTER GEN	300 IN	14859	906.15	44.40	255.20		10595
111000	#STARTER GEN	600 OH	14859	906.15	333.55	266.05		10605#
112000	#BOOST PUMP	500 IN	G0086A	5236.50	171.20	328.40		10668#
113000	#BOOST PUMP	500 IN	G-0012	6946.00	333.55	166.05		10505#
114000	INPUT DR SHAFT	600 IN	ALF-60140	6618.15	2.35	597.25		10937
116100	TRANS-25	2600 OH	BKW-10660	4371.00	2190.00	410.00		10749
117000	FREEWHEEL	2400 OH	B12-5813	UNK	1475.15	924.45		11264
118000	MAST	2600 OH	NJF-51001	4220.35	2167.50	432.10		10772
118800	SWASHPLATE	600 IN	JIJG-51110	4330.25	391.45	208.15		10548
118900	SWASHPLATE	900 IN	JIJG-51110	4330.25	391.45	508.15		10848
119000	SWASHPLATE	1200 IN	JIJG-51110	4330.25	391.45	808.15		11148
119200	SWASHPLATE	2400 OH	JIJG-51110	4330.25	1578.50	821.10		11161
120000	COLL IDLER LINK	4800 RT	J119-2960	4330.25			469.35	10809
120100	COLL LEVER	4800 RT	J119-2740	4330.25			469.35	10809
120300	SWASHPLATE SUPT	4800 RT	TR-003	1578.50			3221.10	13561

Fig. 3-3 Typical computer method for keeping records.

DATE PAINTED 01/76 COMPONENT DESCRIPTION	MODEL CODE 30		SERVICE LIFE	REPORT DATE 9/20/78 COMP S/N	DATE LAST FLIGHT 9/18/78 T.T. OR CYCLE	T.S.I. T.S.O.	TIME TO O/H OR INSP.	MODEL NO. 2068 RETIRE-CYC OR T.T.	REG. NO. N 7612S REMOVE AT A/C HOURS
120500	SW/PLATE SLEEVE	4800	RT	J119-3674	3423.30			1378.30	11716
120600	DUPLEX BRNG	2400	RT	6261	1578.50			821.10	11161
121000	M/R YOKE	1200	OH	JI1-2164	6393.20	938.00	262.00		10801
121100	RET STRAP FIT	1200	RT	J1-2564	938.00			262.00	10601
121105	RET STRAP FIT	1200	RT	J1-5019	938.00			262.00	10601
121300	RET STRAP PIN	1200	RT	A19-19887	938.00			262.00	10601
121305	RET STRAP PIN	1200	RT	A19-19915	938.00			262.00	10601
121500	RET STRAP	1200	RT	3225	660.20			539.40	10879
121505	RET STRAP	1200	RT	3217	660.20			539.40	10879
121700	M/R GRIP	1200	IN	J11-6010	4271.20	938.00	262.00		10601
121705	M/R GRIP	4800	RT	J11-6010	4271.20			528.40	10868
121710	M/R GRIP	1200	IN	J11-6181	4271.20	938.00	262.00		10601
121715	M/R GRIP	4800	RT	J11-6181	4271.20			528.40	10868
122100	M/R BLADE-33	3600	RT	TKK-6012	2741.55			858.05	11197
122105	M/R BLADE-33	3600	RT	TKK-2836	3313.15			286.45	10626
125000	#SERVO-750-17	2400	OH	951	9418.25	21.00	2379.00		12718#
126000	#SERVO-750-009	2400	OH	3353	8362.40	1170.25	1229.35		11569#
127000	#SERVO 750-17	2400	OH	1000	9254.00	1046.25	1353.35		11693#
131000	SHAFT #4-SBC/W	1500	OH	VNLB17280	6805.10	1081.10	418.50		10758
132000	*T/R SHAFT LUB	300	IN		194.15	194.15	105.45		10445#*
132001	SERVO T/R	2400	OH	368	7877.25	1684.15	715.45		11055
133000	T/R GEAR BOX-O/S	2800	OH	ALO-10627	5036.55	789.10	2010.50		12350
134000	T/R HUB	2400	OH	J129-2196	2215.10	21.00	2379.00		12718
136000	T/R BLADE	1200	RT	TKM-6641	21.00			1179.00	11518
136005	T/R BLADE	1200	RT	TKM-6812	21.00			1179.00	11518
143000	TAIL BOOM-11	UL		NNJN-0235	10678.25				
145000	LOWER COLL TUBE	4800	RT	MS-1046	757.20			4042.40	14382
146000	* T/R CNTR TUBE	300	IN	PHIN7612S	10339.50	194.15	105.45		10445 *
147000	FLOAT INSP DUE 12/00/78								
147500	L/FLOAT-13313575								
148000	R/FLOAT-13278475								

74 TOTAL COMPONENTS

Fig. 3-3 Computer sheet continued.

issuance of Service Bulletins. Others send this additional page directly to a computer service which specializes in aircraft maintenance service. These companies perform the same essential services that the operator would in regard to furnishing information for logistical support.

C. Manufacturer's Publications

Besides the necessary records of the helicopter, there is a wide range of materials written by the manufacturer. These include such items as the Operator's Manuals, Maintenance Manuals, Service Bulletins, Overhaul Manuals, Advisory Letters, and Inspection Manuals. It is most unfortunate that at this time no standardization has taken place for all helicopters. An effort is being made, however, by all aircraft manufacturers to standardize the maintenance and parts manuals with the Airline Transport Association (ATA) system format. This appears to be the standardization system that will be adapted throughout the aviation industry. This system has been in use for several years on transport aircraft. It only recently has been adopted by general aviation and the helicopter industry. For this reason both types of manuals will be found in use today with the newer aircraft manuals following the ATA system and the older aircraft following the company system, which was usually adapted from the military format. A change in the manuals on the older aircraft is not likely to occur because of the cost of reproducing this material. Therefore, until the older helicopters are no longer in operation, there will not be a complete standardization accomplished. This slow process will probably take at least twenty years or more to evolve.

1. Operator's manual

The first of the manufacturers publications to be discussed is the *operator's manual* which is sometimes referred to as the *flight manual*. At this time most manufacturers follow about the same format regarding the information contained and the order or sections in which it is presented.

a. First section

The first section contains the operating limitation of the helicopter, which would include the general weight and balance limitations, the engine limitations to include temperatures, RPMs and power, the rotor limitations including minimum and maximum, operating RPM, autoro-

tation RPM, and correction factors if any are required. It will also include any placard information. For example: "Maximum Allowable Weight in Cabin — 440 pounds" or "Protracted Rearward Flight Prohibited."

b. Second section

The second section of the manual contains operating procedures, which would include preflight inspection, servicing requirements, such as fuel and oil, pre-operation cockpit check, starting procedure, warm-up and ground check and shutdown procedure. It will also include emergency procedures such as engine failure, tail rotor failure and hydraulic failure.

c. Third section

The third section includes performance information such as maximum rate of climb with variables like temperature, altitude, and weight; hovering performance charts, airspeed correction charts, and power calculations.

d. Fourth section

The fourth section includes loading instructions with seat occupancy and cargo limitations.

e. Fifth section

Since most helicopters of the same model may be equipped in various configurations, additional information is contained in a fifth section. This section includes all items that are other than a standard configuration, such as external load equipment, floats, non-conventional skid gear, and any other equipment that will affect the flight characteristics or alter the operating limitations.

Maintenance personnel usually have very little to do with the operating manual unless they are allowed to ground operate the helicopter. Some companies have only certain maintenance personnel authorized for operating the machine. Others require a pilot to be at the controls anytime the helicopter is running.

2. Maintenance manuals

The maintenance manuals are of two basic formats — the old manufacturers format and the ATA 100 system. Besides the differences in the way the information is assembled, there is also a difference in the amount of information contained in the maintenance manuals. Some contain only the information necessary for field maintenance while others contain maintenance, overhaul, inspection criteria and structural repair information in one volume. This is the manufacturer's preference and is often influenced by the equipment necessary to perform the various tasks. Some helicopter manufacturers do not allow any overhaul work on their components other than at the factory. Such companies operate exchange programs for such components as transmissions, gearboxes, and rotor heads. For these companies there is no need to add overhaul information to the maintenance manual. Others realize that it is economically unfeasible for everyone to overhaul his own components because of special tooling involved, and so do not include overhaul information.

All of the manufacturers provide a renewal service with these publications. This means that as new material becomes available or text revisions are necessary, this information will be sent to the purchasers of the manual. This is usually done for a period of one year after the purchase of the manual and after that a subscription fee is charged. The price of a maintenance manual varies, but $100 is not unusual. However, some of the larger helicopter maintenance manuals will cost over $1000.

At least one company, other than a manufacturer, furnishes microfiche copies of manuals with a subscription service on updates. This microfiche system has some disadvantages because a viewer must be used and a printer is necessary in order to make copies. The prime advantage of this system is the small space required to store information and the time saved during the revision process.

a. Manufacturers older format

The older type of maintenance manuals are broken down into areas dealing with sections of the helicopter very similar to the manner in which the military manuals or light fixed wing manuals are printed. The beginning includes such general information as inspections, weight and balance computations, and general servicing. Each of the additional sections covers the maintenance of a certain area of the helicopter such as main rotor, tail rotor, electrical system, and airframe sections.

Each of these sections is further broken down with a general description, troubleshooting, removal, teardown inspection, reassembly and installation. This system may have as many sections as required in order to cover the entire helicopter. An alphabetical index is included in the manual for reference purposes. A breakdown per section of a typical maintenance manual follows:

Section I	General Information
Section II	Main Rotor System
Section III	Mast and Controls
Section IV	Transmission System
Section V	Powerplant and Related Systems (Franklin)
Section V	Powerplant and Related Systems (Lycoming)
Section VI	Tail Rotor System
Section VII	Flight Controls (Standard)
Section VII	Flight Controls (Hydraulic)
Section VIII	Instruments
Section IX	Electrical
Section X	Body and Landing Gear
Section XI	Wiring Data
Alphabetical Index	

Old Format

b. ATA system format

The newer manuals that are written in the ATA system format are quite different in construction from the older manuals. Under this system each area is assigned a number which represents a chapter in the manual. For example: fuel systems would be covered in Chapter 28 and hydraulic systems in Chapter 29. These chapter numbers remain the same regardless of the aircraft or the manufacturer. Also, if a helicopter does not have a specific system, that chapter would be excluded from the manual. For example: if there were no hydraulic systems in the helicopter, Chapter 29 would be excluded from the text.

The ATA system is further broken down into subsystems by an additional numbering system. For example: 28-10 designates the fuel storage system while 28-20 designates the fuel distribution system. An additional set of digits is added to designate the details of the subject. For example: 28-10-01 discusses fuel cells and 28-10-02 the auxilliary fuel cells.

The information is broken down still further into three categories for each chapter/section/subject by page number as follows:

A list of chapters is found at the front of the manual through which one can determine which chapter contains the information needed. A typical chapter system sample is as follows:

LIST OF CHAPTERS

Typical ATA System

Although the ATA system appears quite difficult it will soon become apparent through practice that regardless of the helicopter model or the manufacturer, the information desired will be located in the same chapter/section/subject area.

3. *Illustrated parts breakdown*

The illustrated parts breakdown, like the maintenance manual, has different formats. They follow basically the same system as in the

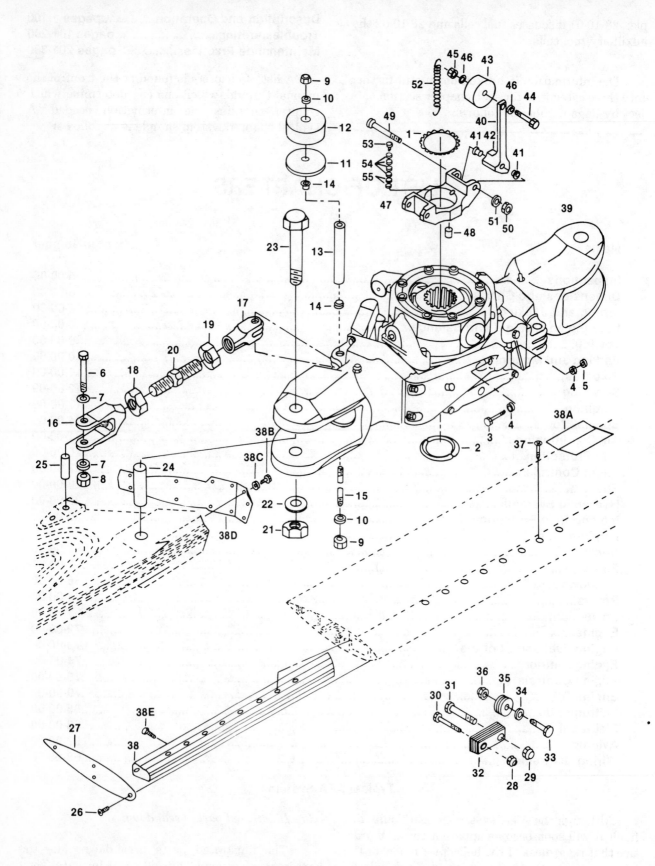

Fig. 3-4 A — Typical IPB breakdown of a rotor head.

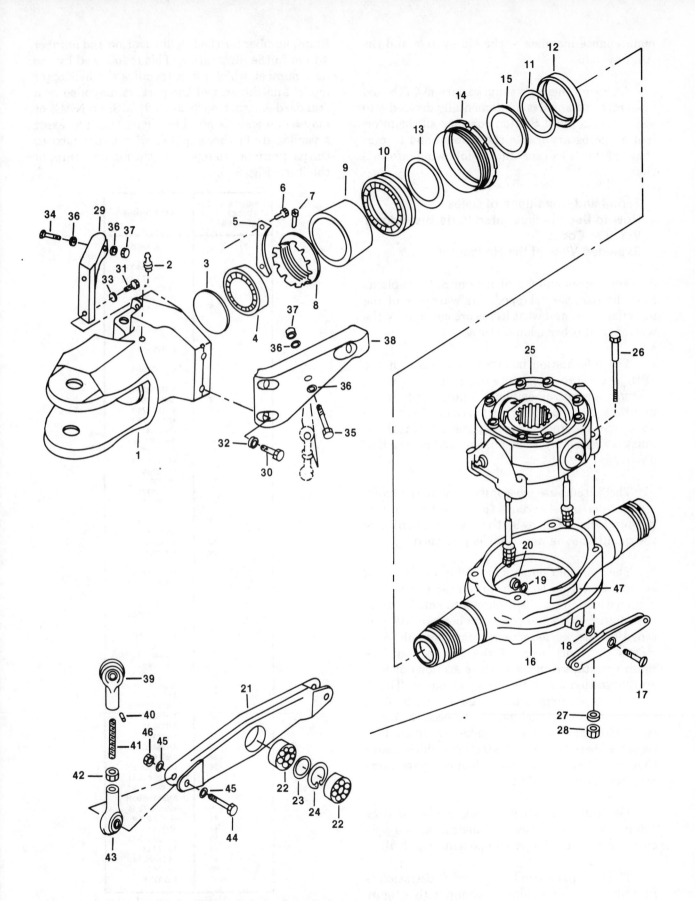

Fig. 3-4 B — Rotor head breakdown continued.

87

maintenance manuals — the old system and the ATA system.

Although there are some variations in the old system, the manual is fundamentally divided into sections. The First Section contains all the information necessary to use the manual and to purchase parts. It will contain the following information:

Terms and Conditions of Sales
How to Use the Illustrated Parts Breakdown
Vendors Codes
Exploded View of the Helicopter

The Terms and Conditions of Sales explains how the parts are shipped, the warranty of the manufacturer, and what items are covered by the warranty of other manufacturers.

The information included in the use of the IPB is the table of contents, page numbering system, group assemblies, figure and index numbers, part numbers, part relationships, oversized parts, alternate parts, special notations, units per assembly, model usage, and how to find a part.

These items are most important to the maintenance personnel because the correct use of this portion helps to increase the speed and enhance the quality of the work that is peformed.

The Table of Contents in the front of the book assigns a section to each large area of the helicopter which in turn is broken into smaller units with figure titles and page numbers always preceded by the section number. For example: 7-10 means the tenth page of the 7th section. The figures contained in the various sections include an illustration and a text page or pages. The illustrations are exploded with guidelines to show relationships with each part numbered to correspond with the text page or pages. There are four page numbers between illustrations which means that some pages have more than one page number. For example: 2-11/2-12.

The first illustration in a section is the large component. Each following illustration is a subcomponent of the larger component (Fig. 3-4).

The text page number for any illustration is first shown in the left-hand column with a figure index number. For example: 5-4 would be the

figure number for the 5th illustration and number 4 item in the illustration. This is followed by the part number which often specifies the helicopter model and the area of the part. It may also be a standard number such as AN, MS, or NAS, or may be a vendor's number. Those that represent a vendor are further supplied with a code next to the part number to represent the manufacturer of the item (Fig. 3-5).

FIGURE & INDEX NUMBER	PART NUMBER
3 ·	47-120-184-31
	47-120-184-33
	47-120-184-29
· 1	47-120-252-7
· 2	MS15002-1
· 3	47-120-113-2
	47-120-113-3
· 4	47-120-418-1
· 5	47-120-265-1
· 6	AN500A10-5
· 7	AN502-10-10
· 8	47-120-178-1
· 9	47-120-179-1
· 10	47-120-417-3
· 11	AN6230B11
· 12	47-120-182-1
· 13	47-120-185-1
· 14	47-120-183-1
· 15	71X7095
· 16	47-120-177-1
	47-120-128-1
· 17	47-120-253-1
· 18	AN960-516L
· 19	AN960-516
· 20	AN320-5
· 21	47-120-128-2
· 22	MS20201KP5A
· 23	47-120-114-1
· 24	MS16625-81
· 25	47-120-184-23
· 26	47-120-155-1
· 27	AN960-716
· 28	NAS679A7
· 29	47-120-259-1
· 30	MS20074-06-10
· 31	AN174H5A
· 32	AN960PD616
· 33	AN960PD416L
· 34	AN173-13
· 35	AN173-14
· 36	AN960PD10
· 37	AN310-3
· 38	47-120-126-5
	47-120-025-11
	47-120-025-5
· 39	AN951REB3N
· 40	100-035-72-14
· 41	47-120-025-9
· 42	AN315-4R
· 43	47-120-025-13
· 44	AN173-11
· 45	AN960PD10
· 46	AN310-3
· 47	100-037-1

Fig. 3-5 Typical figure number/part number breakdown.

FIGURE & INDEX NUMBER	PART NUMBER	DESCRIPTION 1234567	UNITS PER ASSY.	MODELS USABLE ON			NON PROCURABLE	SPECIAL ORDER	CURRENT STOCK
				47 G4	47 G4A				
9 ·	47-150-257-9	Support and Swashplate Assy... See Fig. 8 for next assy	REF	X	X				X
	47-150-175-29	.Swashplate Assy......................	1	X	X		X		
· 1	AN502-10-12	..Screw...............	8	X	X				
· 2	MS20074-04-04	..Bolt.............	8	X	X				
· 3	AN906PD416	..Washer............	8	X	X				
· 4	47-150-206-3	..Shield............	1	X	X				X
· 5	47-150-207-1	..Shield Assy...........	1						
· 6	47-150-183-3	..Ring............	1	X	X				X
· 7	47-150-021-1	..Ring............	1	X	X				X
· 8	47-150-240-1	..Bearing............	1	X	X				X
	30-729-592-5	..Ring Assy............	1	X	X				X
· 9	MS15002-1	...Fitting............	2	X	X				X
· 10	30-729-476-1	...Pin............	2	X	X				X
· 11	30-729-592-7	...Ring............	1	X	X				X
	47-150-184-5	..Swashplate Assy...........	1	X	X				X
· 12	RR81	...Ring (80756)...........	2	X	X		X		
· 13	47-150-214-1	...Seal............	2	X	X				X
· 14	47-150-245-1	...Bearing............	2	X	X				X
· 15	47-150-212-3	...Insert............	2	X	X				X
· 16	22-006-15-30-16	...Bushing............	2	X	X				X
· 17	22-006-15-22-16	...Bushing............	2	X	X				X
· 18	1191-3CNXO-570	...Insert (91767)............	8	X	X				X
· 19	47-150-184-7	...Swashplate............	1	X	X				X
· 20	47-150-213-1	.Pin............	4	X	X				X
	47-150-180-9	.Ring Assy............	1	X	X		X		
· 21	NAS516-1	..Fitting............	4	X	X				X
· 22	AN502-10-20	..Screw............	8	X	X				X
· 23	47-150-180-11	..Ring............	1	X	X				X
		Note 1		X	X				
· 24	47-150-180-3	..Ring............	1	X	X		X		
		Note 1							
	47-150-175-19	.Support Assy............	1	X	X		X		
· 25	MS16624-1087	..Ring............	2	X	X				X
· 26	47-150-034-1	..Seal............	4	X	X				
· 27	47-150-243-1	..Bearing............	2	X	X				X
· 28	47-150-018-1	..Shaft............	1	X	X				X
	47-150-152-10	..Support Assy............	1	X	X				X
· 29	RR81	...Ring (80756)............	2	X	X				X
· 30	45-150-214-1	...Seal............	2	X	X				X
· 31	47-150-245-1	...Bearing............	2	X	X				X
· 32	47-150-212-1	...Insert............	2	X	X				X
· 33	47-150-152-9	...Support............	1	X	X				

Note 1:

47-150-180-11 and 47-150-180-3 cannot be procured separately. as they must be used in matched sets. Procure 47-150-180-9.

Fig. 3-6   Typical parts catalog page showing units per assembly.

The next column of the text page contains the description of the part, including the asembly. The assembly is always listed first with the parts that make it up indented. Parts that are oversized are listed in the description directly below the standard part description with the oversize. Other information such as the use of alternate parts and special notations such as "matched sets" may also be included in the description.

The next column of the text page gives the number of units per assembly that are used (Fig. 3-6).

If the same manual is used for more than one model a usage code is placed in the next column showing to which model the item refers (Fig. 3-7).

When trying to locate a part when the part number is known, one can use the cross reference

Fig. 3-7 — Usage code designating the model.

MODELS USABLE ON				USAGE		
47 G4	47 G4A			NON PROCURABLE	SPECIAL ORDER	CURRENT STOCK
X	X					X
X	X					
X	X			X		
X	X			X		X
X	X					X
X	X					X
X	X					X
X	X					X
X	X					X
X	X					
X	X					
X	X					X
X	X					X
X	X					X
X	X					X
X	X					X
X	X					X
X	X					X
X	X					X
X	X					X
X	X					X
X	X					
X	X					
X	X					
X	X			X		
X	X					X
X	X					X
X	X					
X	X					X
X	X					X
X	X					
X	X					
X	X					X
X	X					
X	X					
X	X					
X	X					
X	X					
X	X					
X	X					X
X	X					X
X	X			X		
X	X					X
X	X					X
X	X				X	
X	X					
X	X					X
X	X					
X	X					
X	X					
X	X					
X	X					
X	X				X	

Fig. 3-7 Usage code designating the model.

Fig. 3-8 — Cross reference indexes

Part Number	INDEX AND FIGURE NUMBER	
	30	20
47-620-234-4	18	
	30	20
47-620-234-5	18	
	30·	20
47-620-235-1	11	74
	12	73
47-620-238-1	18	
47-620-238-2	18	11
47-620-240-1	18	8
47-620-241-3	18	1
47-620-242-1	11	24
	12	19
47-620-243-1	11	20
47-620-246-1	21	1
47-620-247-1	21	2
47-620-249-1	21	5
47-620-250-1	11	58
47-620-251-1	11	56
47-620-252-1	21	
47-620-252-2	21	9
47-620-253-1	21	11
47-620-254-1	12	66
	21	13
47-620-255-1	11	54
47-620-256-1	12	71
	21	8
47-620-256-2	17	17
	19	1
	20	17
47-620-256-3	16	15
	18	10
47-620-278-3	11	29
47-620-280-1	50	52
	50A	52
47-620-280-2	50	52
	50A	52
47-620-280-3	50	52
	50A	52
47-620-280-4	50	52
	50A	52
47-620-280-5	50	52
	50A	52
47-620-287-1	11	57
	21	
47-620-293-2	5	
47-620-297-1	11	55
	21	
47-620-298-1	18	3
47-620-299-1	18	4
47-620-301-1	21	7
47-620-302-1	21	6
47-620-332-1	11	2
47-620-344-2	25	8
47-620-349-2	23	4
47-620-374-1	28	10
47-620-424-1	25	9
47-620-425-1	23	7
47-620-426-1	23	3
47-620-426-2	23	
47-620-426-3	25	7
47-620-426-4	25	
47-620-426-5	23	

Fig. 3-8 Cross reference indexes

index located in the back of the manual. Every part number is listed with the figure index number so that the part may be located in relation to other parts or any other appropriate information may be found (Fig. 3-8).

When the part number is not known but the general location is known, one can use the exploded views of the helicopter shown in the first section of the manual. Each major section is numbered with an appropriate code on the view showing the first illustration number for that area (Fig. 3-9).

In the ATA system manuals the IPB is broken down in the same manner as in the maintenance manual, with each system having chapter numbers that correspond to those in the maintenance manual. For example: Chapter 28 is still Fuel Systems. Each chapter, however, contains an index. The index lists the illustration pages for each view in the chapter. The page numbering system is basically the same as that used in the old system, with page numbers for illustrations every fourth page. The text pages are also set up in the same manner with the figure index number, part number, description, units per assembly, and usage code.

The same methods are used for part location either by part number or by location on the exploded view.

4. Service bulletins

Additional information is given in regard to the maintenance of the helicopter in the form of service bulletins. These are also referred to as service information notices. Although the name varies from one manufacturer to another, the content is always similar. While the service bulletin may deal with any item on the helicopter, it is usually used to inform the operator of a problem area. It may call for an inspection, the replacement of a part, or the reduction of the life of a component (Fig. 3-10).

Due to the seriousness of these matters most manufacturers consider them mandatory and will eventually include them in the maintenance manual. Service bulletins will very often become

airworthiness directives. Like revisions to the maintenance manuals, they are obtained on a subscription basis from the manufacturer, usually on a yearly basis with an annual summary and index.

Additional information is often given to the operator in the form of a service letter or technical bulletin. This may include information on new alternate parts with a longer life, a change in rebuild facilities or any other technical information that may benefit the operator. These items again are available on a subscription basis and are usually included in the cost of the service bulletins.

Manufacturers also furnish service instructions (SIs). These cover many procedures which usually involve modification of the helicopter and kits that are available from the manufacturer, such as a new tail rotor, radio installations, or an alternator kit to replace a generator. These are available on a subscription basis or may be obtained with the kit.

D. Supplemental Type Certificates

The last item available for the helicopter operator is the Supplemental Type Certificate (STC). Although these are not available from the manufacturer of the helicopter, they may be available from the manufacturer of an item, or from an operator who has modified a helicopter and has obtained approval for the STC from the FAA. They could include a number of items including baggage racks, skid gear modifications, different engine installations, or a litter-ambulance configuration. Some of these are available in kit form while others are simply purchased information containing specifications for the modifications.

The helicopter of today will not fly on the paperwork alone. The material that is available to the operator will help insure that the aircraft is maintained in a manner that provides for the safety of the aircraft, if it is used in conjunction with good maintenance practices. Neither the paperwork or the maintenance can accomplish this by itself.

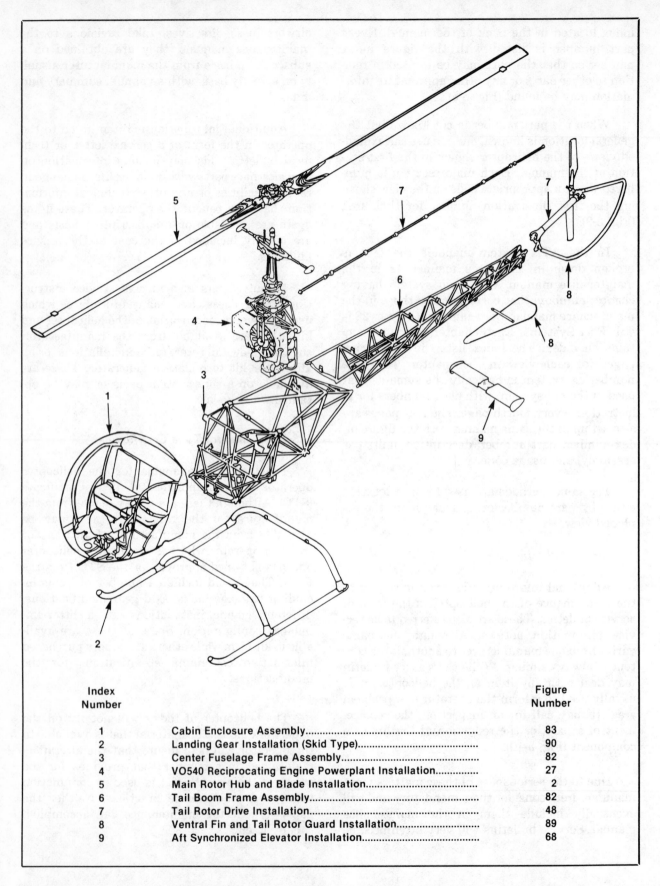

Index Number		Figure Number
1	Cabin Enclosure Assembly	83
2	Landing Gear Installation (Skid Type)	90
3	Center Fuselage Frame Assembly	82
4	VO540 Reciprocating Engine Powerplant Installation	27
5	Main Rotor Hub and Blade Installation	2
6	Tail Boom Frame Assembly	82
7	Tail Rotor Drive Installation	48
8	Ventral Fin and Tail Rotor Guard Installation	89
9	Aft Synchronized Elevator Installation	68

Fig. 3-9   Parts catalog general figure location page.

SERVICE BULLETIN

NO. 47-76-4

DATE 4-5-76

PAGE NO. 1 of 1

**BELL
HELICOPTER** COMPANY
textron

SERVICE APPROVAL	ENGINEERING APPROVAL	FAA/DER APPROVAL
Wm. J. Dahl	*I. O. Pollings*	*SW-179 M. J. McGuGan*

SUBJECT: 1200 HOUR MANDATORY RETIREMENT OF MAIN ROTOR GIMBAL RINGS P/N 47-120-014-5, -6, -7, -9, -11, -13, -15, -17, -19, AND -21.

REASON: Reduction of service life based on field reports of cracked gimbal rings.

HELICOPTERS AFFECTED: All Model 47B, B-3, D, D-1, G, G-2, G-2A, G-2A-1, G-3, G-3B, G-3B-1, G-3B-2, G-3B-2A, G-4, G-4A, G-5, G-5A, H-1, J, J-2 and J-2A helicopters that have the subject P/N gimbal rings installed.

ACCOMPLISHMENT: At the next 1200 hour inspection, but not later than September 1, 1976 regardless of the number of flight hours in service.

DESCRIPTION:

1. Main rotor gimbal rings P/N 47-120-014-5, -6, -7, -9, -11, -13, -15, -17, -19, and -21 must be replaced with gimbal ring P/N 47-120-014-<u>23</u>.

2. The inspection specified in Service Bulletin No. 47-04-1-73-1 dated 4-27-73 <u>does</u> <u>not</u> apply to gimbal ring P/N 47-120-014-<u>23</u>.

3. Add the following data to all Model 47 Mandatory Retirement Schedules:

<u>MAIN ROTOR SYSTEM</u>

Item	Part Number	Replace at
Gimbal Ring	47-120-014 all dash numbers -1 thru -21	1200 hours
Gimbal Ring	47-120-014-23	4800 hours

4. The part required to make this change may be procured from your usual BHT part supply source:

Part Number	Nomenclature	Quantity
47-120-014-23	Ring, Split, Main Rotor	1

Fig. 3-10 Typical service bulletin.

31. Helicopters are not required to carry any additional paperwork to that of the fixed wing aircraft.

    A. True

    B. False

32. A maintenance manual is required when performing inspections on helicopters.

    A. True

    B. False

33. External load operators have to comply with an additional FAR which applies to external loads.

    A. True

    B. False

34. The Aircraft Specifications and Data Sheets are not separated for fixed wing and rotary wing aircraft.

    A. True

    B. False

35. If a helicopter's retirement schedule is lost, times may be estimated.

    A. True

    B. False

36. If a separate list of Service Bulletins and AD notes is kept no log entries are necessary.

    A. True

    B. False

37. New maintenance manuals are written using the ATA format.

    A. True

    B. False

38. The operating limitation of a helicopter can be found in the flight manual.

    A. True

    B. False

39. Renewal service for all manufacturer's publications are furnished free of charge by the manufacturer.

    A. True

    B. False

40. Using the ATA system, Chapter 28 will always be the fuel system.

    A. True

    B. False

SECTION IV

Basic Helicopter Maintenance

The helicopter technician must have a basic understanding of the maintenance practices which are peculiar to the craft. The average A&P may be quite familiar with fixed-wing aircraft, but the helicopter is different in such areas as basic directions, ground handling, and the use of bearings and gears. Although most technicians are aware of some of these areas, additional information should be acquired.

A. Basic Directions

Basic directions on a helicopter may be confusing to the new helicopter mechanic. The right and left are the same as on a fixed-wing aircraft viewed from the rear looking forward. It is not uncommon, however, for the pilot to be placed on the right side rather than the left as is the case in a fixed-wing aircraft. This is because of the relative positon of the cyclic and collective. In some instances the collective arm may be free to do other functions in the helicopter such as tune radios, etc. This is accomplished by setting the tension on the collective.

1. Right and left of engine

Another feature of older aircraft, confusing to the novice with helicopters, is the right and left of the engine. It must be remembered the earlier models of helicopters made use of engines designed for fixed-wing aircraft that were modified for helicopters. For this reason, engines normally mounted horizontally had been mounted vertically or backwards, moving the right and left positions of the magnetos. It would be helpful if a set of rules could be given to the positions on reciprocating engines, but they cannot because the early problems were corrected on the newer reciprocating powered helicopters by the manufacturers. It will always be necessary, therefore, to consult the maintenance manual for the particular helicopter regarding positions prior to working on the older helicopters.

2. Color codes

Since so many of the components on the helicopter rotate, there can be no right or left side established. Because of this situation, color coding is used to determine location and to facilitate removal and installation of parts. Red and white dots and stripes are commonly used on parts of the semi-rigid rotors. Often blue and yellow are used on multi-bladed systems as additional colors for identification purposes.

3. Ground handling

The ground handling of helicopters differs from that of fixed-wing aircraft. Many of the helicopters in use today are equipped with skid gear rather than wheels. In many respects this system is quite practical because helicopters do not require takeoff or landing rolls, but this system does not aid in the ground handling of the aircraft. The skid-gear equipped helicopters use ground handling wheels (Fig 4-1). On the larger helicopters they are often raised and lowered with a hand-operated hydraulic pump. Regardless of whether the wheels are raised manually or hydraulically, the following safety precautions must be observed in order to avoid injury:

1. A bar must be used both for raising and lowering manually operated wheels.

2. This bar must be secured firmly to the ground handling wheel unit.

3. The personnel must stand clear of the bar, in case of slippage, when the helicopter is raised and lowered.

4. Hands or feet must never be placed under the skid gear during the raising or lowering operation.

5. All locking devices and pins must be firmly in place prior to releasing pressure from the bar.

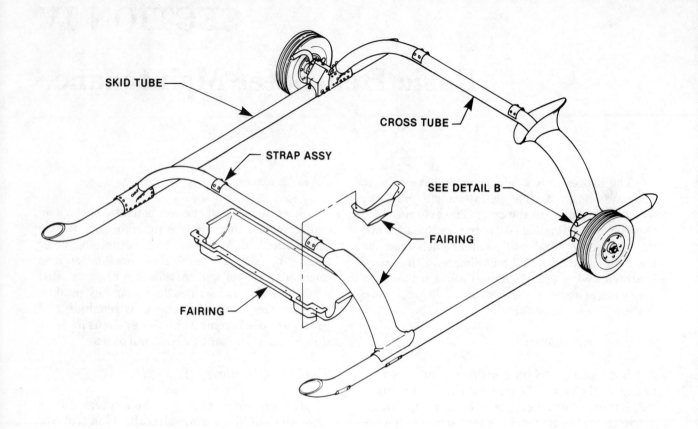

SKID TUBE

CROSS TUBE

STRAP ASSY

SEE DETAIL B

FAIRING

FAIRING

(DETAIL B)

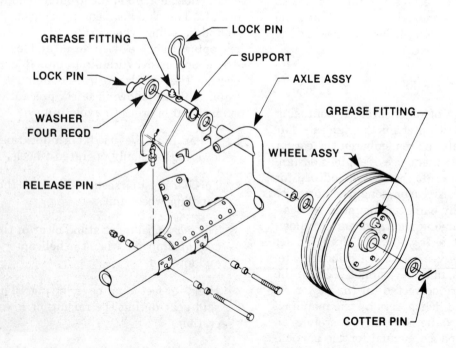

GREASE FITTING

LOCK PIN

LOCK PIN

SUPPORT

AXLE ASSY

WASHER
FOUR REQD

GREASE FITTING

WHEEL ASSY

RELEASE PIN

COTTER PIN

Fig. 4-1   Typical skid gear utilizing ground handling wheels

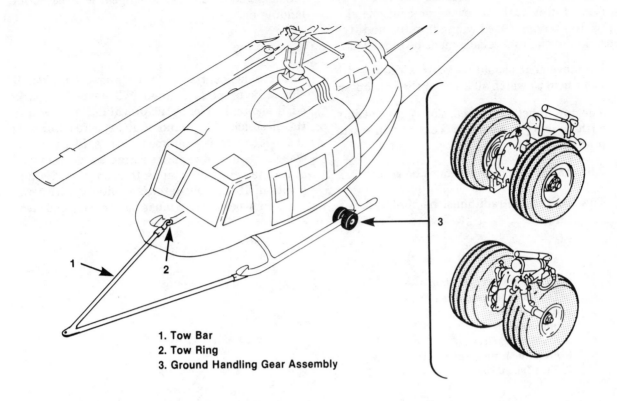

1. Tow Bar
2. Tow Ring
3. Ground Handling Gear Assembly

Fig. 4-2 One method of ground handling using wheels and towbar.

6. *Under no circumstances* should the helicopter be started with the ground handling wheels in the down position.

At best, the ground handling wheels are quite awkward for moving the aircraft. Most of the time the wheels are located near the center of gravity. Because of the wheel locations and differences in aircraft, some upward or downward pressure may be required to keep the skids from scraping while moving the aircraft on the ground handling wheels. Most of the smaller aircraft are moved by hand, pushing or pulling only on prescribed areas. Damage may occur if the tail rotors, antennas, and/or brush guards are used for pushing. The normal pushing points are usually designated in the maintenance manual, but if any doubt exists, the cross tubes of the skids may be used. On some of the larger skid-gear-equipped helicopters provisions are made for towing, with attachments for two bars on the skid gear (Fig. 4-2).

If the helicopter is to be kept inside or if maintenance is to be accomplished, the helicopter may land on a platform or dolly. A number of these are available from various sources. Some are self-propelled, using an electric motor to move the platform, while others are towed. One particular model fits under the helicopter and lifts it at the jackpoints. A typical platform is shown in Fig. 4-3.

Fig. 4-3 Typical platform for skid gear helicopters.

Helicopters having a wheel gear system make ground handling simpler because tow bars may be used. However, the following precautions also apply to moving fixed-wing aircraft and the operation of the tow vehicle must be observed:

1. No movement should be made without sufficient help to watch all areas of the helicopter.

2. The tow must be moved slowly and evenly with no jerky movements occurring on starts or stops.

3. All rotating components must be secure.

4. Tow bar turning radii must be observed.

Even when observing precautions it must be remembered that the landing gear is stressed for landing only.

4. Mooring

If a helicopter is to be stored outside, it should be properly moored. Whenever it is parked, it should be facing the prevailing wind or into the direction of the wind of an expected storm. If the helicopter is equipped with skid gear, the wheels should always be retracted, or removed any time the helicopter is to remain in a static position. If the helicopter is equipped with landing gear wheels, they must be properly chocked.

1. Main Rotor Tiedown Strap
2. Tail Rotor Tiedown Strap
3. Exhaust Cover
4. Intake Cover
5. Aft Mooring Fitting (2)
6. Forward Mooring Fitting (2)
7. Pitot Tube Cover

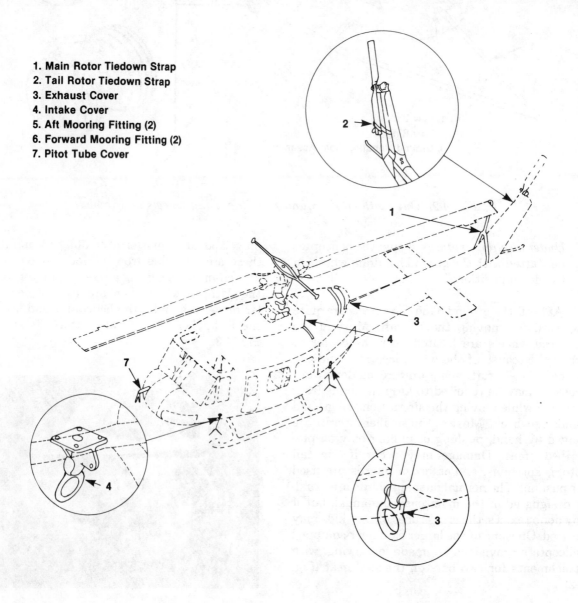

Fig. 4-4   One mooring and tiedown system used on a semi-rigid rotor helicopter.

Most helicopters have provisions for tie-downs on the fuselage (Fig. 4-4). These may also be the jackpoints of the aircraft. These tiedowns or mooring rings on the fuselage may be used to anchor the helicopter to the ramp, if the tiedowns are available.

Any time the helicopter is parked the rotors must be tied down. The tiedown will always include the main rotor, and may include the tail rotor. It will prevent damage from wind and other helicopters landing in the immediate area (Fig. 4-5). The tiedowns should be tight enough to absorb normal blade flexing associated with fully articulated rotors and the hub movement of semi-rigid rotors. If too much flexing of the blade takes

place, the tiedown may come off. Mast damage may be the result if flapping of the rotor occurs. The tail rotor restraint must be strong enough to prevent tail rotor damage.

5. Protection

Most helicopters have covers that can be installed if it is to remain outside overnight. The most commonly used covers are inlet and exhaust covers for the turbine engines and a pitot tube cover. Additional covers may be applied when the helicopter will be exposed to the weather for long periods of time or to severe weather conditions. These include windshield protectors, blade covers, and rotor head protection. Most of the

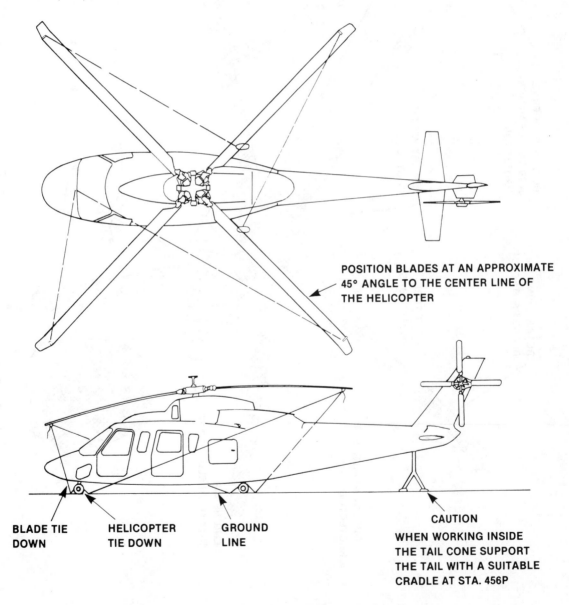

POSITION BLADES AT AN APPROXIMATE 45° ANGLE TO THE CENTER LINE OF THE HELICOPTER

BLADE TIE DOWN

HELICOPTER TIE DOWN

GROUND LINE

CAUTION
WHEN WORKING INSIDE THE TAIL CONE SUPPORT THE TAIL WITH A SUITABLE CRADLE AT STA. 456P

Fig. 4-5   One tiedown system used on a fully articulated rotor system.

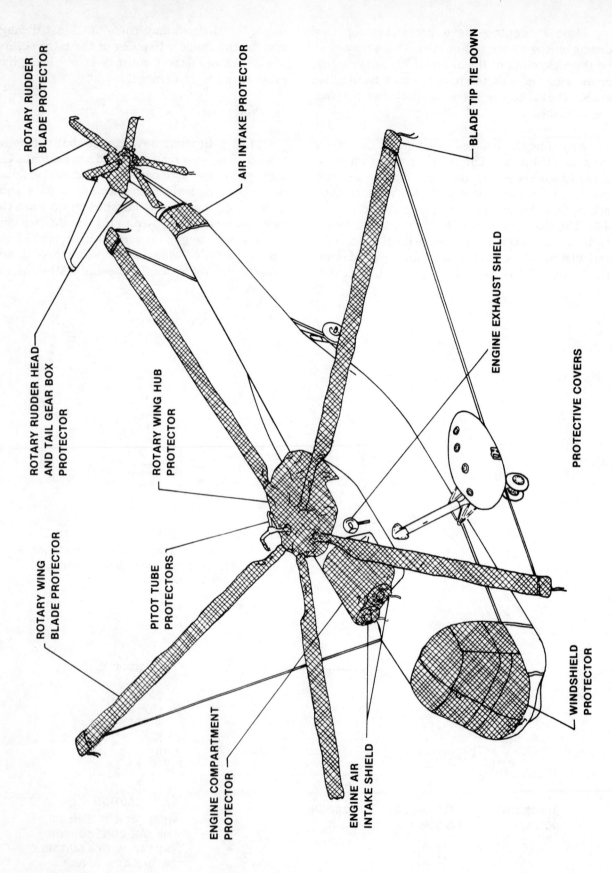

ROTARY RUDDER
BLADE PROTECTOR

AIR INTAKE PROTECTOR

BLADE TIP TIE DOWN

ROTARY RUDDER HEAD
AND TAIL GEAR BOX
PROTECTOR

ROTARY WING HUB
PROTECTOR

ENGINE EXHAUST SHIELD

PROTECTIVE COVERS

ROTARY WING
BLADE PROTECTOR

PITOT TUBE
PROTECTORS

WINDSHIELD
PROTECTOR

ENGINE COMPARTMENT
PROTECTOR

ENGINE AIR
INTAKE SHIELD

Fig. 4-6 A protective covering system used in extreme weather conditions.

100

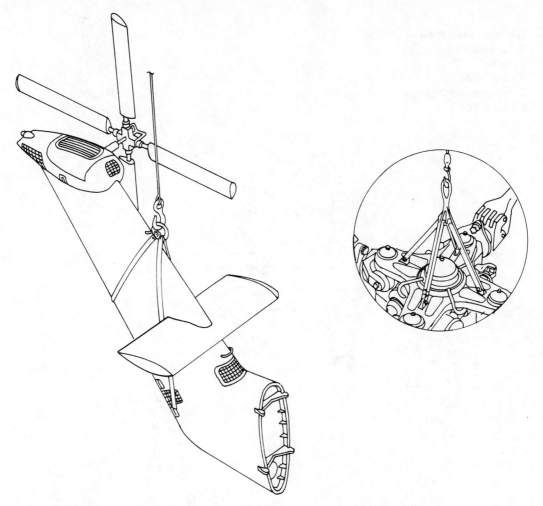

Fig. 4-7   Typical hoisting methods used to lift large components.

time such added protection is not required unless extreme weather conditions exist (Fig. 4-6).

6.   Lifting and leveling

At times it may be necessary to lift the entire helicopter. This would occur when the helicopter was damaged or needed to be retrieved. The most logical point is the mast assembly because it normally supports the helicopter in flight and is very close to the center of gravity. Hoisting eyes which attach to the mast nut are often provided for this purpose (Fig. 4-7).

Additional hoisting areas are provided on large helicopters for removing large components that could not normally be handled by hand. At least one manufacturer provides a work crane that will attach to the helicopter for removal of components (Fig. 4-8).

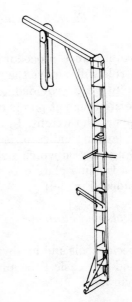

Fig. 4-8   A work crane that attaches directly to the helicopter.

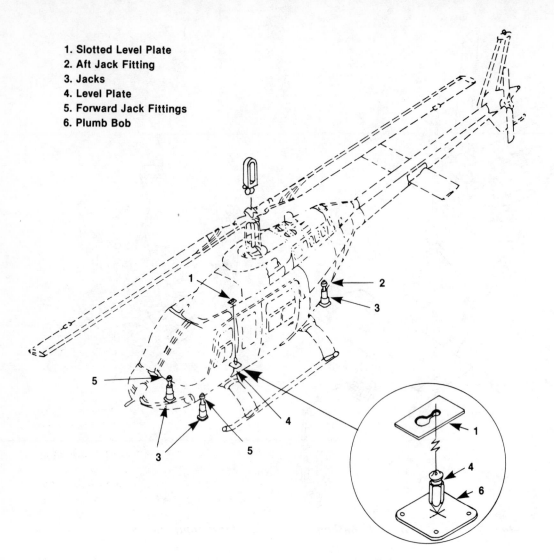

1. Slotted Level Plate
2. Aft Jack Fitting
3. Jacks
4. Level Plate
5. Forward Jack Fittings
6. Plumb Bob

Fig. 4-9 Typical jacking and leveling provisions for helicopters.

Many maintenance procedures such as rigging the controls will require the helicopter to be level. Jackpoints are provided to lift the helicopter. These are found at points of the structure that can support the weight. In addition to the jackpoints, a leveling indicator is provided. This may be leveling lugs on which a spirit level may be placed or a leveling plate over which a plumb bob is suspended (Fig. 4-9).

7. Special tools and hardware

Many special tools and hardware are used on helicopter, and the basic principles of their use should be reviewed.

The maintenance technician should be familiar with torque wrenches and their use. It is quite common that various nuts and bolts on helicopters be assigned special torques. This is the result of their use, the materials involved and the modifications of hardware. Many torques are found in the text of the maintenance manual and should be closely adhered to. It is not always possible, however, to obtain the torque without modifications to the torque wrench. The addition of *crow's feet* will change the effective length of the arm, changing the reading of the wrench. In all such cases, the formula in Fig. 4-10 should be used for computing the torque reading. A great number of special tools are used on helicopters. These often have arm extensions that must be considered in the total torque value. Some manufacturers simplify this by stamping the torque value on the tool. This is not always the case.

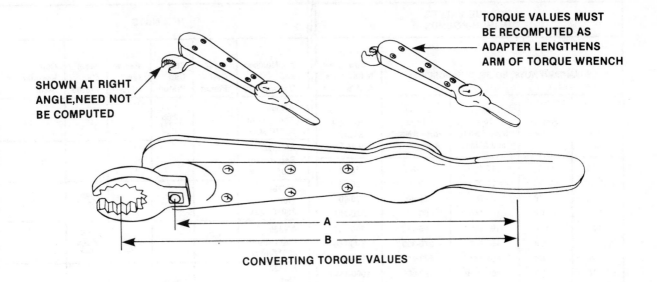

SHOWN AT RIGHT ANGLE, NEED NOT BE COMPUTED

TORQUE VALUES MUST BE RECOMPUTED AS ADAPTER LENGTHENS ARM OF TORQUE WRENCH

A

B

CONVERTING TORQUE VALUES

EXAMPLE · TORQUE VALUE CONVERSION

a. Dimension A on the torque wrench is 12.5 inches. With an adapter installed, demension B is 14.3 inches. A ÷ B = 12.5 ÷ 14.3 = 0.87. This is the conversion factor.

b. Assume that the torque wrench with the adapter installed is to be used to tighten "B" nuts for which the torque value is 1325 inch-pounds. 0.87 × 1325 =

1153, which is the torque reading to be used when this particular adapter is installed on the torque indicating handle and the torque called for is 1325 inch-pounds.

c. If the torque indicating handle and adapter in the preceding example are used, and the torque value is not recomputed, actual torque applied to the nut would be approximately 1516 inch-pounds. With a tolerance of plus or minus 125 inch-pounds, actual torque would exceed the maximum permissible torque by approximately 66 inch-pounds.

Fig. 4-10   Torque wrench extension formula

The helicopter is made up of many different types of materials. It is not unusual to see materials such as aluminum and steel joined by bolts or other fasteners. For this reason dissimilar metal corrosion may occur. To reduce this possibility aluminum washers, etc. may be used. The use of close tolerance bolts is common. It is of the utmost importance that head markings and parts manuals be followed in the replacement of this hardware. If these guidelines are not carefully followed, the result will be the failure of the fastener and very possibly the component itself, or the component may even be damaged beyond repair. Fig. 4-11 shows a chart of standard torques and common bolts used in helicopters.

The safetying of hardware is basically the same as that found on fixed-wing aircraft. However, more of it will be found, because of the vibration levels found in helicopters. As a result, the hardware is safetied with wire, cotter pins, and self-locking nuts. A variation not normally seen on fixed-wing aircraft are castle nuts with a self-locking fiber insert to prevent wearing out the cotter pin due to vibration. In addition to these devices, locking tangs are frequently used to hold nuts or bolts in place. These locking tangs are a one-time-use item and must be replaced each time the bolt or nut is removed.

B.   Bearings

It is most important that the helicopter technician understand the different types of bearings, their function, care, handling, and installation. Improper care of these bearings may lead to catastrophic failure. A great number of bearings are used in the helicopter because of the many ro-

<table>
<tr><th colspan="5">TORQUE VALUES IN INCH-POUNDS</th></tr>
</table>

	STANDARD NUTS, BOLTS, AND SCREWS			High-Strength Nuts, Bolts, And Screws
Bolt, Stud or Screw Size	Wrench Size	Tension-Type Nuts AN310 and AN365	Shear-Type Nuts AN320 And AN364	Any Nut Except Shear Type
8-36	11/32	12-15	7-9	15-18
10-32	3/8	20-25	12-25	25-35
1/4-28	7/16	50-70	30-40	70-90
5/16-24	1/2	100-140	60-85	140-203
3/8-24	9/16	160-190	95-110	190-351
7/16-20	5/8	450-500	270-300	500-756
1/2-20	3/4	480-690	290-410	690-990
9/16-18	7/8	800-1000	480-600	1000-1440
5/8-18	15/16	1100-1300	660-780	1300-2160
3/4-16	1 - 1/16	2300-2500	1300-1500	2500-4500
7/8-14	1 - 1/4	2500-3000	1500-1800	3000-6300
1 - 14	1 - 7/16	3700-5500	2200-3300	5500-9000

HEX NUTS					
An. Number and Description	Steel Cad Plated	Steel Cad Plated	Corr Resistant Steel	Steel Cad Plated	Corr Resistant Steel
AN363 Reg Height 550°F Max		(nut)		(nut)	
AN363C Reg Height 800°F Max			(nut)		(nut)
AN364 Thin 250°F Max		(nut)		(nut)	
AN365 Reg Height 250°F Max	(nut)		(nut)	(nut)	
AN320 Thin 250°F Max		(nut)			
AN310 Reg Height 250°F Max	(nut)				

BOLTS			
Basic Number	Diameter	Threads Per Inch	STEEL ... HEAD ... LENGTH, DIA, GRIP, THD
AN3	10*	32	
4	1/4*	28	
5	5/16	24	
6	3/8	24	
7	7/16	20	UNDRILLED AN6-10A
8	1/2	20	
9	9/16	18	HEAD ONLY DRILLED AN6H10A
10	5/8	18	
12	3/4	16	
14	7/8	14	SHANK ONLY DRILLED AN6-10
16	1	14	*Bolt shank should be without cotter pin hole when used with self-locking nuts

CLOSE-TOLERANCE BOLTS			
Basic Number	Diameter	Threads Per Inch	CLOSE TOLERANCE ... HEAD ... LENGTH, DA, GRIP, THD
AN173	10*	32	
174	1/4*	28	
175	5/16	24	
176	3/8	24	
177	7/16	20	UNDRILLED AN176-10A
178	1/2	20	
179	9/16	18	HEAD ONLY DRILLED AN176H10
180	5/8	18	
182	3/4	16	
184	7/8	14	SHANK ONLY DRILLED AN176-10
186	1	14	*Bolt shank should be without cotter pin hole when used with self-locking nuts

Fig. 4-11   Standard torque tables and hardware identification charts.

tating components. Each of these bearings serves a special purpose carrying rotational loads, thrust loads, or oscillating movements which are associated with the unique flight characteristics of the helicopter.

In order to understand the various functions, it will first be necessary to know the common parts of the bearing and its terminology (Fig. 4-12).

The outer race, or outer ring, provides a surface to retain the bearing and one of the groove areas in which the ball will travel. This may be provided with chamferred corners for installation purposes, and face marking in the form of a part number. The inner race provides the other groove area for the balls, and the bore opening in which is contained the rotating component. The balls are held in their respective positions by the separator or cage. The cages vary considerably in construc-

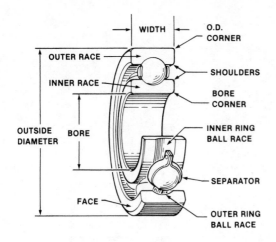

Fig. 4-12 Cut-a-way of a typical ball bearing.

tion, from wire cages to micarta, depending on the application and the lubrication. The grooves may be designed so that more shoulder is given to one side than the other in order to allow thrust loads in one direction. The bearing may be equipped with such features as snap ring grooves, shields for lubrication, self-alignment features and ground faces for duplex arrangements (Fig. 4-13).

1. *Ball bearings*

Ball bearings are used extensively in helicopter construction. Many appear to be standard bearings that might be found in any piece of equipment. However, they will quite often carry the airframe manufacturer's part numbers, which must be adhered to with *no subsitiutions* made. Quite often these bearings are modified or require closer tolerances than those of the bearing manufacturer. The ball bearing is used in so many different functions that although they all use balls to reduce friction, they are designed quite differently for their particular function.

2. *Roller bearing*

The second most widely used bearing in helicopters is the roller bearing. It is normally thought of as carrying radial loads, but by tapering the races it may be used to carry thrust as well as radial loads where more surface area is desirable than that provided by the ball bearing. Roller bearings may also be used in combinations where ball bearings are used to support the thrust loads. The radial loads are carried by the rollers. In lighter load carrying areas, a needle roller is sometimes used. Shown in Fig. 4-14 is a straight

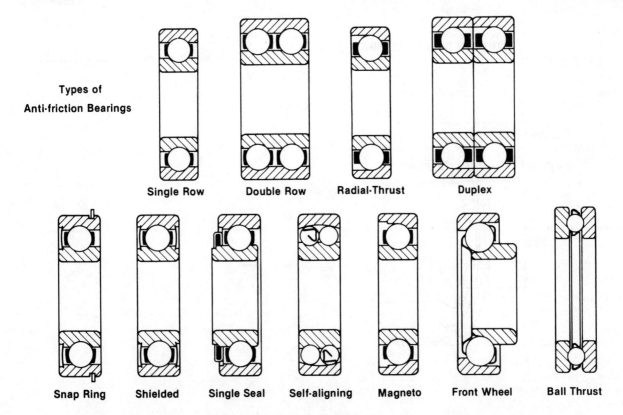

Fig. 4-13 Various types of ball bearings that may be found in helicopters.

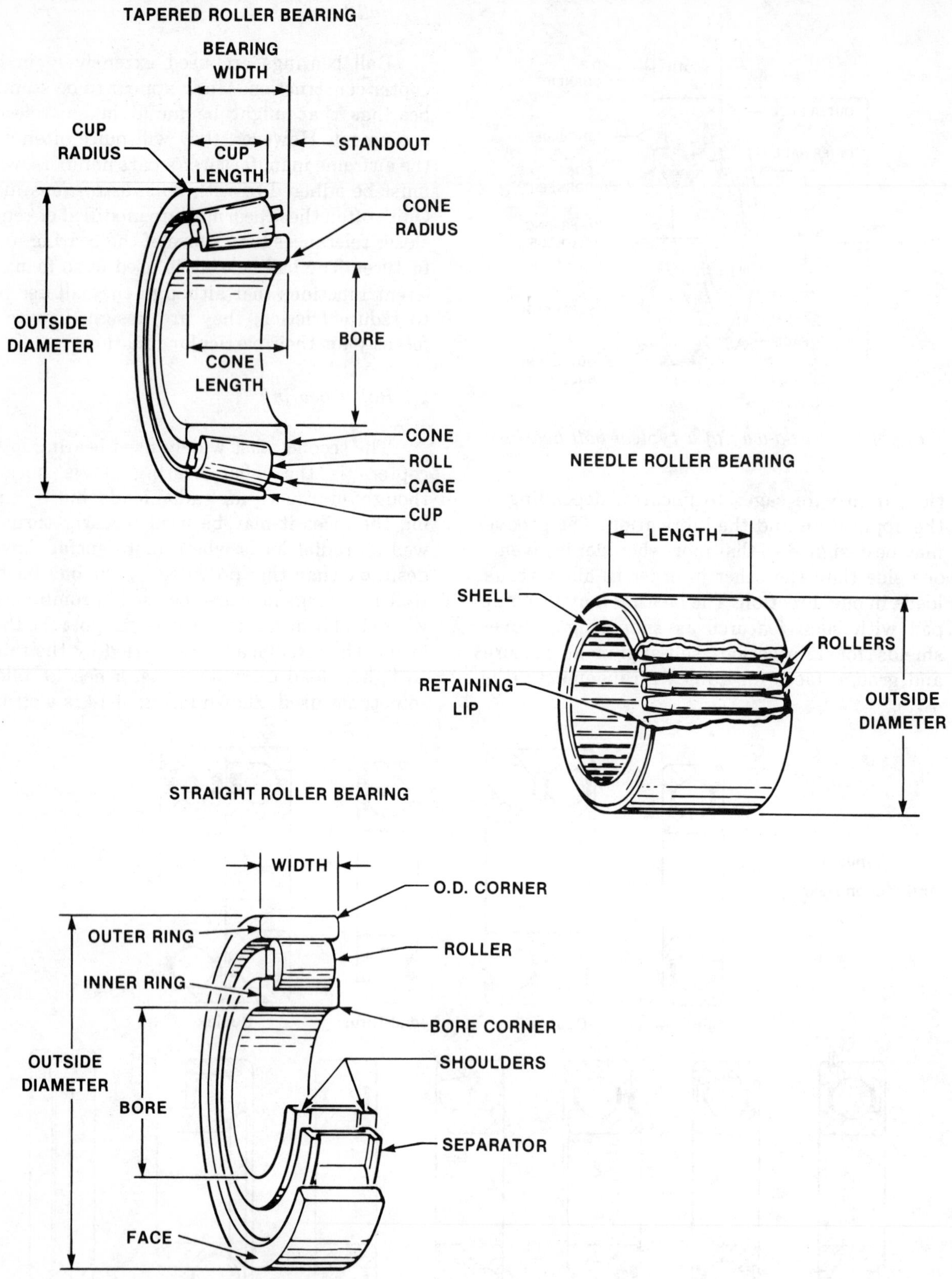

TAPERED ROLLER BEARING

BEARING WIDTH

CUP RADIUS

CUP LENGTH

STANDOUT

CONE RADIUS

OUTSIDE DIAMETER

BORE

CONE LENGTH

CONE

ROLL

CAGE

CUP

NEEDLE ROLLER BEARING

LENGTH

SHELL

ROLLERS

RETAINING LIP

OUTSIDE DIAMETER

STRAIGHT ROLLER BEARING

WIDTH

O.D. CORNER

OUTER RING

ROLLER

INNER RING

BORE CORNER

OUTSIDE DIAMETER

BORE

SHOULDERS

SEPARATOR

FACE

Fig. 4-14 Standard terminology used with roller bearings.

106

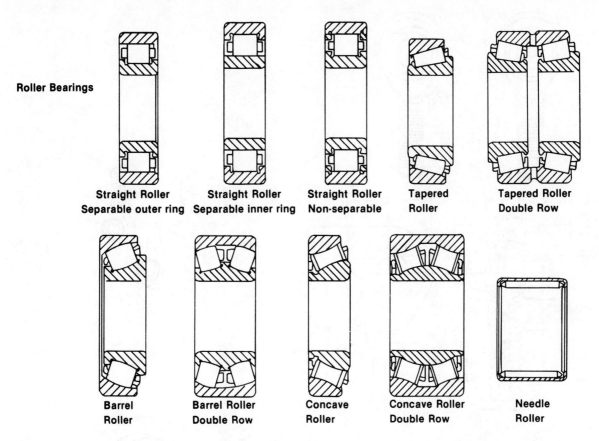

Roller Bearings

Straight Roller
Separable outer ring

Straight Roller
Separable inner ring

Straight Roller
Non-separable

Tapered
Roller

Tapered Roller
Double Row

Barrel
Roller

Barrel Roller
Double Row

Concave
Roller

Concave Roller
Double Row

Needle
Roller

Fig. 4-15 Various roller bearings that may be used in helicopters.

roller, a tapered roller, and a needle roller bearing. These bearings, like the ball bearing, may contain several features such as different styles of cages, removable inner or outer races, barrel, or concave rollers (Fig. 4-15).

The spherical bearings are quite different from the roller or the ball bearings. One of their main uses in helicopters is on control tubes and rods. The spherical bearings are normally referred to as rod ends. They are also finding uses on the pitch change in tail rotors and other areas where some side movement is required or in places that linear motion causes some misalignment.

3. Spherical bearing

One other type of bearing used in helicopters, especially on control linkages, is the spherical bearing. This type of bearing is used where movement in more than one direction is desirable (Fig. 4-16). Like other bearings, they may include such features as lubrication provisions, dry film lubricant, and dust seals.

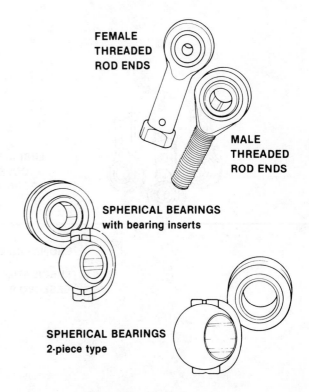

FEMALE
THREADED
ROD ENDS

MALE
THREADED
ROD ENDS

SPHERICAL BEARINGS
with bearing inserts

SPHERICAL BEARINGS
2-piece type

Fig. 4-16 Various spherical bearings used in helicopter applications.

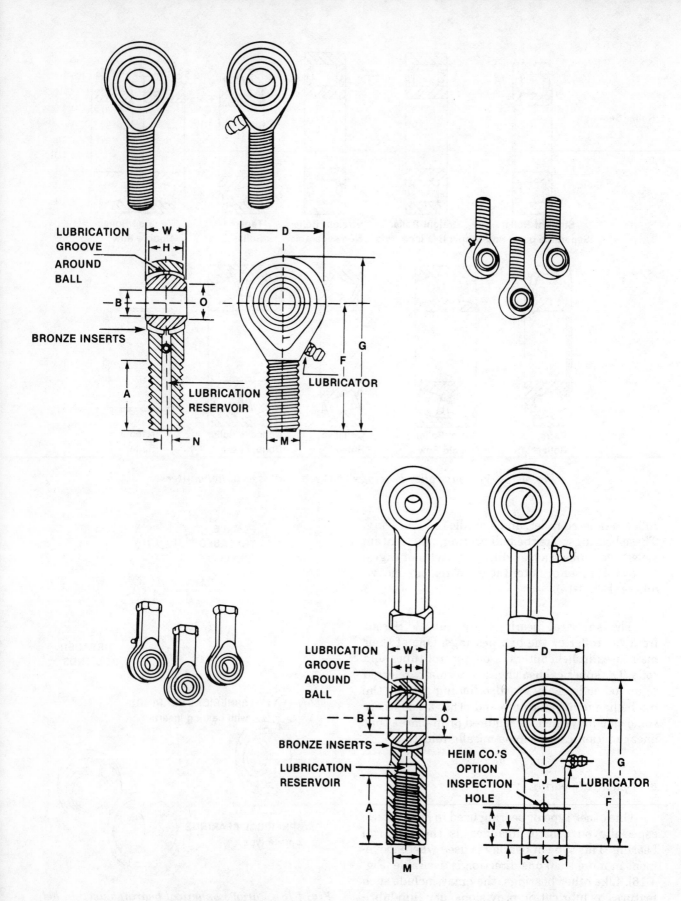

Fig. 4-17 Typical spherical bearings used with control rods.

In their use on rod ends they are often adjustable with a threaded portion to enable the length of the rod to be varied for rigging purposes. Typical rod ends are seen in Fig. 4-17. These rod ends are often high-usage items due to vibrations in the helicopter. Spherical bearings may be inspected by checking for radial movement of the spherical portion of the rod end. In the replacement of rod ends the actual length of the rod is often measured by use of a trammel, or the exposed threads are counted so that the control tube may be returned to its original length without re-rigging the control system (Fig. 4-18). Since spherical bearings are used to compensate for misalignment, it is important that they be properly aligned when installed, because they are often used with forked ends and the movement of the part may be limited as a result of this misalignment (Fig. 4-19).

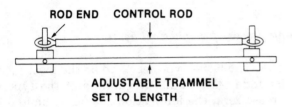

Fig. 4-18 The use of a trammel for adjusting rod length.

a. Roller staking

In other places where spherical bearings are used they often require a process called roller staking for replacement. This process involves pressing out the old bearing and replacing it with a new bearing and sleeve. The sleeve and bearing are held in place by a base with shims laid in the bottom of the base to center the new bearing. The roller stake is placed in a drill press and rotated against the sleeve. This process compresses the sleeve on one side, swagging the bearing in place. The part is turned over and the process is repeated with a different base (Fig. 4-20).

4. Care of bearings

A major consideration of the helicopter technician is the care of bearings. Because of the basic design of these ball and roller bearings, they will require lubrication in order to insure long life and prevent failure of the bearing itself. Many of these bearings may be lubricated by grease. The type of grease will be specified by the manufacturer and may be a high temperature, low temperature, or multi-purpose type grease. This will be dependent upon the temperatures to which the bearing is exposed. In some instances the bearing

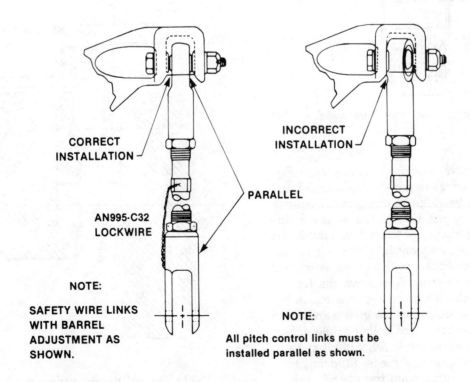

Fig. 4-19 Correct and incorrect methods of installing rod ends.

109

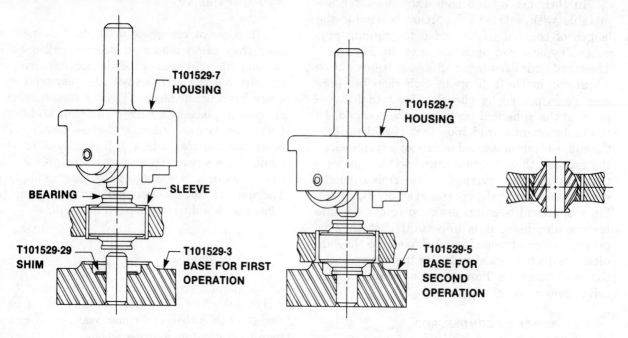

Fig. 4-20   Steps used in the roller staking process for spherical bearings.

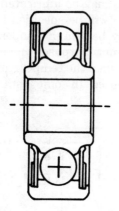

Fig. 4-21   Typical seal bearings used in helicopters.

may be sealed with its own supply of grease (Fig. 4-21). Sealed bearings require no additional lubricant while other bearings require grease frequently. This frequency will be dictated by the manufacturer and should be considered as a minimum requirement. More frequent lubrication is recommended when conditions such as dust, sand, and salt water exist in order to remove the foreign material from the bearings and prevent wear. Dust and dirt will adhere to the grease and cause wear between the races and balls or rollers. Salt water will cause corrosion which will pit the surfaces. Bearings requiring a grease lubricant have various means of lubrication from hand packing to the normal grease zerk or needle-type grease

zerk. The latter type seems to be the most popular today (Fig. 4-22). Regardless of the type of grease zerk, the lubrication should be limited to hand-type grease guns to reduce the possibility of damage to seals.

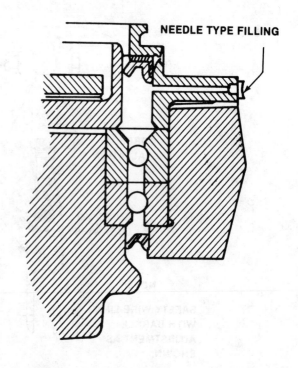

Fig. 4-22   Typical needle type grease filling for hand greasing.

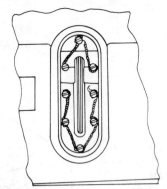

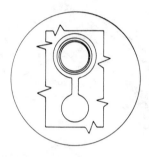

OIL LEVEL SIGHT GAUGE LOCATED
RIGHT SIDE MAIN TRANSMISSION
LOWER CASE

Fig. 4-23   Typical sight gauges used for checking fluid levels.

Other bearings are lubricated with oil. This may be done in different forms to include splash, spray, or pressure feed. The pressure feed system is usually limited to plain bearings or babbitt bearings, which are generally present in reciprocating engines and are not found in helicopter components. The splash system may amount to no more than an oil level maintained in a gearbox which insures that the gears and bearings are lubricated. Lubrication systems require that a certain level of oil be maintained. This is often done with the use of sight gauges to determine the level (Fig. 4-23). Bearings receiving a spray are usually contained in transmissions with a separate oil system consisting of a pump, spray nozzles, and plumbing. This is usually separate from the engine oil system except in older helicopters. This type of system usually makes use of sight gauges to maintain the proper oil level.

Today certain areas of the helicopter may be lubricated by a dry film lubricant placed on bearing surfaces at the time of manufacture. These surfaces are identified by the manufacturer and require no additional lubricant. Other such devices used are Teflon and oil-impregnated

bronze for bushing areas to reduce friction and yet require no lubricant.

Most manufacturers provide a lubrication chart for lubrication of the helicopter (Fig. 4-24). Notice that these charts not only denote the type of lubricant but the method and frequency of its application.

As situations may dictate and during specific inspection it will necessary to remove bearings for inspection purposes. The bearing may be replaced or merely inspected and reinstalled. The utmost care must be taken to insure that no damage is done to the bearing or the mating surfaces of the bearing. Although bearings are built to carry tremendous loads at high speeds, they are quite delicate and must be treated carefully. Any work involving bearings should be performed under clean working conditions. This includes cleaning the area surrounding the bearing prior to removal. It should also include cleaning the tools and equipment used for removal. Removing the bearings may require special tools made by the manufacturer of the helicopter. Other bearings can be removed with universal pullers and splitters (Fig. 4-25). If pullers are not used, the item is usually supported on an arbor press and pressed off. Under no circumstances should a bearing be driven off with a hammer making direct contact with bearing races. This may chip the races, damage the balls or rollers, or destroy the bearing. Proper procedures for removing bearings is shown in Fig. 4-26.

Once the bearing is removed it should be properly cleaned. This is accomplished by washing it with a neutral solvent and drying it. Bearings should never be spun with air while cleaning. After cleaning they should be oiled and stored by wrapping in oil-proof paper if they are to be reused. Often after cleaning, the bearings are inspected. To inspect the bearing, it should be held by the inner race and turned by the outer race slowly to determine roughness. If roughness is felt, it is suggested that the bearing be recleaned before rejection. Some bearings may be separated to facilitate the inspection.

The common defects found in bearings are as follows:

1. Broken or cracked rings.

2. Dented seals and shields.

NOTES:

⚠️1 MIL-G-81322 grease is an authorized replacement for MIL-G-25537 grease, but intermixing of greases is prohibited. When changing from one grease to the other, grease gun purge, or equivalent.

⚠️2 Lubricate with one "shot" of grease from a standard grease gun. CAUTION: Over lubrication will cause bearing to overheat.

SEE DETAIL D

MAIN DRIVESHAFT
REFER TO M&O FOR DETAIL
INSPECTION AND LUBRICATION
INSTRUCTIONS

205-040-004-17

205-040-004-11

SEE DETAIL C

SEE DETAIL B

3 ✋ EP

✋ EP

✋ EP

GWT ⚠️2

204-040-617-15
HANGER BEARINGS

GAP

1

3 ✋ EP

SEE DETAIL A

SYMBOLS

◇	50 HOURS
▢	100 HOURS
⬠	300 HOURS
△	500 HOURS
✦	600 HOURS
○	1000 HOURS
⌓	SIX MONTHS
✋	HAND
🤚	GREASE GUN

1. Collective Servo Actuator Support
2. Driveshaft Hanger Bearings
3. Flex Couplings

LUBRICANTS

Symbol	Specification	
GAP	MIL-G-25537	⚠️1
EP	204-040-755	
GWT	MIL-G-81322	⚠️1

Fig. 4-24 Typical lubrication chart used for a lubrication guide.

112

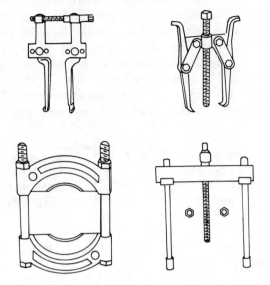

Fig. 4-25 *Standard bearing pullers used for removal of roller and ball bearing.*

3. Cracked and broken separators.

4. Broken or cracked balls or rollers.

5. Flaked areas on balls, rollers, or races.

6. Discoloration due to heat.

7. Brinelled bearings.

When components are torn down in a shop, bearings are often not inspected because shop experience indicates that they should be replaced. This may be due to wear or because the bearing will be damaged when it is removed.

5. Installation

When bearings are to be installed, a number of items must be considered for proper installa-

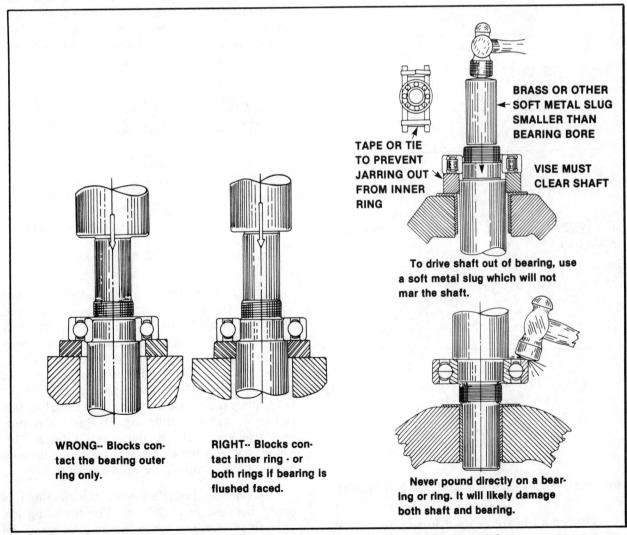

WRONG-- Blocks contact the bearing outer ring only.

RIGHT-- Blocks contact inner ring · or both rings if bearing is flushed faced.

TAPE OR TIE TO PREVENT JARRING OUT FROM INNER RING

BRASS OR OTHER SOFT METAL SLUG SMALLER THAN BEARING BORE

VISE MUST CLEAR SHAFT

To drive shaft out of bearing, use a soft metal slug which will not mar the shaft.

Never pound directly on a bearing or ring. It will likely damage both shaft and bearing.

Fig. 4-26 *Proper and improper procedures for bearing removal.*

tion. All surfaces contacted by the bearing must be clean. If a new bearing is to be installed, it should not be cleaned of grease before installation. Ball bearing installation in helicopters often require two or more bearings used in conjunction with each other. The bearings may be marked as a set or specific part numbers may determine the bearing set. When two bearings are to be used as a specific set, their faces are ground to form the mating surfaces. This is referred to as a duplex bearing. Three matched bearings are called triplex, etc. The matched sets are marked with a large V scribed across the outside surface of the bearing and should be installed in the manner shown in Fig. 4-27.

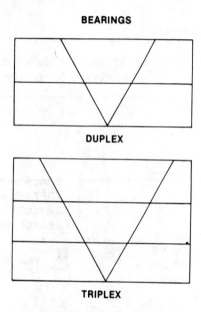

Fig. 4-27 *Proper duplex and triplex bearing installation.*

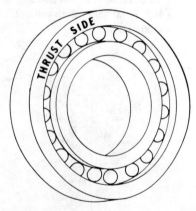

Fig. 4-28 *Thrust side location of a ball bearing.*

Other ball bearings used in sets may be installed in several systems. This is done to allow the bearings to carry thrust loads in one direction or sometimes in both directions. Often a bearing will have "Thrust" stamped on the outer race of the bearing (Fig. 4-28). Some ball bearings may not be marked in this manner but still have a surface which clearly indicates that it is built to carry a thrust load in one direction only. This is indicated by the shoulder of the races (Fig. 4-29).

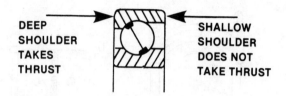

Fig. 4-29 *Thrust shoulder location in relation to the ball and race.*

If such a bearing were installed wrong, it would not be able to withstand thrust loads and could lead to part failure. In most instances the maintenance manual will indicate the correct method of installation, such as face-to-face, back-to-back, or tandem installations (Fig. 4-30).

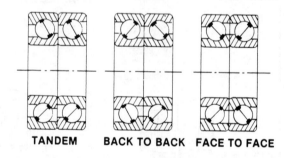

Fig. 4-30 *Typical ball bearing installations*

The two bearing, tandem system carries thrust in the same direction, sharing the load. Both the face-to-face and the back-to-back installations allow thrust loads in both directions. The two systems are used primarily to lock the races. For example: if the installation required that the outer races be held so that no rotation takes places, the bearings would be installed face to face. In other installations the inner race may be stationary while the outer race rotates. This would require a back-to-back installation because more area is available for holding the race.

The actual installation of the bearings is varied because of their uses. The following are general procedures which should be used regardless of the specific installation:

1. Clean the shafts and bearing housings.

2. Clean splines, groves, and keyways. Inspect for burrs, nicks, and slivers.

3. Press bearing on straight and square.

4. A hand-operated arbor press should be used whenever possible.

5. Press only on the race that requires the tight fit.

6. Press bearings until they are seated against the shaft or housing shoulder.

Other methods of installations are used in special installations: heating the bearing in an oil bath to 250 °F so that they will slip over the shaft; placing the outer race in a housing first; using burr marks for the placement of inner races and outer races to maintain close tolerances; and heating the housing before installation. When required, all special procedures are covered in the appropriate maintenance manual.

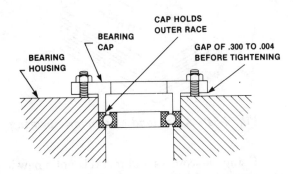

Fig. 4-31 Typical bearing cap installation

Often when bearings are placed in a housing it is desirable to prevent the outer race of the bearing from rotating. This is accomplished by an interference or pinch fit which means the bearing cap pinches the outer race of the bearing. This fit could be .003 to .004 greater than the space the bearing requires (Fig. 4-31). Since the dimensions may vary slightly, this distance is normally set by the use of peelable shims. Two methods are used to determine the pinch. The first method is by placing the bearing in the housing and placing the cap over the bearing. After the cap is placed snugly over the bearing, a feeler gauge is placed between the cap and the housing. The shim is then peeled to obtain this measurement less the desired pinch (Fig. 4-32.)

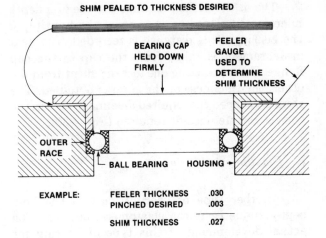

Fig. 4-32 Feeler gauge method of determining bearing pinch.

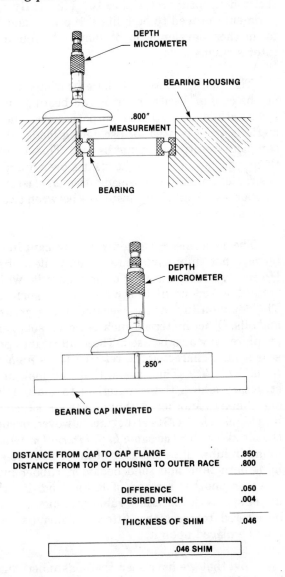

Fig. 4-33 Micrometer method of determining bearing pinch.

115

The other method requires the use of a depth micrometer placed on the top of the housing of the bearing. This distance is recorded. The next measurement is taken from the cap to the cap flange. By subtracting one measurement from the other, the thickness of the shim is obtained. The shim is reduced the required amount to obtain the correct interference fit required (Fig. 4-33).

6. Elastomeric bearing

Another type of bearing used in the helicopter industry is the elastomeric bearing. The actual development of this type of bearing for helicopter use started in the early 1960s. The U.S. Army experimented with elastomeric bearings in their helicopter rotor heads. The early experiments proved to be quite acceptable and led to further development of materials found in rotor systems today.

The characteristics of these bearings should not be confused with roller or ball bearings used for rotational and thrust purposes. The elastomeric bearing is used for oscillating loads where complete rotation is unnecessary. This is why their application to rotor heads has been found so desirable. This type of bearing uses an elastomer (rubber) as the lubricating surface between two or more surfaces.

The elastomer is certainly no lubricant in the terms that lubricants are usually described. However, a lubricant may be any material which is used to reduce friction between two surfaces. The common lubricants used today are greases and oils. Other materials such as water, soap, and graphite may also be used. These lubricants possess a fluid characteristic referred to as *high internal mobility*. This means that the molecular structure allows these materials to move from one shape to another. Although rubber is a solid, it is highly elastic. Its structure, however, is such that it allows for the same *high internal mobility* found in lubricants. Because of this ability to exhibit both fluid and solid behavior, rubber may serve as another method of lubrication. By the use of synthetic materials, rubber compounds can be altered to meet the different demands that may be placed upon it.

Now that we have seen that elastomers may be used as a lubricant, the basic construction of elastomeric bearings may be better understood.

The basic construction is the placement of alternating layers of elastomers and metal laminates (Fig. 4-34). The alternate layers are modified to carry various loads and motion depending upon their application. The elastomers layered between the metal layers are bonded to the metal. This bonding may be to almost any material such as aluminum, stainless steel, or titanium. The material choice will be governed by load factors and other conditions. The bonding of the elastomer to the metal laminates eliminates brinelling, gives structural stability, and forms a seal to keep out dirt and moisture, which affect the life of a conventional bearing.

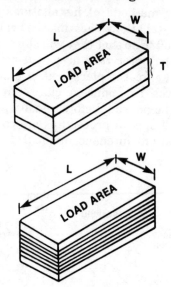

Fig. 4-34 Axial load elastomeric bearing

Using elastomers and metal is not a new idea, these materials are used in the construction of engine mounting, shock mounting of instrument panels, landing gear springs and flexible couplings. It has only been quite recently that new manufacturing techniques have allowed this technology to be extended.

a. Elastomeric bearing types

The elastomeric bearings are sandwich type bearings. The helicopter industry uses this type of bearing because of its wide range of applications. The most common types used are the:

(1) Cylindrical bearings

Cylindrical bearings absorb high radial loads and provide movement in a radial oscillation, such as the teeter-totter motion of a two-bladed main rotor assembly.

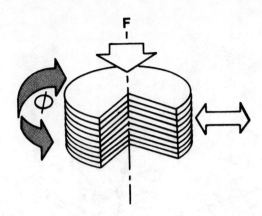

Fig. 4-35 *Typical cylindrical bearing for high radial loads.*

(2) Spherical bearings

Spherical bearings provide movement about the three axes and absorbs heavy torisonal loads. This bearing could be used for the tail rotor pitch change mechanism.

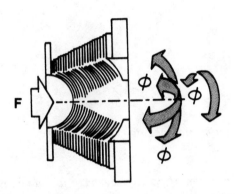

Fig. 4-36 *Typical spherical bearing*

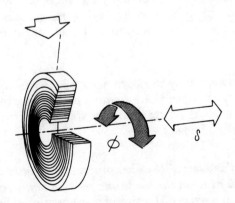

Fig. 4-37 *Typical radial bearing*

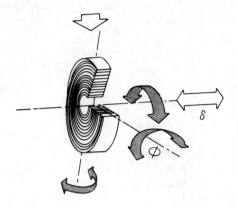

Fig. 4-38 *Typical spherical tubular bearing*

(3) Conical bearings

Conical bearings are capable of absorbing high radial and axial loads with some movement in both directions.

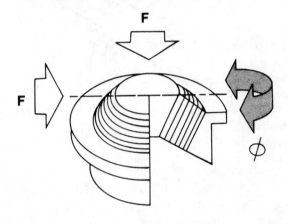

Fig. 4-39 *Typical conical bearing*

These types of bearings used in combinations, can provide the movements necessary and carry the loads required for a complete rotor system (Fig. 4-40).

b. Advantages and disadvantages

The advantage of the elastomeric bearing are numerous.

1. *No lubrication is necessary* because the elastomer is the lubricant.

2. *No disassembly is required for inspections* because the bearing is exposed.

3. *No seizure is possible* because of its design.

117

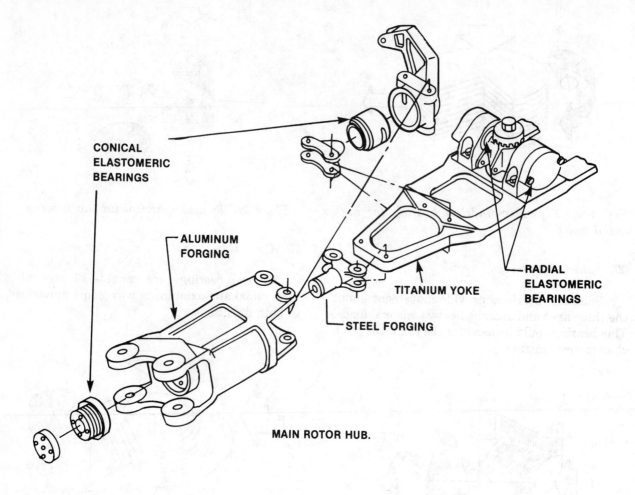

CONICAL ELASTOMERIC BEARINGS

ALUMINUM FORGING

TITANIUM YOKE

RADIAL ELASTOMERIC BEARINGS

STEEL FORGING

MAIN ROTOR HUB.

Fig. 4-40   Semi-rigid rotor using elastomeric bearing

4. *Elimination of the brinelling, pitting, and galling* associated with conventional bearings.

5. *Reduction of vibration and shock* due to the use of the elastomers.

6. *Boots and seals are eliminated* because no grease or oil is required.

7. *Environmental resistance is increased* because the bearing is bonded forming one unit.

8. *Controlled stiffness may be obtained* by the elastomers.

9. *Extended service life is quite common* with a life of five times that of an ordinary bearing.

10. *Reduction of parts necessary for the component has been made* by elimination of close tolerances, seal retainers, and lubrication systems.

However, accompanying these advantages, as in any other mechanical item, certain disadvantages are encountered. These disadvantages are:

1. *The cost of an elastomeric bearing is higher* in most cases than a conventional bearing, but often the extended life will offset the additional cost.

2. *The size of the elastomeric bearing is dependent upon the loads and motion required.* This may exceed the size of a conventional bearing carrying the same load.

118

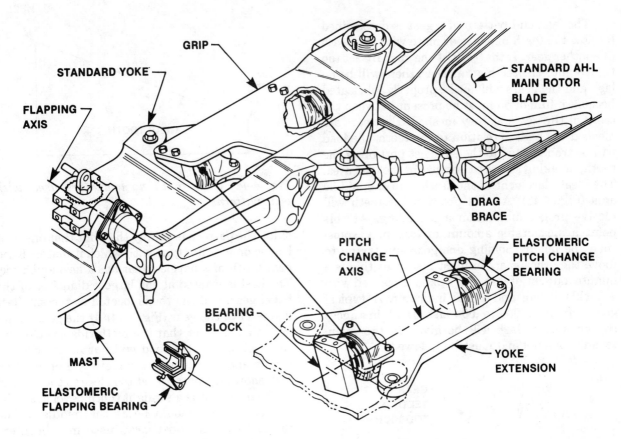

Fig. 4-41 *Rotor head using various elastomeric bearings.*

The elastomeric bearing only requires a visual inspection which can be accomplished quite easily by observing the conditions of the elastomer and its bond to the laminate. This can be accomplished by moving it with its various movements allowed. Often the replacement may be accomplished without complete disassembly. Fig. 4-41 shows an elastomeric bearing typically used in a rotor head.

C. Gears

Gears are used in conjunction with the various bearings and shafts in various components to transmit power, change directions, and to increase or decrease speed. These gears are in various sizes and types doing specific jobs throughout the helicopter. The gear may be a straight tooth gear with which most technicians are familiar. They may also be helicial or spiral bevel gears. Fig. 4-42 shows some typical gears used in a helicopter.

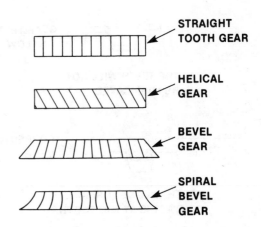

Fig. 4-42 *Types of gears used in helicopters*

Gears are primarily a function of overhaul in regard to replacement, but the helicopter technician should have an understanding of their operation. In order that gears may function properly with each other they must have *lash* and *pattern*.

119

a. Lash and pattern

The lash and pattern of a gear is determined by how the teeth of one gear mate with the teeth of another gear. If the teeth of one gear are set too tightly into the teeth of another, there will be no lash and the gears will not be properly lubricated because a film of oil must be present between the teeth of the gears as they mesh. If the gears are meshed too high in relation to the teeth, the load will be transmitted to the smallest portion of the tooth, breaking the teeth because of the load area. The ideal placement of the teeth is in the middle area (Fig. 4-43). At this position the teeth will receive proper lubrication and loading. At this point a measurable amount of *lash* may sometimes be felt by holding one gear and trying to move the other gear. In most instances this is a minute amount of lash and will be measured with a backlash flag and a dial indicator. A typical gear may have .003 to .004 lash. In all instances the amount of lash will be given in the maintenance manual and must be followed.

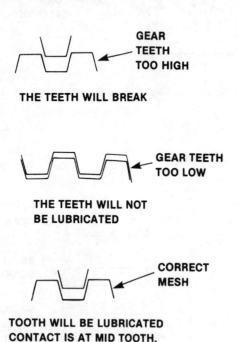

Fig. 4-43 *Various gear tooth positions with mating gears.*

The *pattern* of two gears is also very important and closely related to the lash. The lashes and patterns are generally most critical where directional changes are made with gears, because they are adjustable by moving the gears inward or outward in order to obtain the correct relation-

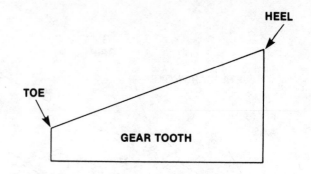

Fig. 4-44 *Gear tooth nomenclature used with gear patterns.*

ship. The pattern is simply the print that one gear leaves on another gear with which it mates. Each gear tooth of a beveled gear has a heel and a toe. The heel is located at the largest diameter of the bevel gear, and the toe is located at the smallest diameter of the gear (Fig. 4-44). If the gears mate in such a manner that the teeth ride too close to the heel or toe, the load will not be distributed evenly and breakage of the teeth will occur. Fig. 4-45 shows the pattern set too close to the toe and to the heel. If it is a straight tooth bevel gear, the proper pattern should be at the middle of the tooth. However, most gears used in helicopters are not straight tooth gears, but are helicial in design. By being helicial more strength may be developed in a smaller gear. With this type of gear a different pattern is developed in a no-load condition than under a load. With this type of gear the ideal no-load pattern is shown in Fig. 4-46.

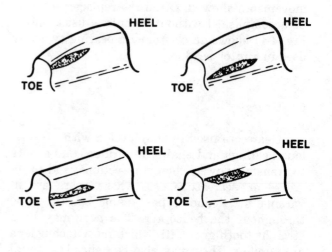

Fig. 4-45 *Gear tooth patterns*

GEAR
HEEL
TOE
PINION
HEEL
TOE
CORRECT

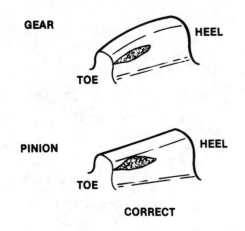

Fig. 4-46 Ideal no load pattern

The patterns of these gears is taken by using Prussian Blue on the gears to leave the imprint of the other gear on the teeth. Shown in Fig. 4-47 are some typical patterns and directions on the movement of the gears. The gears are moved in and out by shims (Fig. 4-48). The thickness of these shims determine the position of the gear and change the lash and pattern.

Often these gears on which lashes and patterns must be obtained are matched sets and are replaced as matched sets. Some of the older gears of this type even have match marks as to what tooth meshes with what tooth with X's and O's scribed in the tooth. This is so that the high and low spots do not come in contact with each other

SHIM TO MOVE
GEAR IN OR
OUT
SHIM
TO MOVE
GEAR IN OR
OUT

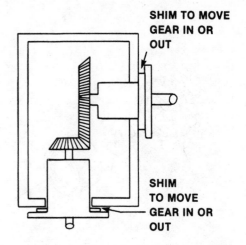

Fig. 4-48 Typical shim method of moving gear positions.

at the same time. Today this system is almost forgotten because more modern methods of manufacturing have eliminated the problem.

Opinions vary considerably as to whether lash or pattern should be determined first. Most technicians prefer to obtain lash first and then check the pattern. The reverse of finding pattern and then determining lash will also work. If either lash or pattern cannot be properly adjusted, it is a good indication of excessive wear in the gear teeth and the gears must be replaced. In such situations it is most probable that if pattern is obtained, the lash will be out; and when the lash is

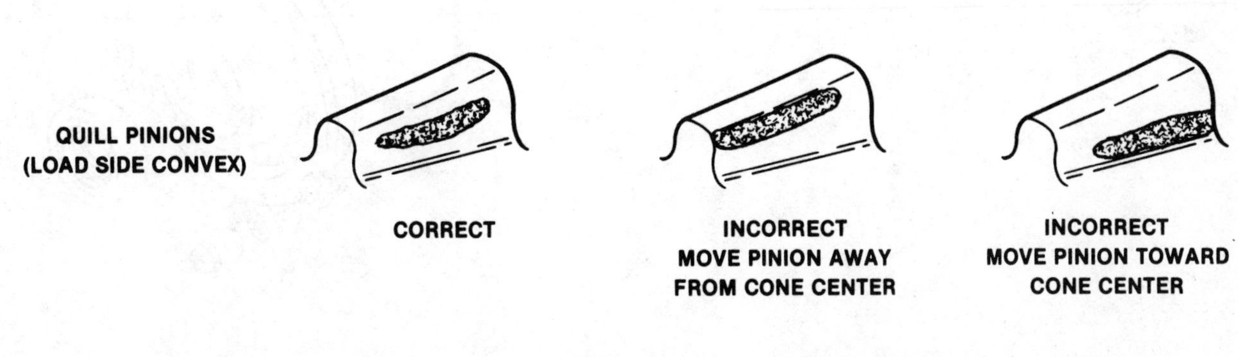

TYPICAL ACCESSORY GEAR TOOTH PATTERN
ACCESSORY GEAR
(LOAD SIDE CONCAVED)
QUILL PINIONS
(LOAD SIDE CONVEX)
CORRECT
INCORRECT
MOVE PINION AWAY
FROM CONE CENTER
INCORRECT
MOVE PINION TOWARD
CONE CENTER

Fig. 4-47 Patterns may be changed by moving the gears.

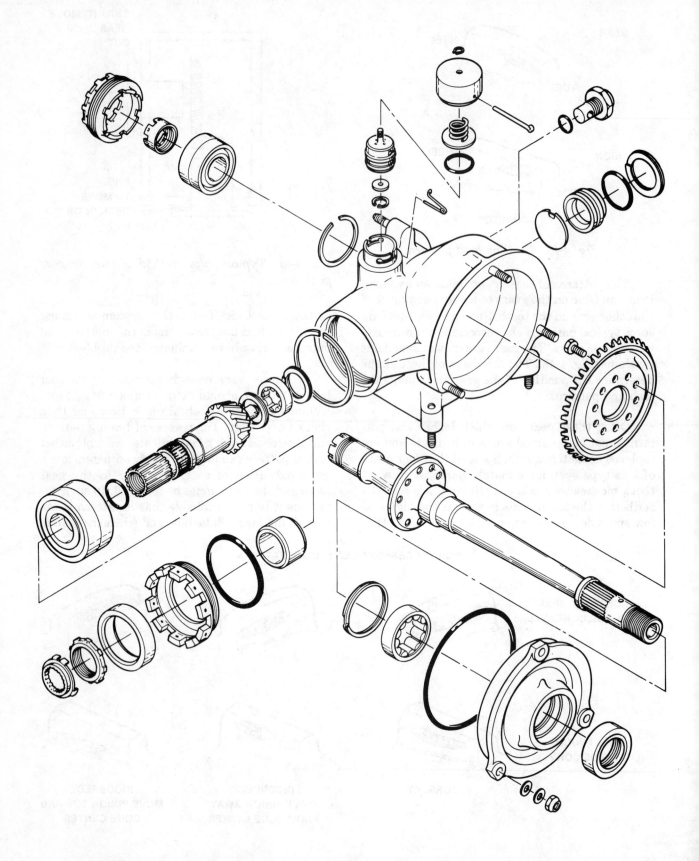

Fig. 4-49 Typical gearbox using control rings to obtain correct gear positions.

set, the pattern will be out. Anytime that one half of a unit such as these is removed, the shim must not be misplaced. If the shim is lost, a new lash and pattern must be taken. Since most of the gears are matched, the mating gears may not be interchanged either.

On most of the newer helicopters only a lash check is taken. This lash check is used as a wear and assembly check only. With new manufacturing techniques control rings are placed in the housings (Fig. 4-49). These rings are ground for a specific case and will control the way the gears will mesh for lash and pattern. This simplifies gear replacement and eliminates the time-consuming process of mating gears. If a control ring is ever removed and lost, the case will have to be returned to the factory for a new ring.

These are a few of the peculiarities that will be found in helicopter maintenance. Most of these items will repeat themselves several times in other maintenance problems as the various systems of the helicopter are studied.

QUESTIONS:

41. The right and the left of the non-rotating components are the same as the directions used on fixed-wing aircraft.

    A. True

    B. False

42. Skid-gear helicopters are moved with ground handling wheels or dollies.

    A. True

    B. False

43. The use of colored dots and stripes on rotating components is for the purpose of:

    A. decoration.

    B. identification.

    C. balance.

44. Rotor blades need not be tied down if a rotor brake is installed.

    A. True

    B. False

45. The helicopter may often be lifted by the mast assembly by the use of hoisting eyes.

    A. True

    B. False

46. A special formula must be used when the arm length of a torque wrench is changed.

    A. True

    B. False

47. Locking tangs may be used several times before replacing.

    A. True

    B. False

48. Most bearings used in helicopters are of a general nature and may be replaced with standard bearings.

    A. True

    B. False

49. Two ball bearings used together are called _____ bearings if they are marked with a "V" and have the races ground for a match set.

    A. Duplex

    B. Matched

    C. Tandem

50. The shoulder of the inner and outer race of a ball bearing determines the thrust side.

    A. True

    B. False

123

51. Spherical bearings are sometimes installed by means of:

   A. locktite.

   B. roller staking.

   C. They can not be changed.

52. Dry film lubricant is normally associated with bronze bearings.

   A. True

   B. False

53. To remove bearings they should be pressed out using the inner race to press on.

   A. True

   B. False

54. Bearings used in a pair to carry a thrust load in one direction are installed:

   A. back-to-back.

   B. face-to-face.

   C. tandem.

55. Bearings may be pinched only at the outer races.

   A. True

   B. False

56. If alignment is not correct on spherical bearing rod ends:

   A. they will self-align.

   B. travel of the component may be limited.

57. The lubricant of an elastomeric bearing is provided by:

   A. dry film lubricant.

   B. the elastomer.

   C. grease.

58. Elastomeric bearings can only carry thrust loads.

   A. True

   B. False

59. Rotational loads cannot be carried by elastomeric bearings.

   A. True

   B. False

60. Gear lash is always associated with gear pattern.

   A. True

   B. False

SECTION V
Main Rotor System

A. Introduction

The main rotor is the wing of the helicopter. In addition to the normal stresses placed on the wing, there are stresses imposed on the rotor system by centrifugal force. This force is coupled with motion which induces vibration, twisting moments, and flexing, placing the rotor system under continuous stress during operation. For this reason, and because of the critical nature of the rotor system, the maintenance and inspection of the helicopter's rotating components must be entrusted to a trained technician who understands the rotor system and its complexity.

Since the inception of the helicopter, it has been the goal of every manufacturer to build the most reliable, maintenance free, and best performing rotor system possible. Through continuous efforts in research and development many improvements have been made in the rotor systems. New improvements have increased the finite life of the components, decreased the maintenance, and increased performance in both lift and speed. Many improvements resulted in various rotor system designs, each one having advantages and disadvantages. The final result is a compromise adapting the greatest advantages with the least adverse characteristics possible. It is only by incorporating these various designs that advances have been made. This has resulted in a number of different rotor systems being produced. The maintenance technician should be familiar with the various systems for proper servicing and inspections. The purpose of this section is to familiarize the technician with some of the rotor systems and maintenance techniques.

B. Rotor Heads

The rotor heads that are in use today are of two basic types — the fully articulated and the semi-rigid rotor. A rigid rotor system has been used experimentally and at least one manufacturer uses a rigid head with blades that bend.

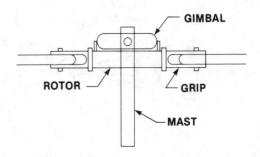

Fig. 5-1   Typical underslung rotor

The semi-rigid rotor heads are of a two-bladed type and are usually underslung. This means that the major portion of the head is below the top of the mast. This is done to increase stability (Fig. 5-1). The head must have a seesaw action or flapping axis using a gimbal or a pillow block trunnion arrangement at the top of the rotor. This equalizes the lift forces of the advancing and retreating blades (Fig. 5-2). The head must also have a feathering axis for changing pitch, provided for by movable blade grips (Fig. 5-3).

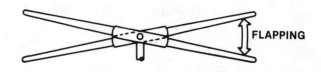

Fig. 2   Flapping axis associated with semi-rigid rotors

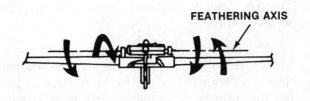

Fig. 5-3   Feathering axis of a rotor system

125

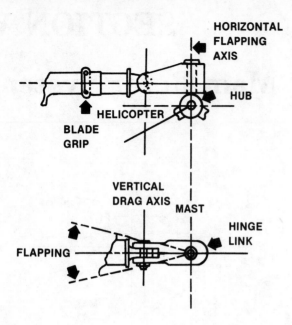

Fig. 5-4 *Fully articulated rotors flap independently*

The fully articulated rotor head has provisions for independent flapping of the rotor blades by using a hinge mechanism for each blade (Fig. 5-4). There must also be a means of allowing the blades to lead and lag independently for equalization of lift of the advancing and retreating blades. Lead and lag are accomplished by another hinge mechanism and a dampener to control the lead and lag of the blade (Fig. 5-5). The head must also provide a pitch change for each blade. Until quite recently this required a rather complex mechanism, but the number of parts has been greatly reduced due to new technology.

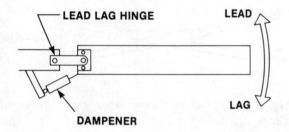

Fig. 5-5 *Lead and lag must be provided on fully articulated rotors*

The different rotor heads may also be classified by the lubrication system used. The original rotor heads needed grease for lubrication of the bearing surfaces, requiring frequent maintenance to insure proper lubrication. The next improvement included an oil system in the head. This allowed the bearing to be enclosed in oil, needing less maintenance. The heads are now classified as *wet* or *dry* heads according to the lubrication requirements. Some heads in the newer technology will require no lubrication.

The rotor heads are usually made of steel and aluminum alloy. As a result many of the parts are time-life limited because of the stresses imposed on the head components. One manufacturer has a new head of fiberglass that presently does not have a retirement life. If this head proves successful in the field, other manufacturers possibly will adopt its' technology.

C. Semi-Rigid Rotor Heads

Due to the different manufacturers and models of helicopters there are many different semi-rigid rotor head designs. One of the early designs is shown in Fig. 5-6. Even though the parts change from design to design the nomenclature of the basic unit remains much the same. A breakdown of the head components is shown in Fig. 5-7.

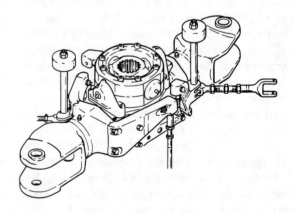

Fig. 5-6 *Bell 47 rotor head*

1. Bell 47

The basic member of the head is the yoke (21). This unit is of steel construction and is used to support the grips (14). The grips are attached to the yoke by an adapter nut that screws into the grip and is held to the yoke by two thrust bearings, a spacer, and a yoke retaining nut (23, 17, and 16 respectively). Shown in Fig. 5-8 is a cutaway view of this relationship. The grip assembly will retain the blade and support the drag brace (2) which is used to prevent fore and aft move-

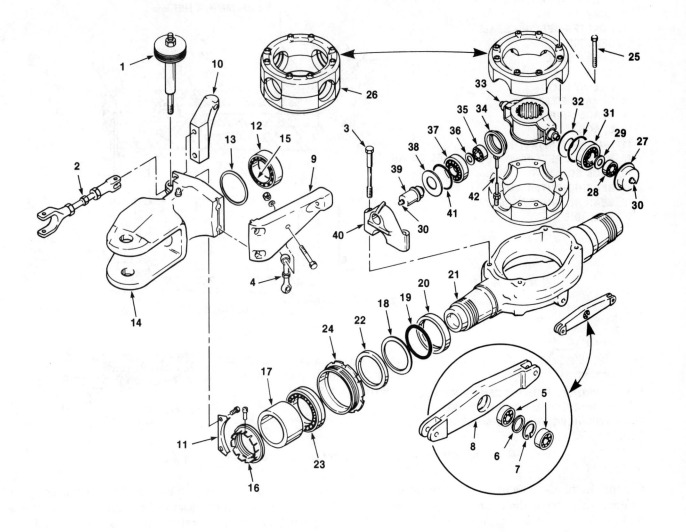

1. COUNTERWEIGHT ASSEMBLIES
2. DRAG BRACES
3. PILLOW BLOCK BOLTS
4. EQUALIZER LINKS
5. BEARING
6. SPACER WASHER
7. SNAP-RING
8. EQUALIZER BEAM
9. PITCH HORN
10. EQUALIZER HORN
11. BLADE GRIP LOCKING PLATE
12. BLADE GRIP BEARING
13. SEAL
14. GRIP

15. BEARING INNER YOKE
16. YOKE BEARING NUT
17. SPACER
18. SHIM
19. O-RING SEAL
20. SEAL RING
21. YOKE
22. SEAL
23. BEARING
24. ADAPTER
25. CAP SCREW
26. GIMBAL RING
27. BEARING CAPS
28. BEARINGS

29. SHIMS
30. FITTINGS
31. BEARINGS
32. SEAL
33. TRUNNION
34. BEARING CAPS
35. BEARINGS
36. SHIMS
37. ROLLER BEARINGS
38. SEALS
39. PILLOW BLOCK PINS
40. PILLOW BLOCK
41. RETAINER RING

Fig. 5-7 Disassembled Bell 47 rotor head

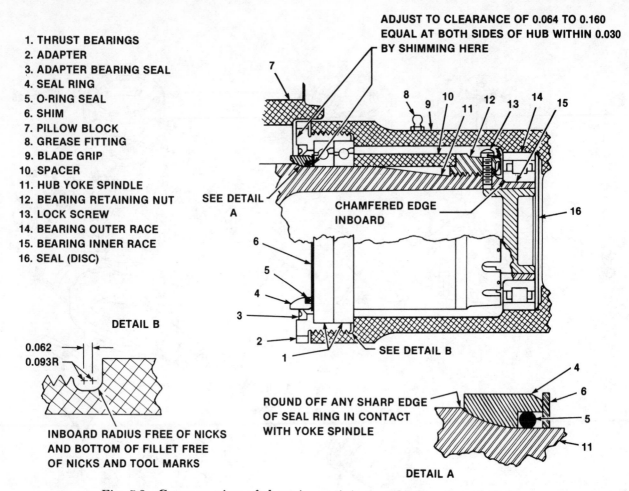

1. THRUST BEARINGS
2. ADAPTER
3. ADAPTER BEARING SEAL
4. SEAL RING
5. O-RING SEAL
6. SHIM
7. PILLOW BLOCK
8. GREASE FITTING
9. BLADE GRIP
10. SPACER
11. HUB YOKE SPINDLE
12. BEARING RETAINING NUT
13. LOCK SCREW
14. BEARING OUTER RACE
15. BEARING INNER RACE
16. SEAL (DISC)

ADJUST TO CLEARANCE OF 0.064 TO 0.160
EQUAL AT BOTH SIDES OF HUB WITHIN 0.030
BY SHIMMING HERE

SEE DETAIL A

CHAMFERED EDGE
INBOARD

DETAIL B

0.062
0.093R

INBOARD RADIUS FREE OF NICKS
AND BOTTOM OF FILLET FREE
OF NICKS AND TOOL MARKS

SEE DETAIL B

ROUND OFF ANY SHARP EDGE
OF SEAL RING IN CONTACT
WITH YOKE SPINDLE

DETAIL A

Fig. 5-8   Cutaway view of the grip retaining method used on Bell 47

ment of the blade. The drag brace is retained to the grip by a rod of the counterweight assembly (1). The purpose of the counterweight is to ease movement of the feathering axis of the main rotor blades. Movement of the blades is accomplished through the pitch horn (9) bolted to the grip. On the rear of the grip is an equalizer horn (10). This, in conjunction with four links (4) and two equalizer beams (8), will ensure that the same pitch angle will be obtained in both blades. On top of the yoke assembly are bolted two pillow blocks (40) used to support the gimbal ring (26) through a set of bearings. The gimbal in turn supports the trunnion (33), which allows the rotor to be driven from the mast and forms a pivot for the rotor system to tilt during flight.

2.   Hiller 12

A rather unique rotor head of early production is shown in Fig. 5-9. This rotor head is used on the Hiller 12. The hub assembly consists of

two major units: the hub unit containing the two main rotor root fork assemblies, each of which is retained by tension-torsion plate assemblies; and a gimbal ring unit which provides the spanwise and chordwise tilt axes for the main rotor hub (Fig. 5-10).

The hub unit (2) is forged aluminum and is designed to permit 2-1/2° preconing of the rotor blades. The elliptical bore of the hub provides a 9° spanwise tilt and a 12° chordwise tilt without striking the mast. Two holes pass through each blade side of the hub. The inboard hole is used for a pin (4) that anchors the hub end on the tension-torsion assembly. The outboard hole or slot allows the incidence arm (9) to pass through the hub. This arm is attached to the tension-torsion plate and is used to change the blade pitch angle. Each blade root fork (1) is mounted in the fork bore of the hub assembly on two needle bearings (26, 28). The steel forks rotate on the bearings forming the blade pitch axis. The outboard tension-

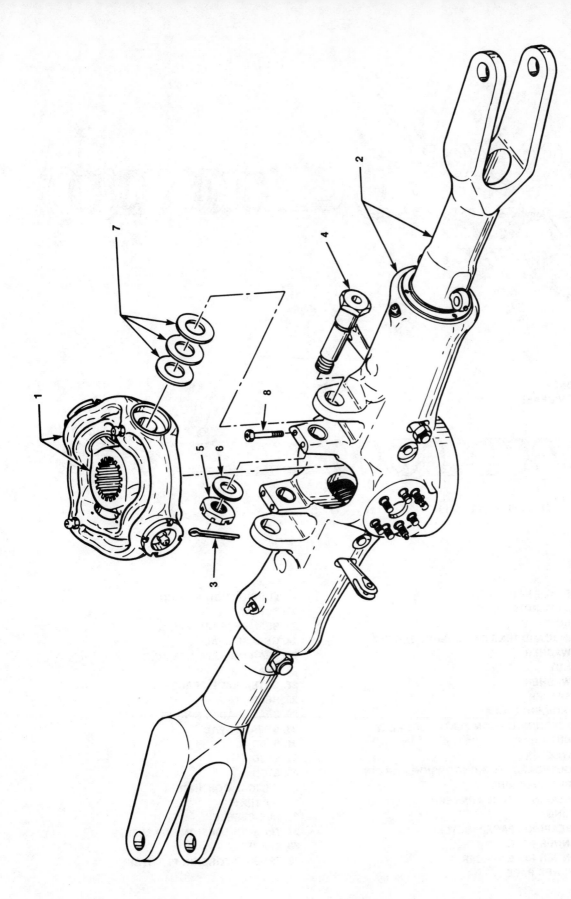

1. GIMBAL RING AND SPLINE FITTING UNIT
2. ROTOR HUB AND BLADE ROOT FORK UNIT
3. COTTER PIN
4. GIMBAL RING BOLT

5. NUT
6. WASHER
7. THRUST WASHER
8. BOLT

Fig. 5-9 Hiller 12 rotor head

129

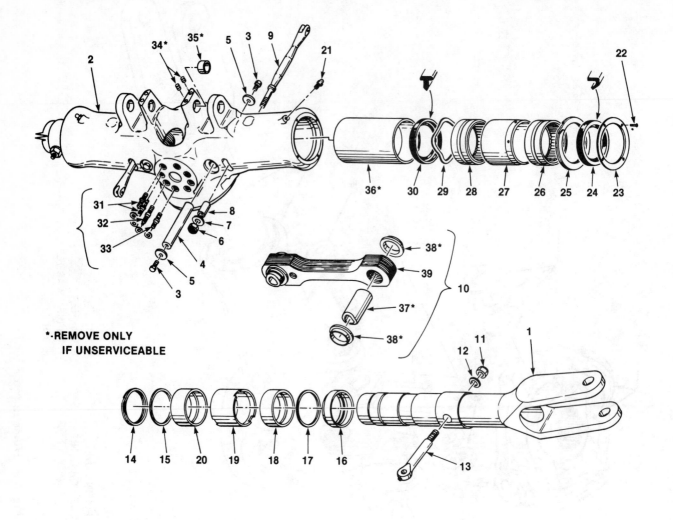

*-REMOVE ONLY
   IF UNSERVICEABLE

1. BLADE ROOT FORK
2. MAIN ROTOR HUB
3. BOLT
4. INBOARD TENSION-TORSION BAR PIN
5. WASHER
6. NUT
7. WASHER
8. SPACER
9. INCIDENCE ARM
10. TENSION-TORSION PLATE ASSEMBLY
11. NUT
12. WASHER
13. OUTBOARD TENSION-TORSION BAR PIN
14. RETAINER RING
15. BEARING SPACER (INNER)
16. RING
17. BEARING SPACER (OUTER)
18. INNER RACE
19. INNER RACE SPACER
20. INNER RACE

21. LUBRICATION FITTING
22. SCREW
23. SEAL RETAINING RING
24. GREASE SEAL
25. BEARING RETAINER RING
26. BEARING
27. OUTER RACE SPACER
28. BEARING
29. SEAL SPACER SPRING
30. GREASE SEAL
31. STUD
32. STUD
33. STUD
34. HELICAL COIL INSERT
35. BUSHING
36. HUB SLEEVE
37. TENSION-TORSION BAR SLEEVE
38. SPACER
39. TENSION-TORSION PLATE SET

Fig. 5-10 Disassembled view of the Hiller 12 rotor head

130

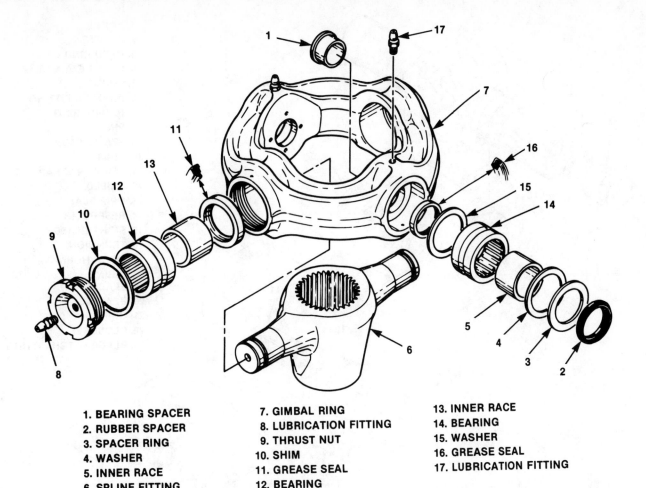

1. BEARING SPACER	7. GIMBAL RING	13. INNER RACE
2. RUBBER SPACER	8. LUBRICATION FITTING	14. BEARING
3. SPACER RING	9. THRUST NUT	15. WASHER
4. WASHER	10. SHIM	16. GREASE SEAL
5. INNER RACE	11. GREASE SEAL	17. LUBRICATION FITTING
6. SPLINE FITTING	12. BEARING	

Fig. 5-11   Hiller 12 gimbal unit assembly

torsion bar pin (13) passes through the fork and the tension-torsion bar (39), holding the fork to the hub, absorbing tension and torsional loads during flight. This system has found wide use on various heads in different forms.

The gimbal ring unit shown in Fig. 5-11 mounts on top of the hub unit by means of four ears on the hub, and a bearing and pin arrangement. A spline fitting with two arms (6) is placed in the center of the gimbal ring. This is driven by the mast assembly and transmits power to the head for rotation.

3. *Bell 206*

A more modern semi-rigid rotor head is that used on the Bell 206 (Fig. 5-12). This head has been designed as a *wet* head, although many have been converted to *dry* heads.

The yoke (1) is the main structural member of the head. This steel unit is shaped to give a 2-1/2° precone angle to the rotor blades. On the inside of the blade bore of the yoke is a cap and pin assembly (6, 7, 8) used to retain a tension-torsion strap (11) to the yoke. This tension-torsion strap, unlike that used in the Hiller, is made of fine wire wrapped around two spools thousands of times. The cap assembly is held in place by the static stops (9) bolted to the yoke. The grip assembly (21) is supported by two bearings (20) on the yoke. It is secured to the yoke by a latch bolt passing through the grip and the tension-torsion strap and is secured to the yoke with the cup and pin. The pitch horn (17) bolts to the grip for pitch change. This is also the attachment point for the oil reservoir (14) and sight glass to lubricate the grips. Another interesting feature of the grips is the hollow blade bolts (25) used for the addition of weight for spanwise balance. It might also be noted that no drag braces are used. The blade is supported by a latch mechanism in place of the drag brace (Fig. 5-13). Placed on the top of the yoke is a trunnion assembly (Fig. 5-14). It is bolted to the yoke with two pillow blocks (10)

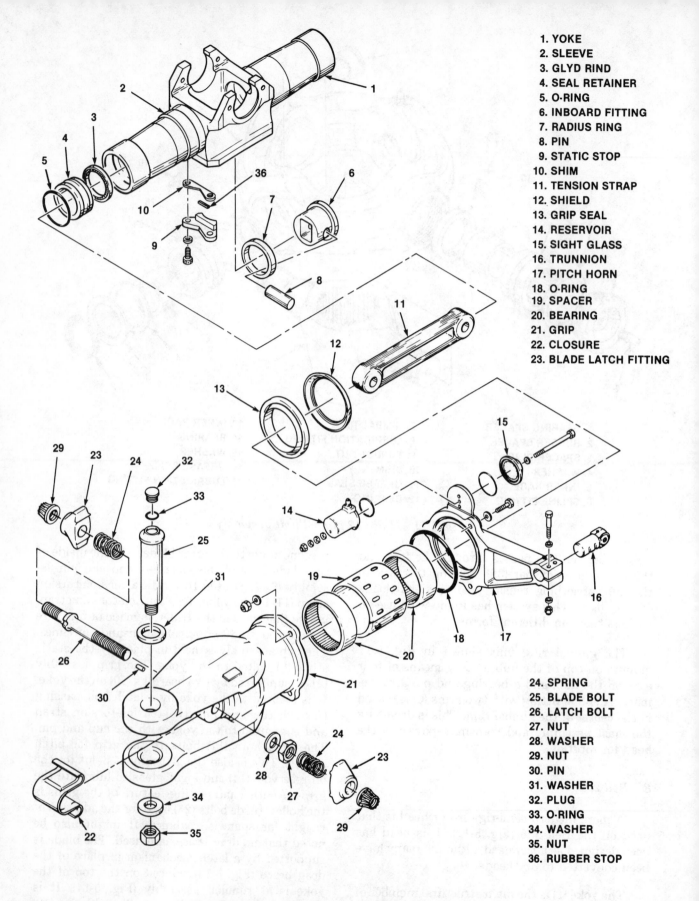

1. YOKE
2. SLEEVE
3. GLYD RIND
4. SEAL RETAINER
5. O-RING
6. INBOARD FITTING
7. RADIUS RING
8. PIN
9. STATIC STOP
10. SHIM
11. TENSION STRAP
12. SHIELD
13. GRIP SEAL
14. RESERVOIR
15. SIGHT GLASS
16. TRUNNION
17. PITCH HORN
18. O-RING
19. SPACER
20. BEARING
21. GRIP
22. CLOSURE
23. BLADE LATCH FITTING

24. SPRING
25. BLADE BOLT
26. LATCH BOLT
27. NUT
28. WASHER
29. NUT
30. PIN
31. WASHER
32. PLUG
33. O-RING
34. WASHER
35. NUT
36. RUBBER STOP

Fig. 5-12   Semi-rigid rotor used on the Bell 206
132

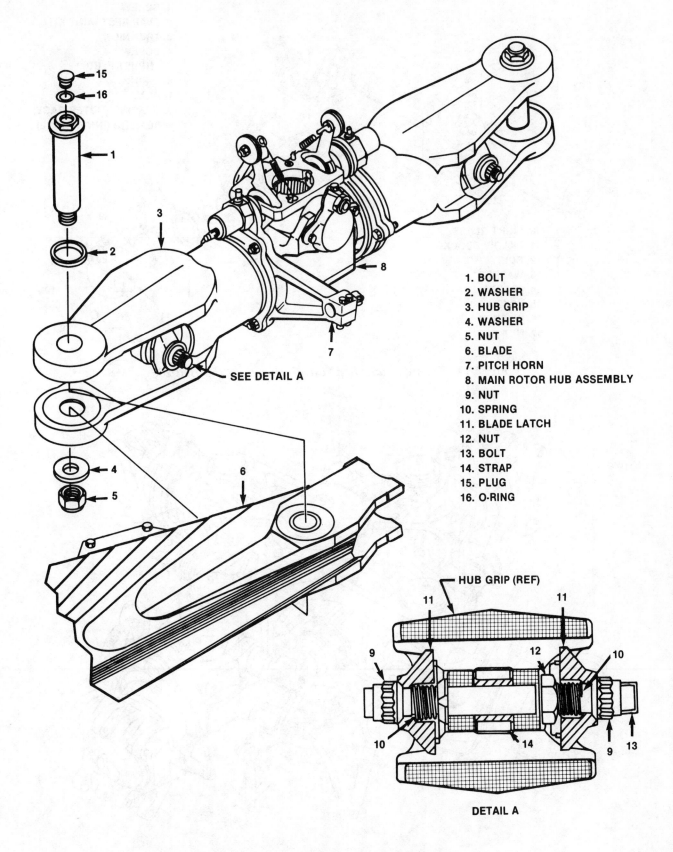

1. BOLT
2. WASHER
3. HUB GRIP
4. WASHER
5. NUT
6. BLADE
7. PITCH HORN
8. MAIN ROTOR HUB ASSEMBLY
9. NUT
10. SPRING
11. BLADE LATCH
12. NUT
13. BOLT
14. STRAP
15. PLUG
16. O-RING

SEE DETAIL A

HUB GRIP (REF)

DETAIL A

Fig. 5-13 Latch assembly used on the Bell 206

133

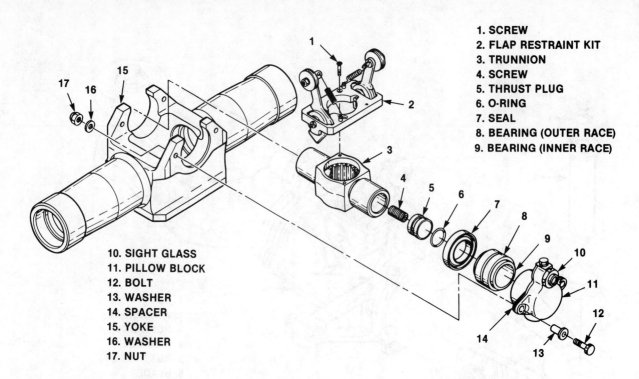

1. SCREW
2. FLAP RESTRAINT KIT
3. TRUNNION
4. SCREW
5. THRUST PLUG
6. O-RING
7. SEAL
8. BEARING (OUTER RACE)
9. BEARING (INNER RACE)

10. SIGHT GLASS
11. PILLOW BLOCK
12. BOLT
13. WASHER
14. SPACER
15. YOKE
16. WASHER
17. NUT

Fig. 5-14   Trunnion and flap restraint used on the Bell 206

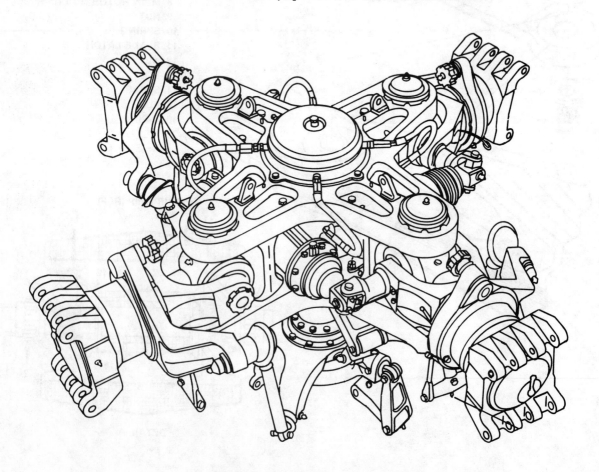

Fig. 5-15   Fully articulated rotor used on the S-58

134

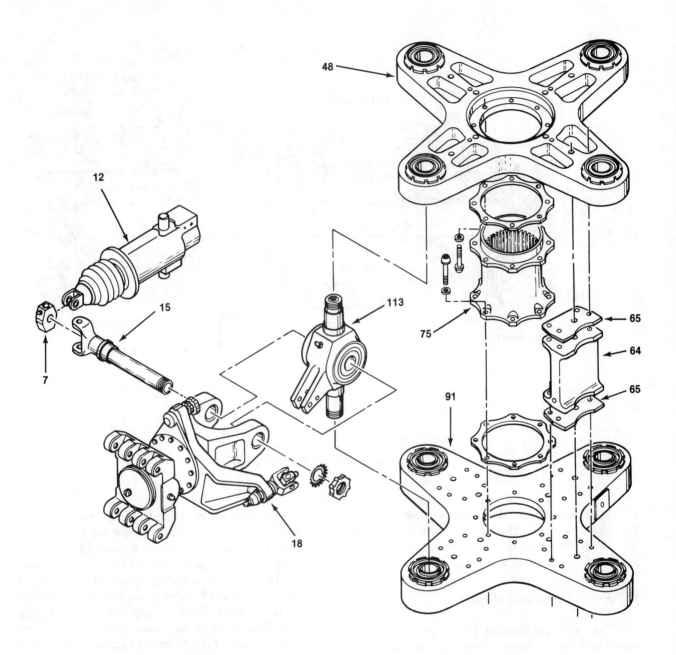

7. TRUNNION
12. DAMPENER ASSEMBLY
15. HORIZONTAL PIN
18. SLEEVE-SPINDLE ASSEMBLY
48. UPPER PLATE

64. SPACER
65. SPACER-SHIM
75. HUB
91. LOWER PLATE
113. HINGE

Fig. 5-16   Disassembled view of the S-58 rotor

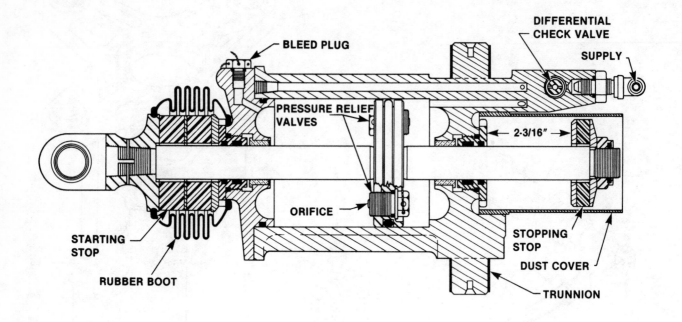

Fig. 5-17 Typical hydraulic dampener used on the S-58

which act as oil reserviors and bearing retainers for the trunnion (3). The flap restraint is placed on top of the trunnion (2) which limits the flapping action of the rotor at low RPM.

D. Fully Articulated Heads

The fully articulated rotor heads, like the semi-rigid heads have many designs. Although they have always given a smoother operation, the number of parts required in the manufacture and maintenance has always been greater until quite recently. With some of the newer designs, the number of parts, as well as the maintenance requirements, have been reduced.

1. S-58

One of the early rotor heads is used on the S-58 helicopter (Fig. 5-15). Although this head is not the earliest, it is similar in design to many of the heads used on Sikorsky helicopters.

Fig. 5-16 shows that the head consists of a hub (75) which is splined to the mast and flanged to accommodate an upper and lower plate assembly (48, 91). The plate assemblies form the support for the four lead-lag hinges (113) that are placed on tapered roller bearings and form the support of the individual flapping hinge for each blade. The sleeve spindle assembly (18) comprises the other half of the flapping hinge and is pinned to the lead-lag hinge by a horizontal pin (15). The forked end of the pin acts as part of a hinge mechanism for the dampeners (12) which control the rate of the lead-lag of the rotor blades (Fig. 5-17). The sleeve spindle assembly also provides the feathering action of the blade (Fig. 5-18). The sleeve (53) attaches to the pitch horn and slides over the spindle (63). The thrust loads of the blade are taken up by a thrust bearing stack (57) which allows pitch change of the blades. The flapping and drooping action of this rotor is limited by flap and droop stops attached to the lead-lag hinge (Fig. 5-19).

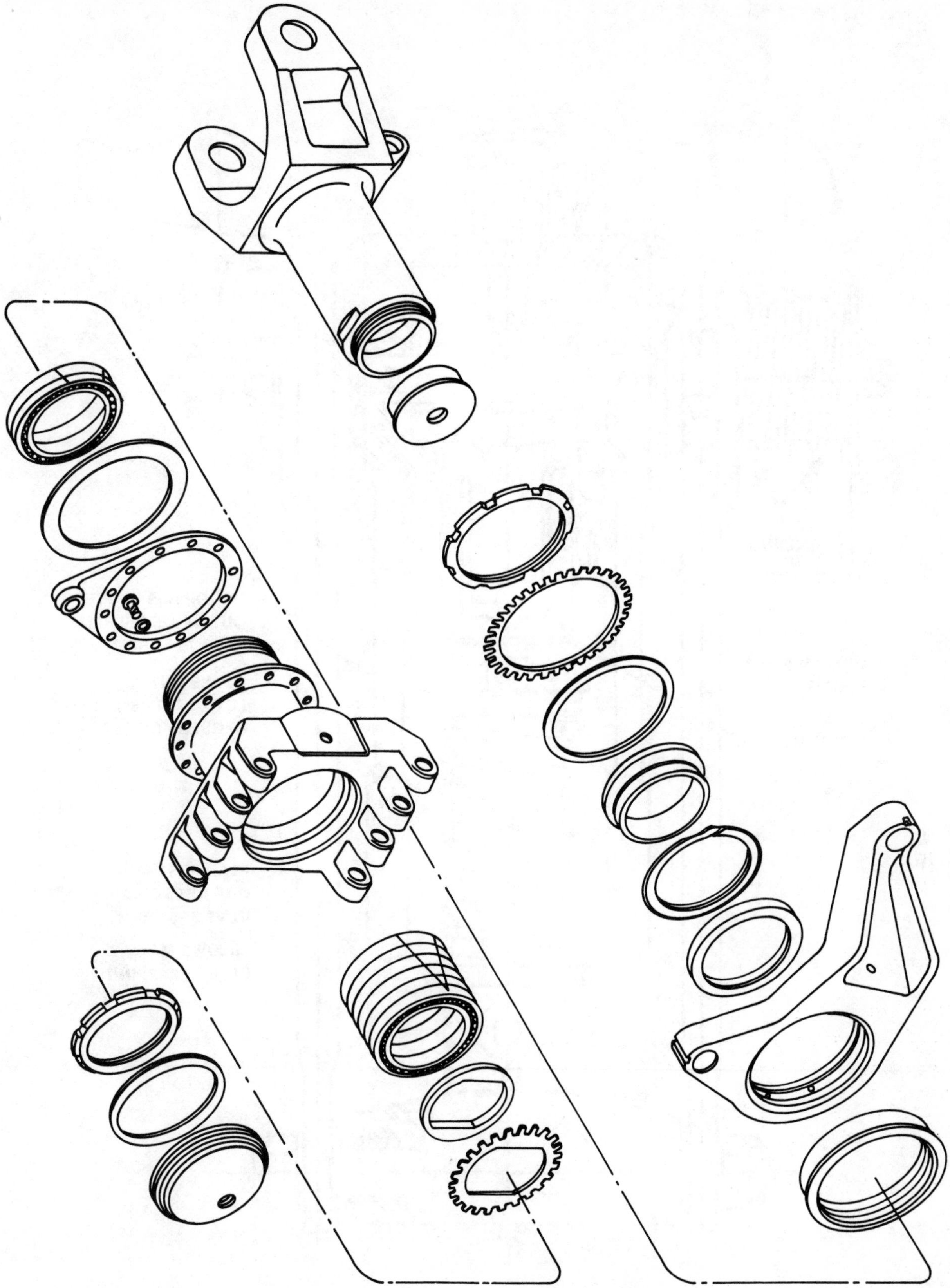

Fig. 5-18 Grip assembly used on the S-58

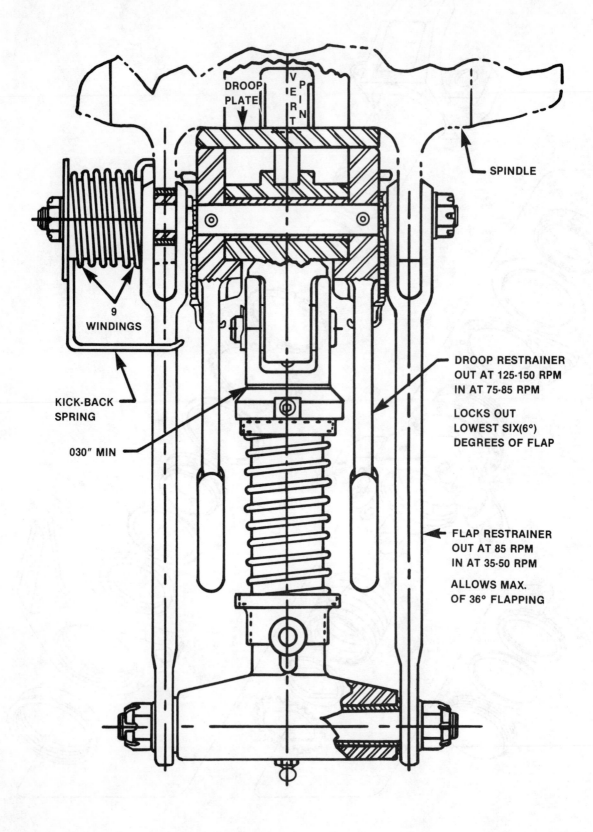

DROOP
PLATE

V
E
R
T

P
I
N

SPINDLE

9
WINDINGS

KICK-BACK
SPRING

030" MIN

DROOP RESTRAINER
OUT AT 125-150 RPM
IN AT 75-85 RPM

LOCKS OUT
LOWEST SIX(6°)
DEGREES OF FLAP

FLAP RESTRAINER
OUT AT 85 RPM
IN AT 35-50 RPM

ALLOWS MAX.
OF 36° FLAPPING

Fig. 5-19   Droop stop assembly used on the S-58

138

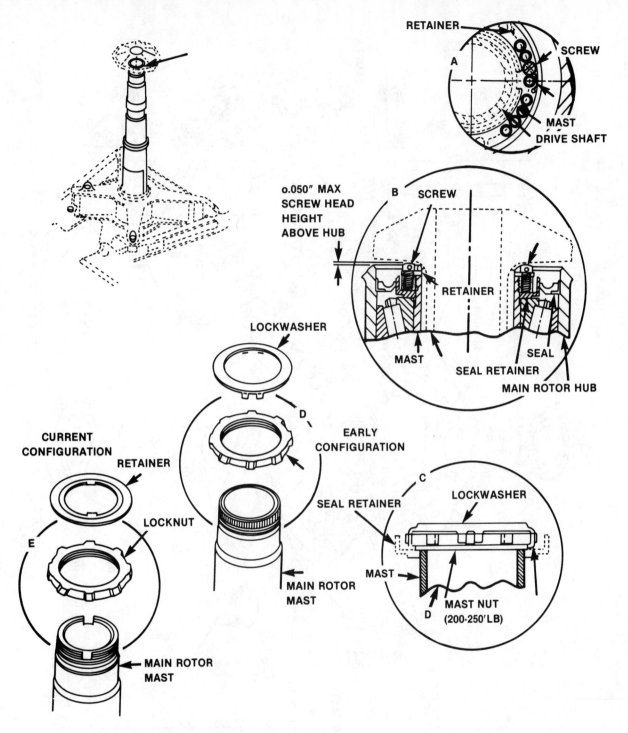

RETAINER

SCREW

A

MAST DRIVE SHAFT

o.050" MAX
SCREW HEAD
HEIGHT
ABOVE HUB

B **SCREW**

RETAINER

MAST **SEAL**

SEAL RETAINER

MAIN ROTOR HUB

LOCKWASHER

D

**EARLY
CONFIGURATION**

**CURRENT
CONFIGURATION**

RETAINER

SEAL RETAINER

LOCKNUT

E

**MAIN ROTOR
MAST**

**MAIN ROTOR
MAST**

C

LOCKWASHER

MAST

D

**MAST NUT
(200-250'LB)**

Fig. 5-20   Mast and driveshaft assembly used on the Hughes 500

2. Hughes 500C

Another fully articulated head of a different style is the head of the Hughes 500C. The head is mounted to a stationary mast and is driven by a driveshaft passing through the center of the mast (Fig. 5-20).

The hub assembly is supported on the static mast by two opposed tapered roller bearings connected with a special lock nut and locking device. The hub assembly consists of the hub, lower shoe, which attaches to the hub, four pitch change housings holding the bearing for pitch change of the blades, and a steel droop stop ring attached to the lower shoe (Fig. 5-21).

139

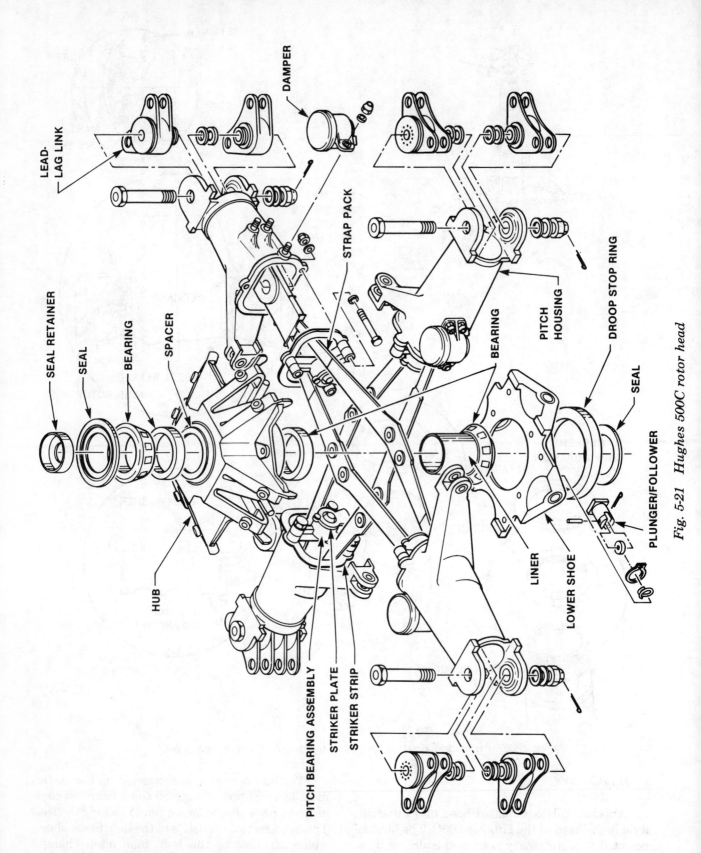

Fig. 5-21 Hughes 500C rotor head

DAMPER

LEAD-LAG LINK

STRAP PACK

DROOP STOP RING

PITCH HOUSING

BEARING

SEAL

SEAL RETAINER

SEAL

BEARING

SPACER

HUB

PITCH BEARING ASSEMBLY

STRIKER PLATE

STRIKER STRIP

LINER

LOWER SHOE

PLUNGER/FOLLOWER

140

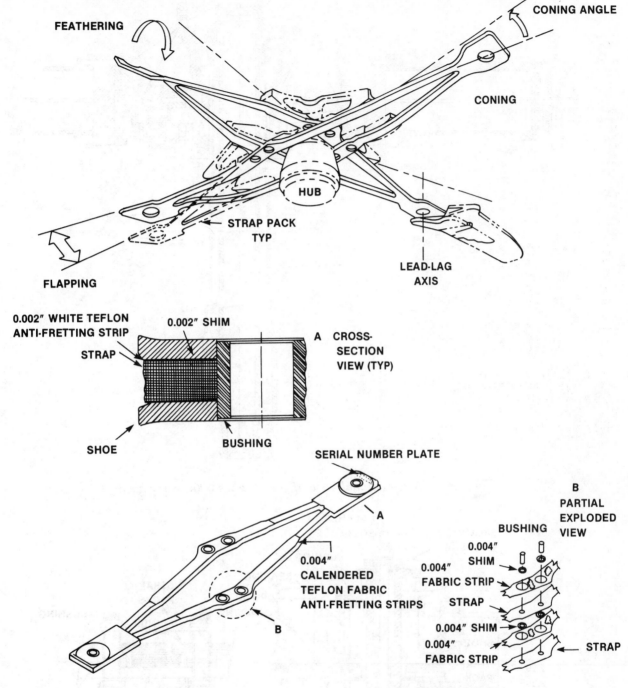

FEATHERING

CONING ANGLE

CONING

HUB

STRAP PACK
TYP

LEAD-LAG
AXIS

FLAPPING

0.002" WHITE TEFLON
ANTI-FRETTING STRIP

0.002" SHIM

A CROSS-
SECTION
VIEW (TYP)

STRAP

SHOE

BUSHING

SERIAL NUMBER PLATE

B
PARTIAL
EXPLODED
VIEW

BUSHING

0.004"
SHIM

A

0.004"
FABRIC STRIP

0.004"
CALENDERED
TEFLON FABRIC
ANTI-FRETTING STRIPS

STRAP

B

0.004" SHIM

0.004"
FABRIC STRIP

STRAP

Fig. 5-22 The strap pack system used in the Hughes 500C

Mounted between the hub and the lower shoe is the strap pack. This unit is the unique feature of the rotor head and is the reason for its light weight and simplicity. It not only reacts to the centrifugal loads imposed on the head by the blades, but also replaces the flapping and feathering hinge found on other fully articulated heads (Fig. 5-22). Each strap assembly is made up of 15 straps of .009 stainless steel with .004 thick

Teflon-impregnated cloth between each strap. The Teflon eliminates fretting corrosion.

The pitch housing arrangement consists of an aluminum housing in which the pitch bearing is held by the striker plate. The spherical pitch bearing has a Teflon lining. The housing itself is secured to a stud in the hub (Fig. 5-23).

141

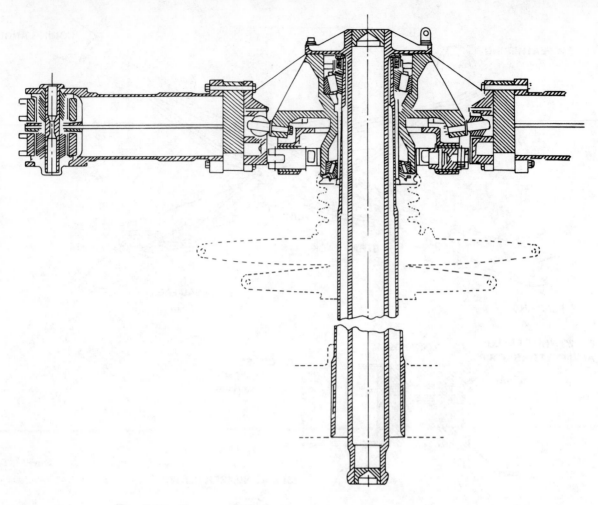

Fig. 5-23   Cross-sectional view of the Hughes 500C rotor head

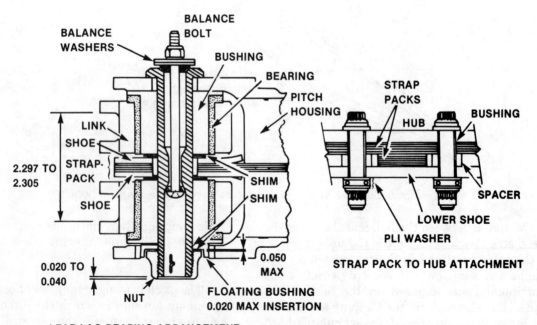

BALANCE WASHERS

BALANCE BOLT

BUSHING

BEARING

PITCH HOUSING

LINK

SHOE

STRAP-PACK

2.297 TO 2.305

SHOE

SHIM

SHIM

0.020 TO 0.040

NUT

0.050 MAX

FLOATING BUSHING 0.020 MAX INSERTION

LEAD-LAG BEARING ARRANGEMENT

STRAP PACKS

HUB

BUSHING

SPACER

LOWER SHOE

PLI WASHER

STRAP PACK TO HUB ATTACHMENT

Fig. 5-24   Lead-lag bearing assembly for the Hughes 500C

142

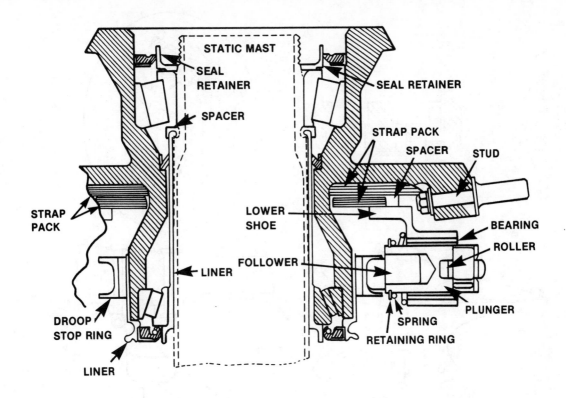

Fig. 5-25   Droop stop system used on the Hughes 500C

The lead-lag bearings are press fitted into the links. The bearings have Teflon-lined shoulders and bores. In the link bearings are steel bushings that bear against the Teflon surfaces of the link bearings. These bushings have a slightly longer length than the link bearings, which allows the bushing to extend from the pitch housing ear to the strap pack shoe, while the lead-lag bolt tightly clamps in the strap pack. At the same time the lead-lag links are free to rotate (Fig. 5-24).

At the bottom of the shoe assembly is the droop stop ring. In the groove of the stop rings are four followers which are pressed into the bodies of the plungers. A roller attached to the plunger rides against the striker plate of the pitch change assembly. This is spring loaded so that during static conditions the striker plate bears against the roller which presses the plunger assemblies against the droop stop ring. At flight RPM the conning angle raises the striker plate off the roller (Fig. 5-25).

Attached at the inboard trailing edge of each blade is a dampener arm which is attached to the dampener. This unit, as the name implies, damp-

ens the hunting action of the lead-lag hinge of the rotor. This particular type is a mechanical unit.

One other rather unique feature of the head is the use of a vibration dampener, a two-part pendulum used to detune the first and second harmonics of the main rotor blade. These vibration absorbers are secured to the root end fitting of the main rotor blades (Fig. 5-26). They are used to absorb 3-per-revolution and 5-per-revolution vibration (Fig. 5-27).

3.   Hughes 500D

The head used on the Hughes 500D is of similar construction to that of the 500C with a few exceptions.

The 500D is a five-bladed rotor. Since the blades cannot be tied to each other as was done in the four-bladed system, they are tied to the hub (Fig. 5-28). The mechanical dampeners are replaced with the elastomeric type, which are discussed in the dampener maintenance portion of this section. The vibration absorbers are also eliminated from the blades because of the blade differences.

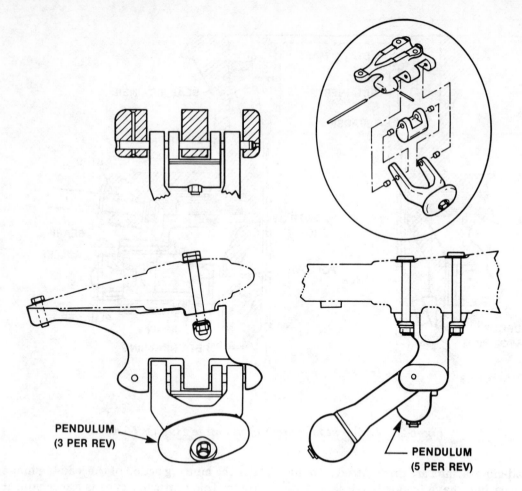

Fig. 5-26   Pendulums used on the Hughes 500C rotor system

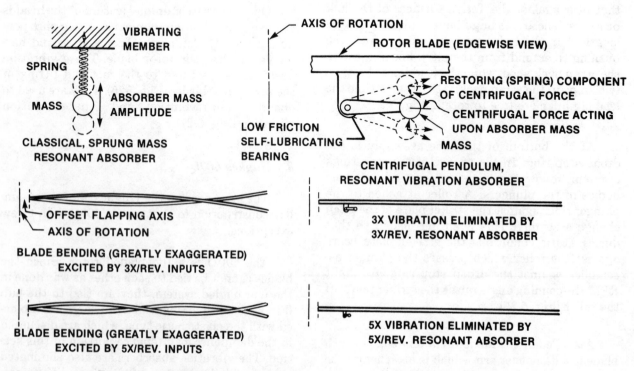

Fig. 5-27   Pendulum theory to eliminate 3 and 5 resonant vibrations

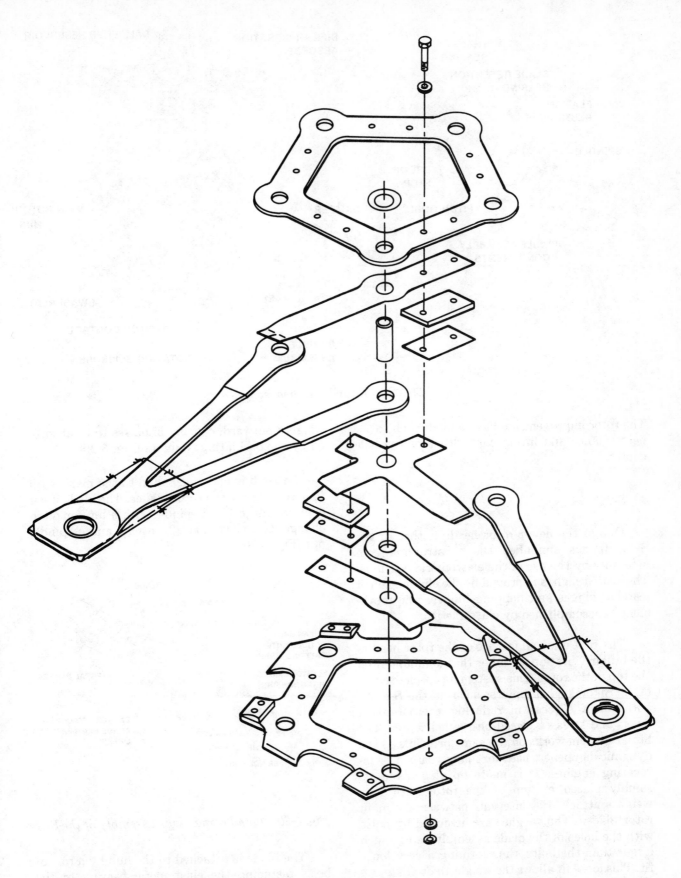

Fig. 5-28 Strap pack system used on the Hughes 500D rotor system

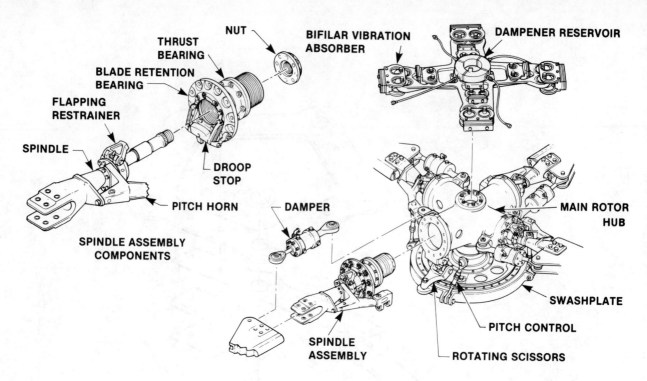

Fig. 5-29 S-76 rotor head disassembled

The rotor improvements have added much to the performance and lifting capabilities of the helicopter.

4. S-76

One of the newer rotor heads is that of the S-76. It has simplified the construction considerably by the use of the elastomeric bearings. The head design is improved by the elimination of lead-lag hinges and flapping hinges. The movement is accomplished by elastomerics.

The first unusual feature of the rotor head is the bifilar vibration absorber that is mounted on the top of the rotor. This system has been used on other Sikorsky helicopters, such as the S-61-N, with much success in reducing the vibration levels and stresses placed on the helicopter. The bifilar system works on the same principle as the dynamic dampeners used for many years in reciprocating engines. It is made up of a blade assembly placed on top of the rotor with four weights attached at intervals between the main rotor blades. The weights are attached by bolts with the holes of the blade assembly being much larger than the bolts, thus forming a very loose fit. This loose fit allows the weight to oscillate. As the rotor turns, centrifugal force holds the

weights outward, causing impulses to be absorbed by the oscillating weights (Fig. 5-29).

The hub is one unit bolted to the mast, with four sockets for the rotor blades. The blade itself contains an integral spindle with a lug for pitch change, two elastomeric bearings, and a spindle nut (Fig. 5-30).

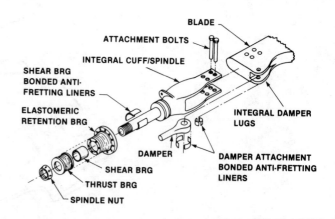

Fig. 5-30 Spindle and blade assembly of the S-76

The blade is attached to the hub by a row of bolts fastening the elastomeric bearing to the hub. This elastomeric bearing is built-up of

TYPES OF ELASTOMERIC BEARINGS

(Solid arrows indicate load)
(Outlined arrows indicate motion)

Polar Spherical

Equatorial Spherical

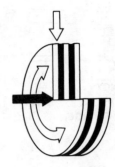

Flat Thrust Pad

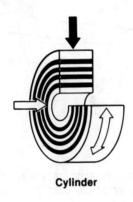

Cylinder

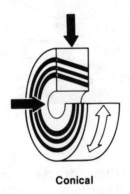

Conical

Typical Helicopter Applications

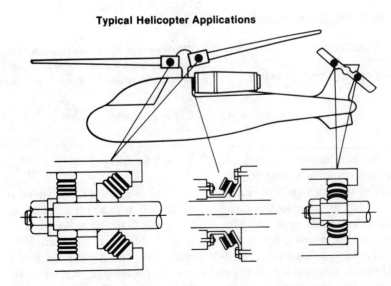

Fig. 5-31   Elastomeric bearing used to give the blade flapping and lead-lag movement

147

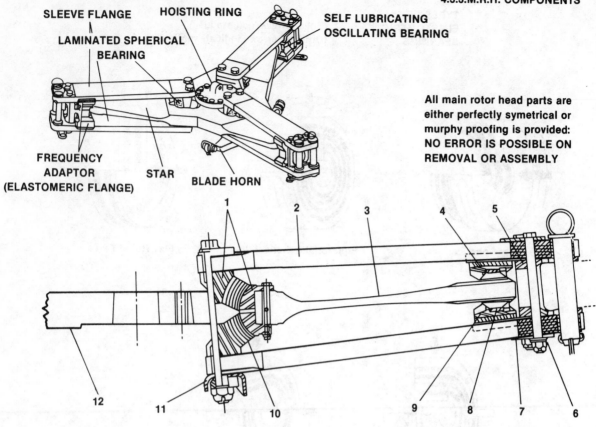

All main rotor head parts are
either perfectly symetrical or
murphy proofing is provided:
NO ERROR IS POSSIBLE ON
REMOVAL OR ASSEMBLY

1 - SPHERICAL BEARING FRAME-ALUMINIUM ALLOY
2 - SLEEVE FLANGE - GLASS/RESIN ROVING
3 - STAR ARM - GLASS/RESIN LAMINATES
4 - BONDING BRAID
5 - ELASTOMERIC FLANGE. FREQUENCY ADAPTOR
6 - SLEEVE SPACER
7 - WASHER (REFER TO NOTE)
8 - PARALLELISM PLATE
9 - SELF LUBRICATING OSCILLATING BEARING

10 - BEARING HOUSING - ALUMINIUM ALLOY
11 - LAMINATED SPHERICAL BEARING
12 - BLADE HORN
13 - LOCATING BOSS

NOTE: Washers (7) can be replaced as required by
balancing plates for head and rotor shaft. The plates are
equally distributed on the upper and lower sleeve flanges.

Fig. 5-32 AStar 350 rotor head

laminations of metal and elastomers bonded together in a soup bowl design with a hole in the
bottom (Fig. 5-31). With this design the blade
may flap, lead and lag. This eliminates the flapping and lead-lag hinge from the system. The
pitch axis passes through this bearing by use of
the integral spindle. The thrust load is carried
from the spindle nut through another thrust type
elastomeric bearing to the retention bearing
which is bolted to the hub. The dampening action
of the blade is accomplished through a conventional hydraulic dampener.

5. AStar 350

The AStar 350 rotor head is the most unusual
design to appear on a helicopter. This rotor head
is made of fiberglass rather than of the conventional metal construction. With this type of construction, the head does not have the finite life
that is found with heads of conventional design.
This head behaves like an articulated head, but is
without the usual articulation mechanisms, thus
eliminating the weight and mechanical complexity of the conventional rotor of this type (Fig 5-32).

148

FLAPPING FUNCTION
(A)

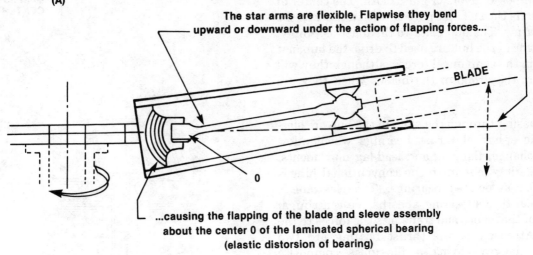

The star arms are flexible. Flapwise they bend upward or downward under the action of flapping forces...

BLADE

0

...causing the flapping of the blade and sleeve assembly about the center 0 of the laminated spherical bearing (elastic distorsion of bearing)

DRAG FUNCTION
(B)

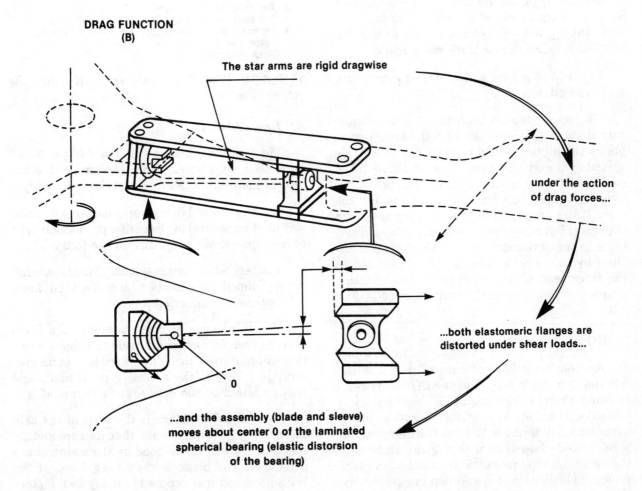

The star arms are rigid dragwise

under the action of drag forces...

...both elastomeric flanges are distorted under shear loads...

0

...and the assembly (blade and sleeve) moves about center 0 of the laminated spherical bearing (elastic distorsion of the bearing)

Fig. 5-33   A — Flapping axis movement of the AStar head   B — Lead-lag movement of the AStar head

149

The hub assembly has three arms made of superimposed layers of glass cloth. The center of the hub is the thickest portion with a taper to the three arms. The hub bolts to the mast assembly. The arms of the hub are used to drive the hub, not support the centrifugal forces, although they will support the droop of the blades when they are static.

Passing through the slots in the hub are elastomeric spherical thrust bearings which allow pitch change, flapping and lead-lag movements. The bearings eliminate the conventional hinges and the associated bearings. The elastomeric spherical thrust bearing absorbs the centrifugal loads of the blades and transmits the forces to the hub. Attached to the thrust bearing are two sleeve flanges having a fiberglass composite structure. The flanges form the sleeve for coupling the flight control linkages and the main rotor blades through a lever. Located between the two sleeve flanges is the frequency adapter consisting of two rubber plates bonded to a housing. This housing accommodates a self-lubricating ball joint which provides a bearing for the fork of the hub which flexes during blade movements.

Fig. 5-33 shows the action of the rotor in flap, drag, and pitch function.

The rotor system also makes use of a dampener system. This operates with the same principle as the bifilar system used on the S-76. This system, however, makes use of a weight installed on top of the rotor head, and the bottom of the weight attached to a ball joint that fits into the mast. Three springs keep the vibrating weight in the center but allow the weight to flap in all directions in the horizontal plane. This system is excited by the periodic alternate loads applied to the rotor head which responds to the excitation frequency that opposes the excitation loads (Fig. 5-34).

6. BO 105

Another rotor head of unusual design is the BO 105. The rotor system of the BO 105 is close to being a rigid rotor system. The head itself is a one-piece titanium forging incorporating provisions for a feathering axis only. The blades are of a reinforced glass fiber with a great amount of elasticity. Due to this elasticity and the forces applied, the blades lead-lag and flap independently. Therefore, although the head is rigid, it is still a fully articulated interaction (Fig. 5-35).

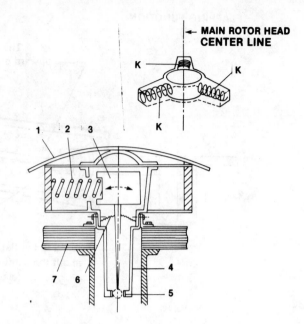

1 · Anti-vibrator fairing
2 · Coil spring (3 springs)
3 · Vibrating weight
4 · Ball joint (5) locating barrel
5 · Ball joint guiding weight (3) in the horizontal plane
6 · Protective boot (preventing ingress of external agents: dust, rain...)
7 · Rotor head star

Fig. 5-34 Vibration absorber used with the AStar head

E. Rotor Blades

The first rotor blades were made of wood and were used on several of the earlier production type of helicopters. Many are still in use today.

The first rotor blades were made of wood and was used on several of the earlier production type of helicopters. Many are still in use today.

The second is the metal blade. This is generally of bonded construction and used on most helicopters in production.

The third type of construction is the fiberglass or composite type of blade utilizing several types of materials including fiberglass in its construction. This is the newest type of blade and may be found on the newer production models.

Since the rotor blade is the wing of the helicopter, it is very important that its care and inspection are well understood by the maintenance personnel. The blade is the lifting force of the helicopter, and it is exposed to many load factors not common to the fixed wing. This includes centrifugal force, twisting moments, and rapid span

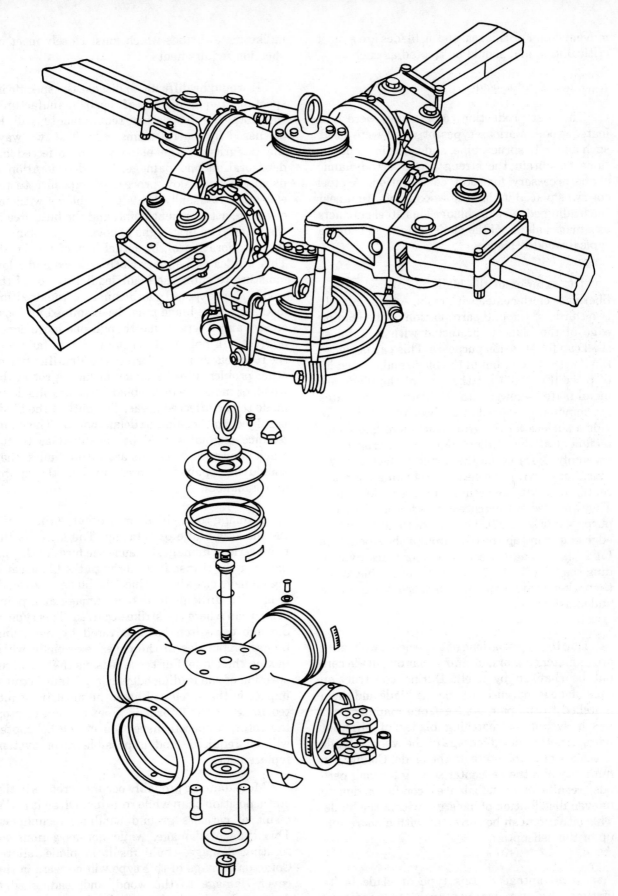

Fig. 5-35   BO105 rotor head using a rigid rotor

151

movements. For this reason the blades are a most critical item and should be treated as such.

1. Wooden rotor blades

The first production rotor blades were laminated wood. Various types of wood were used, such as birch, spruce, pine, and balsa in combinations to obtain the strength and aerodynamic shape necessary for rotor construction. A steel core was placed within the wood lamination near the leading edge of the blade. This steel core acts as a mass balance of the blades. Fig. 5-36 shows a typical wooden blade.

The exterior of the blade is covered with a fiberglass cloth coated with resin. Approximately two-thirds of the outboard portion of the leading edge of the blade is protected with a stainless steel cap for abrasion purposes. This cap is placed flush with the contour of the blade and riveted into place (Fig 5-37). At the butt of the blade are metal plates screwed into the blade. These plates are commonly referred to as cheek plates and provide a surface for the grip attachment and an attachment at the trailing edge for the drag brace assembly. Located on the upper surface are two pins, tacks with the heads protruding, for the center of gravity and center of pressure locations. They are used as reference points for maintenance purposes (Fig. 5-37). On the outboard trailing edge is a trim tab riveted through the wood. The tab is used to adjust each blade for track by bending the tab (Fig. 5-37). At the tip of the blade is a tip pocket used for spanwise balance. Weights are added as necessary.

Due to the variations of the wood, two blades are in matched pairs, meaning that one blade cannot be changed by itself. During construction each blade is matched to a master blade and them matched to the pair. At least one manufacturer has a system of matching blades of different pairs. Another disadvantage of the wooden blade is the effect of moisture on the blade. Changes in humidity and the helicopter setting for long periods, results in an unbalanced condition due to uneven distribution of moisture within the blade. This situation can be corrected with a short run-up of the helicopter.

An advantage of this type of blade is its lifetime. Its use depends upon its condition,

unlike metal blades which must closely meet inspection requirements.

It would be difficult to discuss the specific inspection requirements of each manufacturer, therefore the inspection requirements will be discussed in general terms only. The two ways the integrity of the blade will be affected are deterioration and damage. The deterioration is usually a very slow process of exposure to the elements. It usually leads to problems with the covering, attachement point, and the butt area of the blade. The first signs of covering problems is the deterioration of, or actual loss of the finish. This will leave the glass cloth exposed and allow moisture to enter the blade leading to rot of the wood. Any exposed cloth must be repaired immediately. The blade must be examined for loose screws and rivets. Even though one loose screw or rivet will not result in the ultimate failure of the rotor blade, it may lead to the identification of other problems in the blade, including rot in the wood, or moisture in the blade. Repairs should be made to the affected areas. The butt of the blade is subject to checking or delamination. The maintenance manual should be consulted as to the crack allowance. If cracks are within limits, they should be repaired as prescribed in the appropriate manual.

Damage to the blade may occur, either while the blade is static or rotating. The latter is the more serious damage, because the force of the impact may be transmitted through the blade causing damage elsewhere. Since the blade is covered, it is often difficult to detect damage at a point other than where the strike occurred. This type of damage can often be discovered by observing bulges or buckles in the cover, expecially when flexing the blade. For these reasons the visual inspection of the leading edge is important because impact in that area will have the most transmitted force. If the impact is great enough to stop the rotor, a special inspection of the helicopter will be required, and a possible rotor system replacement.

More damage probably occurs to rotors in the static position than while rotating. Often it is the result of careless ground handling techniques. This type of damage, while not as serious as rotating damage, could result in blade failure. Common damage of this type will be tears in the cover, damage to the wood, and leading edge damage. In most instances, this is repairable by

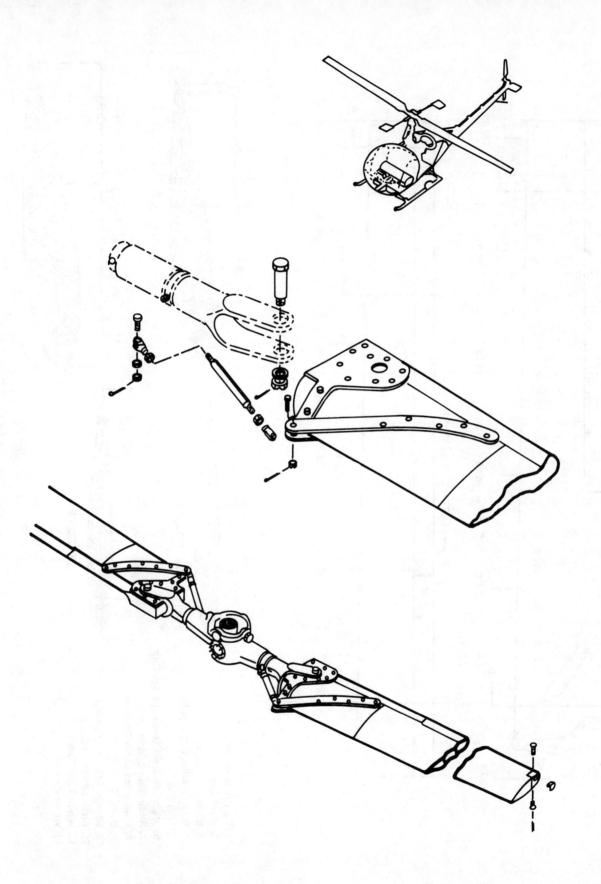

Fig. 5-36 Typical wooden blade installation used on the Hiller 12

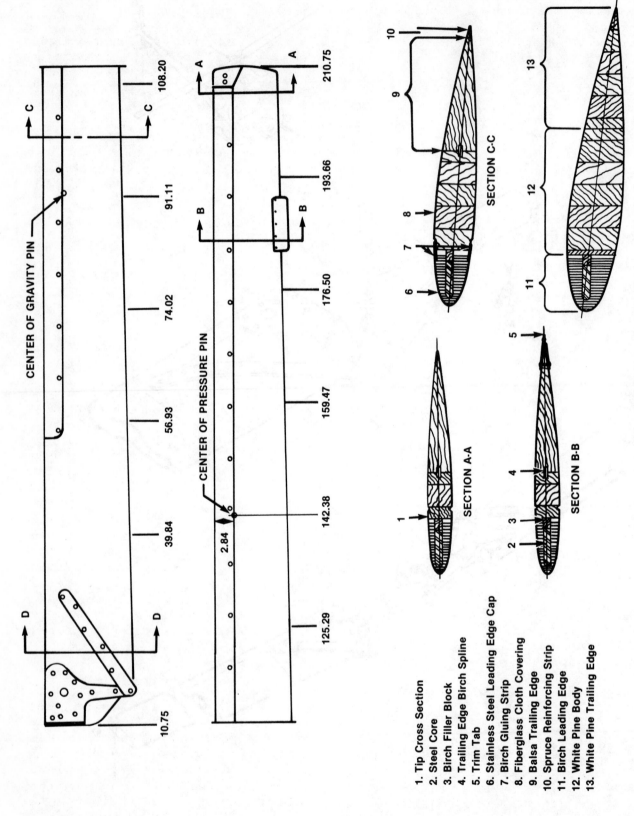

Fig. 5-37 Typical wooden blade construction

1. Tip Cross Section
2. Steel Core
3. Birch Filler Block
4. Trailing Edge Birch Spline
5. Trim Tab
6. Stainless Steel Leading Edge Cap
7. Birch Gluing Strip
8. Fiberglass Cloth Covering
9. Balsa Trailing Edge
10. Spruce Reinforcing Strip
11. Birch Leading Edge
12. White Pine Body
13. White Pine Trailing Edge

154

following the manufacturer's recommendations. Most shops will send the blade out for repair if the damage is extensive. It should be remembered, however, that any damage may be serious and should be taken care of immediately.

Normal maintenance of the wooden rotor blade consists of inspection and blade cleaning. The blades may be washed with soap and water. A soap which is quite often used for this purpose is *flax* soap because it is quite mild and will not corrode the blade. Any caustic solution or solvent may harm the blade and should be avoided. The blades are often waxed after washing. An abrasive cleaner type wax should not be used because this will be detrimental to the finish.

Localized areas may be painted as required, but if refinishing of the entire blade is necessary, rebalancing will be required. Paints for these purposes should be used as directed by the manufacturer for compatability reasons. If new paint is to be applied to the whole blade, precautions should be taken to remove all foreign material from the blades and to distribute the paint evenly over the entire blade. Prior to painting, the paint should be mixed and divided into equal amounts to ensure that each blade receives the same amount of paint. This will simplify the balancing procedure after the painting is completed.

Other maintenance may include the replacement of trim tabs, stainless steel leading edge repairs, cover and wood repairs. If damage is extensive, the blades are sent into a repair facility (Fig. 5-38). Often exchange units are used if the repairs are extensive, depending on the time available.

2. Metal rotor blades

The metal rotor blades have been in production for a period of at least twenty years. Because of construction expense and the various manufacturers involved, the construction varies considerably.

A distinct advantage to the metal blade is the ability to quality control the blade construction. Single blades may be changed without the use of matched sets. All blades are matched to the master blade at manufacture. This system allows additional weight to be added to the blade at manufacture to obtain the best aerodynamic characterisitics and give the blade sufficient weight to develop inertia necessary for autorotation.

Like any other metal component exposed to stresses induced in flight, the blade must be time life limited. This is a disadvantage compared to the wooden blade that has no finite life limitations.

One item that all of these blades have in common is a bonded type of construction. This is done by a heat and pressure process and has some advantages that are very important to the integrity of the rotor blade. They are:

1. Even distribution of stresses

2. Continuous contact between mating surfaces

3. Smoother contours

4. Flexible joints

5. Reduced weight

The disadvantage to this type of construction is the inability to rebond the structure in the field.

The blade construction is usually of aluminum alloy. Fig. 5-39 shows the typical construction of an early type of metal blade. The spar is of box construction running the full span of the blade. This is the main structural component of the blade. The skin is simply a wrap-around giving the blade its aerodynamic shape. This skin is bonded to the spar, I-channel, and the trailing edge strip. A stainless steel strip is attached in the same manner to the leading edge and acts as an abrasion shield to the blade. Without this protection the blade would erode quite rapidly in adverse conditions such as sand and dust.

Grip plates and doublers are added at the root of the blade to spread the attachement stresses over a wide area of the blade. A trim tab is placed on the outboard trailing edge for track adjustment. Weights may be added at the tip pocket for balance purposes. These are mounted directly to the spar and are accessible by removing the tip cap. Additional weights are often placed inboard of the tip weights for inertia. These are sometimes referred to as midspan weights and

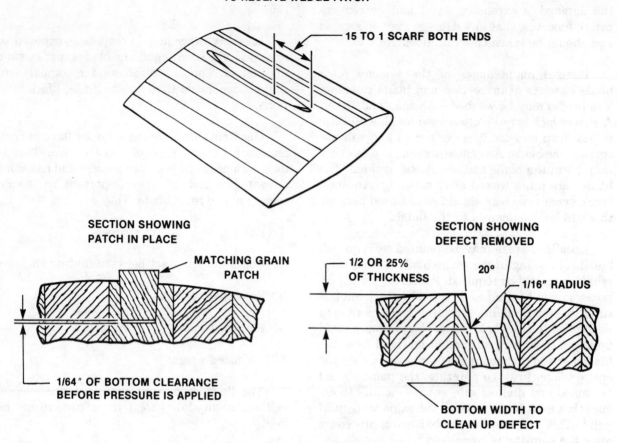

VIEW OF BLADE ROUTED
TO RECEIVE WEDGE PATCH

15 TO 1 SCARF BOTH ENDS

SECTION SHOWING
PATCH IN PLACE

MATCHING GRAIN
PATCH

1/64" OF BOTTOM CLEARANCE
BEFORE PRESSURE IS APPLIED

SECTION SHOWING
DEFECT REMOVED

1/2 OR 25%
OF THICKNESS

20°

1/16" RADIUS

BOTTOM WIDTH TO
CLEAN UP DEFECT

Spruce and Birch Wood Repairs

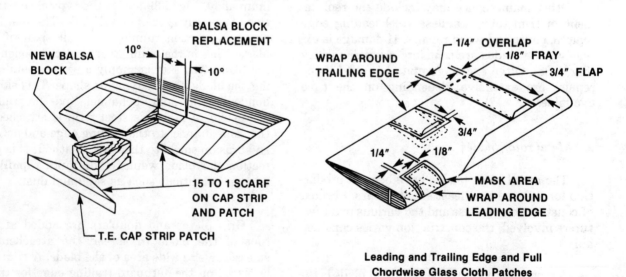

BALSA BLOCK
REPLACEMENT

NEW BALSA
BLOCK

10°

10°

15 TO 1 SCARF
ON CAP STRIP
AND PATCH

T.E. CAP STRIP PATCH

WRAP AROUND
TRAILING EDGE

1/4" OVERLAP

1/8" FRAY

3/4" FLAP

3/4"

1/4"

1/8"

MASK AREA

WRAP AROUND
LEADING EDGE

Leading and Trailing Edge and Full
Chordwise Glass Cloth Patches

Fig. 5-38   Typical repairs permissable to wooden blades

156

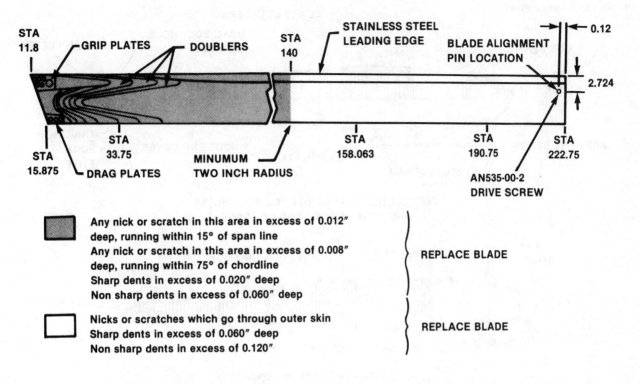

STA 11.8 · GRIP PLATES · DOUBLERS · STA 140 · STAINLESS STEEL LEADING EDGE · BLADE ALIGNMENT PIN LOCATION · 0.12 · 2.724

STA 15.875 · STA 33.75 · DRAG PLATES · MINUMUM TWO INCH RADIUS · STA 158.063 · STA 190.75 · STA 222.75 · AN535-00-2 DRIVE SCREW

Any nick or scratch in this area in excess of 0.012″ deep, running within 15° of span line
Any nick or scratch in this area in excess of 0.008″ deep, running within 75° of chordline
Sharp dents in excess of 0.020″ deep
Non sharp dents in excess of 0.060″ deep

} REPLACE BLADE

Nicks or scratches which go through outer skin
Sharp dents in excess of 0.060″ deep
Non sharp dents in excess of 0.120″

} REPLACE BLADE

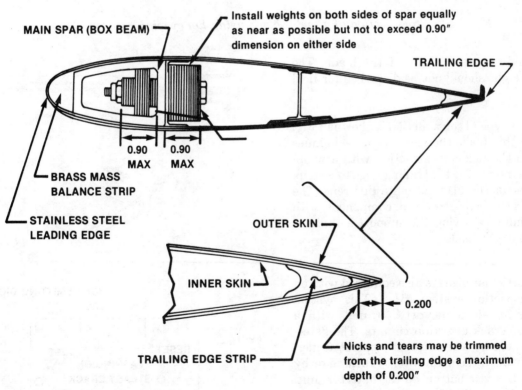

MAIN SPAR (BOX BEAM)

Install weights on both sides of spar equally as near as possible but not to exceed 0.90″ dimension on either side

TRAILING EDGE

0.90 MAX · 0.90 MAX

BRASS MASS BALANCE STRIP

STAINLESS STEEL LEADING EDGE

OUTER SKIN

INNER SKIN

0.200

TRAILING EDGE STRIP

Nicks and tears may be trimmed from the trailing edge a maximum depth of 0.200″

Fig. 5-39   Early metal blade construction as used on the Bell 47

157

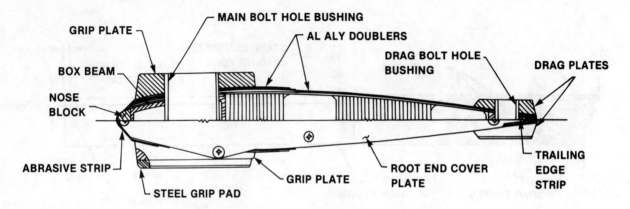

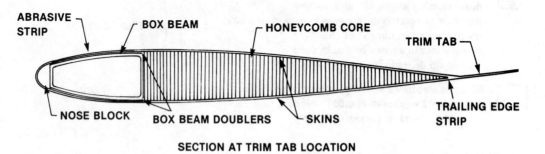

Fig. 5-40   *Cross section of a metal blade using honeycomb construction*

are attached at manufacture of the blade. The midspan weight should not be disturbed for field balancing.

Another type of construction is shown in Fig. 5-40. With this blade the same basic techniques are used in the blade construction with a wrap-around skin bonded at the trailing edge to a strip. The interior of the blade is quite different. The box beam is the main structural component, with a honeycomb core giving the support and shape to the skin of the blade.

This particular blade is also equipped with an integral inspection system (BIS). This system consists of an electronic detector unit with a memory and crack detection circuits. The detector is activated by a centrifugally operated mercury switch when the main rotor is turning or by depressing the *test* button on the detector unit. During testing, a flashing red light indicates a satisfactory condition, and a steady red light indicates a possible blade crack requiring a more detailed blade inspection (Fig. 5-41).

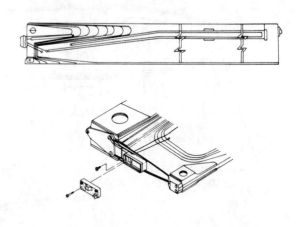

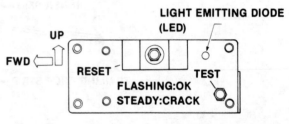

Fig. 5-41   *BIS system used by Bell helicopter*

158

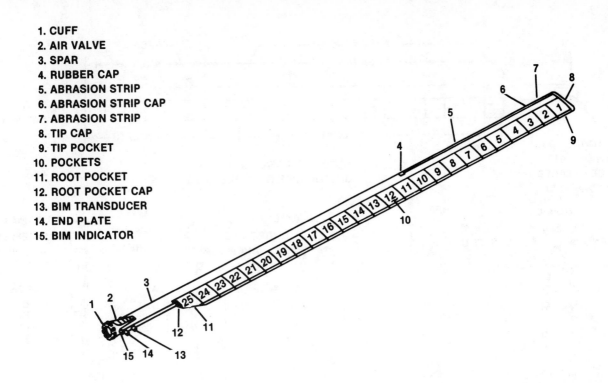

1. CUFF
2. AIR VALVE
3. SPAR
4. RUBBER CAP
5. ABRASION STRIP
6. ABRASION STRIP CAP
7. ABRASION STRIP
8. TIP CAP
9. TIP POCKET
10. POCKETS
11. ROOT POCKET
12. ROOT POCKET CAP
13. BIM TRANSDUCER
14. END PLATE
15. BIM INDICATOR

Fig. 5-42   Sikorski type rotor blade of metal construction

Another type of metal blade construction is shown in Fig. 5-42. This blade is constructed of one spar that serves as the structural support and the leading edge of the blade. Bonded to this main spar are sections of airfoil referred to as pockets. The butt section of the blade is quite unique because a steel cuff section is bolted to the spar. This type of blade also makes use of a blade crack indicator system. This system is referred to as BIM or Blade Inspection Method. The spar is pressurized with an inert gas. An indicator is placed at the blade root. This indicator is nothing more than a pressure switch that moves a striped tube up and down with changes in pressure. A normal indication is shown in Fig. 5-43. If a crack should occur in the spar, the pressure will be lost and the color of the indicator will change (Fig. 5-44).

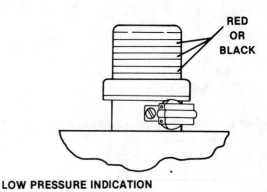

LOW PRESSURE INDICATION

Fig. 5-44   BIM indicator showing low pressure

There are several other types of construction in use but most of these are quite similar to previously mentioned types or a combination of the various types of blade construction.

As with wooden blades, metal blades may be washed with soap and water, and waxed. Some solutions of a caustic base and certain solvents

Fig. 5-43   BIM indicator showing normal pressure

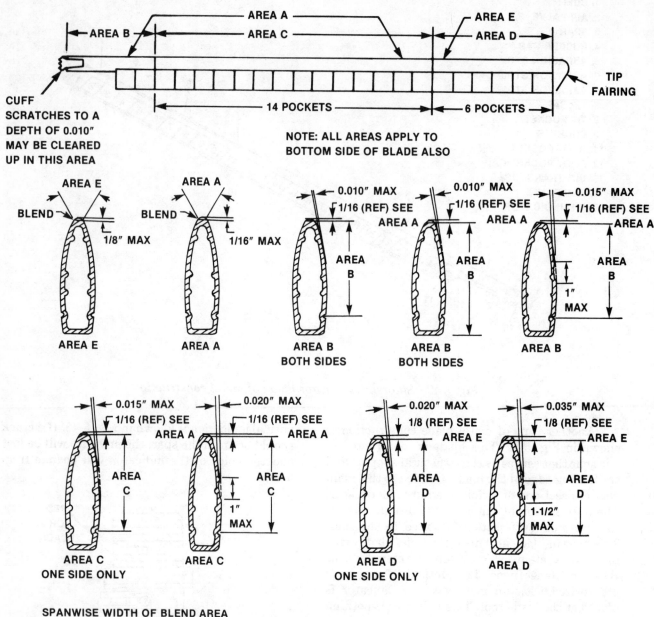

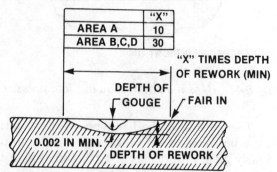

Fig. 5-45   Typical repair limits on a Sikorski metal blade

should be avoided because of their effect on the bonding which will destroy the integrity of the blade. In some areas where the blades are exposed to salt water, the blades are washed daily and a thin film of oil is applied.

Unlike the wooden blade, the exposure to the elements does not lead to rapid deterioration of the blade. The constant exposure, however, will be detrimental to the corrosion factor of the blade. Any corrosion must be carefully removed and the manufacturer's limits must be observed.

The other items of concern in the inspection of the blades are nicks and scratches. They will set up stresses in the blade which can lead to cracks. They may be removed with a smooth contour much as nicks are removed from a propeller blade (Fig. 5-45). The closer to the butt of the blade, the more critical they become. The manufacturer's recommendations must be strictly adhered to in this regard.

Delamination of both the bonding and the skin to the honeycomb may also occur. Some delamination may be field repairable (Fig. 5-46), while others will require that the blade be returned to the factory for repairs. At least one company has a blade rental system whereby blades may be rented while repairs are being made. This is due to the blades being a time-life item which makes exchange units impractical.

3. Fiberglass or composite blades

The newest material for blades is fiberglass. The concept of a fiberglass blade started in the mid 1950s with about four companies being involved in this development. They were Parsons, Aerospatiale, Boelkow, and Boeing-Vertol. Although other manufacturers have become involved, these manufacturers were responsible for much of the early development and research. This type of blade with many variations will undoubtedly be the rotor blade of the future.

The blade is manufactured of several types of materials even though it is covered with fiberglass. Several different construction concepts have been tested or are presently being tested. At present two systems are in use on production-type helicopters. They are a fiberglass spar-type blade and a metal spar blade.

A typical fiberglass spar blade makes use of a precured roving spar. The rovings are strings or strips of glass material. This material is impregnated with epoxy resin (1) (Fig. 5-47). In the figure are rovings (2) wound round a foam core (3). The skins of the blade are preimpregnated glass cloth (4). In addition, root reinforcement plates are added (9). A trailing edge foam filler is shown (5) and the trailing edge is another roving strip (6). The leading edge of the blade is protected with a stainless steel strip covering the span of the leading edge (7). For additional protection polymethane is incorporated in the blade profile,

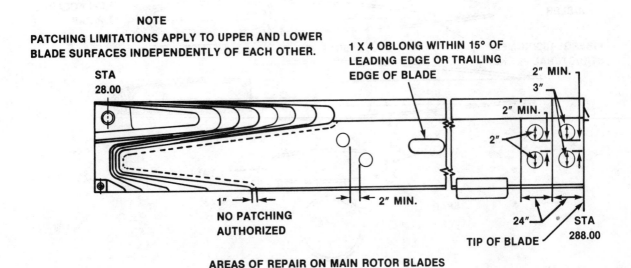

NOTE

PATCHING LIMITATIONS APPLY TO UPPER AND LOWER BLADE SURFACES INDEPENDENTLY OF EACH OTHER.

AREAS OF REPAIR ON MAIN ROTOR BLADES

Fig. 5-46 Typical patch limitations on a Bell metal blade

161

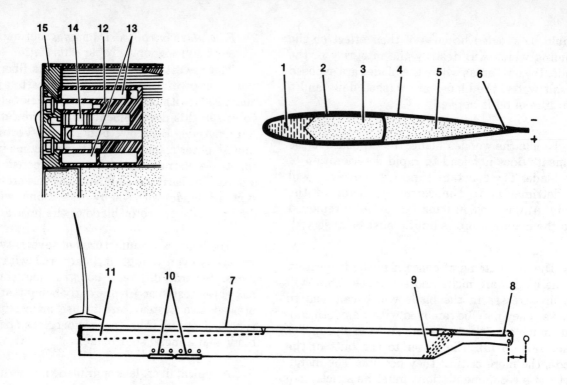

Fig. 5-47   Basic construction of a fiberglass blade

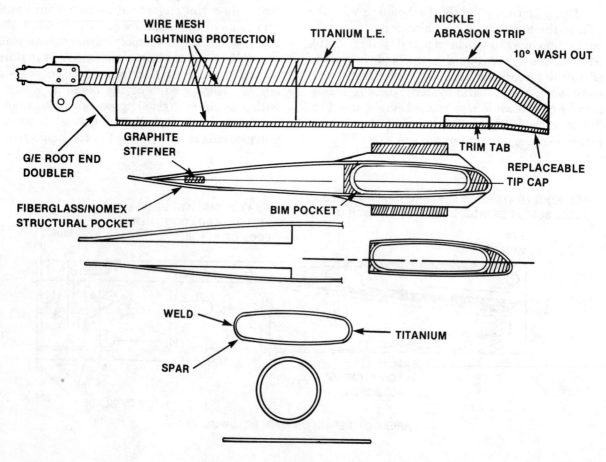

Fig. 5-48   S-76 blade construction

162

on the lower face aft of the stainless steel leading edge strip (11). The balancing weight is added to the tip of the blade (12).

Many other materials may be used with this construction, such as carbon fiber skin, kevlar skin, titanium leading edges and honeycomb fillers. The difference in the construction materials will differ with the manufacturer and the characteristics desired in the blade. The composite blade should not be referred to as a fiberglass blade because it is in reality a metal spar using fiberglass materials to build the remainder of the blade (Fig. 5-48).

There are several apparent advantages of the fiberglass construction over the metal. The major one is the life of the blade. From all indications the fiberglass blade will have no finite life as will the metal blade. In addition, the fiberglass blade will be less susceptible to notch damage (Fig. 5-49), due to the threads of the roving. The corrosion of fiberglass is non-existent. Bonding or delamination problems will often be repaired by epoxy resin injections that may be performed in the field. For these reasons there will be undoubtedly more fiberglass or composites on the market with the new helicopters.

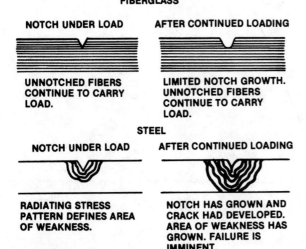

NOTCH DAMAGE CHARACTERISTICS

FIBERGLASS

NOTCH UNDER LOAD	AFTER CONTINUED LOADING
UNNOTCHED FIBERS CONTINUE TO CARRY LOAD.	LIMITED NOTCH GROWTH. UNNOTCHED FIBERS CONTINUE TO CARRY LOAD.

STEEL

NOTCH UNDER LOAD	AFTER CONTINUED LOADING
RADIATING STRESS PATTERN DEFINES AREA OF WEAKNESS.	NOTCH HAS GROWN AND CRACK HAD DEVELOPED. AREA OF WEAKNESS HAS GROWN. FAILURE IS IMMINENT.

Fig. 5-49 Notch damage comparison of metal and fiberglass

F. Rotor Head Maintenance

The rotor head maintenance consists of servicing, inspection, removal, and adjustments at scheduled intervals.

The servicing of the rotor head normally consists of lubrication. Proper lubrication of the rotor head cannot be stressed enough. The greasing of the head is done with a hand-type of grease gun with the manufacturer's specified grease. The intervals are also specified by the manufacturer. However, when operations are conducted in certain areas, more frequent greasing is advisable. For example: a sandy environment would require more frequent lubrication to remove the sand from the greased areas. Although the wet head should require less servicing and lubrication, the problem of leaks may occur. Most systems will have some leakage, but excessive leakage will cause bearing damage.

Leakage of the head is quite obvious and the procedure for locating leaks is the same as in any other rotational item. The head must be clean before the origin of the leak can be discovered. Then the helicopter must be run for a short period and inspected for leakage. Quite often the repair of a leak cannot be accomplished in the field unless teardown capabilities are available. It is quite normal, however, for the greased head to sling grease, especially immediately after greasing. Both the grease and oil should be removed so that no accumulation occurs. This accumulation would not only make visual inspection impossible, but it would retain moisture and dirt that can be harmful to the head.

The normal rotor head inspections are of a visual type. Loose items, such as rod ends, will only add to a more rapid deterioration of the head. The feel of the movements and the possibility of cracks should not be omitted from any inspection criteria.

On certain heads periodic inspections may be requried on the rotor system. These might include such items as *dye check* inspections, partial disassembly and rotation of bearings. These could be required at different intervals of time or as the result of Airworthiness Directives.

The rotor head is a highly stressed unit of the helicopter and usually has many time-change and mandatory retirement items. The constant checking of logbooks, replacement/retirement schedules and historical records prior to each inspection is a time consuming task.

Some manufacturers will allow the major inspections and overhaul to be performed in the

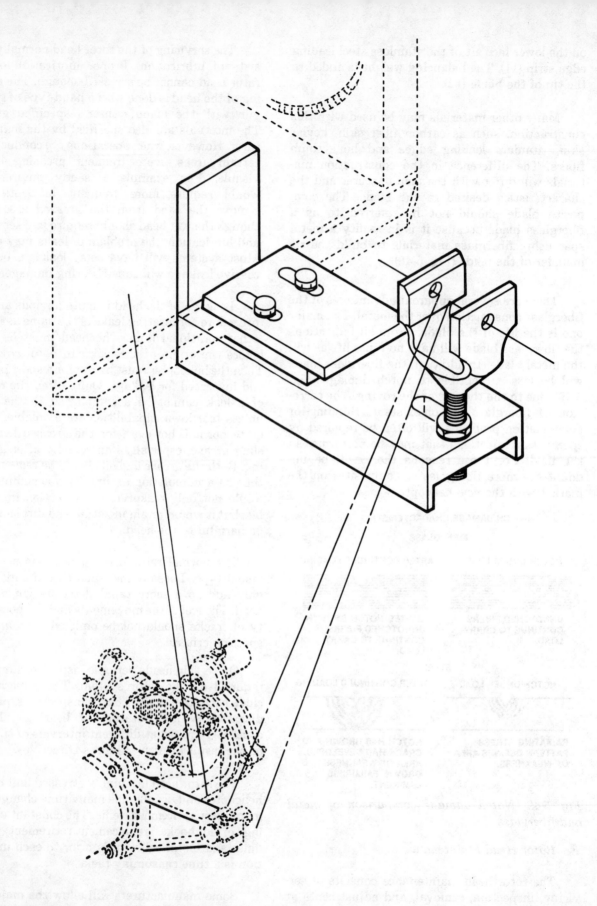

Fig. 5-50 Bracket used to prevent damage to the tension torsion straps during removal and installation

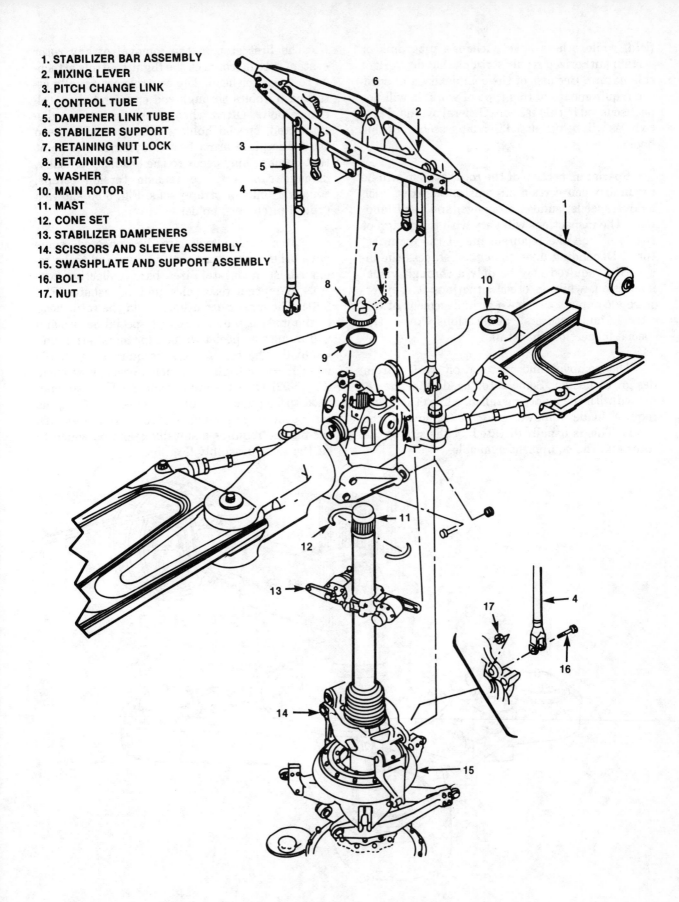

1. STABILIZER BAR ASSEMBLY
2. MIXING LEVER
3. PITCH CHANGE LINK
4. CONTROL TUBE
5. DAMPENER LINK TUBE
6. STABILIZER SUPPORT
7. RETAINING NUT LOCK
8. RETAINING NUT
9. WASHER
10. MAIN ROTOR
11. MAST
12. CONE SET
13. STABILIZER DAMPENERS
14. SCISSORS AND SLEEVE ASSEMBLY
15. SWASHPLATE AND SUPPORT ASSEMBLY
16. BOLT
17. NUT

Fig. 5-51 Typical rotor head removal for a semi-rigid rotor

165

field, while others have exchange programs or certain authorized repair stations that do work of this nature. Because of the complexity and specific requirements of this type of work, it will not be discussed in this section. General overhaul procedures will be discussed in a later section of this book.

Special inspection of the rotor system will be required when certain circumstances exist such as overspeeds, sudden stoppage, and hard landings. The inspections will vary with the design of the head and the requirements of the manufacturer. Depending upon the circumstances the inspection required may be only a through visual inspection, while in other situations it may require a complete teardown or replacement of the rotor. Manufacturers' publications cover the special inspections in detail.

The removal and installation varies from design to design. Some rotor heads may be removed with the blades installed, while others will require blade removal prior to removing the heads. This is usually dictated by the size of the rotor and the equipment available.

The first step in the removal of any rotor system is to disconnect the flight controls attached to the rotor head. The controls are usually attached by bolts through rod ends and close tolerance bolts. Often when pitch controls are disconnected, special holders are required to keep the blade pitch arms from moving to the point that damage may occur to the head. Specifically, damage can occur to tension torsion straps, equalizer links or strap packs. Fig. 5-50 shows a typical pitch horn holder.

After the controls are disconnected, some have other items that may be required to be removed, such as stabilizer bars, collective controls, dampener reservoirs, and driveshafts (Fig. 5-51). The mast nuts used to hold the rotor head to the mast assembly are of a special nature and will require a special wrench for installation and removal. The torques may require a hydraulic wrench or multiplier wrench (Sweeney wrench) (Fig. 5-52). Once the nut is removed, the head may need special hoisting slings or eyes for lifting the rotor system (Fig. 5-53). The rotor, removed with the blades, requires a suitable stand on which to sit the rotor assembly (Fig. 5-54).

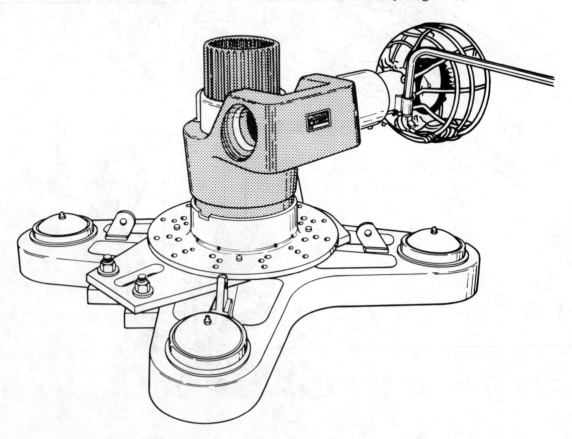

Fig. 5-52 Special multiplier wrench used to remove a rotor head

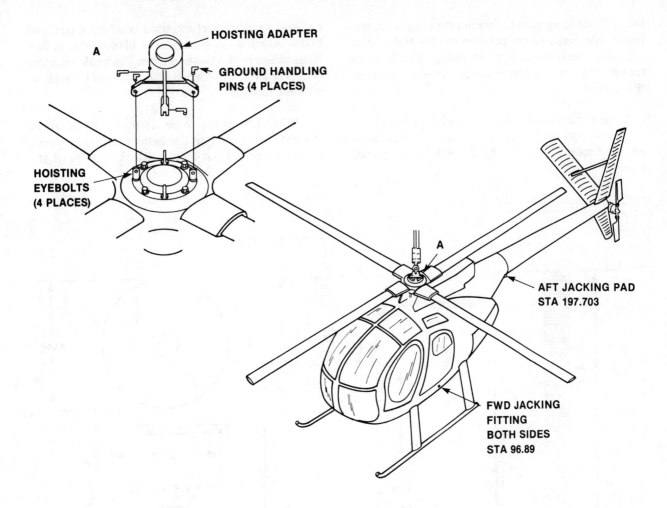

Fig. 5-53   Hoisting eyes are often used to remove the rotor system

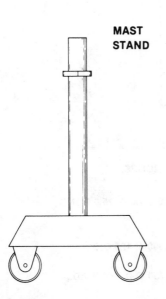

MAST
STAND

Different rotor heads and blade systems have different means of securing the blades to the rotor head. One method is the use of a blade retaining bolt in the grip assembly. Before the blade is removed, it must be properly supported to prevent binding between the grip and the blade. If an attempt is made to remove the bolt without proper support, galling will occur between the bolt and grip. This transfer will elongate the hole and destroy the airworthiness of

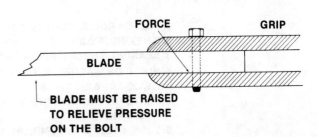

Fig. 5-54   Typical stand used to place the rotor after removal

Fig. 5-55   Blade removal requires lifting the blade

the grip. Damage to the blade retaining bolt, the blade hole, bushing or spreading of the fork of the grip may occur by heavy pounding. The bolt removal should only require moderate pressure (Fig. 5-55).

Some blades required a special puller to remove the bolt (Fig. 5-56). Other blades are retained by taper pins (Fig. 5-57), requiring special pullers. Another method used is where a circle of bolts is used to retain the blade (Fig. 5-58). Regardless of the method used, the blade must be properly supported when it is removed in order to prevent damage.

When blades are to be removed and the rotor system is installed on the helicopter, the support of the blade is even more critical because of the

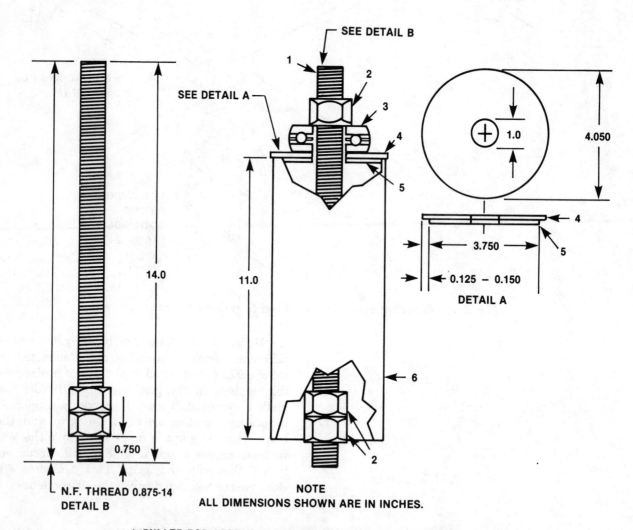

1. PULLER ROD ASSEMBLY 4130 (OR BETTER), 1.0 O.D. — 15.0 LONG
2. 3 HEX NUTS 0.875 NF (14) THREAD
3. BEARING (THRUST) INNER RACE 1.0 I.D.
4. PLATE OR WASHER, STEEL OR ALUMINUM, 4.050-4, 125 O.D., 1,125 I.D., 0.250 THICK
5. PLATE OR WASHER, STEEL OR ALUMINUM, 3.750 O.D., 1.125 I.D., 0.250 THICK
6. TUBE, STEEL OR ALUMINUM, WALL THICKNESS 0.083 - 0.125

Fig. 5-56   Special tool used to remove blade retaining pins

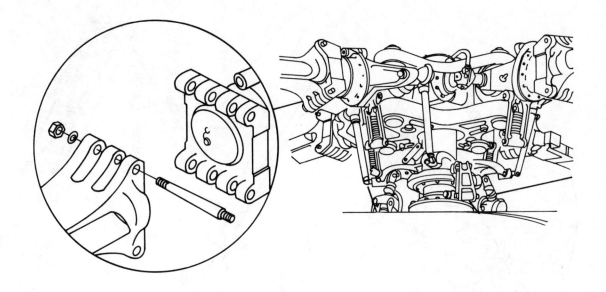

Fig. 5-57   Taper pin method of retaining the blades

height and the damage that may occur during removal. For this reason the blades are usually removed from the aft of the helicopter. This may also require support to the remaining blades when removed.

When the blades are removed, it is important that they be stored on blade racks. This will prevent blade damage during storage. The rotor heads should be placed on a suitable stand to prevent damaging the head.

As previously mentioned, the disposition of the head that has been removed varies with the different manufacturers. If the head is the type requiring a major inspection and return to service, adherence to the overhaul instructions is very critical. The steps are as follows:

First, determine which parts have time lives and if that time has been reached. Parts that have reached maximum life will be discarded without an inspection.

The head will have to be disassembled for inspection. This procedure requires several special tools. No attempt at rebuilding should be attempted without the proper equipment. After disassembly, clean the parts and check part dimen-

sions. Quite often these dimensions are in 10ths of thousandths rather than thousandths. This will require micrometers capable of these readings. Typical dimensional checks are shown in Fig. 5-59.

After these checks are taken, the parts of ferrous metal are magnafluxed and the nonferrous parts are zygloed to locate cracks. Usually the amperages used for magnaflux and areas of concern are given in the overhaul manual. At this point some parts may require rework or updates. This could include adding bushings, changing radii, and removing nicks or scratches. At this time the finish of the part is examined and refinished. Manufacturers do not recommend replacement of plating in the field due to hydrogen embrittlement. If any plating is to be done, it should be done only in accordance with the manufacturer's recommendation. This usually require stress relieving of the part.

After the parts have been inspected, they are ready for reassembly. The disposition of certain items, such as bearings and hardware, is done at the discretion of the operator. Some operators will never use certain items twice while others will. It must be remembered that the rebuilding of components has a direct relationship to the re-

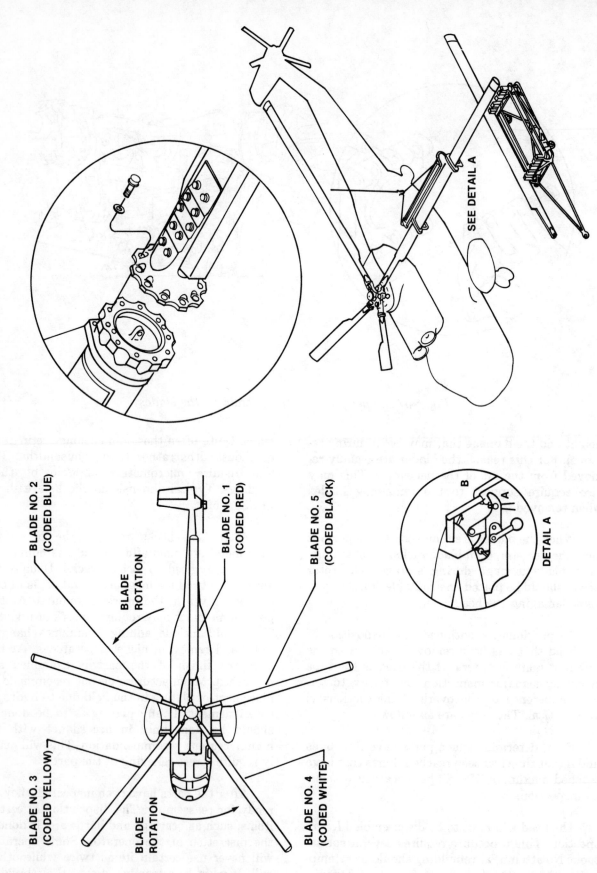

BLADE NO. 2
(CODED BLUE)

BLADE NO. 1
(CODED RED)

BLADE NO. 5
(CODED BLACK)

BLADE ROTATION

BLADE NO. 3
(CODED YELLOW)

BLADE ROTATION

BLADE NO. 4
(CODED WHITE)

SEE DETAIL A

DETAIL A

Fig. 5-58   Blade removal and storage method used on S-76 helicopter

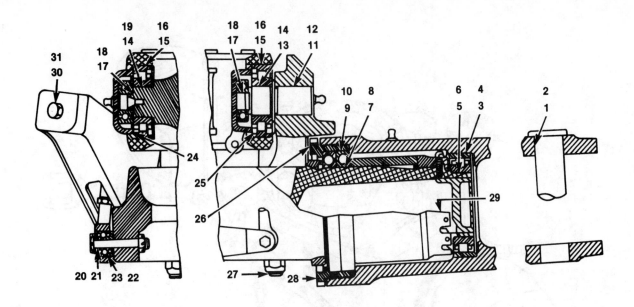

ITEM	NOMENCLATURE		MIN.	MAX.	REPLACE
1	Bolt - Blade Retaining	OD	0.9990	1.0000	0.9980
2	Grip - Blade Bolt Hole	ID	1.0000	1.0010	1.0040
3	Grip - Outer Bearing Bore	ID	3.5423	3.5433	3.5443 (mean)
4	Outer Bearing	OD	3.5427	3.5433	
5	Outer Bearing	ID	2.1648	2.1654	
6	Yoke - Outer Bearing Seat	OD	2.1650	2.1655	2.1638
7	Yoke - Thrust Bearing Seat	OD	2.9519	2.9525	2.9499
8	Thrust Bearings	ID	2.9522	2.9528	
9	Thrust Bearings	OD	4.1331	4.1339	
10	Adapter - Bearing Bore	ID	4.1337	4.1347	4.1352
11	Pillow Block - Pin Bore	ID	0.9995	1.0000	
12	Pin	OD	1.0000	1.0005	
13	Pin - Gimbal Bearing Seat	OD	0.9840	0.9844	0.9835
14	Bearings - Gimbal Ring	ID	0.9839	0.9843	
15	Bearings - Gimbal Ring	OD	2.4404	2.4409	
16	Gimbal Ring - Bearing Bore	ID	2.4400	2.4410	2.4420
17	Pin or Trunnion - Thrust Bearing Seat	OD	0.5840	0.5850	0.5800
18	Thrust Bearings	ID	0.5903	0.5906	
19	Trunnion - Gimbal Bearing Seat	OD	0.9836	0.9840	0.9830
20	Bolt - Equalizer Beam	OD	0.3125	0.3135	
21	Bearing - Equalizer Beam	ID	0.3120	0.3125	
22	Bearing - Equalizer Beam	OD	0.8120	0.8125	
23	Equalizer Beam - Bearing Bore	ID	0.8124	0.8129	0.8134
24	Trunnion Bearing Cap - End Play (each)	in.	0.000	0.002	
25	Pillow Block Bearing Cap - End Play (each)	in.	0.004	0.007	
26	Grip Adapter to Pillow Block - Clearance	in.	0.064	0.160	
27	Bolts - Pillow Block - Torque	in/lb	300	350	*
28	Grip Adapter - Torque	ft/lb	350	375	**
29	Nut - Yoke Bearing - Torque	in/lb	1000	1500	***
30	Hole-Pitch Horn		0.250	0.251	0.255
31	Bolt		0.2487	0.2492	0.2465

*Maximum total for assembly 0.004, recommend 0.002. Slight drag when had turned.
**Equal within 0.002. Total play for assembly 0.008 to 0.014, recommend 0.010.
***Equal both sides of hub within 0.030

Fig. 5-59   Typical dimensional checks that are taken at major inspection intervals

171

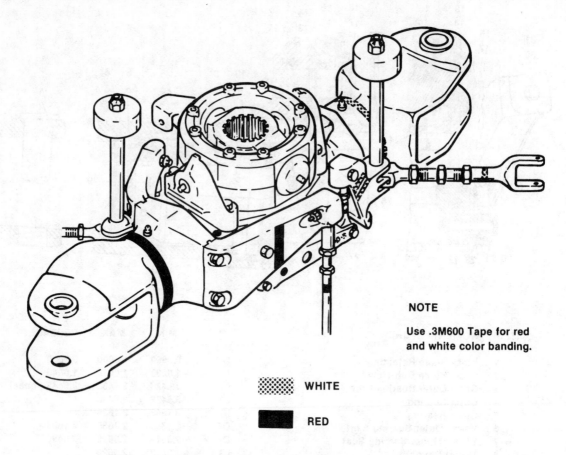

NOTE

Use .3M600 Tape for red
and white color banding.

WHITE

RED

Fig. 5-60   Typical color coding used on rotor heads

quired maintenance during its service life. The reassembly will require such procedures as shimming, bearing pinches, and end play measurements that will be discussed in another section of the text. When the head is reassembled, a color code of the component is usually placed on the parts for identification purposes because no left and right is present (Fig. 5-60).

After the head is reassembled, the blades may be reinstalled, taking the same precautions used in disassembly. At this point a series of maintenance procedures may begin.

1.   Blade alignment

Blade alignment is necessary on semi-rigid rotors. This procedure is sometimes referred to as chordwise balance, but this is really a misnomer. The procedure involves moving the blades about the lead-lag axis held stationary during the operation by the drag brace or latch pins, depending upon the design of the head. This movement is for the specific purpose of placing the blades in cor-

rect relationship with the hub of the rotor. This relationship places the center of gravity and the center of pressure in perspective. If this relationship is incorrect, the stability of the blade will be destroyed. For this reason, correct alignment is critical. The use of a poor procedure or inaccuracy can result in loss of stability of the helicopter. *Always remember that the blades may not go forward of the alignment point.* If static spanwise balance is also to be achieved, as is often the case, the alignment must be done first because the alignment will affect the spanwise balance by changing the weight arm relationship (Fig 5-61).

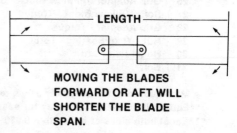

LENGTH

MOVING THE BLADES
FORWARD OR AFT WILL
SHORTEN THE BLADE
SPAN.

Fig. 5-61   Blade alignment moves the blades in relation to the hub

The points to be used in alignment are marked on the blade by the manufacturer. On wooden blades this mark is in the form of a tack referred to as the center of pressure pin. Care must be taken when working with this type of blade because another identical pin is present in each blade. The other pin is used in checking the center of gravity after repairs are made. The C/P pin is always outboard of the C/G pin.

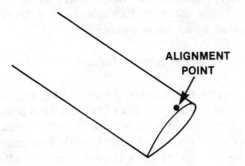

Fig. 5-62 *Typical alignment point on a rotor blade*

On metal blades only one pin exists and is simply referred to as the alignment pin. This pin

will be located very close to the tip of the blade (Fig. 5-62). Additional marks may be placed on the grips of the rotor head for the blade relationship to the head. These marks, if present, are in the form of a scribe mark (Fig. 5-63).

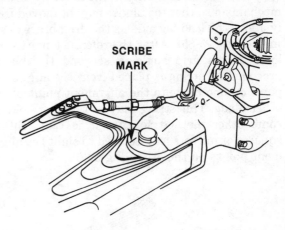

Fig. 5-63 *Typical alignment on a rotor*

Regardless of the method in which the reference points are chosen on the grips, the grip

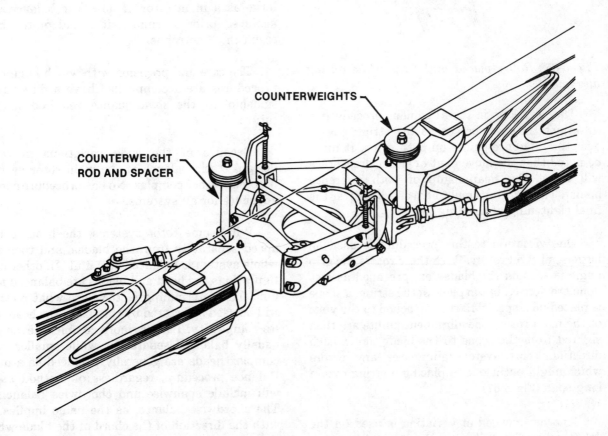

Fig. 5-64 *String and mirror method used in blade alignment*

173

angle must be carefully set to insure accurate sighting. For this purpose different manufacturers use various fixtures to hold the blade angle (Fig. 5-64). During the alignment procedure the blades are held at a precone angle and are usually supported towards the tip of the blade by a roller mechanism so that the blades may be moved freely about the lead-lag axis as the drag brace is adjusted (Fig. 5-65). After the reference marks are located, the grip angle is set and the blades preconed. A string is placed from the alignment point on one blade to the alignment point of the other blade. This string may be taped or held by some other method so that it is taut. Either squares or mirrors may be used to sight the alignment points on the grips (Fig 5-66).

Fig. 5-65 Roller placed under the blade during alignment

The next step in the alignment procedure is to adjust the drag braces so the string passes over the reference points on both grips. It must be noted that the movement of either drag brace will affect the relationship of both reference points. The sightings must be rechecked after the final tightening of the drag brace.

One variation to this procedure is used on large semi-rigid rotors. With these rotors the grip angle is set and the blades are preconed as was done previously, but in place of the string, a scope is placed on a special fixture attached to the yoke of the main rotor. The alignment points are then sighted from the scope to the blade pin in each direction. This system eliminates any errors which might occur due to placing a string over a long span (Fig 5-67).

Another method of variation is used on the Jet Ranger. This helicopter has no drag brace so adjustments are made to the blade latches (Fig.

5-68). In all other respects the same string method is used.

The alignment of the blades is accomplished when major components of the head or blades are replaced and during a major teardown inspection. Blade alignment is sometimes referred to as chordwise balance. It is quite likely that the blades will require further adjustment during static balance and the initial run-up to correct dynamic chordwise imbalance in a procedure referred to as blade sweeping.

2. Static main rotor balance

The main rotor system, like any other rotating object, requires balance. This procedure is accomplished both statically and dynamically in order to insure smooth trouble-free operation of the helicopter. Since the rotor may be affected by either spanwise or chordwise vibrations, it is necessary to balance the rotor in both directions. Although static balance in no way ensures dynamic balance, achieving it first will eliminate problems that would be encountered if dynamic balance was attempted first. With an object as large as a main rotor, if no static balance was achieved prior to run-up, it would quite likely result in catastrophe.

The care and precision with which balancing procedures are accomplished have a direct relationship to the maintenance required in the future.

Because of the wide variations in rotor design, static balance of the main rotor system becomes rather complex. No one procedure can be adequate for all systems.

With some rotor systems, the head is balanced separately from the blades, and then the whole system is balanced as a unit. In other configurations the head and blades are balanced as a unit. The determining factor as to what method will be used is dictated by the size of the head and its complexity. Larger, more complex heads are usually balanced separately, while smaller, less complex heads are generally balanced as a unit. Balance procedure, regardless of method used, will include spanwise and chordwise balancing. The chordwise balance, as the name implies, is with the direction of the chord of the blade while the spanwise balance will be in relation to the span of the blade. In all cases where the head and

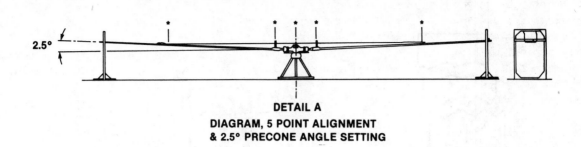

DETAIL A
DIAGRAM, 5 POINT ALIGNMENT
& 2.5° PRECONE ANGLE SETTING

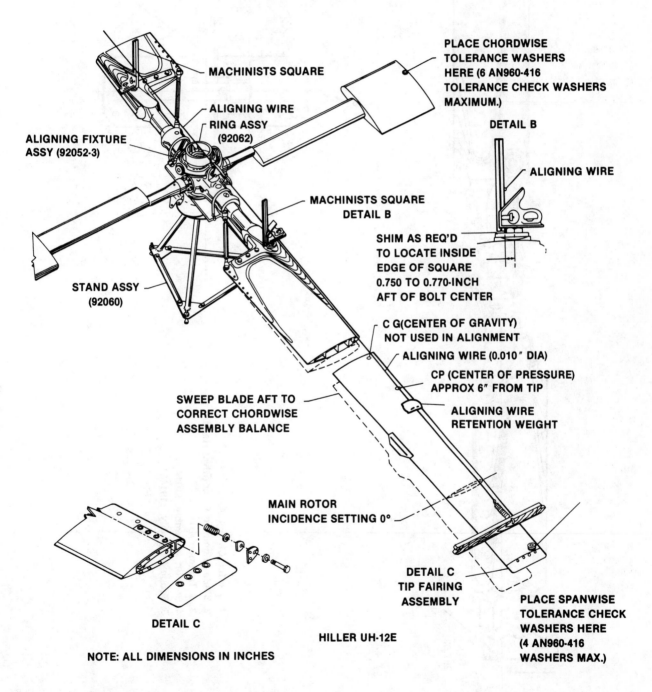

MACHINISTS SQUARE

PLACE CHORDWISE
TOLERANCE WASHERS
HERE (6 AN960-416
TOLERANCE CHECK WASHERS
MAXIMUM.)

ALIGNING WIRE
RING ASSY
(92062)

DETAIL B

ALIGNING FIXTURE
ASSY (92052-3)

ALIGNING WIRE

MACHINISTS SQUARE
DETAIL B

SHIM AS REQ'D
TO LOCATE INSIDE
EDGE OF SQUARE
0.750 TO 0.770-INCH
AFT OF BOLT CENTER

STAND ASSY
(92060)

C G(CENTER OF GRAVITY)
NOT USED IN ALIGNMENT

ALIGNING WIRE (0.010″ DIA)

CP (CENTER OF PRESSURE)
APPROX 6″ FROM TIP

SWEEP BLADE AFT TO
CORRECT CHORDWISE
ASSEMBLY BALANCE

ALIGNING WIRE
RETENTION WEIGHT

MAIN ROTOR
INCIDENCE SETTING 0°

DETAIL C
TIP FAIRING
ASSEMBLY

DETAIL C

PLACE SPANWISE
TOLERANCE CHECK
WASHERS HERE
(4 AN960-416
WASHERS MAX.)

HILLER UH-12E

NOTE: ALL DIMENSIONS IN INCHES

Fig. 5-66   Alignment procedure used on the Hiller 12 using squares

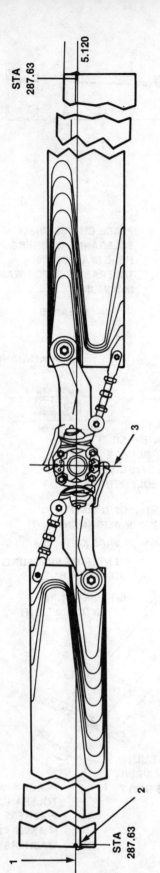

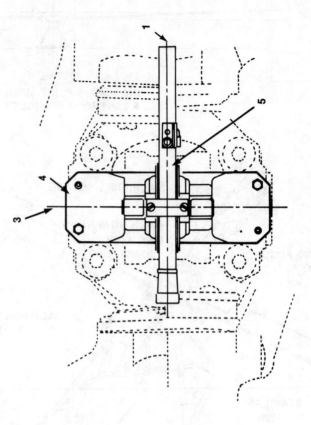

1. ₵ Pitch Change Axis
2. Blade Alignment Point (Rivet Head)
3. ₵ Trunnion Axis
4. Support Assembly, T101400
5. Scope Assembly, T101401

Fig. 5-67   Scope method used on large semi-rigid rotors

176

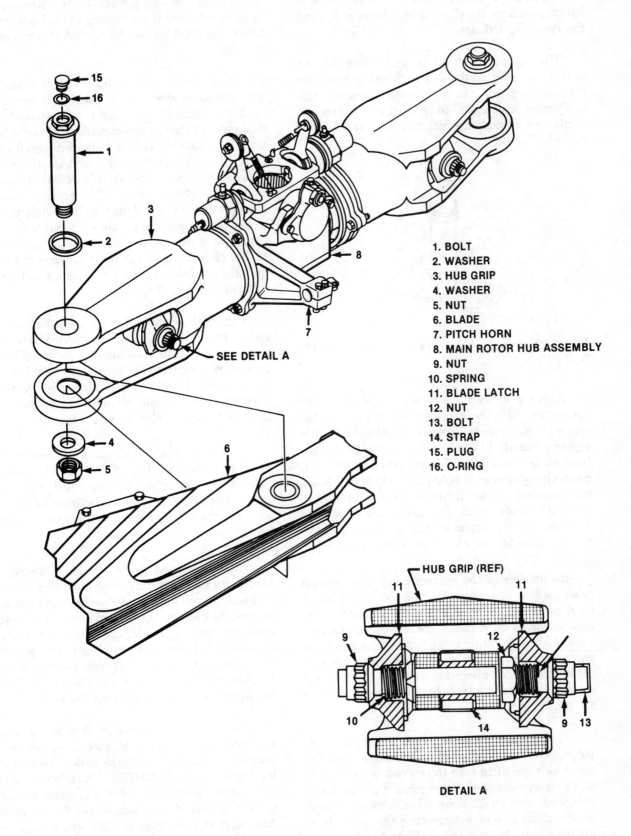

1. BOLT
2. WASHER
3. HUB GRIP
4. WASHER
5. NUT
6. BLADE
7. PITCH HORN
8. MAIN ROTOR HUB ASSEMBLY
9. NUT
10. SPRING
11. BLADE LATCH
12. NUT
13. BOLT
14. STRAP
15. PLUG
16. O-RING

SEE DETAIL A

HUB GRIP (REF)

DETAIL A

Fig. 5-68   Blade latches are used on the Bell 206 to adjust alignment

blades are balanced as a unit, the chordwise balance must be established prior to the spanwise balance because the chordwise balance will affect the spanwise balance.

The equipment used in the balancing procedure varies considerably depending upon the manufacturer of the helicopter. Usually this equipment is designed to be used on the one particular rotor head on which the rotor assembly is placed (Fig. 5-69).

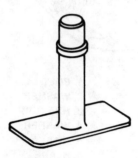

Fig. 5-69 Simple balancing stand used on the Bell 47

Another system made for a specific rotor makes use of a base plate with a post in the center. Resting on the post is a steel ball which is inside a mandrel. The mandrel slides through a base plate which is used in conjunction with the pitch change horns to hold the blade angle. Next, the mandrel passes through the trunnion supporting the rotor head. This places the rotor head assembly on the surface on one ball bearing allowing the head to move in all directions (Fig. 5-70).

Regardless of the system used, the balance procedure is dependent on the rotor seeking a level position, which is the ideal situation. For this reason all balancing work must be carried on under ideal conditions, which includes clean equipment and a work area free of drafts. Balancing is often accomplished in a separate room, or if it must be done in a large hanger area, the rotors are placed in a box.

It is equally important that the rotor heads be properly serviced prior to balancing. Usually *wet heads* are filled with the correct level of oil in all the reservoirs while the *dry heads* are normally balanced prior to greasing. This is done because of the difficulty of determining the amount of grease placed in each point of the head. An un-

even amount of grease would lead to an unbalanced condition which would correct itself by running. In all cases the servicing of the head prior to balancing must follow the manufacturer's recommendations.

If the head is to be balanced as a separate unit due to its size and complexity, it would warrant the addition of weight in manufacturer's designated areas to accomplish a balanced condition. Of course, the unbalanced condition is directly related to the parts and tolerances that make up the rotor head. In this situation the addition of weight is most often accomplished by simply adding the weight required while viewing either the balance indicator or a bull's eye level placed at a designated point on the rotor head. Either chordwise or spanwise balance can be acquired first because the one balance will not affect the other at this point.

Fig. 5-71 shows a typical head balance procedure in which weight is being added to the head in order to obtain a balanced condition. In this procedure weight, in the form of a special washer, is being added to the grip retaining bolt to obtain spanwise balance and washers are added to the paddles to obtain chordwise balance.

A similar type of balancing procedure of the head is shown in Fig. 5-72. In this situation washers are attached to the outer face of the pillow block liner to obtain chordwise balance and lead weight to the inside of the blade retaining bolt to obtain spanwise balance.

After the head is statically balanced, the blades are placed on the rotor head and balanced as a unit. This is accomplished in much the same manner as the head static balance. On semi-rigid rotor systems the blades are moved *aft* to obtain chordwise balance by shortening the drag braces. On semi-rigid rotors the chordwise balance must be obtained first because the effective length of the arm is affected by moving the blade.

The spanwise balance is obtained in one of two manners. Weight is placed either in tip pockets on the blade or in the hollow blade retaining bolts (Fig. 5-73). **NOTE:** The addition or subtraction of weight in other than the manufacturer's approved locations could be dangerous. Although it may appear that weight has been added in these unauthorized areas, these weights

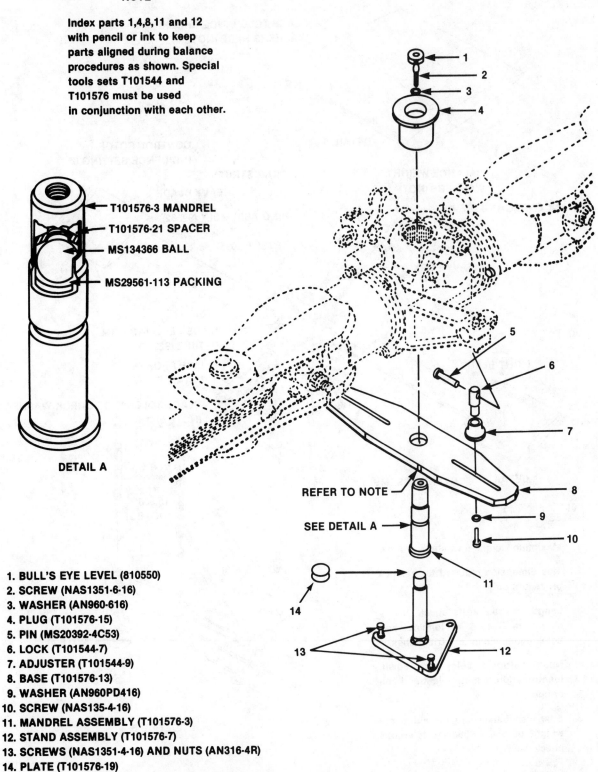

NOTE

Index parts 1,4,8,11 and 12
with pencil or ink to keep
parts aligned during balance
procedures as shown. Special
tools sets T101544 and
T101576 must be used
in conjunction with each other.

T101576-3 MANDREL
T101576-21 SPACER
MS134366 BALL
MS29561-113 PACKING

DETAIL A

1. BULL'S EYE LEVEL (810550)
2. SCREW (NAS1351-6-16)
3. WASHER (AN960-616)
4. PLUG (T101576-15)
5. PIN (MS20392-4C53)
6. LOCK (T101544-7)
7. ADJUSTER (T101544-9)
8. BASE (T101576-13)
9. WASHER (AN960PD416)
10. SCREW (NAS135-4-16)
11. MANDREL ASSEMBLY (T101576-3)
12. STAND ASSEMBLY (T101576-7)
13. SCREWS (NAS1351-4-16) AND NUTS (AN316-4R)
14. PLATE (T101576-19)

REFER TO NOTE

SEE DETAIL A

MAIN ROTOR HUB AND BLADE ASSEMBLY--STATIC BALANCING

Fig. 5-70 Typical special purpose balancing stand

179

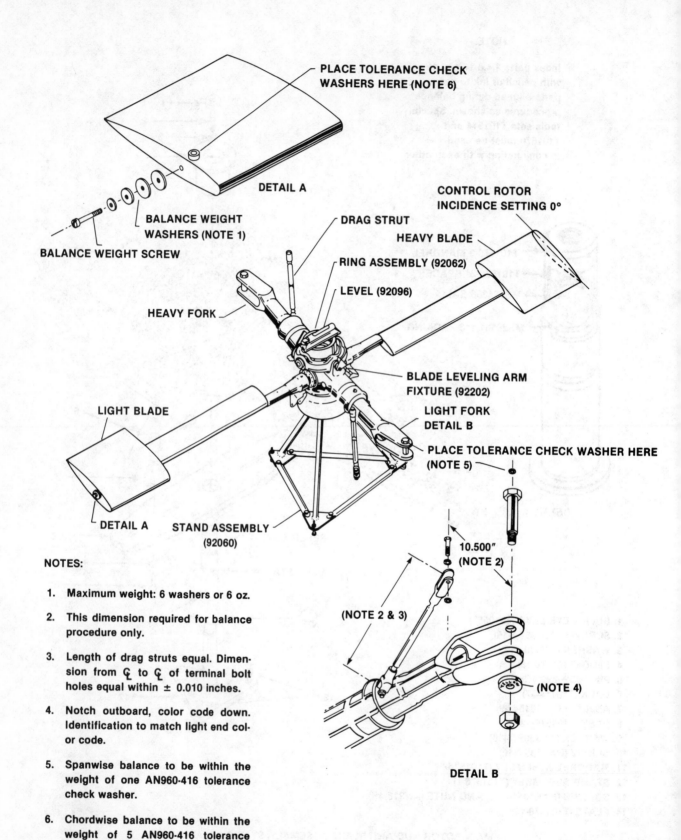

PLACE TOLERANCE CHECK WASHERS HERE (NOTE 6)

DETAIL A

CONTROL ROTOR INCIDENCE SETTING 0°

HEAVY BLADE

BALANCE WEIGHT WASHERS (NOTE 1)

BALANCE WEIGHT SCREW

DRAG STRUT

RING ASSEMBLY (92062)

LEVEL (92096)

HEAVY FORK

BLADE LEVELING ARM FIXTURE (92202)

LIGHT BLADE

LIGHT FORK DETAIL B

PLACE TOLERANCE CHECK WASHER HERE (NOTE 5)

DETAIL A

STAND ASSEMBLY (92060)

10.500" (NOTE 2)

(NOTE 2 & 3)

(NOTE 4)

DETAIL B

NOTES:

1. Maximum weight: 6 washers or 6 oz.

2. This dimension required for balance procedure only.

3. Length of drag struts equal. Dimension from $\mathcal{C}$ to $\mathcal{C}$ of terminal bolt holes equal within ± 0.010 inches.

4. Notch outboard, color code down. Identification to match light end color code.

5. Spanwise balance to be within the weight of one AN960-416 tolerance check washer.

6. Chordwise balance to be within the weight of 5 AN960-416 tolerance check washers.

Fig. 5-71 Balancing the rotor independently of the rotor blades

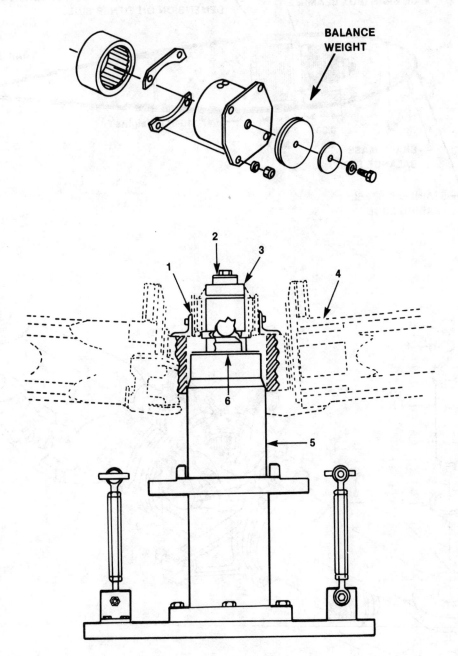

1. T101865 FLAP STOP
2. LEVEL, BULL'S-EYE
3. T101458-3 SOCKET AND T101458-7 SPACER
4. HUB ASSEMBLY
5. T101356 BUILD-UP BENCH
6. T101458-5 PLUG

Fig. 5-72 Balance weight is added to the trunnion caps to obtain chordwise balance

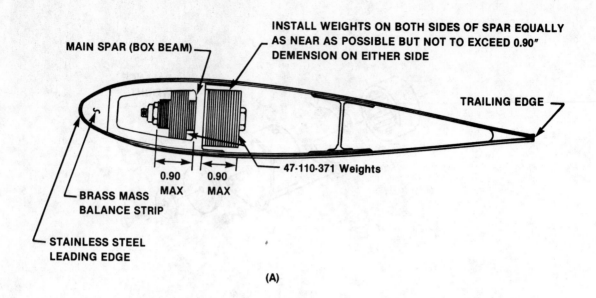

MAIN SPAR (BOX BEAM)

INSTALL WEIGHTS ON BOTH SIDES OF SPAR EQUALLY
AS NEAR AS POSSIBLE BUT NOT TO EXCEED 0.90"
DEMENSION ON EITHER SIDE

TRAILING EDGE

47-110-371 Weights

0.90 MAX   0.90 MAX

BRASS MASS
BALANCE STRIP

STAINLESS STEEL
LEADING EDGE

(A)

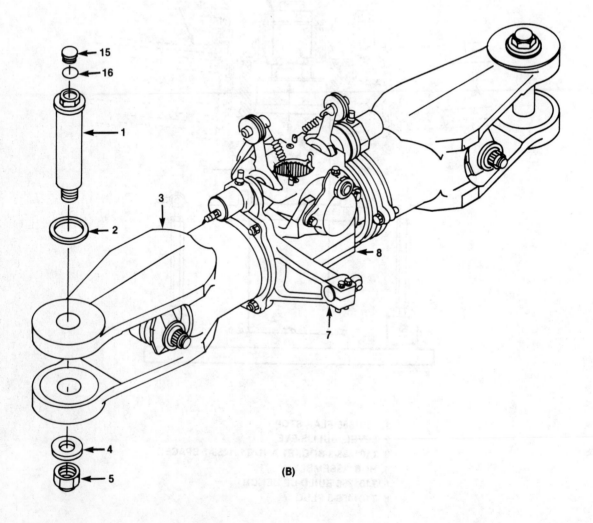

(B)

Fig. 5-73 Weight may be added to the blade tips or blade retaining bolts to obtain spanwise balance

182

were added when manufactured either to act as ballast or to obtain the same characteristics as the master blade and should not be disturbed.

On rotor systems in which the head and the blades are statically balanced as a unit much the same procedure will be used as that used when the head is balanced separately (Fig. 5-74). The head and blades are simply placed on the balance stand and the weight added to the appropriate place in order to obtain balance. In this particular procedure the chordwise balance is obtained by sweeping the blades *aft* while viewing the level placed on the hub yoke. The spanwise balance is accomplished by placing the level on the yoke and adding weight to the tip pocket.

Fig. 5-74 *Head and blades balanced as a unit*

Fig. 5-75 shows another example using the universal balancer. The blades are again balanced chordwise by moving the blade aft by adjustment of the latch pins. However, the weight for spanwise balance is added to the hollow blade retaining bolts.

At present there is one manufacturer of a universal type of balancing equipment. With this equipment several different heads and rotor systems may be balanced with the same basic equipment by using a series of adapters. This system is used to balance not only main rotors, but also tail rotors, propellers, and a variety of other rotating components (Fig. 5-76).

The basis of this equipment is a suspended arbor on which the main rotors or various components may be placed with adapters to adapt the head to the arbor and control the sensitivity (Fig. 5-77). The arbor itself is hollow and suspended by a flexible suspension element placed in the center of the hollow arbor and filled with oil. The oil acts

Fig. 5-75 *Rotor system balanced on a universal balancer*

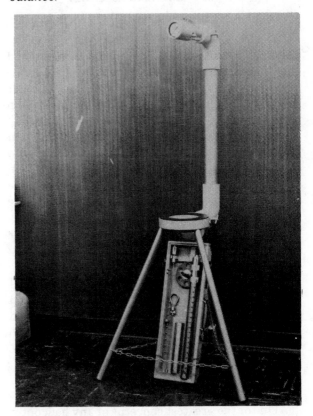

Fig. 5-76 *Universal balancer*

as a dampening device to slow down the movement of the arbor. Attached to the flexible suspension element at the top of the arbor is an indicator bushing. As the arbor is moved by an un-

183

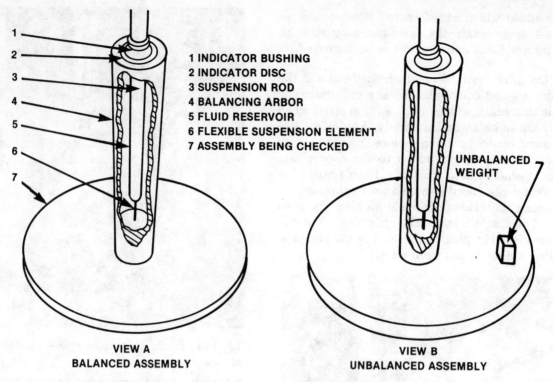

1 INDICATOR BUSHING
2 INDICATOR DISC
3 SUSPENSION ROD
4 BALANCING ARBOR
5 FLUID RESERVOIR
6 FLEXIBLE SUSPENSION ELEMENT
7 ASSEMBLY BEING CHECKED

UNBALANCED WEIGHT

VIEW A
BALANCED ASSEMBLY

VIEW B
UNBALANCED ASSEMBLY

Fig. 5-77   Arbor used with the universal balancer

balanced condition, the suspension element and the indicator bushing will remain in position attached to the arbor. In the area of the indicator bushing is the indicator disc. It is the relationship of the bushing and disc that indicates if a balanced or unbalanced condition exists. If the item is in balance, the relationship of the disc and bushing will be concentric (Fig. 5-78). If the item is slightly out of balance, the relationship of the disc and bushing will be slightly eccentric. If the relationship of the disc and the bushing overlaps, the item has exceeded the measurable tolerances (Fig. 5-78).

The specific type of equipment for individual rotor systems varies considerably in design and sensitivity. This is due not only to the head design but to the sensitivity of the head to vibration.

3.   Vibration

One of the greatest concerns of any helicopter operator and technician should be vibration. No other factor will contribute so much to the general deterioration of the components as will excessive vibration. For this reason it is necessary that the technician understand its causes and effects.

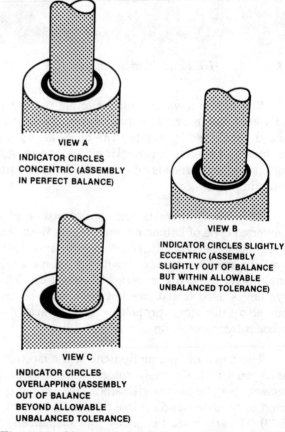

VIEW A

INDICATOR CIRCLES CONCENTRIC (ASSEMBLY IN PERFECT BALANCE)

VIEW B

INDICATOR CIRCLES SLIGHTLY ECCENTRIC (ASSEMBLY SLIGHTLY OUT OF BALANCE BUT WITHIN ALLOWABLE UNBALANCED TOLERANCE)

VIEW C

INDICATOR CIRCLES OVERLAPPING (ASSEMBLY OUT OF BALANCE BEYOND ALLOWABLE UNBALANCED TOLERANCE)

Fig. 5-78   Views of the Arbor indicator showing various balance conditions

The cause of vibration is an unbalanced condition. Regardless of the processes used in manufacture it is almost impossible to obtain a perfect balance of a component.

Suppose that a large wheel was manufactured by casting the disc with the finest material and under the finest casting process available. The casting is machined to the closest tolerances possible and the finest bearing placed in the center. Next this wheel is placed on a shaft (Fig. 5-79). By moving the wheel from Point A to Point B, it may be that it will return to Point A (Fig. 5-80). This is an indication that the wheel is heavier at Point A than at Point B. This wheel may be *statically balanced* by placing weight at Point B or removing weight from Point A. **NOTE:** Usually if the wheel is to be exposed to high RPM and centrifugal forces, material is removed from the wheel rather than material added for weight.

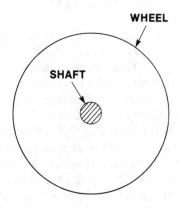

Fig. 5-79   *Wheel placed on an axle*

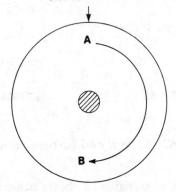

Fig. 5-80   *The wheel will rotate until the heavy spot reaches the bottom*

Even if this wheel is statically balanced, it does not mean that the wheel will be dynamically balanced. To check the dynamic balance, the wheel could be placed on the same axle as used previously with a dial indicator placed on the outer rim (Fig. 5-81). It may be found that as the wheel is moved at a low RPM, the dial indicator will remain at the "O" point but as the RPM is increased a movement will take place on the dial indicator. This movement indicates a dynamic imbalance and is known as displacement or amplitude. The rate at which this condition occurs is known as frequency.

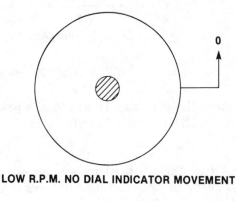

LOW R.P.M. NO DIAL INDICATOR MOVEMENT

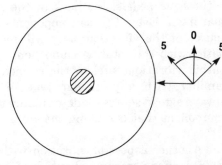

HIGH R.P.M. DIAL INDICATOR MOVEMENT

Fig. 5-81   *A — No dial indicator movement will be shown at low RPM   B — At high RPM the dial indicator will move*

The example of the wheel could be compared to any rotating component of the helicopter such as the main rotor, tail rotor, cooling fans or shafts. Although some vibrations could be of a frequency that they could not be sensed by the human body, most vibrations in the helicopter other than those of the turbine engine can be sensed. In many cases they can not only be sensed but also be distinguished as to the area in which they originate. The amplitude, like the frequency, has limitations in human ability to dis-

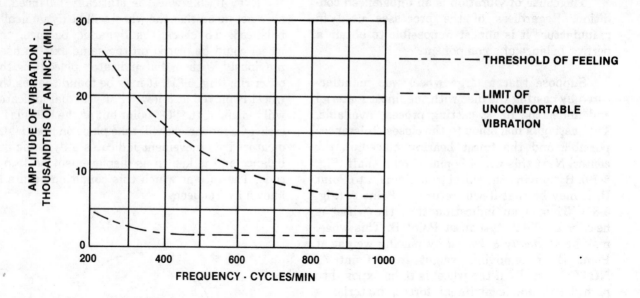

Fig. 5-82 *Points at which vibration may be felt by man*

tinguish the vibration. However, it is possible to distinguish the more harmful vibrations (Fig. 5-82).

Often these vibrations are sensed through stationary or non-rotating components such as anti-torque pedals, the back of the seat, or the seat itself. Even if these components are not the source of the vibration, they will move in sympathy with the rotating component. These sympathic vibrations are, to the trained technician familiar with a particular type of helicopter, always a good source for determining the rotating component that is causing the vibration.

Another aspect of vibration with which the maintenance personnel should be familiar is the fact that all rotating components have a natural frequency at which they are susceptible to vibration. In the design of components, these areas are avoided or the component is redesigned. In some instances when the situation is unavoidable, a transit range is established so that the component is not continuously operated at that speed but merely passes through that range in order to obtain the operating speed. Such areas are denoted in the operations manual and are usually marked on the tachometer by a red arc placed on the instrument in the area of the RPM range.

Vibrations in helicopters are usually classified into three main groups — (1) low frequency, (2) medium frequency, and (3) high frequency.

a. *Low frequency vibrations*

Low frequency vibration is at a rate of 0 to 500 RPM, expressed in terms of cycles per minute (CPM). This range is usually associated with the main rotor, which rotates in a 300 to 500 RPM range. The 1:1 vibration is probably the most common and the easiest to detect. It will be identified as a beat with one beat for each revolution of the rotor. This beat may be either lateral or vertical in nature (Fig. 5-83). The vertical vibration is normally associated with track, while lateral vibration is associated with an unbalanced condition.

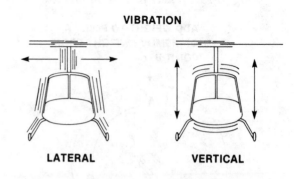

Fig. 5-83 *Lateral and vertical vibrations*

It is also possible to obtain other vibrations such as a 2:1 or 3:1, etc., beats depending upon the rotor system of the helicopter. Although the

186

1:1 and the 2:1 vibrations are easily identifiable, the multiple beats are not. The main rotor vibrations may be caused by numerous features of the main rotor, such as spanwise and chordwise balance, dampeners, lead-lag hinges, and defective head components.

b. Medium frequency vibrations

The medium frequency vibrations are in the area of 500 to 2000 CPM. This wide range is difficult to distinguish as medium frequency. A multiple beat from the main rotor would fall into this category, as well as a cooling fan on certain helicopters. For this reason the medium frequency vibrations may be anything from a distinguishable beat to a buzz. Although the medium frequency vibration exists both in theory and practicality, it is most difficult for the technician to identify a vibration in the medium frequency range. As a result, most vibrations are often simply identified as high and low frequency, with the low frequency having a distinctive beat, and the high frequency an undistinguishable beat resulting in a buzz.

c. High frequency vibrations

The high frequency vibrations are in the range of 2000 CPM and above. As previously described, they are distinguishable only as a buzz and are sometimes felt as a tingling sensation. This type of vibration is often sensed in stationary components such as the anti-torque pedals in sympathy with the tail rotor. The three general areas of high frequency vibration are the tail rotor, engine and drive train systems.

All helicopters are susceptible to vibration because of the great number of rotating components. For this reason, it is most important to keep the vibration level to a minimum because wear factors will be increased. The wear factors will affect not only the life of the rotating components, but also the fatigue life of stationary components that are in sympathy with the rotating components.

It must be observed that these wear factors do not follow a proportional wear rate but actually work in multiples. For instance, if the wear factor on a certain bearing was one thousandth of an inch in 500 hours, it may take no more than 50 hours to accomplish the next one thousandth of an inch wear. In the following 500 hours, 20 to 30 thousandths of an inch of wear may occur. If excessive vibration is allowed to continue, each extra one thousandth of an inch movement that is allowed will occur at a shorter interval. Since each component is attached to another, the wear factor of the adjoining components also increases. One can readily see that this progression may eventually affect a whole system and even cross into another system through sympathetic vibration. Such problems can lead only to high maintenance costs in replacement parts and labor, which is often the difference of operating at a profit or a loss.

4. Tracking

Tracking is a procedure used to check that all blades are traveling within the same tip path plane (Fig. 5-84). If a blade is out of track, the helicopter will have a 1:1 vertical vibration. Track problems can occur on all types of helicopter rotor heads. Usually the helicopter requires tracking when the blades, heads, or pitch change components of the head are replaced. Tracking should always be the first procedure performed when heads or blades are rebuilt or replaced during initial run-up. It will be impossible to correct unbalanced conditions until the track is correct. Often an out-of-track condition will be so outstanding the lateral vibrations will not be felt until the track is corrected.

There are a number of methods used to determine track on helicopters. These vary with the manufacturer and the system which will be most appropriate for the rotor design. Some of these methods are the:

a. Stick Method

b. Flag Method

c. Light Reflector Method

d. Pre-track Method

e. Electronic or Strobe Method

Regardless of the method used, all tracking procedures will begin with ground tracking. In some instances it may be required to do a low speed track as well as a high speed track.

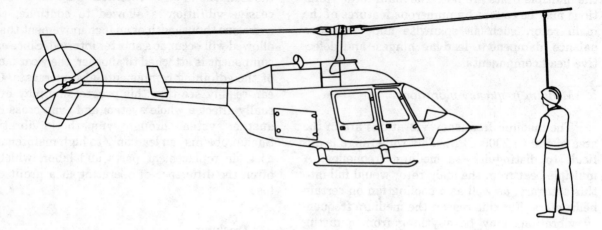

Fig. 5-84   Tracking by the stick method

NOTE: Low speed and high speed track are in relation to rotor RPM.

Many of the helicopters in use today will also require in-flight tracking because of the rotor design. This will require a hover track and track at various air speeds as specified by the manufacturer. It must be remembered that regardless of the method, all tracking must be accomplished in relatively calm air with the helicopter facing into the wind.

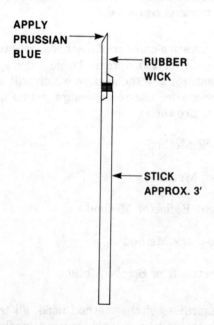

APPLY PRUSSIAN BLUE

RUBBER WICK

STICK APPROX. 3'

Fig. 5-85   Typical tracking stick

a.   Stick method

The first method to be discussed will be the stick method. This system is adaptable only to ground use. A rubber wick of 2 to 4 inches is placed on a stick of sufficient length to touch the rotor (Fig. 5-85). The wick portion is coated with a substance such as Prussian Blue. With the helicopter operating at the specified RPM, the wick attached to the stick will be placed in contact with the rotor blades. When contact is made, the stick is removed. Note the position of the maintenance personnel in relation to the rotor's advancing blade. This position will avoid injury if the stick is placed too high. After shutdown the blades are checked for the mark left by the wick (Fig. 5-86).

If both blades are marked the same amount, the blades are in track as shown in Fig. 5-86A. If one blade carries a heavier mark than the other, the blade with the heavier mark must be raised or the blade with the lighter mark must be lowered. In many instances only one blade will be marked (Fig. 5-86C). This means that only one blade was low enough to receive a mark and the blades will be raised or lowered until all blades are in the same plane of rotation. The disadvantage of this system is that the process may have to be repeated several times before the track can be adjusted correctly, because if only one mark appears, it is not possible to determine the exact position of the other blade.

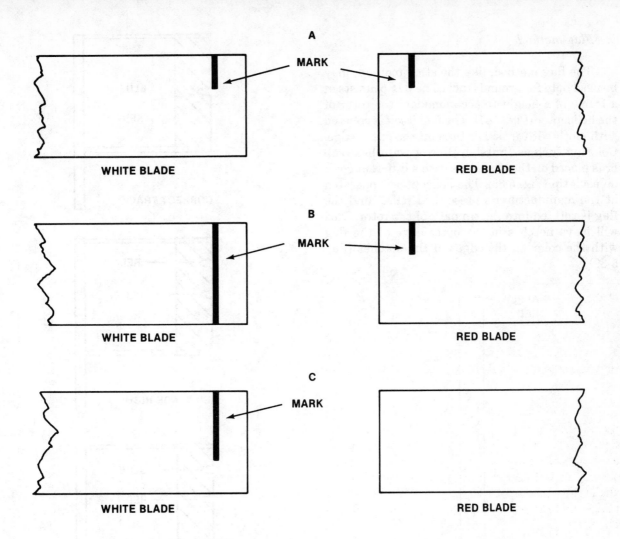

A

MARK

WHITE BLADE **RED BLADE**

B

MARK

WHITE BLADE **RED BLADE**

C

MARK

WHITE BLADE **RED BLADE**

Fig. 5-86 Typical marks made on the rotors by the stick method

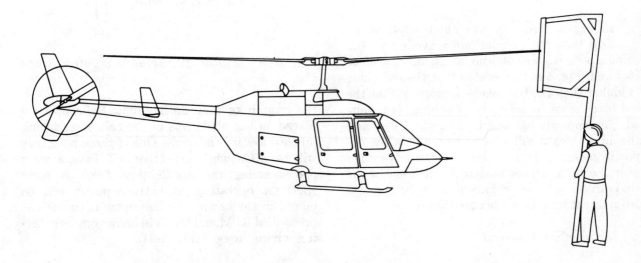

Fig. 5-87 Tracking by the flag method

189

b. Flag method

The flag method, like the stick method, may be used only for ground track. The flag consists of a frame of a height to accommodate the rotor of the helicopter (Fig. 5-87). The flag itself is covered with cloth with masking tape on the outer edge. Coloring such as Prussian Blue or waterbase color is placed on the blade tips with a different color on each tip (Fig. 5-88). The helicopter is operated at the manufacturer's prescribed RPM, and the flag is rotated into the tip path of the rotor. This will leave notches in the outer edge of the flag with the color on the edges of the notches (Fig. 5-89).

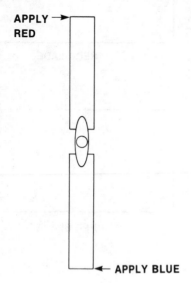

APPLY RED

APPLY BLUE

Fig. 5-88   Marking the blade tips

In Fig. 5-89A, only one notch appears, indicating that both blades are traveling in the same tip path plane and no adjustments will be required. Fig. 5-89B indicates that the red blade is higher than the blue blade, indicating that the red blade must be lowered or the blue blade raised. The opposite has occurred in Fig. 5-89C and the adjustments will have to be made in the opposite manner. This method has an advantage over the stick method in that the distance of the tip path plane is clearly indicated on the flag and adjustment may be made accordingly.

c. Light reflector method

The light reflector method may be used on the ground or in the air. This is a distinct advantage because all blades do not track the same on

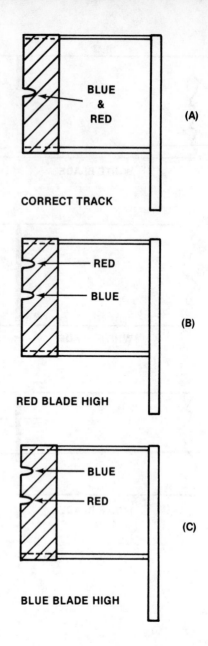

BLUE & RED   (A)

CORRECT TRACK

RED

BLUE   (B)

RED BLADE HIGH

BLUE

RED   (C)

BLUE BLADE HIGH

Fig. 5-89   Typical flag markings after track check

the ground as they do in flight. Reflectors are placed on the blade tips of the helicopter facing inboard toward the cabin. One of these reflectors will be plain while the other will have a strip placed across the middle (Fig. 5-90). A hand spotlight operating on battery power will be placed in the cabin. The helicopter is run at the prescribed RPM and the light shows on the reflectors giving images (Fig. 5-91).

The image in Fig. 5-91A represents an in-track rotor system with the same amount of reflected light showing on both sides. 5-91B

190

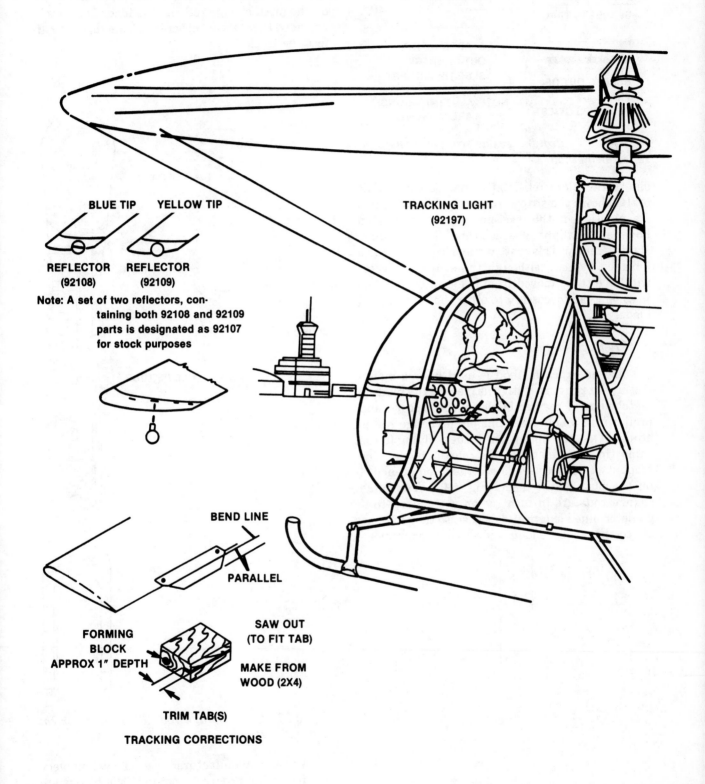

BLUE TIP   YELLOW TIP

REFLECTOR   REFLECTOR
(92108)   (92109)

Note: A set of two reflectors, containing both 92108 and 92109
parts is designated as 92107
for stock purposes

TRACKING LIGHT
(92197)

BEND LINE

PARALLEL

FORMING
BLOCK
APPROX 1" DEPTH

SAW OUT
(TO FIT TAB)

MAKE FROM
WOOD (2X4)

TRIM TAB(S)

TRACKING CORRECTIONS

Fig. 5-90   Light reflector method of tracking

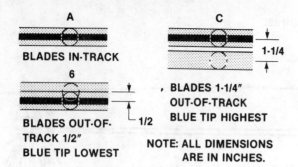

A

BLADES IN-TRACK

6

BLADES OUT-OF-TRACK 1/2″
BLUE TIP LOWEST

C

1-1/4

, BLADES 1-1/4″
OUT-OF-TRACK
BLUE TIP HIGHEST

1/2

NOTE: ALL DIMENSIONS
ARE IN INCHES.

Fig. 5-91 Typical images as seen with the light reflector method

shows the plain reflected blade too high while 5-91C shows the striped reflected blade too high. As mentioned, this system may be used at a hover and in flight, at which time the blades may act differently. This system may also be used on a 3-bladed system, although the striped reflector will have to be moved from blade to blade if adjustments are necessary to other than the striped blade.

d. Pre-track method

The pre-track method is used by one manufacturer at present. With this method the blade is matched to a master blade in the factory and preflown in a spin test. The pitch change rod is adjusted at that time so the blade is flying in the same tip path plane as the master blade. The amount of adjustment is recorded and stenciled on the butt of the blade (Fig. 5-92). The pitch change rods are in turn set on a standard to a predetermined length and decaled so they may be set to the corresponding indicated measurement

TRACK-6

Fig. 5-92 Pretrack adjustment recorded on the blade

stenciled on the blade (Fig. 5-93). When a new blade is installed, the correct length is simply set on the pitch change rod and the blade is in track, provided there are no other problems that may affect the track.

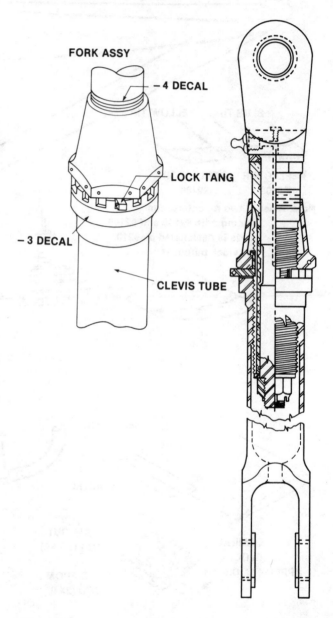

FORK ASSY

– 4 DECAL

LOCK TANG

– 3 DECAL

CLEVIS TUBE

Fig. 5-93 Pitch change rod adjustment for the pretrack method

Another manufacturer uses a system very similiar to the pre-track method. The blades are prespun at the factory and tabbed. At that time the blades are marked on the butt on the blade with the length of the pitch change rod from the centers of the rod ends. In this system no decals are necessary for the pitch change rod adjustment to obtain the correct angle of attack for the particular blade to fly in track.

e. *Electronic strobe system*

The electronic strobe system, like the reflector method, allows the track to be checked not only on the ground but also in flight. Reflectors are placed on the tips of the blades facing the cabin. These reflectors will use a stripe system to identify the blades (Fig. 5-94)

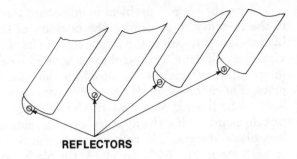

REFLECTORS

Fig. 5-94 Reflectors used for the strobe system of tracking

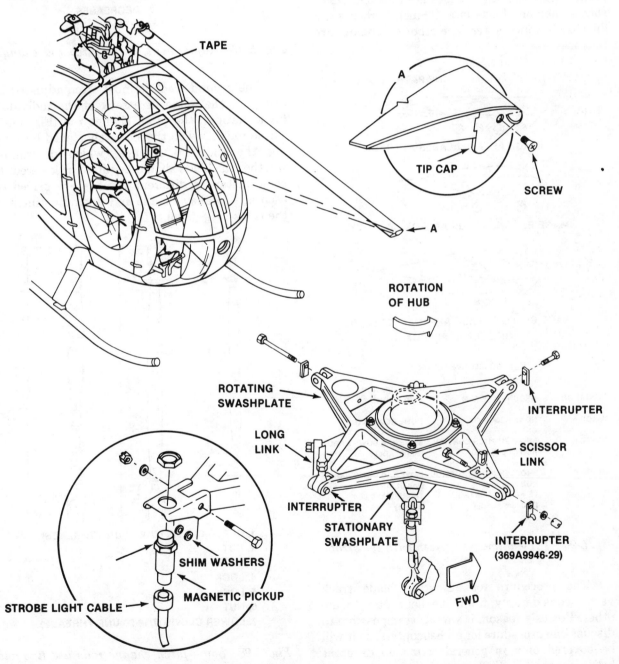

Fig. 5-95 Typical strobe interrupter and pick up installation

Since the biggest problem in adjusting track is the inability to determine the position of the blades during rotation, the strobe light is used to view the reflectors. This strobe is triggered by an interrupter and pick-up mounted on the swashplate (Fig. 5-95). This device allows the strobe light to be flashed each time the blade passes a certain point giving the appearance of a motionless blade showing the reflectors superimposed on each other (Fig. 5-96). In 5-96A, the blades are in track and no adjustment will be necessary, but in 5-96B one blade is approximately 1/2-inch higher while the other blades are in track. 5-96C shows that one blade is a 1/2-inch higher while another is 1 inch lower. The other two blades are in track.

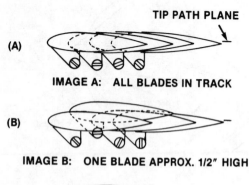

TIP PATH PLANE

(A)

IMAGE A: ALL BLADES IN TRACK

(B)

IMAGE B: ONE BLADE APPROX. 1/2" HIGH

(C)

IMAGE C: ONE BLADE APPROX. 1/2" HIGH;
ONE BLADE APPROX. 1" LOW

CORRECTIVE ACTION

CONDITION	GROUND IDLE RPM	HIGH RPM AND FWD FLIGHT
IMAGE A	NONE REQUIRED	NONE REQUIRED
IMAGE B	SHORTEN PITCH CONTROL ROD (2nd BLADE)	MOVE TAB DOWNWARD (2nd BLADE)
IMAGE C	SHORTEN PITCH CONTROL ROD (2nd BLADE) LENGHTEN CONTROL ROD (3rd BLADE)	MOVE TAB DOWNWARD (2nd BLADE) TAB UPWARD (3rd BLADE)

Fig. 5-96 *Typical images as seen with the strobe*

The procedure for adjusting blade track varies considerably from one helicopter to another. For this reason, it would be impossible to discuss one procedure for all helicopters, so it will be covered only in general terms on different helicopters.

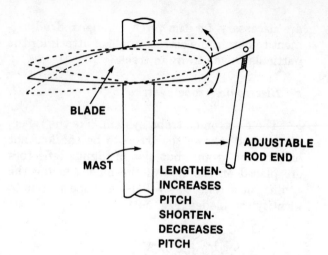

BLADE

MAST

LENGTHEN-
INCREASES
PITCH
SHORTEN-
DECREASES
PITCH

ADJUSTABLE
ROD END

Fig. 5-97 *Adjustment of the pitch rod changes track*

The ground track is most often adjusted by changing the angle of attack of the individual blade through the pitch change rod (Fig. 5-97). These rods are lengthened or shortened by moving the rod end fittings, which determines whether the blade should be raised or lowered. In some instances different threads are placed on each end to allow coarse and fine adjustment of the track (Fig. 5-98).

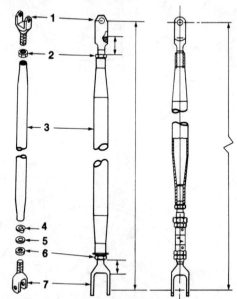

1. UPPER CLEVIS (7/16-14 UNC THREADS)
2. NUT
3. TUBE
4. LOCK
5. LOCK
6. NUT
7. LOWER CLEVIS (7/16-20 UNF THREADS)

Fig. 5-98 *Some pitch change rods use fine and course threads*

f. Trim tabs

Some blades are equipped with stationary trim tabs that may be used in the ground track but are most often limited to flight tracking only (Fig. 5-99). These tabs are fixed to the blade and are simply bent to change the angle of attack of the blade. By bending the tab up the blade will go up. Bending the tab down will force the blade down (Fig. 5-100). During this procedure certain precautions must be observed. The tab should be bent as one unit so that a rippled edge does not occur as often happens if the tab is bent by hand. For this reason a tab bender is often listed as a special tool (Fig. 5-101).

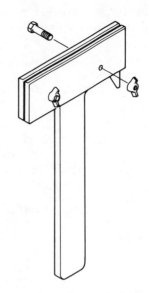

Fig. 5-101 Typical tab bender

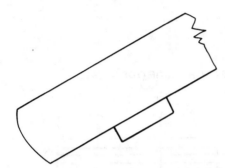

Fig. 5-99 Trim tabs are somtimes attached to the rotor blades

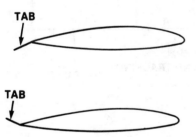

Fig. 5-100 The tab may be bent to adjust track

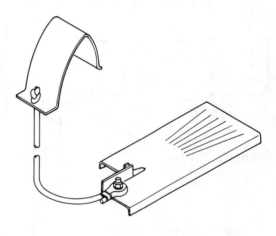

Fig. 5-102 Typical tab protractor

During all initial tracking procedures the tabs should be placed in a neutral position. This will allow adjustment in either direction with a minimum deflection of the tabs which create drag. The number of degrees a tab may be bent is also limited by the manufacturer of the helicopter. If the tab is bent an excessive amount, its effectiveness will be destroyed by disruption of the airflow. For this purpose a protractor-type device is often furnished by the manufacturer (Fig. 5-102). In some instances no trim tabs are present and the trailing edge of the blade is simply bent in designated areas for the specified track speed (Fig. 5-103).

g. Blade crossover or climbing blade

During in-flight tracking, sometimes *blade crossover* or a *climbing blade* occurs. The two terms are synonymous and simply mean that although the blades tracked on the ground and at a hover they do not track during forward flight. One blade flies higher. This is caused by the elasticity of that particular blade. The occurrence of this problem is more common on wood blades than metal.

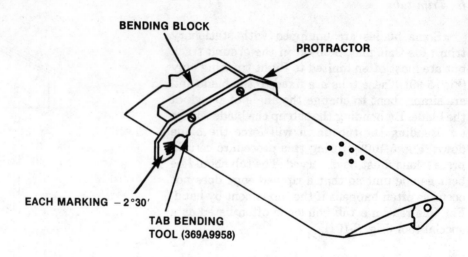

BENDING BLOCK

PROTRACTOR

EACH MARKING – 2°30'

TAB BENDING
TOOL (369A9958)

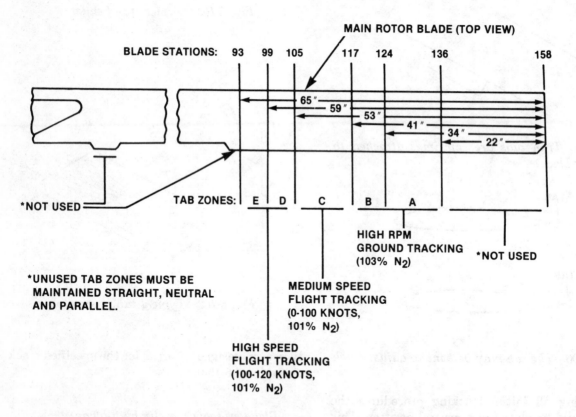

MAIN ROTOR BLADE (TOP VIEW)

BLADE STATIONS: 93 99 105   117 124   136   158

65"
59"
53"
41"
34"
22"

*NOT USED

TAB ZONES: E | D | C | B | A

*UNUSED TAB ZONES MUST BE
MAINTAINED STRAIGHT, NEUTRAL
AND PARALLEL.

HIGH RPM
GROUND TRACKING
(103% N_2)   *NOT USED

MEDIUM SPEED
FLIGHT TRACKING
(0-100 KNOTS,
101% N_2)

HIGH SPEED
FLIGHT TRACKING
(100-120 KNOTS,
101% N_2)

Fig. 5-103 Hughes 500 rotor blade where the trailing edge of the blade is used for tabing.

If no system other than the stick or flag method is available, a low-speed track may be necessary. The helicopter is simply run at the designated speed on the ground and the track is checked. The low blade in the track check is the high blade in flight and will require rolling of the grip in order to fly correctly in forward flight.

Track adjustments, like many of the other adjustments available to the technician, should be used with discretion and should not be thought of as a cure-all for low frequency vertical vibrations. Once the original track has been established and no components that would affect the track have been changed, the need for periodic track adjustment is not necessary. If such vibrations do occur, the components and controls should be carefully inspected for malfunctions before any retracking adjustments are attempted.

5. Spanwise dynamic balance of the main rotor

After the rotor system has been statically balanced, it may be necessary to balance the rotor dynamically after it has been installed. No attempts should be made in dynamic balance without first checking the track. For the most part, if no electronic equipment is available for balancing, the procedure is a trial-and-error situation dependent upon the ability to feel the vibration and its reduction. The skilled maintenance operator who has felt the various vibrations will probably be quicker to reduce the vibration level than the novice.

The system used most often for spanwise balancing is taping the blades and feeling the results of the added weight placed on the blade by the tape. Usually the manufacturer will specify the width of the masking tape and the number of wraps that will be equal to the addition of weight to be added. Even on a two-bladed main rotor system this could involve a number of stops and starts before the optimum vibration level is reached. Even then, this level depends upon the person performing the procedure and his ability to sense vibration. The typical procedure would be to place two or three wraps of masking tape on the blade near the tip (Fig. 5-104). After taping the blade, run the helicopter. If the vibration is reduced, stop the helicopter and add additional wrap. If the vibration becomes worse, remove the

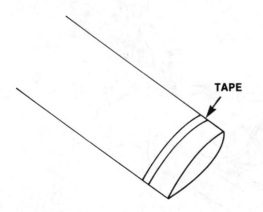

Fig. 5-104   Taping the blade for spanwise balance

tape and tape to the opposite blade. When the lowest vibration level is reached, the weight of the tape is added to the blade — either to the blade pocket or the blade retaining bolt as instructed by the manufacturer.

As previously mentioned, it is often difficult to determine the difference of a spanwise or chordwise balance problem, and it is not unusual to have both vibrations present at the same time. For this reason, it may be necessary to make other corrections after reducing the spanwise vibration. It is also not unusual to have a new vibration appear as this vibration is eliminated. It is usually because the one vibration remained hidden in the presence of the more pronounced vibration.

In any case, the spanwise balance should be accomplished, if required when heads and blades are changed in accordance with manufacturers' recommendations. Like all other adjustments on the helicopter, further balancing should be performed with discretion and should not be attempted as a cure-all of vibration problems.

6. Blade sweeping

Blade sweeping is a procedure used after installation of new blades, head, or major components of the head. This procedure is done only on semi-rigid rotor systems and only after blade alignment has been made. Sweeping is done to obtain chordwise dynamic balance and is not always necessary after obtaining static balance. The indication of the need for sweeping is very similar to that of spanwise balance, a 1:1 lateral vibration from the main rotor is always an indication of an unbalanced condition. It is very difficult for the average technician to determine if the vibration is chordwise or spanwise in nature.

One manufacturer states that if the vibration becomes greater in amplitude with an increase from low to high operating RPM, the problem is spanwise. If the vibration amplitude remains the same throughout the operating range, it is chordwise. This may or may not be obvious to the technician. Other indications of chordwise imbalance are nudging of the cyclic in flight and heavy collective. Either or both of these could indicate the necessity of sweeping the blades.

The procedure for sweeping the blades is quite simple. It involves moving one or both of

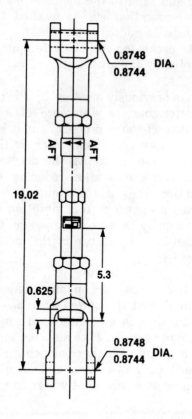

Fig. 5-105 *Typical drag brace with decal showing aft adjustment*

the blades *aft* about the lead-lag axis, which is held stationary by the drag brace or latch pins depending on the type of rotor head, to obtain chordwise balance of the rotor head. Once the initial alignment is achieved, the blades may be moved only in the aft direction without affecting the stability of the helicopter. For this reason, many drag braces are marked with a decal indicating the aft directional movement (Fig. 5-105)

Other than electronic balancing, there is no sure system of determining which blade should be moved or how much movement is necessary. It will be a guess situation and may require more than one adjustment in order to obtain the correct setting. It may also require returning one blade to the original setting and moving the opposite blade. For this reason, it is most important that the original alignment setting be marked (Fig. 5-106). All movement in the sweeping process should be rather small because the movement at the drag brace is multiplied several times at the blade tip.

The basic procedure for adjusting for chordwise balance on a semi-rigid head is as follows:

Step 1: Mark the drag brace with a soft lead pencil or crayon.

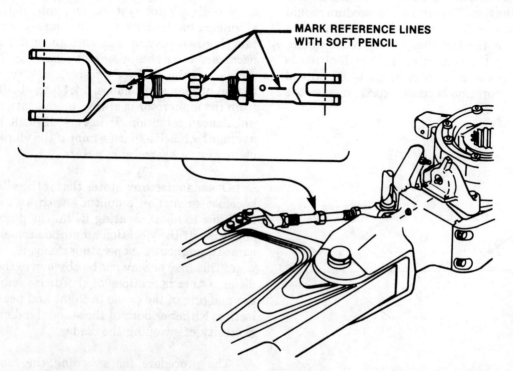

Fig. 5-106 *The drag brace must be marked before adjustments are made*

198

Step 2: Shorten the drag brace by loosening the jam nuts moving the drag brace. *Remember that shortening the drag brace moves the blade aft.* This shortening must be kept in small increments of a flat or less of the brace. Movement of most heads is limited.

Step 3: Retighten the jam nuts and operate the helicopter. If the vibration is reduced to an acceptable level, no further adjustment is necessary. If the vibration becomes worse, return the blade to its original setting and repeat Step 2 with the opposite blade. If the vibration becomes better but still is not acceptable, repeat the process using 1/2 flats until the vibration is reduced.

The same basic procedure is used when an unstable condition exists in the semi-rigid rotor system, due to the blades being too far forward the relationship of the center of gravity and center of pressure is incorrect. This condition is dangerous and can be identified by a nudging of the cyclic in forward flight. To correct this situation, both blades must be moved aft the same amount.

The one semi-rigid rotor helicopter that does not utilize drag braces at this time is the Bell 206, the Jet Ranger. This helicopter has latch pins which were discussed earlier. In adjusting blade sweep on this machine, the same basic principles are used. The blade may be moved only in the aft direction and the latch pin is adjusted rather than the drag brace. These adjustments are most sensitive and are recorded in one-point increments on the twelve-point nut. A total of three points is all that may be utilized without realigning the blades (Fig. 5-107).

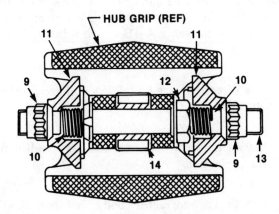

Fig. 5-107 Latch pin used for sweep on the Bell 206

7. *Electronic balancing*

One of the latest developments in the helicopter vibration analysis is in the electronic balancer. This equipment, not only has removed the guesswork from solving vibration problems, but has also enabled the maintenance personnel to establish new lows in vibration levels that would have been previously reached only by accident.

Vibration is sensed through the use of the accelerometer. This device is a piezoelectric type meaning that the sensing element is a special crystal that generates an electrical signal when it is strained or squeezed. The crystals are sandwiched between a base and an internal mass. This particular mass is made of tungsten which is more dense than lead. When the airframe vibrates, the accelerometer moves as a unit causing the mass to pull away from and squeeze the crystal generating an alternating voltage with each vibration cycle. This signal is in turn filtered electronically to eliminate any other vibrations that might be sensed because the accelerometer cannot discriminate. For example, if vibrations of the main rotor were being sought and the main rotor is operated in the 325 RPM range, it would be desirable to eliminate all vibrations that were in other ranges. This is done by filtering out any vibrations of the engine, shafts, and bearings that were also rotating but were of no interest to the operator seeking the vibration level of the main rotor. After the impulse is filtered, it is brought to a meter which shows the vibration in Inches Per Second (IPS) of movement. This movement indicates the intensity of the vibration of the rotor system. The goal is to reduce this vibration to the lowest levels possible. It is not uncommon to bring this level to .1 of IPS or less.

In order to determine the location of the vibration in relation to the rotor, the phase angle (clock angle) must be determined. This determination will indicate the steps necessary to reduce the vibration level. This is accomplished by a signal from a magnetic pick-up pulse and the filtered accelerometer signal. The magnetic pick-up is mounted to the stationary portion of the swashplate with interrupters mounted to the rotating portion. With each revolution of the rotor the magnetic lines of the pick-up are disturbed and an impulse occurs (Fig. 5-108). With the filtered accelerometer signal, this is used to light a ring of 24 lights in the phaser section of the equipment. This ring of lights represents a clock which is in half-hour increments with the 12 and 6 o'clock positions being at the top and bottom respectively. With the intensity of the vibration in IPS and the clock angle in the phaser lights, the vibration can be shown graphically and corrective action can be determined.

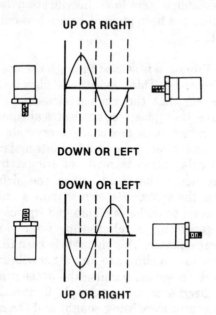

UP OR RIGHT

DOWN OR LEFT

DOWN OR LEFT

UP OR RIGHT

Fig. 5-108   Accelerometers are directional

Using the equipment manufactured by Chadwick Helmuth, charts have been made up for specific helicopters (Fig. 5-109). This chart represents the main rotor of a semi-rigid rotor system. The object is to reduce the vibration level to the center of the chart. The corrective action necessary is given along the side and bottom of the chart. The circular portion is used to record the intensity of the vibration in IPS on the clock angle. For example, if the vibration had an intensity of .5 IPS, it would be charted in the fifth ring. If the phaser placed the clock angle at 4 o'clock, the point of vibration would be charted to a point at 4 o'clock on the fifth ring or the .5 ring of the chart. By moving directly across and down from that point the corrective action indicated would be to add 4 grams to the blade indicated and sweep the indicated blade one increment. These procedures would be repeated until the vibration level is reduced to the desired level and may require three or more moves.

A somewhat different graph is used for a multi-blade rotor but the graphing procedure is

basically the same, but no correction is made for sweep since there are no adjustments with the fully articulated head. All dynamic balancing will be done by addition or subtraction of weight (Fig. 5-110).

At times, after the first move, the vibration becomes worse instead of better. In this situation the chart will need correction. Since the chart represents the best average of many sample readings, the difference from one airframe to another will make a difference in the correction both in the amount of weight and the clock angle. The correction of weight is quite simple. For example, if the weight change brought the move line closer to the center of the graph in a straight line but not far enough, more weight must be added. By the same reasoning, if the move line went past the center, less weight should have been added. The clock angle, however, is not so easy to correct. To be able to correct this situation, one must first understand what the moves should do in relation to the chart.

1. If a pair of moves is made exactly as called for, the move line should go towards the center of the charts.

2. If only one of the two weights is changed, the move line should be parallel to the fine lines extending from the unchanged axis. In other words, the weight on the second axis was not changed, so no change should be indicated.

NOTE: On multi-blade systems, consider only the *presection* in which the first point lies

If the move lines do not follow this order, the clock angle must be corrected. A clock corrector is furnished for this purpose. This is a clear mylar sheet with a movable A—B which rotates abut a rivet at point A

The directions are as follows and are printed on the card:

1. Place the eyelet "A" over the first reading of the move line.

2. Rotate the corrector body so that A—O points in the direction that the move line should go.

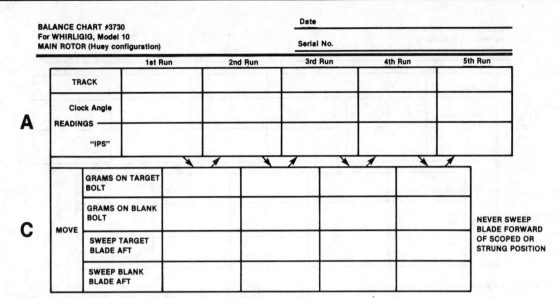

BALANCE CHART #3730
For WHIRLIGIG, Model 10
MAIN ROTOR (Huey configuration)

Date _____

Serial No. _____

NOTES - 1) Set tabs at trail. Adjust for good track at 100%, flat pitch, on the ground, using pitch link only.

2) Set BALANCER to 400 RPM. Push "TEST" button and check that the 12:00 and 6:00 o'clock lights are lighted. Release button.

3) Observe Clock Angle of lighted light, then press "VERIFY TUNE" button. Adjust "RPM TUNE" dial WHILE BUTTON IS PUSHED to return light to angle observed BEFORE BUTTON WAS PUSHED. Release button, observe angle, press and adjust again to match new "unpushed" angle. Repeat until there is NO CHANGE WHETHER BUTTON IS PUSHED OR RELEASED.

4) Record Clock Angle and "IPS" in section A of Chart. Plot in B (label it #1). Note indicated changes in C.

5) Make changes as indicated. Run ship to check result (label it point #2). Repeat as required to reduce "IPS" to .2 or less.

6) If "Move Line" (point #1 to #2) is not in correct direction, use "Clock Angle Corrector" #3597, and assign new numbers to clock. SEE MANUAL FOR DETAILS.

TAKE BALANCE READINGS ONLY
WHEN SHIP IS IN TRACK.

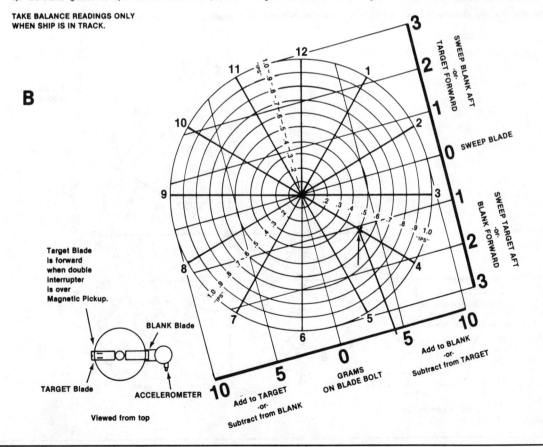

Fig. 5-109 Typical chart used to correct vibration

201

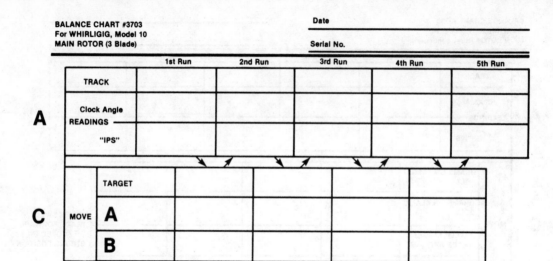

NOTES - 1)Set good ground track, 100%, flat pitch.

2)Set BALANCER to 400 RPM. Run ship 100%, flat pitch, on the ground. Push "TEST" button and check for 12:00, 4:00 and 8:00 o'clock lights.

3)Release "TEST" button and OBSERVE ANGLE OF LIGHTED LIGHT. Then press "VERIFY TUNE" button and adjust "RPM TUNE" dial, WHILE BUTTON IS PUSHED, to return light to angle observed BEFORE button was pushed. Release button, observe angle, press and adjust again to match new "unpushed" angle. Repeat until there is NO CHANGE whether button is pushed or released.

4)Read Clock Angle, and "IPS" with button released, record in Section "A", plot in "B" (label it #1), and note changes in "C".

5)Add weights as indicated. Run ship and repeat readings. (Label 2nd point #2). Repeat until "IPS" is .2 or less.

6)If Move Line (point #1 to #2) is not in the correct direction, use "Clock Angle Corrector" #3597, and assign new numbers to the clock. If two exact weight changes are made, the Move Line should go thru the center. If only one weight is changed, the Move Line should be parallel to the fine lines extending from the other axis of the "pie section".

7)If, after balancing, all blades have weights, remove equally until one or more have no weights.

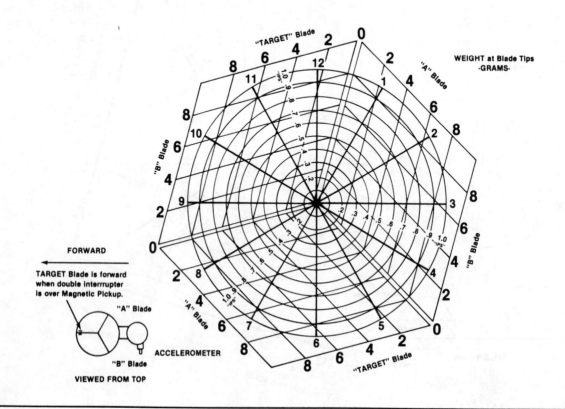

Fig. 5-110   Typical chart used on a multibladed system

202

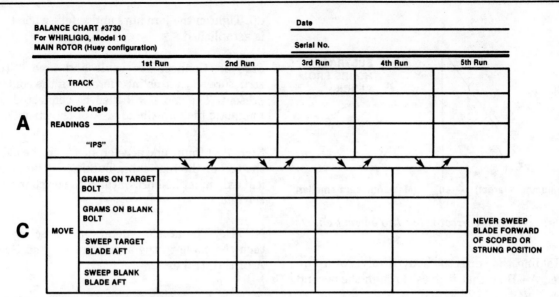

BALANCE CHART #3730
For WHIRLIGIG, Model 10
MAIN ROTOR (Huey configuration)

Date _____

Serial No. _____

		1st Run	2nd Run	3rd Run	4th Run	5th Run
A	TRACK					
	Clock Angle					
	READINGS					
	"IPS"					
C MOVE	GRAMS ON TARGET BOLT					
	GRAMS ON BLANK BOLT					
	SWEEP TARGET BLADE AFT					
	SWEEP BLANK BLADE AFT					

NEVER SWEEP BLADE FORWARD OF SCOPED OR STRUNG POSITION

NOTES · 1) Set tabs at trail. Adjust for good track at 100%, flat pitch, on the ground, using pitch link only.

2) Set BALANCER to 400 RPM. Push "TEST" button and check that the 12:00 and 6:00 o'clock lights are lighted. Release button.

3) Observe Clock Angle of lighted light, then press "VERIFY TUNE" button. Adjust "RPM TUNE" dial WHILE BUTTON IS PUSHED to return light to angle observed BEFORE BUTTON WAS PUSHED. Release button, observe angle, press and adjust again to match new "unpushed" angle. Repeat until there is NO CHANGE WHETHER BUTTON IS PUSHED OR RELEASED.

4) Record Clock Angle and "IPS" in section A of Chart. Plot in B (label it #1). Note indicated changes in C.

5) Make changes as indicated. Run ship to check result (label it point #2). Repeat as required to reduce "IPS" to .2 or less.

6) If "Move Line" (point #1 to #2) is not in correct direction, use "Clock Angle Corrector" #3597, and assign new numbers to clock. SEE MANUAL FOR DETAILS.

TAKE BALANCE READINGS ONLY
WHEN SHIP IS IN TRACK.

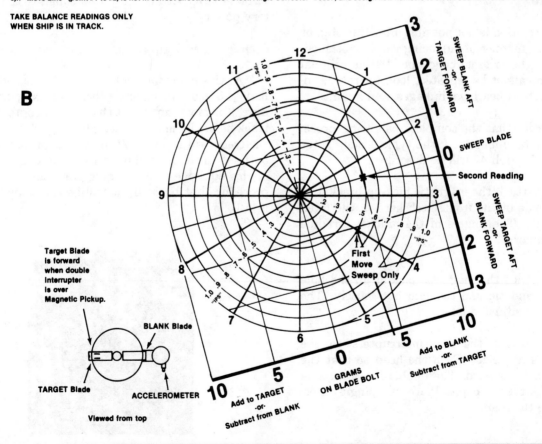

Fig. 5-111   Chart showing first and second corrections

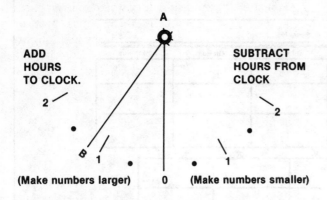

ADD
HOURS
TO CLOCK.

SUBTRACT
HOURS FROM
CLOCK

(Make numbers larger)   0   (Make numbers smaller)

Fig. 5-112 Clock corrector used to correct charts

3. Holding the corrector body firmly, rotate index A—B so that it goes through the second reading.

4. Read the required correction on the scale and change the clock by writing the new numbers on the chart.

5. Replot the second reading and proceed as before.

If correction is not possible after this step or no orderly manner of balancing can be obtained, return to the original condition. If this original condition cannot be repeated, look for rotor problems such as bearings, linkages, and mounts.

In order that the complete balancing procedure may be understood, the typical main rotor balance of a Bell 47 will be described:

Step 1: Attach the magnetic pick-up bracket to the left side of the front pitch horn of the fixed swashplate. The fingers of the bracket straddle the pitch horn.

Step 2: Place the magnetic pick-up in the hole provided and tighten the jam nut loosely. The gap will be adjusted later.

Step 3: Mount the two interrupters to the rotating swashplate. Turn the head so that the red blade is forward. The double interrupter is mounted at that point. Place the single interrupter to the rear.

Step 4: Adjust the pick-up so that a gap of .060 ± .010 is between the interrupters and the pick-

up. Tighten the jam nuts and safety when the gap is established.

Step 5: Connect the cable and tape it to the structure so that no interference of the controls is present. The cable will then be connected to the magnetic pick-up Channel A of the strobex unit.

Step 6: Mount one accelerometer in the cabin at the top of the rear cabin bulkhead. The cylinderical axis must be horizontal with the connector to the left.

NOTE: The accelerometers are directional. Attach the cable to the accelerometer and Channel A of the strobex.

Step 7: Mount the second accelerometer in the vertical position on the right side of the console with the plug facing down. Plug this into Channel B.

Step 8: The strobex unit will operate on either 12 or 24 VDC. Attach the power cables to the battery power.

Step 9: Attach tip targets to the main rotor.

At this point the hook-up is complete and one may proceed. As in any other balancing procedure, it is most important that the helicopter is in track before balance is attempted. For this reason the track will be checked first. This procedure is outlined in the following steps. Different models of this equipment may require variations to this procedure but basically it will be the same (Fig. 5-113).

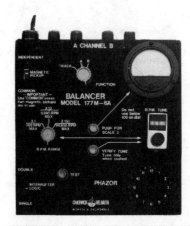

Fig. 5-113 Balancer unit produced by Chadwick Helmuth

The next step is to set the balancer as follows:

Step 10: Set balancer.

    a. Magnetic pick-up to "common"

    b. Interrupter logic to "double"

    c. Function switch to "track"

    d. RPM range to "X1"

    e. RPM tune to "350"

NOTE: When the balancer is powered, the RPM knob should be moved only when the "verify tune" button is depressed.

Step 11: Check the strobex unit with model 135M-11.

Fig. 5-114 Strobex unit

At this time the equipment is set to check the track. It is important that the helicopter is in track prior to any vibration analysis. For this the same basic procedure is used. Tabs are placed in neutral and the helicopter is brought up to operating speed which is 350 rotor RPM. The strobex is triggered by the interrupters so that the light image will be visible at the front of the ship. The ideal image will appear as a (+). If the image looks like this (T) the horizontal target needs to be brought down or the vertical target up. If the image is reversed, the opposite must be done. Adjustments are made until the image is corrected.

Quite often the images will not be superimposed. This may be due to the gap of the interrupter, or the single interrupter may need to be bent slightly. If two images are close enough to verify the blade position, no corrective action will be necessary.

Step 12: Set the hover track by adjusting the pitch link. When the track is adjusted properly at hover, the ship is ready for a vibration check.

Step 13: Set the *function* to channel *A*. This is the lateral accelerometer. The balancer should still be at 350 RPM.

Step 14: Push the test button. Lights should appear at the 12 o'clock and 6 o'clock positions of the phaser while the button is being pressed. Push the "verify to tune" button and adjust the "RPM tune". Release and observe the phaser lights. If the lights remain in the same positions, the tune is correctly set. If not, repeat until they do. This will be rather slow especially on a turbocharged ship because of RPM fluctuation. After tuning is complete, read and record the phaser and IPS on the chart. When this is done — "make only one of the moves indicated." Always take the greater of the moves. Upon completion of the required work, repeat the process and if the IPS becomes lower, continue until an indication of .1 IPS or lower is read. If the move increases the IPS, use the clock corrector.

This equipment may also be used in flight for blade tracking. It is possible to have the track change in forward flight. This is referred to as a climbing blade. It is suggested that it be checked at 50 and 80 MPH. If the blades spread with increased air speed, the tabs should be used. If the spread remains the same, use the pitch links. Remember NOT to tab the blade excessively.

Additional use of this equipment may be desirable for tail rotors and vibrations in various parts of the helicopter. All that is necessary is to know the RPM of the component that is to be checked.

8. *Dampener maintenance*

Although fully articulated heads do not have adjustments of drag braces or blade alignment, blades are hinged for fore and aft movement. These blades do have dampeners which affect the position of the advancing and retreating blade. These dampeners are of three basic types — the hydraulic cylinder, the multiple disk, and the elastomeric bearing. Any of these systems can cause an imbalance of the rotor systems during operation. In fact, it is sometimes hard to distinguish whether the vibration is vertical or lateral in nature. This is due to the position that is sought by the advancing and retreating blade in relation to the lift of the blade (Fig. 5-115). This may result in what would best be described as a shuffle with a 1:1 beat of the rotor.

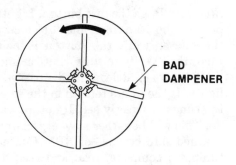

Fig. 5-115 Incorrect blade position on the lead-lag axis

a. Hydraulic dampener

The hydraulic dampener makes use of a cylinder and piston with fluid passing through a controlled orifice. Dampeners of this type of are adjustable so the rate of the dampener can vary

Fig. 5-116). Many of the newer dampeners are sealed units, making field adjustment impossible.

b. Multiple disk dampener

The second type of dampener makes use of a multiple disk arrangement held in a cylinder. The disks are submerged in hydraulic fluid for cooling and lubrication. Passing through the center of the cylinder and disks is a splined shaft. Every other disk is splined to mate with the shaft so that movement of the shaft will rotate the disks. Between each disk is a plate which is splined to the housing so that no rotation takes place. Thus any movement of the shaft which is attached to the blade will cause friction between the disk and plate. The amount of friction will be controlled by spring tension on the top of the stack of disks and plates (Fig. 5-117).

With the use of dampeners, it is sometimes possible to get the blades out of phase through ground handling. This may be corrected by simply moving the blades back into position by hand, thus moving the blade to its relative position of advancing or retreating.

The dampener condition is usually checked by feel, with the maintenance personnel moving the tip of the blade about the lead-lag axis and noting the force required and any bad spots in the travel. The dampeners may also be checked by a bench check (Fig. 5-118). Here a dead weight is used and the time required is noted.

Another type of dampener is checked by disconnecting the dampener from the blade and

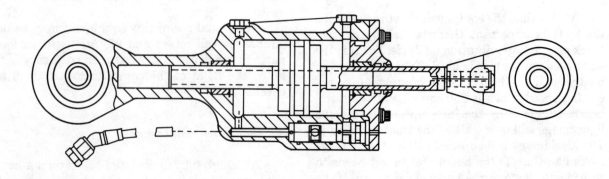

Fig. 5-116 Typical hydraulic dampener

206

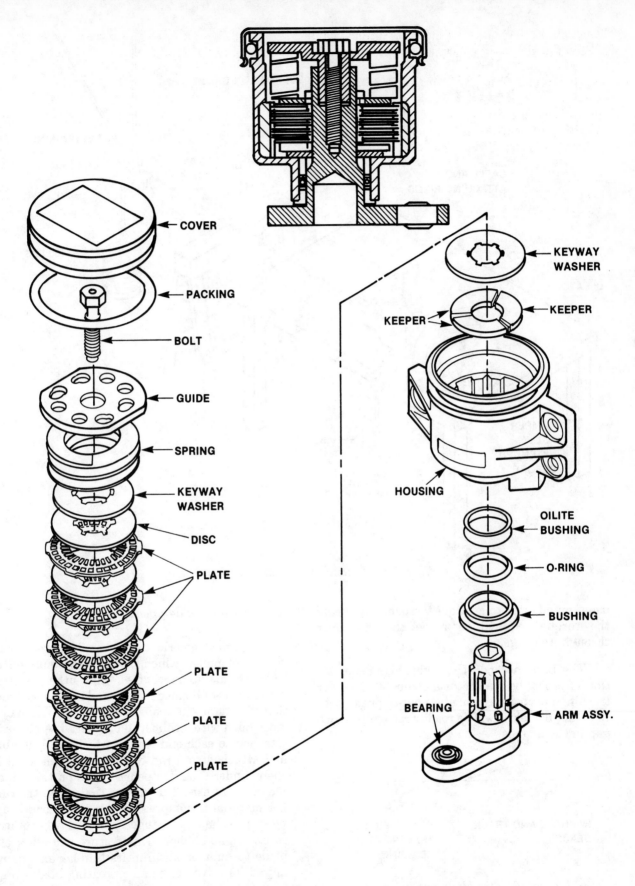

COVER

PACKING

BOLT

GUIDE

SPRING

KEYWAY
WASHER

DISC

PLATE

PLATE

PLATE

PLATE

KEYWAY
WASHER

KEEPER

KEEPER

HOUSING

OILITE
BUSHING

O-RING

BUSHING

BEARING

ARM ASSY.

Fig. 5-117   Multiple disc dampener used on Hughes 500C

207

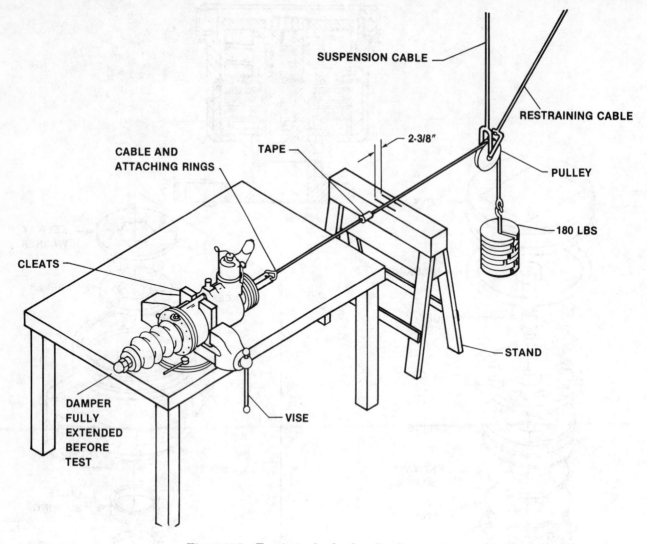

Fig. 5-118 Testing of a hydraulic dampener

using an adapter to a torque wrench, measuring the torque required to move the dampener through its range.

The best method of checking dampener action is probably the use of a strobe as used for tracking purposes. If a blade is out of phase with the other blades, it will be readily recognized by a gap in the images.

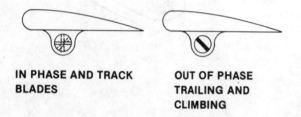

IN PHASE AND TRACK BLADES

OUT OF PHASE TRAILING AND CLIMBING

Fig. 5-119 One blade out of phase

c. Elastromeric dampener

The elastromeric dampener is a relatively new development which should prove quite effective and maintenance free. Like other elastromerics, it is of bonded rubber and metal construction. The dampener consists of an aluminum cylinder filled with a rubber-like material. A clevis is attached to each end, one of which is adjustable and attached to a rod of rubber-like material in the cylinder. The dampener works on the principle of hysteresis. This means that when the rubber material is compressed or a sheer load is applied, the shape is changed and it slowly returns to its original shape. This feature will allow the blade to hunt or move in its lead-lag-axis as required for advancing and retreating blades (Fig. 5-120).

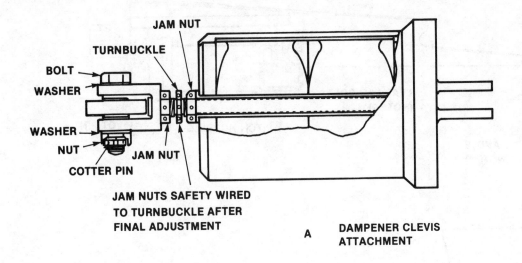

JAM NUT

TURNBUCKLE

BOLT

WASHER

WASHER

NUT

JAM NUT

COTTER PIN

JAM NUTS SAFETY WIRED
TO TURNBUCKLE AFTER
FINAL ADJUSTMENT

A   DAMPENER CLEVIS
ATTACHMENT

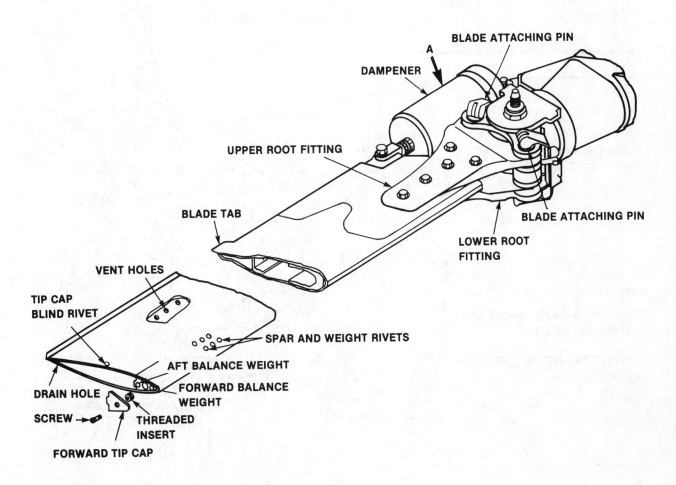

BLADE ATTACHING PIN

A

DAMPENER

UPPER ROOT FITTING

BLADE TAB

BLADE ATTACHING PIN

LOWER ROOT
FITTING

VENT HOLES

TIP CAP
BLIND RIVET

SPAR AND WEIGHT RIVETS

AFT BALANCE WEIGHT

DRAIN HOLE

FORWARD BALANCE
WEIGHT

SCREW

THREADED
INSERT

FORWARD TIP CAP

Fig. 5-120   Elastomeric dampener used on the Hughes 500D

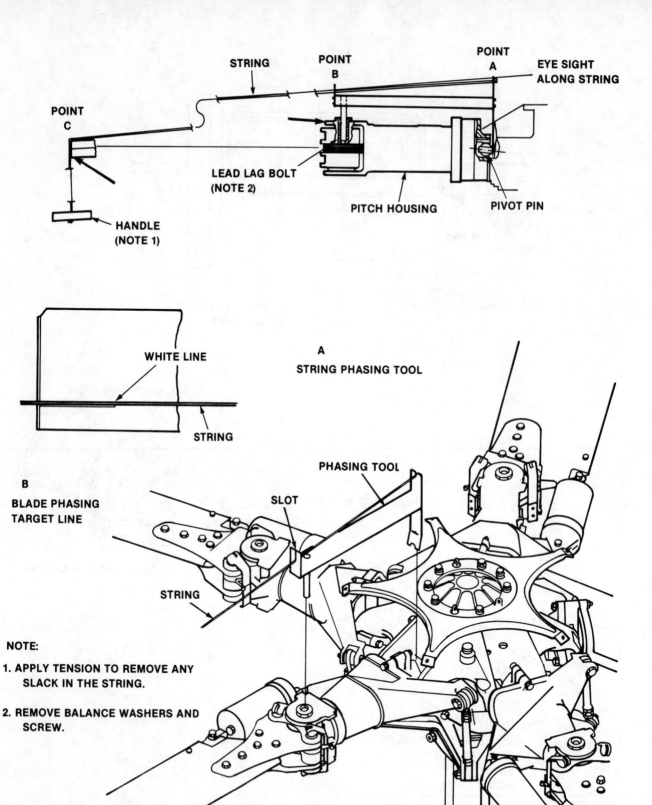

STRING

POINT
B

POINT
A

EYE SIGHT
ALONG STRING

POINT
C

LEAD LAG BOLT
(NOTE 2)

PITCH HOUSING

PIVOT PIN

HANDLE
(NOTE 1)

WHITE LINE

A
STRING PHASING TOOL

STRING

PHASING TOOL

B
BLADE PHASING
TARGET LINE

SLOT

STRING

NOTE:

1. APPLY TENSION TO REMOVE ANY
   SLACK IN THE STRING.

2. REMOVE BALANCE WASHERS AND
   SCREW.

Fig. 5-121 String method of dampener alignment

210

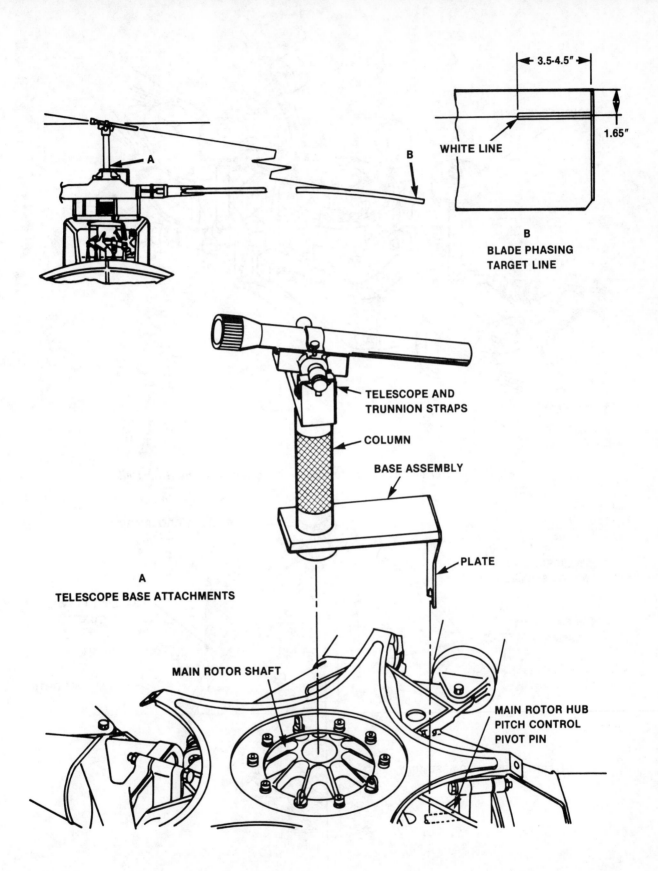

3.5-4.5"

1.65"

WHITE LINE

B
BLADE PHASING
TARGET LINE

TELESCOPE AND
TRUNNION STRAPS

COLUMN

BASE ASSEMBLY

PLATE

A
TELESCOPE BASE ATTACHMENTS

MAIN ROTOR SHAFT

MAIN ROTOR HUB
PITCH CONTROL
PIVOT PIN

Fig. 5-122   Scope method of dampener alignment

211

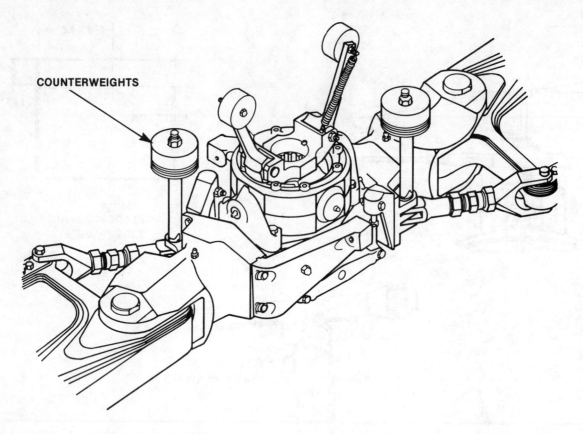

COUNTERWEIGHTS

Fig. 5-123   Counterweights used to assist collective movement on Bell 47

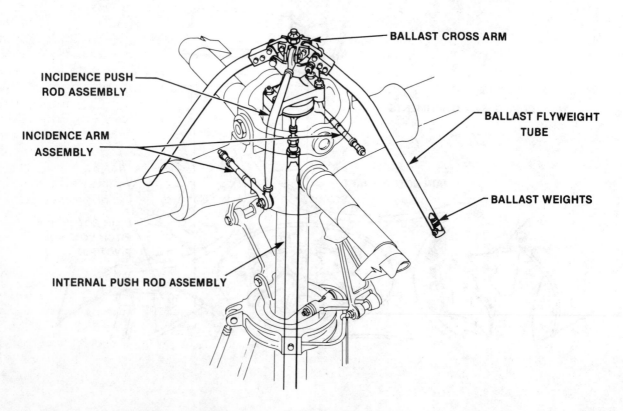

BALLAST CROSS ARM

INCIDENCE PUSH ROD ASSEMBLY

BALLAST FLYWEIGHT TUBE

INCIDENCE ARM ASSEMBLY

BALLAST WEIGHTS

INTERNAL PUSH ROD ASSEMBLY

Fig. 5-124   Ballast arms used on Hiller 12 for collective assist

Actually, no maintenance is performed on the dampener itself. It is simply a replacement item. To obtain correct phasing, however, the adjustable clevis must be moved to obtain the alignment of the rotor. This procedure is not necessary with the hydraulic dampeners because they have no neutral position as the elastromeric type of dampener does. This alignment may be brought about by the string method and the sighting method.

With the string and scope methods, the rotor must be neutralized by placing the cyclic in neutral and placing a protractor on the pitch housing. With the protractor in position, the collective is moved until neutral is established. The string is placed on the phasing tool to the line on the blade (Fig. 5-121). A sighting is taken down the string and the dampener arm is adjusted until alignment is established. The same basic procedure is used when the scope is used. The controls are neutralized and the scope rather than a string is placed in position for sighting (Fig. 5-122).

9. Counterweight adjustment

Some rotor systems, such as the Bell 47 and the Hiller 12, use a counterweight system on the head to aid in raising the collective. Often when the head is rebuilt or the blades are replaced, it is necessary to change the weights so that the collective is not too heavy or too light. In an ideal situation, force on the collective should neutralize at any position, meaning that neither an upward or downward force is required to hold pitch in the rotor. Too much weight will lighten the collective while not enough weight will make the collective heavy. The addition or subtraction of weight on the Bell is simply the addition or subtraction of washers at the top of the head as seen in Fig. 5-123.

The Hiller uses the same type of method with weight being placed inside the pitch tubes until the proper collective weight is established (Fig. 5-124).

10. Autorotation adjustments

When adjustments are made to the main rotor system, the autorotation ability of the helicopter may be affected. This is the reason that any time work is performed that may affect autorotation, it is important to check the autorotation speed. If the rotor is too fast in autorotation, retreating blade stall may occur. If the rotor RPM is too slow, the rotor lift will not support the helicopter. Since autorotation is an emergency procedure, it is most important that the rotor RPM be set prior to the emergency condition because recovey without power is not probable with low rotor RPM.

The autorotation RPM is affected by the gross weight of the helicopter and the density altitude. For this reason the autorotation speed is set in accordance to a chart like the one shown in Fig. 5-125 or by loading the helicopter both heavy and light to check the RPM. The way the adjustment is set will vary from helicopter to helicopter. In most situations the pitch change links are adjusted equally to increase or decrease rotor RPM by changing the pitch of the rotor or by changing the length of the collective pitch rod.

In discussing the various maintenance techniques and adjustments, it must be remembered that most of these are for the purpose of making the initial adjustments to the head assembly. They are not *cure-alls* and no attempt should be made to cure problems by simply adjusting.

For the most part there is no reason, after the initial adjustments are made, that they should not remain as they are unless replacement maintenance is performed on components that will affect the initial settings. Before any readjustment is attempted, a thorough inspection is necessary. While bad dampeners, worn rod ends and mounts can be related to the problem, retrack, rebalance, and sweep adjustments are not. Track, balance, and sweep may improve the problem a little, but will not solve it, and often will do nothing but add to the number of man-hours devoted to maintenance.

It would be most difficult to formulate one troubleshooting guide which would be all-inclusive for all rotor systems because of the variations. For this reason there are two specific guides for general information only on the fully articulated and semi-rigid rotors. These are contained in Fig. 5-126. Always remember that simple logic will be the best procedure in solving problems.

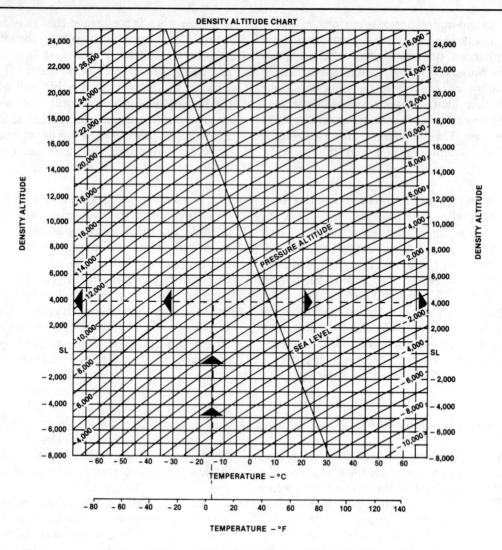

DENSITY ALTITUDE CHART

369 SERIES AUTOROTATION RPM CHART

Gross Weight (lb)	Stabilized Autorotation RPM at Density Altitude					
	Sea Level	1000 Ft.	2000 Ft.	3000 Ft.	4000 Ft.	5000 Ft.
1900	447 - 457	454 - 464	461 - 471	468 - 478	475 - 485	482 - 492
2000	459 - 469	466 - 476	473 - 483	480 - 490	487 - 497	494 - 504
2100	471 - 481	478 - 488	485 - 495	492 - 502	499 - 509	— — — —
2200	483 - 493	490 - 500	497 - 507	504 - 514	— — — —	— — — —

NOTES:
1. Chart values based upon 15° C (59° F) OAT. At sea level, 8° C (14° F) temperature change is equal to 1000 ft. change in density altitude.
2. Perform autorotation rpm checks at gross weight/density altitude combinations for which rpm values are given. Blank spaces indicate that application of collective pitch may be necessary to avoid rotor overspeed.

Fig. 5-125 Autorotation chart used on Hughes 500

TROUBLE SHOOTING MAIN ROTOR

INDICATION OF TROUBLE	PROBABLE CAUSE	CORRECTIVE ACTION
1:1 Lateral vibration		
(a) In hover or forward flight	Spanwise out-of-balance	Dynamically balance with tape
	Chordwise out-of-balance	Dynamically balance by sweeping blade
	"Hub rock"	Adjust equalizer links
(b) Bumping in abrupt maneuvers	One dynamic stop cable too short. (2:1 if both cables short)	Rig Dynamic stop cables
	Sprag mount weak or one safety cable too short. (2:1 if both sides)	Readjust sprag mount system or replace parts
1:1 Vertical vibration (or bounce)		
(a) In hover and forward flight	Rotor out-of-track	Adjust trim tabs
(b) In forward flight but but not hover	Climbing blade	Compare high and low speed track Adjust
2:1 Vibrations		
(a) In hover or forward flight	Mast misaligned	Adjust sprag mounts
	Excessive play in sprag mounting	Replace worn parts. Pre-load lateral sprag rods
	Elevator buffeting	Adjust elevator cable tension
(b) Bumping in maneuvers	See (b) under 1:1 Lateral	
Collective pitch control creeping in normal cruise	Incorrect counterweights	Adjust counterweights
Rotor rpm high or low in autorotation	Minimum pitch blade angle incorrect	Adjust both pitch control rods
Erratic nudging of cyclic control stick	Rotor unstable on longitudinal axis	Sweep both blades aft

Fig. 5-126a Typical semi-rigid rotor troubleshooting chart

Abnormal Vibrations

A. Rotor System - Low-Frequency

    1. Blades - low-frequency. Common low-frequency vibrations are 1:1, 2:1, vibration beat with each revolution of the main rotor

        a. Lateral - 1-per-rev causes lateral motion in seat

            (1) Dampers - setting and phase
            (2) Blades out of balance
            (3) Damaged strap pack
            (4) Binding in lead-lag hinge

        b. Vertical - 1-per-rev causes bounce in seat

            (1) Blade track
            (2) Vibration absorbers malfunctioning - 3- and 5-per-rev
            (3) Tabs improperly adjusted
            (4) Damper out of adjustment and/or phase
            (5) Pitch control bearing worn and/or binding

B. Tail Rotor Vibration - Medium- to High-Frequency

    1. Medium- to high-frequency buzzing vibration felt in pedals and structure; vibration noticeable from low rpm on up through operating (3020) rpm

        a. Causes

            (1) Assembly out of balance
            (2) Tail rotor gearbox output shaft runout excessive
            (3) Stabilizer attach points loose
            (4) Excessive abrasion
            (5) Abrasion strip loose
            (6) Worn gearbox bearings
            (7) Boom attach points loose
            (8) Tail rotor assembly attach nut loose, allowing fork to shift on conical split ring
            (9) Tail rotor swashplate bearing worn (could show as a wobble of swashplate)

Fig. 5-126b Typical fully articulated rotor troubleshooting chart

61. The semi-rigid rotor system makes use of _____ for flapping.

    A. A seesaw system

    B. Individual flapping hinges

    C. Blade bending

62. A tension torsion strap would be found in a _____ rotor head.

    A. Bell 47

    B. Bell 206

    C. Sikorsky S-58

63. The purpose of counterweights attached to the grip assembly of the Bell 47 is:

    A. To aid in raising the cyclic.

    B. To ease in raising the collective.

    C. To insure the rotor returns to the flap pitch stop.

64. Strap packs would be found in the _____ rotor head.

    A. S-58

    B. B0 105

    C. Hughes 500C

65. Elastomeric dampeners would be associated with the _____ rotor head.

    A. Hughes 269

    B. Hughes 500C

    C. Hughes 500D

66. The bifilar system would be associated with the:

    A. S-76

    B. Bell 222

    C Hughes 500D

67. The centrifugal thrust load of the rotor blades of the S-76 are carried by:

    A. Ball bearings.

    B. T T straps.

    c. Elastomeric bearings.

68. The AStar rotor head is made of:

    A. Titanium.

    B. Steel.

    C. Fiberglass.

69. No anti-vibration device is used on the AStar head.

    A. True

    B. False

70. A rigid rotor system is used on the:

    A. S-76

    B. B0 105

    C. AStar

71. Wooden rotor blades may be changed individually.

    A. True

    B. False

72. Metal rotor blades have no finite life.

    A. True

    B. False

73. The big advantage of bonding rather than riveting metal blades is:

   A. Riveting is more costly.

   B. Bonding distributes the stress more evenly.

74. Metal rotor blades with a nitrogen filled spar use the _____ system for crack detection.

   A. BIM

   B. BIS

   C. BIN

75. Damage to the rotor blades is more critical at the root than at the tip.

   A. True

   B. False

76. Replacement of cadmium plating is a common practice in the field.

   A. True

   B. False

77. Blade alignment is a common maintenance practice on:

   A. Semi-rigid rotors.

   B. Fully articulated rotors.

   C. Rigid rotors.

78. Blades set forward of the alignment points are _____ in flight.

   A. More stable

   B. Unstable

   C. Slower

79. For spanwise static balance:

   A. Weight may be added to the blade tip.

   B. The blade may be moved aft.

   C. The blade may be swept forward.

80. Both spanwise and chordwise balance may be accomplished with the universal balancer.

   A. True

   B. False

81. Track is done prior to dynamic balancing.

   A. True

   B. False

82. Track may be checked in the air by the:

   A. Flag method.

   B. Stick method.

   C. Strobe method.

83. Blades are "pre-tracked" on the:

   A. Bell

   B. Hiller

   C. Sikorsky

84. Track may be ajusted by:

   A. Tabs.

   B. Pitch change rods.

   C. Either A or B depending on the helicopter.

85. The dampener system failure may cause:

   A. Vertical vibrations.

   B. Lateral vibrations.

   C. Either A or B or a combination.

86. Vertical vibrations are caused by track.

   A. True

   B. False

87. Lateral vibrations are caused by balance.

   A. True

   B. False

88. The term "sweeping the blade" is associated with:

   A. Semi-rigid rotors.

   B. Fully articulated rotors.

89. When adjustments are made to the main rotor, autorotation speed should be checked.

   A. True

   B. False

90. There is no means of adjusting autorotation speed.

   A. True

   B. False

SECTION VI
Mast and Flight Controls

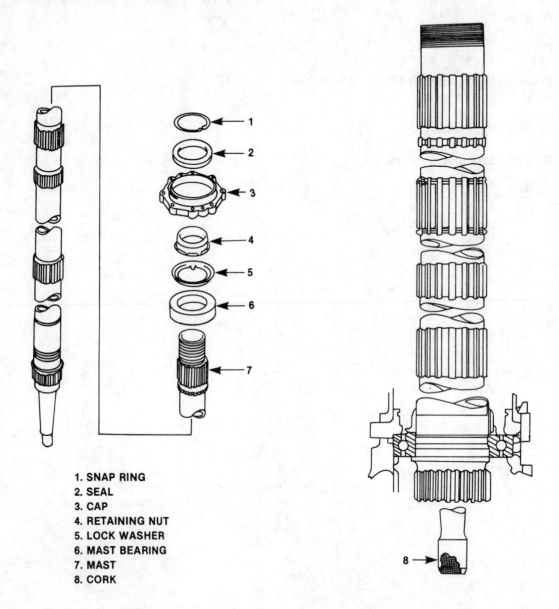

1. SNAP RING
2. SEAL
3. CAP
4. RETAINING NUT
5. LOCK WASHER
6. MAST BEARING
7. MAST
8. CORK

Fig. 6-1   Mast assembly used on the Bell 47

A.   The Mast

The main rotor is attached to the mast assembly. This is a tube that is attached to the helicopter's transmission. It absorbs torsional and tension loads received from the engine torque and the weight of the helicopter in flight.

The mast is a critical item and in some instances has a finite life. The construction of the mast assembly varies considerably from one manufacturer to another. Some masts only support the head assembly, while others may support the stabilizer bar assembly and rotor heads used on many of the Bell products. The mast also drives the swashplate (star assembly) through which the flight controls operate.

We shall first consider the mast of the Bell 47 (Fig 6-1). This mast, mounted in and driven by the transmission, drives the flight control units and the main rotor. For this purpose it is equipped with five sets of splines used as attaching points for the following items from top to bottom:

1. Main rotor

2. Stabilizer bar

3. Dampener bracket

4. Swashplate

5. Transmission

Thread portions are provided for the mast nut at the top, and the mast bearing on the lower end. The mast bearing is a split inner race thrust bearing. The outer race is supported and held in place by a cap on the top of the transmission. The inner race, locked to the flange of the mast by a nut assembly, rotates with the mast. This is the main support for the mast and provides the primary point of rotation and thrust. It is one of the more critical bearings in the helicopter.

Other features of the mast include grooves for snap rings used to hold flight components. Some models of the mast have a cork placed in the bottom preventing oil from the transmission from entering the mast. In addition, an aluminum plug is placed in the top of the hollow mast, preventing distortion of the mast due to the torque applied to the rotor head retaining nut. The

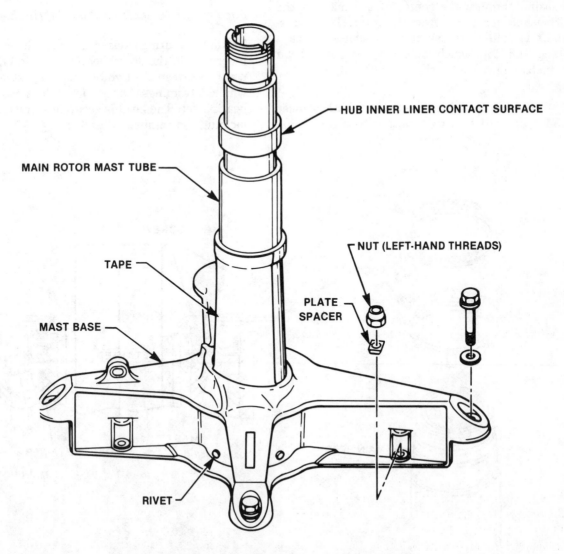

HUB INNER LINER CONTACT SURFACE

MAIN ROTOR MAST TUBE

NUT (LEFT-HAND THREADS)

TAPE

PLATE SPACER

MAST BASE

RIVET

Fig. 6-2 Mast assembly used on the Hughes 500

221

rotor head is supported on a set of split cones at the rotor head trunnion. The trunnion is splined to accept the first set of splines. On top of the rotor are placed the stops for the rotor. The nut is threaded down on the mast, and secured with a locking retainer.

A completely different type of mast assembly is found on the Hughes 500 helicopter series. This is a hollow, stationary mast (Fig. 6-2).

The obvious advantage of this type of system is that the mast may be built lighter because it is not stressed in the same manner as the rotating mast. The rotating mast must not only support and turn the main rotor but also absorb the flight loads. The static mast is attached to the structure of the airframe, eliminating the stresses that would normally be placed on the transmission. Passing through the center of the mast is the driveshaft used to power the rotor. This driveshaft is splined to the transmission and has a flange on top which bolts to the rotor head transferring power to the rotor (Fig. 6-3).

The rotor head is connected to the static mast and supported by two opposing taper bearings.

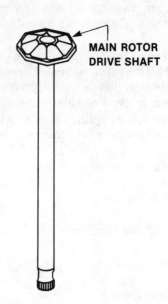

Fig. 6-3   Drive shaft used on the Hughes 500

The lower bearing rides on the mast liner, and the inner race of the upper bearing rides on the mast itself. Between the two bearings is a steel spacer which determines the rotational drag of the roller bearing set. The head is secured to the mast by a locknut and retainer (Fig. 6-4).

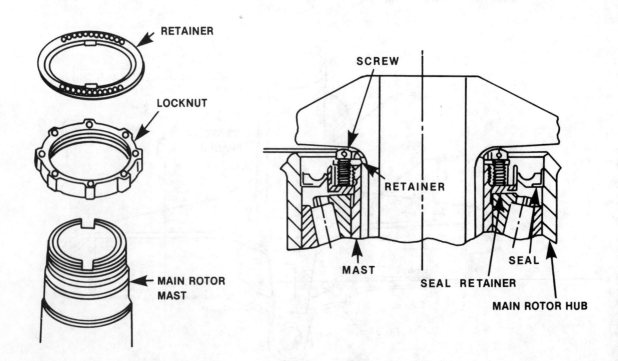

Fig. 6-4   Locknut and retainer system used to secure the rotor head to the mast

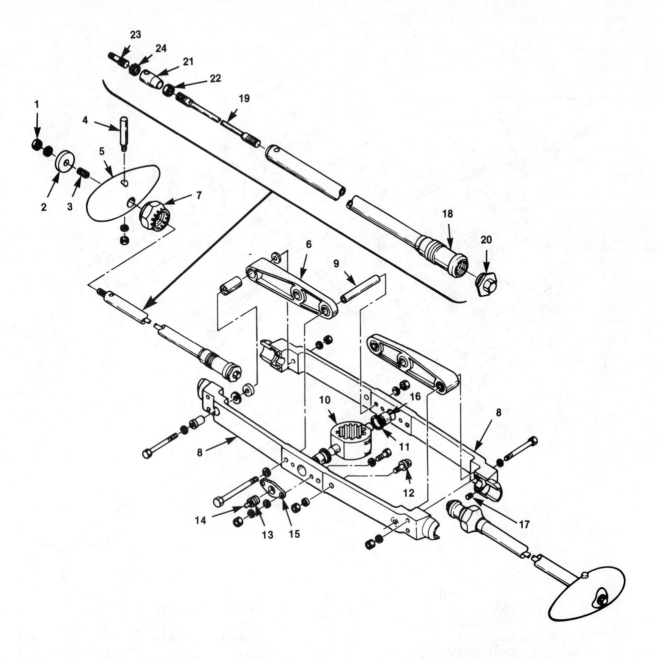

1. NUT - BALANCE ASSEMBLY
2. CAP
3. SPRING
4. TAPER PIN
5. WEIGHT
6. MIXING LEVER
7. RETAINING NUT - TUBE ASSEMBLY
8. FRAME
9. SPACERS
10. CORE
11. THRUST WASHER
12. DYNAMIC STOPS

13. PLUG - CORE ADJUSTING
14. GREASE FITTING
15. PLATE
16. BEARING
17. SET SCREW
18. TUBE
19. TIE ROD
20. NUT
21. ROD - END
22. LOCK-NUT
23. STUD
24. LOCK-NUT

Fig. 6-5   Stabilizer assembly used on the Bell 47

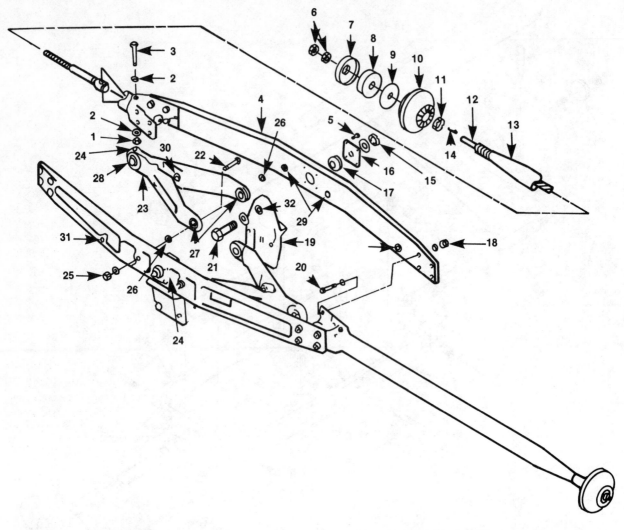

1. NUT	17. PIVOT BEARING SET
2. STAT-O-SEAL	18. NUT
3. BOLT	19. SUPPORT ASSEMBLY
4. CENTERFRAME	20. BOLT
5. SCREW	21. BOLT
6. NUT	22. BOLT
7. RETAINER	23. LEVER ASSEMBLY
8. BUSHING	24. LUBE FITTING
9. WASHER	25. NUT
10. WEIGHT	26. WASHER
11. NUT	27. BEARING (AN201KP-6A)
12. CABLE ASSEMBLY	28. BEARING (BR-5-R)
13. TUBE ASSEMBLY	29. BUSHING
14. KEY TYPE LOCK	30. BUSHING
15. NUT	31. BUSHING
16. PIVOT BEARING RETAINER	32. BUSHING

Fig. 6-6 Stabilizer assembly used on later Bell Models

Other mast assemblies may include other features such as control tubes passing through the center, an assortment of means to secure the head to the mast, and other such features. However, each must be treated in a careful manner on all helicopters. All masts are made of machined steel forgings, making them susceptible to corrosion, stresses, scratches, and other damage associated with steel parts. As with all critical parts rotor masts are to be inspected in accordance with the manufacturer's recommendations contained in their maintenance manuals.

These masts are plated with cadmium to prevent corrosion from forming on the steel. As with so many parts of a highly stressed nature, they cannot be replated in the field. Electroplating sets up internal stresses that cannot be relieved without special equipment.

All scratches, nicks, and gouges in the mast must be carefully examined. In some instances they may be reworked to relieve any possible stress concentration.

Masts used on semi-rigid rotors of certain helicopters are most susceptible to damage from mast bumping due to the underslung head striking the mast. This area must always be inspected carefully. Damage in the radial direction is most critical.

At overhaul, masts are checked dimensionally, magnafluxed and may require a run-out check for concentricity.

Most masts will contain a main mast bearing. This bearing is important and must be inspected and installed following specific procedures. A failure of this single bearing will result in possible shearing of the mast or stoppage of the main rotor. This bearing may be damaged by improper installation or lack of care when the mast is removed. The maintenance manual must always be followed.

B. Stabilizer Bar

Several models of the Bell helicopter use a stabilizer bar system. The bar is either mounted on the mast or on the trunnion cap of the rotor. This system, as mentioned in Section 2, provides stability to the helicopter. Its principle of operation is quite simple.

If the helicopter rotor is disturbed by wind forces in a hover, the stabilizer bar tends to remain in its same plane of rotation due to the gyroscopic action of rigidity even though the mast and the helicopter fuselage are tilted. Since the stabilizer bar is connected by linkage to the feathering axis of the rotor, the relative movement between the mast and the stabilizer bar will cause the blades to feather. This feathering of the blades will cause the rotor to return to its original position.

When extreme movements of the cyclic control are made, the main rotor will change its plane of rotation. This in turn will move the helicopter and mast. The stabilizer bar, however, will remain in its same plane of rotation. As this angular relationship changes between the mast and the stabilizer bar, centrifugal force will cause the bar to seek a new position perpendicular to the mast. This will, however, take place after a slight delay which must be controlled. If the delay is not controlled, a corresponding delay would take place in the control response, removing the control from the pilot. Dampener units are used to achieve the desired response.

The *dampeners* are linked to the stabilizer bar regulating its movement. Any movement of the mast will be transferred to the stabilizer bar. Its position will then become perpendicular to the mast at a predetermined rate. The bars and dampeners vary somewhat in construction and placement. Basically there are two types: one that is used on the Bell 47, and the other found on the Bell 205 and 212 series of aircraft.

On the Bell 47 model, the stabilizer bar is attached to the mast assembly on the second set of splines at 90° to the rotor. The stabilizer bar is made up of seven major items. These are the:

1. core,

2. centerframe,

3. mixing levers,

4. core plug,

5. outer tube,

6. weight,

7. tie rod assembly.

The core is splined internally to the splines of the mast and has two ears used as stops for the bar travel. The core slides over the mast assembly and is held in place by two snap rings, one at the bottom of the splines and one at the top. Attached to the core by two bearings is the frame assembly made of two matched halves. The frame holds the outer tube and surrounds the core. It also provides a point for the dampeners to attach and for an attachment of the mixing levers. The outer tubes are held by the frames and have the weights attached to the outboard end. Inside the outer tube is the tie rod, a safety device, in case the outer tube breaks. No load is carried by the tie rod under normal conditions. The plug core is attached to the frame and provides a means of greasing the pivot point of the center frame and the core as well as a centering adjustment (Fig. 6-5).

The general makeup of the other stabilizer bars is quite similar to that of the 47 with the exception of being mounted above the main rotor, attaching to the hub trunnion. This eliminates the need for splines on the mast. The other great difference is that a cable, rather than a tie rod, is placed in the outer tube (Fig. 6-6).

To insure smooth operation both stabilizer bars require static balance. On the model 47 bar this is accomplished on the helicopter by disconnecting the dampener links, pitch change rods, and the linkage from the mixing levers. A small spirit level is placed on the upper surface of the center frame. If the bar is not balanced, washers are added to the light side.

On the other type of bar, the balance is checked with the bar removed. A balancing rod is run

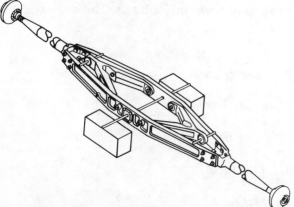

Fig. 6-7 Static balancing system used on stabilizer bars

through the support bearings and the bar is suspended on two level surfaces. If the bar is not balanced, the weight on the heavy side is moved inboard until balance is achieved (Fig. 6-7).

This balancing of the stabilizer bar is a routine item at the major inspection periods when the components are torn down and built up. Other maintenance performed would include bearing changes and shimming of the mixing levers. Other normal inspection and overhaul requirements are followed including magnetic inspection and dye penetrant inspection at overhaul.

C. Dampeners

The dampener units used in conjunction with the stabilizer bars differ in design. Both types use a hydraulic dampener, which is double action, restricting the travel rate of the stabilizer in both directions.

The Bell 47 utilizes two dampeners mounted in a frame attached to the mast and located on a set of splines below the stabilizer bar (Fig. 6-8).

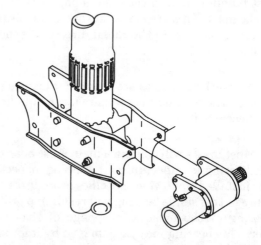

Fig. 6-8 Dampener assembly used in conjunction with the stabilizer bar

The dampeners themselves consist of a cylindrical housing divided into four chambers by a wing shaft. The wing shaft has passages which allow fluid to pass from one chamber to the other when the shaft is turned. An attached arm is connected to the stabilizer bar through the linkage. Since the rate of movement of the bar is important, a metering valve is used to control the flow. This valve is adjustable and temperature compensated to control the flow rate. This is done by use of a plexiglass tube that expands and contracts with changes in termperature.

The other dampeners work in much the same manner. They too are attached to the mast by a frame assembly below the rotor head. The metering valve, however, is somewhat different, utilizing a cam and slider valve assembly. This gives the dampener a variable orifice resulting in a difference in the rate of movement. Slow movement of the dampener causes low fluid flow through the orifice, which offers little resistance. Rapid movement increases the resistance.

The maintenance of these dampeners is somewhat limited. Both dampeners require fluid level checks and occasionally need additional fluid. A sight gauge and a filler plug are provided for that purpose. Problems may be encountered in filling the fluid level if too much air is present in the dampener. The timing of the dampener is one of the primary concerns. The Bell 47 dampener may be checked for timing by disconnecting the linkage and attaching a special arm and weight to the arm. This is then raised and let fall free. It should take four seconds plus or minus 1/2 second for the dampener to return to its neutral position (Fig. 6-9). If the timing is not correct, the dampener may be adjusted by moving the plexiglass tube in and out. At times it will not be possible to correct the timing. In this situation the dampener must be removed and replaced. Often the dampener movement can be felt for soft and hard spots in order to determine its condition.

The other dampeners are checked for timing by raising the stabilizer to the stops and returning it to neutral position. It should take five seconds plus or minus 1 second (Fig. 6-10). There is no possible adjustment for this dampener; it can only be replaced.

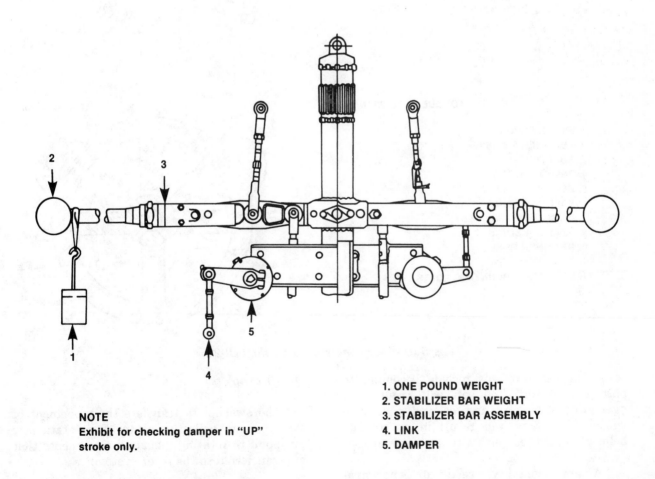

NOTE
Exhibit for checking damper in "UP"
stroke only.

1. ONE POUND WEIGHT
2. STABILIZER BAR WEIGHT
3. STABILIZER BAR ASSEMBLY
4. LINK
5. DAMPER

Fig. 6-9 Timing check for proper dampener action

227

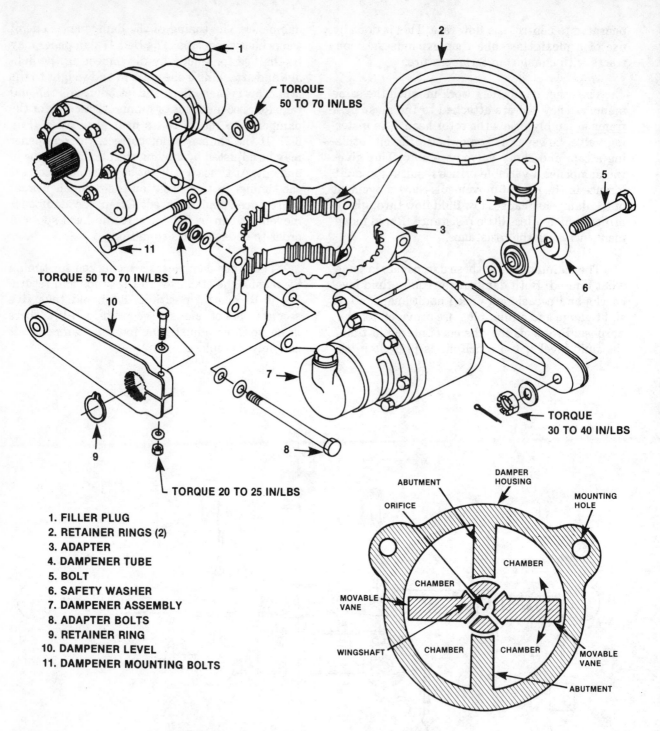

TORQUE
50 TO 70 IN/LBS

TORQUE 50 TO 70 IN/LBS

TORQUE 20 TO 25 IN/LBS

TORQUE
30 TO 40 IN/LBS

1. FILLER PLUG
2. RETAINER RINGS (2)
3. ADAPTER
4. DAMPENER TUBE
5. BOLT
6. SAFETY WASHER
7. DAMPENER ASSEMBLY
8. ADAPTER BOLTS
9. RETAINER RING
10. DAMPENER LEVEL
11. DAMPENER MOUNTING BOLTS

ABUTMENT
DAMPER HOUSING
ORIFICE
MOUNTING HOLE
CHAMBER
CHAMBER
MOVABLE VANE
WINGSHAFT
CHAMBER
CHAMBER
MOVABLE VANE
ABUTMENT

Fig. 6-10 Dampeners used on the bell 205

Dampener problems include becoming too hard or too soft. Too soft will result in an overstable helicopter and delayed control response. Too hard will result in an unstable helicopter with too quick a control response.

A supplemental type certificate is now available to remove the stabilizer bar system from the Bell 47.

D. Swashplate

The swashplate transfers the movement of the cyclic and collective control from stationary push-pull to rotating push-pull movements that are transferred to the rotor system.

Each manufacturer has a different method of performing this operation. Basically, the function and movements that must take place are the same regardless of who manufacturers it.

When collective is applied, all the rotor blades collectively change pitch, which means that the swashplate must be able to move up and down as it rotates. Fig. 6-11 shows this operation.

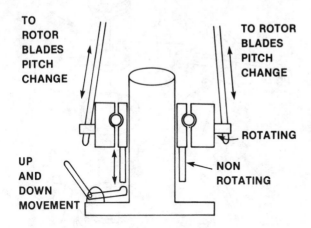

Fig. 6-11 Basic collective swashplate movement

The cyclic movements are somewhat more complicated because they tilt the whole rotor

system left, right, fore, and aft. This requires universal joint movement of the swashplate. The non-rotating part moves in the same direction as the desired rotor movement. However, the action must be applied 90° to the force to move the rotor due to gyroscopic precession (Fig. 6-12).

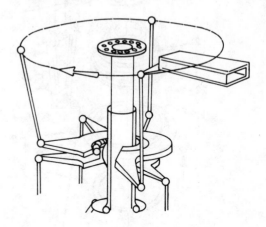

Fig. 6-12 Basic swashplate movement

From this general information about the swashplate and the two types of movement, it is evident that one movement takes place in con-

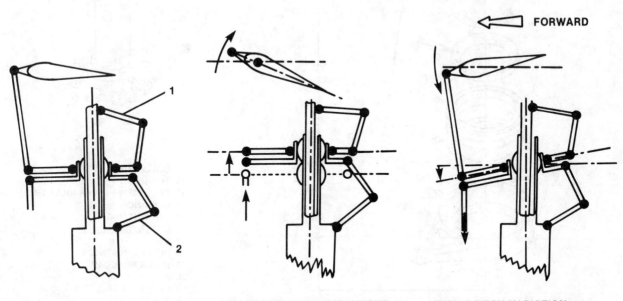

The upper scissors (1) attached to the rotor shaft drive the rotating star.
The lower scissors (2) attached to the housing restrain the fixed star.

COLLECTIVE PITCH VARIATIONS

The ball joint slides along the rotor shaft. The pitch variation is equal on all 3 blades. In the above view pitch is increasing.

CYCLIC PITCH VARIATION

The ball joint is not moving but the swashplate pivots about it. In the view above the pitch decreases in front and increases at the rear.

Fig. 6-13 Basic swashplate movements of pitch and cyclic movements

229

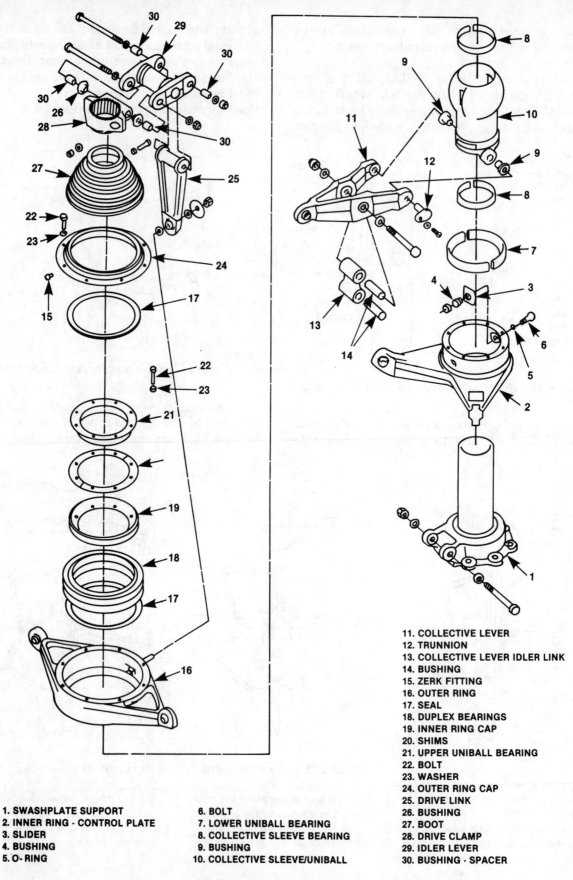

1. SWASHPLATE SUPPORT
2. INNER RING - CONTROL PLATE
3. SLIDER
4. BUSHING
5. O- RING
6. BOLT
7. LOWER UNIBALL BEARING
8. COLLECTIVE SLEEVE BEARING
9. BUSHING
10. COLLECTIVE SLEEVE/UNIBALL
11. COLLECTIVE LEVER
12. TRUNNION
13. COLLECTIVE LEVER IDLER LINK
14. BUSHING
15. ZERK FITTING
16. OUTER RING
17. SEAL
18. DUPLEX BEARINGS
19. INNER RING CAP
20. SHIMS
21. UPPER UNIBALL BEARING
22. BOLT
23. WASHER
24. OUTER RING CAP
25. DRIVE LINK
26. BUSHING
27. BOOT
28. DRIVE CLAMP
29. IDLER LEVER
30. BUSHING - SPACER

Fig. 6-14 Swashplate assembly of the Bell 206

230

junction with the other. Fig. 6-13 shows typical movements of a swashplate. Each manufacturer uses his own system of performing these functions.

One swashplate type is on the Bell 206 (Fig. 6-14) and it contains the following major components:

1. Swashplate support

2. Collective sleeve

3. Control plate inner ring

4. Control plate outer ring

5. Collective lever

6. Swashplate thrust bearings

7. Swashplate drive link

The swashplate support is a one-piece aluminum forging through which the mast passes. This support bolts to the transmission at the base. The outside surface is anodized to provide a wear-resistant surface.

Sliding over the support is the collective sleeve. The sleeve is a forging with the upper portion forming a uniball. The uniball has a hardened surface on which Teflon bearings ride. In addition, there are two grooves in the base portion of the sleeve to accommodate two Teflon bearings which provide the surface for the sleeve movement up and down on the support asembly. This movement performs the collective function.

The control plate inner ring contains the lower Teflon bearing which contacts the uniball. Attached to this plate is an inner ring cap which holds the shims, one of which is the upper uniball bearing. The shims are used to set the tension of the uniball. The movement of the inner ring is a tilting action with no rotation.

The outside of the inner ring is the thrust bearing surface retained by the inner ring cap. The thrust bearing's outer races make contact with the control plate outer ring. The thrust bearing connecting the inner plate to the outer plate is a duplex set of angular contact ball bearings. The outer ring tilts with the inner ring and also ro-

tates with the mast because it is driven from a drive link attached to the mast. Two additional ears are provided on the outer ring for the attachment of the pitch change rods.

A collective lever is attached to the support assembly through a link at about midpoint on the lever arm. One end of the lever is attached to the sleeve and the other to the collective linkage. The drive link is attached to a set of splines at the mast and the outer plate. This provides the rotation of the outer ring without putting undue stress on the control rods. The assembled swashplate is seen in Fig. 6-15.

Another swashplate system in use today is the type used on the Hughes 500D (Fig. 6-16). Like all other swashplates it has two types of control movements — the cyclic and the collective. The collective input raises and lowers the swashplate as a unit. This changes the movement of the ball and socket from which the pitch on all blades is changed. The cyclic input is actually two inputs — the longitudinal and the lateral. The two inputs move the helicopter fore and aft, left and right by tilting the swashplate on the ball and socket.

The stationary swashplate is secured to the inner race of a double row ball bearing while the outer race of the bearing is held by the rotating swashplate. The center of the inner or stationary swashplate is the receptacle for the uniball which fits over the stationary mast and rides up and down on a polished sleeve. Both the ball and the socket are lined with Teflon for ease of movement.

The rotating swashplate is connected to the pitch change arms of each individual blade. This rotating swashplate is driven by a scissors assembly attached to the rotor because the mast is stationary. Because of the eccentric action of the scissors, counterweights are placed on the opposite sides of the scissors to rotating swashplate connection points.

Although other manufacturers and models of helicopters use different components and materials, the basic operation of the swashplate is much the same. Possibly, the most complex swashplate is the Bell 47. It does not utilize a uniball design but a series of gimbal rings to obtain the tilt that is needed.

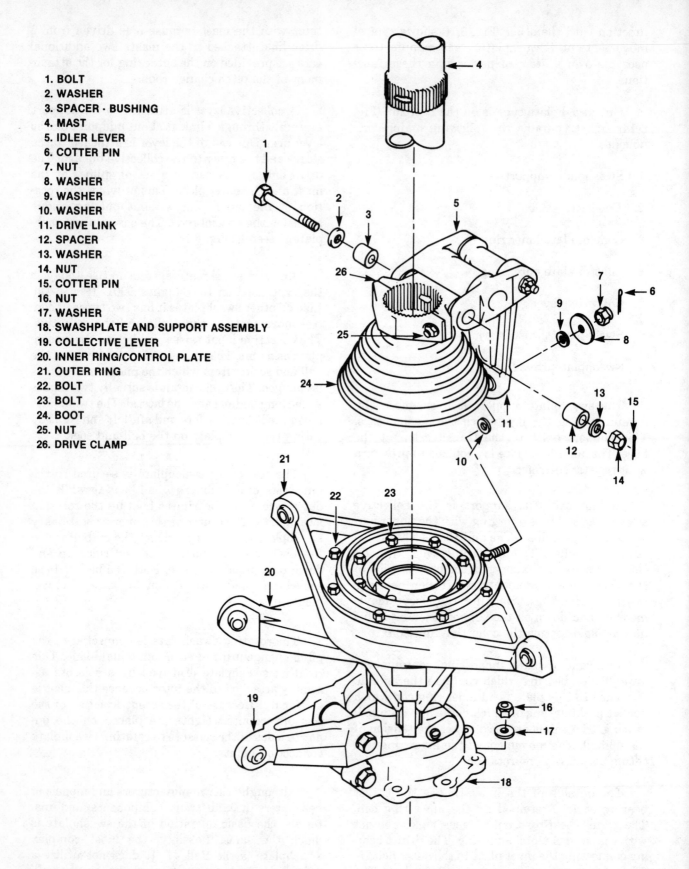

1. BOLT
2. WASHER
3. SPACER - BUSHING
4. MAST
5. IDLER LEVER
6. COTTER PIN
7. NUT
8. WASHER
9. WASHER
10. WASHER
11. DRIVE LINK
12. SPACER
13. WASHER
14. NUT
15. COTTER PIN
16. NUT
17. WASHER
18. SWASHPLATE AND SUPPORT ASSEMBLY
19. COLLECTIVE LEVER
20. INNER RING/CONTROL PLATE
21. OUTER RING
22. BOLT
23. BOLT
24. BOOT
25. NUT
26. DRIVE CLAMP

Fig. 6-15 Assembled swashplate and drive link assembly

232

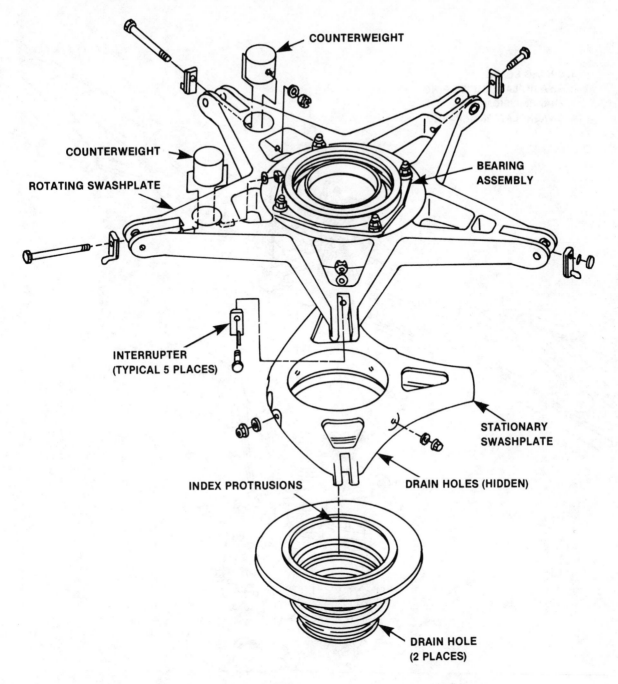

COUNTERWEIGHT

COUNTERWEIGHT

ROTATING SWASHPLATE

BEARING ASSEMBLY

INTERRUPTER (TYPICAL 5 PLACES)

STATIONARY SWASHPLATE

INDEX PROTRUSIONS

DRAIN HOLES (HIDDEN)

DRAIN HOLE (2 PLACES)

Fig. 6-16   Swashplate and star assembly used on the Hughes 500D

The most important maintenance procedure of the swashplate assembly is to keep its movable surfaces clean. For this purpose boots and seals are almost always installed to keep out dust that may injure the bearing surfaces. It is necessary to keep the swashplate properly lubricated. Instructions for proper lubrication are contained in the maintenance manual. There is a tendency to minimize the lubrication requirements by using sealed bearings or using Teflon on the bearing surfaces. The Teflon surfaces must be kept clean or they will score with grit between the surfaces.

One of the standard maintenance procedures on swashplates is to check the tension on the uniball and the rotating plate. This is usually accomplished as follows:

Disconnect the control rods from the swashplate assembly. Attach a spring scale to one of

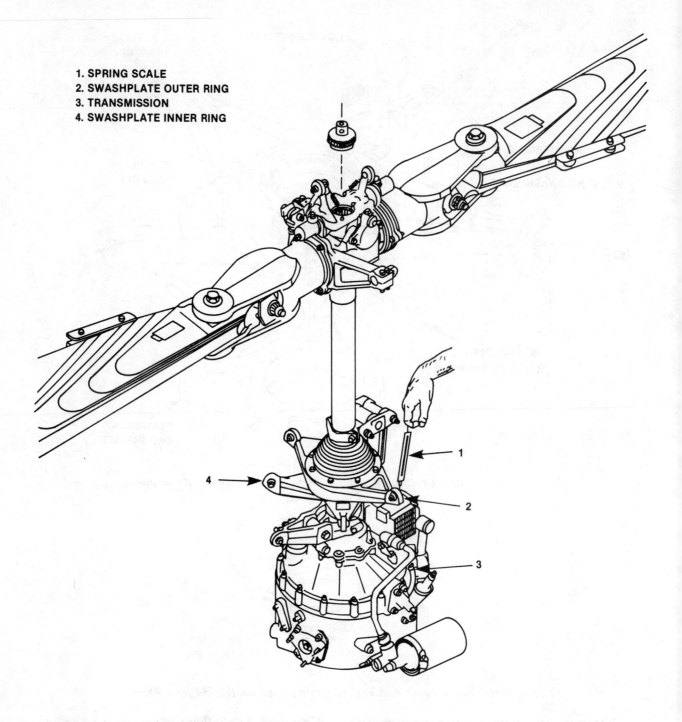

1. SPRING SCALE
2. SWASHPLATE OUTER RING
3. TRANSMISSION
4. SWASHPLATE INNER RING

Fig. 6-17   Checking the swashplate tension

the pitch change horns and pull the scale to check the required tension (Fig. 6-17). If the tension is incorrect, it may normally be adjusted by shims which determine the pressure of the Teflon bearing on the ball. If it is too loose, feedback through the cyclic will occur. If the ball is too tight, jerky cyclic movements will be the result. Other main-

tenance includes changing bearings, many today are spherical and will require roller staking.

The overhaul procedures are quite similar to those found on other components — dimensional checks, magnetic particle inspection, and dye penetrant inspection. It is not unusual to find

234

parts that have finite lives in the swashplate assembly.

Since the swashplate utilizes both cyclic and collective inputs, it is necessary to discuss these inputs.

The controls are usually made of push-pull tubes, torque tubes, bellcranks, mixer boxes, gradient springs, magnetic brakes, bungee springs, counterweights, hydraulic servos, and trim mechanisms. The larger the helicopter, the more complex the control system. On some small helicopters, the pilot may be able to move all the controls without any assistance, while the larger helicopters require a hydraulic boost and often artificial feel to aid the pilot. Some of the large machines would be completely unmanageable without assistance.

E. Flight Control Systems

It is necessary to understand some of the components that make up the system prior to discussing the whole system.

1. The collective

The collective stick is usually located on the left side of the pilot. It normally pivots from one end and is raised and lowered to raise and lower the aircraft. This is usually the standard system. However, one new design has changed its function to a push-pull type mechanism by repositioning the collective.

It is common for additional items to be contained on the collective, among them a twist grip. This twist grip of reciprocating engine helicopters is the throttle. It must be remembered when using this throttle, that the closed position is towards the thumb as the collective is normally held. This is just the opposite on a motorcyle even though their operation is the same. The throttle was placed in that position because on the early helicopters it was necessary to adjust engine power as the collective was raised and lowered.

The twist grip is used to control the compressor RPM on helicopters having free turbine engines and to operate the engine when the emergency fuel system is used.

A switch box is also often placed on the top of the collective. The early helicopters had a starter

button so it could easily be reached without removing the hand from the control during starting. Today, with turbine powered aircraft the box usually contains the trim switches for the engines, landing lights, and searchlights, plus the starter button. It may include other items that might be used while the pilot had his hand on the collective (Fig. 6-18).

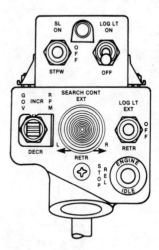

Fig. 6-18 Typical switches contained on the collective

All collectives are also provided with a tension or friction adjustment. In theory the collective should not be so heavy that it has a tendency to move down nor should it be so light that it moves upward. However, in order to free the hand that is used for the collective for brief periods of time, it will be necessary to place tension on the collective. This is also done during run-up maintenance checks to insure that the collective does not come up. See Fig. 6-19 for a typical friction device on the collective.

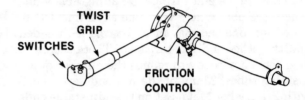

Fig. 6-19 Typical friction adjustment for collective

2. The cyclic

The cyclic control is located in front of the pilot. It is used to tilt the rotor in all directions as the control is moved. Like the collective, switches are usually provided on the cyclic grip for items that may be used while the pilot's hand is on the cyclic control. This would include the microphone for communication and the trim switches for the aircraft. The trim switch is used to alter the flight controls for the load. It will normally operate fore and aft, and left-right trim. A friction lock is provided for the cyclic so the force required to move it may be set (Fig. 6-20).

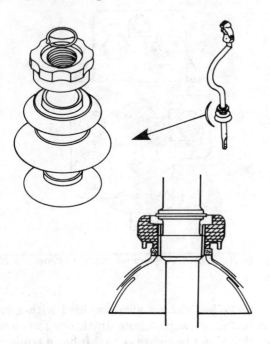

Fig. 6-20 Typical friction control for cyclic

3. Push-pull tubes

The push-pull tubes used in a cyclic or collective system may vary in construction. Some have forked rod ends installed on both ends. Others use combinations of forked ends and spherical bearing ends. Some end fittings are adjustable while others are not. Where very fine adjustments are called for, one end may often be coarse-threaded and the other end fine-threaded. There seems to be a tendency today to reduce the number of adjustable tubes. Many of the rod ends are sealed with Pro-Seal or Metal Set on the adjustable ends providing a good moisture seal which prevents corrosion on the inside of the tube. When the rod ends are removed maintenance shops will often make a policy of flushing the tubes with a primer.

Rod ends may be a high usage item on some helicopters and in some operations, depending on the type of operation, the environment, and the vibration level under which the helicopter is operated. A little play in each rod end can be excessive when multiplied by twenty or more rod ends in a system. Therefore they are inspected and cleaned at periodic inspection intervals. Rod ends that would be acceptable on fixed-wing aircraft would not be on helicopters mainly because of the number involved and the vibration levels. If wear can be felt in a rod end such as a fork or spherical bearing, it is time to change it.

It must be remembered that wear factors do not progress on a straight-line curve. For example, .001 of an inch wear that occurred in 500 hours of operation may quadruple in the next 500 hours of operation. As the wear factor increases in one area, it will add to the wear factor in units connected to it. Since every unit is connected to another, the whole helicopter is connected in this progression. The replacement of one worn rod end is *good cheap maintenance*.

Replacement of these rod ends may amount to no more than loosening a jam nut and unthreading the old one. If materials such as Pro-Seal have been used, it may require some heat and MEK to remove the old rod end. In an effort to save time the rod is usually measured, or the exposed threads counted, or a trammel is used to ensure that the rod stays the same length. This

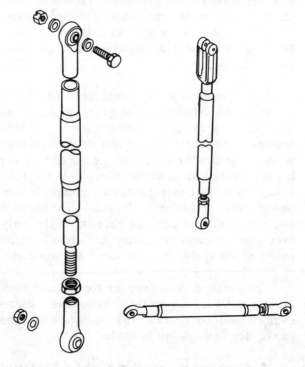

Fig. 6-21 Various types of push-pull tubes

type of system will avoid re-rigging the flight control system. However, all major rigging points should be checked before returning the helicopter to service.

Some rod ends may be riveted into place. This type requires careful drilling to remove the old rivets prior to replacement. Elongated holes in the tube are cause for rejection. The rivets used in these tubes and rod ends are usually steel, which does not ease the removal or replacement. The maintenance manual and parts catalog must be strictly followed regarding the type of rivet to be used. Usually the riveted ends are sealed with a recommended compound such as Pro-Seal. See

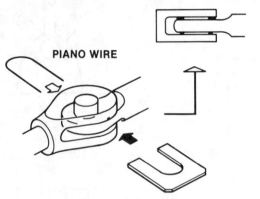

Fig. 6-22 *One method to insure alignment of spherical bearings*

Fig. 6-21 for typical rod ends installed in tubes. When spherical bearings are used, they must always be properly aligned. It is very easy to get the bearing misaligned when adjusting the rod length in place. A handy homemade tool, such as seen in Fig. 6-22, will be most beneficial.

Most push-pull tubes require close tolerance bolts and cotter pins for safety. It is not unusual to find fiber-lock castle nuts in these locations.

4. *Torque tubes*

Other items found in flight control systems are torque tubes. Used for several different purposes in a system, they usually lie perpendicular to the center line of the aircraft. Torque tubes are usually attached to each end of the structure by a bearing so that partial rotation of the shaft may take place. The type of bearing used varies considerably: oilite bronze bushings, Teflon bearings, or sealed prelubricated ball bearings. The tube is usually held by a saddle (Fig. 6-23). The torque tube may in some instances be used to convert a rotary motion to a linear motion such as the movement of the collective. It may also be used to transfer the motion to two points such as the rotor and the engine, to change direction or mechanical advantages, or to transfer a movement from one place to another.

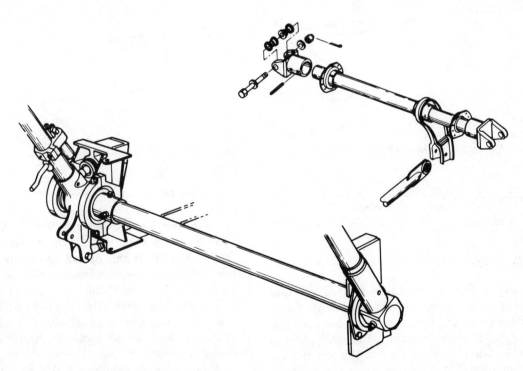

Fig. 6-23 *Typical torque tubes found in a control system*

237

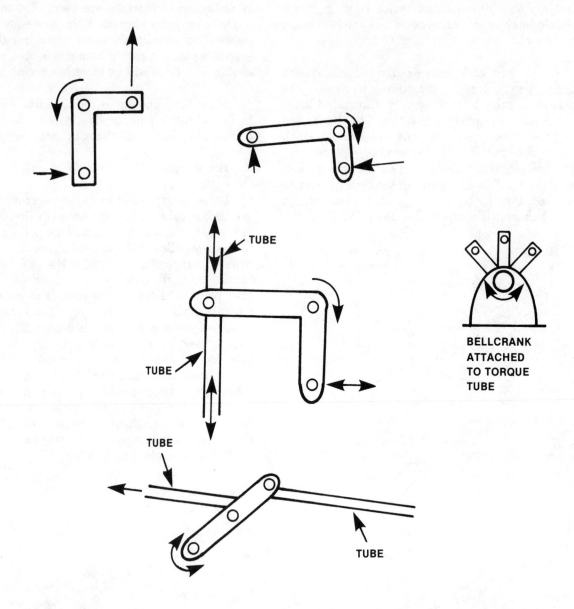

Fig. 6-24   Bellcranks may be used to change directions and mechanical advantage

Torque tubes are inspected periodically for security, bearing wear and cracks, especially at the horn attachment point and rod attachment point.

5.   Bellcranks

Closely related to the function of the torque tube is the bellcrank mainly used to change direction with a push-pull tube. The bellcrank may not be used to change direction, but will always change the travel of the tube and the mechanical advantage. See Fig. 6-24 for some typical bellcranks.

6.   Mixer box

Another closely related item to the torque tube and the bellcrank is the mixer box (Fig. 6-25). Usually all helicopters use a mixer box for the cyclic and collective inputs prior to the swashplate. The purpose of the mixer is to prevent the collective input from affecting the cyclic input as they move together or in relation to each other. If such a device were not installed, movement of the collective would change the height of the cyclic setting on the swashplate and the cyclic setting would alter the collective.

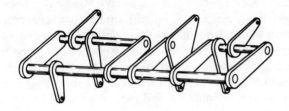

Fig. 6-25 Mixer box used to transmit cyclic and collective control movements

In viewing Fig. 6-26, note that when the collective is pulled upward, the swashplate will move upward and the cyclic control movement

that was already present will move the same amount in the same direction. This will move the swashplate up parallel to its original position. As the collective is lowered, the swashplate will lower, staying parallel to its position. In viewing the mixer unit control linkages at points A, B, and C, the same distance is in the same direction.

In Fig. 6-27, the fore and aft cyclic is moved. As the cyclic is moved forward, the input goes only through B which moves the servo and tilts the swashplate in the same manner.

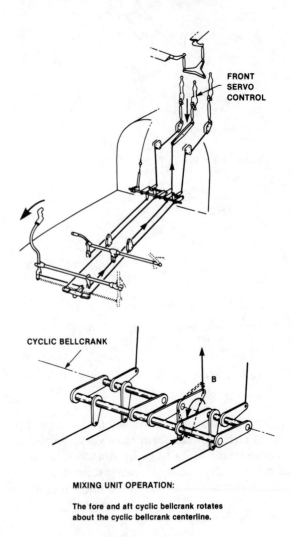

FRONT SERVO CONTROL

CYCLIC BELLCRANK

MIXING UNIT OPERATION:

The fore and aft cyclic bellcrank rotates about the cyclic bellcrank centerline.

Fig. 6-27 Fore and aft mixer unit movements

SUMMING BELLCRANKS

R

A.B.C.

A

B

C

SUMMING BELLCRANKS

RH LATERAL CYCLIC BELLCRANK

FORE AND AFT CYCLIC BELLCRANK

LH LATERAL CYCLIC BELLCRANK

MIXING UNIT OPERATION:

The summing bellcranks and levers assembly, when actuated by the collective pitch lever, rotates about the summing bellcrank center-line. Control linkage points A, B, and C move the same distance in the same direction.

Fig. 6-26 Mixer box operation

It can easily be seen in Fig. 6-28 that lateral movements of the cyclic will move bellcranks A and C in equal and opposite directions allowing the swashplate to tilt in the desired direction.

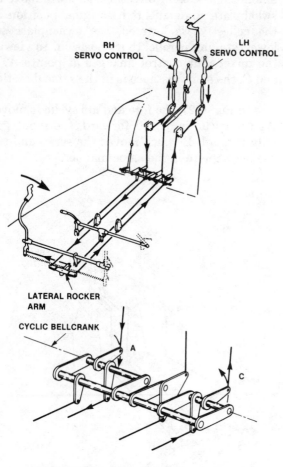

RH SERVO CONTROL

LH SERVO CONTROL

LATERAL ROCKER ARM

CYCLIC BELLCRANK

A

C

MIXING UNIT OPERATION:

The two lateral cyclic bellcranks rotate by the same value but in opposite directions about the cyclic bellcrank centerline.

Fig. 6-28   Lateral cyclic movements to the mixer unit

Such mixing units may be found in most helicopters although the form may vary. Variations of these mixer units have been used to increase tail rotor pitch as collective was added in addition to the coordination of the cyclic and collective.

7. Gradient unit

Since many of the helicopters today use a hydraulic boost on the controls, the feel of the movement of the control is removed. This feel is quite necessary to keep the pilot from over-controlling the machine. This feel is artificially added. This is accomplished by using what is commonly referred to as a gradient unit (Fig. 6-29). Gradient units may be found on all inputs to the cyclic and are sometimes found with the

tail rotor system and collective. Basically these gradient units are spring units that are compressed and released as movement of the control is made. This spring compression takes place in both directions. These units are usually made for each input and are not interchangeable. They are, however, adjustable and can be adjusted for the required spring tension.

The units are always installed in conjunction with the control system but never as an integral part of the system. In addition to their use as an artificial feel, they are often used to help trim the helicopter, in conjunction with a magnetic brake unit. The helicopter, like the fixed-wing aircraft, may require trimming to hold the helicopter in proper flight attitude. This is commonly due to the load distribution. Unlike the fixed-wing aircraft, however, it would be most difficult to install movable trim tabs that could be used to adjust flight characteristics of the helicopter. For this reason the pilot is forced to use the cyclic for these corrections. This means that if the aircraft flew somewhat nose heavy, a constant back pressure would be required during flight. If the aircraft flew one side low as well, both back pressure and side pressure would be required. This could become very tiring in a very short time.

With the gradient system and a magnetic brake, the cyclic may be moved to make the required attitude change and to engage the magnetic brake. From that point the gradient spring will relieve the required force to hold the cyclic so that the aircraft remains in the trimmed attitude. It must be observed that the aircraft may still be flown working against the gradient unit as usual. See Fig. 6-29 for a view of this unit.

A trim motor is quite similar to a gradient unit. Basically it works on the same principle except that the trim or movement of the cyclic is done by use of a linear actuator in conjunction with a switch on the cyclic. This linear actuator moves the stick against spring pressure to trim the helicopter (Fig. 6-30).

8. Control boosts

Helicopters not using hydraulics for boosted controls may make use of such items as bungee springs to assist the pilot in moving the controls. Other assists include counterweights that were used on the rotor heads of the Bell 47 and the

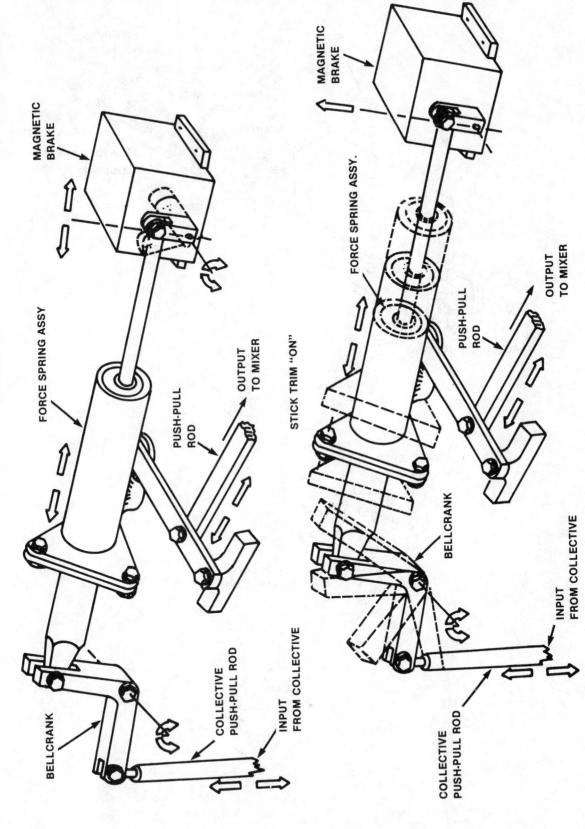

MAGNETIC BRAKE

STICK TRIM "OFF"

FORCE SPRING ASSY

PUSH-PULL ROD

OUTPUT TO MIXER

BELLCRANK

COLLECTIVE PUSH-PULL ROD

INPUT FROM COLLECTIVE

MAGNETIC BRAKE

FORCE SPRING ASSY.

STICK TRIM "ON"

PUSH-PULL ROD

OUTPUT TO MIXER

BELLCRANK

COLLECTIVE PUSH-PULL ROD

INPUT FROM COLLECTIVE

Fig. 6-29   Magnetic brake and gradient movements for helicopter trim

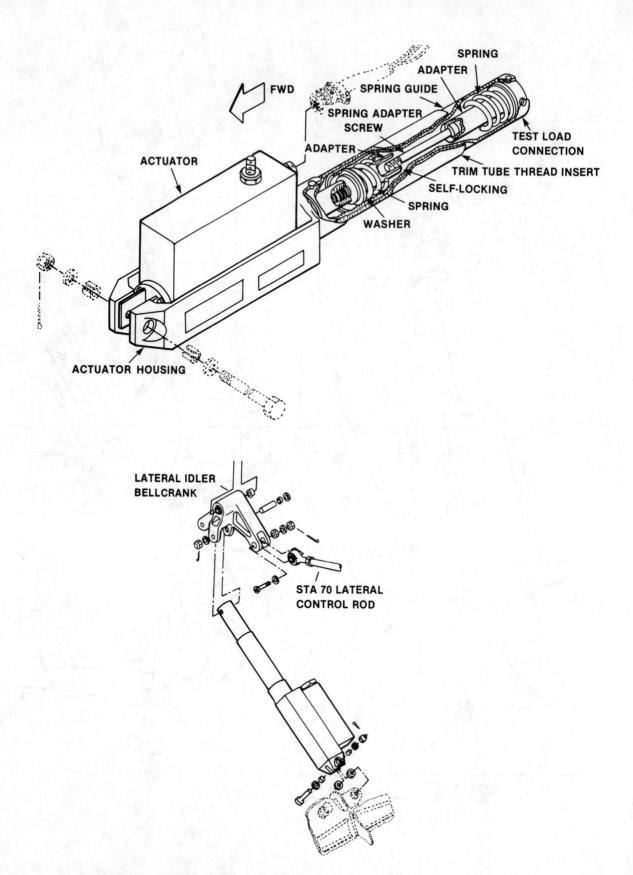

Fig. 6-30   Trim motor and gradient as found on the Hughes 500

Hiller 12 to assist the pilot in raising the collective.

One system of rather unique design is that of the Hiller 12 where the flight controls for the cyclic moved paddles attached to the main rotor. These in turn move the rotor. This system worked quite well but was slow in reaction time.

Today practically all new helicopters use a hydraulic boost system for the controls. These systems are necessary on some helicopters while on others they simply aid the pilot and improve the flying ability of the machine. On aircraft requiring boosted controls, two systems are used — the main and a backup system, just in case of emergencies. Most helicopters utilize hydraulic systems only for control boost. Few helicopters are equipped with retractable gears and other items that would require hydraulic power. In addition to the ability to aid the pilot in moving the rotor, most of the actuators are built to absorb rotor feedback. This improves the smoothness of the controls and eliminates annoying vibration in the controls.

The hydraulic systems contains all the components normally found in a hydraulic system. The system includes the following items:

1. Hydraulic pump

2. Reservoir

3. Relief valve

4. Filters

5. Accumulators

6. Actuators

Additional items may be added depending upon the size of the system and its requirements.

The hydraulic pumps are normally driven by the transmission to ensure that hydraulic power will be available during autorotation in the event of engine failure. The pumps are usually of the gear or piston type.

The reservior contains a screen in the filler cap and a sight gauge to check the level of the fluid.

The system pressure is set with a conventional type relief valve. The pressures vary considerably from one system to another. Some systems are 250 psi while others are 2000 psi. With the higher pressures the components may be built lighter.

Many newer filtering systems are using pop-out warning buttons to indicate bypassing of the filter. Most of these filters are either a throwaway type or require ultrasonic cleaning.

The accumulators are of a conventional piston type. On many of the smaller systems no accumulator will be found.

The hydraulic actuators differ from those on other hydraulic systems. Some move the piston while others move the cylinder. The cylinders are also equipped with pilot and irreversible valves. Some of the actuators are dual actuators with the cylinders being fed by two seperate hydraulic systems. To understand the types of actuators and their function, note the typical unit as used on a Bell 47 as seen in Fig. 6-31.

When the cyclic is moved, the linkage moves the servo valve. This opens the valve ports and applies pressure to one end of the cylinder and releases trapped fluid in the opposite end of the cylinder. This causes movement of the piston, actuator shaft, and the attached control linkage. As the movement of the cyclic is stopped, the actuator movement stops and the valve port closes. This causes the swashplate to be held in its new positon by the fluid trapped in the cylinder. The irreversible portion of the actuator consists of four valves which will be called A, B, C, and D, to correspond with Fig. 6-31.

1. Valve *A* is a 10 psi pressure inlet check valve.

2. Valve *B* is a return to pressure check valve operating on 2 psi.

3. Valve *C* is a return line relief valve operating on 35 psi.

4. Valve *D* is a return line relief valve operating on 340-370 psi.

In normal operation fluid passes through check valve A to the servo valve. The relief valve *D* and the check valve *B* prevent fluid from pass-

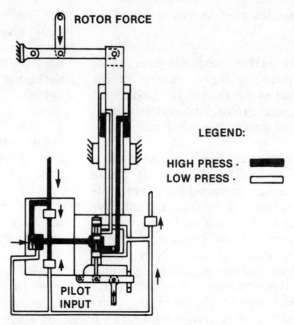

ROTOR FORCE

LEGEND:

HIGH PRESS - ■■■■
LOW PRESS - ▭

PILOT
INPUT

**DETAIL 1. NORMAL SYSTEM ON OPERATION SHOWING
VALVE OPEN DUE TO ROTOR FORCE OR PILOT INPUT.**

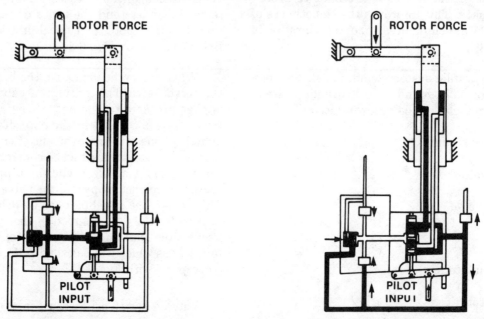

ROTOR FORCE

PILOT
INPUT

**DETAIL 2. SYSTEM OFF OPERATION SHOWING
VALVE OPEN DUE TO ROTOR LOAD.**

ROTOR FORCE

PILOT
INPUI

**DETAIL 3. SYSTEM OFF OPERATION SHOWING PILOT
MOVING CYLINDER TO OPPOSE ROTOR FORCE.**

Fig. 6-31 Hydraulic servoes as found on the Bell 47

ing to the return side of the cylinder. When the cyclic is moved, the control head valve directs fluid to the piston in the direction of the control movement. This forces the fluid on the opposite side of the piston to the return line through valve *C*. If the hydraulic pressure should fail, the fluid will remain trapped because check valve *A* and relief valve *C* will prevent its escape. The input line has no pressure and no pressure is being developed for the fluid to pass through relief valve *C*. Therefore a closed circuit is formed. The irreversibility is obtained independently of the hydraulic pressure for all fixed cyclic positions. The hydraulic fluid, being incompressible, is locked in the cylinder by check valve *B* and relief valve *D*. On the return side the fluid is also trapped because there is no pressure to operate relief valve *C*.

With boost pressure on, flight loads are restricted by the boost pressure. After the pressure has failed and the cyclic is moved, the servo valve is opened and fluid is directed to the piston. The fluid on the opposite side of the piston is forced out by the piston movement. This routes the fluid around the closed circuit through the low pressure check valve B and back to the servo valve.

The locking feature of the irreversible valve is safeguarded from excessive loads by the relief valve D. If D should open, this would be im-

mediately sensed by the pilot and should act as a warning device. With this lock and load valve system, feedback from the rotor may be well hidden until the hydraulic power is turned off or hydraulic failure has occurred.

Most of the actuators are built on this principle of operation, and may be found on all of the controls, including the collective and tail rotor on some helicopters. There is also a tendency today to use compact units that contain many of the components of a hydraulic in one unit. This may

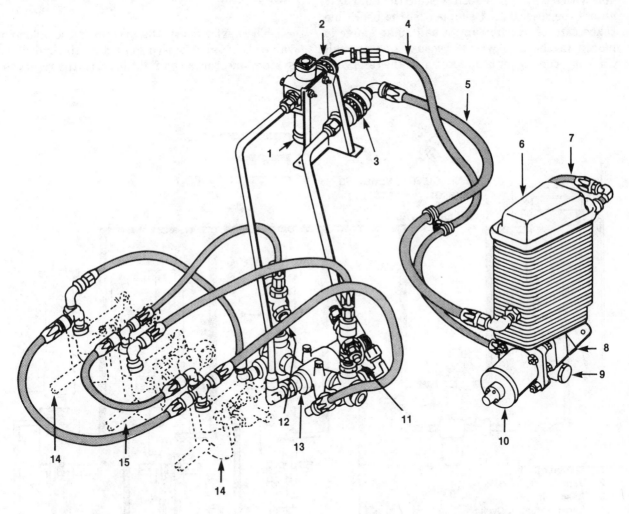

1. FILTER
2. QUICK-DISCONNECT SOCKET (PRESSURE)
3. QUICK-DISCONNECT SOCKER (RETURN)
4. HOSE (PRESSURE)
5. HOSE (RETURN)
6. PUMP AND RESERVOIR
7. VENT LINE
8. VENT

9. PRESSURE REGULATOR VALVE
10. TACHOMETER GENERATOR
11. CAP
12. CAP
13. SOLENOID VALVE
14. SERVO ACTUATOR (CYCLIC)
15. SERVO ACTUATOR (COLLECTIVE)

Fig. 6-32   Bell 206 hydraulic unit

include in one unit the reservoir pump and the relief valve. One aircraft that utilizes such a system is the Bell Jet Ranger (Fig. 6-32). Because of its relative simplicity it will be used as a typical example of a system used on a light helicopter.

The hydraulic system consists of a reservoir, pump, regulator, filter, solenoid valve, and three servo units. The reservoir pump and regulator are contained in one unit attached to the transmission. A filler cap is placed at the top of the reservoir with a tray-type screen to stain the fluid as it enters the reservoir. A scupper on the back side takes care of overfills and a ball sight gauge is placed in the side where, because of its small capacity, cooling air is directed over the reservoir.

The fluid is fed by gravity to the pump which is contained in the same unit and is driven from the transmission. The pressure regulator for the pump is housed in the same unit and is set for 600 ± 50 psi. A schematic of the system is shown in Fig. 6-33. The fluid leaves the pump unit across the cabin roof to the filter unit. The filter unit itself is replaced or ultrasonically cleaned at specified maintenance periods. A by-pass system is included in the filter assembly with a red pop-out indicator unit on the top. Any time the button has popped out the filter must be replaced and the button reset.

The next item in the system is the solenoid valve. This valve is used to turn off the hydraulic system and route the fluid back to the reservoir

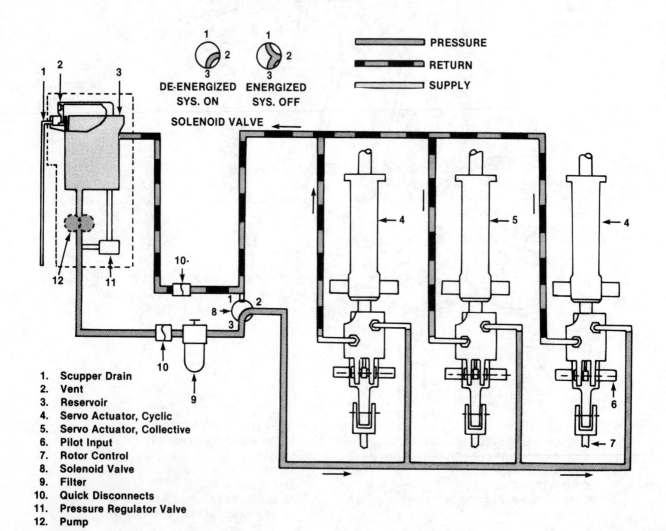

1. Scupper Drain
2. Vent
3. Reservoir
4. Servo Actuator, Cyclic
5. Servo Actuator, Collective
6. Pilot Input
7. Rotor Control
8. Solenoid Valve
9. Filter
10. Quick Disconnects
11. Pressure Regulator Valve
12. Pump

Fig. 6-33   Schematic of Bell 206 hydraulic system

246

when desired. The valve is activated by a switch on the console by the pilot. The solenoid is energized when *off*.

From the solenoid valve the fluid is routed to three servo cylinders located on the roof. One cylinder is the collective while the other two are for fore-and-aft and lateral cyclic. A schematic of a typical servo cylinder is seen in Fig. 6-34. The servos, like those on the 47, contain irreversible valves. If hydraulic pressure is lost to the servo actuator, the plunger in the sequence valve is pushed up by the lower spring and poppet valve. This action closes the hydraulic return port and maintains irreversibility, keeping the pilot control even with the system inoperative.

The sequence valve also acts as a thermo relief valve if pressure should build up while the system is inactive. As the fluid is moved from the servos it returns to the reservoir.

Larger systems in their operations become more complex. A dual system used on the Bell 212 is seen in Fig. 6-35. It consists of two separate systems which do not make contact with each other. The components in each system are exactly alike except for the pumps and locations. The systems are referred to as System 1 and System 2, each powering the cyclic and collective controls through dual servo controls. System 1 additionally powers the tail rotor servo.

System 1 supplies fluid power to the top portion of the dual servo actuators while System 2 supplies the lower portion of the servos.

The following components are included in each system:

1. Reservoir

2. Temperature bulb and switch

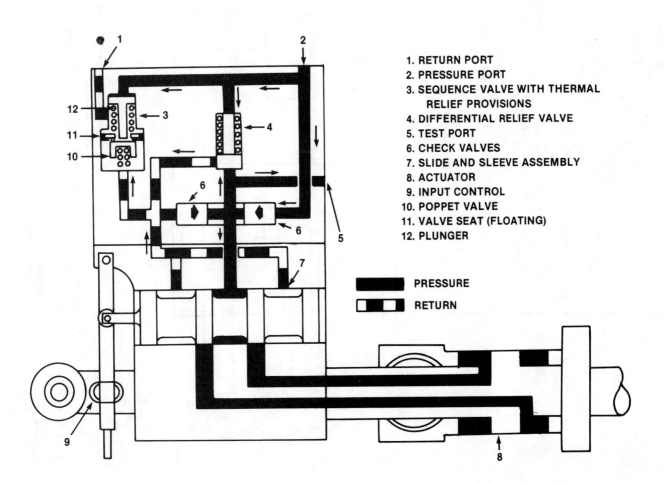

1. RETURN PORT
2. PRESSURE PORT
3. SEQUENCE VALVE WITH THERMAL
   RELIEF PROVISIONS
4. DIFFERENTIAL RELIEF VALVE
5. TEST PORT
6. CHECK VALVES
7. SLIDE AND SLEEVE ASSEMBLY
8. ACTUATOR
9. INPUT CONTROL
10. POPPET VALVE
11. VALVE SEAT (FLOATING)
12. PLUNGER

PRESSURE
RETURN

Fig. 6-34 Typical servo unit used on the Bell 206

247

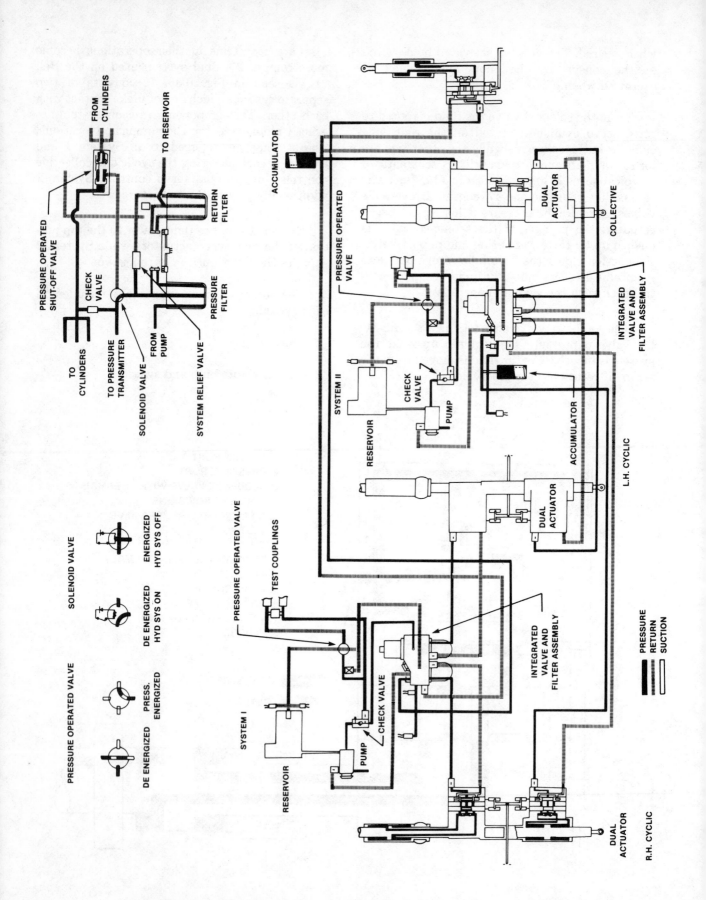

Fig. 6-35 Dual hydraulic system utilizing two independent systems

248

3. Pump

4. Check valve (pressure supply line)

5. Integrated valve and filter

6. Pressure transmitter and switch

7. Accumulator

8. Test couplings

9. Restrictor fittings

10. Check valves

11. Lines

12. Servo actuators

Since the fluids from the two systems do not contact each other, two separate reservoirs are provided. Each reservoir is in a different location. The System 1 reservoir is on the right aft edge of the cabin roof with the filler scupper aft while System 2 reservoir is located on the left aft edge of the cabin roof with the scupper and filler cap forward. A sight gauge is visible through the holes in the transmission cowling provided for each reservoir. The levels may then be checked without removal of the cowling.

A cap and filler neck are provided on each reservoir for servicing. A vent opening to the atmosphere is located at the top. Three hydraulic lines and a drain plug are connected to the reservoir. One line is a gravity feed to the pump; one a return; and the third is the overboard drain for the scupper. At the return line is a cross fitting containing a temperature bulb, temperature switch, and a screen baffle. This baffle speeds up the de-aeration of the fluid returning to the reservoir. The temperature bulb is conected to an indicator in the cockpit and the temperature switch lights a caution light when the fluid overheats.

The two variable delivery, axial piston-type pumps have different locations. The System 1 pump is located on the right side of the transmission accessory and sump case. System 2 pump is located on the forward side of the main transmission case. Each pump is driven from a different part of the transmission reducing the chances of failure of both systems. Even though the pumps are driven at different speeds, they deliver the same pressure of 1000 psi at no flow and 900 psi at full flow.

In each system, check valves are placed in the pump pressure outlet lines. Each check valve has four ports. Three ports connect to pump pressure, system pressure, and a pressure test coupling. The fourth is simply plugged off. The check valve assembly allows fluid flow in the system when the pump is in operation. An additional check valve is installed in the pressure test line to prevent the pump from pressurizing the line during pump operation. The check valve assembly prevents motorizing the pump and overfilling the reservoir during test operations in which external hydraulic power is used.

Fluid flows under pressure from the check valve assembly to the integrated valve and filter assemblies. Both are identical but are mounted in different locations, with one unit rotated 180° as compared to the other unit. Each of these units incorporates two filters, two differential pressure indicators and switches, a system relief valve, a solenoid valve, check valve, and pressure-operated shutoff valve.

The two filters are installed in the bottom of the check valve assembly. One of is the pressure filter and the other the return fluid filter. Both filter elements are a metal type and are interchangeable with others of the same filtering capabilities.

The pressure filter does not incorporate a bypass. This means that if the filter becomes clogged, the fluid flow will be restricted. The return filter, however, does have bypass capabilities and will do so with a pressure differential across the filter element allowing fluid to return to the reservoir.

Both filter elements are provided with differential pressure indicators which will extend a red indicator button when a restriction causes a pressure differential across the filter element. The movement of this button also activates an electrical switch causing a red dot to be displayed on an indicator. This, however, does not indicate which system or which filter is clogged. This can be determined only by viewing the individual filter buttons. The buttons are reset manually when the differential no longer exists.

The fluid passing through the pressure filter passes through the system relief valve and the solenoid valve located on the top of the assembly. The system relief valve protects the system from excessive pressure should the pump malfunction, by returning the excessive pressure to the return side.

The solenoid valves are three-way, two-position, electrically operated valves. Each valve is controlled by a switch marked HYDSYS1 and HYDSYS2. The valves are spring loaded to the system "ON" position and electrically energized to the system "OFF" position. When the valve is electrically deenergized, the fluid is directed through the system; and when electrically energized, the fluid is bypassed to the return. This provides a means of shutting off either hydraulic system in case of system malfunction.

In addition to passing through the solenoid valve, fluid must pass through a check valve in each assembly. This check valve directs fluid under pressure to the servo actuator ports and prevents flow in the opposite direction. Accumulator pressure is maintained in the servo lines when pump pressure is lost. After the fluid under pressure passes through the check valve, it must go through a pressure switch and transmitter before leaving the system. The pressure switch is used to activate a caution light when the pressure is low, and the pressure transmitter relays the system pressure to the indicator on the instrument panel.

Parallel with the system pressure line in each system is an accumulator. The accumulators are a piston-type utilizing a spring force. They are charged by the system pressure compressing the spring. If the system pump pressure should fail the accumulators will partially charge the servos.

Two test couplings are provided each system. The pressure coupling and return line coupling are used in checking the systems with external hydraulic power. In each test coupling line is a pressure-operated valve. The valves are three-way, two-position valves and connect the system return to the test return when test pressure is applied. When the test pressure is reduced, the fluid returns to its normal flow back to the reservoir. A restrictor is also placed between the system return and test pressure. This is used to relieve any thermal pressure that might build up in the line.

Unable to relieve the pressure, it could open the pressure-operated valve.

Check valves are installed at various points throughout the system. The check valves allow flow in one direction and prevent flow in the opposite direction. One check valve is located in the test lines between the return and pressure test lines for thermal relief. Another is in the pump by-pass port preventing pressure build-up in the pump case. Additional check valves are placed in each servo actuator return line at the integrated valve to prevent system return pressure from pressuring the servo return line.

By-pass type check valves are installed at each pressure port of the dual servo actuators. These provide an irreversible feature by retaining fluid in the actuator when system pressure is lost. These valves, however, allow fluid to flow from the actuators when the system is in operation.

Four servo actuators are installed in the system to assist the pilot in the movement of the controls and prevention of rotor feedback. Three are dual servo actuators, one for the collective and two for the cyclic. A single smaller actuator is used for the tail rotor and is operated by System 1 only.

The dual servo actuators located on the cyclic and collective system are powered by both or either system. The upper portion is supplied by System 1 while the lower portion is supplied by System 2. Details of the dual servo actuators can be seen in Fig. 6-36.

The upper and lower portions of each dual actuator is equipped with its own servo and by-pass valve. The servo valves are actuated by linkage from a common input.

The upper servo valves direct fluid to the upper or lower side of the piston of the upper chamber moving the piston in the desired direction with the cylinder staying stationary.

The lower servo valve directs fluid to the top or bottom of the piston in the lower chamber. This moves the cylinder rather than the piston in the required direction.

The linkage for both the upper and lower servo and by-pass valves incorporate springs. The springs allow movement of one servo in the event

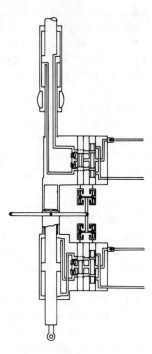

Fig. 6-36 Dual type actuator utilizing two systems

the other becomes jammed. For example, if the upper servo became jammed, the lower servo would continue to function and move the controls.

In normal operation hydraulic pressure under 100 psi acts on the top or the bottom of the pistons to move the controls in the desired direction as determined by the servo valves. With the servo valves in neutral, pressure is directed to both sides of the piston.

If System 1 is not functioning, the upper piston is moved by the lower actuator.

If System 2 is not functioning, the lower cylinder is moved by the upper actuator.

If both systems are not functioning, the upper piston and lower cylinder are moved manually.

The upper and lower servo actuators function much the same during manual operation. Check valves in the actuator prevent liquid lock. Cavitation of the actuator is prevented by a check valve at the pressure inlet port and the pressure-operated shutoff valve in the integrated valve. Seal leakage loss is replenished by the accumulator. In this system the actuator is irreversible as long as

fluid is retained in the system between the actuator and the integrated valve.

The tail rotor servo actuator works in much the same manner as the dual servo actuators except that it is powered by only one system. Therefore only one servo, piston and cylinder are required. When System 1 does not function, the same check valve provisions are provided so that the tail rotor control may function manually as the other actuators function in a manual position.

9. Maintenance and Inspection

Regardless of the systems used, one of the most important items with any hydraulic system used in a flight control system is proper servicing. This starts with checking the fluid levels and adding the proper fluid to the reservoir. Usually Mil 5606 fluid is used, but in all circumstances, the maintenance manual must be consulted to insure that the proper fluid is used. The systems seldom require the addition of large amounts of fluid. High usage of fluid is an indication of leakage and all components and lines should be checked before more fluid is added.

All actuators should be cleaned periodically to remove any foreign matter from the actuator rods. Dirt and sand will increase the wear factors and induce leakage. If the helicopter operates under adverse conditions such as sandy environments, this may become part of the daily maintenance of the helicopter.

At specified periods of time the filters are either cleaned or replaced depending on the type of filters used and the facilities available for cleaning the filter units. Often this is done when the fluid is changed or during routine maintenance without changing the fluid. In either situation after cleaning or replacement, the filters must be checked under pressure for leaks.

The usual inspection of the systems consists of visual inspections for leakage, cleanliness, and mounting of the actuators including alignment. These inspections are usually done with hydraulic power on the system. This power is most often produced by external hydraulic power through test lines in the system. External power may also be used for other maintenance procedures and should always be in accordance with the manufacturer's instructions especially regarding the pressure required and the position of the system switches. If such precautions are not observed, the system may be damaged, may not function properly, or may be overfilled.

Maintenance of the components is usually quite limited to removal and replacement of tubing, hoses, valves, and pumps. Components such as pumps, valves, and actuators will require special equipment for rebuilds, limiting the repair of such items to removal and replacement. When such items are removed, normal hydraulic safety practices must be observed, including bleeding the pressure from the system before opening lines and capping all openings so that the system is not contaminated. With internal breakdown of components, it may be necessary to drain and flush the complete system prior to replacement.

Although it is quite rare that any hydraulic components would have a finite life, most of the components will have recommended overhaul times.

The other components in a flight control system will also require some service, inspection, and maintenance.

The flight controls will usually require periodic lubrication in the form of oil or grease. The introduction of sealed bearings and Teflon bushings has reduced this servicing considerably. At least one system, which does not use hydraulic boost on the controls, has one-way locks that require a small amount of hydraulic fluid at routine servicing.

Since most systems make use of push-pull tubes and bellcranks, the inspection must include the rod ends and spherical bearings. All loose rod ends and bearings must be replaced. The importance of the condition of these items cannot be over-emphasised because wear factors will affect the control movements and the feedback of the rotor system. The novice helicopter technician may feel that a couple of thousandths of play will make very little difference. However, when this is multiplied fifteen times by each rod end in the system, it is a sizable amount of excessive movement. Coupled with vibration it will increase the wear factors at a rapid rate. Although it is not uncommon to replace rod ends, an excessive amount of replacement is always a good indication of excessive vibration in the rotor system.

Most rod ends are attached with close tolerance bolts which are subject to wear as much as the rod end, and may require replacement. The rod end bolts are checked for safeties, which in most instances are cotter pins.

One of the items to be considered in the inspection of push-pull tubes is corrosion. They have been known to corrode from the inside out although such precautions as sealing the ends is a common practice.

During inspection the controls should be moved to their extreme positions checking all the control stops. Such items as gradient systems, magnetic brakes, and trim motors must also be checked for operation and condition.

A few items in the control system may be assigned a finite life. This sometimes involves control tubes but is quite often true of swashplate items. Other items such as trim motors and magnetic brakes, control tubes, etc. will have recommended overhaul times assigned.

10. Control rigging

Maintenance is usually confined to removal and replacement for items other than rod ends and bolts. However, many of the items in a control system are adjustable and control movements are quite critical. For this reason it is often necessary after removal and replacement of components that the particular control system be rigged, meaning that the system must be adjusted so that the correct amount of pitch is present on the collective and the cyclic travel is within tolerances.

This is done by a number of methods. Most of the early helicopters became quite complex in regards to rigging the controls. This was mainly due to the little thought that was given to maintainability at the time of manufacture and the fact that the fuselages were often built with such tolerances as + or −1/8-inch. These machines had adjustments on both ends of each push-pull tube and bellcranks were set at a number of degrees from the center line of the bellcrank.

It must be remembered that regardless of the type of helicopter, the rigging procedures must be done in accordance with the manufacturer's instructions to insure that the helicopter acquires no unsafe flight characteristics from the rigging procedure. This, however, does not mean that minor adjustments will not be required after the initial flight. Even these minor adjustments must be done in accordance with the maintenance manual and in small increments to avoid unstable flight characteristics.

In order to perform rigging of the flight controls, some equipment will be necessary and in many instances special tools such as jigs, rigging pins, and holding fixtures will be required. Other items of the helicopter such as mast alignment which would adversely affect the rigging often require checking.

The equipment required for rigging the cyclic and collective varies with the type of helicopter to be rigged. In addition to common hand tools, because it may be necessary to level the helicopter, suitable jacks of sufficient capacity for the leveling operation may be needed. This situation, however, is seldom experienced with the newer helicopters. If leveling is required, instructions will be given in a separate section of the maintenance manual.

Other common equipment used in rigging procedures are a measuring scale used to obtain required dimensions and a universal protractor (prop protractor). The protractor is used to obtain predetermined degrees on the bellcranks, swashplates, etc., when required.

Some of the helicopters manufactured today make use of rigging jigs and pins to aid in the rigging procedure. The pins are placed in predetermined locations to hold bellcranks so rods may be adjusted according to a set length. The jigs may be used for a variety of rigging tasks, as a holder for the swashplate, or as a template to determine the degrees of travel.

Usually the rigging procedure of the cyclic would consist of placing the cyclic control in the neutral position which would be straight up or perpendicular to the floor. A number of devices have been made for the specific helicopters for centering the cyclic in this position. Once the cyclic is centered the rods are adjusted to the

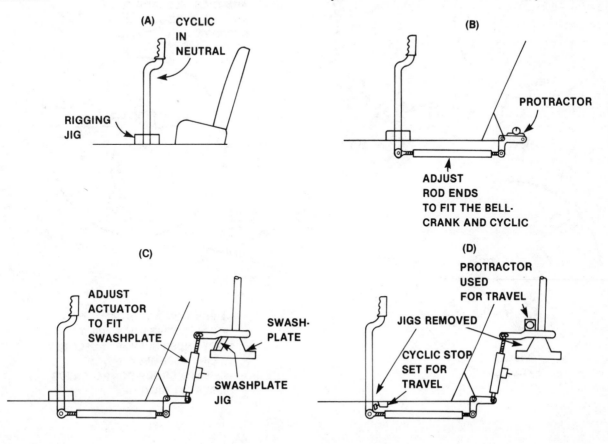

Fig. 6-37 Basic rigging procedures

253

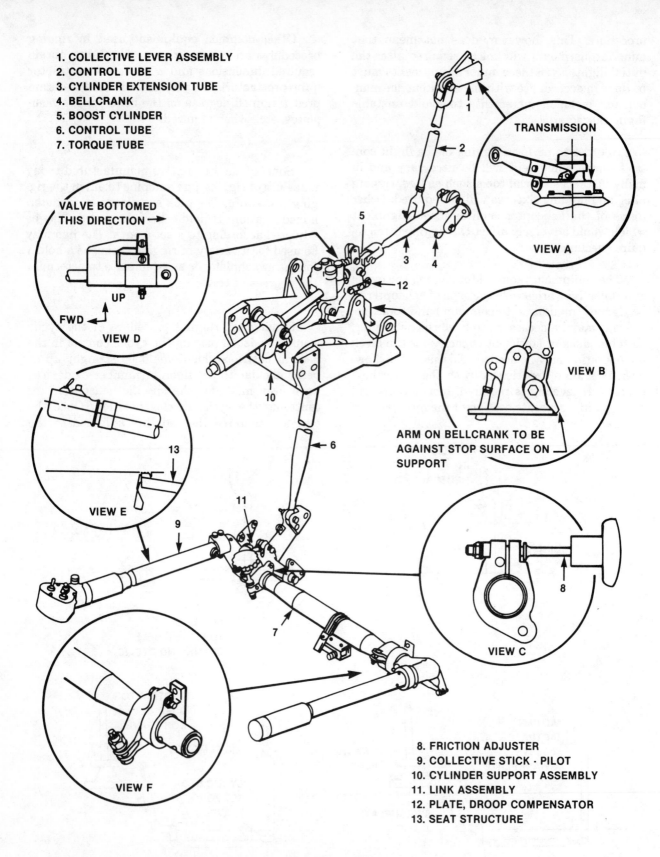

1. COLLECTIVE LEVER ASSEMBLY
2. CONTROL TUBE
3. CYLINDER EXTENSION TUBE
4. BELLCRANK
5. BOOST CYLINDER
6. CONTROL TUBE
7. TORQUE TUBE

TRANSMISSION

VIEW A

VALVE BOTTOMED
THIS DIRECTION →

UP
FWD ←

VIEW D

VIEW B

ARM ON BELLCRANK TO BE
AGAINST STOP SURFACE ON
SUPPORT

13

VIEW E

VIEW C

VIEW F

8. FRICTION ADJUSTER
9. COLLECTIVE STICK · PILOT
10. CYLINDER SUPPORT ASSEMBLY
11. LINK ASSEMBLY
12. PLATE, DROOP COMPENSATOR
13. SEAT STRUCTURE

Fig. 6-38   Bell 206 collective rigging

254

next check point. This may be a bellcrank that is either held in place by a rigging pin or is to have a preset angle determined by a protractor. When the bellcrank is in the correct position, the next reference point may be the hydraulic servo unit. Normally these are adjustable in length and the servo valve is set in neutral. The actuator may be attached to the swashplate which must be set to a fixed number of degrees by a protractor or another rigging fixture. From this point the control rods which go to the rotor are set. The rotor may be held in position or be checked with a protractor for its neutral position. After this neutral position is established, the extreme positions are set by stops which may be located on the bellcranks or on the swashplate (Fig 6-37). Although oversimplified, these would be typical basic steps that would be taken in the rigging of a cyclic system.

To understand the rigging procedure we shall use a Bell 206 to show the steps required. The steps involving the engine and the tail rotor will be covered in their respective sections.

In addition to the normal hand tools the following additional tools will be required:

1. One 6-inch scale with increments of .01″

2. A fish scale of 0 to 10 pounds capacity

3. One 5/16-inch rigging bolt with the threads removed

4. One feeler gauge

NOTE: *The following procedure is for training purposes only. Do not attempt to rig to these specifications. They may vary with different models and may change. Only use the manufacturer's up-dated maintenance manual.*

The collective and cyclic which are interconnected on the Bell 206, are shown in Figs. 6-38 and 6-39.

Assuming that all non-adjustable control tubes are in place in the collective and cyclic system, the 5/16-inch rigging bolt will be placed through the bottom of the fuselage through the cyclic stick (Fig. 6-39C). This will center the cyclic stick. When the bolt is in place, the cyclic is frictioned down to hold it in place.

The collective control is raised to a position of 2.40 inches above the pilot's seat structure as seen in Fig. 6-38E. This is also locked into position by the collective friction adjustment.

The next step is to position the bellcrank stop assembly at the hydraulic cylinder support casting so that the bellcrank contacts the minimum collective stop (Fig. 6-38B). This must be held in this position. The vertical push-pull tube must be adjusted and connected between the bellcranks as seen in Fig. 6-38, item 6. When this is accomplished, the servo must be bottomed out in the aft direction with the cylinder pushed forward (Fig. 6-38D). The collective lever on the swashplate is then positioned to obtain a dimension of 1.98 inches between the spotface on the swashplate support base and the centerline of the collective lever trunnion pins and held in that position. This dimension is shown in Fig. 6-38A. At this time the tube between the transmission and the swashplate collective lever may be adjusted. The bolt may then be removed from the cyclic, and the collective system must be checked for proper clearances of all parts before hydraulic power is applied. At this time the minimum angle of the blade grips will also be checked.

Rigging of the cyclic will require the same tools used with the collective except a 12-inch scale will be necessary for some of the measurements. The 5/16-inch bolt is again placed through the bottom of the fuselage to center the cyclic as was done when rigging the collective (Fig. 6-39C). Again the cyclic may be held in place by the friction. The collective is placed in the full down position and locked with the friction adjustment.

When this is completed, place the two bellcranks on the cabin roof 3.09 inches above the center line of the aft bellcrank control rod attachment holes and hold in that position (Fig. 6-39B). Next, place both pilot valves in the forward position with the cylinders placed aft (Fig. 6-39D) and hold in that position while the tunnel tubes are adjusted to fit (Fig. 6-39, item 7). When this is accomplished, position the swashplate 8.83 and 8.87 inches between the spot face on the upper case and centerline of the bolt holes in the bearing on both control plate horns (Fig. 6-39A). Adjust the vertical push-pull tubes to fit between the aft bellcrank and the swashplate control horns. The last step is to connect the rotor pitch links to the swashplate and check the minimum blade angle.

1. SWASHPLATE INNER RING · CONTROL PLATE
2. CONTROL TUBE
3. CONTROL TUBE
4. BELLCRANK
5. BELLCRANK
6. CYLINDER SUPPORT ASSEMBLY
7. CONTROL TUBE
8. CONTROL TUBE
9. YOKE
10. TORQUE TUBE
11. CYCLIC FRICTION ADJUSTER
12. CYCLIC CONTROL STICK
13. COTTER KEY
14. NUT
15. BOLT · RIGGING WORK AID
16. RIGHT HORN
17. LEFT HORN
18. CYLINDER EXTENSION TUBE
19. SPRING
20. MIXING BELLCRANK
21. TRANSMISSION

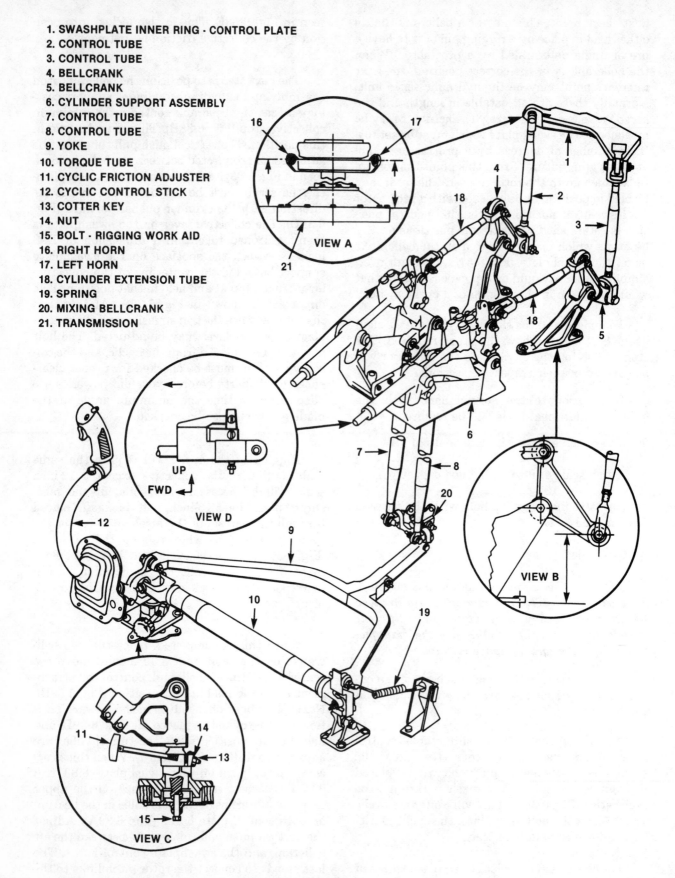

VIEW A

VIEW D

UP

FWD

VIEW B

VIEW C

Fig. 6-39 Bell 206 cyclic rigging

256

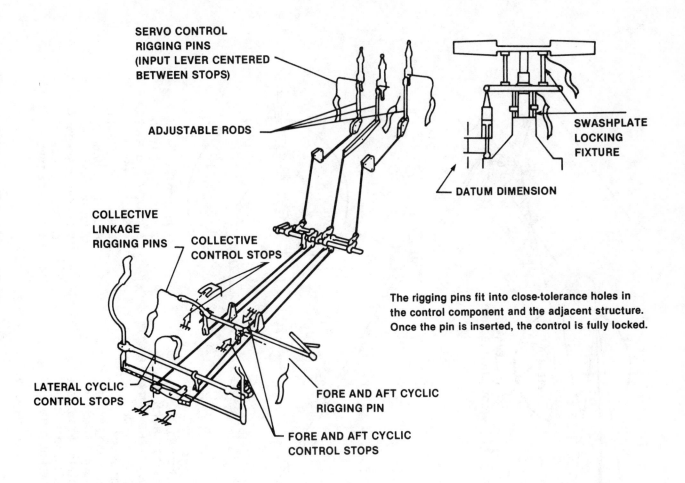

SERVO CONTROL
RIGGING PINS
(INPUT LEVER CENTERED
BETWEEN STOPS)

ADJUSTABLE RODS

SWASHPLATE
LOCKING
FIXTURE

DATUM DIMENSION

COLLECTIVE
LINKAGE
RIGGING PINS

COLLECTIVE
CONTROL STOPS

The rigging pins fit into close-tolerance holes in
the control component and the adjacent structure.
Once the pin is inserted, the control is fully locked.

LATERAL CYCLIC
CONTROL STOPS

FORE AND AFT CYCLIC
RIGGING PIN

FORE AND AFT CYCLIC
CONTROL STOPS

Fig. 6-40   AStar using rigging fixtures

A complete interference check must be made again of the cyclic system prior to the use of hydraulic power.

A quite different rigging procedure is shown in Fig. 6-40. This is the AStar 350 which makes exclusive use of rigging pins to determine positions of the various components in the control systems in order to establish the distances and relationships between the controls and the main rotor.

The rigging pins are fitted to the cyclic system in the neutral position and when the collective is in the mid-travel position six pins are used. One is placed in the fore and aft cyclic, one in the lateral cyclic to neutralize the cyclic control stick, one in the collective system to hold the collective at its mid-travel position, and three additional pins are placed in the three servos of the ac-

tuators. In addition, the swashplate is locked into position by a rigging fixture, leaving the adjustment to be made at the actuators. After all the linkage is set to these established points, the stops on the cyclic and collective are set. These limits are set to a predetermined length of the actuator arm, referred to as dimension "X" in Fig. 6-40.

Although this type of system simplifies rigging considerably, it is not always possible to do. This is especially true as helicopters are made larger and items such as trim motors, magnetic brakes and gradients are used. The system may become even more complex if stabilization equipment is used in the control system.

In most rigging procedures the items mentioned are not connected to the basic control system until it is rigged. They are added after the basic rigging is completed. It is at that time that

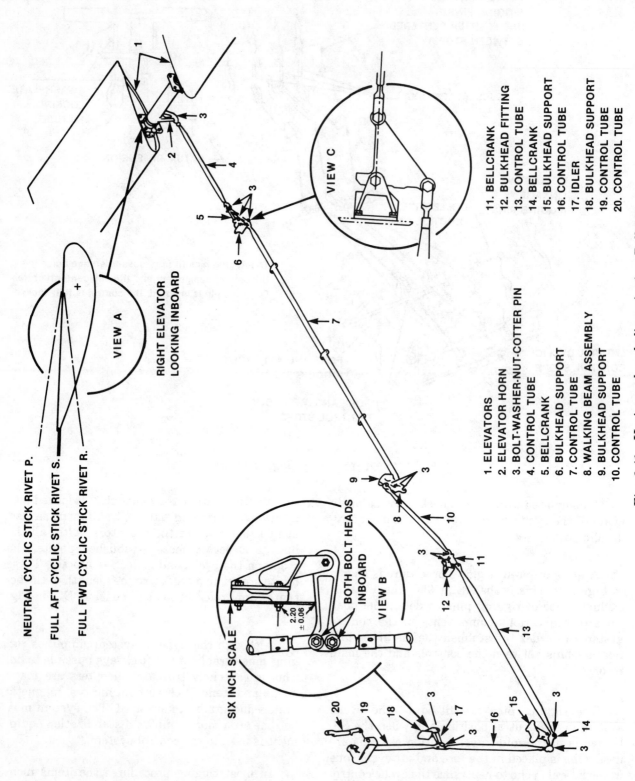

NEUTRAL CYCLIC STICK RIVET P.

FULL AFT CYCLIC STICK RIVET S.

FULL FWD CYCLIC STICK RIVET R.

VIEW A

RIGHT ELEVATOR
LOOKING INBOARD

VIEW C

VIEW B

SIX INCH SCALE

BOTH BOLT HEADS
INBOARD

2.20
± 0.06

1. ELEVATORS
2. ELEVATOR HORN
3. BOLT-WASHER-NUT-COTTER PIN
4. CONTROL TUBE
5. BELLCRANK
6. BULKHEAD SUPPORT
7. CONTROL TUBE
8. WALKING BEAM ASSEMBLY
9. BULKHEAD SUPPORT
10. CONTROL TUBE

11. BELLCRANK
12. BULKHEAD FITTING
13. CONTROL TUBE
14. BELLCRANK
15. BULKHEAD SUPPORT
16. CONTROL TUBE
17. IDLER
18. BULKHEAD SUPPORT
19. CONTROL TUBE
20. CONTROL TUBE

Fig. 6-41 Horizontal stabalizer rigging Bell 205

258

the control friction will be adjusted. In addition to these items a number of helicopters are equipped with a movable elevator control surface which will be rigged to work with the fore and aft cyclic.

Such a system is installed on the Bell 205. It consists of two negative lift airfoils mounted on the tail boom. The fore and aft movement of the cyclic stick changes the angle of attack of the elevator, increases the controllability of the helicopter, and lengthens the CG range. The movements of this elevator are not in direct relationship to the movements of the cyclic control. The trailing edge of the elevator moves down when either the fore or aft cyclic is moved from the neutral position. This non-linear movement is made possible by an over-center bellcrank (Fig. 6-41).

The rigging procedure for this system, like that for the cyclic and collective controls, is accomplished with the hydraulic boost turned "OFF" with only the adjustable tubes disconnected.

The first step is to position the cyclic stick in the neutral (vertical) position. Move the servo valves to the top of their travel by pressing down on the servo actuator extension tubes without moving the control tubes below. Once this is accomplished, adjust the second control tube in the system to position the idler lever (Fig. 6-41A), and adjust the last control tube in the system to the minimum length to reach the bellcrank. Then place the cyclic stick full forward against the stop and move the servo valves to the total of their travel without moving the tubes below the actuators. Position the trailing edge of the elevator .50 below the rivet R (Fig. 6-41A). At this point the aft bellcrank must be above the centerline as shown in Fig. 6-41C. If it is not, adjust the third control tube to fit. When the cyclic is moved to the extreme aft position the elevator should pass through rivet S.

The final rigging is accomplished with the hydraulic boost "ON" only after the control system is thoroughly checked for travel and interference. Moving the cyclic full forward should place the elevator in line with rivet R. If it does not, the third tube must be adjusted.

It may easily be seen that there are many different models used to rig flight controls, but it must be remembered that, regardless of the system, the controls are being adjusted across fixed points. The manufacturer's instructions must be followed if the helicopter is to fly correctly. Improper rigging can lead to a great number of flight problems including partial or complete loss of control. Some of these problems may not even be evident until certain flight attitudes are attempted or when the helicopter if loaded in a certain manner.

QUESTIONS:

91. All mast assemblies carry tension and torsion loads during flight.

   A. True

   B. False

92. Stabilizer bars are found on all semi-rigid rotor systems.

   A. True

   B. False

93. Stabilizer bars require static balance.

   A. True

   B. False

94. Dampeners used in conjunction with stabilizer bars require timing checks.

   A. True

   B. False

95. The swashplate is used to transfer cyclic movements only to the main rotor.

   A. True

   B. False

96. The rotating part of the swashplate is driven by the pitch change links.

   A. True

   B. False

97. The force required to move the swashplate is never checked.

   A. True

   B. False

98. The collective stick is usually given an up-and-down movement.

   A. True

   B. False

99. The cyclic must be moved to bank the helicopter.

   A. True

   B. False

100. Neither the cyclic or collective give directional control to the helicopter.

   A. True

   B. False

101. Movement of the cyclic will not affect the collective setting because of the:

   A. gradient system.

   B. magnetic brake.

   C. mixer assembly.

102. The gradient system is used on all helicopters.

   A. True

   B. False

103. The magnetic brake is used to trim some helicopters.

   A. True

   B. False

104. Hydraulic boost systems sometimes incorporate more than one system.

   A. True

   B. False

105. Hydraulic failure makes most helicopters impossible to fly.

   A. True

   B. False

SECTION VII

Main Rotor Transmissions

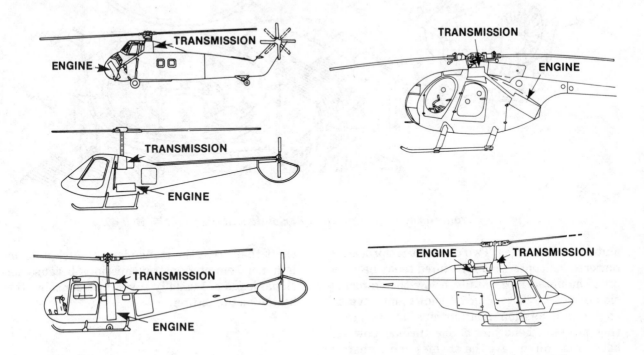

Fig. 7-1 Typical relationships of engines and transmissions used in helicopters.

The main rotor turns at speeds of three to four hundred RPM on most helicopters. At the same time the engines that power these rotors are turning at a much higher RPM. For example: an average reciprocating powerplant may run in a range of 3000 to 3200 RPM while the rotor turns at 340 RPM. A typical powerplant on turbine helicopters may operate at 6600 output shaft RPM while the main rotor rotates at 325 RPM.

There are two reasons for these speed reductions: (1) the engines which produce the greatest amount of power are high RPM and, (2) the rotor cannot operate at the high RPMs because of the tip speed and retreating blade stall. Although shorter blades and supersonic blade tips have been tried with some success, they would not allow the speeds of 3000 or 6000 RPM which would be required for direct drive from the engine.

For these reasons the helicopters require transmissions to reduce the engine speed to a

speed that can be handled by the main rotor. As with all other components used on helicopters, each manufacturer has different ways of designing the transmission, mounting and powering it. These have also changed considerably as the technology of the helicopter has developed from reciprocating power to turbine power.

The powerplants and their relationship to the transmission are quite important to the basic design of the transmission and to the requirements of the transmission and related components.

A. Transmissions

Most of the early light helicopters had a reciprocating engine hung vertically and coupled to the transmission which drove the rotor. Some of the older heavier helicopters located the reciprocating engine in the nose of the helicopter and drove the transmission by shafting. At least one military helicopter had the engine in the rear

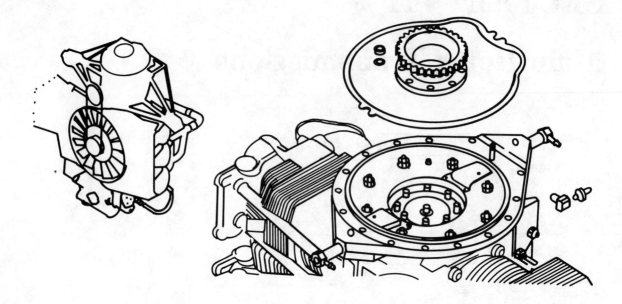

Fig. 7-2   Transmission to engine adapter plate and gear on the Bell 47.

and utilized shafting. Two different reciprocating powered helicopters manufactured today have engines mounted horizontally below the transmission driven by belts. Fig. 7-1 shows some typical engine-transmission relationships in reciprocating powered helicopters. The turbine powered helicopters often have the engines and transmissions in different locations.

In either case the power from the engine must be transferred to the transmission. This is done in a number of different ways depending upon the location of the engine and the transmission.

The first of these systems will be that of the Bell 47. To all outside appearances, the engine and transmission are joined into one unit. Actually, the engine is bolted to the transmission by an adapter plate, and a gear that meshes with the transmission is placed on the engine (Fig. 7-2). This is a very simple system and it requires a minimum of maintenance.

The Hiller 12 looks quite similar because of the mounting of the transmission and engine. However, the internal portion is quite different (Fig. 7-3). In this system, a flexible rubber and steel coupling is bolted to the engine drive flange. The purpose of this coupling is to absorb torsional vibrations imposed on the clutch and drive train. Mounted on the top of this unit is the clutch system which in turn has a small splined

shaft that drive the transmission. Such a device is not uncommon on transmissions because torsional loads are usually taken into consideration by the manufacturer.

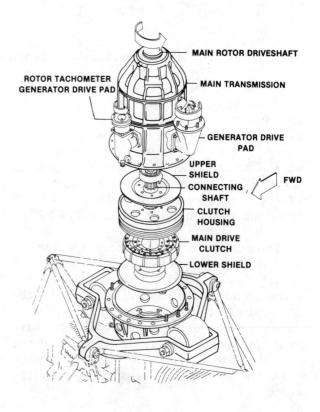

Fig. 7-3   Hiller 12E transmission installation.

262

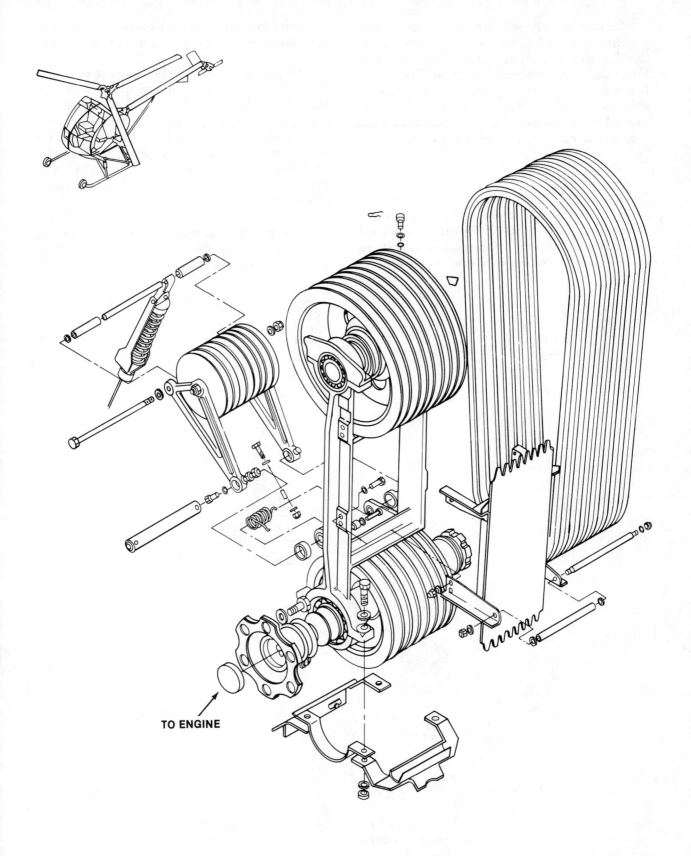

TO ENGINE

Fig. 7-4 Belt drive system used on the Hughes 300 engine to transmission.

On two other light helicopters a belt system is used to transmit the power from the engine to the transmission. One system utilizes eight V-belts placed on a pulley that adapts to the flange of the engine crankshaft. Another pulley is attached directly to the transmission (Fig. 7-4). The other system is quite similar in design but uses one single belt of a multiple V-type.

1. Driveshaft

Still another system on some reciprocating powered helicopters, the driveshaft is equipped with a rubber coupling to absorb torsional shock loads and is placed between the engine and the transmission. Items, such as a clutch assembly, are usually placed in line with this shaft (Fig. 7-5).

Most turbine helicopters make use of a *short shaft* system to deliver power to the transmission. These short shafts vary in design from helicopter to helicopter, but all have some way to correct for misalignment and for movement of the transmission. Some of these shafts operate with no lubrication while others require it. This lubrication is usually in the form of grease and is often hand-packed.

The first of these systems to be discussed will be that of the Bell 206, which is typical of those used on several Bell models.

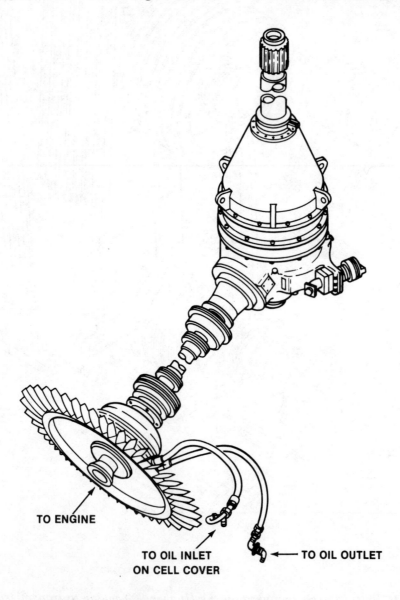

TO ENGINE

TO OIL INLET
ON CELL COVER

TO OIL OUTLET

Fig. 7-5 Sikorsky S-58 engine to transmission drive unit.

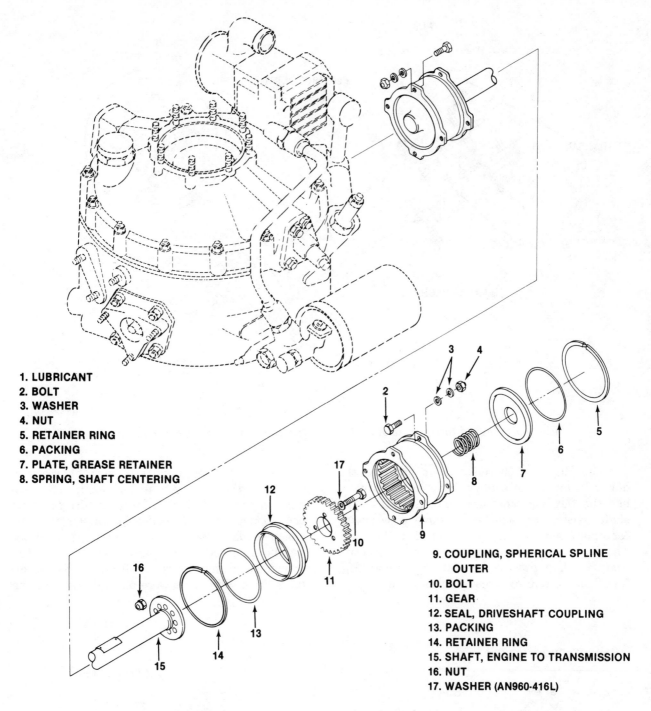

1. LUBRICANT
2. BOLT
3. WASHER
4. NUT
5. RETAINER RING
6. PACKING
7. PLATE, GREASE RETAINER
8. SPRING, SHAFT CENTERING

9. COUPLING, SPHERICAL SPLINE
   OUTER
10. BOLT
11. GEAR
12. SEAL, DRIVESHAFT COUPLING
13. PACKING
14. RETAINER RING
15. SHAFT, ENGINE TO TRANSMISSION
16. NUT
17. WASHER (AN960-416L)

Fig. 7-6   Engine to transmission shaft assembly used on the Bell 206.

The driveshaft consists of a shaft with two flexible couplings attached at each end. The shafts may be placed with either end to the transmission or engine. The shaft turns at a rather high rate of speed (6600 RPM). Therefore, balance is quite important. Two data plates are attached to the shaft 180° apart. The couplings are made up of interchangeable parts. Flexibility is obtained by a crowned tooth gear that rides on the splines of the outer coupling. The shaft and gear are centered by the use of springs on each end. The purpose of these flexible couplings is to correct for momentary misalignment of the shaft caused by movement of the transmission during flight. This type of shaft requires lubrication by hand-packing with grease (Fig. 7-6).

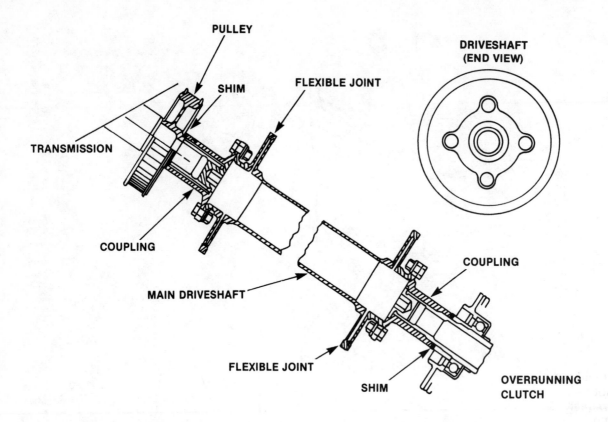

Fig. 7-7 Engine to transmission driveshaft assembly used on the Hughes 500.

The Hughes 500 series shaft provides the power in much the same manner as the others, but the flexible joints are quite different. The shaft itself is constructed in three pieces with each piece having a flange attached to the ends. The flanges are welded together by an electro-beam welding process for a flexible joint (Fig. 7-7). This system requires no lubrication.

One of the most unique driveshaft systems is that found on the AStar. An engine-to-transmission coupling in addition to the driveshaft is used to insure that the driveshaft only carries torsional loads. Like most transmissions, it is not rigidly mounted to the airframe. In fact, the transmission may move in all directions during flight. If a solid shaft were used, there would be

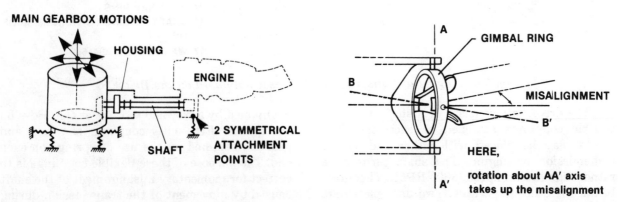

Fig. 7-8 Drive system used by the Aerospatiale AStar. Similar systems are used on other Aerospatiale products.

266

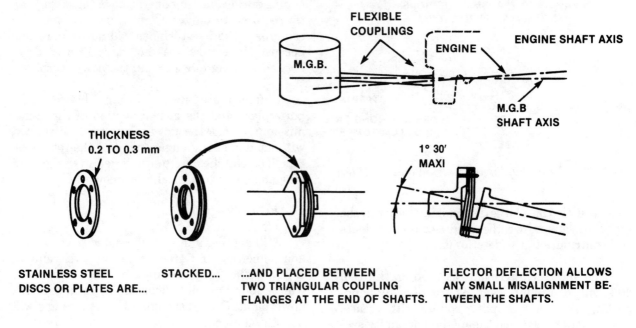

FLEXIBLE COUPLINGS

M.G.B.

ENGINE

ENGINE SHAFT AXIS

M.G.B SHAFT AXIS

THICKNESS 0.2 TO 0.3 mm

1° 30' MAXI

STAINLESS STEEL DISCS OR PLATES ARE...

STACKED...

...AND PLACED BETWEEN TWO TRIANGULAR COUPLING FLANGES AT THE END OF SHAFTS.

FLECTOR DEFLECTION ALLOWS ANY SMALL MISALIGNMENT BE-TWEEN THE SHAFTS.

Fig. 7-9 Drive coupling used on some Aerospatiale products.

stresses placed on the shaft by this movement. To correct for this movement, the engine and transmission are joined as a unit by a housing. To insure that adequate movement of the transmission may take place, a universal joint connection is provided at the transmission on the housing (Fig. 7-8). Inside this housing is the driveshaft. The driveshaft itself must also be provided with flexibility for the deflection caused by the transmission movements, but will not carry any tension or compression loads because of the housing. The flexibility is provided by a coupling made up of stacks of stainless steel discs bolted to the shafts to form a flexible joint (Fig. 7-9). The shaft requires no servicing with a lubricant. Because of the slow deterioration rate of the stainless steel discs, inspection is all that will be required.

B. Maintenance

The maintenance of these systems will be just as varied because of the various systems that are used.

In the system used on the Bell 47 with the gear installed on the engine crankshaft flange, the gear is lubricated from the oil system of the engine, eliminating the need of servicing with lubricant. Inspections are limited to major ones because the gear is not accessible except by removal of the transmission. The inspection of the gear will be quite similar to those for other gears and include the use of magnetic particle inspection and visual inspection of the teeth for wear. Since there is no repair criteria for the gear or its mating surfaces, they are only to be removed and replaced with normal procedures.

The Hiller 12, however, with its steel and rubber coupling, will require additional inspection. No lubrication is given in that area because a dry clutch is located there. Holes are provided, however, for viewing the rubber coupling and its condition. It must be examined for deterioration of the rubber, separation of the rubber from steel bonding, and deformation of the rubber. Any of these will require replacement of the coupling. This deformation is checked as shown in Fig. 7-10.

The helicopters with belt drive will require inspection of the belts and pulleys. The pulleys may require greasing for lubrication at specified periods. As for any other component requiring lubricant, the periods may be shortened due to adverse conditions. The belts must be inspected for cracks and deterioration. Belts are usually assigned an finite life. However, as with other materials of this type, deterioration is also dependent upon age as well as use. Lack of use can affect the life as greatly as high usage. The environ-

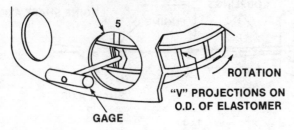

"PORT HOLES"
IN ENGINE TO TRANSMISSION HOUSING
1-7/16" DIA. APPROX. (TYP.)

5

ROTATION

"V" PROJECTIONS ON
O.D. OF ELASTOMER

GAGE

Fig. 7-10 Drive coupling inspection on the Hiller 12.

ment will also be a large determining factor in the life. Exposure to weather and cleaning solvents will contribute to the deterioration.

The shaft arrangement, as used on the Bell 206, will require lubricant. This is done by hand-packing the outer coupling splines with grease. The type of grease and the method are quite specific in the maintenance manual and must be followed to avoid failure of the unit. This unit is subject to visual inspections daily and particular attention must be given to the grease seals. Failure of these seals will result in the loss of the grease by centrifugal force, causing shaft failure. At the required lubrication times the unit is to be disassembled, cleaned, and inspected. Any of the coupling parts may be replaced as required, normally the result of wear.

Some shafts of this type also require alignment procedures between the engine and transmission. Once the initial alignment is made with the installation of the engine, it will not be necessary to repeat it until the major components are again changed. The procedure will require shimming of the engine mount to obtain correct alignment of the shaft. Details of this procedure will be covered in the engine section of the text.

The drives used to transmit power to the transmissions vary considerably in design. The drive must always be considered a critical item. Manufacturer's inspection and maintenance procedures must always be followed.

C. Clutch

The clutch is another unit closely associated with the drives. This unit, not found in all helicopters, is used in reciprocating engine and turbine powered helicopters that do not use a free

turbine. The clutch is necessary to unload the engine during starting operation because the inertia required to move the rotor system would be too great. The free turbines will not require this because the engine does not have a direct drive between the compressor and the power turbine.

Clutches are always located between the powerplant and the gear reduction of the transmission so that the powerplant may be started without immediate engagement of the rotor system. The clutches are quite varied in design and may engage automatically or manually.

D. Free Wheeling Unit

Still another unit closely related to the clutch and sometimes referred to as the over-running clutch is the free wheeling unit. This component will be found on all helicopters regardless of the powerplant. On multi-engine helicopters one will be located on each engine.

The purpose of this free wheeling unit will allow the engine to drive the transmission and prevent the rotor from driving the engine. Without this unit the engine would be driven by the rotor any time an autorotation is attempted. In addition, any seizure of the engine would prevent the possibility of autorotation. For this reason the helicopter, equipped with two engines, must have a free wheeling unit on each engine output.

Although practically all helicopters use the same type of unit, their location and size vary from one helicopter to another. The operation of the units will always be automatic.

E. Automatic Clutches

The automatic clutch systems vary somewhat in design. The Bell 47 clutch is a centrifugal clutch using a set of shoes and a drum (Fig. 7-11). The set of shoes is splined to the drive gear fastened to the powerplant. As the engine increases in speed, the shoes move outward by centrifugal force making contact with the drum which drives the transmission. As the centrifugal force becomes great enough, the drum, through the transmission, turns the rotor. This engagement should be quite smooth with the rotor RPM lagging slightly behind the engine until the two attain the same speed. At that time the engine and rotor speed remain constant with the shoes riding with the drum. This process should take

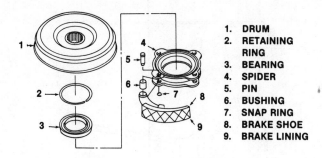

1.	DRUM
2.	RETAINING RING
3.	BEARING
4.	SPIDER
5.	PIN
6.	BUSHING
7.	SNAP RING
8.	BRAKE SHOE
9.	BRAKE LINING

Fig. 7-11   Clutch assembly used on the Bell 47.

place in a few seconds. If a longer period of time is required, the clutch is slipping.

Another centrifugal type clutch is used on the Hiller 12 (Fig. 7-12). This type of clutch is often referred to as a mercury clutch because mercury is used for the weight of the centrifugal force. The drive clutch assembly is the clutch housing or drum that is attached to the transmission drive train. The clutch assembly is surrounded by segments of shoe that will make contact with the drum when the engine is running at 500 RPM with positive engagement at approximately

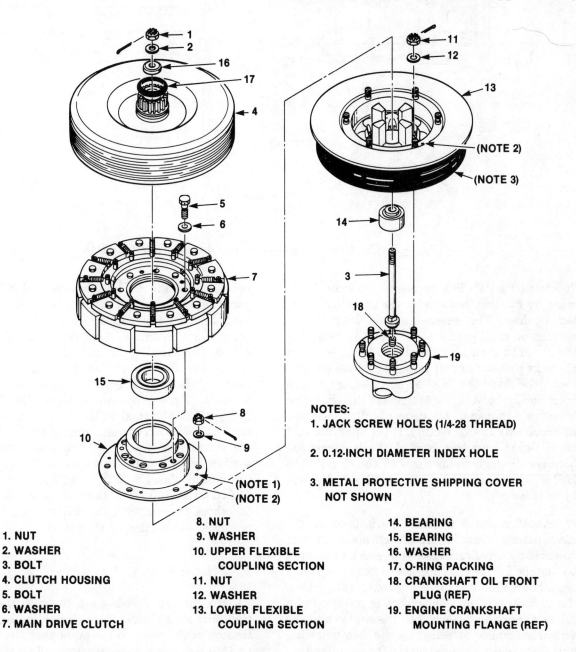

NOTES:
1. JACK SCREW HOLES (1/4-28 THREAD)

2. 0.12-INCH DIAMETER INDEX HOLE

3. METAL PROTECTIVE SHIPPING COVER NOT SHOWN

1.	NUT
2.	WASHER
3.	BOLT
4.	CLUTCH HOUSING
5.	BOLT
6.	WASHER
7.	MAIN DRIVE CLUTCH
8.	NUT
9.	WASHER
10.	UPPER FLEXIBLE COUPLING SECTION
11.	NUT
12.	WASHER
13.	LOWER FLEXIBLE COUPLING SECTION
14.	BEARING
15.	BEARING
16.	WASHER
17.	O-RING PACKING
18.	CRANKSHAFT OIL FRONT PLUG (REF)
19.	ENGINE CRANKSHAFT MOUNTING FLANGE (REF)

Fig. 7-12   Mercury clutch used on the Hiller 12.

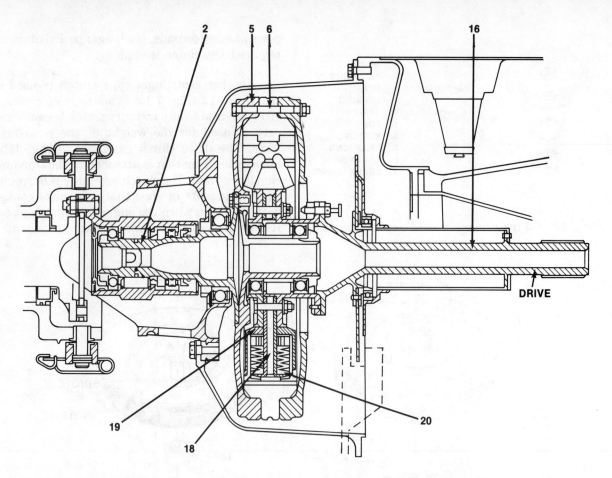

Fig. 7-13   Clutch system used on the Aerospatiale Gazelle.

700 to 900 RPM. The segments are moved outward by mercury held under the shoes by a rubber bladder. The shoes are held in place by springs on each segment and assist in returning the shoes to their static position. Because of the slippage that does occur prior to positive engagement, the drum is cooled by air passing through holes in the base of the transmission. The same holes used to inspect the drive coupling mentioned previously in this section. It is important that no oil leaks into this area of the transmission because slippage will occur with the clutch. The Bell 47 clutch, however, runs in oil and depends upon it for cooling.

Another clutch of this type is used on the Aerospatiale Gazelle. This helicopter is not powered by a free turbine engine, so a clutch must be installed. This clutch is also a centrifugal dry type, but is mounted in the horizontal rather than the vertical position. The clutch is made up of a driving assembly attached to the engine and the driven assembly attached to the free wheeling unit (Fig. 7-13). Mounted on the forward flange is the driving portion made up of a support ring (19)

and ten lined shoes. The shoes are held in the support ring by tie rods (18). These same tie rods are used to keep the support assembly concentric with the driveshaft (16). A stack of spring washers is placed under each shoe to set the tension of the shoe for the correct engagement and return of the shoe. The driven assembly is a drum (6) held in place by two flanges. The forward flange (5) is attached to the free wheeling shaft (2). The operation is quite similar to those of the other clutches. Upon starting, the driving assembly immediately starts to rotate. However, the clutch shoes will not move outward until 29,000 to 33,300 RPM is reached. At that time the shoes engage with the driven assembly and power is transmitted to the rotor.

F. Belt Tighteners

Helicopters utilizing a belt drive use a belt tightener as a clutch. This simply increases the tension of the belts to the point that the pulleys on the engine and transmission will rotate. With this type of system the clutch must be engaged by the pilot rather than automatically. In one system the clutch is manually engaged by a lever. The other system utilizes a solenoid to move the belt tightener into position. Although these systems are very simple mechanically, they require some skill of the pilot to engage and disengage at the proper time for a smooth engagement and to avoid an overspeed with disengagement. Since the load is being removed by disengagement, the engine must be brought to low power setting before it is attempted. With the pilot operated clutch mechanism, the operator's manual must be closely followed.

G. Hydromechanical Clutch

Another type of clutch that has been used on helicopters is the hydromechanical clutch. This particular unit also incorporates a fan for cooling the engine and a free wheeling unit. The hydromechanical clutch assembly makes it possible to start the engine and operate at any RPM without engaging the rotor. Because of the fluid coupling,

the engagement is always smooth and provides a positive lock of the engine to the rotor. Additional provisions are made for free wheeling and disengagement for stopping the engine.

The fan assembly that is attached to the clutch assembly provides cooling air for the engine. It acts as a flywheel for the engine when the clutch is not engaged and forces ram air in the carburetor. The lower end of the clutch assembly is bolted to a hub that is splined to the engine and the upper end is bolted to a rubber coupling on the main driveshaft.

The main components of the clutch are the fluid coupling consisting of a vaned driving disc attached to the engine shaft and a vaned driven disc attached to the main driveshaft. The mechanical coupling is composed of a roller and cam type free wheeling unit controlled by a fly ball governor, actuator and blocker plate. The clutch pump utilizes engine oil for the fluid coupling and associated hoses.

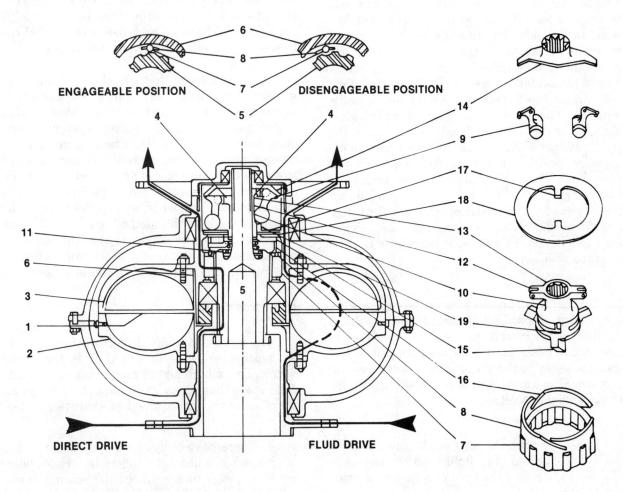

Fig. 7-14 Hydromechanical clutch and free wheeling unit used on the S-58.

271

Using Fig. 7-14, the principles of operation are as follows: the fluid coupling (1) consists of a driving member (2) and a driven member (3). The torque capacity of this coupling is in a row and can accelerate the rotor in low pitch at approximately 130% of idle speed. A free wheeling unit (4) is connected in parallel with the fluid coupling. A driving cam member (5) is integrally connected with the driving member of the fluid coupling (2). The driven housing (6) is integrally connected with the driven member of the fluid coupling (3). The intermate rollers (7) are housed in the roller retainer (8). The angular position of the roller retainer and the rollers in relation to the cam, as shown in both the engaged and disengaged positions, is determined by the interaction of the two systems.

This interaction is as follows: the flyball governor flyweights (9) are restrained against the inboard stop (10) by the action of the spring (11) until a speed of 1250 RPM is reached. After this speed is reached and as speed is increased, the weights will move out until the free wheeling unit is engageable. If the speed is decreased the weights will move inward under spring force and return it to the disengaged position. When the flyweights are permitted to move, the flyweight (9) and the actuator sleeve (12) move on the spline (13) due to the flyweight force on the actuator stop (14). The fingers (15) engage with the helical slots (16) in the roller retainer (8). This rotates the roller retainer which moves the rollers into an engageable position as the actuator sleeve moves downward. The blocker plate (18) has tangs (17) extending into the "L" shaped slot (19) of the actuator sleeve. In all modes of operation the tangs remain in the slots. This prevents the blocker from moving on the splines. It remains in the disengaged position.

On the other hand, as soon as the engine is decelerated to a speed below that of the driveshaft, the drag on the blocker is reversed and the tang is moved into position with the actuator slot. If the speed is below 1250 RPM, the force will move the actuator sleeve and butt the free wheeling unit into the engaged position.

When starting the engine, the rotor will remain disconnected until fluid from the engine is allowed to flow into the fluid coupling because of the following:

a. The free wheeling unit is held out of engagement at speed below 1250 RPM because of the spring action against the flyweights.

b. The free wheeling unit is held out of engagement at speeds above 1250 RPM whenever engine RPM exceeds rotor RPM because the speed differential causes drag on the blocker plate preventing motion of the actuator sleeve.

The clutch is engaged by filling the coupling with oil. The fluid passing through the coupling makes a smooth engagement of the rotor. When rotor speed is attained, the mechanical coupling through the free wheeling unit is accomplished by decelerating the engine. At this point, the torque on the blocker plate reverses allowing the free wheeling unit to engage. By advancing the throttle again, the mechanical coupling is engaged through the free wheeling unit. After engagement the oil from the fluid coupling returns to the engine and the fluid coupling remains dry. From this point on the helicopter may be flown with the free wheeling unit operating in a normal mode. If the engine is throttled back below 1250 RPM the free wheeling unit will become disengaged.

It is fortunate that all clutches and free wheeling units are not as complex. The free wheeling unit is necessary on helicopters, even though a clutch is installed in the drive system. A few older helicopters have free wheeling units as an integral part of the transmission. Others have the free wheeling unit located at the end of the main drive from the engine to the transmission. The location of the free wheeling unit depends on the manufacturer and the method used to drive the tail rotor. It is quite necessary that the tail rotor be driven by the main rotor during autorotation. If it is not, directional control would be lost.

H. Sprag Clutch

The most commonly used free wheeling unit on helicopters made in the U.S. is the sprag clutch. This clutch allows movement in only one direction by having an inner and outer race which are often at the end of the driveshaft (Fig. 7-15).

The sprag assembly is made up of a number of sprags resembling the rollers in a roller bearing. The sprags, unlike the circular bearings, have a figure 8 shape. The vertical height of each of

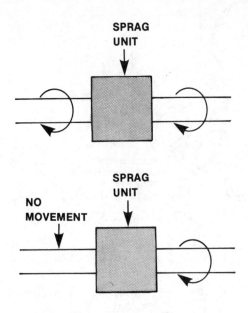

Fig. 7-15 Sprag unit operation.

these sprags is slightly greater than the gap between the ID of the outer race and the OD of the inner race. They are held in position by a double cage assembly that is spring loaded into the engaged position. This engaged position places the sprags against both races at a slight angle. Rotation from the engine on the outer race jams the sprags between the outer and inner races and this interference fit drives the inner race which is attached to the driveshaft. If the driveshaft attempts to drive the engine, the sprags will be relieved and the driveshaft will rotate without the engine. The same would happen if the engine stopped. A typical sprag clutch is seen in Fig. 7-16.

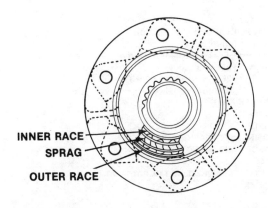

Fig. 7-16 Typical sprag unit.

It may be noticed that sprags may be designed to drive in either direction or on the inner or outer race. The actual application of these units varies considerably from one installation to the next, but the operation is the same.

Both the Bell 47 and the Hiller have the free wheeling unit as an integral part of the transmission so those systems will be discussed with the gear system.

The belt-driven helicopters, however, utilize the sprag system in the upper pulley of the belt drive.

The Bell 206 has a sprag system installed at the engine output end (Fig. 7-17). This system operates as follows: a shaft from the power turbine drives the power takeoff gear shaft through the engine reduction gearbox. The free wheeling unit is mounted on the engine gearbox and its shaft is splined directly to the power takeoff of the gear shaft. The engine power is transmitted to the outer race of the free wheeling unit, then through the sprags to the inner race which is attached to the transmission driveshaft. The forward short shaft of the tail rotor drive system connects through a flexible coupling to a splined adapter on the aft end of the free wheeling shaft that passes through the engine gear reduction box. During autorotation the main rotor drives the power input shaft. At this time, the free wheeling unit provides a disconnect from the engine but continues to drive the tail rotor and transmission accessories such as the hydraulic pump, which is necessary for boosted controls.

It might also be noted that at times, such as during autorotation, the sprags make minimal contact between the inner and outer races. The sprag clutch must be lubricated on the Bell 206 for this reason. This lubrication is furnished from the transmission system which is still in operation during autorotation.

The Hughes 500 sprag unit operates in a similar manner but is different in installation. The sprag clutch is mounted on the front of the engine between the forward power takeoff and the main driveshaft. The clutch assembly is attached to the engine output pad by bolts. No gasket is placed between the two surfaces, but a drain hole is provided in the housing to allow any seal leakage to drain overboard. The clutch may be repaired by the removal of the clutch sub-

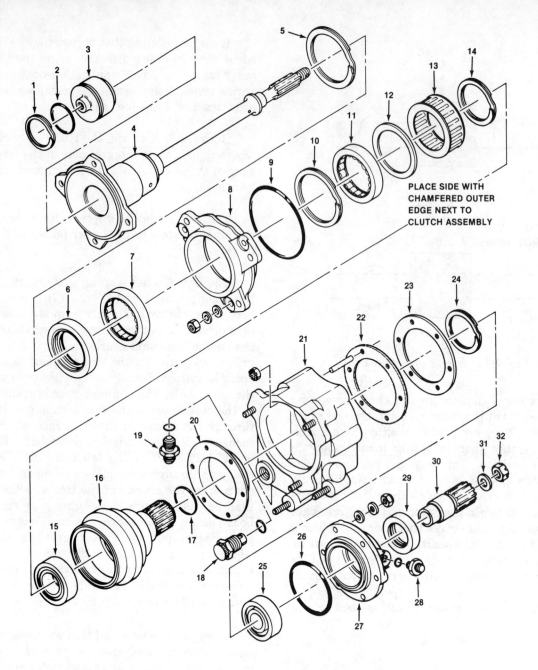

PLACE SIDE WITH
CHAMFERED OUTER
EDGE NEXT TO
CLUTCH ASSEMBLY

1. RETAINER RING
2. O-RING
3. VALVE HOUSING
4. SHAFT, FREE WHEELING UNIT INNER RACE
5. RETAINER RING
6. SEAL
7. BEARING, ROLLER
8. CAP, FORWARD BEARING AND SEAL
9. O-RING
10. RETAINER RING
11. BEARING ROLLER
12. PLATE, OUTER RACE GUIDE
13. CLUTCH ASSEMBLY, ONE WAY
14. RETAINER RING
15. BEARING, BALL
16. SHAFT, FREE WHEELING UNIT OUTER RACE

17. O-RING
18. DRAIN PLUG AND CHIP DETECTOR
19. UNION AND O-RING
20. PILOT RING, FREE WHEELING HOUSING
21. HOUSING, FREE WHEELING
22. GASKET, FREE WHEELING HOUSING
23. SHIM, AFT BEARING HOUSING
24. RETAINER RING
25. BEARING
26. O-RING
27. HOUSING, AFT BEARING
28. REDUCER AND O-RING
29. SEAL
30. ADAPTER, FREE WHEELING TAIL ROTOR DRIVE
31. WASHER
32. NUT

Fig. 7-17A   Sprag unit installation as used on the Bell 206.

274

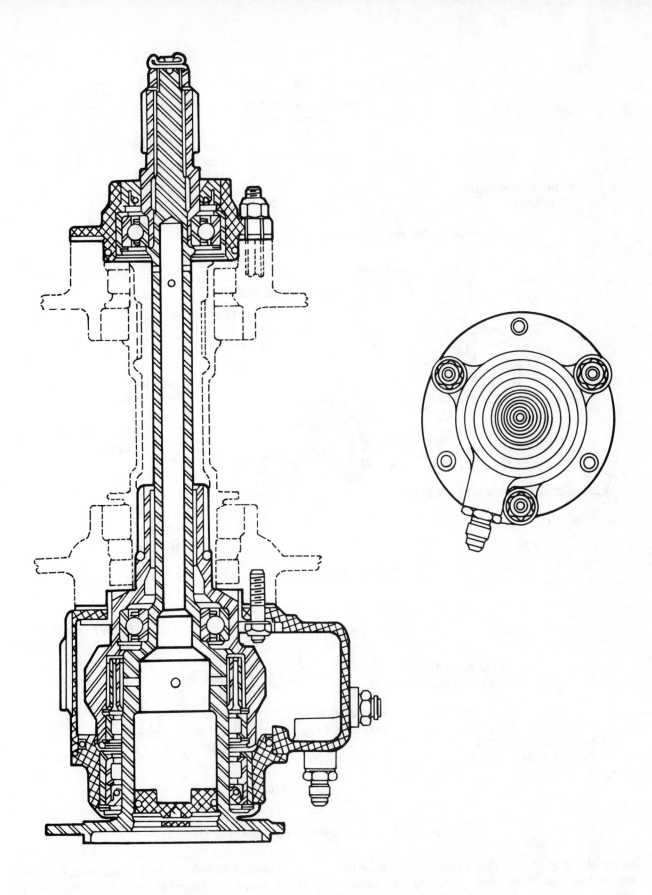

Fig. 7-17B Cross-sectional view of the Bell 206 sprag unit.

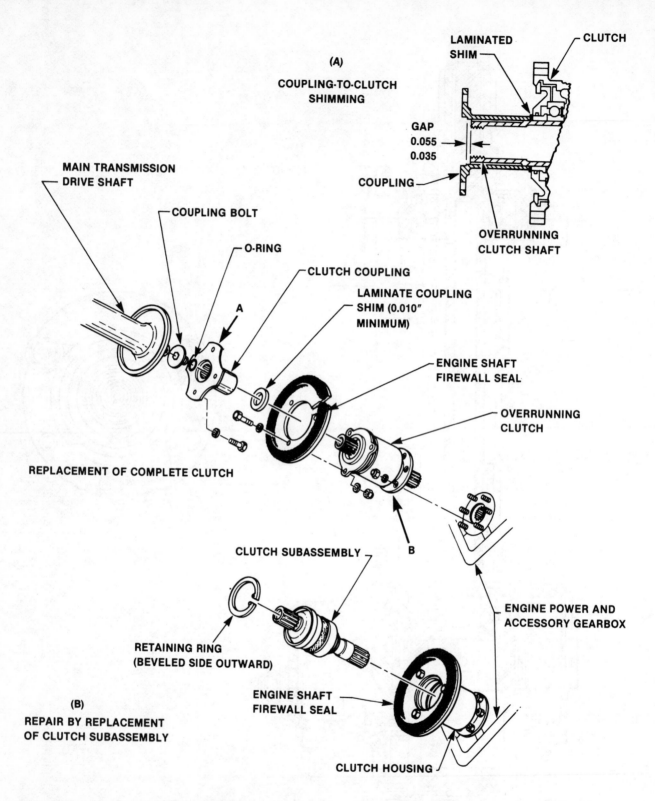

(A)

COUPLING-TO-CLUTCH SHIMMING

LAMINATED SHIM

CLUTCH

GAP 0.055 0.035

COUPLING

OVERRUNNING CLUTCH SHAFT

MAIN TRANSMISSION DRIVE SHAFT

COUPLING BOLT

O-RING

CLUTCH COUPLING

LAMINATE COUPLING SHIM (0.010" MINIMUM)

ENGINE SHAFT FIREWALL SEAL

OVERRUNNING CLUTCH

A

B

REPLACEMENT OF COMPLETE CLUTCH

CLUTCH SUBASSEMBLY

ENGINE POWER AND ACCESSORY GEARBOX

RETAINING RING (BEVELED SIDE OUTWARD)

ENGINE SHAFT FIREWALL SEAL

(B)

REPAIR BY REPLACEMENT OF CLUTCH SUBASSEMBLY

CLUTCH HOUSING

Fig. 7-18   Sprag unit installation on the Hughes 500.

assembly (Fig. 7-18). This makes it possible to repair the clutch without removing the whole unit.

The unit has shafts projecting from each end of the housing. One of these is the inner race of the sprag unit and the other is the outer race of

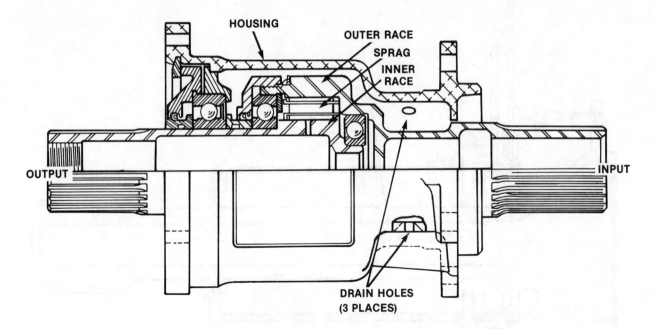

Fig. 7-19 Sprag unit with self-contained oil system on a Hughes 500.

the sprag. The outer race is the engine side and the inner race is the transmission side. The inner and outer races are separated by two ball bearings and the sprag unit. This bearing arrangement is locked by a large nut and lock washer (Fig. 7-19).

The sprag assembly and bearings are lubricated quite differently from those of the Bell 206. The housing bearing on the output side of the sprag unit is in constant rotation. This bearing is hand-packed with grease. The two bearings and

sprag unit, however, operate in oil which is kept within the unit. Since no supply of outside oil is available, the level must be checked regularly and the unit must be inspected for leakage. Sprag units cannot operate dry.

I. Roller Unit

Another type of free wheeling unit is shown in Fig. 7-20. This particular unit is used on the Aerospatiale Gazelle.

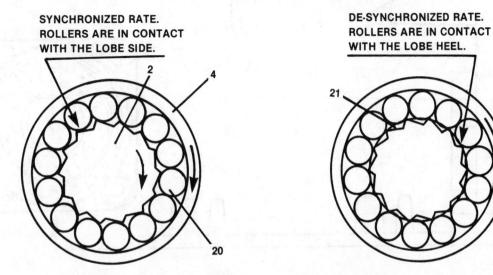

Fig. 7-20 Roller free wheeling used on the Aerospatiale Gazelle.

277

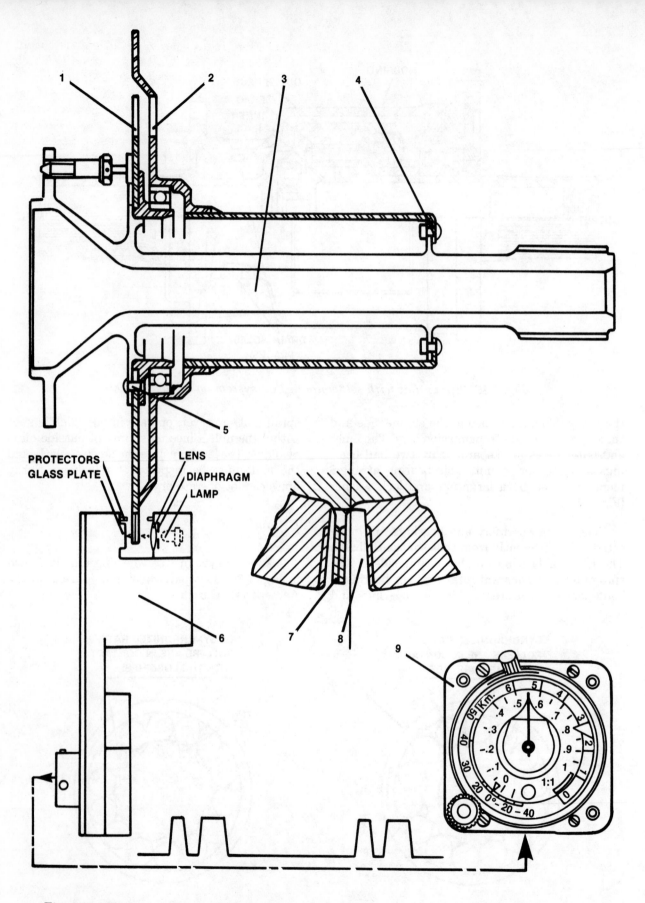

Fig. 7-21   *Electronic torquemeter system used on the Aerospatiale Gazelle driveshaft.*

278

The operation of this unit is quite similar to that of the sprag unit, but rollers are used rather than sprags. The rollers are trapped between a lobed shaft and the free wheeling head. These rollers are held in contact with the free wheeling head by a spring. When rotation of the lobe shaft occurs from the engine, the rollers make contact with the lobe side and wedge the rollers to the driver and the driven portions, forming a solid unit. When the rotor goes to autorotation, the rollers change position and make contact with the lobe heel. In this position the lobed shaft may remain still with the outer free wheeling head in rotation. This unit is sealed with oil in manufacture.

J. Torquemeter

Another item that may be included in the engine to transmission drive system is a torquemeter. The torquemeter used on turbine powered helicopters is usually located within the turbine. This system measures the power output of the engine. The torquemeter may be a limiting factor for the transmission on some helicopters because some engines are capable of producing more power than the transmission can absorb. This may be due to ambient conditions or the engine may be capable of these power outputs in almost any condition.

Additional information about torque and torquemeters will be given in the engine portion of this text.

One helicopter utilizing such a system is the Aerospatiale Gazelle. The torquemeter is located between the engine and transmission, on the engine side of the shaft, prior to the clutch and free wheeling unit. This unit is quite unique in design because it uses an optical-electronic detection device rather than the hydromechanical unit (Fig. 7-21). It measures the angular deviation between two discs (1) and (2). The two discs are attached to the ends of (4) and (5) the shaft that drives the transmission from the engine. A torque sensor (6) surrounds the two discs. This sensor emits a light beam that passes through a window (8) in the one disc. This beam is alternately cut by a tooth in the other disc. The beam is then picked up and transformed into an electronic signal which in turn is given to the indicator which reads in percent of torque. In actuality this measurement is the amount of twist in the shaft. As can be noted in the view, both discs are attached to the shaft, but one disc is attached near the engine output, while the other disc is attached near the clutch. The shaft between these two discs is built to deflect or twist as power is applied. Although both discs rotate with the shaft, the view through the three windows in relation to the three teeth changes as power is applied and the shaft twists (Fig. 7-22). The transmitter senses this view change and sends the signal to the indicator.

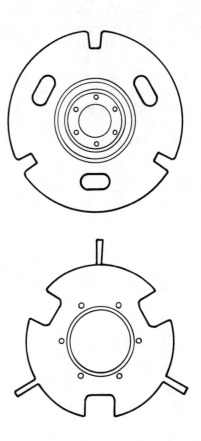

Fig. 7-22 Disc used in the Aerospatiale Gazelle torquemeter.

The indicator is a computer indicator and gives a readout in percent of torque from −5% to 110% on the face of the instrument. A control knob is placed on the instrument, the pilot presets the given torque value in relationship to the outside air temperature. This moves a red index marker for the maximum torque. The indicator also has a press-to-test button to check the servo mechanism and a warning light for overtorque conditions.

K. Rotor Brake

Another component that may be located between the engine and transmission is the rotor brake. This component is used to stop the rotor on shutdown after the engine has ceased to power the rotor. Because of the inertia of the main rotor it takes a few minutes for the rotor to come to a complete stop. When loading passengers or fueling operations, a safety hazard exists during rotor coastdown. Wind gusts will add to the hazard because the blades can suddenly dip to within four feet of the ground. For this reason, rotor brakes are often installed on helicopters, either as standard or optional equipment. Their use, however, is usually limited. Most operators confine their use to necessity rather than convenience because of the wear factors to the unit. It must be remembered that the rotor has a very high inertia requiring a great amount of braking force. For this reason the brake is never applied until the rotor has slowed down considerably on its own.

Usually these brakes are a disc type, attached to the input to the transmission. They may be either hydraulic or manually operated. Fig. 7-23 has a view of the rotor brake system used on some Bell 206 models. This system is hydraulically operated with a master cylinder installed on the cabin roof. The master cylinder is equipped with a handle which the pilot pulls to apply brake pressure. The brake unit itself is a single disc unit with a dual brake pad system similar to what might be found on many general aviation aircraft for wheel brakes. The disc attaches to the short shaft between the transmission and the engine so the free wheeling unit does not affect the braking action. This system with its master cylinder will require servicing with fluid because it does not utilize the hydraulic system of the aircraft.

A manually operated rotor brake is used on the Aerospatiale AStar 350 (Fig. 7-24). This sytem consists of a fixed housing secured to the transmission (2) and a movable housing (4) that slides into the fixed housing and supports the brake linings. The movement of this housing is in

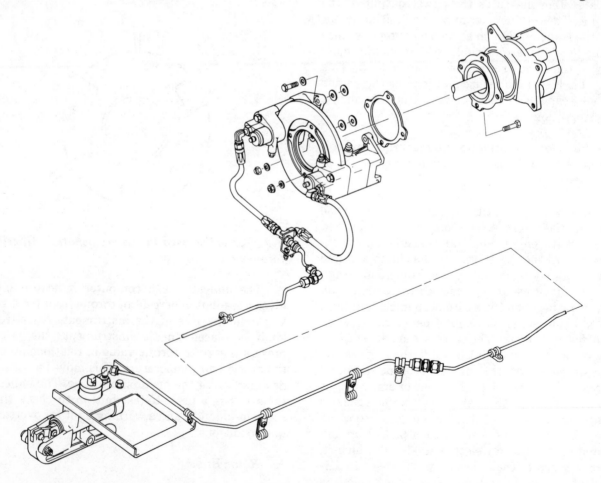

Fig. 7-23 Typical rotor brake installation.

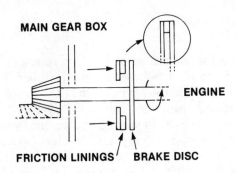

MAIN GEAR BOX

ENGINE

FRICTION LININGS   BRAKE DISC

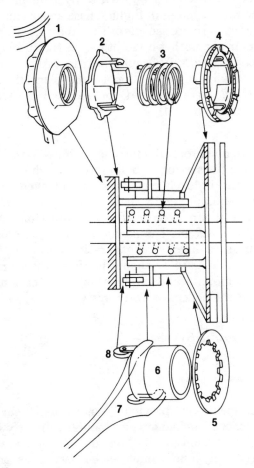

Fig. 7-24 Mechanical rotor brake system.

the fore and aft direction only. Between the fixed housing and the movable housing is a spring (3) to keep the movable housing off the disc when the brake is not applied. The brake itself is actuated by a control fork (7). The fork slides over the fixed housing and through a sleeve (8), and a diaphragm (5) moves the movable housing against the disc attached to the input of the transmission.

L. Maintenance

The maintenance practices applied to these components located between the engine and

transmission are as varied as the components themselves. Maintenance procedures must be performed in accordance with the manufacturer's recommendations. The operation of the clutch and free wheeling unit must be checked in each preflight run-up as both items are critical to the safety of flight.

The clutch engagement should be smooth and positive. To check the clutch engagement, the tachometer is used. Most helicopters make use of a dual type instrument. One needle indicates rotor RPM and the other indicates engine RPM. In normal operation the two needles stay superimposed or *married*. During starting or until the clutch is engaged, the engine RPM will be ahead of the rotor. After actual engagement takes place the rotor RPM should increase rapidly until the two needles are superimposed. The amount of time required for this to happen is the engagement time. Since the clutch is actually slipping during this period, it is critical. Some helicopters are placarded to warn the pilot of the maximum engagement time. If this time is longer or the two needles do not *marry*, the clutch is slipping. No flight should be attempted under these conditions.

The free wheeling unit is as critical to flight as the clutch. In the situation of engine failure or seizure, it is the free wheeling unit that will allow the helicopter to autorotate. It too is checked with the use of the tachometer during preflight run-up. This is done by suddenly reducing the RPM of the engine while the two needles are superimposed. At that time the two needles should split, with the rotor RPM remaining at its present position and the engine RPM rapidly decreasing. If this does not happen, the free wheeling unit is inoperative and the process should be discontinued. This would mean that the unit is frozen and autorotation is impossible. Slippage could occur between the engine and transmission giving the same indication as a slipping clutch.

If the clutch units are used properly and overhaul procedures are followed, they will normally last from major inspection to major inspection or recommended overhaul.

The centrifugal clutch used on the Bell 47 may require new shoe linings. The drum may have to be turned to return its surface to a serviceable condition because it is subject to wear from the shoe contact and warpage from frictional heat. The shoe linings and drums are often replaced by specialty shops. If shoes or drums are to be replaced, the contact area of the two is critical and must be checked to insure that the contact area of the shoe covers the area of the drum. Quite often they must be lapped in place with sandpaper and checked with Prussian Blue.

The Hiller 12 makes use of a mercury centrifugal clutch. This type of clutch has replaceable linings and a drum, both of which are susceptible to the same wear factors of Bell 47. In addition, the mercury level is quite important because it is the weight of this mercury coupled with centrifugal force that engages the clutch. Leakage of the mercury is very corrosive to metal. The loss of mercury will be noticed by clutch slippage.

The sprag unit, which is the most widely used free wheeling unit, requires servicing if it contains its own oil supply. The units must be checked for the quantity oil leakage periodically. The Hughes 500 unit is checked with a ruler. This can be done only after the removal of the driveshaft as shown in Fig. 7-25.

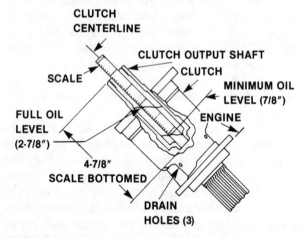

Fig. 7-25 Sprag unit servicing on the Hughes 500.

The units are subject to overhaul unless the manufacturer provides exchange units. Some units may be disassembled for inspection, such as the unit on the Bell 206. Any components in this unit not meeting inspection criteria will be replaced. A wear factor is always created between the sprags, the driver, and driven races of these units. Replacement of parts in these areas is not uncommon.

M. Vibrations

The transmissions of helicopters are usually mounted to the fuselage on semi-flexible mounts. This helps dampen vibration that would be transmitted from the main rotor system to the fuselage. With the balancing equipment available for rotor systems, very low levels of dynamic vibration may be reached. However, the levels may be increased and aggravated by loads placed on the rotor system in flight. These levels can be annoying to the passengers. They may start harmonic or sympathetic vibrations in the fuselage and components. This may lead to fatigue and wear factors that would not take place if the vibrations were isolated, or reduced by the transmission mounting.

Two main rotor dampening systems were discussed in the section on main rotors which reduce the vibration levels considerably, but even helicopters equipped with these systems also have isolation mountings on the transmission. Although the mount has some flexibility, it must also possess high strength ratios because the helicopter is actually suspended from the transmission mounts and is absorbing the torsional loads of the helicopter rotor system.

N. Mounting Systems

1. Bell 47

As mentioned previously, some of the early light helicopters had engines mounted directly to the transmission forming one unit. This system required only one mount which served as the engine and transmission mount. The Bell 47 mount system consists of an adapter plate, a basket assembly, rubber lord mounts, and a mount system on the bottom of the engine (Fig. 7-26). This mount is usually referred to as an engine mount, but it essentially carries both the engine and transmission as a unit. The adapter plate is bolted to the engine and suspended by two trunnion pins. This gives the engine and transmission some flexibility from side to side. The trunnions pass through the tubular steel mount, often referred to as the basket, which is attached to the center section of the helicopter through two rubber lord mounts. The mounts allow some flexibility in the fore and aft direction and a slight amount of movement for torque.

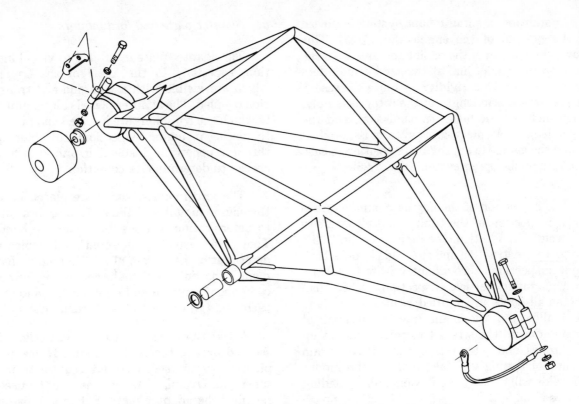

Fig. 7-26   Engine-transmission mount used on the Bell 47.

1. ENGINE SUMP(REF)
2. FITTING
3. ROD (2)
4. RH MOUNT ASSEMBLY
5. AFT MOUNT ASSEMBLY
6. LORD MOUNT
7. LARGE WASHER
8. BOLT (4)

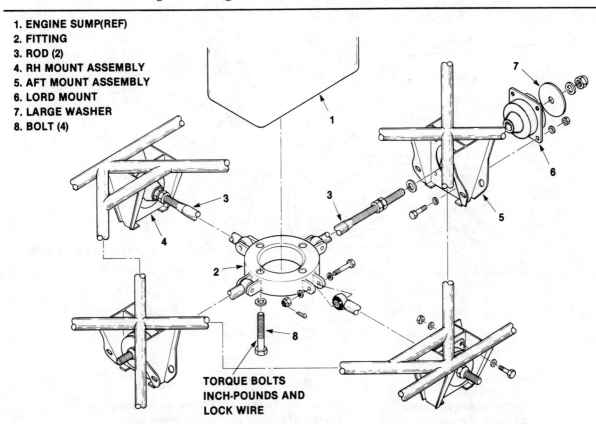

TORQUE BOLTS
INCH-POUNDS AND
LOCK WIRE

Fig. 7-27   Sprag mount system used on the Bell 47.

In addition, a sprag mount system is placed on the bottom of the engine (Fig. 7-27). This allows the bottom of the engine to move with the trunnion movement and at the same time offers some rigidity. This rigidity is quite necessary because of the arm length of the rotor assembly, which includes the mast, transmission, and the engine length. A safety cable system is installed to hold the engine in approximate position in case of failure of the sprag system (Fig. 7-28).

The inspection of the engine mount requires visual inspection of the tubing and all intersection welds. In addition, the item has a finite life due to its construction and the loads imposed. At major inspections throughout its life it will require magnetic particle inspection. Other than very small dents in specified locations, no damage is allowed in the mount, nor is the repair of damage due to the stress concentrations set up by patches and intersection repairs. A certain amount of flexing will take place in the mount and welds will destroy the flexing ability, leading to stress build-up.

a. Adapter plate and lord mounts

The adapter plate is subject to visual inspection, especially in the areas of the trunnions which are visible with the engine and transmission coupled. The adapter plate is aluminum alloy in which the trunnions are inserted and pinned into place. At major inspections this plate goes through penetrant inspection and dimensional checks to determine its condition.

The lord mounts, which are placed between the engine mount and the helicopter, are subject to deterioration of the rubber and the bonding. They are visually inspected and replaced if deterioration has taken place. No repairs may be made. The only real maintenance performed is component removal and replacement, and the attachments to the engine and transmission.

When the adapter plate is reinstalled, it is secured first to the engine mount. If new pinion pins are to be used, they are reamed to fit the taper pin. Oversized taper pins may be used by reaming the adapter plate. Shims are also used

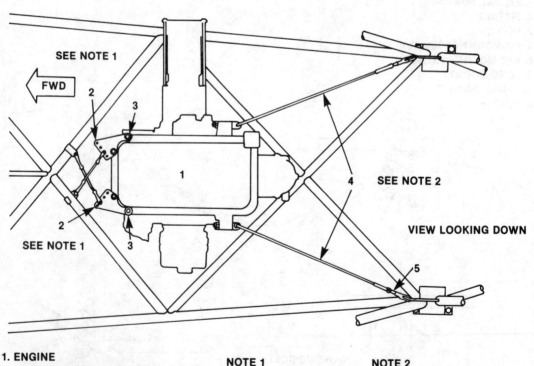

1. ENGINE
2. FORWARD SAFETY CABLES
3. HEADS OF BOLTS DOWN
4. AFT SAFETY CABLES
5. TURNBUCKLES

NOTE 1
Provide to slack in length of cable.

NOTE 2
Tighten cables snug, then loosen clevis turns.

Fig. 7-28 Safety cable system used on the Bell 47.

between the adapter plate and mount to obtain proper clearance. The installation of the adapter plate requires the correct height be placed on the engine studs before installation. After this height is set, a metal gasket is placed between the engine and the adapter plates and the studs are torqued and safetied.

To remove the lord mounts, simply unbolt the clamp. The installation is much the same with special attention given to the gap in the clamp. This gap determines the number of retainers to be used in holding the lord mount (Fig. 7-29).

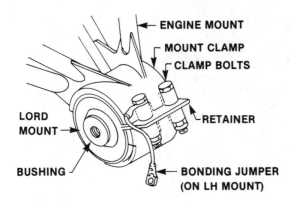

Fig. 7-29 *Isolation mount used on the Bell 47.*

b. *Sprag mounts*

The sprag mount system is subject to visual inspection. The mounts, like those used in the engine mount, should be checked for rubber cracks and loose bonding of the rubber. The rod ends are subject to wear. The components, other than lord mounts, are appropriately checked by magnetic particle and penetrant inspections at all major inspections.

In the view of the sprag mount the rod ends of the mount are threaded, making them adjustable. The movement of these rods will position the mast of the helicopter. This particular mast is positioned to the vertical position. This is done by leveling the helicopter and the mast using the sprag mounts. If a rod end or rods are changed, the mast alignment must be checked. Likewise, the changing of the lord mount could affect the mast alignment. Incorrect alignment can affect the flight characteristics of the helicopter. Such misalignment has also been known to cause vibration problems in the helicopter, especially when tipped slightly aft where the transmission coupling makes contact with the tail rotor shaft.

It must also be remembered that although the Bell 47's mast is vertical, some masts using a sprag system may be tilted to the side, as it was mentioned in the aerodynamics section of this text. Always consult the maintenance manual before attempting any adjustments of the mast alignment (Fig. 7-30).

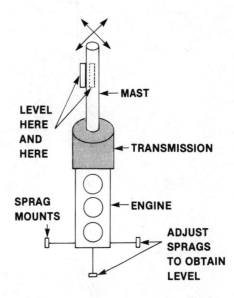

Fig. 7-30 *Mast alignment system used on vertical installations.*

c. *Safety cables*

The safety cables are visually inspected for condition and are subject to the same conditions as a control cable. The cables are adjustable and should be set in accordance with the manufacturer's recommendations. The cables will be loose in all normal conditions so that all normal movements may take place. A cable set improperly will cause abnormal vibrations during certain maneuvers, such as turns, etc. This is because the normal movement will be restricted by the cables.

2. *Bell 206*

An entirely different system is used on the Bell 206. The 206, unlike the 47, has the engine located aft of the transmission with the power passing through a short shaft to the transmission. The transmission is mounted to the fuselage by two pylon mount links attaching at two points to the cabin roof. The apex of the "A" frame link

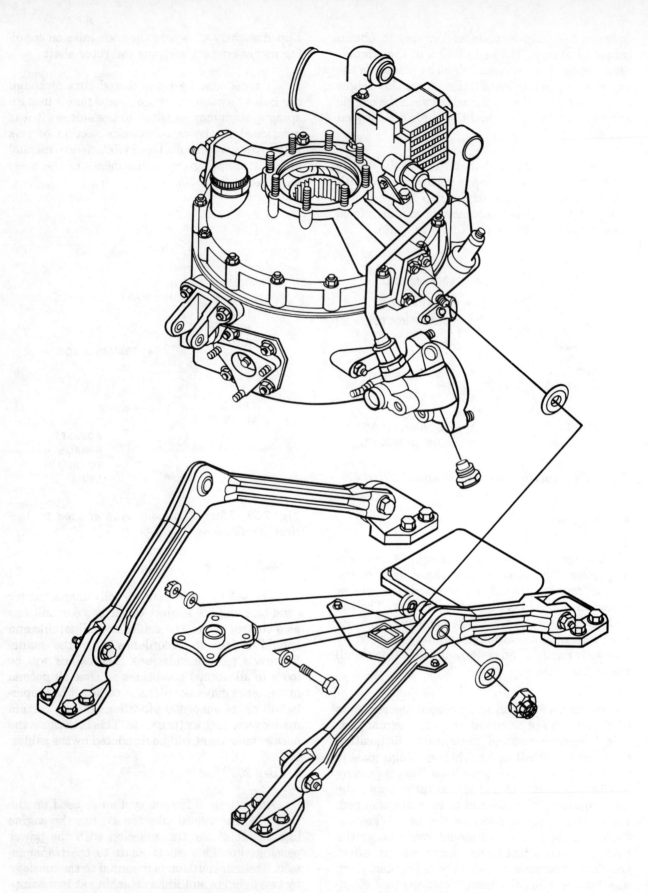

Fig. 7-31 Bell 206 transmission mounting system.

contains a spherical bearing attached to a spindle on the transmission case (Fig. 7-31).

Fore-and-aft movement must be restricted. To restrict this movement, an isolation mount is attached, through a plate with a spherical bearing to the bottom of the transmission. This mount is made up of layers of elastomer and metal, any fore-and-aft movement will place the elastomer in tension and compression. Because of this elasticity, the transimmison and mast will return to its original position when the load is relieved. In addition to the isolation mount, a spike is attached to the same plate as the isolation fitting. This spike passes through a hole surrounded by a stop plate in case of failure of the isolation mount and prevents unlimited movement of the transmission and mast assembly. Fig. 7-32 shows the attachment of the transmission at the bottom with the isolation mount and spike.

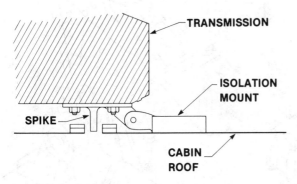

Fig. 7-32 Spike and isolation mount system used on the Bell 206.

The pylon mount links carry the load of the helicopter and should be examined for nicks and scratches. The pylon mount links may be reworked in specified areas because of the loads imposed. The pylon mounts are shimmed by the manufacturer to assure the alignment of the transmission. The shims are to remain with the helicopter or interchanging of shims will require re-alignment at a major overhaul facility. The isolation mount is visually inspected like other elastomeric items and may be replaced as required. The mounts are subject to deterioration due to solvents. A cover is placed over the mount and should be in place at all times.

a. Nodal beam system

The nodal beam system, is used on the Bell 206L, 222, and 214 models. The nodal beam vir-

tually eliminates the two-per-revolution vibrations normally felt in semi-rigid rotor systems. This is accomplished by the flexing of the nodal beam, tuned for the two-per-revolution vertical vibrations (Fig. 7-33). The transmission, mast, and rotor are isolated from the fuselage by the nodal beam and the transmission restraint. The nodal beam uses four link attachments and two stop mounts bolted to the transmission. The four link assemblies are secured to the four support assemblies and the flexture assemblies. The support assemblies are attached to the cabin roof and contain elastomeric bearings to isolate and balance the vibration inputs into the flexture assemblies. The assemblies are the primary vibration absorbing unit and are provided with tuning weights for the fine turning of the nodal beam system.

O. Transmission

The transmission's movement is restricted through the use of the transmission restraint. The restraint consists of an elastomeric bearing secured to the transmission restraint support. The restraint support is attached to the cabin roof and two drag pins. Two stop mounts are bolted to the transmission and are installed over the drag pins. The stops mounted to the drag pins restrict the up movement and all oscillatory movement of the transmission (Fig. 7-34).

Many other helicopter transmissions mount to the structure of the airframe and use rubber mounts between the airframe and the transmission as a vibration dampeners.

A few systems make use of a lift link in addition to the bolts and dampening devices. This lift link is a means of tranferring the loading during flight to the structure of the aircraft. See Fig. 7-35 for a view of a lift link mounting system.

In a situation such as the Hughes 500 series the lifting load is transferred through the stationary mast rather than being carried by the mast through the transmission.

Regardless of the means used to attach the transmission, careful inspection will be required of the mounting system to insure the integrity of the helicopter. Because of the stresses imposed on the mounts, nicks or scratches must be reworked, in accordance with manufacturer's recommendations.

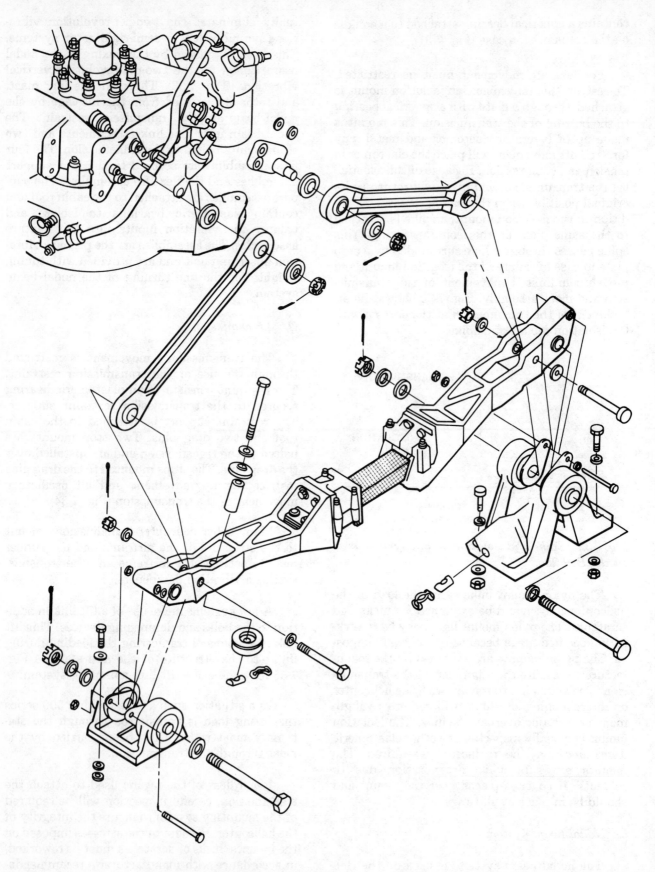

Fig. 7-33 Nodal beam system used on several Bell models.

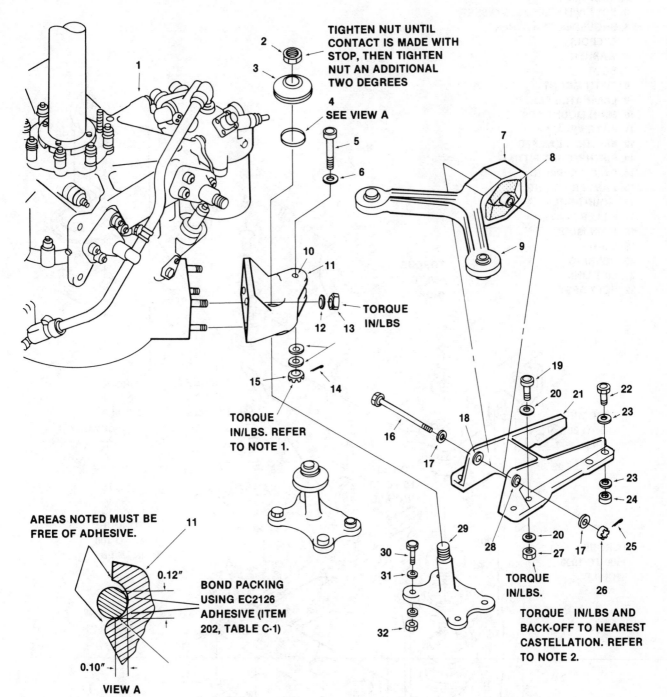

2 TIGHTEN NUT UNTIL CONTACT IS MADE WITH STOP, THEN TIGHTEN NUT AN ADDITIONAL TWO DEGREES

3
4 SEE VIEW A
5
6
7
8
9
10
11
12 13 TORQUE IN/LBS

15 TORQUE IN/LBS. REFER TO NOTE 1.
14

16
17
18
19
20 21 22
23
23
24
20
27 17 25
26
28
29
30
31
32

TORQUE IN/LBS.

TORQUE IN/LBS AND BACK-OFF TO NEAREST CASTELLATION. REFER TO NOTE 2.

AREAS NOTED MUST BE FREE OF ADHESIVE.
11
0.12"
BOND PACKING USING EC2126 ADHESIVE (ITEM 202, TABLE C-1)
0.10"
VIEW A

Fig. 7-34   Bell 206L isolation mount.

The transmissions themselves vary considerably in construction. This is due to the manufacturer's preference, the power absorbed, and the accessories driven by the transmission. The transmission is built as small and lightweight as possible to reduce the overall helicopter weight. Due to the strength-to-weight ratio, spiral bevel and helical gears are used for directional changes.

Some of these transmissions will make use of planetary gear reduction and in a few instances a double planetary system is utilized.

1. Bell 47

The first transmissions to be covered will be the Bell 47, 900 series (Fig. 7-36 A & B). The

1. TRANSMISSION SUPPORT CASE
2. BOLT ASSY.
3. BOLT (WITH LOCKING INSERT)
4. SHOULDERED WASHER
5. EYEBOLT
6. WASHER
7. BOOT
8. FIFTH MOUNT
9. LAMINATED PLATES
10. MAIN MOUNT ASSY.
11. FILLER PLATE
12. FRICTION DAMPER
13. FIFTH MOUNT FITTING
14. PYLON SUPPORT
15. DAMPER FITTING
16. MOUNT BOLT
17. FILLER PLATE
18. MAIN MOUNT
19. BOOT
20. BUSHING
21. LIFT LINK
22. BOLT ASSY.

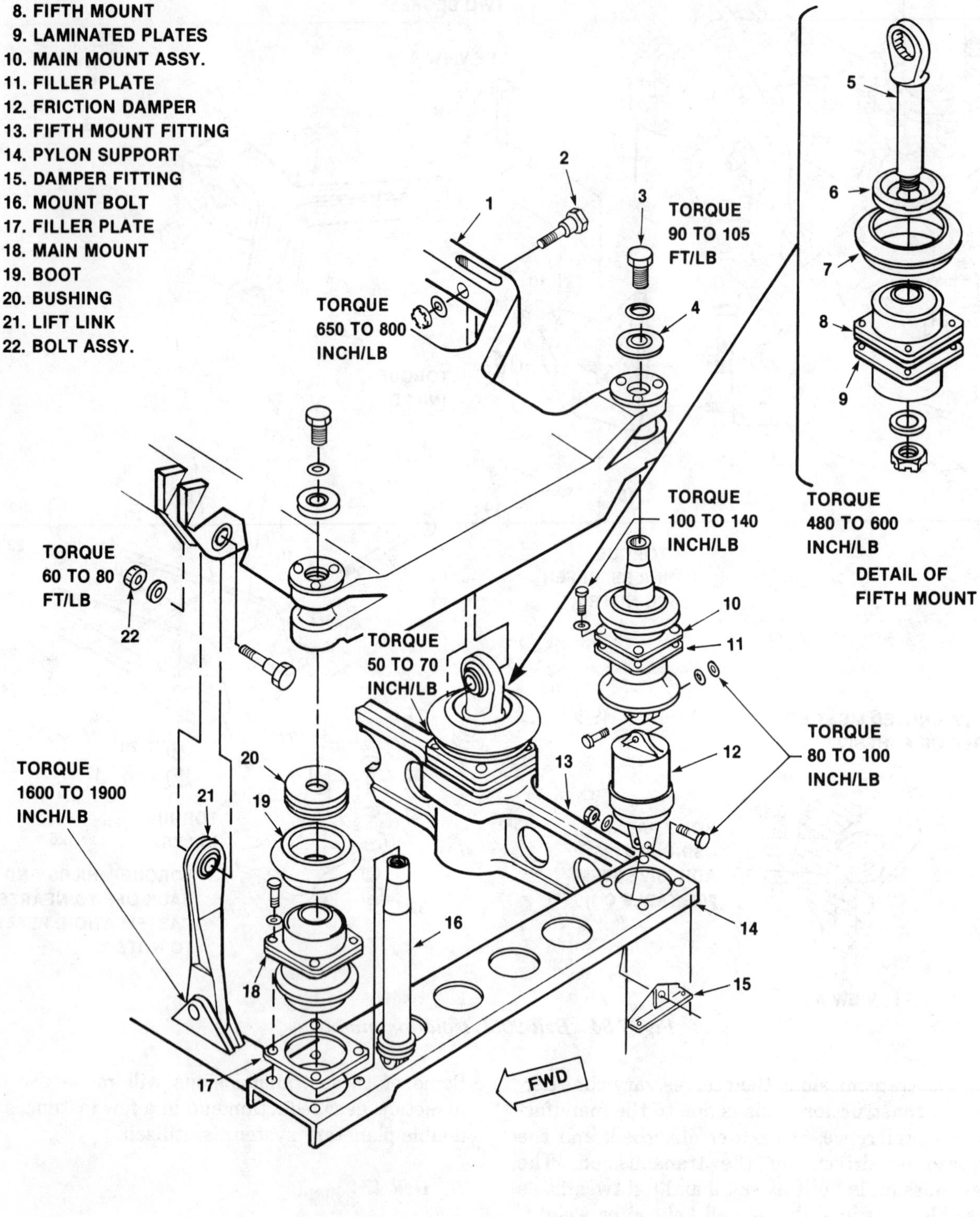

TORQUE 90 TO 105 FT/LB

TORQUE 650 TO 800 INCH/LB

TORQUE 480 TO 600 INCH/LB

DETAIL OF FIFTH MOUNT

TORQUE 100 TO 140 INCH/LB

TORQUE 60 TO 80 FT/LB

TORQUE 50 TO 70 INCH/LB

TORQUE 80 TO 100 INCH/LB

TORQUE 1600 TO 1900 INCH/LB

FWD

Fig. 7-35 Lift link and isolation mount system.

290

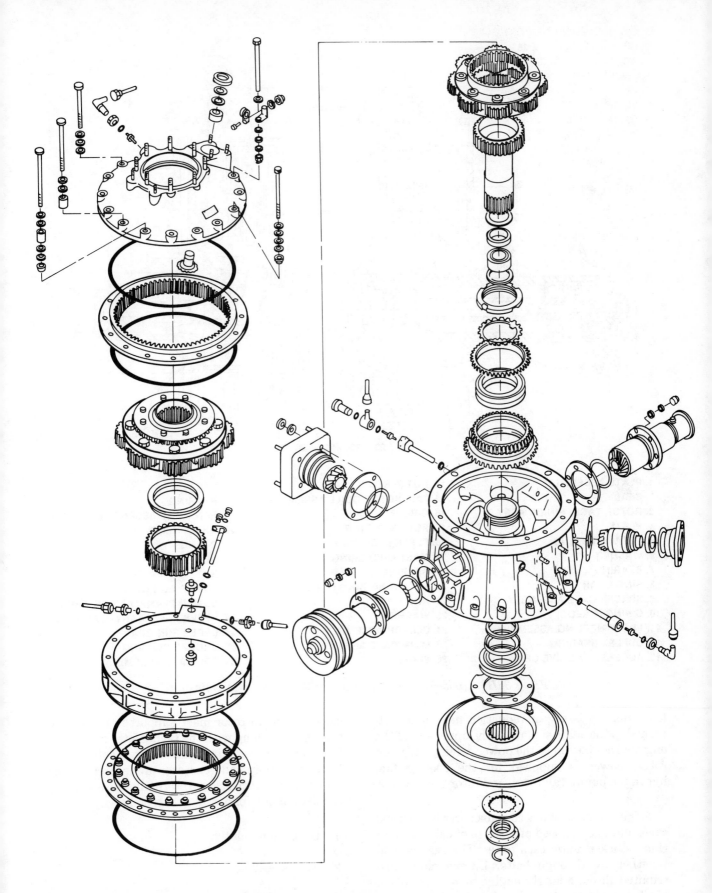

Fig. 7-36A   Bell 47 900 series transmission

291

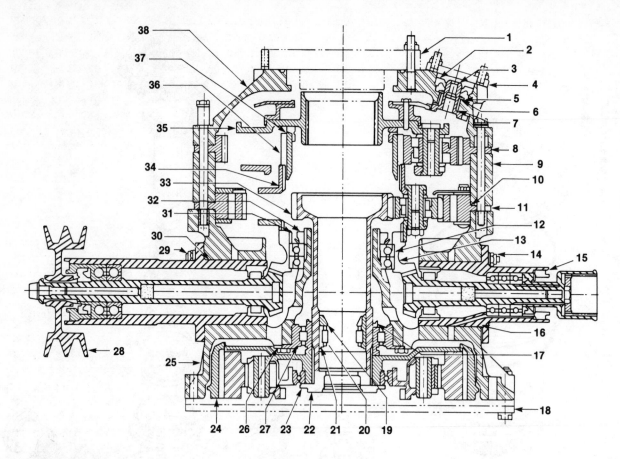

1. PLATE ASSEMBLY	14. NUT (6 REQD)	
2. SEAL	15. TAIL ROTOR QUILL ASSEMBLY	
3. ROTOR TACH. PINION ASSY.	16. O-RING	27. BEARING
4. PLATE	17. RETAINER RING	28. FAN QUILL ASSEMBLY
5. RETAINING RING	18. PLATE ASSEMBLY	29. NUT (6 REQD)
6. WASHER	19. MAST GUIDE RING	30. O-RING
7. BEARING	20. BEARING	31. NUT
8. RING GEAR	21. RETAINING RING (2 REQD)	32. NUT
9. SPACER CASE ASSEMBLY	22. NUT	33. LOWER SUN GEAR
10. O-RING (4 REQD)	23. WASHER	34. LOWER PLANETARY ASSEMBLY
11. FREEWHEELING ASSEMBLY	24. CLUTCH ASSEMBLY	35. UPPER PLANETARY ASSEMBLY
12. DUPLEX BEARING	25. MAIN CASE ASSEMBLY	36. UPPER SUN GEAR
13. ACCESSORY DRIVE GEAR	26. PLATE	37. BRONZE BEARING
		38. TOP CASE ASSEMBLY

Fig. 7-36B   Cross-sectional view of the 900 series transmission.

transmission is a gear reduction mechanism attached to the adapter plate at the upper end of the engine. In addition to the power driving the main rotor, power is supplied for the cooling fan, hydraulic pump, tail rotor, and rotor tachometer.

The transmission is contained in a cylindrical case, and is composed of a series of castings and rings stacked upon each other. The case is held together by through bolts. Engine oil is distributed throughout the engine by a distribution block located on the right aft side of the center

case. The main rotor mast support is located on the top case along with the tachometer drive. The four drive assemblies, tail rotor, cooling fan, hydraulic pump and generator are located on the lower section of the case. Internally, the assembly consists of the following subassemblies:

1. Centrifugal clutch

2. Free wheeling unit

3. Two stage planetary reduction gears

4. Four spiral bevel gears for accessory drives

The centrifugal clutch relieves the engine starting load by the separation of the rotor system from the engine.

The free wheeling unit provides for autorotation with an idling or dead engine.

The accessory pads of the transmission receive power as long as the rotor is turning with power on or off. This makes it possible for the pilot to have complete control during autorotation.

The speeds of the various drives are as follows for normal operation:

Engine	3200 RPM
Mast	355.20 RPM
Tail Rotor Drive	3840 RPM
Fan Drive	3840 RPM
Tachometer Drive	1600 RPM
Generator Drive	3840 RPM
Hydraulic Drive	3840 RPM

The *clutch assembly* located at the bottom of the transmission is a centrifugal type that operates in oil. The shoes are a matched set and are pinned to the spider assembly. The spider, splined to the crankshaft adapter gear drives the clutch. In the center of the spider is a deep groove ball bearing having its outer race locked to the spider and its inner race locked to the clutch drum. This bearing rotates only when the clutch is not fully engaged. When full engagement occurs, the drum and spider will turn as a unit. The clutch drum is splined to the lower sun gear and seats against the lower case bearing. Three holes are provided in the top of the drum at 120° intervals to provide an oil bath for the clutch.

The lower case of the transmission is cast aluminum. Steel liners are inserted for the lower case bearing, fan quill sleeve, hydraulic pump quill, tail rotor quill, and generator quill. In addition, the interior is provided with a threaded steel pedestal for accessory drive gear mounting, four large holes in the webbing for oil drainage and lightening, and four holes on the exterior for the accessory drives. The lower sun gear passes through the lower case pedestal and the lower case bearing and is splined to the clutch drum which is retained by a nut threaded to the sun gear. The lower case bearing, a three-piece roller bearing, carries the load of the sun gear. On the inside of the sun gear is a needle bearing, the mast alignment bearing for the lower end of the mast, that passes through the inside of the sun gear. The upper teeth of the sun gear mesh with the teeth of the pinion gear of the lower planetary spider.

Mounted on the lower case pedestal are two angular contact bearings. The bearings have locked interraces and support the accessory drive gear. The accessory drive gear provides power for the four drive quills located in the lower case.

The lower spider has a top and a bottom flange with a set of splines. Both spline sets are indexed for mating. The bottom splines are narrow and fit over the accessory drive gear holding the retaining nut. The upper splines are wider and drive the upper sun gear. The lower spider holds eight planetary gears that are pinned to the spider. Each of these planetary gears contain roller bearings in nylon cages.

Surrounding the lower planetary system is the *free wheeling unit* which permits the uncoupling of the engine during autorotation (Fig. 7-37). The inner ring acts as a fixed gear for the lower pinion gears while the engine is driving the rotor and as a free gear when the rotor is driving the unit. The outer ring provides a rolling surface during autorotation and a locking surface during engine engagement. Between the two rings are forty rollers placed in inclined slots with spring assemblies to hold the roller in the high incline portion of the slot. They allow locking action in the clockwise direction and unlocking in the counterclockwise direction. The rollers and springs are held in place by two guide rings held by bolts and act as an oil deflector for the lower spider.

The *upper sun gear* is splined to the top of the lower spider and meshes with the upper spider pinion gears. The gear splines have a retainer shoulder to prevent the sun gear from interfering with the pinions of the lower spider. A bronze thrust bearing is provided for a soft surface between the upper sun gear and the mast drive

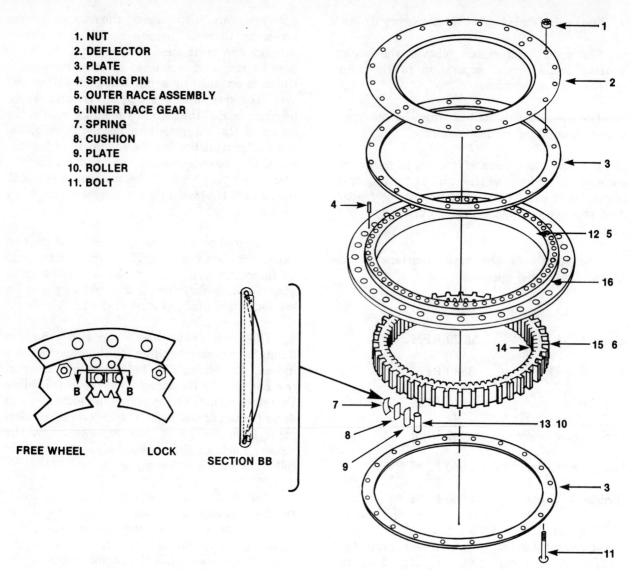

1. NUT
2. DEFLECTOR
3. PLATE
4. SPRING PIN
5. OUTER RACE ASSEMBLY
6. INNER RACE GEAR
7. SPRING
8. CUSHION
9. PLATE
10. ROLLER
11. BOLT

FREE WHEEL   LOCK

SECTION BB

Fig. 7-37 Free wheeling unit that is an integral part of the transmission.

flange. The upper spider has top and bottom flanges and supports the gear for the rotor tach drive on the upper flange. The top flange is bored to accept the pins for the pinion gears and splined to drive the mast.

The pinion gears are of similar construction to those used in the lower spider and utilize roller bearings. However, the rollers are held in micarta rather than nylon cages. The pinion gears rotate about a fixed ring gear driving the spider which in turn drives the mast. The drive flange which is the upper spider is bolted into place.

The *fan drive quill* is driven from the accessory drive gear. The gear itself is a bevel gear with a hollow shaft plugged with a cork. The shaft is supported on the gear end by a roller

bearing using the gear shaft as the inner race. The outer race of this bearing makes contact with the quill sleeve assembly. This sleeve provides the bearing support and a flange for mounting the quill to the transmission case. Two ball bearings are on the opposite end of the sleeve supporting the gear shaft for axial loads. The bearings are locked on the outer race by a nut and shoulder in the sleeve. The nut also holds an oil seal for the gear shaft. At the end of the shaft is the fan pulley. It is placed on cones and retained by a bolt in the end of the shaft.

The *tail rotor quill* is driven from the accessory drive gear. It is a bevel gear with a shaft. It is supported by three ball bearings placed in a sleeve of similar to the construction of the fan

294

quill, with a splined coupling placed on the end to accommodate the tail rotor driveshaft.

The *generator drive quill* is of similar construction, with a gear shaft supported by bearings in a sleeve bolted to the transmission.

The *hydraulic drive quill* is driven by the accessory drive gear with the same type of arrangement of sleeve gear shaft and bearing as the other drives from the accessory drives.

The *tachometer drive quill* is located on the top of the transmission and is driven by a gear attached to the upper spider. The driven gear is placed in the top case of the transmission with a square drive to accomodate a tachometer or drive cable. The gear is supported by a needle bearing.

The *center case* is a magnesium casting which provides space for the free wheeling unit and the fixed ring gear. Oil is distributed to the transmission from the engine in this area.

The *upper case* is a dome-shaped aluminum casting which provides a receptacle for the main mast bearing, an oil inlet for the mast bearing and a tachometer pad. The three sections of transmission are all held together by through bolts passing through the three sections from the upper case.

The power progression of the transmission is as follows:

1. Crank shaft gear

2. Clutch spider

3. Clutch shoes

4. Clutch drum

5. Lower sun gear

6. Lower spider pinions

7. Free wheeling ring

8. Lower spider

   a. Accessory drive gear

      1. Generator quill

      2. Hydraulic quill

      3. Tail rotor quill

      4. Fan quill

9. Upper sun gear

10. Upper spider pinions

11. Fixed ring gear

12. Upper spider

13. Mast drive flange

14. Tachometer drive

The transmission oil is actually supplied from the engine oil system. The oil pases through oil jets on the lower case of the engine and around the mast bearing at the top of the engine. It drips through the transmission and returns to the engine. This system has an obvious disadvantage in that any contamination of the oil by either the engine or the transmission will pass through both. For this reason, transmissions built today separate the oil systems of the engine and transmission. This transmission can be completely disassembled in the field for repair and major inspection.

a. Maintenance

During operation the transmission oil temperature is monitored by an indicator. This one indicator will read the oil temperature of either the engine or transmission depending upon the position of the selector. Temperature is always a good indicator of the condition of the transmission.

Like any other component that utilizes oil, it is subject to oil leakage. The leakage will appear on the outside of the transmission. O-rings are used to seal the parting surfaces of the cases. The O-rings may be changed by separating the transmission section cases. Conventional lip seals are used on all the accessory drive quills. These will often require the removal of the quill for replacement and, in some instances, the disassembly of the quill package. It must be remembered that the quill assemblies have shims located between the sleeve flange and the transmission case. The shims determine the lash and pattern of the gears. If a quill is removed for inspection or seal replacement, the shims must be returned as originally placed, or the lash and gear pattern will be destroyed. If this should occur, the lash and gear pattern must be re-determined, and and the proper shims installed.

To check the condition of the shoes and drums the clutch assembly may be removed by lifting the transmission from the adapter plate, without complete disassembly of the transmission. This is normally done at 600-hour inspections or whenever the clutch operation is questionable.

The major inspections of the transmission require complete disassembly of the transmission. All steel parts are subject to magnetic particle inspection and all nonferrous component will receive flourescent penetrant inspection (Zyglo). Besides visual inspection for wear, parts are dimensionally checked and gears are measured for wear using gauge pins. See Fig. 7-38 for the typical use of gauge pins.

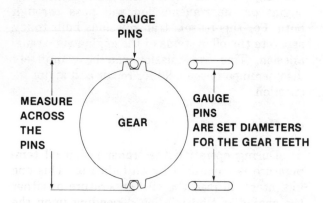

Fig. 7-38 *Gauge pins are used to measure toothwear.*

During the major inspection it is not uncommon to replace certain parts such as bearings, rollers, and springs without inspection. These items are replaced at the discretion of the shop performing the work. When various parts are replaced, the lash and pattern of the accessory gears and quills may be disturbed. Lash and gear patterns are always checked on reassembly.

2. Bell 206

The trend today is to simplify the transmission as much as possible. This will reduce the operating and manufacturing costs. In some instances, this is possible, especially on the light

turbine helicopters being built today. One transmission of this type is that of the Bell 206 (Figs. 7-39 and 7-40).

This transmission is mounted in front of the engine receiving the engine power through a short shaft from transmission input. The engine used is a free turbine, no clutch is necessary. A sprag unit is mounted at the engine output, therefore no free wheeling unit is necessary in the transmission.

The transmission case is made up of a main case and a top case. The main case provides a housing for the input quill, accessory drive quill, transmission oil pump, and supports the spiral bevel gear and shaft. The lower mast bearing and support mount are placed in the bottom of the lower case and serves as a reservoir for transmission oil. The lower case also provides mounting bosses for:

1. Sight gauge

2. Drain plug and chip detector

3. Oil filter head

4. Pressure line "IN"

5. Pressure and return line for the free wheeling unit

6. Pressure regulating valve

7. Drag link

8. Oil strainer

9. Oil jet #1

10. Internal passages for pressure oil

The *input quill* transmits engine power to the transmission. The quill consists of a steel pinion gear supported by a set of tri-plex thrust bearings and one radial alignment bearing (Fig. 7-41). These bearings are positioned on steel liners in the main case and the outer races are pinched by means of a cap and shim.

A *spiral bevel gear* and shaft mesh with the input gear reducing the RPM 3.26 to 1, and changes the direction of the power train 90°. The assembly is made up of a main gear shaft and a

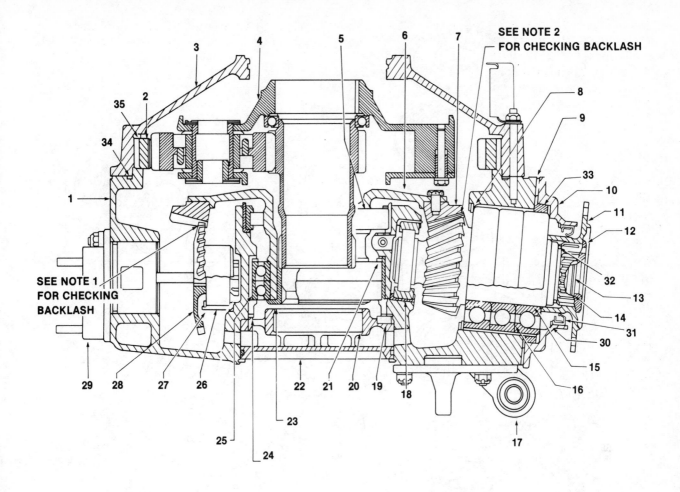

1. TRANSMISSION CASE
2. RING GEAR, PLANETARY FIXED
3. TOP CASE, TRANSMISSION
4. PLANETARY ASSEMBLY
5. BEARING, MAIN INPUT GEAR SHAFT ROLLER
6. GEAR SHAFT, MAIN INPUT
7. SPIRAL BEVEL GEAR, MAIN INPUT
8. GROUND SHIM RING, INPUT PINION
9. LAMINATED SHIM
10. HOUSING, INPUT PINION BEARING AND SEAL
11. ADAPTER, INPUT PINION
12. NUT
13. COVER, PINION NUT
14. LOCK SPRING, INPUT PINION NUT
15. PINION GEAR, INPUT
16. TRIPLEX BEARING, INPUT PINION
17. DRAG LINK ASSEMBLY
18. BEARING, INPUT PINION ROLLER

19. KEY · LOCK
20. BEARING, MAIN ROTOR LOWER MAST
21. GROUND SHIM RING, MAIN INPUT SPIRAL BEVEL GEAR
22. SUPPORT ASSEMBLY, LOWER MAST BEARING
23. NUT, GEAR SHAFT BEARING INNER
24. NUT, GEAR SHAFT BEARING OUTER
25. DUPLEX BEARING, INPUT GEAR SHAFT
26. DOUBLE ROW BEARING, ACCESSORY DRIVE
27. BEARING HOUSING, ACCESSORY DRIVE
28. GEAR, SPIRAL BEVEL ACCESSORY DRIVE
29. OIL PUMP
30. RETAINER RING
31. SEAL
32. O-RING
33. O-RING
34. O-RING
35. SPACER RING

Fig. 7-39 Bell 206 transmission cross section.

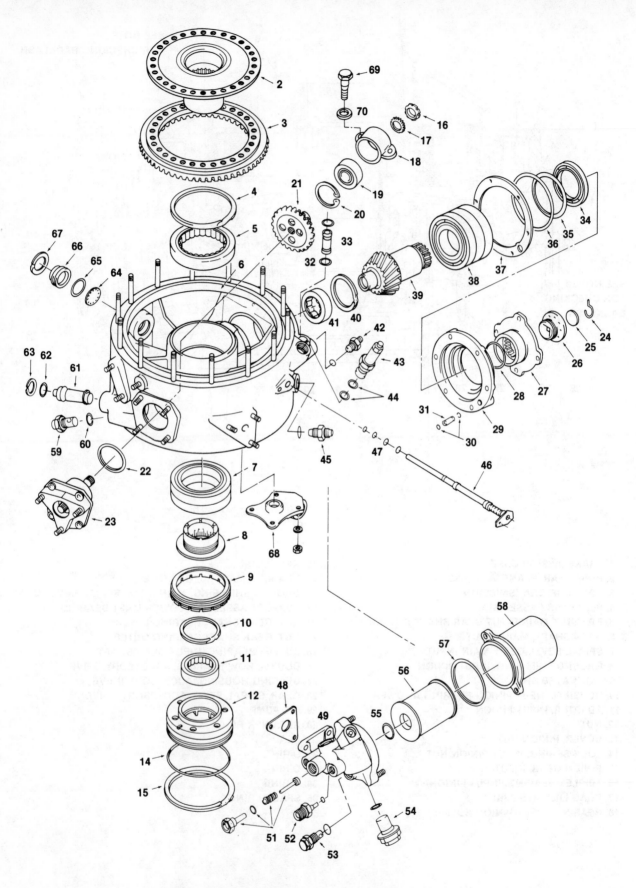

Fig. 7-40A Expolded view of the 206 transmission.

1. BOLT
2. MAIN RING GEAR SHAFT
3. RING GEAR
4. RETAINER RING
5. ALIGNMENT BEARING · MAIN RING GEAR SHAFT
6. TRANSMISSION LOWER CASE
7. DUPLEX BEARINGS · MAIN RING GEAR SHAFT
8. NUT · MAIN RING GEAR SHAFT
9. NUT · MAIN RING GEAR SHAFT BEARINGS
10. RETAINER RING
11. BEARING · MAST ALIGNMENT
12. SUPPORT · MAST ALIGNMENT BEARING
13. LOCK KEY
14. O-RING
15. RETAINER RING
16. SPANNER NUT · ACCESSORY DRIVE GEAR
17. LOCK PLATE
18. HOUSING · ACCESSORY DRIVE BEARING
19. BEARING · ACCESSORY DRIVE
20. RETAINER RING
21. ACCESSORY DRIVE GEAR
22. O-RING
23. OIL PUMP · TRANSMISSION
24. LOCK RING
25. COVER
26. NUT · INPUT PINION
27. ADAPTER
28. O-RING
29. COVER · INPUT PINION
30. O-RING
31. OIL TRANSFER TUBE
32. O-RING
33. OIL TRANSFER TUBE
34. SEAL
35. RETAINER RING

36. O-RING
37. SHIMS
38. TRIPLEX BEARINGS · INPUT PINION
39. INPUT PINION
40. RETAINER RING
41. BEARING · INPUT PINION ALIGNMENT
42. UNION · FREEWHEELING PRESSURE OIL
43. REGULATOR VALVE · OIL PRESSURE
44. O-RING
45. UNION · FREEWHEELING RETURN OIL
46. OIL JET · NO. 1
47. O-RING
48. GASKET
49. OIL FILTER HOUSING
50. THERMO SWITCH
51. BY-PASS VALVE—FILTER
52. TEMP BULB
53. DRAIN VALVE
54. OIL MONITOR
55. O-RING
56. FILTER ELEMENT
57. O-RING
58. FILTER HOUSING
59. CHIP DETECTOR
60. O-RING
61. FILTER SCREEN
62. O-RING
63. RETAINER RING
64. INDICATOR PLATE · OIL LEVEL
65. O-RING
66. SIGHT GLASS · OIL LEVEL
67. RETAINER RING
68. DRAG LINK
69. BOLT
70. WASHER

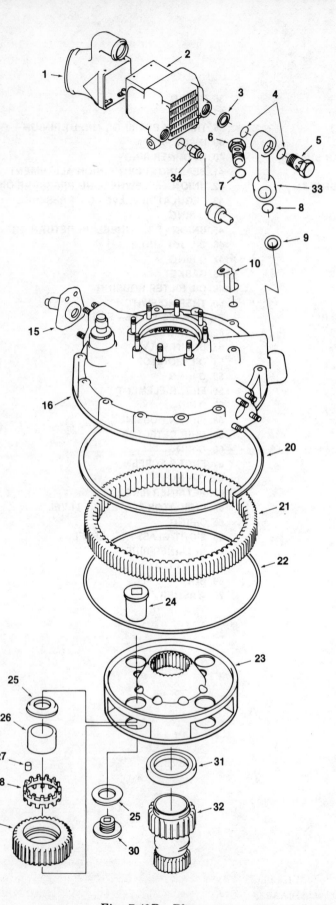

1. DUCT · COOLING AIR
2. RADIATOR · OIL COOLER
3. GASKET
4. O-RING
5. BOLT
6. BOLT
7. O-RING
8. O-RING
9. GASKET
10. BRACKET
11. ADAPTER
12. CLIP
13. FILLER · BREATHER CAP
14. O-RING
15. SPINDLE
16. TOP CASE
17. JET · NO. 2
18. O-RING
19. OIL TRANSFER TUBE
20. SPACER RING
21. FIXED RING GEAR
22. O-RING
23. PLANETARY CARRIER ASSY.
24. SHAFT
25. WASHER
26. INNER RACE
27. ROLLER
28. RETAINER · CAGE
29. GEAR · PLANETARY
30. NUT
31. BEARING · SUN GEAR
32. SUN GEAR
33. TRANSFER TUB
34. UNION · OIL "IN"

Fig. 7-40B   Planetary system of the Bell 206 transmission.

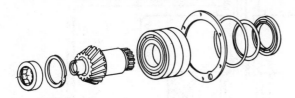

Fig. 7-41 Pinion gear system used in the Bell 206.

main gear. The gear is secured to the shaft by bolts. The gear shaft is supported by one roller bearing at the top of the shaft and two angular thrust bearings at the base.

The sun gear is splined to the inside of the main gear shaft and drives the pinion gears of the planetary system. At the top of the sun gear is an angular thrust bearing which supports the planetary system.

The planetary system consists of four planetary gears with rollers and cages which are pinned in the planetary carrier assembly. The gears walk around a fixed ring gear mounted in the upper case with splines on the outer diameter. The center of the carrier is splined to accommodate the mast which fits through the carrier and the sun gear.

The sun gear engages all four planet gears at their centerpoint. As the sun gear rotates, the motion is transmitted to the planets. The planets in turn rotate or walk around the fixed ring gear. This will rotate the carrier assembly which will turn the mast.

Only one *accessory drive quill* is used in the Bell 206 transmission. This quill is mounted in the lower case and is positioned under the spiral bevel gear. The accessory gear is driven from this bevel gear and turns the following:

1. Transmission oil pump

2. Hydraulic pump

3. Rotor tachometer generator

The items are placed in piggyback with each other in that order.

The top case houses the fixed ring gear and the upper end of the sun gear. The center bore houses the mast bearing assembly and has studs for the mast and swashplate. This transmission,

like all of the helicopters in production today, has its own separate oil system to supply lubrication to the various components of the transmission and the free wheeling unit. Fig. 7-42 shows a schematic of the oil system. The oil pump is mounted internally in the transmission lower case and is driven from the accessory drive quill. The pump is a vane type which produces a constant volume. It picks up oil from the strainer outlet in the bottom of the case and moves the oil through internal passages to the oil filter head which is mounted on the outside of the lower case.

The *filter head* provides an attachment point for the filter and incorporates a thermoswitch, temperature bulb, and an oil by-pass valve. As the oil enters the head, temperature is sensed by the temperature switch, used for a temperature bulb, operating an instrument in the cockpit. In normal operation the oil then enters the filter. If, however, the filter should become clogged to the point that a differential of pressure exists, the oil will be bypassed rather than entering the filter unit. The oil flows to the *oil cooler*. This unit is used to regulate the temperature of the oil entering the transmission. The cooler is located outside the transmission and is cooled by a fan driven from the tail rotor drive shaft. The cooler itself is a radiator equipped with a by-pass system. During starting and cold weather the oil bypasses the cooler. As the oil warms up, however, the by-pass valve starts to open and oil flows through the core of the cooler before it is directed through the lubrication points and pressure regulated.

The pressure regulating valve limits the system pressure. This is a common relief type valve which bleeds off pressure when oil pressure overcomes the spring setting. This valve is located in back of the filter and is field adjustable. Bypass oil is returned to the sump.

Two *oil jets* are located on the upper and lower case. Oil flows from the oil cooler to the case through an external fitting where it is distributed to both jets and the free wheeling unit. The oil passing through the jets flows through the transmission and returns to the lower case. The oil going to the free wheeling unit, however, goes out of the case through an external fitting and a restrictor fitting. The restrictor fitting also contains a low pressure warning switch and an oil pressure tap for a continuous reading indicator. Oil leaving the free wheeling unit is returned to the sump.

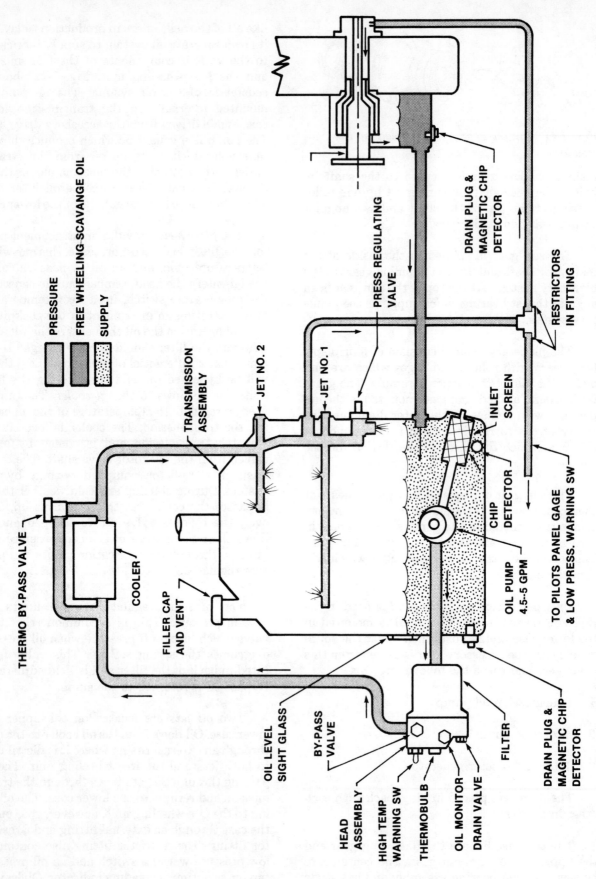

PRESSURE

FREE WHEELING SCAVANGE OIL

SUPPLY

DRAIN PLUG & MAGNETIC CHIP DETECTOR

PRESS REGULATING VALVE

RESTRICTORS IN FITTING

TRANSMISSION ASSEMBLY

JET NO. 2

JET NO. 1

INLET SCREEN

CHIP DETECTOR

TO PILOTS PANEL GAGE & LOW PRESS. WARNING SW

OIL PUMP 4.5-5 GPM

THERMO BY-PASS VALVE

COOLER

FILLER CAP AND VENT

DRAIN PLUG & MAGNETIC CHIP DETECTOR

OIL LEVEL SIGHT GLASS

BY-PASS VALVE

HEAD ASSEMBLY

HIGH TEMP WARNING SW

THERMOBULB

OIL MONITOR

DRAIN VALVE

FILTER

Fig. 7-42 Bell 206 Transmission oil system

302

a. Maintenance

From a maintenance standpoint this transmission is much simpler than that of the Bell 47 even though it has its self-contained oil system. The probability of oil leaks is greatly reduced with only one parting surface and two quills. The upper case is sealed with an O-ring and lip seals are used on the quills. The jets which are mounted externally are sealed with O-rings. The transmission is equipped with a sight gauge in the lower case for checking the oil level. The oil and filter are changed at recommended intervals. At this time the chip detector is checked and the filter is cut open for examination. Any excessive metal will require the replacement of the transmission and cooler.

The 206 transmission, like that of the 47, may be disassembled in the field for major inspection and parts replacement. Because of the fewer parts, this is somewhat simplified, but the same basic checks are made of the ferrous and nonferrous parts. The lash and pattern requirements have been somewhat simplified with a *lash only check* being made.

The reason for lash only check is that shim rings are placed in the case by the manufacturer to determine the lash and pattern requirements of the gears. The lash check is really only an indication of the gears and the assembly procedures. If the rings are removed and lost from the case, new ones must be ground by the manufacturer for that particular case. These rings are not interchangeable.

3. Hughes 500

Another transmission is that of the Hughes 500. It is located below the stationary mast and access may be gained from the inside of the cabin. The power is transmitted from the engine through a shaft to the transmission input. Like the Bell 206, no clutch is required. The free turbine engine does not use a clutch and the sprag

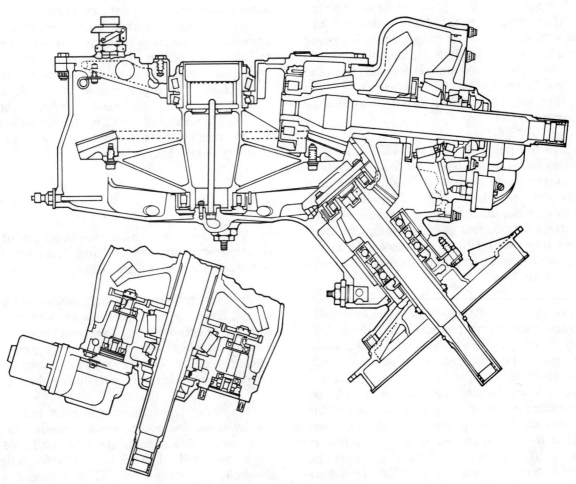

Fig. 7-43 Hughes 500 transmission cross section

unit located near the engine, eliminating the need of a free wheeling assembly in the transmission.

The *power input* is made through a pinion gear shaft supported by two ball bearing and two roller bearings, with the loads carried by the rollers and the thrust carried by the ball bearing. This input is placed on the same angle as the engine and the pinion gear engages the tail rotor output pinion gear.

The *tail rotor output* gear and shaft are supported by two thrust bearings and a roller bearing. The input gear and the tail rotor gear reduce the tail rotor output to 2160 RPM from 6180 RPM which enters the engine. Attached with the tail rotor drive gear is the *output pinion gear*. This meshes with the output bevel gear and further reduces the output RPM to 485 at which speed the rotor is driven by the driveshaft passing through the output bevel gear (Fig. 7-43). All of these gears are spiral bevel gears because of their strength and tooth contact area.

Two accessory drive pads are mounted on the rear of the transmission, at the right- and left-hand side of the tail rotor output shaft. These are driven by a spur gear pinned to the tail rotor output shaft driving two pinions for the right and left side. The right-hand pad drives the oil pump and filter unit while the left pad drives the rotor tachometer.

Like the Bell 206 transmission the Hughes 500 also has a transmission lubrication system. This system, however, is considerably different in design but not in function. The lubrication utilizes an external oil cooler, a scavenge system, an externally mounted pressure pump, an internal oil filter, an oil filter by-pass valve, an oil temperature switch and miscellaneous lines and fittings (Fig. 7-44).

Pressure is obtained in the externally mounted gerotor type pressure pump. From this pump the oil goes directly to the oil cooler externally mounted on the engine side of the firewall. A thermostatic by-pass valve is located at the cooler. Oil will bypass the cooler when the oil temperature is too low. As the temperature of the oil increases, the oil passes through the cooler where it is exposed to cooling air from a blower powered by the main driveshaft. If the cooler should become clogged, a differential of pressure bypass is incorporated which will eliminate the

cooler from the system. As the oil leaves the cooler, it passes through a temperature switch, which is the temperature sensor for the warning light on the instrument panel. The oil then returns past the pressure pump to the filter. This filter element is a 12-micron throwaway type filter. If the filter should become clogged, oil is bypassed around the filter by a differential of pressure valve. After flowing through the filter, the oil is directed to the relief valve where the pressure is controlled. As the oil enters the internal passages, it makes contact with a minimum pressure switch which will activate a pressure warning light if the pressure drops below minimum. The oil is directed to the various passages to supply the bearing and gears with oil. The oil collects in the input sump and is picked up by a scavenge pump. The pump is a gerotor pump mounted on the end of the input gear shaft. The pressure from the scavenge pump is used to lubricate the upper cylindrical roller bearing of the input shaft.

Although the transmissions used in the various helicopters today vary considerably in construction most of them will use the same basic principles of the transmissions covered. This will include input pinion rotating bevel gears, planetary gear reductions of various kinds and accessory gears. The big variation in the different transmissions is the number of accessories driven. This is usually in direct relationship with the complexity of the helicopter in regard to electrical systems, hydraulic power and other such items.

a. Maintenance

The standard maintenance practices of the transmissions involve servicing, replacement of seals, changing the oil and filters.

The inspections of the transmission are quite varied, from major inspections of the transmission where complete teardown and rebuilding is done to simple remove-and-return transmissions (exchange units). The exchange units may be dictated by the manufacturer or by the shop itself.

On many transmissions a great number of special tools and equipment are needed to perform overhaul. The costs are only justifiable if a large amount of this work is to be performed or if the helicopters are involved in seasonal work where the maintenance personnel would have a

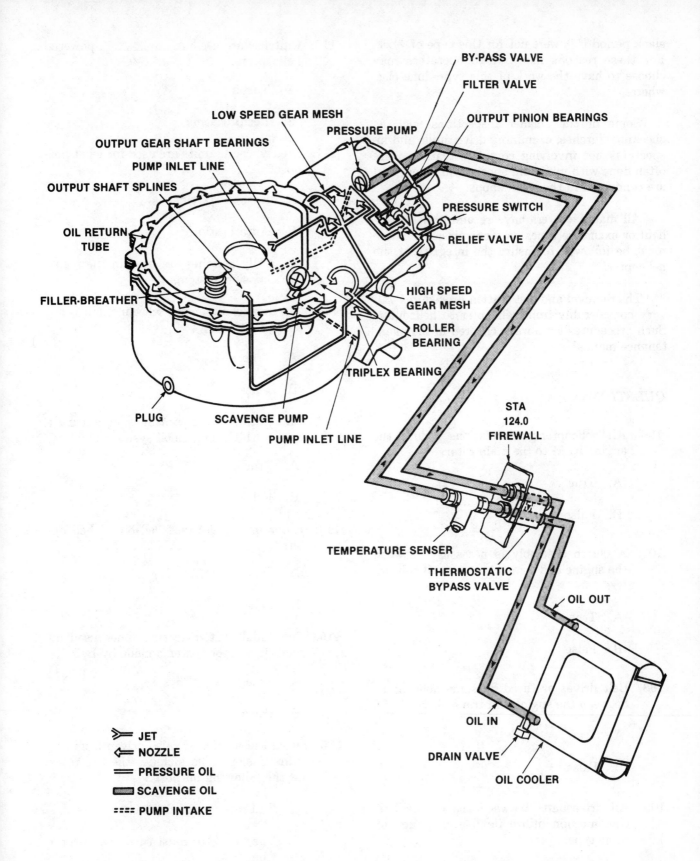

Fig. 7-44 Hughes 500 transmission lubrication system

305

slack period if it were not for this type of work. For these reasons many small operators may choose to have the work of this type done elsewhere.

Some of the smaller inspections such as checking clutches, examining drive quills and inspections not involving complete teardown are often done with minimum special equipment and are conducted in the small shops.

All manufacturers have recommended overhaul or exchange times on transmissions. These must be followed to ensure the integrity of the helicopter.

The removal and installation procedures will vary considerably from helicopter to helicopter. Such procedures are always covered in the maintenance manual.

QUESTIONS:

106. All helicopter transmissions reduce the engine RPM to the main rotor.

    A. True

    B. False

107. A clutch assembly is necessary between the engine and transmission on all helicopters.

    A. True

    B. False

108. Belt drives are used on some helicopters between the engine and transmission.

    A. True

    B. False

109. All driveshafts between the engine and transmission utilize flexible couplings of some type.

    A. True

    B. False

110. Clutches are used on all _____ powered helicopters.

    A. Turbine

    B. Reciprocating

111. Free wheeling units are used for what purpose?

    A. Ease in starting

    B. Autorotation

    C. Only clutches are used in the transmission system.

112. The most common free wheeling unit is the sprag unit.

    A. True

    B. False

113. Lubrication of the transmission is usually done with the engine oil system.

    A. True

    B. False

114. Rotor brakes are installed on all helicopters.

    A. True

    B. False

115. The nodal system is sometimes used on semi-rigid rotor systems made by Bell.

    A. True

    B. False

16. Often accessories are also driven from the transmission. This includes the tail rotor for the following purpose.

    A. Tail rotor speed must be decreased.

    B. The tail rotor must turn in autorotation.

    C. The tail rotor is always driven from the engine.

117. No accessory drives will require a lash and pattern check.

    A. True

    B. False

118. Hydraulic pumps are often driven from the transmission.

    A. True

    B. False

119. Planatary gear reductions are often used in transmissions.

    A. True

    B. False

120. The transmission gears are often lubricated by spray.

    A. True

    B. False

SECTION VIII

Powerplants

The powerplants used in helicopters are the result of 45 years of technology and development. The helicopter, however, is much younger than that because the powerplants used on the early helicopters were all adaptations of existing fixed wing powerplants. In order to adapt these engines several changes had to be made.

A. *Fixed Wing Powerplant Changes*

Most of the powerplants had to be mounted vertically rather than horizontally (the normal manner). This brought about changes in the lubrication system, especially in the scavenge system, because the sump system had to be relocated.

Another change was the speed at which the engine must operate due to the horsepower requirement of the helicopter. One method used to increase the power was to increase the speed. Some engines were increased approximately 800 RPM.

The next change was the cooling system. The engine in the fixed wing aircraft was cooled with airflow from the propeller, routed through the cowling and a series of baffles. Since the propeller was no longer present, a fan was installed to develop the airflow required for cooling. This sometimes involved more gearboxes for the cooling fans and more drive quills from the transmission. The method of controlling power had to be changed because the rotor remained at a constant RPM. Unlike the fixed wing aircraft, power cannot be controlled by the propeller because the rotor pitch is used to control the height at which the helicopter flies. This means the RPM of the engine must be controlled rather than the rotor.

The operation of the engines, other than the higher RPM, changed very little with the same instrumentation, warm-up and shutdown procedures used. However, the idle RPM was increased considerably. 1700 RPM was not an unusual idle speed. This was mainly due to the lack of a flywheel on most applications.

On the fixed wing aircraft the propeller acts as a flywheel to keep the engine rotating and no clutch is present between the propeller and the engine. However, because of the freewheeling unit being present, no such flywheel action is available on a helicopter application. This lack of flywheel action also led to a wider use of carburetor heat on carburetor-equipped engines because ice leads to sudden loss of power without the usual warnings associated with ice and fixed wing induction systems.

Other systems such as superchargers and fuel injection systems were also adapted to the helicopter powerplants. The operational procedures remained basically the same.

Another change in the operation was the establishment of transient ranges of RPM due to harmful vibration ranges in the airframe components. This means continuous operation at certain power settings may cause failure of components due to vibration. This sometimes occurs between the engine and the propeller on fixed wing aircraft but not so extensively as is in helicopter operations.

B. *Modifications*

Often the life of these engines has been shortened as a result of modifications, due to the high power setting at which the helicopter is required to operate. As these weaknesses have shown up they have been corrected, helping to extend the life. Helicopter engines usually have 1200 hour TBO (time before overhaul) times established.

1. *Installation*

The early models of the Bell 47 and the Hiller 12 used horizontally opposed engines requiring an engine installation modification. Both helicopters used Franklin engines followed by Lycoming engines. The Franklin engines were of the 6V4 series, and the Lycoming engines were the 0-435 and 0-540 series. Some modifications

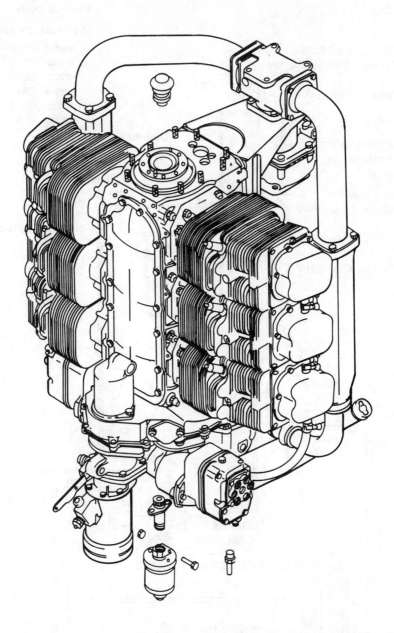

Fig. 8-1   Typical reciprocating engine used on the Bell 47 and Hiller 12

had to be made for the helicopter applications because both of the engines were used on fixed wing aircraft. First, the engines were placed vertically and backward from their original positions. This movement resulted in the relocation of the oil sump to the bottom of the engine (Fig. 8-1). This also required moving the carburetor and modification of the oil scavenge system.

Rather than relocating the sump on many of the Lycoming engines, the engine became a dry sump oil system with a separate oil tank (Fig. 8-2).

2. *Separate air cooler*

A separate air cooler was installed that did not depend on ram airflow for cooling. For this reason, the coolers were usually larger and utilized air from the cooling fan which passed around the core of the radiator.

3. *Maintenance problems*

The directions in relation to accessory installation became confusing. For example: the right magneto was on the left side of the fuselage.

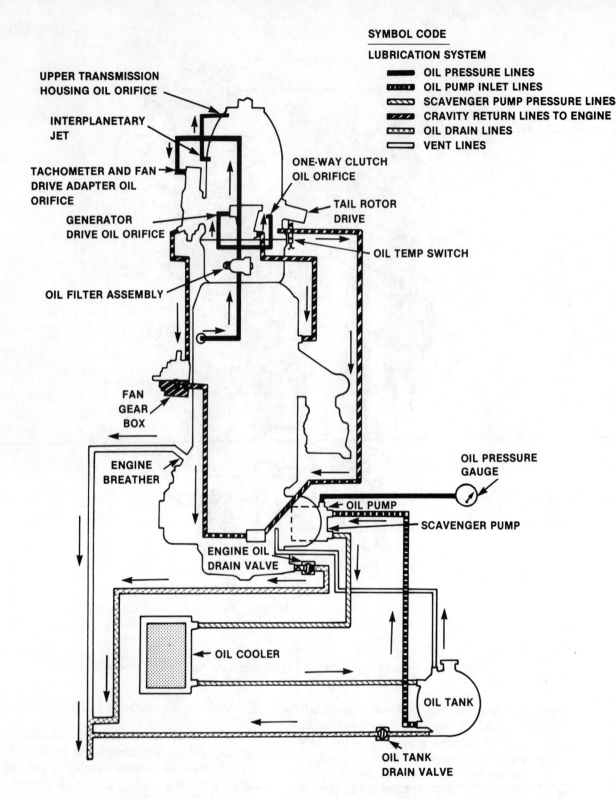

SYMBOL CODE

LUBRICATION SYSTEM

- OIL PRESSURE LINES
- OIL PUMP INLET LINES
- SCAVENGER PUMP PRESSURE LINES
- CRAVITY RETURN LINES TO ENGINE
- OIL DRAIN LINES
- VENT LINES

UPPER TRANSMISSION HOUSING OIL ORIFICE

INTERPLANETARY JET

TACHOMETER AND FAN DRIVE ADAPTER OIL ORIFICE

GENERATOR DRIVE OIL ORIFICE

OIL FILTER ASSEMBLY

ONE-WAY CLUTCH OIL ORIFICE

TAIL ROTOR DRIVE

OIL TEMP SWITCH

FAN GEAR BOX

ENGINE BREATHER

OIL PRESSURE GAUGE

OIL PUMP

SCAVENGER PUMP

ENGINE OIL DRAIN VALVE

OIL COOLER

OIL TANK

OIL TANK DRAIN VALVE

Fig. 8-2   Oil system used on some models of the Hiller 12

The directions were changed on the newer helicopters because of the confusion. However, for some of the older models, the directions in the older maintenance manuals must be used.

Because of the vertical location and the presence of a clutch and transmission, the engine's crankshafts could not be rotated easily by hand, as was done with the fixed wing aircraft by

Fig. 8-3   Radial engine installation on the S-55

rotating the propeller. This complicates some maintenance procedures such as timing or compression tests. To eliminate this problem, some engines were provided with a crank engagement. This engagement point was on the side of the engine and could also be used for starting. The Franklins, however, have a cover that is removable for turning the engine with the aid of a special tool. Many of the maintenance personnel working on the engines have built turning tools to aid in maintenance. This is often a quill placed in an unused accessory pad on the engine.

C. Radial and Opposed Engines

Some of the older large helicopters used radial engines. The two most widely used powerplants were the Pratt and Whitney R1340 series and the Curtis Wright 1820 series. The engines were used in the S55 and S58 respectively. Both powerplants were located in the nose of the aircraft with the output shafts facing inward at an upward angle (Fig. 8-3). This placed the accessory sections next to the access doors. The power-

plants also went through extensive modifications to adapt to the new position in the helicopter, especially the lubrication system.

Other radial engines were also used in helicopters. They were constructed with the engine in several different positions. Most of these helicopters were never used as civilian aircraft or the production was quite limited.

Two of the newer reciprocating powered helicopters placed the engines in the middle of the fuselage in a horizontal position below the transmission. Both use belt drives to the transmission and the engines facing forward. Both are Lycoming powered using the 036 series engines.

All these engines have certain things in common. One item is cooling. The aircraft engines commonly used are air-cooled, and it is necessary that they receive their cooling air from a fan. As with other items used on helicopters, each manufacturer approaches this problem in different ways. In all cases the fan must be powered by the

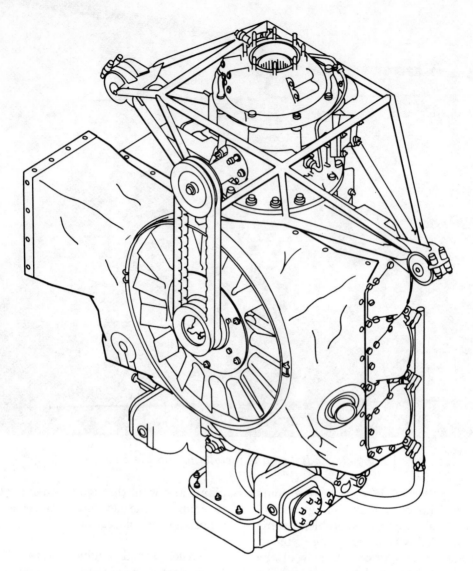

Fig. 8-4 Engine transmission installation of the Bell 47

engine and ducted around the cylinders to dissipate the heat.

D. Cooling Systems

1. Bell 47

The cooling fan is mounted on the front side of the engine, powered by two matched V-belts, driven from the fan quill assembly of the transmission (Fig. 8-4).

The fan turns at a higher speed than the engine so it may distribute the necessary cooling air to the engine. The major components of the cooling assembly are as follows:

1. Fan quill

2. Fan

3. Index plate

4. Shroud

5. Cylinder baffles

The *fan quill*, located on the forward side of the transmission, turns at a 1:2 ratio to the engine. Attached to the end of the quill is a double pulley accommodating two matched V-belts. This transmits the power from the transmission to the fan.

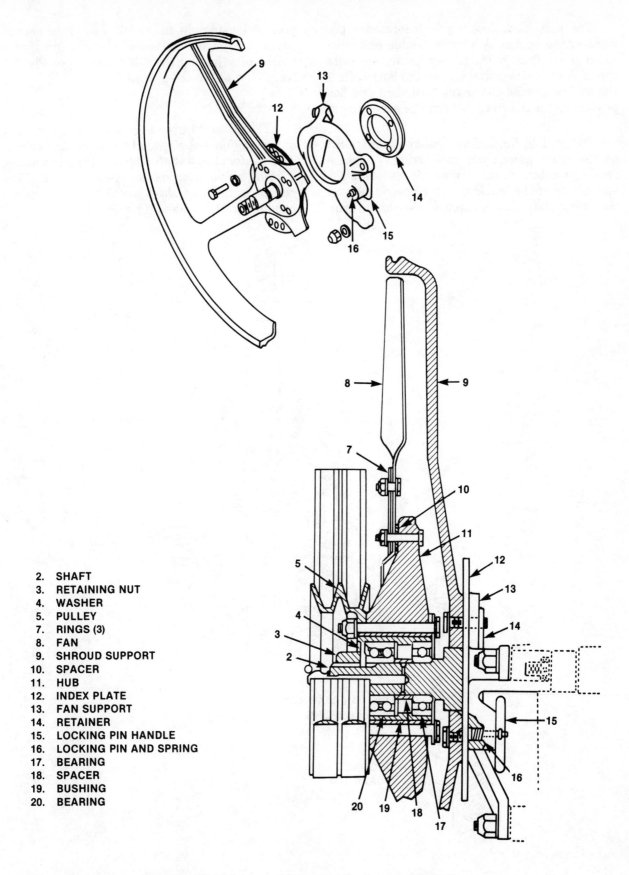

2. SHAFT
3. RETAINING NUT
4. WASHER
5. PULLEY
7. RINGS (3)
8. FAN
9. SHROUD SUPPORT
10. SPACER
11. HUB
12. INDEX PLATE
13. FAN SUPPORT
14. RETAINER
15. LOCKING PIN HANDLE
16. LOCKING PIN AND SPRING
17. BEARING
18. SPACER
19. BUSHING
20. BEARING

Fig. 8-5 Belt-driven cooling fan used on the Bell 47

The multi-bladed cooling *fan* is located on the front of the engine. A smaller double pulley located on the front of the fan further increases its speed. A *shroud* is placed around the fan to direct the airflow around the engine cylinders and has provisions for the oil cooler and the generator.

The cooling fan and fan pulley are installed on the *index plate* shaft ballbearing. A grease zerk is located in the center of the shaft for lubrication of the bearings. An eccentric cam on the index plate passes through the shroud sup-

port. A locking pin on the left side of the shroud support engages the index plate to provide a means of adjusting the belt tension. See Fig. 8-5 for a view of the fan assembly.

2. Hiller 12

The Hiller 12 uses a cooling fan on the front of the engine and a shroud to direct the airflow. This system has a shaft from the transmission to a right angle gearbox to power the fan. The shroud is made of sheet metal or fiberglass depending on the model (Fig. 8-6).

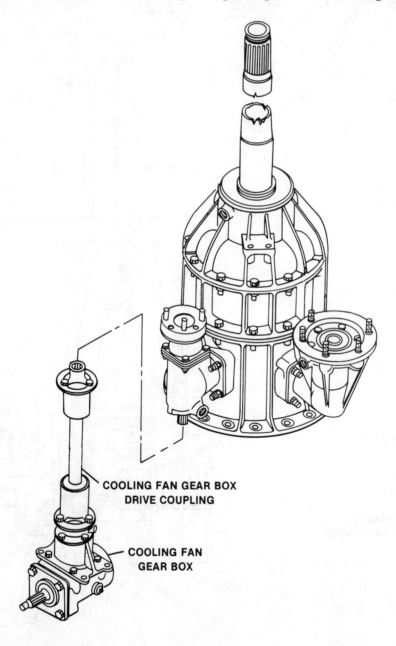

COOLING FAN GEAR BOX DRIVE COUPLING

COOLING FAN GEAR BOX

Fig. 8-6   Shaft-driven cooling fan system used on the Hiller 12

3. Maintenance

The cooling systems are subject to routine maintenance and inspection. The system used on the Bell 47 requires manual lubrication, while systems using gearboxes are supplied with oil from either the transmission or the engine.

Cooling fans are subject to cracks often occurring at the root of the blade areas. Such cracks may be caused on a helicopter by operating the engine in the wrong RPM range for extended periods of time. See Fig. 8-7 for a view of the crack area.

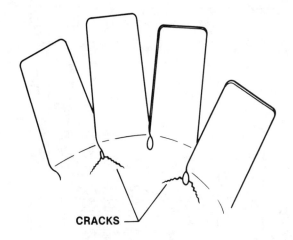

CRACKS

Fig. 8-7 Typical cracks in the cooling fans

Like other rotating items on the helicopter, cooling fans are subject to balance problems. The fans are usually statically balanced before installation. This is done by placing the fan on a mandrel and knife edges and adding weight to the light side of the fan in the form of washers. Where a single unit fan is used, it is normally statically balanced at the time of manufacture. The dynamic imbalance can often be felt in the helicopter as a buzz. In the Bell 47 this is normally felt in the back of the pilot during operation. On many of the other helicopters it is not so easily distinguished because of the relatively high speed of the fan. Often when a vibration is suspected, it may be checked with electronic balancing equipment or by disconnecting other items of the same frequency during operation. This may include generators and hydraulic pumps, although both items may often be eliminated as a vibration source by unloading the systems.

The cooling fans will have recommended overhaul periods and may have finite lives on some of the items.

E. Correlation Systems

The power application of the helicopter, with a reciprocating engine, is quite different from that of a fixed wing aircraft. Rather than a throttle lever, as is found in the fixed wing, a twist grip is used on the collective. This throttle grip is similar to the grip found on motorcycles except the action is in the opposite direction. An easy way to remember the throttle action is that the decrease position is toward the thumb as the collective is gripped. On the earliest helicopters, it was necessry for the pilot to add throttle while raising or lowering the collective. Few helicopters that were built with this system are still in existence.

In order to eliminate this problem the correlation box came into use. This system provides a means of increasing or decreasing the throttle opening as the collective is raised and lowered. The final adjustment of the power is usually still done by the twist grip because no correction factor is built in for atmospheric conditions.

For a typical throttle correlation system, the system on the Bell 47 will be used. This system makes use of a twist grip which rotates a shaft in the collective. This shaft has a gear attached at the bottom end of the collective shaft. The gear meshes with a gear attached to a shaft within the collective jackshaft. Attached to this shaft is a clevis which moves the throttle linkage. Either the movement of the twist grip, or the changing of the collective, repositions the clevis and in turn the throttle. See Fig. 8-8 for their positions and movements.

This rotary movement of the twist grip and the collective is changed to a linear movement at the clevis by a push-pull tube. The push-pull tube is attached to another jackshaft which transfers the movement to the right side of the helicopter where another push-pull rod is attached from the jackshaft to a cam box. The cam box transforms the push-pull movement back to a rotary motion and is attached to the throttle of the carburetor by linkage (Fig. 8-9).

The cam box is used to correlate the movements of the collective and twist grip into throt-

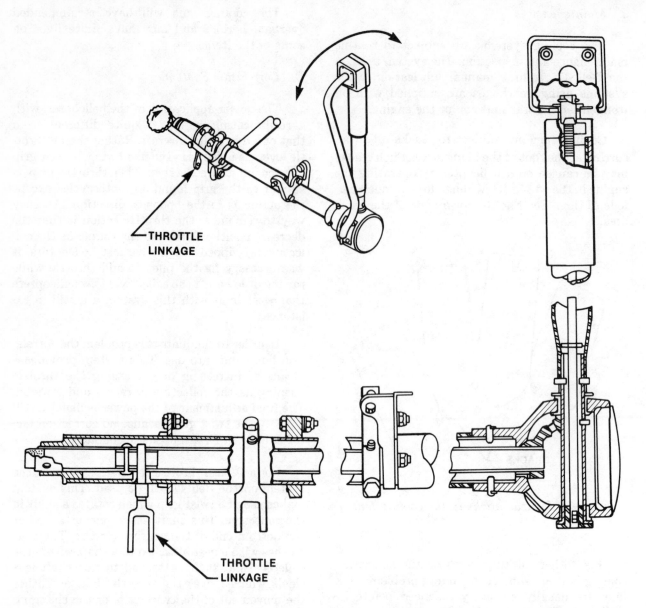

THROTTLE
LINKAGE

THROTTLE
LINKAGE

Fig. 8-8 Typical throttle linkage used on the Bell 47

tle. This is necessary because throttle-to-power output is not a straight-line movement. In other words, the engine power is not increased with the same throttle movement throughout its operation. The same power increments are not required for each degree of pitch change of the main rotor. For this reason a cam is used to establish the correct movement of the throttle in relationship to the pitch of the blades.

This cam, however, is not the usual type of cam. It is an irregular slot cut in a flat piece of metal. The slot with its irregular shape represents the various power outputs of the engine at dif-

ferent blade pitch settings. The cam is rotated by the input of the twist grip and collective. This in turn moves a cam follower connected to the cam box output which is connected through linkage to the throttle valve of the carburetor.

It may be noted that almost all of this linkage is adjustable. The replacement of any of the linkage will require re-rigging of the throttle control. The replacement of an engine may also lead to at least a partial re-rigging. The collective rigging will also affect the throttle rigging. Throttle rigging should never be attempted until the collective is properly rigged.

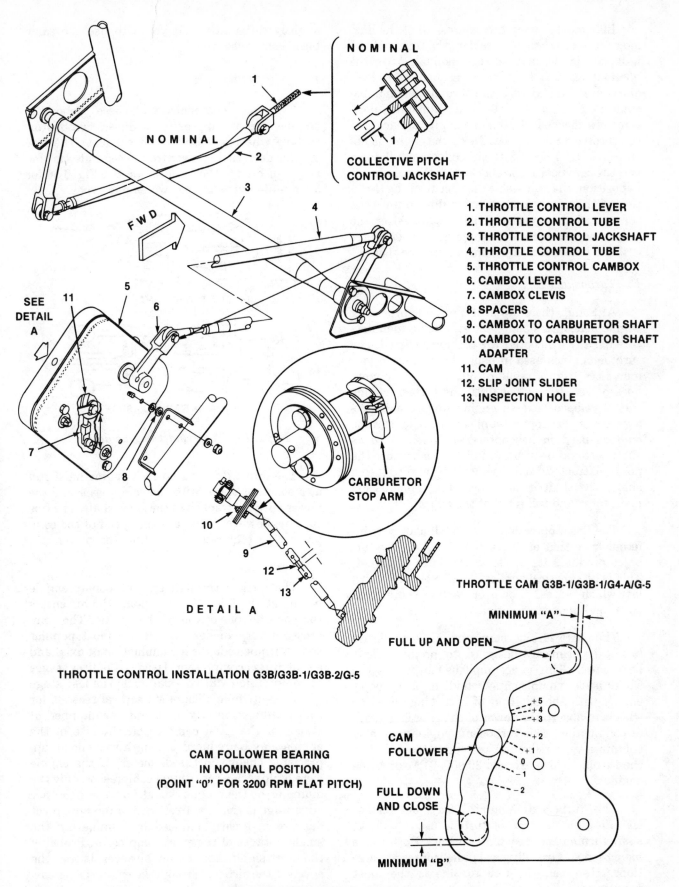

NOMINAL

NOMINAL

NOMINAL

COLLECTIVE PITCH
CONTROL JACKSHAFT

1. THROTTLE CONTROL LEVER
2. THROTTLE CONTROL TUBE
3. THROTTLE CONTROL JACKSHAFT
4. THROTTLE CONTROL TUBE
5. THROTTLE CONTROL CAMBOX
6. CAMBOX LEVER
7. CAMBOX CLEVIS
8. SPACERS
9. CAMBOX TO CARBURETOR SHAFT
10. CAMBOX TO CARBURETOR SHAFT
    ADAPTER
11. CAM
12. SLIP JOINT SLIDER
13. INSPECTION HOLE

FWD

SEE
DETAIL
A

CARBURETOR
STOP ARM

DETAIL A

THROTTLE CAM G3B-1/G3B-1/G4-A/G-5

THROTTLE CONTROL INSTALLATION G3B/G3B-1/G3B-2/G-5

MINIMUM "A"

FULL UP AND OPEN

+5
+4
+3
+2
+1
0
-1
-2

CAM
FOLLOWER

CAM FOLLOWER BEARING
IN NOMINAL POSITION
(POINT "0" FOR 3200 RPM FLAT PITCH)

FULL DOWN
AND CLOSE

MINIMUM "B"

Fig. 8-9   Throttle cam and linkage

317

Like most rigging procedures, all of the linkages are set to their nominal lengths which will be indicated in the maintenance manual. After the nominal lengths have been reached, the clearances are checked with the throttle linkage disconnected. After the full-up and full-down positions are checked, the linkage is placed back and the throttle stops are set. Next, the engine is operated at 3200 RPM with the collective full-down and the cam position is checked. If the cam is not in position, the adjustable disc between the throttle and the cam box must be readjusted until the zero position is reached on the cam. After the ground adjustments are completed, the helicopter is flown before fine adjustments may be made.

F. Turboshaft Engines

Although there are still many reciprocating engine helicopters and some still being manufactured, many helicopters are turbine powered. The turbine engines used in helicopters come in various sizes from a range of 300 to 3000 or more horsepower. It was not until the turbine engine was developed that an engine was actually designed for helicopter application. The turbine engines used in helicopters are referred to as shaft turbines or turboshafts. This is because the power extracted from the engine is used to turn a shaft. The shaft in turn turns the transmission main rotor and tail rotor of the helicopter.

The basic operation is quite similar, yet different from that of the turbojet engine. The turbojet produces its power in the form of thrust. This is by practical application of Newton's third law which states, "For every action there is an equal and opposite reaction."

The shaft turbine may produce some thrust but it is primarily designed to produce shaft horsepower. This is accomplished by using the same basic components found in a turbojet engine with the addition of a turbine wheel or wheels to absorb the power of the escaping gases of combustion. This turboshaft engine may also contain a gear reduction to reduce the speed of the turbine which exceeds 30,000 RPM on some engines.

The turboshaft engines may be further classified by the type of turbine used — direct shaft turbine and free shaft turbine. Both types have been successfully used in helicopter applications. However, the free turbine is the most popular in use today. The two turbines operate slightly differently and yet both use the same basic components.

1. Components

The basic components of these turboshaft engines are a compressor, diffuser, combustor, turbine wheel or wheels, and exhaust. The free turbine derives its power from a separate turbine not connected to the compressor. See Fig. 8-10 for a simplified view of the two engine types.

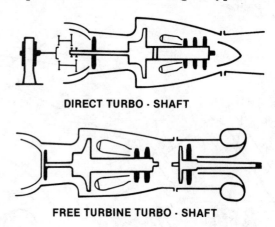

DIRECT TURBO - SHAFT

FREE TURBINE TURBO - SHAFT

Fig. 8-10   Turboshaft engine design

The direct drive turboshaft engine must run at a constant speed with the compressor and the power output attached to the same shaft. The free turbine, however, can vary the speed of the compressor as required to maintain the power turbine.

The airflow through the turboshaft engine begins at the inlet. At that point the air enters the compressor section of the engine. The compressors vary in design, but the most popular shaft turbine today is a combination of axial and a centrifugal compressor. Usually the first stages of compression will be axial while the last stage will be centrifugal. There are several reasons for this combination. By reducing the number of stages of the axial compressor, the size of the engine may be reduced in length without an appreciable change in the diameter. If the engine were built with a centrifugal compressor, only the diameter of the engine would increase. Another advantage is that the likelihood of foreign object damage is greatly reduced by eliminating the smaller stages of the axial compressor. Probably the most significant reason, however, is that the speed of the airflow through the engine is increased by using this combination of axial and cen-

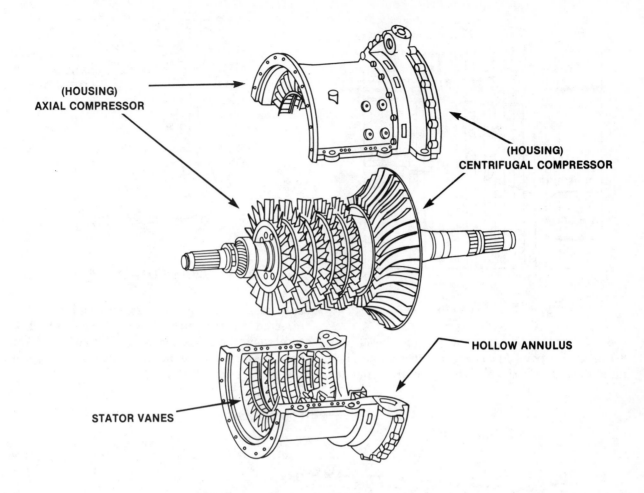

(HOUSING)
AXIAL COMPRESSOR

(HOUSING)
CENTRIFUGAL COMPRESSOR

HOLLOW ANNULUS

STATOR VANES

Fig. 8-11   Mixed compressor assembly

trifugal compressors. Fig. 8-11 shows this combination compressor.

The theory of operation of the compressors is quite simple. The axial compressor is made up of stages, each stage consisting of one stator and one rotor. The rotor is a multi-bladed disc with

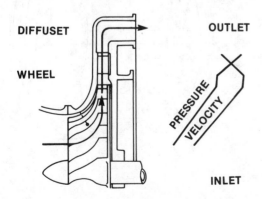

DIFFUSET

OUTLET

WHEEL

PRESSURE

VELOCITY

INLET

Fig. 8-12   Centrifugal compressor

each blade being an airfoil. The rotating airfoils speed up the airflow and force the air through the stator. This converts the airflow velocity into pressure by reducing the area in which the air flows (an application of Bernoulli's Principal). This process is repeated at each stage of the axial compressor (Fig. 8-12).

The centrifugal compressor is a large curved disc with blades. The blades are larger at the inlet than at the outlet. The air is simply picked up by the inlet and forced into a smaller area as the compressor rotates (Fig. 8-13).

The air is then directed to the diffuser section where it is straightened and enters the combustion area of the engine where some is used to support combustion and the rest used for cooling purposes.

Although different types of combustors may be used, the most popular for the turboshaft is

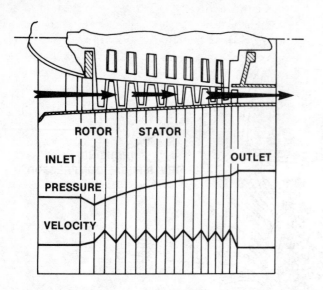

Fig. 8-13   Axial compressor

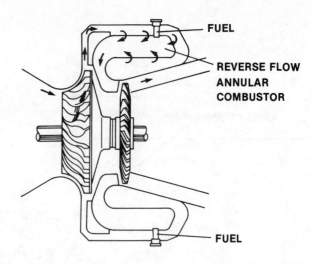

Fig. 8-14   Fuel enters the combustor

the annular combustor using reverse flow (Fig. 8-14). At this point fuel is added to the air and ignited. This heats the air which rapidly expands and passes through a nozzle assembly and is directed to the turbine wheel. This wheel is rotated by the gases passing over it and turns the compressor which generates more air to repeat the process (Fig. 8-15).

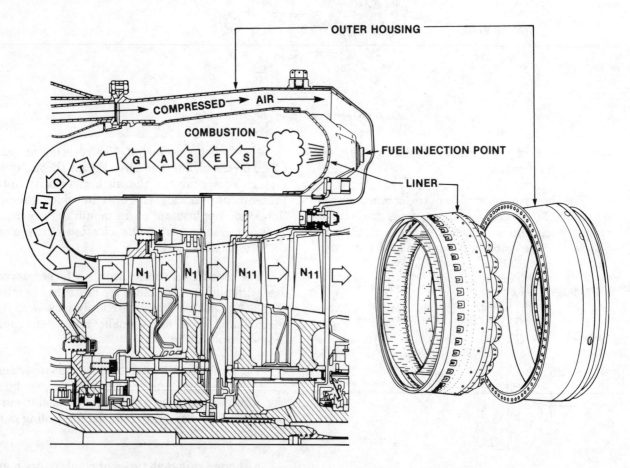

Fig. 8-15   Turbine wheels are turned by the expanded gases.

At this point the two turboshafts vary in operation. In the free turbine another turbine is placed behind the compressor turbine called the power turbine. This turbine drives a shaft to power the helicopter. The direct drive turbine may also have another turbine wheel but this is fixed to the compressor and also drives a power shaft used to power the helicopter. The way the shaft and turbine are used for power varies from engine to engine. Some engines drive from the compressor end (cold end) while others drive from the combustor end (hot end). Both have advantages and disadvantages. The main advantage of driving from the hot end is that less shafting is required. However, the gear reduction is exposed to more heat in this area. Two typical hot end and cold end systems are seen in Fig. 8-16.

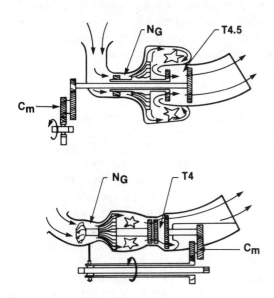

Fig. 8-16 Turboshafts may be driven from the cold end or hot end.

2. Weight and power

As in reciprocating powered helicopters, a number of items must be considered in the design and development of the engines built specifically for the helicopters.

The one consideration is the power-to-weight ratio. With the reciprocating engine a weight ratio of one pound per horsepower was considered ideal. Today it is not unusual to produce a turbine with ratio in excess of four horse-power per pound. This increases the payload of the helicopter, provides extra power for emergency conditions and under certain atmospheric conditions that require increased power.

The power an engine produces is measured in horsepower, which takes many forms. This horsepower produced by the turboshaft is usually expressed as *shaft horsepower (SHP)*, the power the engine was specifically built to produce. Another term sometimes used to indicate the power of a turboshaft engine is *equivalent shaft horsepower (ESHP)*. This takes into consideration the thrust that is produced by the engine and is calcuated as additional power. Thrust, however, is of very little benefit for helicopter operations. The horsepower produced is usually calculated under standard day conditions — meaning a 59° with a barometric pressure of 29.92 inches of mercury. This is also done with no accessories other than those necessary to sustain the engine operation. For example, no generator would be necessary because the engine will run without it.

a. Flat rated

It is quite easy to see the standard day is not a usual day for helicopter operations. It is known that both the engine performance and the helicopter performance will deteriorate with increases in atmospheric conditions such as density altitude. For this reason many turbines are referred to as *flat rated*. This means that a given horsepower may be reached to a given temperature such as 80 degrees. Some engines are even flat rated to higher temperatures such as 100 degrees.

b. Torque limited

Another term used in the discussion of power in regards to helicopters is *torque limited*. The term is not used in regards to the engine but the power the engine may deliver to the transmission. It is the transmission that is torque limited or capable of withstanding only so much of the engine's potential power output. This can, however, be of some benefit during operations when engine power deteriorates. If all the power is not used, additional power may be available because of the torque limitations. This often occurs with the single engine operation of a twin engine helicopter.

3. Power output

It must also be understood the helicopter engine produces only the power demanded of it by the helicopter operator. This is equally true of the turbine and reciprocating powerplant. The helicopter rotor operates at a constant RPM, but the pitch of the blades determines the power required to maintain the RPM. As the pitch increases more power is required to maintain the same RPM. On the reciprocating engine this power is measured by the manifold pressure. While operating on the ground at 3200 RPM the manifold pressure may be no greater than 10 inches of mercury. During a hover, however, the manifold pressure may reach close to atmospheric pressure to maintain the same 3200 RPM.

a. Torquemeter

Power output on the turbine engine is measured by a torquemeter. This device measures the force produced by the engine and may be expressed in the form of foot-pounds of torque, pounds of oil pressure, or any other convenient measurement. The most convenient measurement is foot-pounds of torque. Regardless of the measurement, this will increase with the pitch of the rotor to maintain the same RPM. The actual power produced by the engine is the output RPM times the torque in foot-pounds divided by a constant of 5252. Therefore, both the RPM and the torque are the determining factors in the power output of any engine. An engine that is capable of producing a very high RPM is not necessarily a powerful engine nor is a low RPM engine with high torque necessarily powerful, but the combination of the two factors will determine the power output of the engine.

b. Tachometer

To measure RPM on a shaft turbine, a tachometer is used. If the engine is a free turbine, two tachometers are used. One tachometer is used for the compressor (N_1 or N_g) and the other for the power turbine (N_2 or N_f). Tachometer designations are dependent of the engine, because no standard has yet been established. The fixed shaft turbine will require only one tachometer because the engine has only one rotating unit.

Tachometers often read in percent of maximum RPM instead of RPM due to the speed at which the turbine operates. For example: if a particular turbine reached a maximum speed of 24,500 RPM, this would be considered a percentage of the 100%. In some instances of a free turbine N_1 will be given in percent and N_2 in output shaft RPM. Since the N_2 system is attached to the main rotor, the N_2 tachometer is a dual

tachometer indicating the engine and main rotor output similar to tachometers used on reciprocating engine powered helicopters. This dual tachometer is also used with the fixed shaft turbines.

Free turbines can operate with different tachometer readings on both the N_1 and N_2 system. For example: a helicopter may operate on the ground at 100% N_2 with 60% N_1 because very little power is required to turn the rotor at an almost flat pitch. However, as collective is added, the N_1 must increase its speed to produce more gases for the N_2 system as more power is required. This same helicopter may require 85% of N_1 to maintain 100% N_2 in forward flight or 88% for hover and 98% for climb. If the N_2 RPM cannot be maintained or lags behind as collective is increased, it is referred to as *droop*. This may be the result of an overloaded helicopter, a worn engine, or incorrect adjustment.

c. Exhaust gas temperature indicator

Another instrument important to the operation of the turboshaft engine is the *exhaust gas temperature indicator*. This may be referred to by several names, dependent on the sensing unit location. It may be Exhaust Gas Temperature (EGT) or Inter Turbine Temperature (ITT). In either case it is related to the temperature of the gases passing through the turbine area. If these gases are too hot, the metal of the hot section of the engine may be damaged. This is especially true in the areas of the nozzles and turbine wheels. Such overheating may lead to a burning of the metal or a turbine wheel stretch because of the combination of the heat and centrifugal force. This instrument must be carefully monitored during starting and may be a determining factor during takeoff with heavy loads and high ambient temperatures in some helicopters even though the torque is within limits.

4. Oil system

Like the reciprocating engine, the shaft turbine will contain an oil system. This will require an oil pressure gauge and an oil temperature gauge. Both will operate in the same manner as that of the reciprocating engine. However, the oil warm-up period will not be as critical as the piston engine. This is due to the use of roller and ball bearings receiving their lubrication by spray rather than by pressure as required with plain

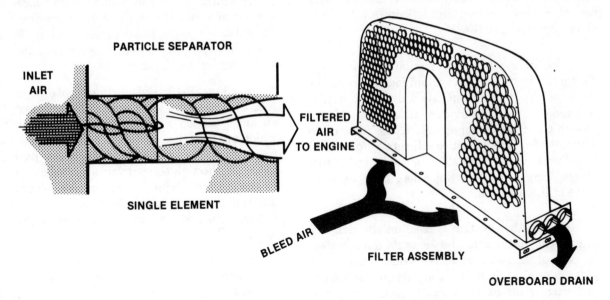

PARTICLE SEPARATOR

INLET AIR

SINGLE ELEMENT

FILTERED AIR TO ENGINE

BLEED AIR

FILTER ASSEMBLY

OVERBOARD DRAIN

Fig. 8-17   Particle separator used on the Bell 206

babbit bearings. The oil pressure is critical, because of the increased oil flow through the engine for cooling purposes as well as lubrication.

5. Particle separators

The turboshaft has eliminated a few of the requirements necessary to the reciprocating engine, while adding a few necessary for the turbine engine. With the piston engine, cooling air was a requirement for engine operation. The turbine engine has no such requirement, but it will require a larger airflow for the operation of the engine. One of the most critical requirement of this air is that it be clear of foreign objects. This can be difficult in helicopter operations where landings are often conducted in unimproved areas with dust and sand being blown into the air by the downwash of the main rotors. This often re-

quires the use of a particle separator on the inlet of the engine. Most separators are available as optional equipment. Some helicopters have them as standard equipment.

There are several particle separator systems in use today, and they all operate on two principles. For this reason only three systems will be discussed. The first will be the Bell 206 system. On this aircraft a total of 283 individual elements are used for the inlet filter. Each of these filter elements is a swirl chamber (Fig. 8-17). As the air passes through each element, it is swirled and any dirt particles are thrown to the outside of the tube by centrifugal force, causing the particles to drop to the bottom of the filter unit. Compressor bleed air runs into the bottom of the unit to scavenge the particles overboard through three holes on each side of the filter unit. Since the openings are

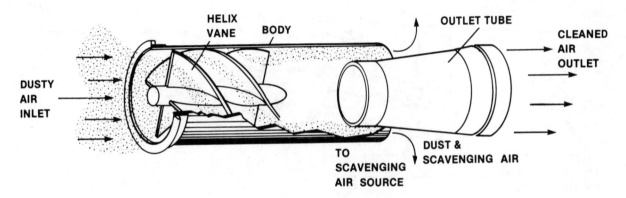

HELIX VANE   BODY

OUTLET TUBE

CLEANED AIR OUTLET

DUSTY AIR INLET

TO SCAVENGING AIR SOURCE

DUST & SCAVENGING AIR

Fig. 8-18   Large single unit particle separator

rather small, some problems are experienced with wet snow. For this reason, deflectors have been placed on the inlet cowling.

Another system quite similar to the 206 is shown in Fig. 8-18. This system makes use of the same swirling action but has a different frontal arrangement with individual filter units placed around an octagon shaped unit. These filter units have also been found quite efficient as one large filter unit rather than 200 or more individual filters. This large tube inlet has been used on some military aircraft.

Still another system is used on the Bell 212 (Fig. 8-19). It consists of a separate duct system for each of the two engines. This duct system provides for inlet air particle separation and cools and carries off exhaust gases. Each system is composed of an air inlet system, a forward duct, engine induction baffle, particle separator valve, transition duct, power section exhaust duct and ejector.

Each particle separator valve is controlled by a 28-volt actuator. The particle separator valve is open under normal conditions of operation to provide inertia separation. The door, however, will close under two conditions. One of these conditions occurs anytime the N_1 drops below 52% RPM. The other occurs when the fire extinguisher handle is pulled.

A switch is also provided which places the system in automatic in the normal position, and the valve is open in the override position. Whenever the valve is closed, the caution particle separator light will illuminate.

In Fig. 8-19 the airflow pattern is as follows: air enters the forward duct through the air inlet section and has two paths of airflow which are into the engine inlet and into the ejector. A portion of the air and the heavy particles move aft through the particle separator valve into the ejector, giving inertia particle separation. The remaining air enters the compressor through a wire mesh screen and is consumed by the engine.

On many other helicopters, an inlet screen is used with no particle separation. The screens will prevent large foreign objects from entering the engine. They are particle separators, also able to collect material such as grass and leaves. They must be checked frequently for accumulation especially if the helicopter is operated in an area where this type of material may be picked up during landings. The accumulation of this type of material will limit the airflow to the engine. This may result in higher temperatures and could lead to a condition of compressor stall.

6. Guide vanes

A set of guide vanes are located prior to the compressor, usually fixed airfoils placed around

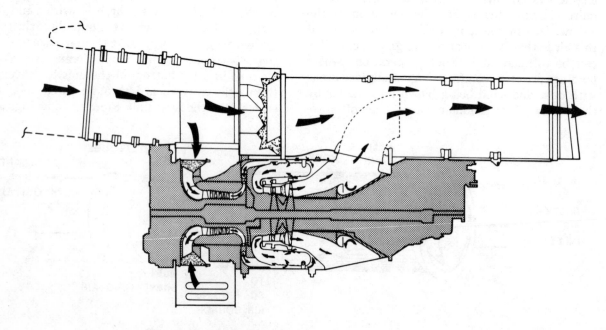

Fig. 8-19 Particle separator used on the Bell 212

the circumference of the inlet. They are used to straighten the airflow and prepare the air for the compressor. In a few instances the inlet guide vanes may be movable if a transonic airfoil is used in the compressor. The purpose of the variable inlet guide vanes is to provide a surge margin for the engine by directing the air at various angles at the various compressor speeds.

7. Compressor damage

The compressors in turboshaft engines are often axial flow during the first stages of compression and then pass through a centrifugal compressor for the final compression stage. Both the axial and centrifugal compressors have been used in turbine engines for many years. The small engine compressors are subject to several factors.

a. FOD damage

Foreign object damage (FOD) may be caused by anything other than air passing through the compressor. This is one reason a particle separator is placed on the inlet of many of the helicopter engines. Foreign objects may be quite varied and the damage they may cause will also be quite varied.

b. Erosion

If the damage is caused by sand, which in certain operations would be quite common, the compressor components will erode, allowing the engine to continuously ingest sand particles with the rapid airflow. Material will be removed from the compressor blades and stators as if the compressor was sandblasted.

This removal of metal will eventually change the shape of the airfoil sections since the blades are actually airfoils. This erosion of the airfoil might be compared to the formation of ice on a wing because both will change the shape and efficiency of the airfoil. Once this efficiency is changed, the compressor cannot supply the required airflow. The first result of this is higher operating temperatures because so much of the airflow is used for cooling in a turbine engine. As the erosion continues, the next result will be in compressor surge or stall. This is the result of the combustor pressure, becoming greater than the compressor pressure and having reverse flow. This may be a loud report or a rumbling sound

and will more often occur when the engine is developing high power.

c. Nicks, scratches, and blade deformation

Larger items passing through the compressor can result in severe damage such as scratches, nicks, and deformation of the blades. And, under the right circumstances, may result in blades breaking off, passing through the rest of the compressor, doing still more damage. The nicks and scratches may not in themselves be harmful to the airflow but will result in stresses to the blade. The blades of the compressor rotor are highly stressed as the result of centrifugal force because of the rotational speeds. This, coupled with the stress area caused by FOD, can result in failure with the blade passing through the compressor and doing more damage. The loss of a blade will also cause a balance problem resulting in total failure of the engine.

Such damage can be greatly reduced by a particle separator but even with such a precaution, care of the inlet section is required by the maintenance personnel. This includes the removal of safety wire clippings and other objects that may be ingested by the engine. Safety wire and soft materials such as rags are most damaging.

d. Dirt

Another concern with compressors is dirt. Dirt, like erosion, will change the shape of the airfoils and reduce the efficiency of the compressor. This will increase the operating temperatures. This buildup of dirt is rather gradual and the temperature increase will also be gradual. Dirt buildup may be accelerated by the area of operation and any oil that may be on the compressor blades. The removal of dirt is usually done by injecting a cleaning solution in the inlet of the engine in a liquid form. It is not unusual for this to drop the operating temperature as much as 40 °C on some engines. In any cleaning, the maintenance manual must be carefully studied and followed.

e. Blockage

Blockage or partial blockage of the airflow is critical as it limits the airflow through the engine. If enough of the airflow is restricted, stall and flameout of the engine may result. This blockage may be the result of several factors including ice, weeds, and grass or leaves collecting in the inlet area of the engine. Most helicopters have some protection from ice and snow by the location of the inlet air and sometimes by deflectors in the area. Additional protection is usually given to the engine by using compressor discharge air to prevent ice buildup at the inlet guide vanes. This heats the hollow vanes with *bleed air* which may be 400° from compression.

The blockage that occurs from vegetation usually collects during landings and hovering operations. It requires cleaning of the inlet area and careful consideration of landing areas where this problem might be minimized. Such a buildup may occur at the particle separator or on the inlet screen.

8. Acceleration time

One of the earliest problems encountered with turboshaft engines in helicopters is the acceleration time of the engine. The acceleration, or response, time is instantaneous with reciprocating engines, while the response time of the turbine is not. Today acceleration times have been increased appreciably from that of the earliest turboshaft engines but even today an acceleration time of 2-1/2 seconds from flight idle to maximum power is not unusual.

An aid to assist the acceleration, such devices as bleed valves, bleed ports and variable stators are used in conjunction with the compressor section of the turboshaft engine. These devices simply unload the compressor during acceleration so that the compressor may turn faster more quickly.

With the bleed systems, compressor air is simply dumped overboard from the latter stages of compression. On engines equipped with variable stators the stator angle changes allowing the air to pass through without being as fully compressed. Without the aids the turboshaft would be very slow in acceleration and would almost certainly reach a state of compressor stall when rapid response is required. The systems are all designed to fail in the open position, resulting in a power loss at the highest power outputs. The devices are usually operated by the fuel control and the air pressure ratio of the compressor.

9. Combustion

The air passes through the compressor and diffuser which prepares it for the combustor section. As previously mentioned, the most widely used combustor for the turboshaft engine is the annular combustor utilizing the reverse flow system. The air brought into the combustion section is used for two different purposes. The smaller portion is used for combustion, while the larger portion is used for cooling and protecting the combustor components from the heat developed by combustion.

It is in this part of the engine that fuel and ignition are introduced and combustion takes place. The fuel is furnished by the fuel control unit to discharge nozzles at strategic locations around the combustor.

Ignition is initated by a spark plug-like ignitor, but is sustained by the continuous flow of air and fuel. In many engines the ignition system may be deactivated once the engine is operating.

10. Fuel controls

A typical fuel metering system is shown in Fig. 8-20. The fuel enters the fuel control unit through the inlet screen equipped with a by-pass in the event the screen should become blocked. The fuel is then directed to the pump. This particular pump is a dual element gear-type pump driven through the compressor accessory gear box. The fuel is then routed through a servo filter. Most of the fuel will pass around the filter unit while some will enter the filter and be used to operate a hydraulic system within the control unit. This fuel will be used to operate the computer portion of the fuel control. The fuel that passes around the filter unit takes one of two paths. One path leads to the high pressure relief valve, excessive pressure is returned to the inlet side of the pump. The other fuel proceeds to the change-over valve. The change-over valve directs fuel to either an automatic or manual mode. The manual mode, normally referred to as the *emergency system*, is only used when the automatic system malfunctions.

The change-over valve is manually activated by the pilot through a switch and solenoid. In the schematic the change-over valve is in the automatic mode. In this position the fuel travels to the pressure regulator valve, a differential

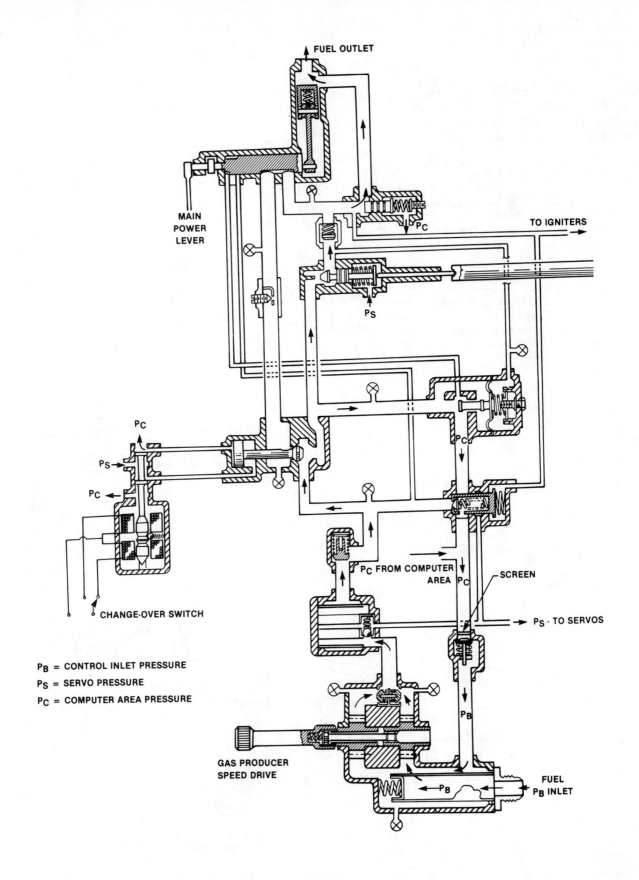

FUEL OUTLET

MAIN
POWER
LEVER

TO IGNITERS

P_C

P_S

P_C

P_S

P_C

P_C

P_C FROM COMPUTER
AREA P_C

SCREEN

P_S · TO SERVOS

CHANGE-OVER SWITCH

P_B = CONTROL INLET PRESSURE

P_S = SERVO PRESSURE

P_C = COMPUTER AREA PRESSURE

P_B

GAS PRODUCER
SPEED DRIVE

P_B

FUEL
P_B INLET

Fig. 8-20   Typical hydromechanical fuel control

327

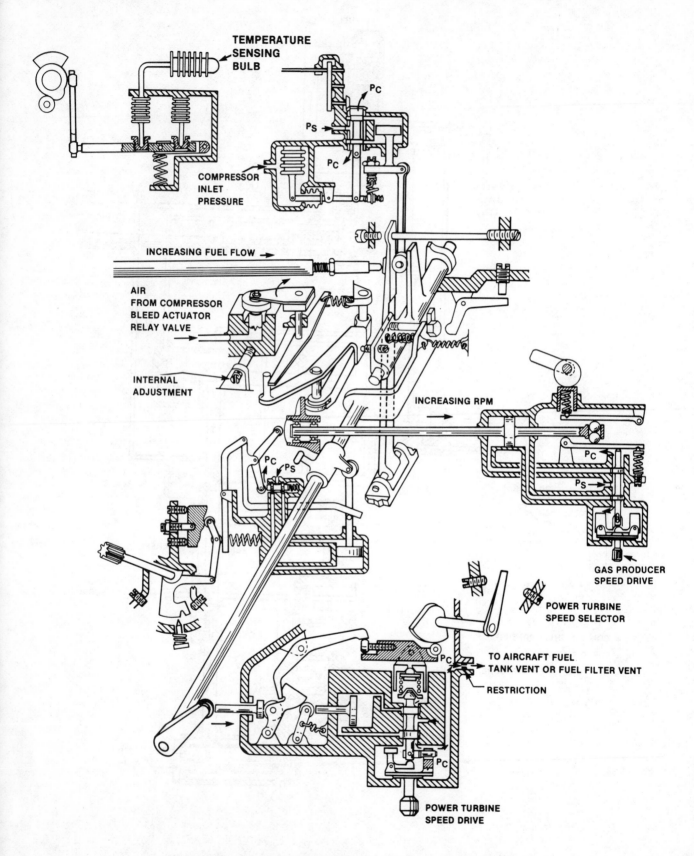

Fig. 8-21 Hydromechanical fuel control computor section

328

pressure valve. This valve may bypass fuel to the inlet side of the pump if excessive pressure has built up in that portion of the system. The fuel flows through the metering valve. The position of this valve is determined by the mechanical computer portion of the fuel control. Ths is the automatic portion of the fuel control. After passing through the metering valve, the fuel comes in contact with the foot valve, actually a minimum pressure valve, which prevents fuel from leaving the fuel control without minimum pressure as would occur on starting. The next valve fuel makes contact with is the shut-off valve. This is simply used to turn the fuel on and off.

In the manual or emergency position the fuel is directed past a restrictor as a means of limiting pressure because the regulator valve is not in this system. The fuel is metered by a manual metering valve and then returns to the normal fuel path to the engine.

Other fuel controls may operate differently. The pump may be a separate unit and the valves may have different locations, but the basic principles are almost always the same.

a. Computer portion

The computer portion of fuel controls varies considerably depending on the manufacturer. As on the carburetor of a reciprocating engine, the purpose of a fuel control is to direct the correct proportions of fuel to the engine meeting the demands of that engine. However, with the turbine several items must be considered to determine the quantity of fuel to be placed in the combustor at a given time. This amount of fuel is governed by several factors that ensure that the correct ratio of fuel and air are obtained. The items shown in Fig. 8-21 will govern the fuel-air ratios and position the metering valve so the ratio is obtained. These items are:

1. A temperature compensator

2. A barometric pressure compensator

3. An N_1 governor*

4. An N_2 governor

5. A power control actuator

6. A 3-D cam

*This particular fuel control is used on a free turbine engine. For this reason both the N_1 and N_2 have governors. In systems with direct drive turbines, only one governor would be present.

The temperature of the air will affect the operation of the engine and the amount of fuel the engine should receive. For this reason temperature compensation is corrected by the fuel control. This is done by placing a temperature bulb at the inlet of the engine. The bulb is filled with a liquid that expands and contracts with changes in temperature. As it expands and contracts, it moves through a tube attached to a bellows in the fuel control. The bellows acts through linkage and positions the metering valve in the correct position for the temperature.

In a like manner the ambient air pressure must be considered for the proper ratio. Because the proper ratio is obtained by mixing fuel with air by density rather than volume. Compressor inlet pressure is sensed through a line to the fuel control. Inside the fuel control is a chamber containing an aneroid. Like the aneroid in a barometer it will expand and contract with changes in pressure. The changes will be weaker than would be required to move the mechanical linkage. For this reason the aneroid simply operates a servo valve using fuel pressure to activate a piston that will move the linkage to position the metering valve.

The N_1 governor is used to control the speed of the N_1 system or compressor section. It is a mechanical governor operating from the N_1 accessory gearbox rotating a set of flyweights which sense the speed of the system. The flyweights raise and lower a servo valve utilizing fuel pressure to activate the piston that moves the linkage to position the metering valve.

The N_2 governor operates in much the same manner except the governor is driven from the N_2 or power turbine system. The flyweights move the servo valve which in turn moves the piston and positions the metering valve. The power control works in much the same manner, movements being transferred to the linkage to position the metering valve.

It is quite easy to see all of these movements must in some way be correlated to obtain the correct amount of fuel for the engine in all modes of operation. A mathematician with the help of an engineer could figure out each conceivable fuel ratio required for the speeds, power, temperature, barometric pressure, acceleration and deceleration. These in turn may be plotted on a curve. In fact, this is what is done. The plotted curves are ground into the three faces of the cam. No movements of the various components of the computer section will take place without affecting or being affected by the cam position. The movement of the metering valve must be in harmony with all aspects of the computer.

b. *Operational procedures*

Now that the basic operation of the fuel control has been discussed, its relation to the helicopter and the engine may be discussed.

The engine's N_1 system is rotated by a starter. As the rotational speed increases, the pump in the fuel control builds up pressure. This pressure is tapped off for starting fuel next to the foot valve and flows to the starting fuel nozzles. When the pressure is sufficient and the compressor has reached proper operating speed ignition takes place. This means the airflow and ignition system must be in operation prior to fuel flow through the starting system and the fuel control must be in the proper position.

Positioning the fuel control is accomplished with the twist grip which positions the N_1 governor, power control actuator of the fuel control, and the stopcock.

Once combustion has occurred, the hot gases passing through the turbine with the assist of the starter accelerate the engine to the point that it is self-sustaining without the aid of the starter. The foot valve then opens to deliver fuel to the main nozzles. At this time the engine accelerates until the twist grip position is reached. Once the twist grip is placed in the proper position, the engine may develop the proper rotor RPM.

The rotor RPM may be varied by changing the fuel requirements through the N_2 governor, which has a linear actuator connected to a speeder spring arrangement on the governor. The linear actuator is moved by a switch on the collective, increasing or decreasing the tension of the speeder spring. Tension of the speeder spring controls the flyweights of the governor placing them in an overspeed or underspeed condition. The position of the flyweights determines the need for more or less fuel.

The linear actuator movement is necessary to set the rotor RPM at a constant speed for the particular condition. Once this fuel ratio is established and the RPM set, it will remain in that state. On the ground this may be 66% N_1 speed and 325 rotor RPM.

The collective is connected to the N_2 governor by linkage through the linear actuator. As the collective is raised, the pitch of the rotor increases and the governor receives an underspeed signal from the tension of the speeder spring. The demands for more fuel repositions the metering valve to maintain the fuel required for constant rotor RPM. If the collective is lowered, the reverse action takes place.

For all practical purposes, it may be said that the engine maintains a constant RPM through the N_2 governor once the RPM is established.

11. *Ignition systems*

The ignition systems of turbine engines is only used during starting. Once combustion occurs the system is not in use. Most of the ignition systems are high capacitance discharge systems and are commonly used on all jet engines. They consist of an exciter, igniter, and appropriate wiring. Many of these ignition systems have automatic relight systems in the event of a flameout.

After combustion has occurred, the air in the combustor is heated very rapidly. This expands the air and it moves to the nozzle assembly where it is directed to the turbine wheel. At this point the turbine wheel rotates the compressor. In the direct-drive shaft turbine, it also turns the power shaft. On the free turbine the air passing through the compressor turbine is redirected to a power turbine which drives the output shaft. The use of more than one turbine wheel is not unusual in either type of engine. The air then passes through the exhaust system and overboard.

G. *Powerplants*

There are many helicopters in operation today using basically the same turboshaft engines. At the present time approximately six different turboshaft engines are widely used in civilian

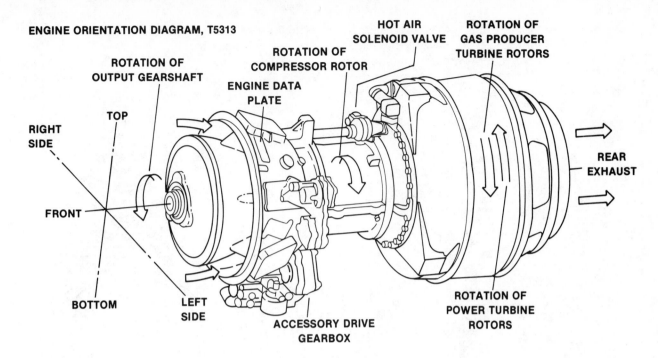

ENGINE ORIENTATION DIAGRAM, T5313

ROTATION OF
OUTPUT GEARSHAFT

ROTATION OF
COMPRESSOR ROTOR

ENGINE DATA
PLATE

HOT AIR
SOLENOID VALVE

ROTATION OF
GAS PRODUCER
TURBINE ROTORS

TOP

RIGHT
SIDE

FRONT

REAR
EXHAUST

BOTTOM

LEFT
SIDE

ACCESSORY DRIVE
GEARBOX

ROTATION OF
POWER TURBINE
ROTORS

Fig. 8-22   T53 turboshaft engine

helicopters, although possibly another six are in other applications that are not as widely used. We will only discuss the more widely used engines.

1. Lycoming T53 series

One of the oldest turboshaft engines is the Lycoming T53 series. This engine has been built in several different models and used by military and civilian helicopters. It was probably the first engine built specifically for a helicopter.

The two models most widely used are the T5311 and the T5313. Earlier models of this engine were used by the military and had a few civilian applications. Because the T5313 is a later engine and will be in service, it will be used in the discussion.

a. T5313 engine

The T5313 is a turboshaft engine with a two-stage free-power turbine and a two-stage gas-producer turbine. It has a combination axial-centrifugal compressor and an annular atomizing type combustor. It is torque limited in horse-power to 1250 SHP for 5 minutes and 1100 SHP for maximum continuous operation.

All directions and rotations are referenced as if seated in the pilot's seat — front, rear, forward,

aft, right, left, up and down. Rotations are clockwise and counterclockwise. The first stage turbine turns counterclockwise. The second stage turbine and the output shaft turn clockwise (Fig. 8-22).

There are five major sections of the engine. They are the:

1. Air inlet section

2. Compressor rotor section

3. Diffuser section

4. Combustion section

5. Exhaust section

A view of the disassembled engine is shown in Fig. 8-23.

The flow of air through the engine and basic operation is shown in Fig. 8-24. The air passes through the struts that support the inner and outer portions and rearward across variable inlet guide vanes to the compressor. The air is compressed by a five-stage axial compressor and a single-stage centrifugal compressor. The air then passes through the diffuser where the high-velocity air is converted to high pressure and the

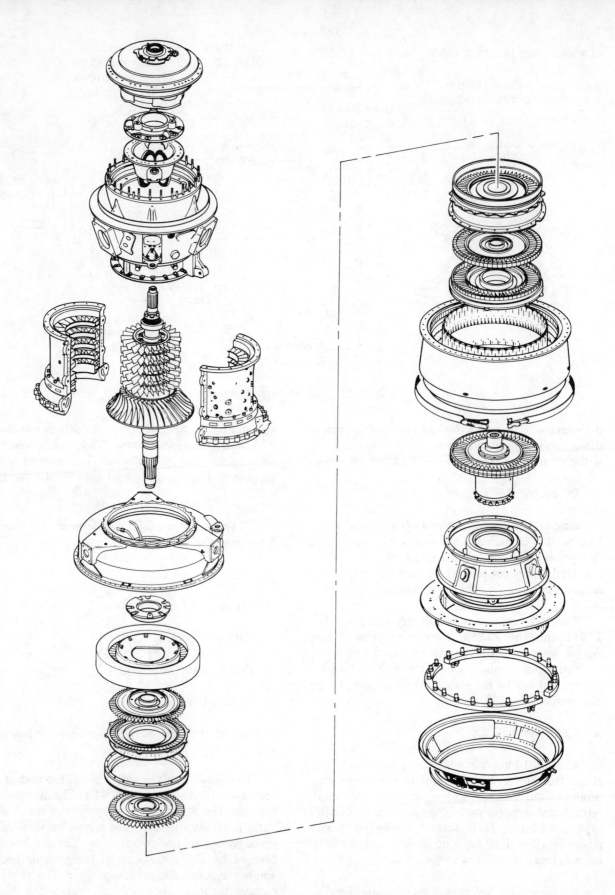

Fig. 8-23   Exploded view of T53 engine

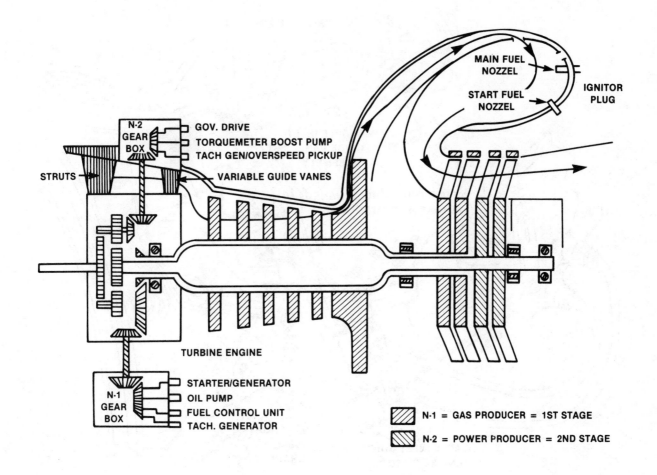

Fig. 8-24 Basic T53 operation

air flow is returned to a radial flow. Provisions are made on the diffuser for bleeding air from the compressor. This air may be used for a number of purposes including a cabin heater, an oil cooler blower, and engine anti-icers.

As the air leaves the diffuser, it enters the combustion area where the pressure is reduced, the velocity is decreased, and the direction is changed. The air is used for two purposes — to cool the combustion area and to support combustion. The fuel is introduced into the chamber by 22 atomizers at the aft end of the combustor. As combustion takes place, the temperatures will reach 3500°F. Flowing out of the combustor, the gases again reverse direction and flow across the two-stage gas producer turbine and two-stage power turbine. The power turbines drive a shaft passing through the compressor turning the gear reduction, the engine output shaft, and the N_2 gearbox.

The gas producer turbines turn the compressor which extracts approximately 2/3 of the energy to produce more air for combustion. In addition to driving the compressor it also turns the N_1 accessory gearbox on the bottom of the engine.

(1) Major operating systems

The major operating systems of the engine are:

1. Variable inlet guide vanes

2. Interstage bleed system

3. Anti-icing system

4. Ignition system

5. Fuel system

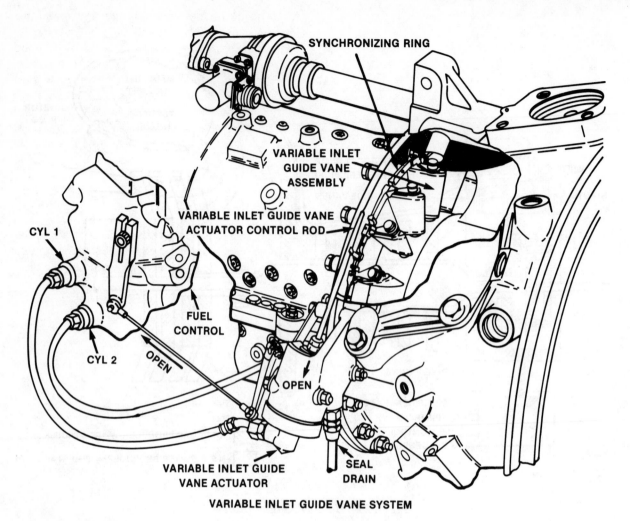

VARIABLE INLET GUIDE VANE SYSTEM

Fig. 8-25   Variable guide vane operation

6. Oil system

(a) Variable inlet guide vanes

The variable inlet guide vanes provide a surge margin. The angle of incidence of the inlet air to the first compressor rotor must be within the stall-free operating range of the transonic airfoil. The first two stages of the compressor have sonic-type blades. Because of the sonic blades it is necessary to vary the angle of attack with the speed of the compressor. The angle of attack is changed by the guide vanes.

The inlet guide vanes consist of a series of hollow blades positioned by a synchronizing ring through the inlet guide vane actuator (Fig. 8-25).

The actuator is positioned by a pilot valve in the fuel control. The pilot valve position is the function of N_1 speed and compressor inlet temperature. From 0 to 80% RPM, the vanes are at a minimum open position. The vanes start to open at 80% N_1 and are fully open by 95% N_1 speed. For a steady state operation between 80% and 95% N_1 the vanes will assume a steady position.

(b) Interstage air bleed

The interstage air bleed (Fig. 8-26) improves the compressor acceleration by the automatic release of air during acceleration. This is accomplished by bleed holes around the fifth stage of compression.

Compressor discharge pressure is taken from the diffuser housing and connected to the actuator control-air dump valve, through an orifice to the control valve in the fuel control. The con-

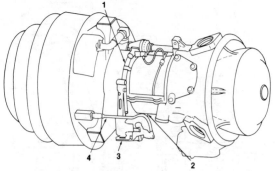

1. BLEED BAND ASSEMBLY
2. FUEL CONTROL TO INTERSTAGE BLEED ACTUATOR
   AIR PRESSURE HOSE
3. INTERSTAGE BLEED ACTUATOR
4. AIR DIFFUSER TO INTERSTAGE BLEED ACTUATOR
   AIR PRESSURE HOSE

Fig. 8-26   Bleed band position

trol valve in the fuel control is operated as a function of N_1 speed. When the valve is open, the compressor air is dumped overboard. The bleed band will remain open because of the spring in the actuator, up to speeds of 80% N_1 and during acceleration. The band will be closed at steady-state condition above 80%. This will close the control valve in the fuel control, causing the dump valve to close. When the dump valve closes, pressure in the cylinder will force the piston to move and close the band (Fig. 8-27).

(c) Anti-icing system

The anti-icing system supplies hot air under pressure to prevent icing of the inlet housing and the inlet guide vanes during operations.

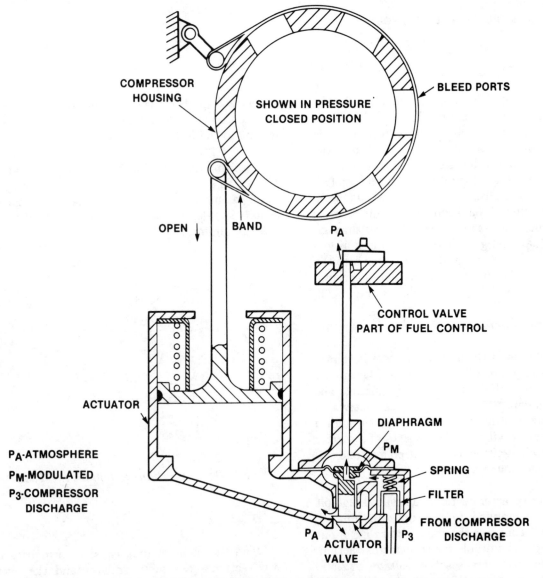

Fig. 8-27   Schematic of the bleed band system of the T53

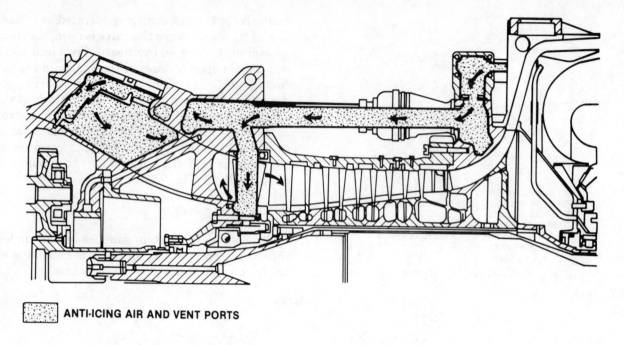

ANTI-ICING AIR AND VENT PORTS

Fig. 8-28 Anti-icing system

Air is collected from an air chamber on the top of the diffuser section. This air has been heated by the compression. The heated air is directed to the anti-icing valve on the top of the engine. This inline valve is operated by a solenoid and is spring loaded to the open position for a fail-safe system. The air is directed from the valve to the inlet housing of the engine. From this point, it passes through an annular passage and through the individual inlet guide vanes. The bleed air exits the individual vanes and passes back into the compressor. Other bleed air is circulated through the inlet struts and dumped overboard (Fig. 8-28).

(d) Ignition system

The purpose of the ignition system is to provide high energy, medium voltage to four igniter plugs located in the combustor for starting. The system is a capacitor discharge type unit which converts low voltage to high voltage through a transformer and vibrator. It consists of a starter trigger switch, ignition unit, ignition lead and coil assembly, and four igniter plugs.

When the starter switch is activated, 24-volt DC power is applied to the ignition unit. A vibrator unit converts the steady-state DC input to pulsating DC suitable for transformer action. The transformer increases the voltage to 2500 volts used to charge the capacitor. When the

stored voltage becomes sufficient, it will jump a gap and travel to the dividers where the voltage is sent to the four igniters.

Ignition is accomplished at approximately 12% of N_1 speed with starting fuel and is shut off at aproximately 40% of N_1 when the starter switch is released. At that time combustion is self-sustaining (Fig. 8-29).

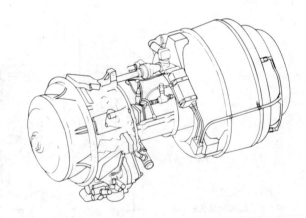

Fig. 8-29 Ignition system on the T53

(e) Fuel system

The fuel control unit consists primarily of two sections—the fuel regulator and the over-speed governor. The purpose of the fuel control is

336

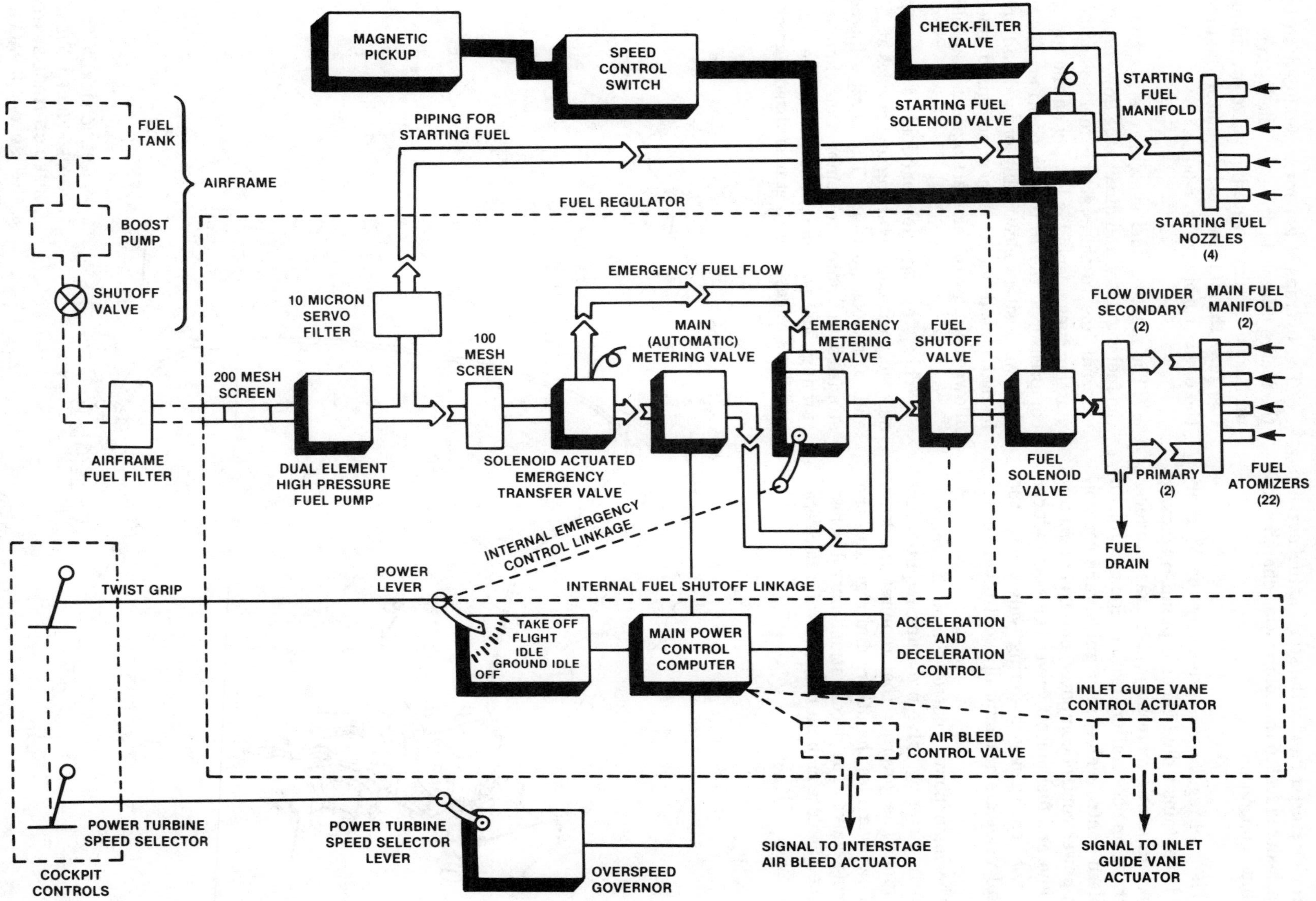

Fig. 8-30 T53 fuel system

337

to provide starter fuel for the starting fuel nozzles and scheduled fuel to the combustion chamber for continued operation.

The fuel regulator is driven by the N_1 gearbox. It contains a dual element pump, a transfer valve, automatic metering valve, gas producer governor, an acceleration-deceleration control, an air bleed control valve, inlet guide vane control, main power control computer, emergency metering valve and fuel shutoff valve. The gas producer governor, emergency metering valve, and the shutoff valve are mechanically controlled units.

The main power control computer controls the main metering valve providing required fuel to engine. The governor that requires the least fuel flow overrides the others and regulates the metering valve. The deceleration control schedules the absolute minimum fuel flow for deceleration.

The overspeed governor, mounted on top of the fuel regulator, is driven by the N_2 gearbox. It positions the main metering valve providing the fuel flow through the fuel regulator required for the power turbine (Fig. 8-30).

The starting fuel system receives fuel from the fuel regulator and directs the flow through an external line to the starting fuel solenoid. The starting fuel solenoid is located on the top of the compressor in the 10 o'clock position. The valve is a two-position electrically opened and spring-loaded closed valve. When energized open, it allows fuel flow to the starting fuel manifold.

This starting fuel manifold is a two-piece assembly with four starting fuel nozzles at 2, 4, 8, and 10 o'clock positions. The nozzles introduce atomzied fuel into the combustion chamber for starting. The solenoid, activited by the starting switch, is released with starter disengagement.

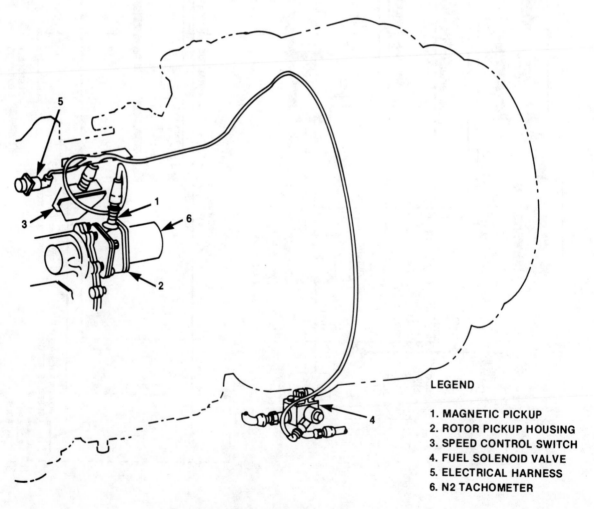

LEGEND

1. MAGNETIC PICKUP
2. ROTOR PICKUP HOUSING
3. SPEED CONTROL SWITCH
4. FUEL SOLENOID VALVE
5. ELECTRICAL HARNESS
6. N2 TACHOMETER

Fig. 8-31 Speed control system

The main fuel system consists of the over-speed trip system solenoid, the flow divider, main fuel manifold, and main fuel atomizers.

/1/ Overspeed trip system

The components of the system include a rotor pickup housing, magnetic pickup, speed control switch and fuel solenoid valve (Fig. 8-31).

The overspeed trip system was designed as a means of preventing engine failure due to excessive N_2 speed. The excessive speeds could be the result of loss of output shaft load or a sudden increase in fuel flow due to a fuel control malfunction. In these situations, the overspeed trip system will restrict fuel flow if the N_2 RPM reaches 110%.

The pickup housing for this system is located between the N_2 gearbox and the N_2 tachometer generator. Inside the box is a 60-tooth gear which is driven from the gearbox. A magnetic pickup is placed in close proximity to the gear teeth producing a voltage signal as each tooth passes the pickup. The pulses will increase in frequency as the speed of N_2 increases. The pulses govern a speed control switch, designed to provide 28-volts DC to the solenoid valve when 110% N_2 RPM is reached. At 110% the valve closes and limits the fuel flow to the engine. Main fuel flows through the solenoid valve from the fuel control to the flow divider and dump valve assembly mounted on the bottom of the engine (Fig. 8-32).

/2/ Flow divider

The flow divider and dump valve assembly are designed to provide correct fuel atomization throughout the engine's operation. This is ac-

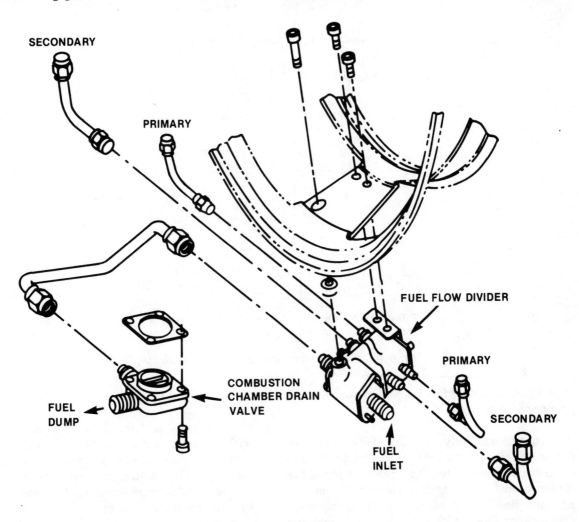

SECONDARY

PRIMARY

FUEL FLOW DIVIDER

PRIMARY

FUEL DUMP

COMBUSTION CHAMBER DRAIN VALVE

SECONDARY

FUEL INLET

Fig. 8-32 Fuel flow divider and combustor drain valve

339

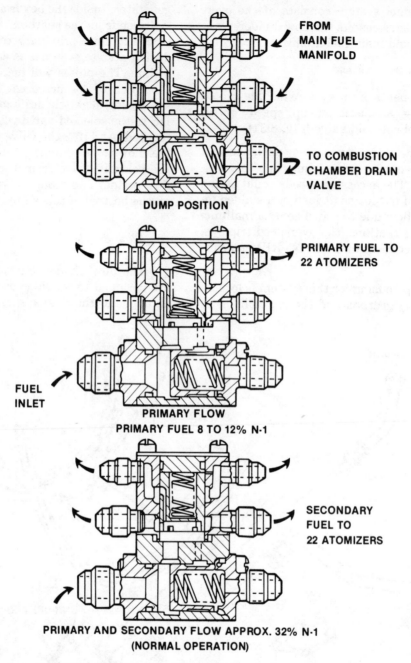

FROM MAIN FUEL MANIFOLD

TO COMBUSTION CHAMBER DRAIN VALVE

DUMP POSITION

PRIMARY FUEL TO 22 ATOMIZERS

FUEL INLET

PRIMARY FLOW
PRIMARY FUEL 8 TO 12% N-1

SECONDARY FUEL TO 22 ATOMIZERS

PRIMARY AND SECONDARY FLOW APPROX. 32% N-1
(NORMAL OPERATION)

Fig. 8-33   Fuel divider primary and secondary flow

complished by a dual flow capability consisting of primary and secondary.

At approximately 8 to 13% of N_1 and above, fuel is delivered from the fuel control to the flow divider and dump valve. At a predetermined fuel pressure, fuel flows through the top aft lines for primary flow to 22 atomizers. With increased pressure the flow dividers provide additional flow through the forward lines for secondary flow (Fig. 8-33).

/3/ *Main fuel manifold*

The main fuel manifold is a two-piece unit with 11 dual atomizers in each section. Each section has primary and secondary flow to each atomizer. The 22 atomizers are directly attached to the manifold and discharge the atomized fuel into the combustion chamber.

After shutdown the flow divider and dump valve drain the fuel from the manifold through a

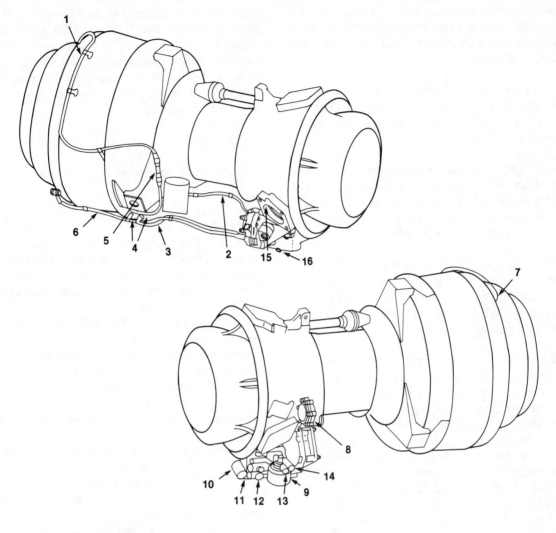

1. NO. 3 AND 4 BEARING PRESSURE LINE
2. PRESSURE LINE TO MANIFOLD
3. NO. 2 BEARING SCAVENGE LINE
4. NO. 2 BEARING PRESSURE LINE AND INLET STRAINER
5. PRESSURE MANIFOLD
6. NO. 3 AND 4 BEARING SCAVENGE LINE
7. NO. 3 AND 4 BEARING INLET STRAINER
8. TORQUEMETER BOOST PUMP

9. MAIN OIL FILTER
10. OIL PUMP
11. OIL PRESSURE ADJUSTMENT
12. OIL TEMPERATURE BULB
13. OIL PRESSURE TRANSMITTER AND PRESSURE SWITCH PRESSURE TAP
14. IMPENDING BY-PASS POP-OUT BUTTON
15. TORQUE PRESSURE TAP
16. CHIP DETECTOR

Fig. 8-34   Exterior lubrication system of T53

line to the combustion chamber drain valve. The combustor drain valve is spring loaded open when the engine is static and closed from pressure in the combustor.

(f)   Oil system

The engine oil system consists of a main oil pump, oil filter, torquemeter rotary boost pump and the lines (Fig. 8-34).

The oil is supplied from an airframe mounted tank to the oil pump mounted on the N_1 gearbox.

It is a dual element vane-type pump using one element to deliver lubricating oil under pressure and the other element for scavenge oil. Two alternate gear-type pumps may be used. The pump has an inlet and outlet hose connection, a pressure relief valve, and an oil temperature bulb.

The oil filter is a reusable wafer-disc type element enclosed in a housing and bolted to the gearbox. The filter contains a by-pass valve operating on a differential of pressure. In the event that the filter becomes clogged, oil will continue to flow to the engine.

Separate strainers are located at the number 3 and 4 bearings and the number 2 bearing. Both of these strainers are cleaned at the same frequency as the oil filter.

A magnetic chip detector is installed in the lower right-hand side of the accessory gearbox to provide an indication of metal particles in the engine lubrication system.

A torquemeter boost pump is mounted on the front of the N_2 gearbox. The pressure element receives engine oil at 80 - 100 psi and delivers it to the torquemeter at 120 - 125 psi through the oil filter to the engine by two paths.

One path is internal to the front section lubricating the gearing, torquemeter, the accessory drive gear, and the number 1 main bearing. The second path is through external lines lubricating bearings number 2, 3, and 4.

When the various points of the engine are lubricated, the oil from the inlet housing drains back into the accessory gearbox. Scavenge oil from number 2 main bearing is pumped back to the gearbox by an ejector pump through an external line. Bearings 3 and 4 return the scavenge oil by external lines and two paddle pumps to the accessory gearbox. The scavenge oil is picked up by the scavenge element and returned to the oil tank via an oil cooler (Fig. 8-35).

2. Allison 250 series

The most widely used engine in helicopters is probably the Allison 250 series of engine. Various models of this engine have been and are presently being installed in new helicopters. This engine is used on the Bell Jet Ranger, Long Ranger, and Hughes 500 C and D, plus several conversions of reciprocating engine helicopters. The Allison 250 has also been used in twin engine applications such as the BO-105 and the S76. Although these engines are basically the same they must operate as one unit in a helicopter since they are both supplying power to the same components with equal power. There are several different dash numbers of these engines even though all have the same basic construction except for the C28 and C30 engines. This major difference will be discussed later.

The Allison 250 series are turboshaft engines featuring a free power turbine. The engine consists of a combination axial-centrifugal compressor (except the C28 and C30 which have a centrifugal compressor only) a single *can* type combustor, a turbine assembly which incorporates a two-stage gas producer turbine, a two-stage power turbine, an exhaust collector, and an accessory gearbox.

a. Definitions

The following definitions apply to this engine:

N_1: Gas producer
N_2: Power turbine
front: The compressor end of the engine
rear: The combustion end of the engine
top: The exhaust gas outlet side of the engine
bottom: Determined by the scavenge oil outlet and burner drain plug
right and left: Determined by facing the accessory mounting pad
direction of rotation: Rear looking forward
accessories rotation: Determined by facing the accessory mounting pad.
compressor stage: One rotor and one stator
turbine stage: Consists of one stator and one rotor
compressor and turbine stage numbering: The compressor is numbered 1 through 6 in the direction of airflow — the turbines are numbered 1 through 4 with the first stage at the rear and the fourth at the front.
main bearing numbering: 1 through 8 in a front-to-rear direction.

b. Major assemblies

The major engine assemblies are (Fig. 8-36):

1. Compressor

2. Combustion Section

3. Turbine

4. Accessory Gearbox

5. Accessories

(1) Compressor

The compressor has six axial stages of compression feeding air into one centrifugal compressor. (Except for the C28 and C30 which have only a centrifugal compressor.)

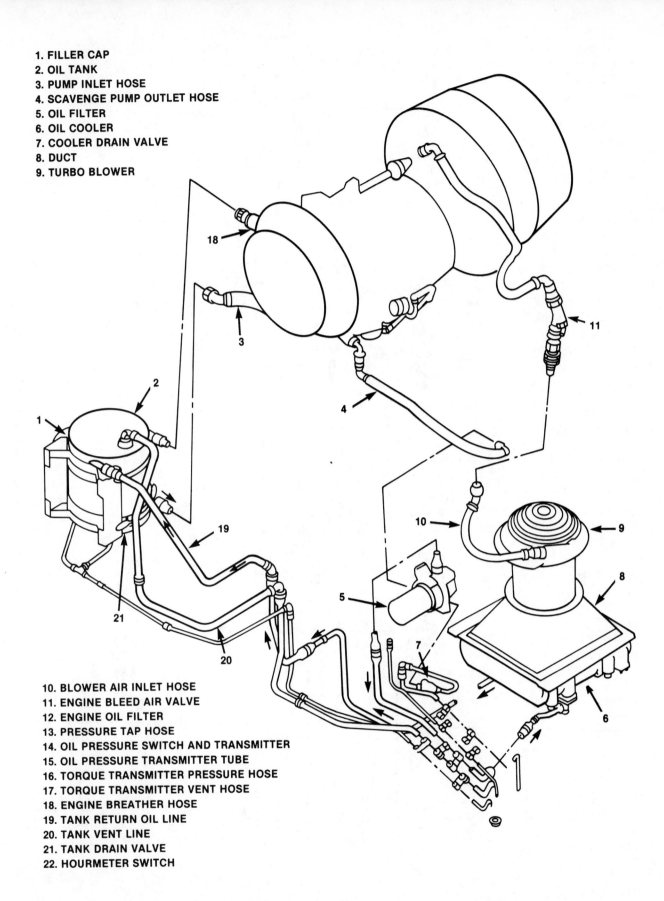

1. FILLER CAP
2. OIL TANK
3. PUMP INLET HOSE
4. SCAVENGE PUMP OUTLET HOSE
5. OIL FILTER
6. OIL COOLER
7. COOLER DRAIN VALVE
8. DUCT
9. TURBO BLOWER

10. BLOWER AIR INLET HOSE
11. ENGINE BLEED AIR VALVE
12. ENGINE OIL FILTER
13. PRESSURE TAP HOSE
14. OIL PRESSURE SWITCH AND TRANSMITTER
15. OIL PRESSURE TRANSMITTER TUBE
16. TORQUE TRANSMITTER PRESSURE HOSE
17. TORQUE TRANSMITTER VENT HOSE
18. ENGINE BREATHER HOSE
19. TANK RETURN OIL LINE
20. TANK VENT LINE
21. TANK DRAIN VALVE
22. HOURMETER SWITCH

Fig. 8-35 Lubrication system including airframe components

343

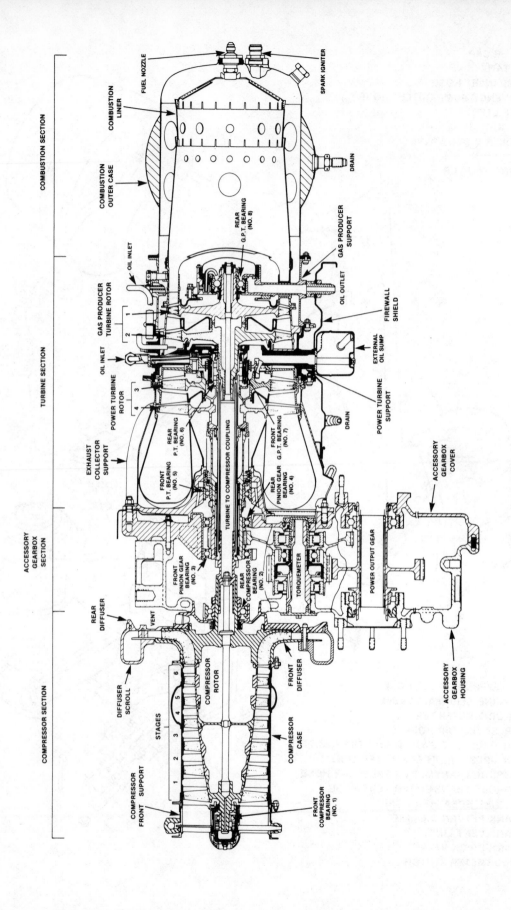

Fig. 8-36 Cross-sectional view of the Allison 250 engine

Air enters the engine through the compressor inlet and is compressed by six axial compressor stages and one centrifugal stage. As the air leaves the seventh stage of compression, it is directed into the scroll assembly. Air is tapped off the scroll assembly for various systems requiring bleed air. The bleed air has attained a temperature of 500+ degrees during compression. The compressed air leaves the compressor section through two external ducts transfering the air to the rear of the engine for combustion.

The compressor in the C28 and C30 engines is a centrifugal compressor with a single stage of compression. When the air is compressed, it is directed to the diffuser section. At this point air is tapped off to operate various accessories. See Fig. 8-37 for a view of the compressor section.

(2) Combustion section

The combustion section consists of an outer combustion case and a combustor liner. A spark igniter and a fuel nozzle mounted on the aft end of the outer combustion case is seen in Fig. 8-38.

Air enters the single combustion liner at the aft end through holes in the liner. The air is mixed with fuel sprayed from the nozzle and combustion takes place. This expands the gases which move forward and out of the combustor to the turbine assembly converting heat energy into mechanical energy.

(3) Turbine assembly

The turbine assembly is mounted between the combustion assembly and the accessory gearbox. It consists of the two-stage gas producer turbine, a two-stage shrouded power turbine, the exhaust collector support, and the necessary supporting structure (Fig. 8-39).

The expanding gases move out of the combustion assembly passing through the first stage nozzle where they are accelerated to a high velocity by the turbine nozzle. This high velocity air passes through the first stage turbine. As the air leaves the first stage turbine, it enters the second stage nozzle where the velocity is increased again before passing over the second stage turbine. These first two stages are used to power the N_1 system and part of the accesory gearbox.

The power turbine is a two-stage free turbine having no physical connection to the gas producer turbine.

As the expanding gases leave the gas producer turbine, they pass over the thermocouple and enter the third stage nozzle. The third and fourth stages of the turbine operate in the same manner as stages one and two, and are shrouded to prevent the loss of gases over the blade tips. When the gas leaves the fourth stage, it is directed overboard through two exhaust ducts. The power turbines drive the gearbox assembly and a portion of the accessory drives.

(4) Gearbox assembly

The gearbox assembly consists of the gearbox housing, gas producer gear train, power gear train, oil pump assembly, and the necessary oil tubes to provide pressure and scavenge oil to the lubrication system (Fig. 8-40).

The gas producer gear train is driven by the N_1 turbine. The accessories driven by the system are:

a. Gas producer tachometer

b. Fuel pump assembly

c. Starter-generator

d. Gas producer fuel control

The power turbine gear train is driven by the N_2 turbine. This is provided with a gear reduction to gear the turbine speed down to the output shaft speed. Accessories driven from the power turbine are as follows:

a. Power turbine tachometer generator

b. Power turbine governor

c. Torquemeter.

In the strictest sense the torquemeter is not an accessory but an integral part of the power turbine gear train. Through the use of axial thrust, developed by a set of helical splined gears acting on an oil chamber piston, engine oil under pressure is used to reflect the amount of torque developed by the power turbine (See Fig. 8-41).

c. Lubrication system

The lubrication system receives oil from an airframe mounted tank. This is delivered to the

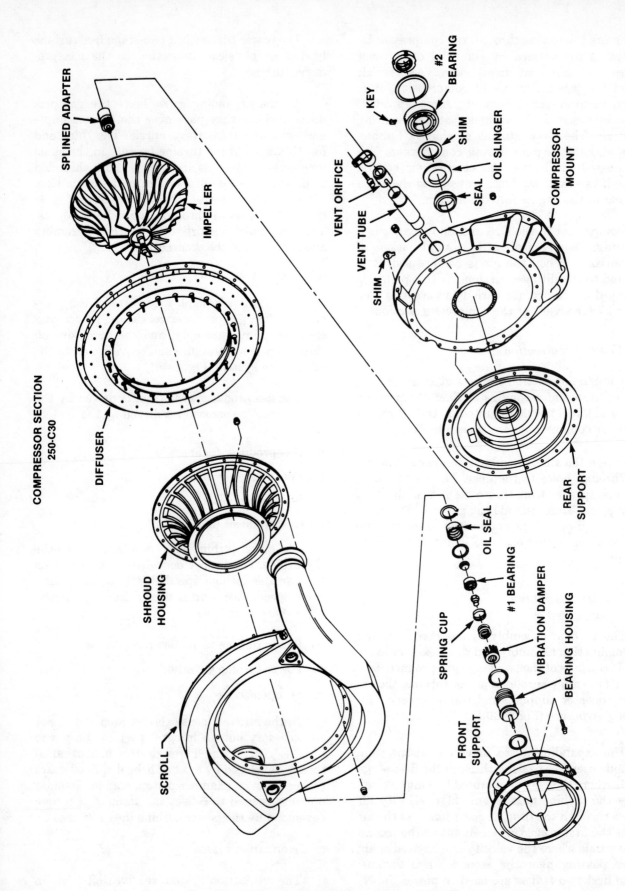

COMPRESSOR SECTION
250-C30

SPLINED ADAPTER

IMPELLER

DIFFUSER

SHROUD
HOUSING

SCROLL

VENT ORIFICE

VENT TUBE

SHIM

KEY

#2
BEARING

SHIM

SEAL

OIL SLINGER

COMPRESSOR
MOUNT

REAR
SUPPORT

OIL SEAL

SPRING CUP

#1 BEARING

VIBRATION DAMPER

BEARING HOUSING

FRONT
SUPPORT

Fig. 8-37 Compressor section of the Allison 250-C30

346

COMBUSTION ASSEMBLY

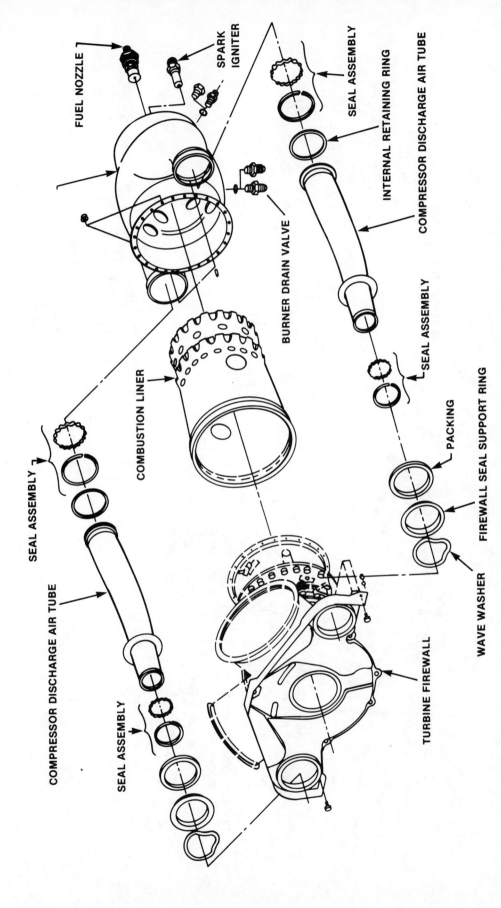

FUEL NOZZLE

SPARK IGNITER

SEAL ASSEMBLY

INTERNAL RETAINING RING

COMPRESSOR DISCHARGE AIR TUBE

BURNER DRAIN VALVE

COMBUSTION LINER

SEAL ASSEMBLY

SEAL ASSEMBLY

COMPRESSOR DISCHARGE AIR TUBE

SEAL ASSEMBLY

PACKING

FIREWALL SEAL SUPPORT RING

WAVE WASHER

TURBINE FIREWALL

Fig. 8-38 Combustor section of the Allison 250

347

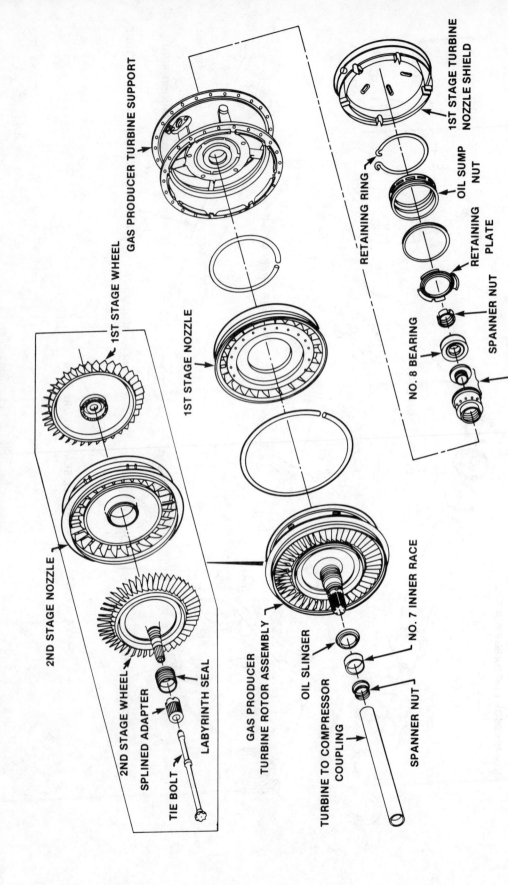

GAS PRODUCER TURBINE ASSEMBLY

GAS PRODUCER TURBINE SUPPORT

1ST STAGE WHEEL

1ST STAGE NOZZLE

1ST STAGE TURBINE NOZZLE SHIELD

RETAINING RING

OIL SUMP NUT

RETAINING PLATE

SPANNER NUT

NO. 8 BEARING

LABYRINTH SEAL

2ND STAGE NOZZLE

2ND STAGE WHEEL

SPLINED ADAPTER

TIE BOLT

LABYRINTH SEAL

GAS PRODUCER TURBINE ROTOR ASSEMBLY

OIL SLINGER

NO. 7 INNER RACE

TURBINE TO COMPRESSOR COUPLING

SPANNER NUT

Fig. 8-39a   Gas producer turbine section of the Allison 250 engine

348

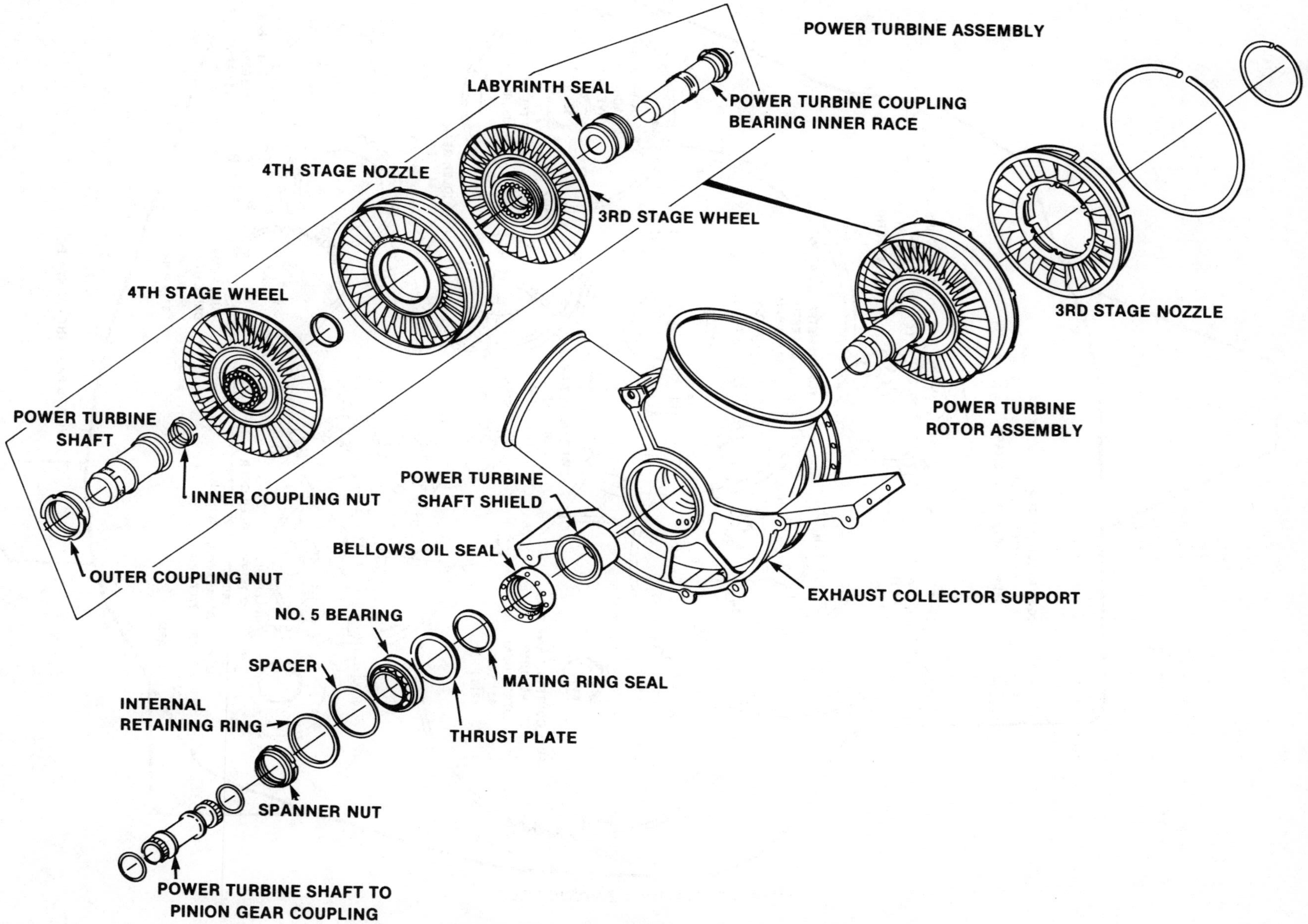

POWER TURBINE ASSEMBLY

3RD STAGE NOZZLE

POWER TURBINE COUPLING
BEARING INNER RACE

POWER TURBINE
ROTOR ASSEMBLY

EXHAUST COLLECTOR SUPPORT

LABYRINTH SEAL

3RD STAGE WHEEL

4TH STAGE NOZZLE

4TH STAGE WHEEL

POWER TURBINE
SHAFT SHIELD

BELLOWS OIL SEAL

MATING RING SEAL

THRUST PLATE

NO. 5 BEARING

SPACER

INTERNAL
RETAINING RING

SPANNER NUT

POWER TURBINE SHAFT TO
PINION GEAR COUPLING

INNER COUPLING NUT

OUTER COUPLING NUT

POWER TURBINE
SHAFT

Fig. 8-39b Power turbine section of the Allison 250 engine

349

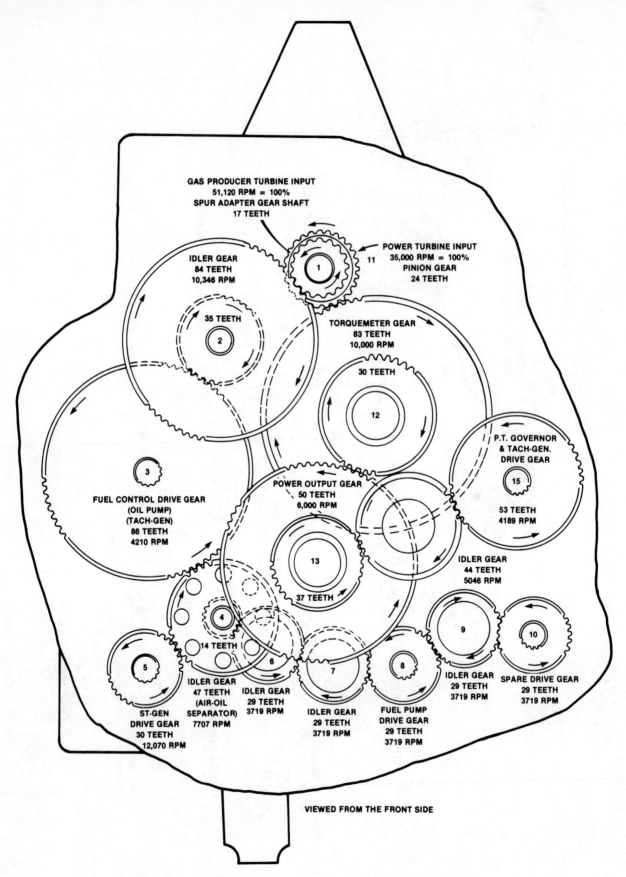

Fig. 8-40 Accessory drive section of the Allision 250 engine

350

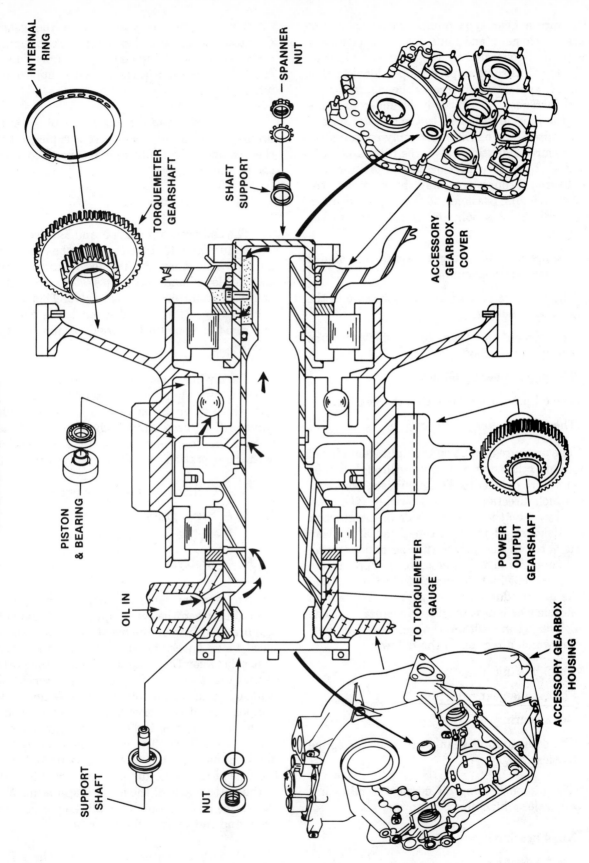

TORQUEMETER SCHEMATIC

INTERNAL RING

TORQUEMETER GEARSHAFT

SHAFT SUPPORT

SPANNER NUT

ACCESSORY GEARBOX COVER

PISTON & BEARING

POWER OUTPUT GEARSHAFT

OIL IN

TO TORQUEMETER GAUGE

ACCESSORY GEARBOX HOUSING

SUPPORT SHAFT

NUT

Fig. 8-41 Hydromechanical torquemeter Allison 250 engine

oil pump, a gear type pump consisting of one pressure element and four scavenge elements. The pump is operated by the N_1 gear train (Fig. 8-42). It will turn at a speed proportional to that of the N_1 system and increases the volume as the speed increases. The oil travels under pressure from the pressure element to the oil inlet port of the oil filter. The oil filter assembly contains the oil pressure regulating valve, the filter and a differential of pressure filter by-pass. The filtered oil is delivered through a one-way check valve to the gearbox housing passage and the oil pressure sensing port. At this point oil is delivered to the following:

1. The pressure oil port on the right front side of the gearbox housing.

2. The pressure oil port on the right side of the gearbox housing.

3. The screen and then an oil delivery tube within the gearbox.

4. The pinion bearing oil nozzle.

5. The oil pressure tube within the gearbox.

6. The torquemeter assembly.

The pressure oil port on the right front side of the gearbox housing delivers oil through a tube and pressure reducer to the compressor front support which directs oil to No. 1 bearing. The pressure oil port on the right rear side of the gearbox cover delivers oil through tubes and a one-way check valve to the power turbine and gas producer supports. The power turbine support contains a nozzle which directs oil to bearings 6 and 7. The gas producer turbine support delivers oil to a nozzle which directs oil on No. 8 bearing. The oil delivery tube within the gearbox has four nozzles which direct oil to the following:

1. No. 2 bearing

2. First stage gear reduction

3. No. 3 bearing

4. The spur adapter gear shaft holes for spline lubrication.

The pinion bearing oil nozzle assembly has three nozzles which direct oil to the:

1. No. 4 bearing

2. No. 5 bearing

3. No. 5 bearing oil seal

The oil pressure tube within the gearbox directs oil into the 2nd stage gear reduction. Oil delivered to the torquemeter not only fills the cavity but also lubricates the two support bearings.

The oil from the various points of the engine drains to the sump areas where it is picked up by the scavenge elements and returned to the oil cooler and tank.

(d) Bleed air system

The compressor bleed air and anti-ice system is seen in Fig. 8-43. Like the T53, the compressor must be unloaded during acceleration. Rather than a bleed band and port system, the Allison 250 uses an airbleed control valve. This valve is open during starting and ground idle operation and remains open until a pre-determined ratio is reached.

The air bleed valve consists of an evacuated bellows, two diaphragm assemblies, a poppet type servo valve, bleed valve, bleed orifice, bleed valve orifice, bleed valve body and a bleed valve cover. The following pressures are associated with the operation of the air bleed control valve:

1. P_e — Compressor discharge pressure

2. P_x — Servo pressure

3. P_i — 5th stage pressure

4. P_a — Ambient pressure

An annular shaped diaphragm retainer, located between the two diaphragms, retains the diaphragms between the bleed valve body and the bleed valve cover. The two diaphragms, with a spacer between them, are retained to the bottom of the evacuated bellow by a nut. The servo valve is attached to the bottom of this assembly. Thus the position of the servo valve is determined by the forces acting on the two diaphragms and the evacuated bellows. The cavity between the two diaphragms is ported to P_a. P_e is ported to the top side of the upper diaphragm and P_i is ported to the bottom side of the lower diaphragm. When the engine is not in operaton, all the pressures are equal and the valve will remain open.

When P_e increases to the point where $P_e - P_a$ force overcomes the $P_i - P_a$ plus the bellows force, the servo valve will begin to close. As it

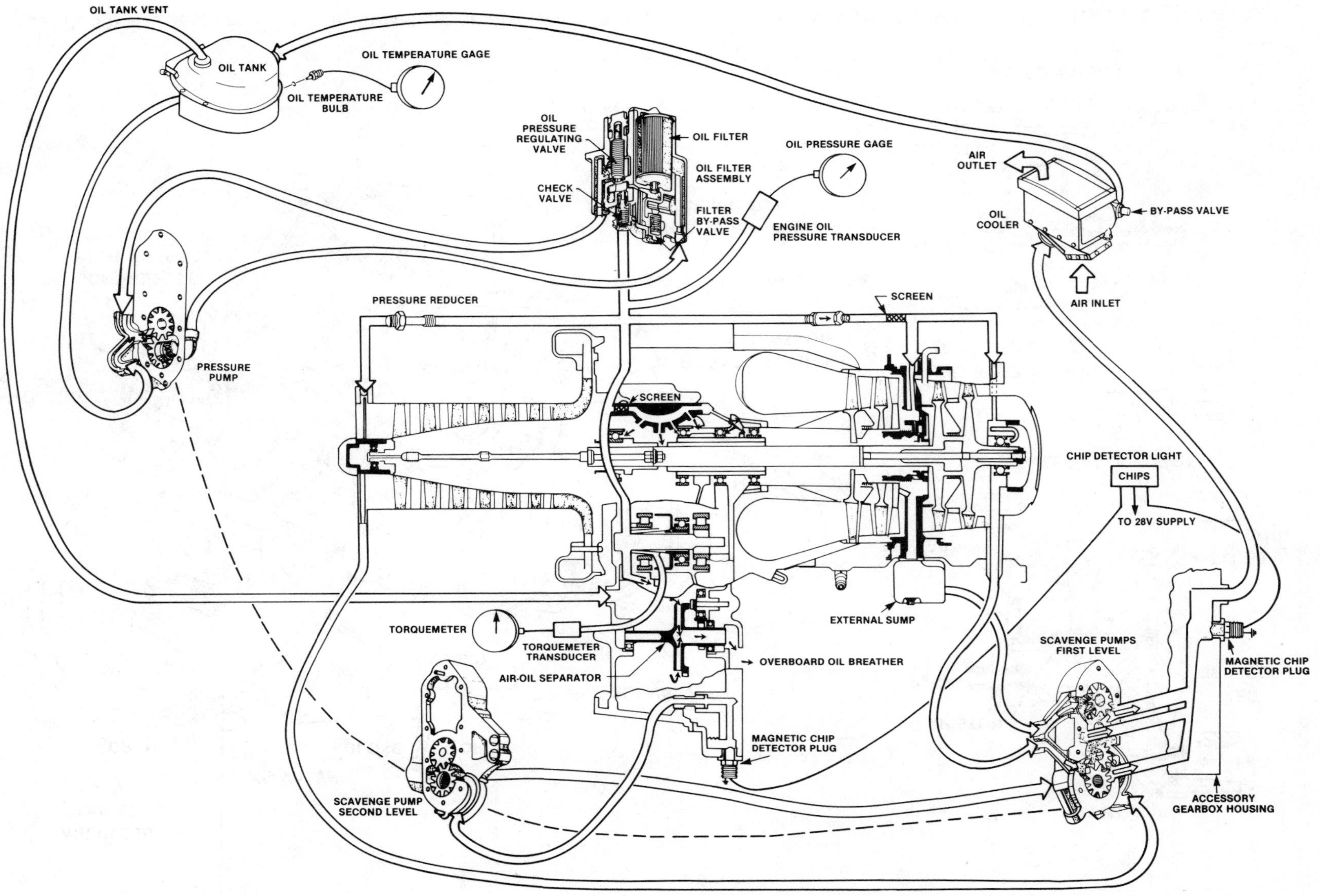

Fig. 8-42 Allison 250 lubrication system

353

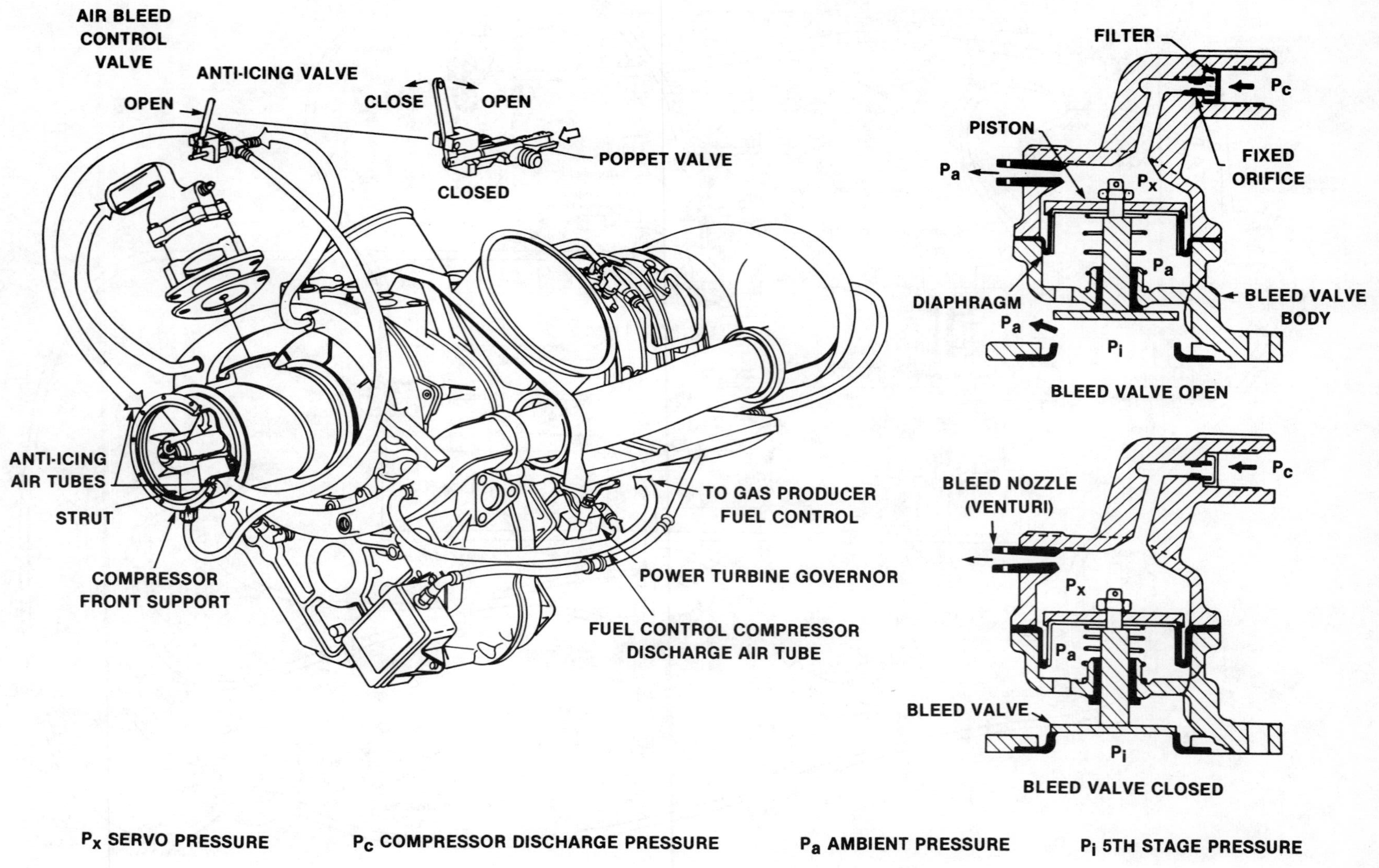

AIR BLEED CONTROL VALVE

ANTI-ICING VALVE

POPPET VALVE

OPEN

CLOSE — OPEN

CLOSED

ANTI-ICING AIR TUBES

STRUT

COMPRESSOR FRONT SUPPORT

TO GAS PRODUCER FUEL CONTROL

POWER TURBINE GOVERNOR

FUEL CONTROL COMPRESSOR DISCHARGE AIR TUBE

FILTER

P_c

FIXED ORIFICE

BLEED VALVE BODY

P_x

P_a

PISTON

DIAPHRAGM

P_a

P_a

P_i

BLEED VALVE OPEN

P_c

BLEED NOZZLE (VENTURI)

P_x

P_a

P_i

BLEED VALVE

BLEED VALVE CLOSED

P_x SERVO PRESSURE

P_c COMPRESSOR DISCHARGE PRESSURE

P_a AMBIENT PRESSURE

P_i 5TH STAGE PRESSURE

Fig. 8-43   Anti-icing and compressor bleed system — Allison 250

354

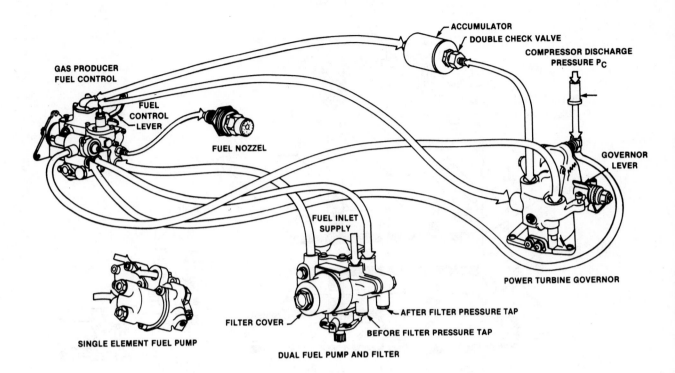

GAS PRODUCER
FUEL CONTROL

FUEL
CONTROL
LEVER

FUEL NOZZEL

ACCUMULATOR

DOUBLE CHECK VALVE

COMPRESSOR DISCHARGE
PRESSURE P_C

GOVERNOR
LEVER

FUEL INLET
SUPPLY

POWER TURBINE GOVERNOR

SINGLE ELEMENT FUEL PUMP

FILTER COVER

AFTER FILTER PRESSURE TAP

BEFORE FILTER PRESSURE TAP

DUAL FUEL PUMP AND FILTER

Fig. 8-44   Fuel system Allison 250

does, there is increased restriction to the flow from P_x into P_i; and P_x becomes greater than P_i but remains less than P_e. The bleed valve will be placed in some intermediate position between full open and full closed. It is only when P_x becomes equal to P_e that the bleed valve will be fully closed.

e.   *Anti-icing system*

The anti-icing system provides hot air for the compressor front support areas. This system must be operated by the pilot when anti-icing is required.

Hot air is extracted from the diffuser scroll and passes through the anti-icing valve which is a poppet type valve. The position is determined by a lever on the side of the valve. This delivers air to two anti-icing tubes at the compressor inlet.

The compressor front support consists of a double wall. During the anti-icing operation, the hot air enters the supports flowing into an annular passage. The hot air flows through the struts and the nose and is exhausted through slots in the struts. The remaining hot air is exhausted through the nose.

f.   *Fuel system*

The fuel system components are (Fig. 8-44):

1.   Fuel pump assembly

2.   Gas producer fuel control

3.   Power turbine governor

4.   Accumulator and check valve

5.   Fuel nozzle

Fuel is supplied by the helicopter fuel system to the inlet of the engine driven pump. Two different types of pumps are used — either a single or a dual element pump.

The dual element pump consists of two spur gear pumps, filter, filter by-pass valve, regulator valve and two check valves. As the fuel enters the pump, it normally flows through the filter. If the filter should become clogged, the fuel will be bypassed. The two pumps are parallel with each other with shear points on each element. Either element is capable of supplying enough fuel to meet all the requirements of the engine. A check valve is placed on the outlet port of each element in case of failure of one element. The pump

355

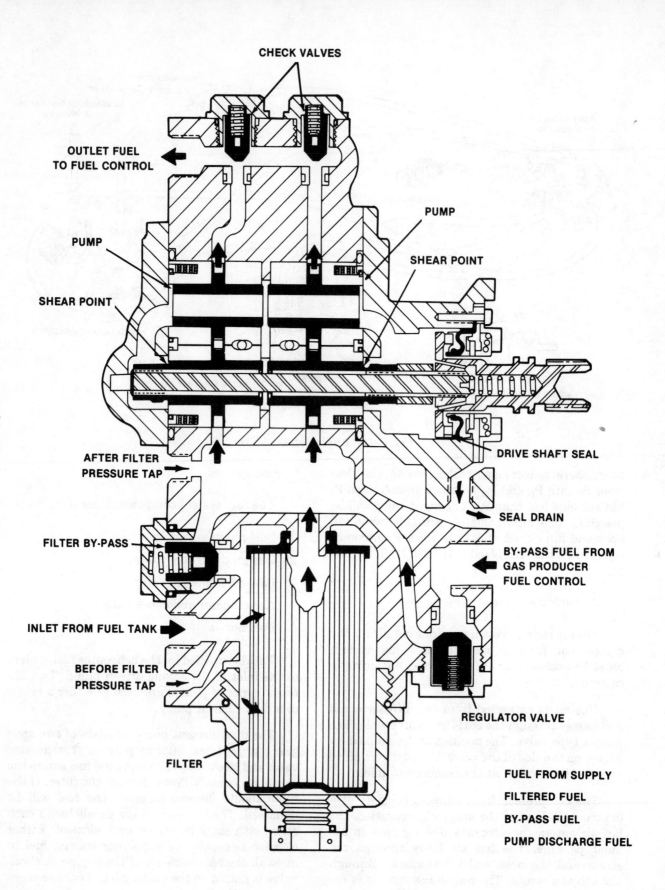

CHECK VALVES

**OUTLET FUEL
TO FUEL CONTROL**

PUMP

PUMP

SHEAR POINT

SHEAR POINT

DRIVE SHAFT SEAL

**AFTER FILTER
PRESSURE TAP**

SEAL DRAIN

FILTER BY-PASS

**BY-PASS FUEL FROM
GAS PRODUCER
FUEL CONTROL**

INLET FROM FUEL TANK

**BEFORE FILTER
PRESSURE TAP**

REGULATOR VALVE

FILTER

FUEL FROM SUPPLY

FILTERED FUEL

BY-PASS FUEL

PUMP DISCHARGE FUEL

Fig. 8-45   Fuel pump Allison 250

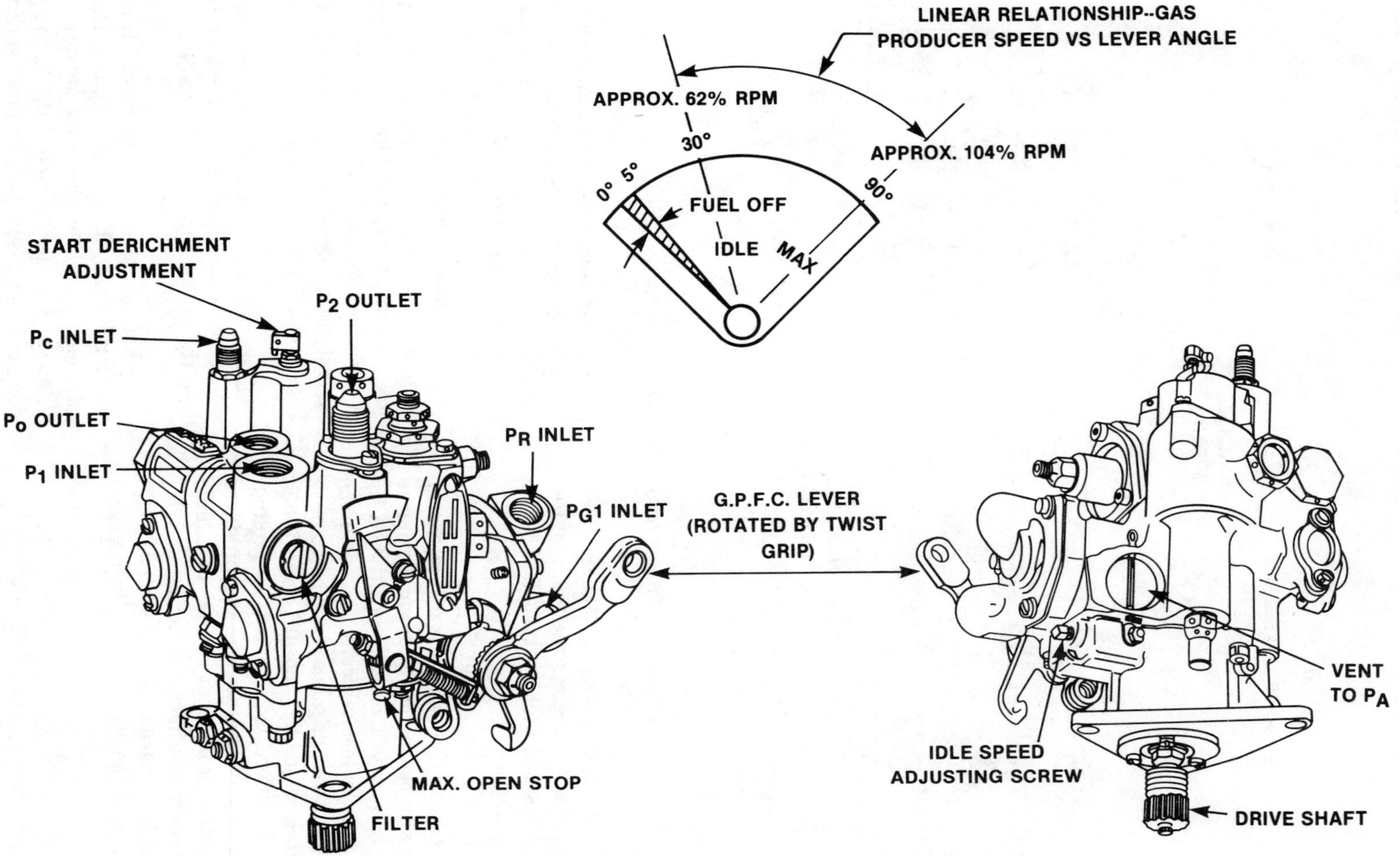

LINEAR RELATIONSHIP--GAS
PRODUCER SPEED VS LEVER ANGLE

APPROX. 104% RPM

APPROX. 62% RPM

90°

30°

0.5°

FUEL OFF

IDLE

MAX

VENT TO PA

DRIVE SHAFT

IDLE SPEED ADJUSTING SCREW

G.P.F.C. LEVER
(ROTATED BY TWIST GRIP)

PG1 INLET

PR INLET

MAX. OPEN STOP

FILTER

P2 OUTLET

START DERICHMENT ADJUSTMENT

PC INLET

PO OUTLET

P1 INLET

Fig. 8-46 Fuel control units — Allison 250

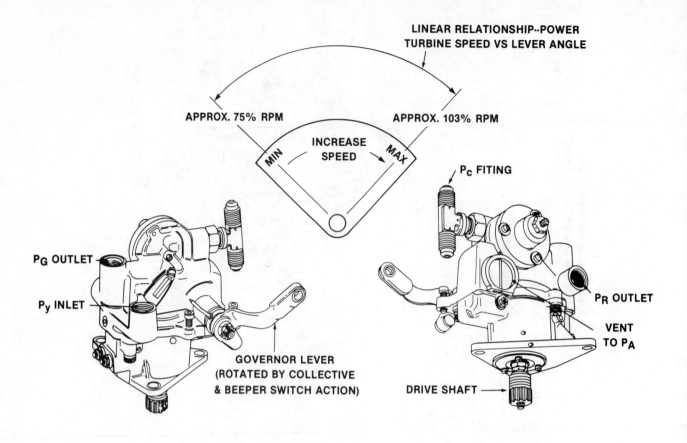

LINEAR RELATIONSHIP--POWER TURBINE SPEED VS LEVER ANGLE

APPROX. 75% RPM   APPROX. 103% RPM

MIN   INCREASE SPEED   MAX

P_C FITING

P_G OUTLET

P_y INLET

P_R OUTLET

VENT TO P_A

GOVERNOR LEVER
(ROTATED BY COLLECTIVE
& BEEPER SWITCH ACTION)

DRIVE SHAFT

Fig. 8-47   Power turbine governor — Allison 250

discharge pressure is delivered to the gas producer fuel control which meters the fuel required by the engine. All excess fuel is returned to the inlet of the pump (Fig. 8-45).

The gas producer fuel-control is driven by the N_1 gear train and senses compressor discharge pressure. The fuel-control lever is positioned by the twist grip and is mechanically linked to the cut-off valve. The twist grip has three basic positions — cut-off, ground-idle, and full open. When the twist grip is moved from cut-off to ground-idle, as during an engine start, the gas producer fuel-control automatically meters fuel as a function of compressor discharge pressure and N_2 RPM. The fuel flow during this phase of operation is controlled by the gas producer fuel-control (Fig. 8-46).

The power turbine governor is not required for starting or ground-idle operation but is required for speed governing the power turbine. The gas producer and the power turbine governor are interconnected by three lines—regulated air

pressure, governor reset pressure, and the governor servo pressure. The power turbine governor is driven by the N_2 gear train and also senses compressor discharge pressure (Fig. 8-47).

The governor lever is positioned by the droop compensator and beeper button. The power turbine governor is required for controlling the speed of the power turbine. The N_2 RPM is under the control of the beeper system and set by the pilot. This is usually 100% N_2.

The droop compensator moves the governor any time the collective is raised or lowered to keep the power turbine at 100% N_2.

When the twist grip is moved from ground-idle to full open, the power output of the engine is sufficient to drive the rotor system to 100%. When the N_2 tries to exceed 100%, the power turbine governor resets the gas producer fuel control and limits the fuel flow. When the collective pitch is increased, the power requirements are increased and the governor resets the fuel control again, thus maintaining a constant rotor RPM.

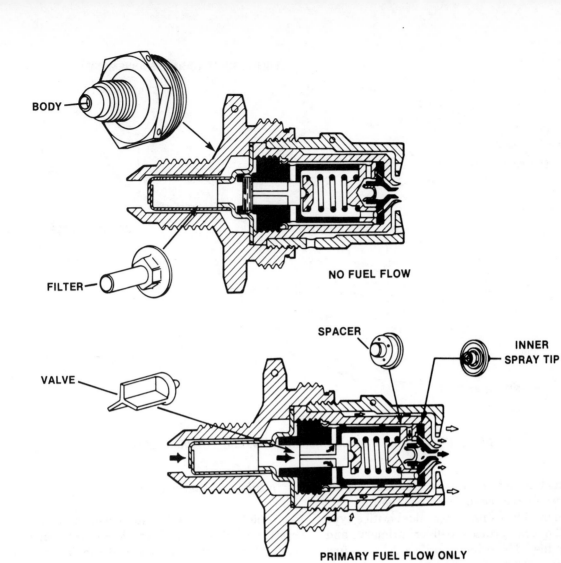

NO FUEL FLOW

PRIMARY FUEL FLOW ONLY

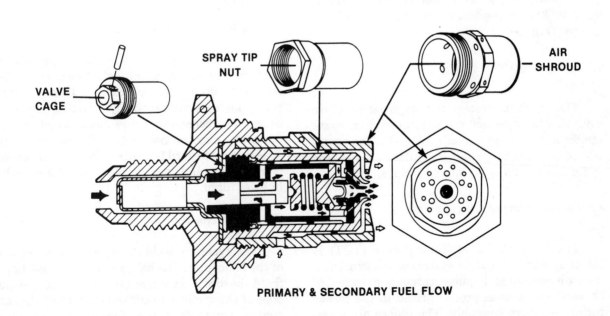

PRIMARY & SECONDARY FUEL FLOW

Fig. 8-48   Fuel nozzle used in the Allison 250

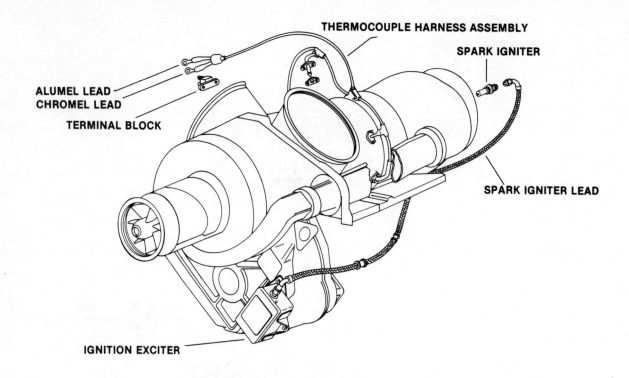

Fig. 8-49 Ignition and thermocouple system — Allison 250

The fuel nozzle located in the rear of the engine receives regulated fuel from the fuel control. The nozzle is a single-entry dual-orifice type nozzle. The two orifices deliver primary and secondary fuel. The primary orifice delivers fuel at all times of operation, but the secondary is open only when the fuel nozzle pressure exceeds 150 psi (Fig. 8-48).

g. Ignition system

The ignition system is composed of three components—a capacitor discharge exciter, spark igniter lead, and an igniter (Fig. 8-49). The operation of this discharge unit is similar to that of the systems used on other shaft turbines.

h. Turbine temperature system

The Turbine Outlet Temperature (TOT) is taken by a thermocouple system which generates its own electrical impulse through a series of chromel and alumel probes placed in the power turbine support assembly. The probes are wired in parallel and will read the average temperature of that area of the engine.

i. Flight and engine control

The flight control system consists of the aircraft collective control, cyclic control, tail rotor control, twist grip control, and the N_2 governor control switch (Fig. 8-50).

(1) Collective control system

The collective control system controls the vertical movement of the helicopter. The collective adds pitch to or subtracts it from the main rotor blades simultaneously. Raising the pitch causes an increasing blade angle which creates more lift, and the helicopter will rise vertically. This control is used to control the aircraft takeoff, climb, hover, and descent; plus the air speed while in level flight.

(2) Cyclic control

The cyclic controls the directional movement of the helicopter. The helicopter has a tendency to fly in the direction of main rotor disc tilt. The purpose of the cyclic is to tilt the main rotor disc and control horizontal flight, forward, backward, or sideways. Cyclic movement causes the opposite main rotor blades to change angle equally and op-

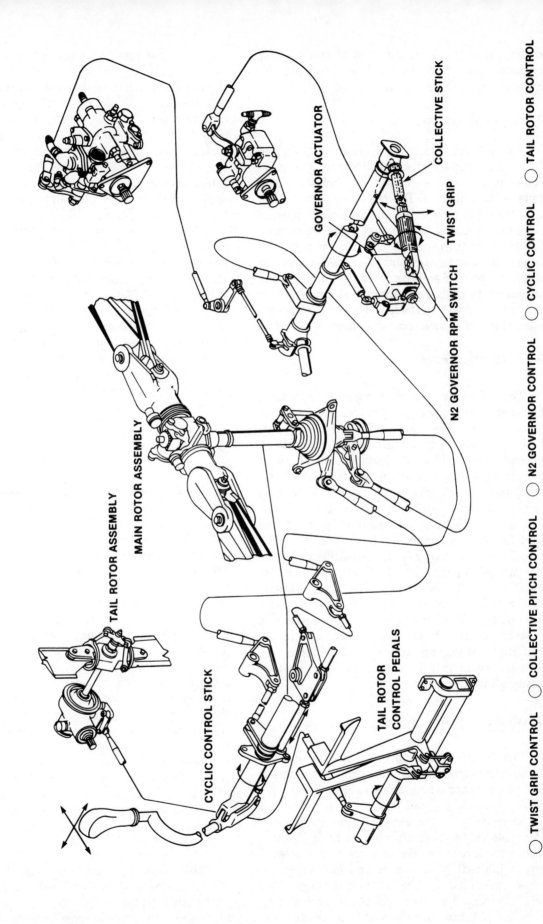

GOVERNOR ACTUATOR

COLLECTIVE STICK

TWIST GRIP

N2 GOVERNOR RPM SWITCH

TAIL ROTOR ASSEMBLY

MAIN ROTOR ASSEMBLY

CYCLIC CONTROL STICK

TAIL ROTOR CONTROL PEDALS

Fig. 8-50   Airframe and fuel control relationship — Allison 250

○ TWIST GRIP CONTROL   ○ COLLECTIVE PITCH CONTROL   ○ N2 GOVERNOR CONTROL   ○ CYCLIC CONTROL   ○ TAIL ROTOR CONTROL

positely, creating a lift differential and causing the main rotor disc to tilt. Application of this control is called *cyclic* or *cyclic change*.

(3) Tail rotor system

The tail rotor control system controls the directional heading of the helicopter. The anti-torque pedals in the cockpit control the blade angle of the tail rotor. The tail rotor functions as an anti-torque device. As the collective pitch is raised, more power is supplied from the engine. This tends to turn the helicopter to the right. To correct this turning tendency, left pedal must be added. When power is reduced, a simultaneous movement of the right pedal is required, or the helicopter will yaw to the left. This system is also called the anti-torque control system.

(4) Twist grip control

The twist grip control changes the setting of the lever arm on the gas producer fuel control which affects the fuel flow, TOT, and consequently, N_1 RPM and torque. The twist grip mounts on the end of the collective. Rotation of the twist grip changes the fuel control setting. Three basic positions—cut-off, idle, and maximum—are used for the twist grip setting. The twist grip is fitted with a spring-loaded idle stop to prevent the throttle from inadvertently being placed in the cut-off position during flight. An adjustable friction control is used with the twist grip to maintain it at the selected position. Raising and lowering the collective pitch has no effect on the twist grip position. To change the twist grip setting, it must be rotated. It is seldom necessary to coordinate twist grip and collective pitch operation, since the twist grip is in the full open position during all flight operation.

(5) N₂ governor control switch

The N_2 governor control switch is used to change the setting of the lever arm on the power turbine governor which affects the fuel flow, N_1 RPM, TOT, and torque. Movement of the switch to the increase or decrease position energizes a reversible motor that through aircraft linkage, rotates the lever arm. The total travel of the lever arm is limited by minimum and maximum set screws provided in the aircraft linkage. The switch is located on the end of the collective pitch stick and is commonly referred to as the *beeper*.

The rotor speed on a helicopter must be kept within certain limits. If rotor RPM is too high, the resultant centrifugal forces can overstress the rotating parts. If the rotor RPM is too low, excessive rotor blade coning (upward bending) will result. The engine control system for helicopter installations must control the power output of the engine so that the rotor RPM remains within established limits. The device, which allows the engine to drive the rotor but prevents the rotor from driving the engine, is generally called a free-wheeling unit or overrunning clutch. When the engine delivers power to the rotor system, the percentage of rotor RPM (N_2) will be the same; N_2 RPMs are indicated on the same instrument. When N_2 and N_R (rotor RPM) percentages are the same, the tachometer indicator N_2 and N_R needles are "locked." *Split needles* describes a condition where the percentage of N_R is greater than the percentage of N_2. When the needles are split, the engine delivers no power to the helicopter rotor, and the helicopter rotor delivers no power to the engine.

j. Clutch system

When starting an engine, it is always desirable to have a minimum starter load; thus, it is necessary that an engine be able to be cranked without the helicopter rotor's imposing any load on the starter. Helicopters powered by reciprocating engines, incorporate a clutch system which enables the starter to crank the engine without cranking the rotor. This clutch system provides a gradual stress-free pickup of rotor momentum while the system is being engaged. Helicopters, powered by the 250 series engine do not incorporate a clutch system because the free turbine design permits the starter to crank the gas producer system without any helicopter rotor load on the starter. When a 250 series engine is started, $N_2 N_R$ speed will not begin to increase when the starter cranks the engine. $N_2 N_R$ speed gradually increases as N_1 speed increases to idle RPM; thus, a free turbine allows for stress-free pickup of rotor momentum and permits the cranking of an engine with the rotor imposing no load on the starter.

Let's assume that the engine has been started, is running at stabilized ground-idle, and that takeoff power is required. The operator must move the twist grip from ground-idle to full open.

When this is done, the gas producer fuel control governor spring is reset from the N_1 ground-idle RPM setting to the N_1 overspeed governor setting. This results in an increase in N_1 RPM, an increase in N_2 RPM to 100% and approximately 70 SHP with the collective pitch stick in minimum. On free turbine installations, it is not necessary for the operator to co-ordinate the twist grip with the collective pitch stick. As the collective pitch stick is pulled up, the rotor pitch changes such that the rotor power requirements increase, so the rotor RPM will tend to droop. As N_2 droops, the power turbine governor senses the droop and initiates the necessary action causing the gas producer fuel control to increase fuel flow. As the fuel flow increases, N_1 RPM increases and expansion through the power turbine increases. The power turbine develops more power which is delivered to the rotor system to prevent excessive N_2 RPM droop.

k. Power turbine governor

The characteristics of the power turbine governor are such that as the helicopter rotor system power requirements increase, N_2N_R RPM tends to decrease, and if the rotor system power requirements are decreased, then N_2N_R tends to increase. On helicopters, it is highly desirable to vary rotor system power requirements without having a change in N_2N_R RPM as described in the previous paragraph. Therefore, in order to prevent N_2N_R RPM variation when a power change is made, the helicopter manufacturer provides a droop compensator. The compensator acts on the power turbine governor such that the N_2N_R RPM will be held constant as power to the rotor system is varied. The droop compensator *resets* the power turbine governor spring during power changes so that the resulting stablized N_2N_R following a power change is the same as it was before the power change. Thus, when the operator increases collective, the power delivered to the rotor system will increase and the stabilized N_2N_R will remain the same. In the event it is desired to operate at a different N_2N_R RPM, it is necessary to *reset* the power turbine governor by some means other than the droop compensator. The helicopter manufacturer provides an electrical *beeper* system. By means of manually positioning the beeper, the system resets the power turbine governor so the N_2N_R RPM will be governed at a different speed.

3. PT6 engine

The PT6 is a twin pack configuration. This engine is used in the Bell 212 and the Sikorsky S58 conversions. The PT6 twin pack installation is manufactured by the United Aircraft of Canada and designated as the PT6-3 turboshaft engine. The engine consists of three major sections — two identically free power turbine turboshaft power sections and a single common power output reduction gearbox with a single output shaft (Fig. 8-51).

a. Power section

Inlet air from the air management system enters each power section through a circular plenum chamber formed by the compressor inlet case and is directed to the compressor. The compressor consists of a three-stage axial compressor and a single-stage centrifugal compressor. Air passes through the compressor, through diffuser pipes and straightening vanes to the combustion chamber.

The combustion chamber is an annular-reverse-flow type unit with various sized perforations for entry of the air into the combustion chamber. The expanding gases of combustion move forward and change direction 180° to pass through the compressor turbine nozzle to the compressor turbine.

From the compressor turbine the gases pass rearward through the power turbine nozzle and the power turbine. The exhaust gases are directed out through the exhaust plenum into the atmoshpere (Fig. 8-52).

An accessory gearbox section mounts to the front of each power section, and houses the input shaft from the power section, the reduction gearing for the tachometer generator, fuel control unit, and the starter-generator. Each gearbox contains oil reservoir and pumps for the lubrication system of the accessory gearbox, the power section, and the power input section of the reduction gearbox (Fig. 8-53).

The two power sections are identical free-power turbine engines. Each power section uses two separate turbines, a gas producer turbine to drive the compressor and an accessory gearbox, a free power turbine which drives the turbine shaft

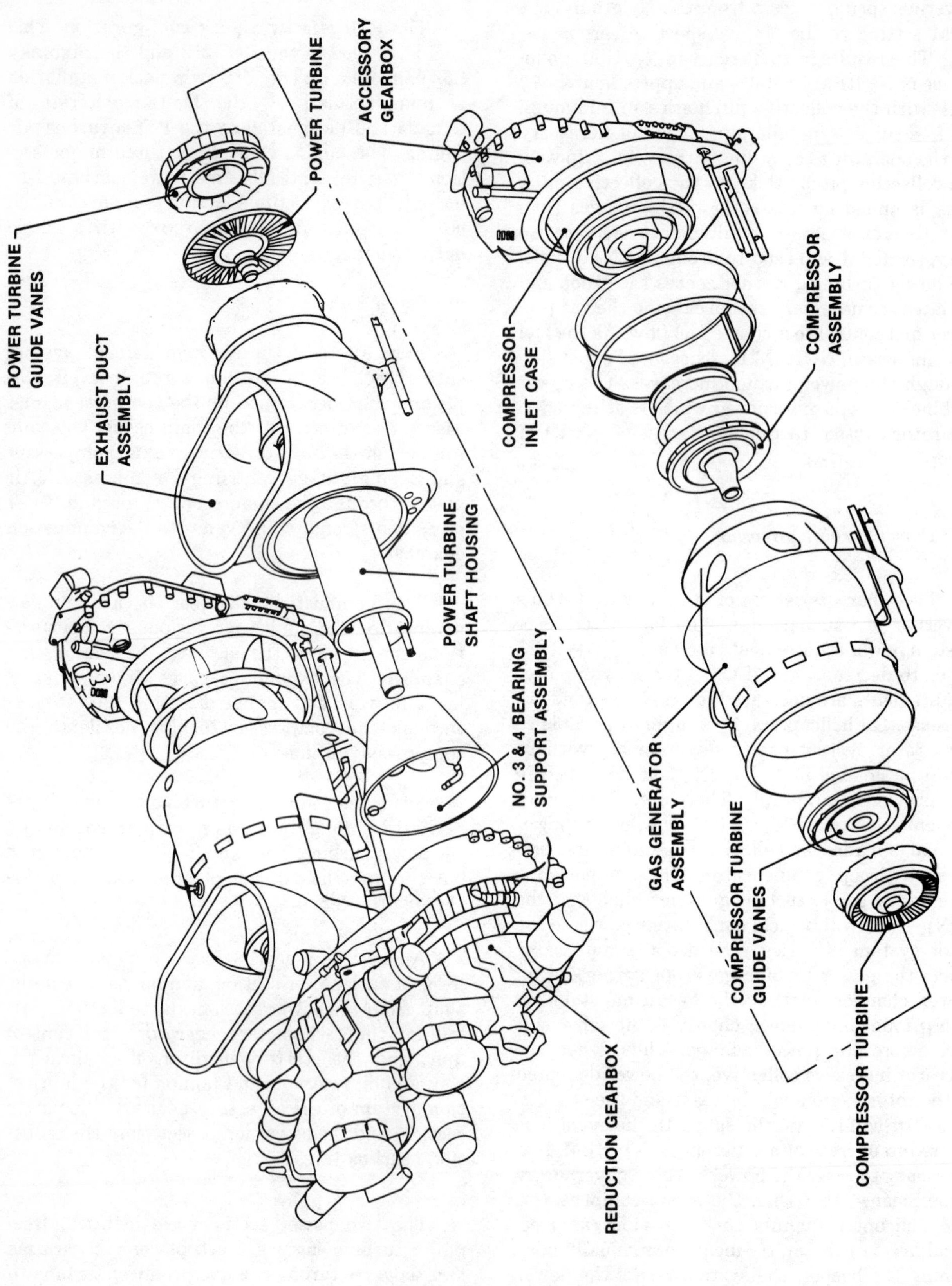

POWER TURBINE GUIDE VANES

POWER TURBINE

ACCESSORY GEARBOX

POWER TURBINE GUIDE VANES

EXHAUST DUCT ASSEMBLY

COMPRESSOR INLET CASE

COMPRESSOR ASSEMBLY

POWER TURBINE SHAFT HOUSING

COMPRESSOR ASSEMBLY

NO. 3 & 4 BEARING SUPPORT ASSEMBLY

GAS GENERATOR ASSEMBLY

COMPRESSOR TURBINE GUIDE VANES

REDUCTION GEARBOX

COMPRESSOR TURBINE

Fig. 8-51 PT6 twin pack

364

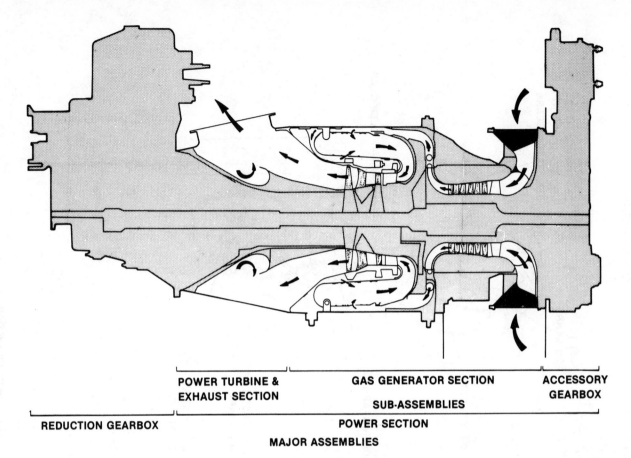

POWER TURBINE &
EXHAUST SECTION

GAS GENERATOR SECTION

SUB-ASSEMBLIES

ACCESSORY
GEARBOX

REDUCTION GEARBOX

POWER SECTION

MAJOR ASSEMBLIES

Fig. 8-52   PT6 airflow

coupled to the power output shaft to the reduction gearbox. Each power section is made up of the accessroy gearbox, gas generator section, and the power turbine-exhaust section.

The two power sections drive a single gearbox ouput shaft to the transmission through separate halves of a common reduction gearbox, often referred to as a combining gearbox, combining the output of both power sections into one. The reduction gearbox provides a 5:1 reduction of the power turbine speed to output shaft speed by means of a three-stage gear train for each power section. Each power section reduction contains a sprag clutch that drives in one direction only. This prevents driving one power section with the other in an engine-out situation (Fig. 8-54).

b.   Fuel system

The powerplant fuel system consists of separate but identical power sections, hydropneumatic fuel control systems and fuel pumps, with a common torque control unit. Each power section fuel system is made up of a fuel pump, a

manual fuel control unit, power turbine governor, flow divider, manifolds, and nozzles.

(1)   Fuel pump

The fuel pump is a positive displacement gear-type unit, with a 10-micron pleated paper filter mounted on the pump body. The output of the pump in excess of the power section requirement is returned to the inlet.

(2)   Manual fuel control unit

The manual fuel control unit is mounted with the fuel pump and the automatic fuel control unit is on the accessory gearbox. The function of the manual fuel control unit is to pass fuel from the pump to the automatic fuel control, and from the automatic fuel control to the flow divider. It has a transfer valve, combination metering valve and shut-off valve controlled by the power control lever, a pressurizing valve and a by-pass valve. The automatic fuel control establishes the proper fuel schedule, in response to the power requirements, by controlling the speed of the gas producer turbine.

365

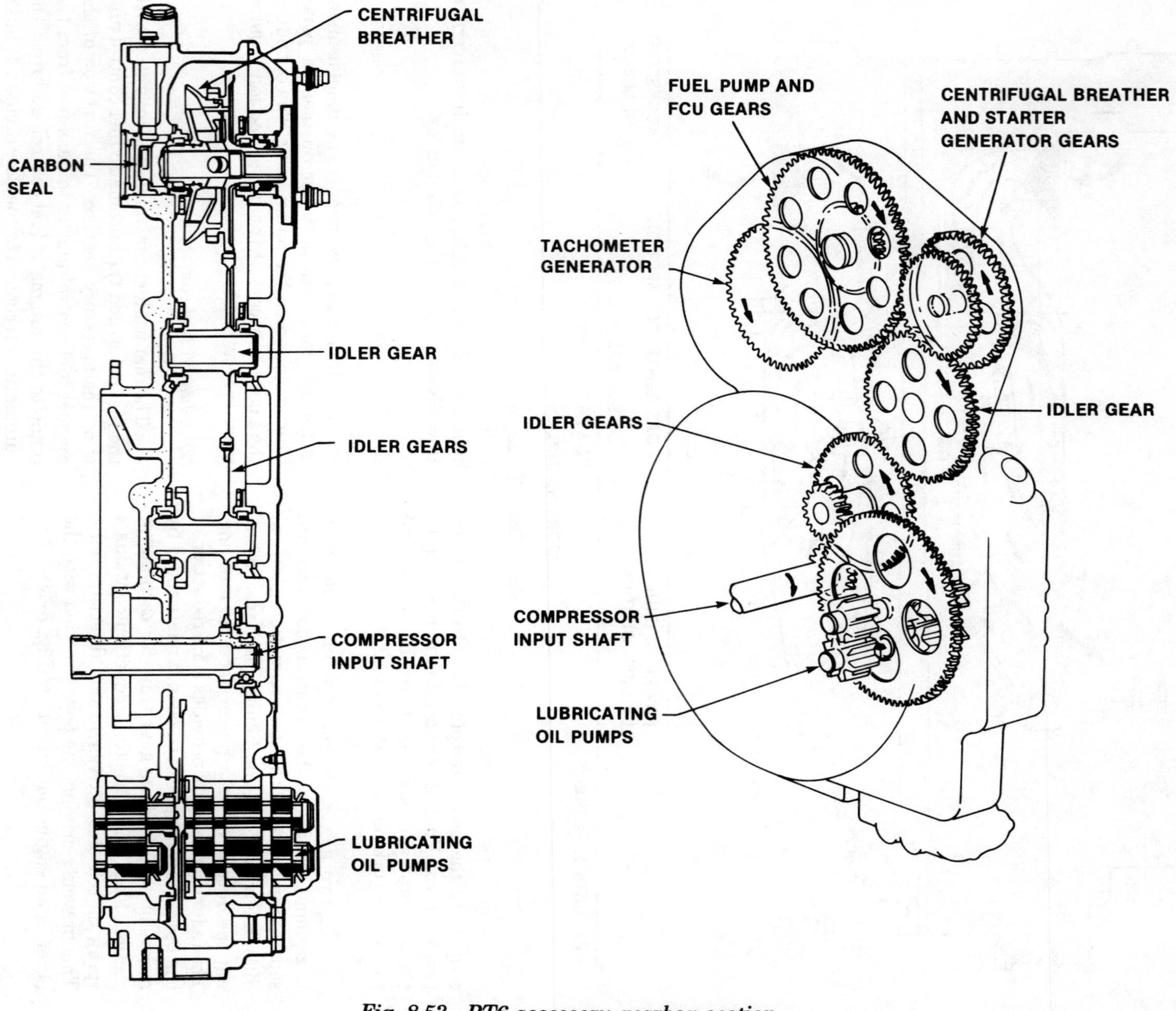

CENTRIFUGAL BREATHER AND STARTER GENERATOR GEARS

IDLER GEAR

FUEL PUMP AND FCU GEARS

TACHOMETER GENERATOR

IDLER GEARS

COMPRESSOR INPUT SHAFT

LUBRICATING OIL PUMPS

CENTRIFUGAL BREATHER

IDLER GEAR

IDLER GEARS

COMPRESSOR INPUT SHAFT

LUBRICATING OIL PUMPS

CARBON SEAL

Fig. 8-53 PT6 accessory gearbox section

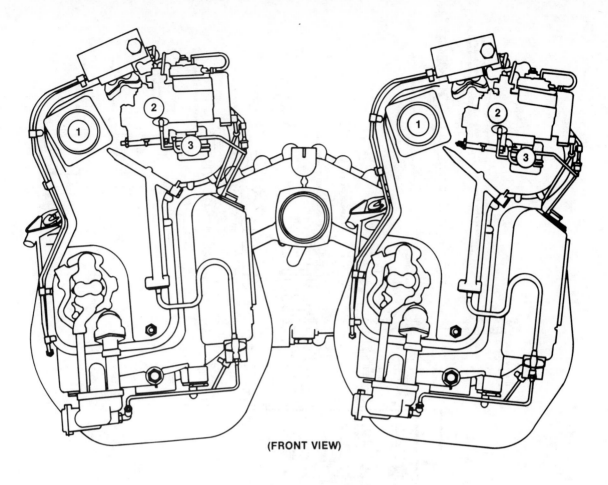

(FRONT VIEW)

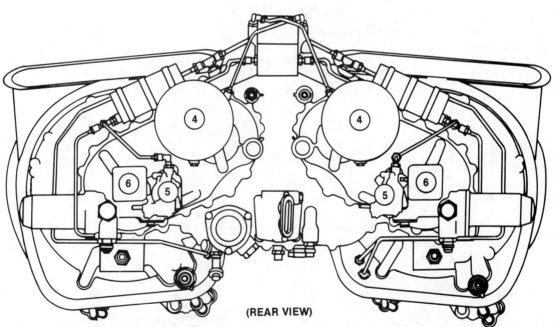

(REAR VIEW)

1. STARTER GENERATOR
2. FUEL PUMP & FCU
3. N_g TACHOMETER GENERATOR

4. BLOWER
5. Nf GOVERNOR
6. Nf TACHOMETER GENERATOR

Fig. 8-54   Front and rear view of PT6-3 engine

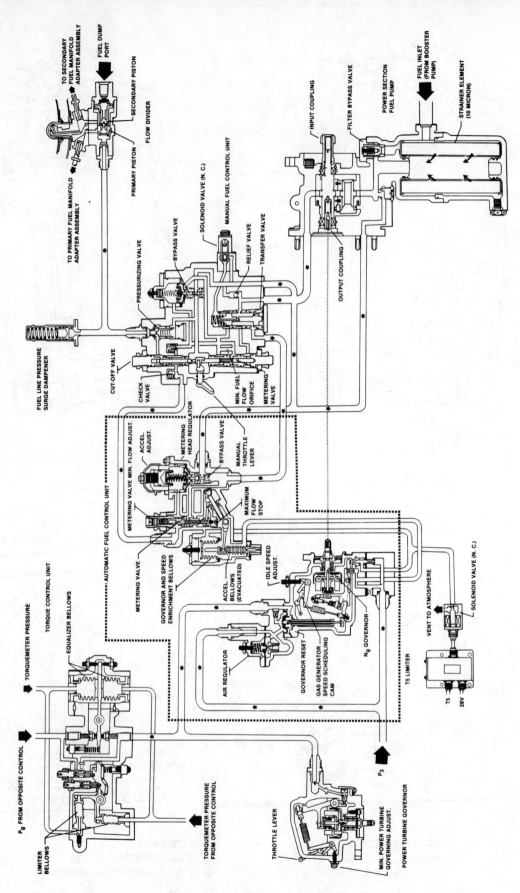

Fig. 8-55 Fuel control unit PT6-3

368

(3) Power turbine governor

The power turbine governor for each power section is mounted on the rear of the reduction gearbox, driven at a speed proportional to the power turbine speed. It causes a change in governor reset air to the automatic fuel control to change the compressor speed when it senses a power turbine speed change.

A single torque control unit mounted on the reduction gearbox receives torquemeter pressure from each power section. By controlling the governor reset air it limits the total torque output and maintains equal torque output of the two power sections.

(4) Flow divider

A flow divider is mounted on the gas generator case providing metered fuel to the primary and secondary manifolds and the 14 simplex fuel nozzles.

c. Oil system

The powerplant has three separate oil systems. Identical systems provide lubrication for the two power sections, accessory gearbox sections, and their respective input sections of the reduction gearbox. A third oil system provides lubricaion for the output sections of the reduction gearbox. Integral oil tanks and oil pumps, oil filters, visual oil level indicators, filters and drain facilities are provided for each system with two blowers driven by the reduction gear train of each power section.

d. Power section

Each power section contains an interstage air bleed system to provide anti-stall characteristics dumping part of the compressed air from the compressor 3rd-stage vane. A bleed valve mounted on the gas generator case at the 5 o'clock position controls the dumping of the air.

Each power section has its own separate ignition system consisting of an ignition exciter, shielded igniter plug cables, and two igniters.

The power lever controls system consists of two parallel mechanical linkages connecting the dual control twist grip of the collective stick to the manual fuel control units on the accessory drive sections. The upper twist grip is No. 1 engine control and the lower twist grip is No. 2 control. A flight idle stop is provided on each twist grip to prevent an inadvertent shutdown of the power section when retarding the twist grip.

The linkage for the power turbine governors of each power section consists of a mechanical input from the collective pitch control through a droop compensator, an electrical linear actuator control for speed selection, and a jackshaft to the power turbine governors for control of the power turbine speed of both power sections. The droop compensator maintains and stabilizes the pre-selected N_f (N_2 or rotor) RPM by changing governor control as collective pitch is increased or decreased. The linear actuator provides control of the N_f RPM selection by changing the postion of the lever on the power turbine governor.

e. Twin pack coupling

The PT6 twin pack is somewhat unique in its design with one output shaft for the two engines. This is not always the design in all twin engine applications. Other helicopters may have two input shafts to one transmission, but each engine must be able to function by itself. This means each engine must have its own free wheeling unit and the transmission must be able to turn with the one engine inoperative (Fig. 8-56). The twin engine applications requires the power output of the two engines be matched during operation. On the twin pack the power outputs are matched by the torque control unit. This unit senses the torque from both engines and matches the two through the fuel control, and acts as a torque limiting device.

On other twin engine applications the torque of the two engines must be matched by using the beep system.

f. Torque output limits

It is possible to exceed the torque limits of the helicopter in some instances. The torque is the measurement of power output of the engine. In some instances the engine is capable of producing more power than can be handled by the airframe. This would be especially true under certain weather conditions. For this reason the torquemeter is assigned a maximum limit. It must be remembered the engine will produce only the power demanded of it by the rotor system. If the

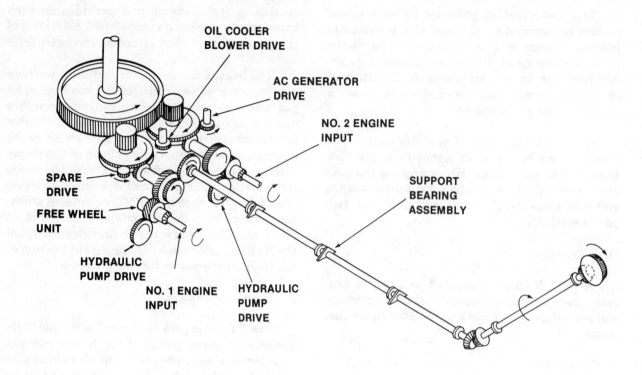

OIL COOLER
BLOWER DRIVE

AC GENERATOR
DRIVE

NO. 2 ENGINE
INPUT

SPARE
DRIVE

FREE WHEEL
UNIT

SUPPORT
BEARING
ASSEMBLY

HYDRAULIC
PUMP DRIVE

NO. 1 ENGINE
INPUT

HYDRAULIC
PUMP
DRIVE

Fig. 8-56   Geartrain using two engines — S76

demand is too great the power output may also be too great. An engine capable of producing 1000 horsepower will produce it only on demand.

g. Ignition system

On some helicopters using turbine engines the twist grip arrangement has been eliminated in favor of a lever for the free turbine. The N_1 usually has three positions: ground-idle, flight-idle, and full N_1. The N_1 system will speed up and slow down as a function of N_2 so a steady rotor RPM may be maintained during all flight conditions. However, under a manual operation N_1 would have to be controlled. Fig. 8-57 shows such a lever being used on N_1.

This type of situation also exists on the direct shaft turbine. On these engines a set RPM is maintained by the governor of the fuel control. No linkage such as a droop cam is used. When the collective is raised or lowered, the power is simply increased or decreased to maintain the steady RPM. This system is used in many helicopters

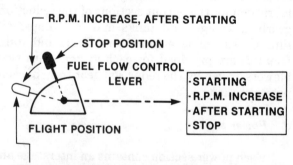

R.P.M. INCREASE, AFTER STARTING

STOP POSITION

FUEL FLOW CONTROL
LEVER

· STARTING
· R.P.M. INCREASE
  AFTER STARTING
· STOP

FLIGHT POSITION

FOR SUCH A POSITION OF THE FUEL FLOW CONTROL LEVER, THE ENGINE IS CONTROLLED BY ITS GOVERNING SYSTEM.

Fig. 8-57   Power lever as used in some turbine engine installations.

manufactured by Aerospatiale which often use a direct shaft turbine.

4. Autorotation landing

In the event of an engine failure during flight, a helicopter can usually make a safe autorotational landing without injury to personnel or damage to the helicopter. An autorotation is a condition of flight in which the helicopter rotor (N_R) speed and the resultant lift are derived entirely from the airflow up through the rotor system.

If an engine fails or power loss is such that powered flight is no longer possible, the pilot must immediately initiate autorotation. This is done by moving the collective pitch lever down to select minimum rotor pitch. As the helicopter descends, the airflow up through the rotor will maintain N_R speed, the overrunning clutch will prevent the rotor system from delivering power to the engine, and the N_2N_R tachometer indicator needles should split.

During the descent, the pilot maintains the desired airspeed and controls the directional movement of the helicopter with the cyclic control stick. As the helicopter approaches the desired touchdown point, the pilot *flares* the helicopter to slow it down. This normally results in a slight increase in N_R speed. As the forward speed decreases, the upward flow of air through the rotor decreases and N_R speed again decreases. The helicopter will settle at a slightly increased rate, but with reduced forward speed.

When the helicopter is at the prescribed height above the touchdown point, the pilot increases collective pitch by pulling the collective pitch lever upward. At this time, the inertia of the rotor is the driving force for the rotor system. With the increased collective pitch, there will be a downward flow of air through the rotor to decrease the sink rate, and the helicopter can make a *soft* touchdown.

The N_R speed decays rapidly when the collective pitch is increased. If increased collective pitch is initiated too soon on an autorotational landing, a *hard* touchdown will result.

Practice autorotational landings can be made by simulating an engine failure. This is accomplished by moving the twist grip to ground-idle, which results in the engine output to the helicopter rotor being reduced to zero. Thus, the overrunning clutch can function, and the N_2N_R tachometer indicator needles can *split*.

The natural pilot response to loss of altitude is to increase the collective pitch. If the loss of altitude is due to an engine failure, and the pilot increases collective pitch, N_2N_R RPM will rapidly decrease and a *soft* autorotational landing may be impossible. When an engine fails on a helicopter powered by a reciprocating engine, there is a significant change in sound level.

On gas turbine powered helicopters, an engine failure in flight is not easily detected. There is very little sound level variation at the time of power loss. For this reason, it is desirable that helicopters powered by this turbine engines be equipped with an engine failure warning system. The warning system consists of a red engine-out light, located on the instrument panel, and an audio horn that comes on simultaneously with the red light as the N_1 RPM drops below the idle setting.

5. *Maintenance*

The turbine engine has complimented the helicopter in many ways, but it has also brought about some maintenance practices that are different than those used on reciprocating engines.

Most of the work performed on the turbines is limited to routine servicing, inspection, removal and replacement maintenance. Servicing includes cleaning, changing oil, adding oil, and changing filters in accordance with the manufacturer's recommendations. Usually the servicing instructions are contained in the engine manual rather than the airframe manual unless related to the airframe.

These general servicing techniques are sometimes changed by adding additional requirements by operators. This is especially true where the operation involves different environments such as salt water. With a salt water environment the cleaning requirements are more stringent due to corrosion problems and may include frequent internal as well as external cleaning.

The life of turbine engines is not only based on time of operation but on cycles of the engine. It is not unusual to see items such as turbine wheel life limited to cycles. Other items on the engines are generally given overhaul or replacement times.

a. *Modular concept*

Many turbine engines are maintained on a modular concept regarding overhaul. This means the hot section will have one life, the compressor another, and the gear reduction still another life. Any of the modules can be removed and overhauled separately. In some instances the module may be exchanged. However, in most instances the whole engine is exchanged or a rental engine is used, while the other engine is rebuilt. This is due to finite life components. Large operators have spare engines for exchange and may do their own major repair work. The small operator will usually have the major work done by an authorized repair station, the manufacturer, or his representative.

b. Engine change

The removal and replacement of the engine is compared to some of the reciprocating engine helicopters because in most installations nothing has to be removed except the engine. On some of the larger turbine helicopters a work crane that can be attached to the helicopter is provided as special ground support equipment. This is an advantage when engines must be changed in the field where hoists are not available.

In most situations the engines are preserved before removal. This may include spraying the inlet area with oil while motoring the engine and preserving the fuel system. Only the type of preservative recommended by the manufacturers and their procedures should be used. On most engines the hoses and electrical connections will utilize quick disconnects and electrical plugs for easy removal and installation.

All large operators will have engines built-up for the specific installation including plumbing,

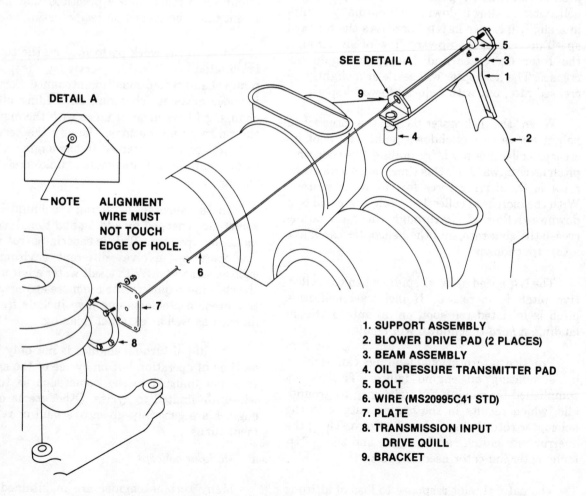

DETAIL A

NOTE — ALIGNMENT WIRE MUST NOT TOUCH EDGE OF HOLE.

SEE DETAIL A

1. SUPPORT ASSEMBLY
2. BLOWER DRIVE PAD (2 PLACES)
3. BEAM ASSEMBLY
4. OIL PRESSURE TRANSMITTER PAD
5. BOLT
6. WIRE (MS20995C41 STD)
7. PLATE
8. TRANSMISSION INPUT DRIVE QUILL
9. BRACKET

Fig. 8-58   Engine to transmission alignment — Bell 212

electrical system and accessories. The changing of smaller items can be time-consuming, often requiring several more hours of labor than the actual removal and replacement.

c. Engine alignment

After a new or replacement engine is installed, it may be necessary to check the alignment of the engine to the transmission so that the main input shaft does not have any undue stresses placed on the couplings. Misalignment will result in shaft failure in a very short time. The alignment is normally done by shimming the legs of the mount between the fuselage and the mount.

This procedure is not required at each engine change unless the mount is also changed or the helicopter has been structurally damaged or driveshaft wear is excessive. However, some operators check the alignment with the installation of an engine.

The particular installation that will be discussed is the Bell 212 as seen in Fig. 8-58.

For this procedure special tools are used. A support assembly is positioned on the engine's blower assembly. This is used to hold the beam assembly in which a knurled nut and safety wire are installed. The wire passes through a target on

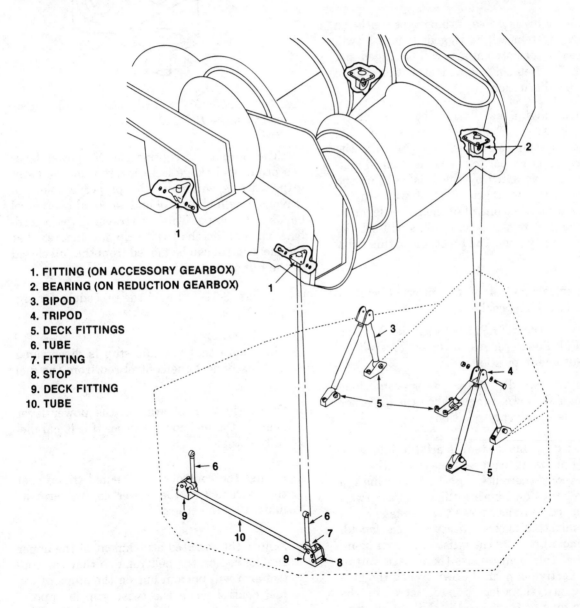

1. FITTING (ON ACCESSORY GEARBOX)
2. BEARING (ON REDUCTION GEARBOX)
3. BIPOD
4. TRIPOD
5. DECK FITTINGS
6. TUBE
7. FITTING
8. STOP
9. DECK FITTING
10. TUBE

Fig. 8-59 Engine mount system — Bell 212

373

the beam and is attached to the transmission input shaft by means of a plate. When the wire is taut, it should pass through the hole of the target without touching the side of the hole. If it does touch, the mounts must be shimmed until the correct alignment is obtained (Fig. 8-59).

d. Control rigging

Probably the most difficult procedure in the installation of an engine is the rigging of the controls. The first step is the preliminary rigging. The actual fine adjustments, in most instances, cannot be made until the engine is in operation and flight tests can be made.

If the engine is a free turbine type, both the N_1 and N_2 system will be rigged. If it is a twin engine helicopter both engines will be rigged and matched. The Bell 205 engine installation will be used in this discussion.

On this engine installation there will be N_1 and N_2 controls. The N_1 controls the fuel regulator portion and the N_2 controls the overspeed governor portion. The mechanical linkage portion is actuated by the twist grip on the collective. This twist grip control will provide manual, mechanical control of the power lever on the fuel control regulator unit. This will set the fuel for the N_1 system. The functions of this twist grip are:

1. Mechanical control of the internal shutoff valve of the fuel control.

2. Govern or control RPM between the Off, Idle and Full Power ranges, with the governor in the automatic position.

3. Maintain steady state power conditions through all power ranges when the governor is in the Emergency position.

Included in this system is a flight-idle stop. The stop purpose is to prevent the twist grip from being moved to the shut-off position, causing the engine to shut down during flight. As the twist grip is moved to reduce power, the linkage has a cam attached that makes contact with a solenoid. This solenoid prevents the twist grip from being moved past this point unless the release button on the collective is pushed down. When the button is engaged, the solenoid is retracted and the twist grip may be moved to the shut-off position (Fig. 8-60).

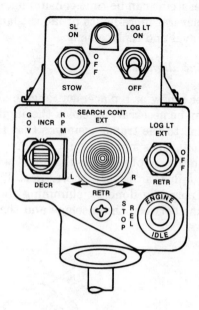

Fig. 8-60 *Collective controls placed at the top of the collective — Bell 205*

The purpose of rigging the N_1 power lever gas producer linkage is to insure that the twist grip controls will have the proper amount of travel at the fuel control and an equal overtravel beyond the stops. This overtravel gives a feedback cushion on the twist grip and insures that the fuel control can be moved from the full closed to the full open position.

Using Figs. 8-61 and 8-62 the procedure for rigging the N_1 is:

1. Make sure that the idle stop is disengaged and disconnect the control rod from the fuel control.

2. Check the control arm on the power lever shaft of the fuel control to see if it is parallel to the stops.

3. Adjust the control rod for equal travel past the extremes of the power control arm as limited by the stops.

4. Adjust the serrated attachment of the upper control rod on the bellcrank so that the control arm will bottom out on the stops of the fuel control when the twist grip is approximately 5° short of its extreme position. This will give the necessary cushion.

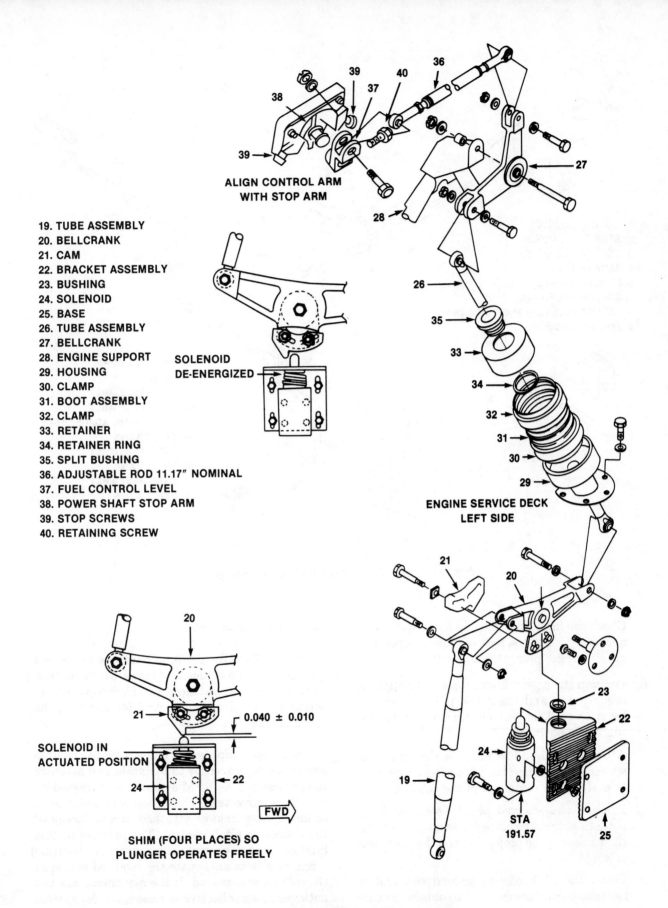

ALIGN CONTROL ARM
WITH STOP ARM

19. TUBE ASSEMBLY
20. BELLCRANK
21. CAM
22. BRACKET ASSEMBLY
23. BUSHING
24. SOLENOID
25. BASE
26. TUBE ASSEMBLY
27. BELLCRANK
28. ENGINE SUPPORT
29. HOUSING
30. CLAMP
31. BOOT ASSEMBLY
32. CLAMP
33. RETAINER
34. RETAINER RING
35. SPLIT BUSHING
36. ADJUSTABLE ROD 11.17" NOMINAL
37. FUEL CONTROL LEVEL
38. POWER SHAFT STOP ARM
39. STOP SCREWS
40. RETAINING SCREW

SOLENOID
DE-ENERGIZED

ENGINE SERVICE DECK
LEFT SIDE

0.040 ± 0.010

SOLENOID IN
ACTUATED POSITION

FWD

SHIM (FOUR PLACES) SO
PLUNGER OPERATES FREELY

STA
191.57

Fig. 8-61   Bell 205 flight idle stop system

375

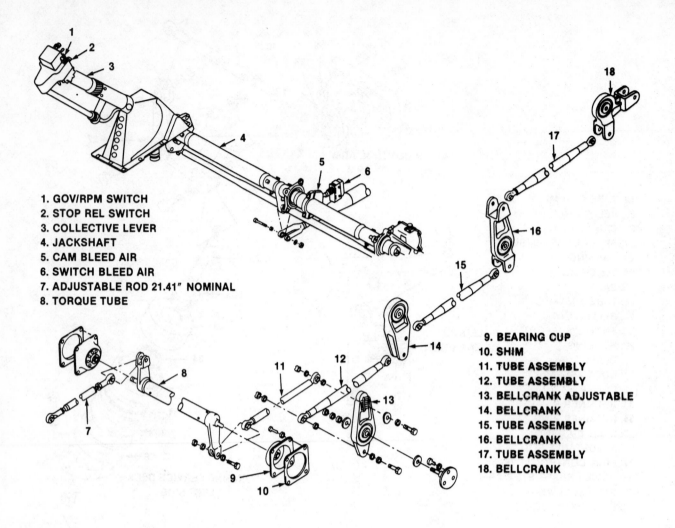

1. GOV/RPM SWITCH
2. STOP REL SWITCH
3. COLLECTIVE LEVER
4. JACKSHAFT
5. CAM BLEED AIR
6. SWITCH BLEED AIR
7. ADJUSTABLE ROD 21.41″ NOMINAL
8. TORQUE TUBE

9. BEARING CUP
10. SHIM
11. TUBE ASSEMBLY
12. TUBE ASSEMBLY
13. BELLCRANK ADJUSTABLE
14. BELLCRANK
15. TUBE ASSEMBLY
16. BELLCRANK
17. TUBE ASSEMBLY
18. BELLCRANK

Fig. 8-62   Bell 205 collective engine linkage

5. Check the flight-idle solenoid for operation. If necessary, shim the four mounting screws to obtain proper plunger alignment.

6. Position the power lever stop arm to approximately 44° and mark the position on the twist grip. This will be approximately the flight-idle position.

7. Attach the flight-idle stop on the extended spacer of the bellcrank, with the stop projection aft of the centerline of the solenoid.

8. Position the solenoid on the serrated base plate to obtain the correct clearance between the surface of the projection and the tip of the solenoid.

9. Check the flight-idle in ground run and if necessary readjust the stop to obtain the correct N_1 speed.

(1) Droop compensator

The linkage for the power turbine overspeed governor section consists of two areas of control. There is a mechanical input for the droop compensation and an electrical control for selecting the speed setting.

A droop compensator is installed in the linkage of the N_2 governor to maintain and stabilize the preselected N_2 RPM as power is increased by collective movement. This droop compensation is achieved by a linkage attached to a bellcrank of the collective pitch control. The purpose of this linkage is to change the governor position mechanically to anticipate the required action as the collective is moved. If the movement was not anticipated as collective is raised, the N_2 system would slow down, thus the term droop.

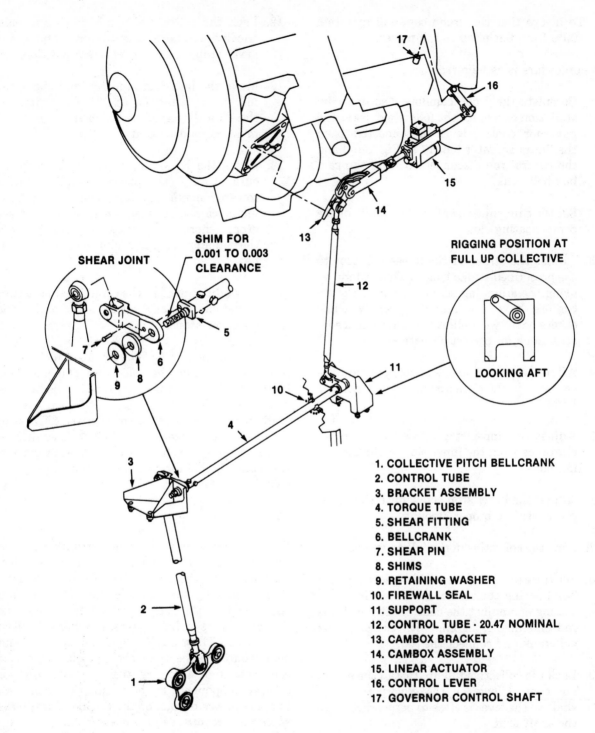

SHIM FOR 0.001 TO 0.003 CLEARANCE

SHEAR JOINT

RIGGING POSITION AT FULL UP COLLECTIVE

LOOKING AFT

1. COLLECTIVE PITCH BELLCRANK
2. CONTROL TUBE
3. BRACKET ASSEMBLY
4. TORQUE TUBE
5. SHEAR FITTING
6. BELLCRANK
7. SHEAR PIN
8. SHIMS
9. RETAINING WASHER
10. FIREWALL SEAL
11. SUPPORT
12. CONTROL TUBE - 20.47 NOMINAL
13. CAMBOX BRACKET
14. CAMBOX ASSEMBLY
15. LINEAR ACTUATOR
16. CONTROL LEVER
17. GOVERNOR CONTROL SHAFT

Fig. 8-63 Bell 205 compensating cam and liner actuator system

The electrically operated portion consists of a linear actuator and a RPM increase/decrease switch (beep button) on the collective. By moving the switch, the linear actuator is lengthened or shortened. Since this is attached to the lever of the governor the N_2 speed is changed (Figs. 8-63 and 8-64).

The purpose of rigging the N_2 system is:

1. To insure the correct spread is available on the tachometer by means of the *beep* button and that it is positioned in the right area of speed.

2. To insure that the droop cam will maintain 100% from flat pitch to full power.

The procedure is as follows:

1. Complete the droop cam/linear actuator installation except for the following: leave the governor control lever disconnected from the linear actuator (no. 17 in Fig. 8-64) and the control rod disconnected from the cam box bellcrank.

2. Set the cam adjustment to the middle of the compensating slot.

3. Adjust the stroke of the linear actuator to the prescribed stroke length. This is done by using the adjusting screws. Some of the actuators have one adjusting screw while others have two. Follow the maintenance instructions for correct adjustment.

4. After the proper stroke is set, position the actuator to the retracted position. (Increase RPM)

5. Adjust the upper stop screw to the proper clearance from the inner side of the mounting boss.

6. Adjust the lower stop screw until the screw protrudes the proper amount.

7. Lock the collective in the full-down position.

8. Set the cam slot to be visible below the cam box housing the correct distance. Hold this setting and adjust the control tube until the rod end hole is in line with the cam box bellcrank and connect the rod.

9. Lock the collective full up. Install the governor control lever on the governor control shaft so the lever is close to perpendicular to the shaft arm.

10. Rotate the governor control lever until the correct clearance is met between the governor shaft arm and the upper stop screw.

11. Hold in this position, adjust the actuator rod end to line up with the hole in the governor control lever and connect the actuator rod end.

12. Lock the collective in full down and electrically extend the actuator. Adjust the lower stop screw to its correct position.

13. Make the initial ground run and check the full range using the INC/DECR switch. If the spread cannot be reached the rod end must be repositioned.

14. Check the RPM droop. If RPM droop occurs, rotate the cam counterclockwise towards maximum compensation. If maximum cam compensation does not correct droop, shorten the control rod to decrease the amount of cam visible below the cam box.

15. Any adjustment to the cam, linear actuator, or rod end makes it necessary to adjust the governor stops.

This particular helicopter also includes a bleed air switch on the collective. This shuts off bleed air when maximum power is pulled on the collective. This bleed air is used to heat the aircraft. Since this air is taken from the diffuser of the engine, it is necessary to have this additional air for full power. When the collective is rigged or the engine is installed, it is necessary to rig this switch (Fig. 8-65).

(2) Engine trimming

The engine may also need trimming at this time. The adjustments should be made only in accordance with the manufacturer's recommendations. Generally they include idle and maximum speed only on the engine. The adjustments, like so many others on helicopters, should not be used as cure-all. They have a specific purpose and should only then be used. These would include the replacement of a fuel control, a new engine, or critical components in the engine that might affect the power output of the engine. *The engine should not require sudden adjustments.*

The rigging of different engines will vary from the procedure described. On a twin engine helicopter a similar procedure would be required of both engines with the two engines matching.

On the direct-drive turbines, no compensating cam or linear actuator controls would be found. On other free turbines, similar procedures would be followed.

12. CONTROL TUBE - 20.47 NOMINAL
13. CAMBOX BRACKET
14. CAMBOX ASSEMBLY
15. LINEAR ACTUATOR
16. CONTROL LEVER
17. GOVERNOR CONTROL SHAFT
18. SHAFT STOP-ARM
19. HIGH RPM STOP
20. LOW RPM STOP

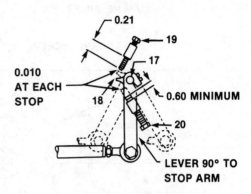

DETAIL AT GOVERNOR
VIEWED FROM TOP

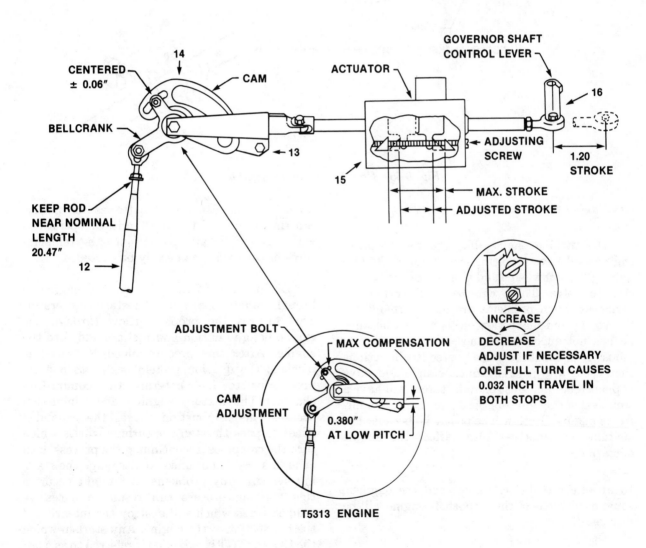

Fig. 8-64 Bell 205 cam and actuator adjustment

379

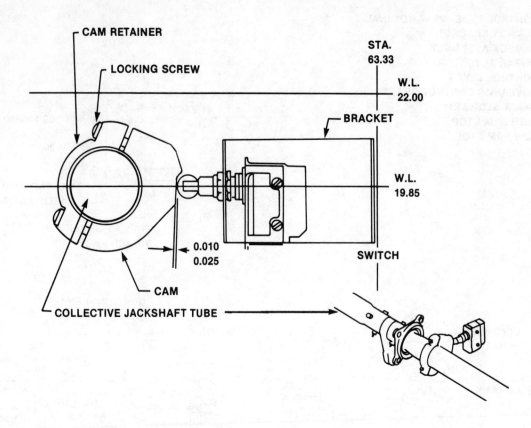

CAM RETAINER

LOCKING SCREW

STA.
63.33

W.L.
22.00

BRACKET

W.L.
19.85

0.010
0.025

SWITCH

CAM

COLLECTIVE JACKSHAFT TUBE

Fig. 8-65   Bell 205 bleed air switch

(3) Engine problems

The turbine engine, like the reciprocating engine, will have problems from time to time requiring the knowledge and abilities of the technician to solve. These can be most trying experiences. Such problems are most difficult for the young and inexperienced technician because he has not encountered the same problem previously. It must be remembered malfunctions that occur are generally quite simple and have happened before. Most manufacturers will have a troubleshooting guide in the engine manual or airframe manual. Both will be beneficial because the airframe systems can often affect the engine operation.

In an effort to better understand the engines, some basic areas of the turboshaft engine will be discussed.

(a) Turboshaft starting procedures

Most turboshaft engines use a starter-generator with battery power used for starting.

Most systems use *ni-cad* batteries for power. Starting is one of the most critical operations with any turboshaft engine since the temperatures of the engine can easily be exceeded.

During a normal operation the engine is brought up to speed by the starter-generator. This insures the proper airflow through the engine before ignition and fuel are added to the engine. After this predetermined N_1 speed is reached, the ignition system begins to operate just prior to fuel entering the combustion chamber. The mixture is ignited and combustion occurs. This combustion causes the expanded gases to pass through the turbine wheels which turn the compressor, continuing the process until enough speed is obtained to disengage the starting system. Any problems that might occur in this starting process can result in excessive temperatures which will destroy the integrity of the hot section of the engine. Any start in which the EGT or TOT is exceeded is referred to as a *hot start*. Generally hot starts are specified by temperature and time limits in the manual. These items will determine the maintenance action to be taken.

Other poor starts that may occur may be described as a *hung start* and a *torch start*. Either of these may not be a hot start but can result in one.

The *hung start* occurs when the engine is not capable of accelerating after combustion has occurred.

The *torch start* occurs when flames are visible from the tail pipe during starting.

Any of the three starts, hot, hung, or torch, require immediate attention from the maintenance personnel. If an over-temperature condition occurs, damage will occur to the engine. The damage that does occur may either be apparant immediately or become evident only after many more hours of operation.

To solve the problem, it must be determined which system has failed, resulting in this starting problem. The systems are similar and yet are different from those of a reciprocating engine. The same basic elements are still necessary — air, fuel, and ignition.

Air is developed by the compressor. This can be affected by the starting system because it is used to develop the compressor speed that is necessary for starting. Fuel is supplied in the correct manner by the starting fuel system. This means the fuel must be atomized as it enters the combustor. Ignition must be active prior to any fuel entering the combustor preventing accumulation of fuel prior to ignition.

These following areas could result in a hot start:

1. *Faulty ignition* — the operation can normally be heard. If the system is to be checked while on the aircraft the engine should be turning.

2. *Faulty starting system* — under battery power the engine should be able to obtain at least starting RPM. The engine should be motored over without fuel and ignition.

3. *Faulty fuel* — the nozzles should spray in a definite pattern and on shutdown fuel should be dumped overboard. Ignition should not occur in either circumstance while testing the system.

After careful examination each system may be eliminated one by one until the problem area is self-evident. It is only through such a described process that engine problems may be solved because each system is related to the engine as a whole.

The same type of process may be used for all malfunctions. The difference between technicians is often their ability to troubleshoot. Whether it is an engine or an airframe problem, the basics must be understood and a system used to solve the problems that occur. It is only in this manner that problems may be solved in a most economical and swift manner.

The engines used in the helicopters are the finest technology can provide, but they must be operated and maintained in the manner recommended by the manufacturer to insure safe reliable operation.

QUESTIONS:

121. There is no flywheel action on a reciprocating engine used in a helicopter due to the free wheeling unit.

   A. True

   B. False

122. A reciprocating engine in a helicopter runs _____ than in a fixed-wing aircraft.

   A. Faster

   B. Slower

123. The reciprocating engines used in helicopters were all modified fixed-wing engines.

   A. True

   B. False

124. Cooling fans are used on all reciprocating engine helicopters.

   A. True

   B. False

125. Power of the engine is changed with the movement of the collective by the corrolation box.

    A. True

    B. False

126. The most widely used type of shaft turbine in helicopters is the free turbine.

    A. True

    B. False

127. The free turbine may operate at different compressor speeds while the output shaft is turning at a constant speed.

    A. True

    B. False

128. Bleed valves are used to improve acceleration without stall.

    A. True

    B. False

129. The output shaft may be located on the hot or cold end.

    A. True

    B. False

130. The N_2 RPM may be adjusted for the conditions of the day with the "beep" button.

    A. True

    B. False

131. Particle separators make use of the fact that dust is heavier than air.

    A. True

    B. False

132. The fuel controls on free turbines use an N_2 governor.

    A. True

    B. False

133. Movement of the collective will move the N_2 governor on a free turbine.

    A. True

    B. False

134. On a free turbine the twist grip would set the N_1 RPM only.

    A. True

    B. False

135. On twin engine application the two engines are mated by the torquemeter.

    A. True

    B. False

The tail rotor (sometimes referred to as an anti-torque rotor) is used for directional control of the single main rotor helicopters. This system, like other systems on the helicopter, has as many variations as there are helicopters.

For many years the tail rotor was one of the areas that plagued the would-be inventors of the helicopter. The absence of the tail rotor brought about co-axial main rotors, tandem rotors, rotors located side-by-side, and intermeshing main rotors. Even after Sikorsky used the tail rotor, these other designs continued. The majority of helicopters are equipped with tail rotors. Those not utilizing a tail rotor are used primarily by the military. One model of the tandem rotor helicopter is presently used in the civilian fleet and more will go into production in the future.

Even though the tail rotor has disadvantages, the main rotor, tail rotor system seems to be the best compromise at this time. The tandem main rotor being second best because of the complexity of design.

A. Operation

The tail rotor, like the main rotor, must be able to perform in much the same manner, with the blades being able to change pitch and flap either independently or as a unit. However, no system of lead-lag has been built into the tail rotor. The tail rotor blades must have a negative and positive pitch capability to supply directional control under powered conditions and autorotation. Directional control is done by foot pedals similar to those used on fixed-wing aircraft to control the rudder. In fact, they are often referred to as rudder pedals even though they aren't. They serve the same function of supplying directional control.

B. Tail Rotor System

The drive for the tail rotors is supplied from the transmission of the helicopter, or at least by connection with the transmission. It is necessary for the tail rotor to rotate at all times during helicopter flight, even if the engine is not operational. The tail rotor may be driven by either the engine or the transmission during autorotation.

1. Tail rotor driveshaft

The tail rotor is driven through shafting from the transmission down the length of the tail boom. Tail booms generally have some limited flexibility, which means the shafting must also have some ability to move in a fore-and-aft direction. This movement may be supplied by splined shafts or flexible couplings and sometimes a combination of the two is used. The shafting must be supported throughout the length of the tail boom. This is normally accomplished by the use of hanger bearings, which not only support the shaft, but also provide shaft alignment. Alignment is very important from a vibration standpoint. At times it may be necessary to divert the shaft if the tail rotor is mounted at the top of a tail boom pylon (Fig. 9-1). In this type of situation an intermediate gearbox is used, or in some instances a universal joint. The majority of manufacturers utilize the intermediate gearbox, which will be used to change direction and will not increase or decrease the speed.

2. Tail rotor gearbox

The tail rotor gearbox changes direction and increases or decreases the speed. Some manufacturers prefer to increase the speed while others decrease the output shaft. In either situation the tail rotor turns faster than the main rotor. On some helicopters the speed in excess of 3000 RPM with other operating over 2000 RPM is not unusual.

3. Tail rotor blades

The tail rotors themselves are made of a number of different materials and designs. Many of the newer blades are composites with some

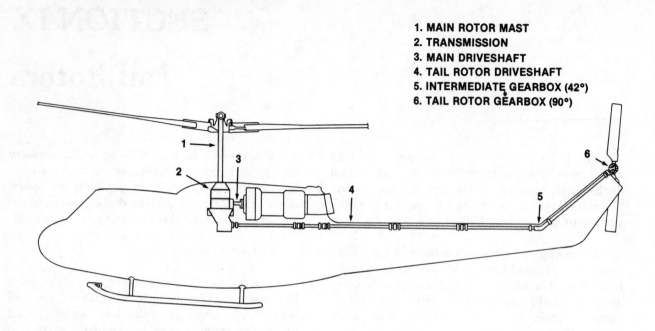

1. MAIN ROTOR MAST
2. TRANSMISSION
3. MAIN DRIVESHAFT
4. TAIL ROTOR DRIVESHAFT
5. INTERMEDIATE GEARBOX (42°)
6. TAIL ROTOR GEARBOX (90°)

Fig. 9-1   Typical tail rotor shafting using an intermediate gearbox and tail rotor gearbox.

metal blades still in use. Some helicopters will use a two-bladed system while others use a multi-blade system.

4. *Pitch-change mechanism*

For the pitch-change mechanism a number of different systems are used. Most of the newer helicopters utilize push-pull tubes to the tail rotor, while a few use cable. The pitch-change system may also have a hydraulic boost on the control system operated from the same system used for the cyclic and collective.

C. *Bell 47 Tail Rotor System*

The tail rotor driveshaft assembly provides the mechanical connection between the main transmission, tail rotor output quill and the tail rotor gearbox. The driveshaft assembly consists of three tubular sections connected by splined couplings with one universal joint (Fig. 9-2).

In addition to the three driveshafts and one universal joint, an extension drive is placed at the end of the shaft assembly. The extension drive assembly consists of an extension shaft, a housing, and a gearbox. The extension drive is attached through a yoke to the upper end of the tail boom. The gearbox provides for a 90° directional change, and a gear reduction to the tail rotor.

The major components of the tail rotor driveshaft system are:

1. Forward shaft section

2. Middle (mid) shaft section

3. Aft shaft section

4. Eight bearing assemblies

5. One universal joint

6. Extension shaft

7. Forward bearing and housing

8. Center bearing and housing

9. Extension housing

1. *Forward shaft*

The forward shaft incorporates fixed splines at each end of a hollow sealed shaft. The splined couplings are placed on the output quill of the transmission and the midshaft into which the forward shaft couples. The couplings allow for misalignment that may take place between the transmission and the mid shaft. The forward shaft is held in place by snap rings in each coupling.

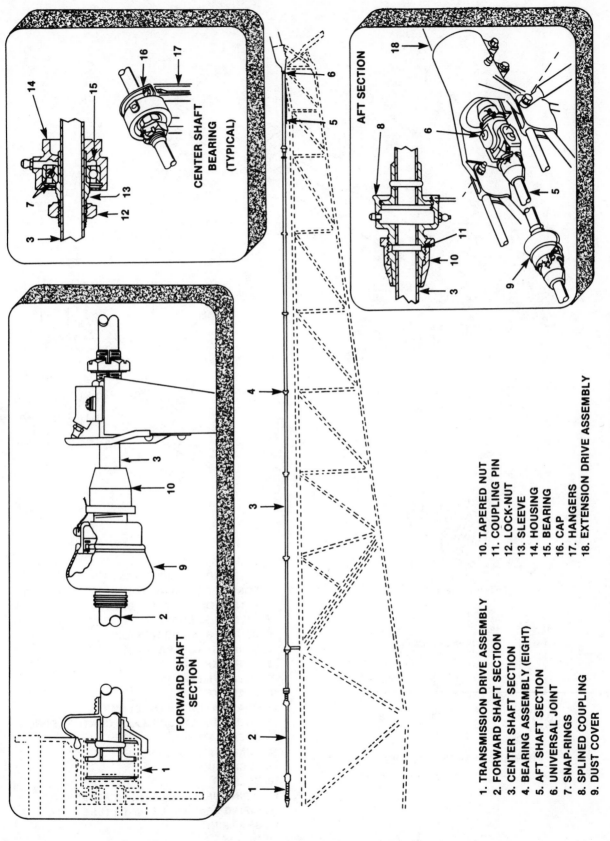

CENTER SHAFT
BEARING
(TYPICAL)

FORWARD SHAFT
SECTION

AFT SECTION

1. TRANSMISSION DRIVE ASSEMBLY
2. FORWARD SHAFT SECTION
3. CENTER SHAFT SECTION
4. BEARING ASSEMBLY (EIGHT)
5. AFT SHAFT SECTION
6. UNIVERSAL JOINT
7. SNAP-RINGS
8. SPLINED COUPLING
9. DUST COVER

10. TAPERED NUT
11. COUPLING PIN
12. LOCK-NUT
13. SLEEVE
14. HOUSING
15. BEARING
16. CAP
17. HANGERS
18. EXTENSION DRIVE ASSEMBLY

Fig. 9-2 Tail rotor shafting used on the Bell 47.

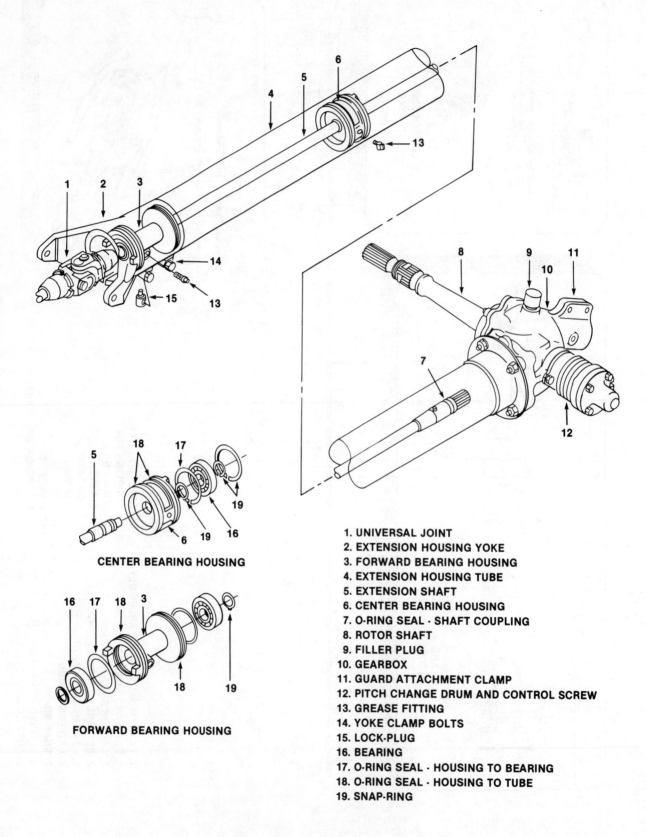

CENTER BEARING HOUSING

FORWARD BEARING HOUSING

1. UNIVERSAL JOINT
2. EXTENSION HOUSING YOKE
3. FORWARD BEARING HOUSING
4. EXTENSION HOUSING TUBE
5. EXTENSION SHAFT
6. CENTER BEARING HOUSING
7. O-RING SEAL · SHAFT COUPLING
8. ROTOR SHAFT
9. FILLER PLUG
10. GEARBOX
11. GUARD ATTACHMENT CLAMP
12. PITCH CHANGE DRUM AND CONTROL SCREW
13. GREASE FITTING
14. YOKE CLAMP BOLTS
15. LOCK-PLUG
16. BEARING
17. O-RING SEAL - HOUSING TO BEARING
18. O-RING SEAL - HOUSING TO TUBE
19. SNAP-RING

Fig. 9-3   Extension tube used on the Bell 47.

386

2. Middle or mid shaft

The middle shaft, or mid shaft, is hollow and sealed. It is supported by seven bearing packages placed along the top of the tail boom and one on the center section of the helicopter, making a total of eight. At each end of the mid shaft is a coupling — one to connect the forward shaft and one to connect the aft shaft. The couplings are secured to the shaft by tapered sleeve locknuts and pins. The support bearings use deep groove ball bearings capable of taking loads in both directions. The bearings are secured to the shaft by tapered sleeves and nuts. Each of the bearing packages has provisions for greasing as do the couplings.

3. Aft shaft

The aft shaft, like the forward and the mid shaft, is a hollow sealed shaft. It has a fixed set of splines attached to one end. The other end is straight in order to accept the universal joint which is held in place by a pin and tapered sleeve locknut.

4. Universal joint

The universal joint provides a coupling between the aft shaft and the extension tube shaft. It also provides a directional change of appproximately 15 degrees between the aft shaft and the extension tube shaft. This end of the universal joint is also held by a tapered sleeve and pin as was used to hold the opposite end of the universal joint to the aft shaft.

5. Extension tube

The extension tube (Fig. 9-3) has the universal joint attached at one end of the shaft. The opposite end of the shaft is splined for connection to the tail rotor gearbox which attaches to the extension tube which supports the gearbox. An O-ring is installed at the splined end to dampen any vibration that might occur between the splined shaft and the tail rotor gearbox input.

The extension tube housing is a one-piece aluminum alloy tube with a flange on one end and is bolted to the tail rotor gearbox. The forward end has a yoke assembly attached. This clamps to the housing and is pinned to the housing, preventing rotation. This tube provides a housing for three-deep groove ball bearings which are con-

tained in their own housings. The housings are held in the tube by their snug fit against the inner wall of the tube. Between the housing and the wall are O-rings.

The forward bearing housing incorporates two bearings. These are retained by snap rings and lubricated by a grease zerk which protrudes through the extension tube.

The center bearing housing has one bearing held by snap rings and lubricated in the same manner.

6. Tail rotor gearbox

Attached to the extension tube by the flange on the aft end is the tail rotor gearbox. This gearbox is driven by the extension tube shaft and acts as a gear reduction as well as a directional change for the tail rotor, mounted on the output shaft of the tail rotor gearbox.

Major components of the tail rotor gearbox are (Fig. 9-4 A and B):

1. Gearbox housing

2. Input sleeve

3. Output shaft and front cap

4. Pitch-change mechanism

The tail rotor gearbox housing attaches to the extension tube flange by bolts. The housing is made of cast aluminum and is equipped with a filler plug, a drain plug, a sight gauge, and a mounting point for the brush guard.

a. Input sleeve

The input sleeve, made of an aluminum casting, fits into the gearbox housing. The sleeve houses the input shaft, thrust bearings, and alignment bearing.

The angular contact bearings are installed face-to-face and are held in the sleeve by a retaining nut with a steel washer against the outer races. The retaining nut has a garlock seal in the center where the input shaft passes through and is sealed on the outer threads by an O-ring. The bearing inner races are secured against a flange on the input shaft, a thrust washer and spacer.

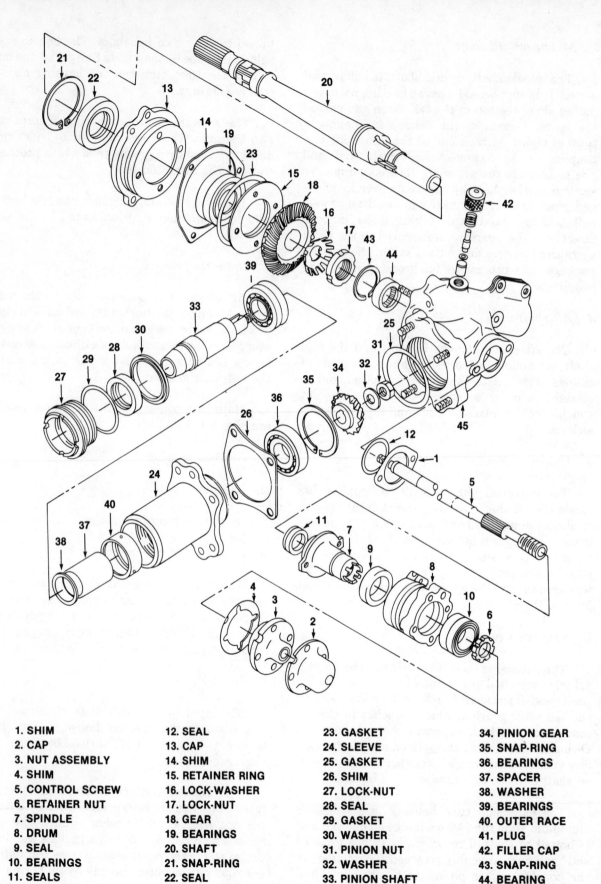

1. SHIM	12. SEAL	23. GASKET	34. PINION GEAR
2. CAP	13. CAP	24. SLEEVE	35. SNAP-RING
3. NUT ASSEMBLY	14. SHIM	25. GASKET	36. BEARINGS
4. SHIM	15. RETAINER RING	26. SHIM	37. SPACER
5. CONTROL SCREW	16. LOCK-WASHER	27. LOCK-NUT	38. WASHER
6. RETAINER NUT	17. LOCK-NUT	28. SEAL	39. BEARINGS
7. SPINDLE	18. GEAR	29. GASKET	40. OUTER RACE
8. DRUM	19. BEARINGS	30. WASHER	41. PLUG
9. SEAL	20. SHAFT	31. PINION NUT	42. FILLER CAP
10. BEARINGS	21. SNAP-RING	32. WASHER	43. SNAP-RING
11. SEALS	22. SEAL	33. PINION SHAFT	44. BEARING
			45. GEAR CASE

Fig. 9-4A   Exploded view of the Bell 47 gearbox.

388

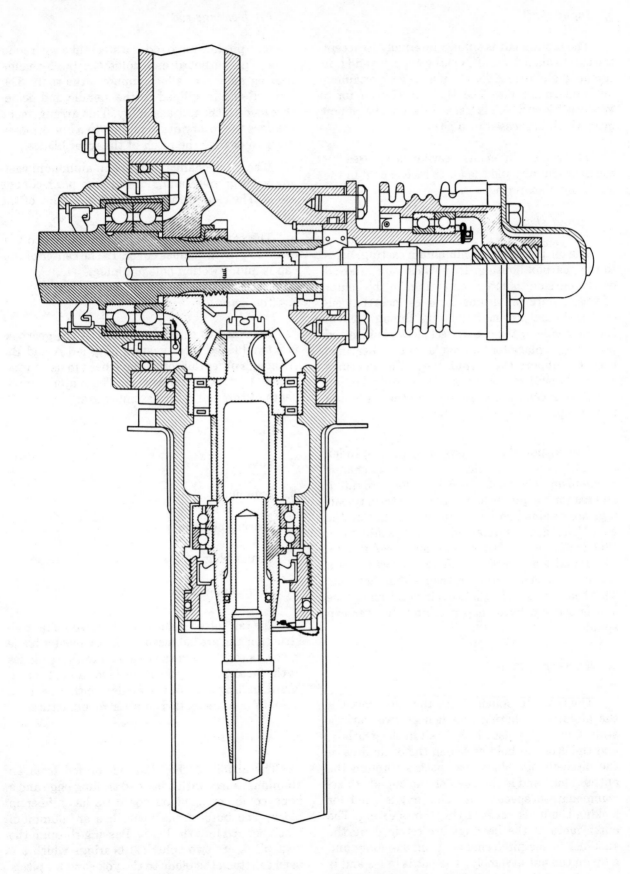

Fig. 9-4B   Cross-sectional view of the Bell 47 tail rotor gearbox.

b. Input shaft

The input shaft is splined internally to accept the extension driveshaft. On the opposite end it is threaded and drilled for the pinion gear retaining nut and cotter pin. The shaft is slotted for a Woodruff key which is used to retain the pinion gear which is pressed into position.

The roller alignment bearing is secured by the gear and nut and the outer race is held in the sleeve by a snap ring.

c. Output shaft

The output shaft, an aluminum casting, bolts to the gearbox housing. Its surfaces are grooved on the outside to accept an O-ring. In the center of the cap are provisions for a garlock that encircles the output shaft passing through it. On the back side of the cap a steel sleeve is inserted providing a place for an angular thrust bearings used to support the output shaft. The bearings are also installed face-to-face and are locked on the outer races by a retaining ring that is bolted to the cap.

The output shaft is master splined to index the tail rotor controls on the pitch-change mechanism. The shaft itself is hollow providing an area for the pitch-change rod. The thrust bearings are retained on the shaft by a flange and the gear. The gear is retained on the shaft by a Woodruff key, a retaining nut, and a safety clip. The radial loads of the shaft are absorbed by a roller alignment bearing in the gearbox housing. This bearing uses the shaft itself as the inner race and is secured by a snap ring and the rear cap spindle.

d. Rear cap spindle

The rear cap spindle locks the outer races of the alignment bearing and houses two garlock seals. One seal is used to hold oil in the gearbox, and the other to hold grease in the drum area of the pitch-change shaft that passes through the output shaft and is threaded on the outside to accommodate a special nut. This nut is used for locking the inner races of the drum bearing. The outer races of the bearings are retained by the shoulder in the pitch-change drum assembly and a lip on the nut assembly. The nut is brass and is acme-threaded to the pitch-change rod.

e. Pitch-change rod

The pitch-change rod is a steel tube with solid ends. The outboard end holds the pitch-change bearing inner race which supports the shaft. The inboard end is splined to the spindle and acme-threaded to the nut assembly. This arrangement changes the rotary drum motion to a linear movement to change the pitch of the rotor blades.

The pitch-change drum is an aluminum casting with grooves and slots for the pitch-change cable. The cable wraps around the outside of the drum.

The cap and nut assembly are bolted to the drum to provide a dust cover. In the center of the cap is an inspection hole and plug.

7. Tail rotor

Attached to the output shaft of the gearbox is a two-bladed rotor system (Fig. 9-5 A and B). Although other tail rotors have been in use on the Model 47, this is the newest. The major components of this tail rotor assembly are:

1. Blades

2. Yoke

3. Trunnion

4. Bearing housing

5. Thrust plug

6. Pitch-change horn

The tail rotor blades are of bonded metal construction and are balanced against a master blade in the factory. Weights are added to these blades at the factory, at the tip of the blade and at the inboard trailing edge of the blade. Neither of these weights is to be disturbed after manufacture.

a. Construction

The airfoil of the blade is formed from an aluminum sheet with a bonded trailing edge and a honeycomb core. The outboard tip has a fibertip block. The butt of the blade has an aluminum block bonded into the blade. Passing through the butt block are two spherical bearings which are used to attach the blade to the yoke and for pitch-change.

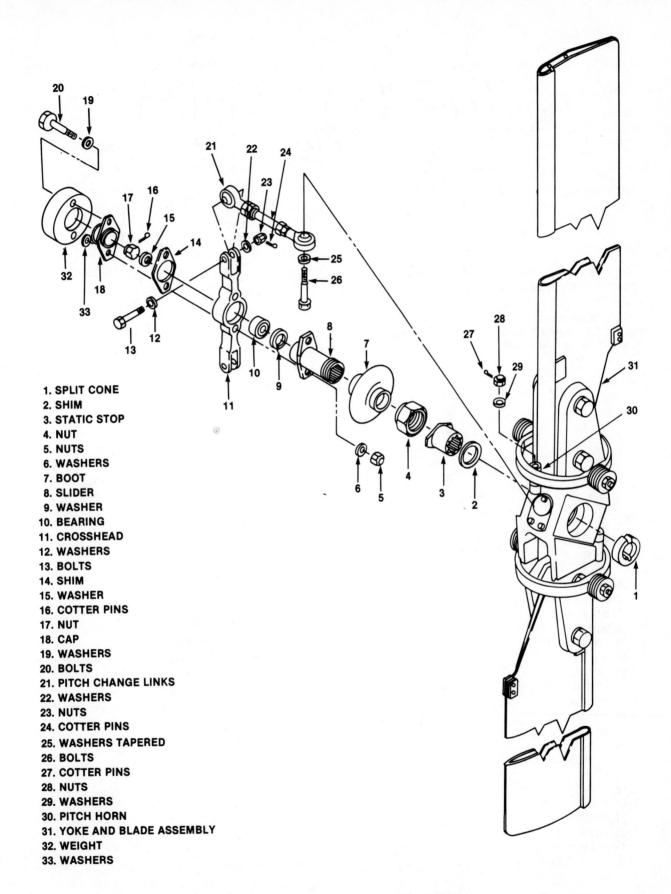

1. SPLIT CONE
2. SHIM
3. STATIC STOP
4. NUT
5. NUTS
6. WASHERS
7. BOOT
8. SLIDER
9. WASHER
10. BEARING
11. CROSSHEAD
12. WASHERS
13. BOLTS
14. SHIM
15. WASHER
16. COTTER PINS
17. NUT
18. CAP
19. WASHERS
20. BOLTS
21. PITCH CHANGE LINKS
22. WASHERS
23. NUTS
24. COTTER PINS
25. WASHERS TAPERED
26. BOLTS
27. COTTER PINS
28. NUTS
29. WASHERS
30. PITCH HORN
31. YOKE AND BLADE ASSEMBLY
32. WEIGHT
33. WASHERS

Fig. 9-5A   Tail rotor used on the Bell 47.

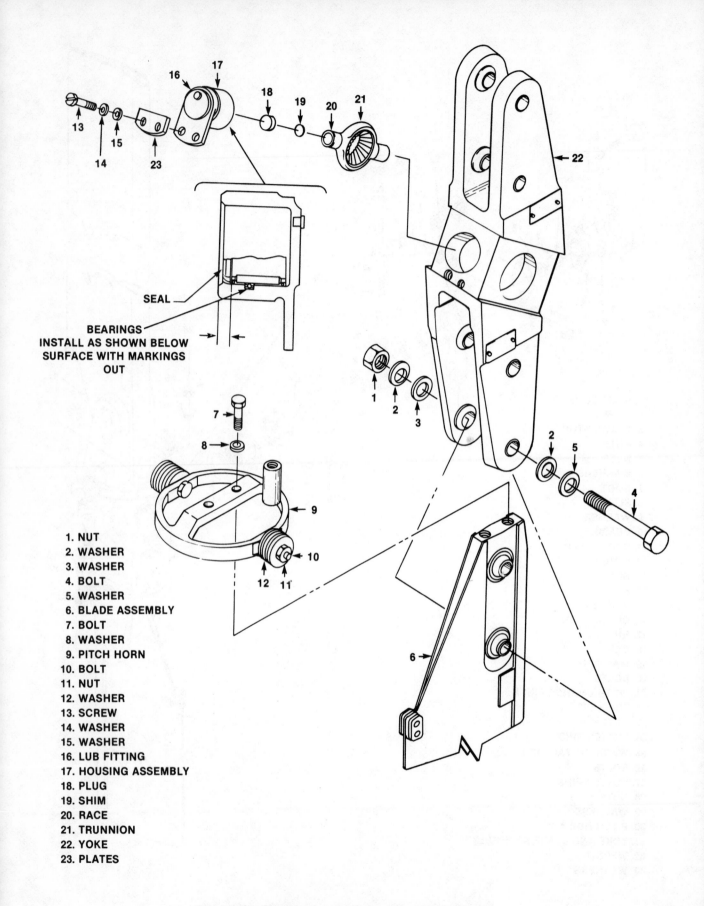

SEAL

BEARINGS
INSTALL AS SHOWN BELOW
SURFACE WITH MARKINGS
OUT

1. NUT
2. WASHER
3. WASHER
4. BOLT
5. WASHER
6. BLADE ASSEMBLY
7. BOLT
8. WASHER
9. PITCH HORN
10. BOLT
11. NUT
12. WASHER
13. SCREW
14. WASHER
15. WASHER
16. LUB FITTING
17. HOUSING ASSEMBLY
18. PLUG
19. SHIM
20. RACE
21. TRUNNION
22. YOKE
23. PLATES

Fig. 9-5B   Hub and trunnion used on the Bell 47.

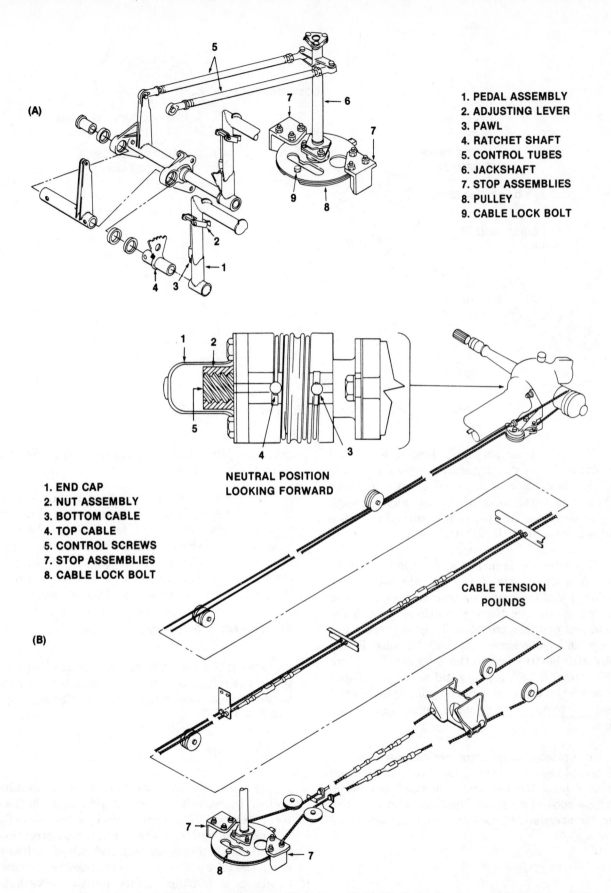

(A)

1. PEDAL ASSEMBLY
2. ADJUSTING LEVER
3. PAWL
4. RATCHET SHAFT
5. CONTROL TUBES
6. JACKSHAFT
7. STOP ASSEMBLIES
8. PULLEY
9. CABLE LOCK BOLT

NEUTRAL POSITION
LOOKING FORWARD

1. END CAP
2. NUT ASSEMBLY
3. BOTTOM CABLE
4. TOP CABLE
5. CONTROL SCREWS
7. STOP ASSEMBLIES
8. CABLE LOCK BOLT

CABLE TENSION
POUNDS

(B)

Fig. 9-6   A — Bell 47 pedal assembly.   B — Bell 47 pitch change mechanism.

393

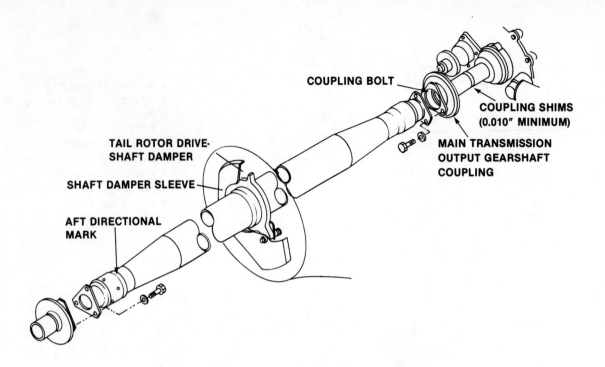

COUPLING BOLT

COUPLING SHIMS
(0.010" MINIMUM)

TAIL ROTOR DRIVE-
SHAFT DAMPER

MAIN TRANSMISSION
OUTPUT GEARSHAFT
COUPLING

SHAFT DAMPER SLEEVE

AFT DIRECTIONAL
MARK

Fig. 9-7   Tail rotor driveshaft used on the Hughes 500.

The yoke is an aluminum forging with steel inserts for blade attachment. Provisions are made for the installation of two steel bearing housings which attach the yoke to the trunnion through needle bearings. The position is such that it provides a delta hinge for the tail rotor.

The trunnion is master splined to receive the tail rotor driveshaft. A taper at the face of the splines holds the trunnion against the split cones on the shaft. The bearing housings fit into the yoke and over the trunnion. They are secured to the yoke by two screws for each housing. Plates may also be attached to these screws for chordwise balance. Teflon plugs and shims are placed between the outer ends of the yoke spindles and bearings to provide a means of centering the trunnion.

The pitch-change horns are circular rings attached to the root of the blade with two bolts and have a boss for the attachment of the pitch-change rods. Two other holes are also provided for counterweight washers used to set pedal creep.

b.   Control system

The tail rotor is controlled through pedal cables, a pitch-change mechanism, and the tail rotor blades (Fig. 9-6)

The pedals located on the floor are adjustable to the pilot's leg length. The pedals act through push-pull tubes to move a jackshaft on the box beam. The jackshaft is connected to a cable drum from which cables go to the pulley on the tail rotor gearbox. The movement of the drum moves the pitch-change mechanism of the blades.

D.   Hughes 500 Tail Rotor System

This system is much different from other systems that might be seen. The Hughes 500 has a very simple system but it is quite different from the Bell 47.

1.   Driveshaft

The tail rotor driveshaft is a one-piece unit installed between the transmission and the tail rotor gearbox. The driveshaft is a dynamically balanced tube of bonded and riveted construction with flange coupling on each end. About halfway down the tube a steel sleeve is bonded to the tube to act as a bearing surface for the driveshaft dampener (Fig. 9-7)

2. Splined couplings

Splined couplings are provided at the output of the transmission and input to the tail rotor gearbox. The couplings are steel and are of the Bendix flexible type as used on the main driveshaft. These couplings allow for any misalignment that may occur. The balancing of the shaft is accomplished by brass weights bonded to the shaft in three locations.

3. Dampener

The driveshaft dampener (Fig. 9-8) mounted in the aft fuselage boom, surrounds the steel sleeve which is bonded to the shaft.

The dampener consists of a graphite centered Teflon block held in place by bolts, springs, and washers. This block requires a set friction which is set by spring tension.

4. Tail rotor gearbox

The tail rotor gearbox, mounted on the tail boom, is used to increase the tail rotor speed and change the direction 90° (Fig. 9-9). It contains a mesh ring gear and a pinion spiral bevel gear. The input shaft has two ball bearings on the aft end and one of the front end. The output shaft has a roller bearing on the inboard end and a duplex bearing set on the outboard end. The bearings of the input and output shafts are lubricated by the oil supply contained in the gearbox. The gearbox is equipped with a sight gauge and a chip detector.

5. Tail rotor installation

The tail rotor installation consists of a pitch control assembly, a drive fork assembly, two pitch control links. The two blade assemblies are connected to a tension torsion strap and mount over the hub.

The pitch is controlled collectively by the pitch control assembly consisting of link assemblies connecting the pitch control arms to a swashplate that slides axial on the tail rotor output shaft. The movement of the swashplate is controlled through a series of bellcranks and rod assemblies connected to the pedals.

a. Tail rotor blades

The tail rotor blades are aluminum skin wraparounds with a honeycomb spar and doublers at the root of the blade. The root fittings are aluminum forgings bonded and riveted to the blade. The fittings are bored to accommodate the feathering bearings that ride on the yoke spindle, and incorporate a pitch change horn.

b. Tail rotor hub

The tail rotor hub consists of a drive fork, conical teetering bearings, strap pack, hub, flap restrainer, and attachment hardware.

The strap pack ties the blades together. The strap pack is made of stainless steel straps held together in the center and secured to each blade by a single bolt.

The hub is a stainless steel forging bored through the center to accommodate the strap pack. The hub is attached to the drive fork using a single bolt and cone shaped bearings. Shims are used to center the drive fork in the hub (Fig. 9-10).

The drive fork transfers torque from the gearbox output shaft to the tail rotor assembly. The drive fork is held on the output shaft by split cones and a retaining nut.

The flap restrainer assembly consists of an aluminum cup with an extension for insertion into the tail rotor gearbox output shaft. The cup accepts a 2-inch rubber stop.

c. Pitch control assembly

The pitch control assembly consists of a rotating swashplate and pitch control housing. The pitch control housing is a machined casting fitted with two sealed ball bearings. The bearing's outer race is secured in the housing by a swage ring. A spherical bearing, pressed into a bore of the housing, is the attachment point of the pitch-control bellcrank that provides control input to the swashplate. The swashplate slides into the two ball bearings in the pitch control housing and is secured to the inner race of the bearings by a locknut. Two bronze liners are situated in the swashplate, one is splined, and the other smooth. The splined liner mates with the splined portion

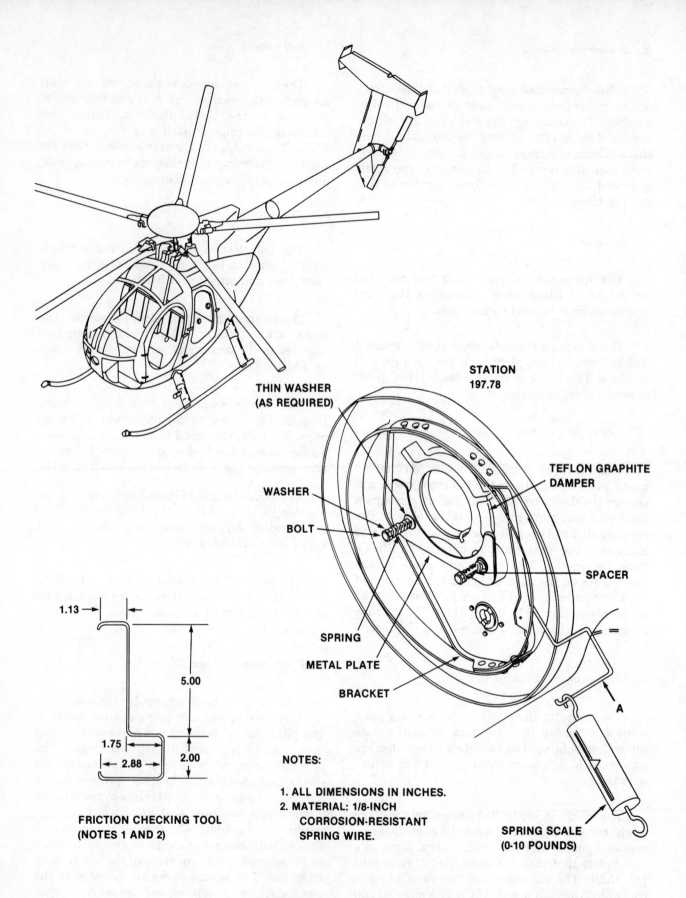

STATION 197.78

THIN WASHER (AS REQUIRED)

TEFLON GRAPHITE DAMPER

WASHER

BOLT

SPACER

SPRING

METAL PLATE

BRACKET

A

SPRING SCALE (0-10 POUNDS)

1.13

5.00

1.75

2.88

2.00

FRICTION CHECKING TOOL (NOTES 1 AND 2)

NOTES:
1. ALL DIMENSIONS IN INCHES.
2. MATERIAL: 1/8-INCH CORROSION-RESISTANT SPRING WIRE.

Fig. 9-8 Driveshaft dampener used on the Hughes 500.

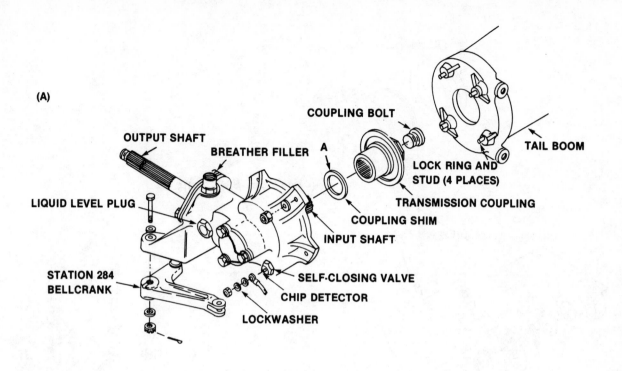

(A)

OUTPUT SHAFT
BREATHER FILLER
A
COUPLING BOLT
TAIL BOOM
LOCK RING AND
STUD (4 PLACES)
LIQUID LEVEL PLUG
TRANSMISSION COUPLING
COUPLING SHIM
INPUT SHAFT
STATION 284
BELLCRANK
SELF-CLOSING VALVE
CHIP DETECTOR
LOCKWASHER

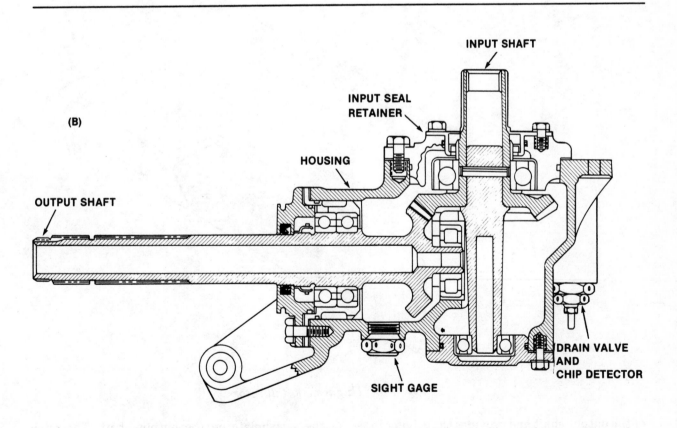

(B)

INPUT SHAFT
INPUT SEAL
RETAINER
HOUSING
OUTPUT SHAFT
DRAIN VALVE
AND
CHIP DETECTOR
SIGHT GAGE

Fig. 9-9 Hughes 500 tail rotor gearbox A — Exploded view. B — Cross-sectional view.

397

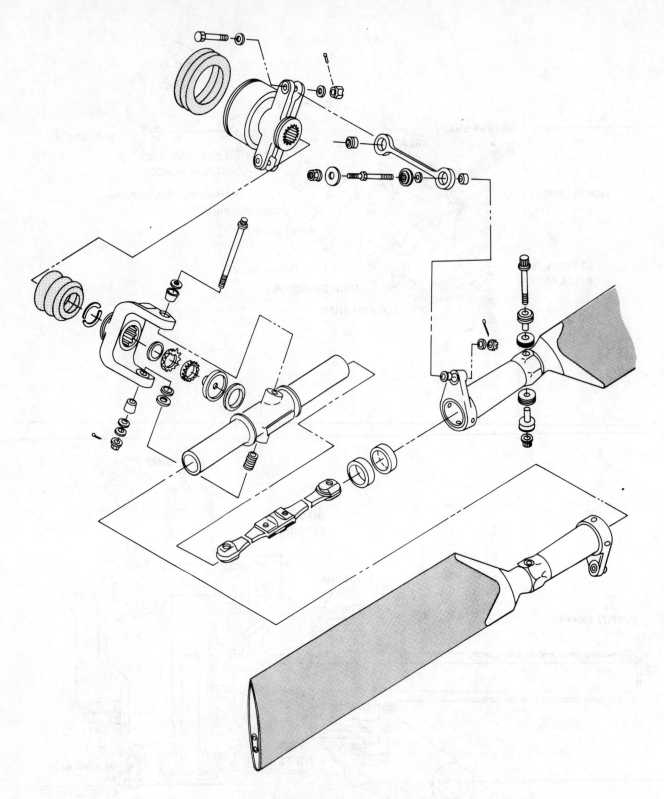

Fig. 9-10 Hughes 500 tail rotor

of the output shaft and provides the driving force for the swashplate. The smooth liner is roller staked and serves as a second bearing surface for the swashplate on the output shaft. The pitch links are forged aluminum, and have replaceable swaged spherical bearings (Fig. 9-11).

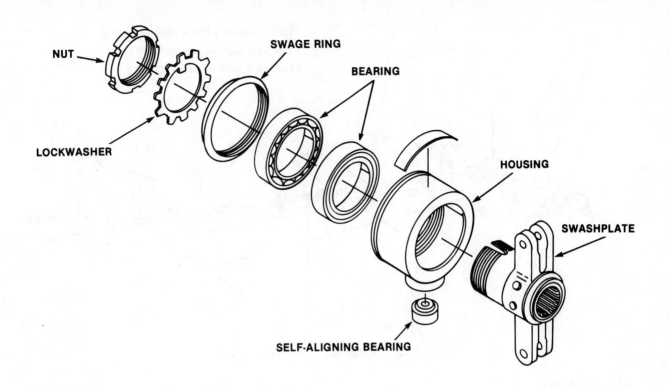

NUT

LOCKWASHER

SWAGE RING

BEARING

HOUSING

SWASHPLATE

SELF-ALIGNING BEARING

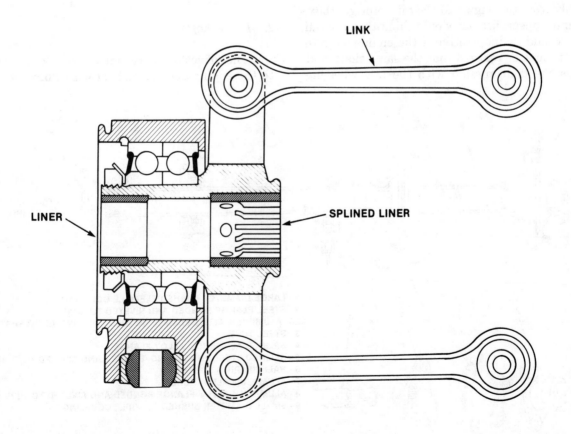

LINK

LINER

SPLINED LINER

Fig. 9-11   Hughes 500 pitch change mechanism

399

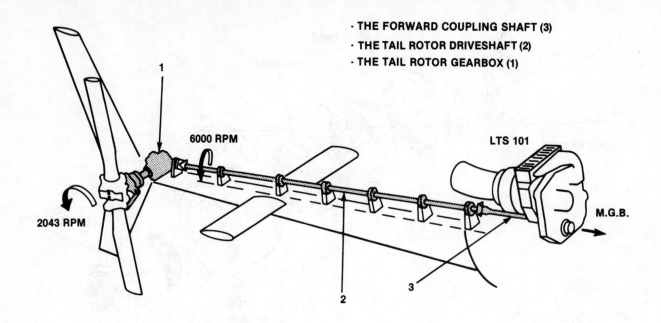

· **THE FORWARD COUPLING SHAFT (3)**
· **THE TAIL ROTOR DRIVESHAFT (2)**
· **THE TAIL ROTOR GEARBOX (1)**

Fig. 9-12   AStar tail rotor drive system

E.   AStar 350

The AStar 350 uses a two-section shaft assembly from the engine to the tail rotor gearbox. At first appearance one would think that the tail rotor would be inoperative if the engine were to fail. It must be realized that the same shaft that drives the transmission with the free wheeling unit, will transmit power from the transmission to the tail rotor in the event of an engine failure (Fig. 9-12).

1.   Driveshafts

The driveshafts are connected to each other, to the engine and the tail rotor gearbox by flex-

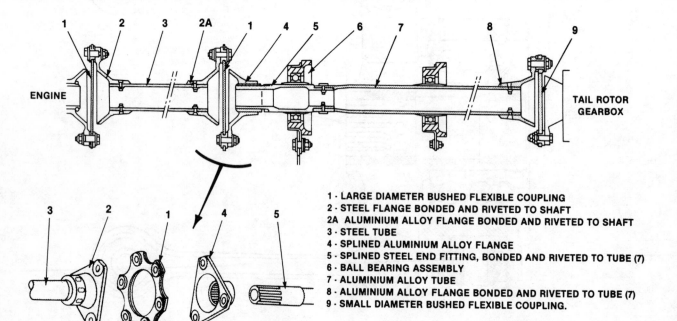

1 · LARGE DIAMETER BUSHED FLEXIBLE COUPLING
2 · STEEL FLANGE BONDED AND RIVETED TO SHAFT
2A ALUMINIUM ALLOY FLANGE BONDED AND RIVETED TO SHAFT
3 · STEEL TUBE
4 · SPLINED ALUMINIUM ALLOY FLANGE
5 · SPLINED STEEL END FITTING, BONDED AND RIVETED TO TUBE (7)
6 · BALL BEARING ASSEMBLY
7 · ALUMINIUM ALLOY TUBE
8 · ALUMINIUM ALLOY FLANGE BONDED AND RIVETED TO TUBE (7)
9 · SMALL DIAMETER BUSHED FLEXIBLE COUPLING.

Fig. 9-13   Driveshaft and coupling system used on the Aerospatiale AStar.

400

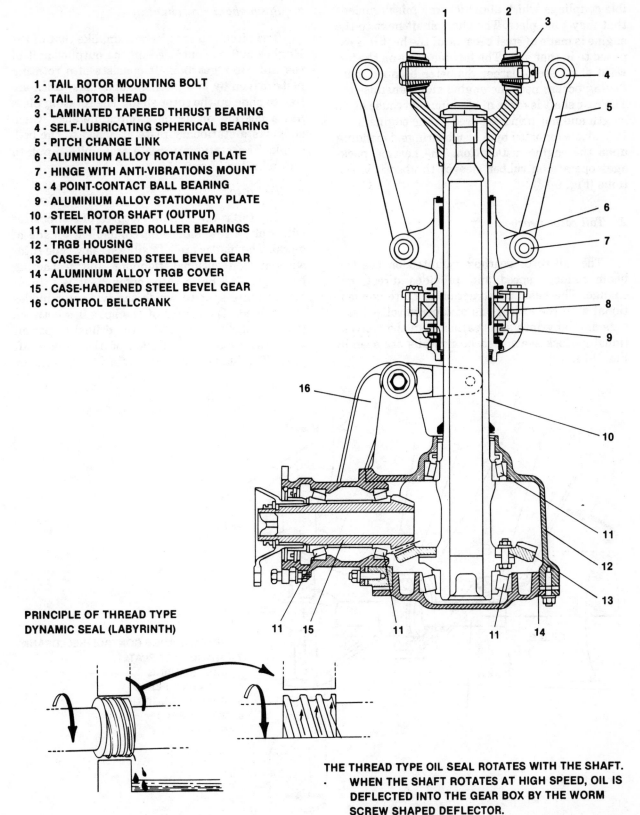

1 - TAIL ROTOR MOUNTING BOLT
2 - TAIL ROTOR HEAD
3 - LAMINATED TAPERED THRUST BEARING
4 - SELF-LUBRICATING SPHERICAL BEARING
5 - PITCH CHANGE LINK
6 - ALUMINIUM ALLOY ROTATING PLATE
7 - HINGE WITH ANTI-VIBRATIONS MOUNT
8 - 4 POINT-CONTACT BALL BEARING
9 - ALUMINIUM ALLOY STATIONARY PLATE
10 - STEEL ROTOR SHAFT (OUTPUT)
11 - TIMKEN TAPERED ROLLER BEARINGS
12 - TRGB HOUSING
13 - CASE-HARDENED STEEL BEVEL GEAR
14 - ALUMINIUM ALLOY TRGB COVER
15 - CASE-HARDENED STEEL BEVEL GEAR
16 - CONTROL BELLCRANK

PRINCIPLE OF THREAD TYPE
DYNAMIC SEAL (LABYRINTH)

THE THREAD TYPE OIL SEAL ROTATES WITH THE SHAFT.
- WHEN THE SHAFT ROTATES AT HIGH SPEED, OIL IS
  DEFLECTED INTO THE GEAR BOX BY THE WORM
  SCREW SHAPED DEFLECTOR.
- AT REST, THERE IS NO LEAKAGE SINCE THE OIL LEVEL
  IS BELOW THE SEAL.

Fig. 9-14   Tail rotor gearbox and seal system used on the Aerospatiale AStar.

401

ible couplings which allow for any misalignment that may take place. The short shaft next to the engine is made of steel because of the heat it is exposed to in that area. The flexible discs on the forward shaft are of larger diameter because more flexing occurs near the engine and transmission. The rear shaft is made of aluminum because of its length and not being exposed to the engine heat. It is also supported by 5 or 6 bearings depending upon the engine installation. The bearing packages operate on rubber sleeves to absorb vibrations (Fig. 9-13).

2. Tail rotor gearbox

The tail rotor gearbox mounted on the tail boom reduces speed and provides directional change. The basic construction is quite conventional with the exceptions of tapered roller bearings and labyrinth seals rather than the conventional garlock seals. Gearbox details are seen in Fig. 9-14.

3. Pitch change mechanism

The pitch change mechanism, like that of the Hughes 500, is contained on the output shaft of the tail rotor gearbox. It consists of a rotating plate driven by two pitch change links which are free to slide on the rotor shaft. The rotating plate has a bearing on its outer circumference which supports a stationary plate attached to the bellcrank. The stationary plate transmits input to the tail rotor (Fig. 9-15).

4. Tail rotor

The tail rotor is manufactured of composites with only a few mounting components made of metal. The blades are a flexible seesaw type rotor without conventional flapping and feathering bearings. The basic rotor component is a fiberglass roving spar to which the two rotor blades are molded. The center of the spar fits between two half-shells, one of which is drilled to permit the seesaw blade installation on the rotor shaft yoke. The blade is covered by a fiberglass skin.

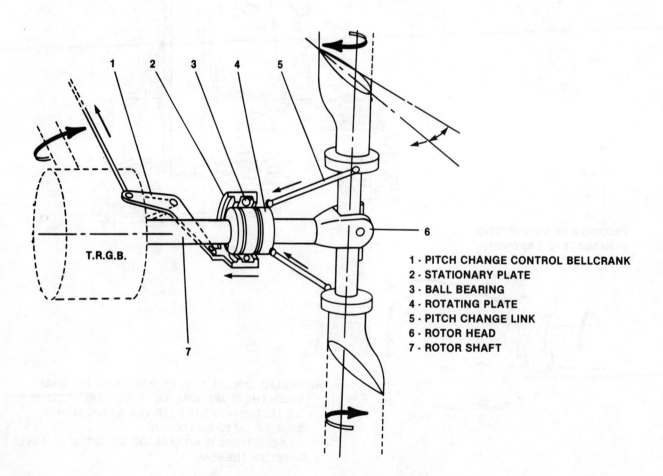

1 - PITCH CHANGE CONTROL BELLCRANK
2 - STATIONARY PLATE
3 - BALL BEARING
4 - ROTATING PLATE
5 - PITCH CHANGE LINK
6 - ROTOR HEAD
7 - ROTOR SHAFT

Fig. 9-15 Aerospatiale AStar pitch change system

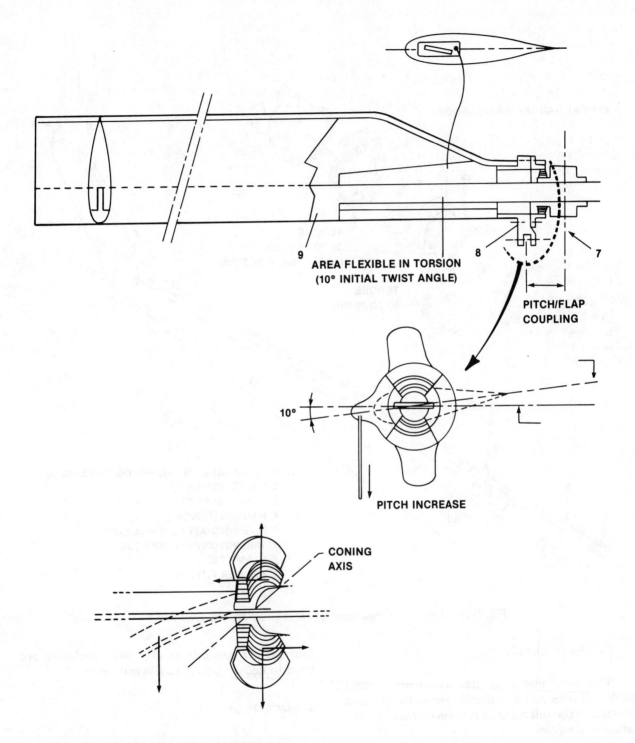

AREA FLEXIBLE IN TORSION
(10° INITIAL TWIST ANGLE)

PITCH/FLAP COUPLING

10°

PITCH INCREASE

CONING AXIS

Fig. 9-16   Blade system utilized on the Aerospatiale AStar

The main rigid section is filled with a foam between the skin and the spar. At the blade root the skin is secured by an aluminum flange. This flange includes the blade horn to which the pitch change link is connected. It also has two large eccentric bosses which are sometimes referred to as Chinese weights — two metal half-shells support the spar at the center. Between these half-shells are elastomeric bearings capable of carrying tension and sheer loads. In the blade torsion area is a cavity with foam filler which allows the blade spar to distort freely (Fig. 9-16).

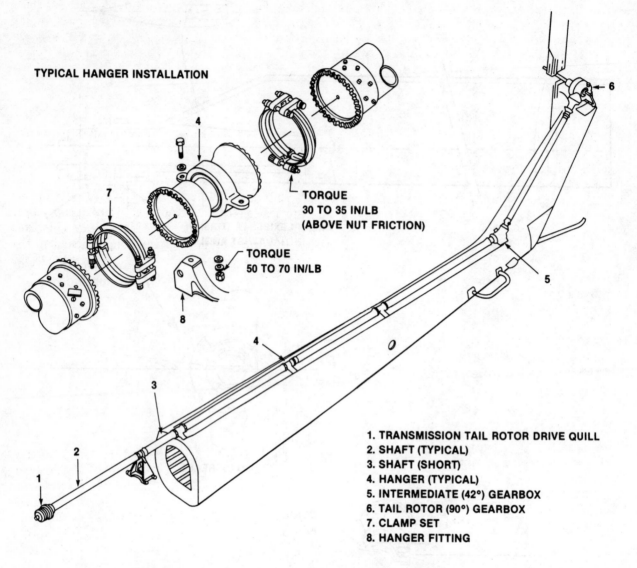

TYPICAL HANGER INSTALLATION

TORQUE
30 TO 35 IN/LB
(ABOVE NUT FRICTION)

TORQUE
50 TO 70 IN/LB

1. TRANSMISSION TAIL ROTOR DRIVE QUILL
2. SHAFT (TYPICAL)
3. SHAFT (SHORT)
4. HANGER (TYPICAL)
5. INTERMEDIATE (42°) GEARBOX
6. TAIL ROTOR (90°) GEARBOX
7. CLAMP SET
8. HANGER FITTING

Fig. 9-17   Drive and coupling system used on the Bell 212.

5.   Tail rotor controls

This particular helicopter uses conventional push-pull rods and a hydraulic servo for boosted control on the tail rotor as is done on many of the larger helicopters.

F.   Bell 212

The Bell 212 has a drive system from the transmission rather than the engine.

In this system a total of six shafts are used — five of which are the same length and one that is shorter. In addition to the use of the six shafts,

four hanger assemblies and two gearboxes are used to deliver power to the tail rotor.

1.   Driveshafts

The forward shaft extends through a tunnel beneath the powerplant to a hanger assembly on the engine deck. This shaft is connected to the tail rotor output quill of the transmission. The second, third, and fourth driveshafts connect between hanger assemblies with the second shaft being the short one. The fifth driveshaft connects between the hanger assembly and the 42° gearbox with no hangers in between (Fig. 9-17).

Each shaft is made of aluminum alloy and has a curvic coupling riveted to each end that mates with the hangers and gearboxes. Each of these shafts are statically balanced with weights bonded to the shaft near the center. Each end is attached to the couplings by V-band type clamps to secure the curvic couplings. The clamps must be replaced as a set because the two halves are manufactured together. The clamps are bolted with the heads in the direction of rotation. The clamps installed 90° to the bolts on the preceding clamp for balance purposes. This is one of the few areas in which friction torque is used. This means the assigned torque value must have the torque of the locknut added to it for the correct value.

2. Driveshaft hangers

Each of the hanger assemblies is used to support the shafts and allow flexing of the tail boom. The hanger assembly consists of a short splined shaft mounted on a single row of ball bearings to a ring-shaped hanger with mounting lugs. Couplings are splined to each end of the shaft. The front coupling is a flex coupling and the rear coupling is rigid.

3. Flexible coupling and mounting lugs

The flexible coupling consists of an inner and an outer coupling. The outer coupling is retained to the inner coupling by a seal. Both couplings are lubricated by hand-packed grease. The ball bearing assembly is permanently lubricated.

The mounting lugs are bolted to the airframe. The bases of the lugs are master shimmed at the factory with the shims bonded to the airframe. The shims should not be removed because they determine the alignment (Fig. 9-18).

4. 42° gearbox

Located at the base of the tail fin is the 42° gearbox. This is used to change the direction of the shafting as it goes up the tail fin. The gearbox consists of a case with a quill attached at each end. There is no change of speed with this gearbox. The case serves as a reservoir for the oil used to lubricate the gears. It is equipped with a sight gauge, filler cap, chip detector, and drain plug. The case, flange mounted to the tail boom, is master shimmed to the boom as are the hangers.

The two quills are removable and may be changed without disturbing the lash and pattern because the case is permanently shimmed. Both quills are equipped with flexible couplings similar to those used on the hangers (Fig. 9-19). A single shaft connects the 42° gearbox to the 90° gearbox.

5. 90° gearbox

The 90° box, mounted at the top of the tail fin, provides a gear reduction, and a 90° change in direction. The gearbox case houses the meshing input and output quill assemblies. This case, like that of the 42° box, acts as a reservoir for the lubrication and is equipped with a cap, sight gauge, chip detector, and drain plug. This case uses ground shim rings for the placement of the quills. The components may be replaced without disturbing the lash and pattern (Fig. 9-20).

6. Tail rotor

Attached to the output of the 90° gearbox is a two-bladed tail rotor. The hub is preconed and underslung as was the main rotor.

a. Yoke

The yoke is a steel flex beam with a total of six Teflon lined, self-aligning uniball type bearings. The two bearings near the yoke center adapt the trunnion yoke to the center and provide the flapping axis. The two outboard bearings on each side provide the attachment points for each rotor blade and the pitch-change axis of the blade (Fig. 9-21).

b. Blades

The blades are of a conventional bonded honeycomb construction very similar to previous blade construction. Each blade is balanced with a master blade at manufacture although additional balancing as a unit will be required when blades are changed (Fig. 9-22).

c. Pitch change

The pitch change is conventional with push-pull tubes and hydraulic assist on the controls for assistance in pedal movement.

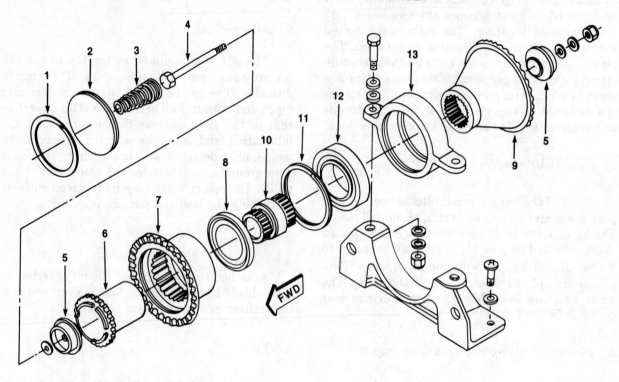

1. RETAINING RING
2. COVER PLATE
3. SPRING
4. RETAINING BOLT
5. RETAINING PLATES
6. INNER(SPHERICAL) COUPLING
7. OUTER COUPLING
8. SEAL
9. REAR COUPLING
10. SHAFT
11. RETAINING RING
12. BEARING
13. HANGER

FWD

CROSS-SECTIONAL VIEW

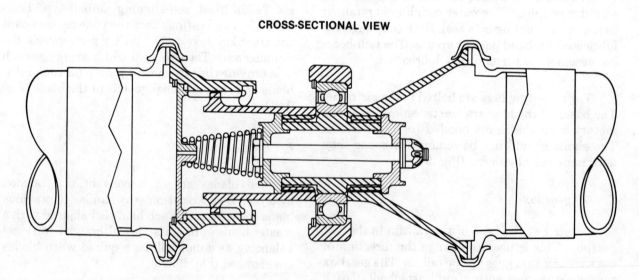

Fig. 9-18 Drive coupling utilized on the Bell 212.

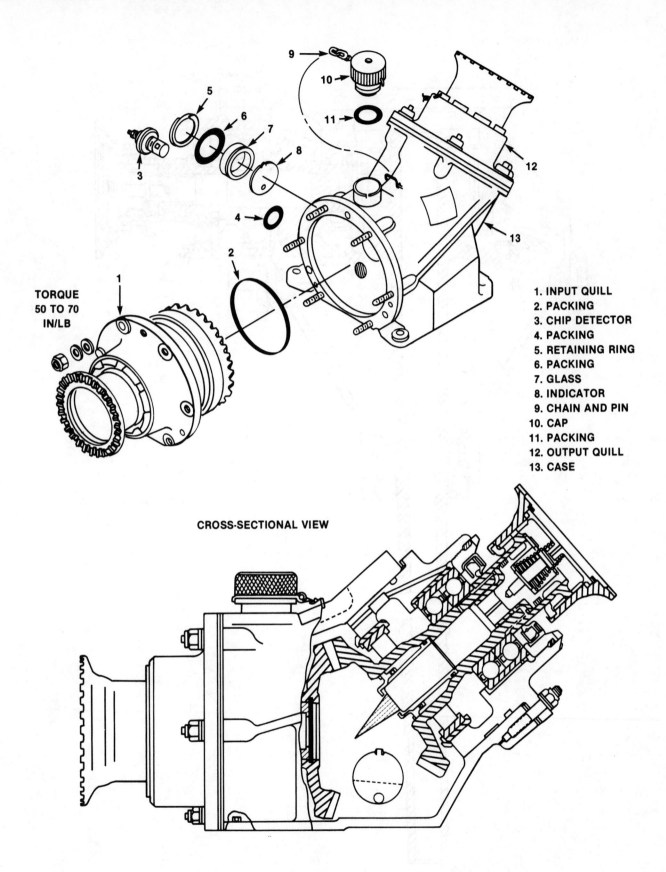

TORQUE
50 TO 70
IN/LB

1. INPUT QUILL
2. PACKING
3. CHIP DETECTOR
4. PACKING
5. RETAINING RING
6. PACKING
7. GLASS
8. INDICATOR
9. CHAIN AND PIN
10. CAP
11. PACKING
12. OUTPUT QUILL
13. CASE

CROSS-SECTIONAL VIEW

Fig. 9-19   Intermediate gearbox used on the Bell 212.

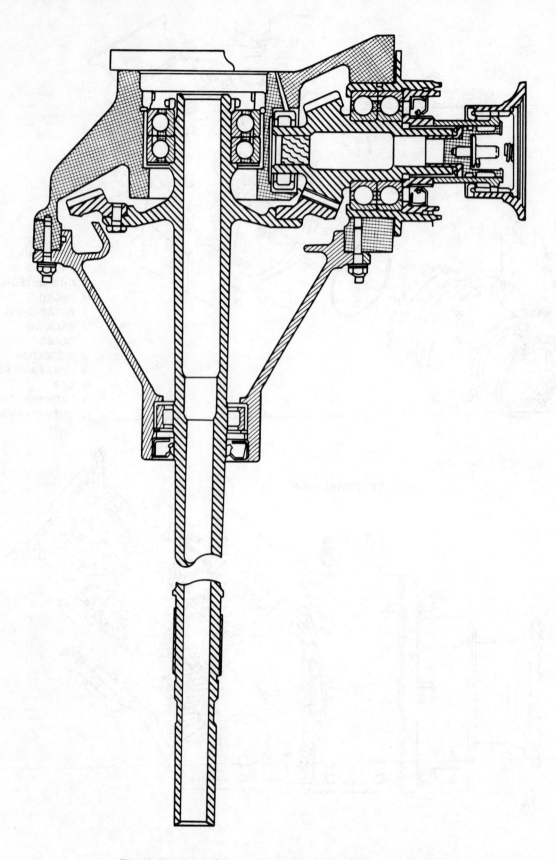

Fig. 9-20 Cross-sectional view of the Bell 212 gearbox.

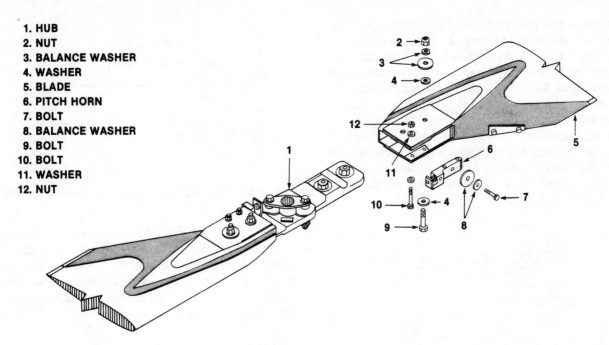

1. HUB
2. NUT
3. BALANCE WASHER
4. WASHER
5. BLADE
6. PITCH HORN
7. BOLT
8. BALANCE WASHER
9. BOLT
10. BOLT
11. WASHER
12. NUT

Fig. 9-21   Bell 212 rotor blade system

Like the other systems, the tail rotor drive system requires servicing, inspection, and maintenance.

G.   Servicing

The servicing has been reduced considerably on the newer helicopters because of the use of hanger bearings that are permanently lubricated.

However, many of the older helicopters require grease in these bearings. The greasing periods and the type of grease are specified by the manufacturer.

1.   Temperature

Impending failure of any bearing will be indicated by a rise in the temperature of the bearing

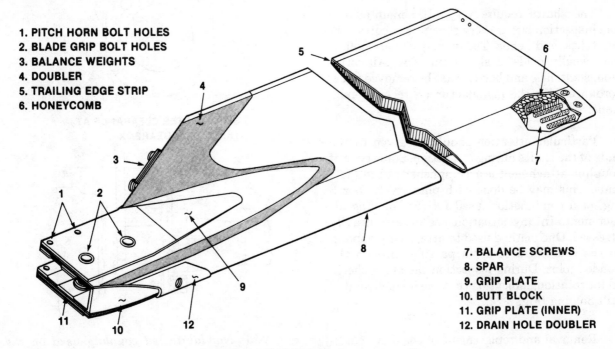

1. PITCH HORN BOLT HOLES
2. BLADE GRIP BOLT HOLES
3. BALANCE WEIGHTS
4. DOUBLER
5. TRAILING EDGE STRIP
6. HONEYCOMB

7. BALANCE SCREWS
8. SPAR
9. GRIP PLATE
10. BUTT BLOCK
11. GRIP PLATE (INNER)
12. DRAIN HOLE DOUBLER

Fig. 9-22   Bell 212 blade construction

409

package and may result in high frequency vibrations as the failure progresses. For this reason, on shafting that is not enclosed, the bearing packages are touched by hand during the post flight inspection to determine the temperature. On some of the enclosed shafting, a heat sensitive sticker is placed on the bearing package to indicate increased temperatures. At least one helicopter is using a hanger which allows the bearing to rotate in the housing in case the bearing should freeze rather than the possibility of the shaft failure (Fig. 9-23).

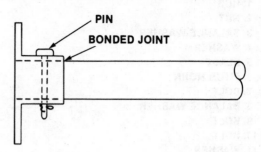

Fig. 9-24 Typical pin used on check bonded joint.

maintenance practices. When removing shafting, care must be taken that the shafts are not nicked, scratched, or bent. Damage to the shafts can result in rejection of the shaft. If there are several shafts, and they are of different lengths, it may be advisable to mark their locations.

3. Couplings

The couplings are of several varieties and may be all interchangeable on one aircraft, while another aircraft may have different types at dif-

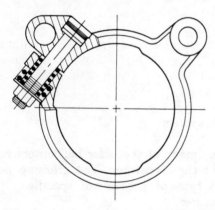

Fig. 9-23 Bearing hanger system used on the Bell 206.

2. Driveshaft inspection

The shafts require very little maintenance and inspection but are very sensitive to corrosion, scratches, and bends. The driveshafts are hollow and usually made of aluminum alloy. All corrosion, scratches, and bends must be removed in accordance with the manufacturer's recommendations.

Particular attention should be given to the ends of the shafts during inspection. Some type of coupling attachment is accomplished at the shaft ends. This may be done with pins, rivets, bonding, or a combination, used for the coupling attachment. In any situation the area is heavily stressed. One method used to attach the coupling to the shaft utilizes a pin passing through the bonded joint. During inspection the pin is checked for rotation, indicating that the bonded joint is still holding (Fig. 9-24).

Removal and replacement of the drive shafting requires special attention and some special

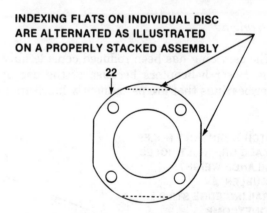

SLIP ADAPTER CLEARANCE AT TAIL ROTOR GEARBOX

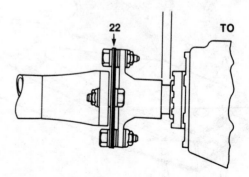

Fig. 9-25 Non-lubricated coupling used on the Bell 206.

ferent locations. Some of the couplings will require lubrication. This is done with grease and may require hand packing or the use of a grease gun. On certain helicopters, a coupling such as seen in Fig. 9-25 may be used. This coupling does not require lubrication. The coupling consists of a stack of indexed stainless steel discs and it is important that the stack be properly indexed. Once the stack is used, it should never be restacked. It will require removal as a stack and must be replaced as a stack.

4. Alignment

The alignment of the tail rotor driveshaft is very important. When the alignment is incorrect, the vibration level increases, resulting in an increase in the wear factors throughout the whole system and especially in bearing areas. Most of the newer helicopters are aligned at manufacture and have shims permanently bonded to eliminate

alignment on shafts of this type. A runout check may be all that is required unless structural damage has occurred to the airframe. This runout check is normally done with a dial indicator with the shaft installed.

a. Alignment check

Older helicopters may require an alignment check in addition to a runout check of the shafts. If alignment problems are encountered, the hanger bearings are shimmed to obtain correct alignment.

(1) Bell 47 alignment check

One helicopter that requires an alignment check is the Bell 47 (Fig. 9-26). This alignment is checked by inserting a special plug in the transmission drive quill with a target and a rod through the extension tube fittings with a string

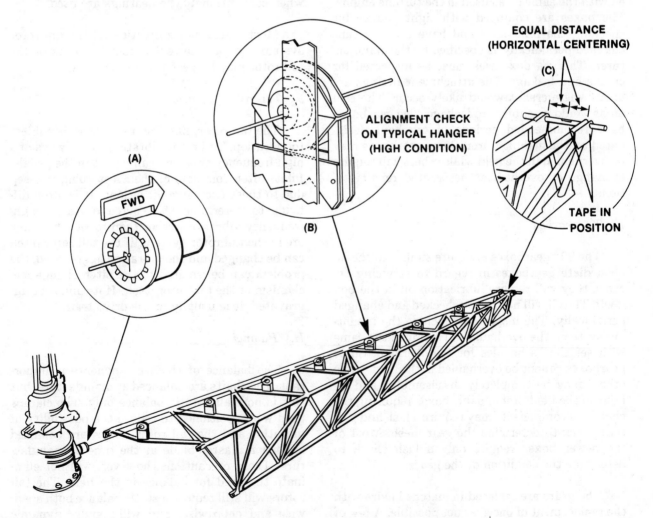

Fig. 9-26 Driveshaft alignment of the Bell 47

411

attached at the centerpoint of the rod. A dummy bearing is placed in the various hangers and the string is brought through the dummy bearing and held taut against the target plug. The position of the string passing through the dummy bearing is then checked for position. If the alignment is incorrect, corrective action must be taken (Fig. 9-27).

5. Intermediate gearboxes

If intermediate gearboxes are used in the system, they will require servicing with lubricating oil. The type of oil used will vary from helicopter to helicopter.

6. Types of lubricants

The trend with the newer helicopters is to service as many of the components with the same lubricant as possible. As a result many are serviced with the same oil as used in the turbine engine. The boxes are equipped with sight gauges for checking the fluid level and have the lubricant changed periodically as specified by the manufacturer. The gearbox cases must be inspected for cracks and leakage. The attachment fittings are areas where cracks would likely occur. The seal areas would be subject to leakage. The gearboxes have recommended periods of overhaul designated by the manufacturer. Some gearboxes may be overhauled in the field while others will require exchange or overhaul at designated repair stations.

7. 90° gearbox

The 90° gearboxes are quite similar to the intermediate gearboxes in regard to servicing because they will require lubrication oil in the box itself. The oil will need to be checked and changed periodically. The inspections include the mounting system. The overhauls will be much the same with set time schedules for the overhaul. Some gearboxes cannot be overhauled in the field, while others may be completely disassembled and rebuilt in the field. Rebuildable boxes requiring the change of components may require a lash and pattern check to determine the gear mesh. Most of the newer boxes require only a lash check to determine the condition of the gears.

The gears are replaced in matched pairs with the replacement of one gear not possible. A few of the old gears may have match marks on the teeth for placement but such practices have become quite rare.

8. Tail rotors

The tail rotors have provisions for greasing. The newer designed tail rotors have eliminated the need for grease by the use of permanently lubricated bearings and elastomeric bearings.

The inspection requirements are quite varied but always include critical dimensions for damages such as cracks, nicks, and gouges. The fitting and bearing areas are checked for looseness. All movements of the blades must also be checked for smoothness of motion.

Many parts used in the tail rotor are assigned a finite life due to the stresses placed on them. Typical time change items may include yokes and blades. Bearing replacements are quite common when conventional type bearings are used.

Most maintenance practices of the tail rotor system such as the replacement of parts or the tail rotor may be performed in the field.

9. Tail rotor vibrations

The tail rotor, like the main rotor, is subject to vibration. Tail rotor vibrations are always of a high-frequency type and can be felt in the pedals. Pilots often complain of their feet going to sleep due to these excessive vibrations. It is often difficult to determine the source of these high-frequency vibrations other than to say that they are in the tail rotor system. If the tail rotor pitch can be changed and the vibration aggravated, the problem can be isolated to the pitch change mechanism or the tail rotor itself. If it cannot be aggravated, it is usually in the drive train.

H. Balancing

The balance of these components is important. The shafts are balanced at manufacture, but this is normally static balance only. The clamps used were positioned to reduce the possibility of vibration and the tail rotor blades are balanced against a master blade at the time of manufacture. These precautions, however, will not eliminate the need for balance in the field. The tail rotors will still require a static balance both spanwise and chordwise, and will require dynamic balance as well.

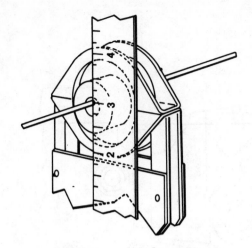

BEARING HANGER OUT OF ALIGNMENT · LOW

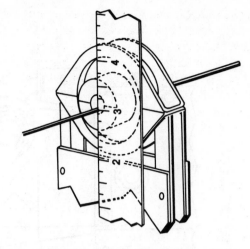

BEARING HANGER OUT OF ALIGNMENT · HIGH

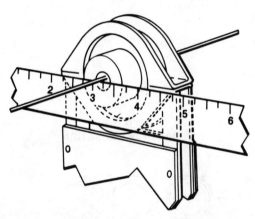

BEARING HANGER OUT OF ALIGNMENT · SIDEWISE

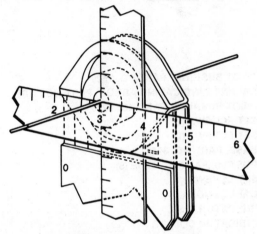

BEARING HANGER IN ALIGNMENT

TYPICAL SHIM FOR LOW HANGER

Fig. 9-27   Shimming Procedure used on the Bell 47

413

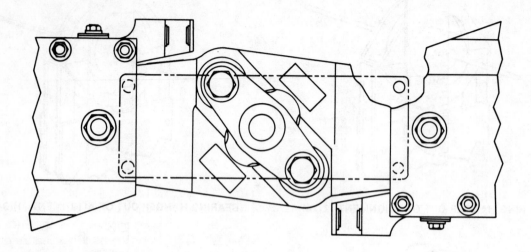

1. PILOT BUSHING, PART NO. 2529
2. BALANCE INDICATING ARBOR, PART NO. 3165
3. PILOT BUSHING, PART NO. 3285
4. SET SCREWS (2)
5. SET SCREWS (2)
6. BASE, PART NO. 3152
7. POST (4), PART OF BASE (8)
8. SET SCREWS (2)
9. CABLE LOOP
10. INDICATOR DISK
11. INDICATOR COLLAR
12. WASHERS, CHORDWISE BALANCE
13. BOLT
14. WASHERS, SPANWISE BALANCE
15. BOLTS, BLADE ATTACHING

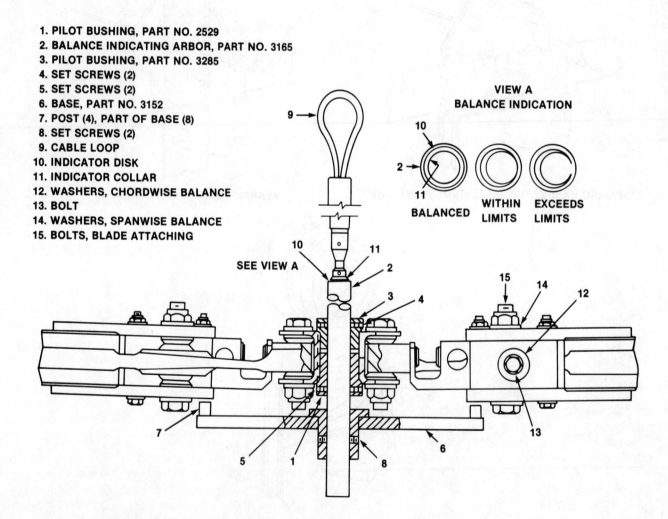

VIEW A
BALANCE INDICATION

BALANCED   WITHIN LIMITS   EXCEEDS LIMITS

SEE VIEW A

Fig. 9-28   Universal balancer being utilized on the Bell 212 tail rotor.

414

The static balance will be accomplished in several different ways. As on the main rotor, balancing equipment for the specific tail rotor is often available from the manufacturer. Universal balancing equipment is also available for a number of tail rotors. The actual balancing points of the tail rotor vary from one helicopter to another and the addition of weight in areas other than those authorized would be dangerous. Basically the balance procedure for the tail rotors are similar except for the placement of the weight.

Many of the older blades had the spanwise weight placed on the blade tips and chordwise weights added to the blade itself. Most of the newer blades have the weight added to the hub of the blade rather than to the blade itself.

1. Balancing procedures

Balancing procedures require the blade in either a vertical or a horizontal position. Fig. 9-28 shows a tail rotor placed in a universal balancer. This balancer operates in the same manner as the universal balancer used on the main rotors. The bushings, etc., are made for the specific rotor while the balancing arbor with the correct bushing and holders may fit several different tail rotors. Like the arbor used on the main rotor, the arbor utilizes a disc attached to a cable and dampened in oil. Weight is added to the blade at the predetermined locations until a perfect circle is visible between the disc and the collar of the balancer as shown in view A of Fig. 9-28. This type of balancer is very sensitive and will be disturbed by any air currents. All static balancing must be accomplished in a closed room to insure accuracy of the procedure.

2. Bell 206 balancer

Another type of balancer used for a specific rotor is shown in Fig. 9-29. This particular one is used on the Bell 206 with some of the items being interchangeable with the main rotor. Therefore, the basic balancer is used for both the main and tail rotor. The balancer makes use of a large ball bearing in the mandrel on which the stand rests. This gives the tail rotor, which is placed on the mandrel, movement in all four directions so that the tail rotor may be checked both spanwise and chordwise at the same time. A bubble bull's eye level is placed in the center of the mandrel so that weight may be added to place the bubble in the center.

3. Knife edge balance

Some older models of helicopters balanced the tail rotors on knife edges or a roller stand similar to what is used on fixed pitch propellers. A knife edge stand is shown in Fig. 9-30.

In a knife edge stand, to insure accuracy, the knife edges must leveled in conjunction with each other and the blades must be locked in the same pitch during the balancing procedure. Rather than having blade pitch holders, as were used on the other two balancers, wedges are used to hold the blade in a zero pitch condition during balancing. By placing the blades vertical, the chordwise balance may be checked. With the blades in a horizontal position the spanwise balance is checked. Normally in this type of procedure tape is used for the weights until the balance is achieved in both directions. The tape is then used to determine the exact weight to be added. At that time the washers will be added for spanwise balance and the chordwise weight will be secured to the blade.

4. Dynamic balance

Normally one more check will be made before the chordwise weight is secured to the blade. Even after the tail rotor blade is statically balanced it may not be dynamically balanced. For this reason it is necessary to balance dynamically the tail rotor as well as statically. The better the static balance the less dynamic balance problems will arise when the tail rotor is placed on the helicopter.

I. Tail Rotor Track

The balance problem, like that on the main rotor, may be solved only after the tail rotor is in track. This track may be established either by hand or electronically and on a few helicopters no provisions will be made for track adjustment.

1. Stick method

The stick method is usually used when no electronic equipment is available. The procedures for this method are quite simple. A small diameter stick with a sponge rubber tip is used. The sponge rubber tip has Prussian blue applied. With the helicopter at operating speed, the maintenance personnel places the stick on the structure of the airframe from the opposite side

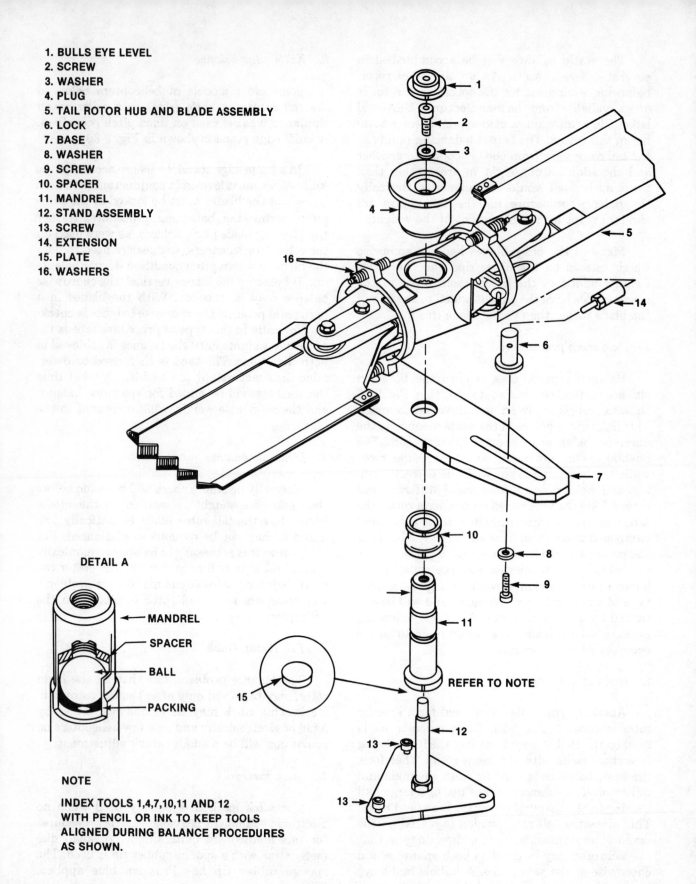

1. BULLS EYE LEVEL
2. SCREW
3. WASHER
4. PLUG
5. TAIL ROTOR HUB AND BLADE ASSEMBLY
6. LOCK
7. BASE
8. WASHER
9. SCREW
10. SPACER
11. MANDREL
12. STAND ASSEMBLY
13. SCREW
14. EXTENSION
15. PLATE
16. WASHERS

DETAIL A

MANDREL

SPACER

BALL

PACKING

NOTE

INDEX TOOLS 1,4,7,10,11 AND 12
WITH PENCIL OR INK TO KEEP TOOLS
ALIGNED DURING BALANCE PROCEDURES
AS SHOWN.

REFER TO NOTE

Fig. 9-29 Bell 206 tail rotor balancer

416

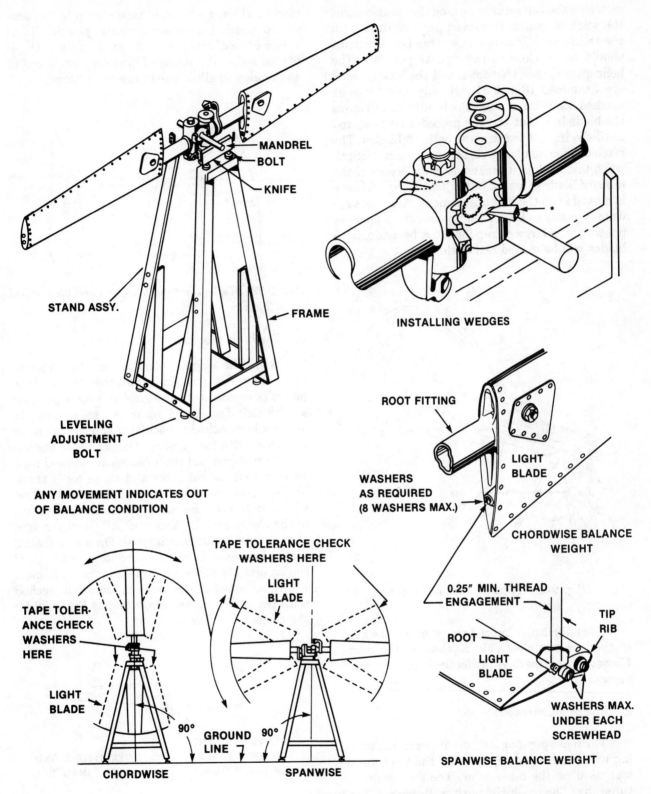

MANDREL

BOLT

KNIFE

STAND ASSY.

FRAME

INSTALLING WEDGES

LEVELING
ADJUSTMENT
BOLT

ROOT FITTING

LIGHT
BLADE

WASHERS
AS REQUIRED
(8 WASHERS MAX.)

CHORDWISE BALANCE
WEIGHT

ANY MOVEMENT INDICATES OUT
OF BALANCE CONDITION

TAPE TOLERANCE CHECK
WASHERS HERE

LIGHT
BLADE

TAPE TOLER-
ANCE CHECK
WASHERS
HERE

LIGHT
BLADE

90°

GROUND
LINE

90°

CHORDWISE

SPANWISE

0.25" MIN. THREAD
ENGAGEMENT

TIP
RIB

ROOT

LIGHT
BLADE

WASHERS MAX.
UNDER EACH
SCREWHEAD

SPANWISE BALANCE WEIGHT

*INSERT WEDGES ON BOTH SIDES OF EACH END OF HUB
USING EQUAL PRESSURE TO MAINTAIN OR ESTABLISH
APPROXIMATE CHORDWISE CENTER OF YOKES.

Fig. 9-30   Balancing stand using the Hiller 12 tail rotor.

417

on which the tail rotor is located. From this point the stick is gradually moved until contact with the tail rotor blades is made. This contact point should be as close to the tips as possible. The helicopter is then shutdown and the blade marks are examined (Fig. 9-31). If only one blade is marked, the pitch change link is adjusted to move the blade in or out and the procedure is repeated until the inprint is the same on both blades. The pitch change link length is set to a nominal length when installed so it makes little difference if the inboard blade is moved out or the outboard blade is moved in on the first adjustment. Attempts are usually made to keep the movements as close as possible. If a large correction must be made, both blades will be moved rather than one.

Fig. 9-31   Tracking the tail rotor

The adjustment procedure for either the stick method or the electronic method is the same. However, the method of determining the track varies.

2. Electronic method

The most popular method of electronic tracking uses the same equipment for the tail rotor as was used on the main rotor. The unit manufactured by Chadwich-Helmuth will permit both tracking and balancing of the rotor.

The track is checked with the strobex unit of the equipment. Reflective tape is placed on one of the blade tips in the vertical position. The other blade will have a piece of tape placed in the horizontal position in the same relative position if it is a two-bladed rotor (Fig. 9-32). If it is a three-bladed rotor, the strips of tape may be placed at 45° angles to allow one image for each blade.

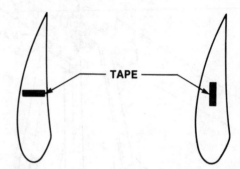

Fig. 9-32   Reflector tape being placed on the tail rotor blades.

a. Tracking procedure

With the engine running at the required speed and the strobex connected, the maintenance personnel with the strobex take a position at the side facing the rotor. At this point the strobex is switched to oscillator and the tail rotor is viewed with the strobex. The oscillator knob is tuned until four tail rotor blades are viewed for a two- or four-bladed rotor and three for a three-bladed rotor. When the correct images are viewed, move toward the cabin section where the tips of the blades may be observed. All the tip images should appear sumperimposed. On a two-bladed rotor, they should appear in the form + or −1. If the images are not superimposed, the pitch links will be adjusted as was done by the stick method until the correct image appears. See Fig. 9-33 for the correct viewing positions.

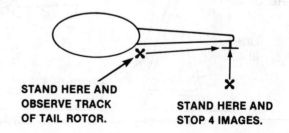

STAND HERE AND OBSERVE TRACK OF TAIL ROTOR.

STAND HERE AND STOP 4 IMAGES.

Fig. 9-33   Correct position for track check

b. Dynamic balance

The tail rotor may also be dynamically balanced with the Chadwick equipment. This is done

418

with both the Strobex and Vibrex units. However, the phazor portion of the Vibrex unit is not used because the interrupter cannot be installed as it was on the main rotor. The one blade is marked with a piece of reflector tape. This target will designate that blade as the target blade.

(1) Accelerometer

One accelerometer is placed on the gearbox in the location prescribed. The cable from this accelerometer must be placed in such a manner that it will not become entangled in the rotor or driveshaft. The accelerometer is then plugged into Channel B of the Vibrex. A DC power cord is run from the helicopter to the observation point (Fig. 9-34).

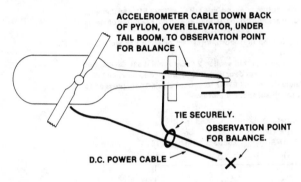

Fig. 9-34   Cable installation for dynamic balance check.

The balancer is set to the operating RPM on the tune dial and the range to the X10 position. The switch to the "ACCB" and the strobex oscillator to the OFF position. See Section 5 for a view of the balancer and strobex for button locations.

(2) Viewing target

The tail rotor is viewed with the strobex. The target will show the clock angle when viewing. Do not check the phazor, it is not functional. While viewing the tail rotor with the strobex, push the verify-to-tune button. If the image moves to a new clock angle, adjust the RPM scale until the verify-to-tune button has no effect on the position of the target image.

At this point the target image is the o'clock position for the chart and IPS scale will indicate the vibration level. The chart will be followed in the same manner as the chart used on the main rotor with weight being added as indicated on the chart. If errors in the move line occur, the clock

corrector may also be used as was done with the main rotor. Fig. 9-35 shows a typical chart to be used on a two-bladed tail rotor.

3.   Feel-and-guess method

If no balancing equipment is available, the tail rotor balance on the helicopter will be most difficult to achieve. The feel-and-guess method can be used to obtain the smoothest feel. Of course, neither track nor balance should be attempted except when calm weather conditions are present.

J.   Tail Rotor System Rigging

Equally important to the operation of the tail rotor system as the balance and track is the rigging of the tail rotor system. Although the system varies from helicopter to helicopter, most of the helicopters will use a push-pull tube system for pitch control. In addition to the push-pull system, hydraulic servos may be used, and gradients for fuel may also be added to the system as required. Many of the older light helicopters also use a cable system for moving the tail rotor.

The Bell 212 anti-torque system consists of a set of control pedals, pedal adjuster assembly, a servo actuator, force gradient assembly, a magnetic brake, pitch change mechanism, and connecting linkage.

The operation of the pedal provides hydraulic boosted pitch change to the tail rotor blades. The pedal position may be changed by depressing and turning a knob on the cabin floor. The force trim system is linked to the directional controls, and is controlled by a switch on the cyclic. To rig the directional control system, follow the views in Fig. 9-36.

All of the fixed length tubes in the system should be installed at the beginning of the procedure. The following links must be disconnected:

a. The pitch links from the blade pitch horns.

b. The link lever on the left side of the 90° gearbox.

c. The control tube from the bellcrank above the servo actuator.

d. The force gradient from the pedal adjuster.

419

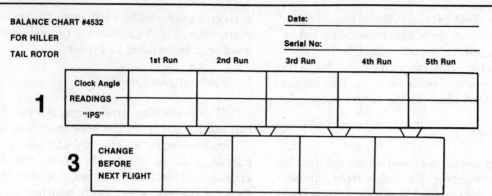

BALANCE CHART #4532
FOR HILLER
TAIL ROTOR

Date: _____

Serial No: _____

	1st Run	2nd Run	3rd Run	4th Run	5th Run
1 Clock Angle READINGS "IPS"					

3 CHANGE BEFORE NEXT FLIGHT					

NOTES: 1) Track tail rotor. Viewing rotor disc from side, adjust Strobex oscillator so the single grip target appears as a STOPPED image of four. Then, view rotor disc edge-on, from near cabin door, and observe track of Tip Targets. Adjust track as required.

2) Set Balancer to 2210 RPM ("RPM Tune" to 221 and "RPM Range" to "X1"), switch to Channel "B", and Strobex oscillator "OFF". View "Clock Angle" of grip target from side of tail rotor disc.

3) Now, press "Verify Tune" Button and adjust "RPM Tune" Dial, WHILE BUTTON IS PUSHED, to return target to angle observed before button was pushed. Release, observe angle, press and adjust again to match new "unpushed" angle. Repeat until there is NO CHANGE WHETHER BUTTON IS PUSHED OR RELEASED. TUNE ONLY WITH BUTTON PUSHED.

4) Read "Clock Angle" with button released, and "IPS" without Strobex flashing, and record in section 1 of chart. Plot in section 2 (label it point #), and note required changes in 3.

5) Make one change only for the first move, either tip or pitch link weight — whichever is farthest from the zero axis line.

6) Run ship and repeat readings, plot in section 2 (label it point #2). Check that the "Move Line" (point #1 to #2) is in the correct direction. If it is, proceed to balance to 0.2 "IPS" or less. If not, use "Clock Angle Corrector" #3597 to correct clock. Then, proceed to balance using the corrected clock for all subsequent moves.

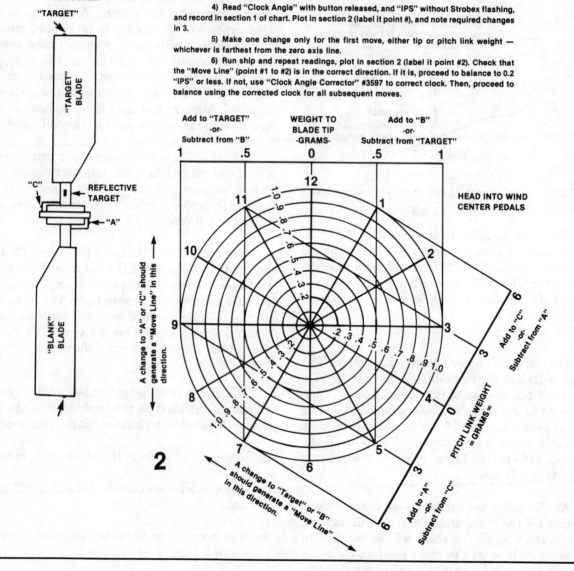

2

Fig. 9-35 Chart used for tail rotor balancing check.

420

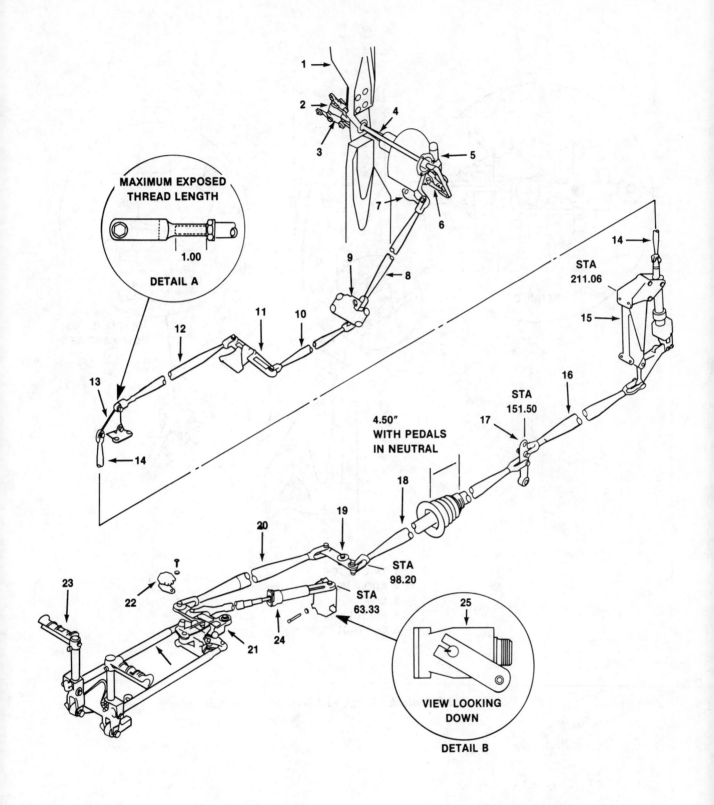

MAXIMUM EXPOSED THREAD LENGTH

1.00

DETAIL A

STA 211.06

STA 151.50

4.50″ WITH PEDALS IN NEUTRAL

STA 98.20

STA 63.33

VIEW LOOKING DOWN

DETAIL B

Fig. 9-36A   Typical tail rotor pitch change linkage.

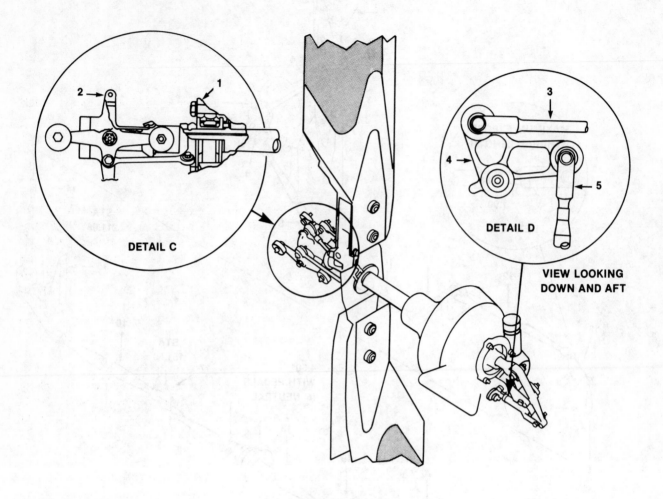

DETAIL C

DETAIL D

VIEW LOOKING
DOWN AND AFT

1. TAIL ROTOR
2. CROSSHEAD
3. LINK
4. BELLCRANK
5. CONTROL TUBE

Fig. 9-36B   Bell 212 pitch change mechanism at the tail rotor.

1. Bell 212 rigging procedure

1. Check the length of the clevis on the servo actuator and set to the specified length if necessary.

2. If dual controls are installed, place both the pilot's and copilot's left pedals against the stops and adjust the interconnect rod to fit.

3. Adjust both pitch change links to the required length which is given from the center line of each rod end and connect them.

4. Position the crosshead to obtain the specified dimension between the inboard face of the crosshead and the outboard face of the trunnion.

5. Holding the position of the crosshead, adjust the link assembly to obtain the correct clearance between the bellcrank and link assembly. Connect the link.

6. Position the left pedal full forward and push the servo actuator to bottom the servo and by-pass valves. Check the crosshead and link assembly to see that they are still positioned and adjust the tube assembly to fit. Then shorten the tube 1/2-turn and connect it.

7. With the pedals placed in neutral, position the bulkhead boot the specified distance and clamp the boot to the tube.

8. With the hydraulic boost off, check the control movement for smoothness and clearance.

9. With the pedals in neutral, position the arm on the directional brake in the center of travel and adjust the force gradient to fit between the control system and the magnetic brake arm.

The system will require a track check when the whole system has been rigged in this manner.

a. Overview of tail rotor rigging

Some anti-torque systems are more difficult to rig than others. Like other flight control systems, some systems use rigging pins, protractors, and jigs to position the controls while rigging. All of these devices are used to help simplify the system. It may have been noticed that the pitch of the tail rotor was set for left pedal only in this procedure. The right pedal is assumed to be set in this system by the extreme left pedal position.

Many of the newer helicopters are using this type of system of setting for the extreme position while the older helicopters are rigged for a neutral position and then checked for the extreme position. The use of protractors is becoming rare with manufacturers more interested in fixed lengths rather than degrees. This is probably due to the desire to eliminate a maintenance error with the protractor.

From time to time, it may be necessary to install a tail rotor. The tail rotor, like other components, is installed in various ways. Usually the tail rotor is splined to the output shaft of the gearbox and rests on a set of split cones. If it is a two-bladed rotor, flap stops are incorporated in the attachment and may be adjustable by shims to limit the flap travel. In such situations, the blade flap angle must be set as shown in Fig. 9-37. The rotor itself will be held to the shaft by a nut. If the same tail rotor is to be removed and replaced, no other maintenance procedures will be required. However, if it is not the same tail rotor track, balance and pedal creep may have to be set in addition to the installation procedures.

On some tail rotor systems pedal creep may be adjusted. This is done through counterweights attached to the tail rotor. Pedal creep may be adjusted by adding or subtracting washers from the arms or rings. To check pedal creep the pedals are set to neutral when the helicopter is at the designated power setting. When the feet are taken off the pedals, the pedals should remain in neutral. If the left pedal moves forward, the weights are too heavy and weight must be removed. If the right pedal creeps forward, more weight must be added. The weight of these washers must be equal at all times or balance will be affected. Pedal creep should always be checked in a no-wind condition. See Fig. 9-38 for a typical counterweight installation.

Many other maintenance procedures may be included on specific tail rotors. For this reason all maintenance should be done in strict accordance with the maintenance manual.

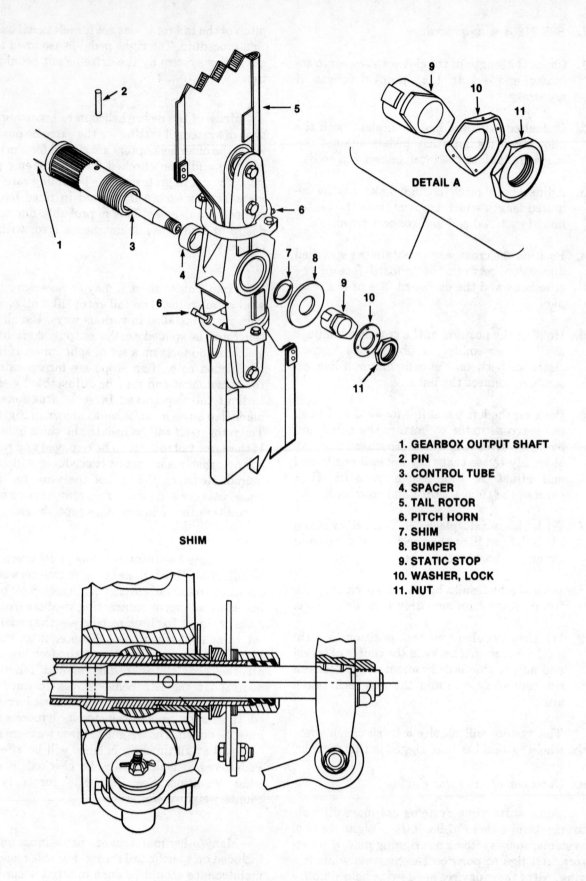

DETAIL A

SHIM

1. GEARBOX OUTPUT SHAFT
2. PIN
3. CONTROL TUBE
4. SPACER
5. TAIL ROTOR
6. PITCH HORN
7. SHIM
8. BUMPER
9. STATIC STOP
10. WASHER, LOCK
11. NUT

Fig. 9-37 Flap restraint system used on the Bell 206.

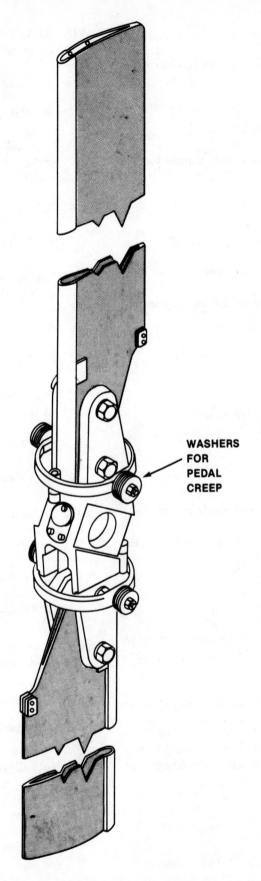

WASHERS FOR PEDAL CREEP

Fig. 9-38   Washer system used to control pedal creep on the Bell 206.

425

QUESTIONS:

136. Helicopters built with co-axial main rotors:

    A. have tail rotors.

    B. do not require tail rotors.

137. The tail rotor provides anti-torque for the main rotor and:

    A. directional control.

    B. added speed.

    C. high altitude preformance.

138. During forward flight the tail rotor will utilize negative pitch.

    A. True

    B. False

139. The tail rotor is controlled by:

    A. the cyclic.

    B. foot pedal.

    C. The pitch is set and needs no control.

140. Both negative and positive pitch is provided for by the tail rotor.
    A. True

    B. False

141. The tail rotor obtains its power directly from the engine.

    A. True

    B. False

142. Alignment of the tail rotor shafting is not important because flexible couplings are provided.

    A. True

    B. False

143. All tail rotor drives utilize an intermediate gearbox to reduce the speed.

    A. True

    B. False

144. The tail rotor gearbox may be used to increase or decrease the speed of the output shaft.

    A. True

    B. False

145. Tail rotor blades do not require a flapping axis as do main rotor blades.

    A. True

    B. False

146. Only spanwise balance needs to be checked on tail rotors.

    A. True

    B. False

147. Track of the tail rotor may be changed by:

    A. adjusting the pitch change links.

    B. changing the pedal travel.

    C. tabing the blade.

148. The tail rotor cannot be balanced dynamically with the electronic balancer.

    A. True

    B. False

149. Not all tail rotors may be adjusted for track.

    A. True

    B. False

150. Tail rotor vibrations are always:

A. low frequency.

B. medium frequency.

C. high frequency.

SECTION X

Airframes and Related Systems

The airframes of the helicopter cover a wide range of materials, mainly due to the advances in technology that have taken place in the last 40 years since the first helicopters were manufactured. For the most part, the materials used in helicopter construction have remained the same as those used on fixed-wing aircraft.

A. Tubular Construction

Some of the early helicopters used the typical tubular fuselage construction with trusses. Although construction type had a high strength-to-weight ratio, manufacturing such an airframe was quite costly. Each tube was cut, fitted, and welded into place. In addition to this disadvantage, it was difficult to hold dimensions to a close tolerance.

The big advantage of this type of construction was the way in which it could be repaired in the field unless there was severe airframe damage which would require jigging in order to hold the alignment.

The criteria of these repairs are all contained in the maintenance manual and the FAA's AC 43 series Advisory Circulars. A typical fuselage of this type is seen in Fig. 10-1.

B. Sheet Metal Construction

At the same time several of the manufacturers went to aluminum structures. These were of monocoque and semi-monocoque design.

This construction type had a high strength-to-weight ratio. In fact, the ratio was higher than the tubular construction of the same size.

Sheet metal construction had some advantages in the manufacturing process. Parts could be stamped out, and compound curves made at a more rapid rate. Helicopters could be constructed in jigs with closer tolerances than those of the tubular fuselage construction.

In the field, few additional tools were required for repairs. In general, the structure was slightly more delicate. If large repairs were re-

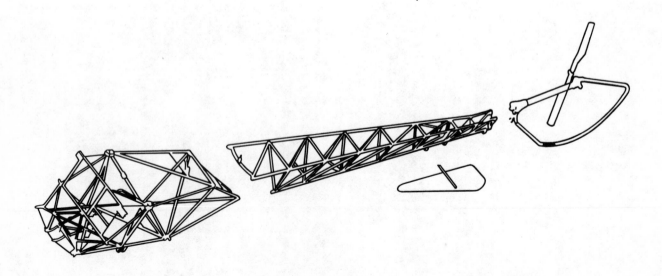

Fig. 10-1   Bell 47 fuselage utilizing tubular steel construction.

428

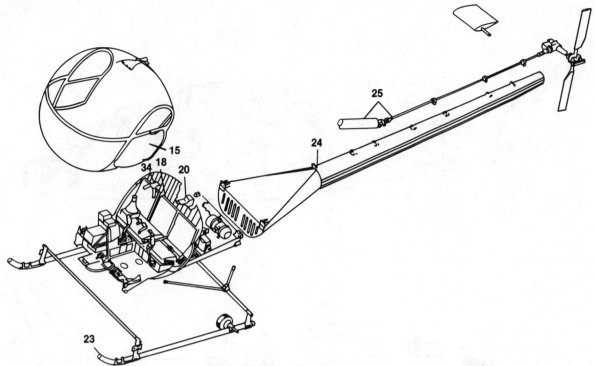

Fig. 10-2   Hiller 12 fuselage utilizing semi-monoque construction.

quired, the fuselage required jigs to obtain proper alignment for the various sections.

A few helicopters were built using a combination of the sheet metal construction and the tubular construction. Tubular design was used in areas where high strength was a requirement. Sheet metal was used when the strength requirements were not so critical. Fig. 10-2 shows a typical monocoque and semi-monocoque design.

C.   Bonded Construction

The third type of construction used in helicopter fuselages is the use of fiberglass, honeycomb, and bonded structures. All of these materials and methods are of high strength-to-weight ratios. Honeycomb and bonded structures have reduced construction costs. The bonding eliminated some of the riveting and welding. Today most airframes are a combination of various materials and methods of construction obtaining the greatest advantages of each (Fig. 10-3).

D.   Stress and Loads

The basic structure of the helicopter varies somewhat from that of a fixed-wing aircraft although they both use the same construction tech-

niques. This is due to the areas of load and stress that are placed on the airframes in different locations. It is these differences that should be understood by helicopter maintenance personnel in order to inspect and repair the helicopter airframe properly.

The typical single-engine fixed-wing airframe has two areas that must be built for the primary stress loads of lift and thrust (Fig. 10-4). These are at the engine attachment points which carry the thrust loads and the wing attachment points which carry the lift forces. Although other points of the fuselage will be designed to carry other loads, these two points will be the primary load carriers during flight.

The helicopter fuselage carries both the lift and thrust forces at the same point (Fig. 10-5). This means that the center area of the helicopter must be built to carry and propel the helicopter from this point. Like the fixed-wing fuselage, the helicopter fuselage must also carry other loads. The lift and thrust area has the highest load factors applied in flight because the main rotor is both the wing and propeller in flight.

1.   Landing

Another load factor in the fuselage is in landings. While the fixed-wing must depend on for-

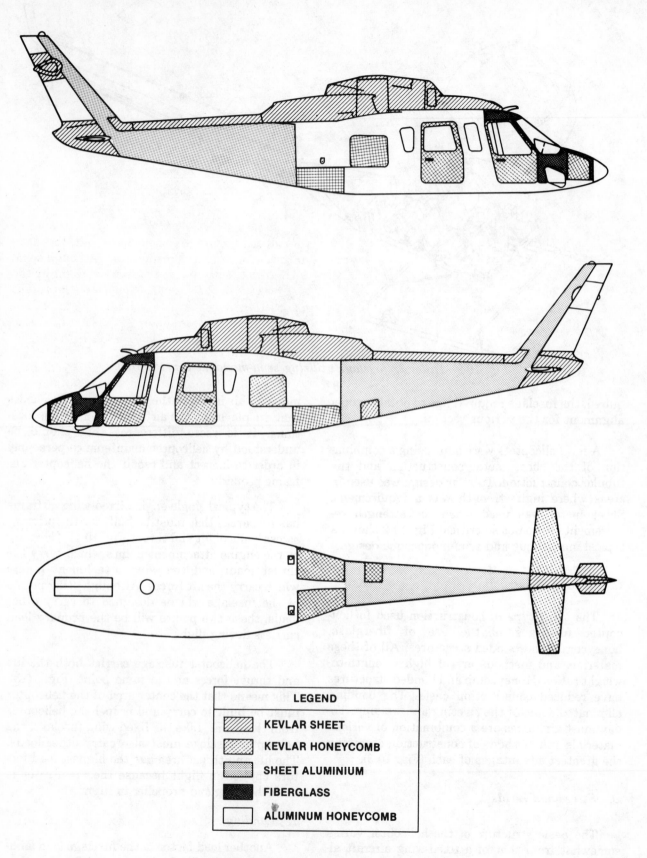

LEGEND

	KEVLAR SHEET
	KEVLAR HONEYCOMB
	SHEET ALUMINIUM
	FIBERGLASS
	ALUMINUM HONEYCOMB

Fig. 10-3 S-76 fuselage utilizing multiple materials.

430

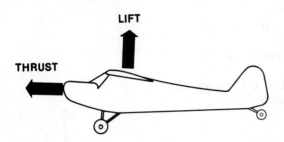

Fig. 10-4   Fixed wing fuselage takes thrust and lift loads at separate points.

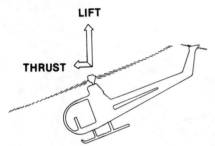

Fig. 10-5   Helicopters carry both thrust and lift at the same point.

ward speed for flight and to land smoothly, the helicopter does not require forward speed to maintain flight. For this reason, many of the helicopters are equipped with skid gear rather than wheels. While the fixed-wing will carry a landing load in two directions, the helicopter will usually carry the load in only one direction (Fig. 10-6).

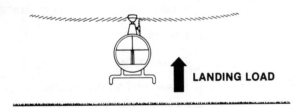

Fig. 10-6   Landing loads are transmitted upward.

There are times, however, that the helicopter may carry both loads such as in an autorotation landing and a tail rotor failure landing. Therefore, some construction for these stresses must be made. Even the helicopters equipped with wheel landing gears will not be required to carry the same load levels as their fixed-wing counterpart.

2.   Vibration levels

The vibration levels of these airframes are also quite different. The helicopter has the highest level of vibration due to the use of so many rotating components. Great strides have been taken in recent years to reduce the vibration levels with the bifilar system and the nodal beam. However, these vibration levels are transferred throughout the airframe and must be considered by the maintenance personnel who are inspecting the airframe.

3.   Tail section

Tail sections of the helicopter must also be considered as different from those of the fixed-wing. Attached to the tail boom at the end is the tail rotor. As we know, this is not only the directional control for the helicopter but the anti-torque control for the main rotor. Although some of these loads are relieved in forward flight by the use of a vertical fin, the side load is still present on the tail boom during all modes of flight. In addition to the side load, many of the helicopters today also have a horizontal stabilizer, which is pushing downward in cruise flight conditions. These loads are usually carried by a cantilevered tail boom that attaches to the main cabin section of the fuselage. These attachment areas are subject to inspection because of the loads induced on them.

E.   Wheel and skid gear

Both the skid gear and wheel gear have advantages and disadvantages. The skid gear is less complex and requires less maintenance than the wheel gear. However, it is much easier for ground handling with wheel gear than it is with skids. The helicopter with wheels may also move under its own power on the ground without actually having to fly.

F.   Visibility

Because of these differences in flight characteristics, other construction criteria must also

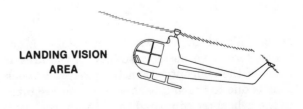

Fig. 10-7   Vision requirements differ in helicopters.

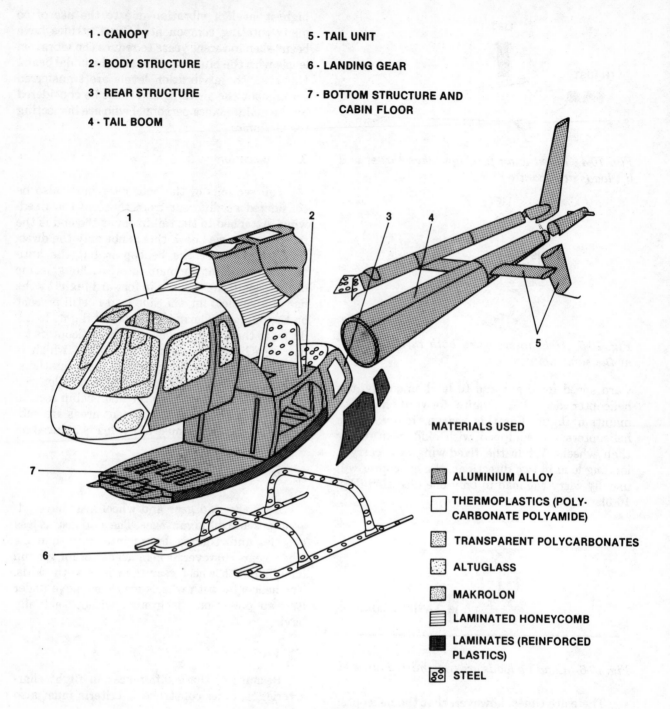

1 - CANOPY

2 - BODY STRUCTURE

3 - REAR STRUCTURE

4 - TAIL BOOM

5 - TAIL UNIT

6 - LANDING GEAR

7 - BOTTOM STRUCTURE AND
   CABIN FLOOR

MATERIALS USED

- ALUMINIUM ALLOY
- THERMOPLASTICS (POLY-CARBONATE POLYAMIDE)
- TRANSPARENT POLYCARBONATES
- ALTUGLASS
- MAKROLON
- LAMINATED HONEYCOMB
- LAMINATES (REINFORCED PLASTICS)
- STEEL

Fig. 10-8   AStar 350 fuselage

be considered in the way of visibility. Many helicopters have better visibility in the area in front of the helicopter than the fixed-wing does. This is due to the approach angles that are made in the helicopter compared to the approach angle of the fixed-wing and also due to to the type of work done by the helicopter. See Fig. 10-7 for this difference in approach.

G.   Structural Components and Materials

Since there are so many different aircraft it would be impossible to look at the airframe of each and every fuselage, so we will discuss the airframe of the AStar 350. The AStar, like so many of the newer helicopters, uses a combination of material and a semi-monocoque type of construction.

The basic structural components and their materials are shown in Fig. 10-8. Notice in this view that the materials used are aluminum or synthetic materials of the thermosetting type of resins. Steel is used only where it is absolutely necessary.

As the view separates the airframe into various sections, it is quite easy to see that they are also manufactured in these different sections before the helicopter is assembled.

1. Body structure

The body structure (Fig. 10-9) is the main structural member of the fuselage. It not only carries the lift and thrust loads, but also the landing loads. The body structure will support all the other members of the fuselage either directly or indirectly. All the forces applied to these other members will be transmitted to the body structure. In actuality this section is a reinforced box with "X" members placed in each side. The transmission assembly, which is connected to the main rotor and absorbs all the lift of the aircraft, is placed on top of this box. The skid gear which absorbs the compression loads of landing is attached to the bottom of the box. In the middle of this structure is placed the fuel tanks which should be in the most protected area of the helicopter.

2. Bottom structure

Attached to the body structure on the front of the box is the bottom structure and cabin floor (Fig. 10-10). This section is made of two cantilevered beams extending from the box that are connected to the cross members of the box. These two beams will actually carry the weight of the cabin and transmit it to the box. Cross members are added to these two beams to support the floor

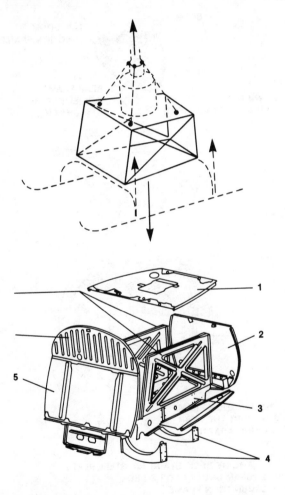

1 - TRANSMISSION PLATFORM
2 - REAR BULKHEAD. ATTACHMENT OF REAR STRUCTURE
3 - LATERAL BEAMS (L.H. SIDE AND R.H. SIDE). ATTACH-
    MENT OF BOTTOM STRUCTURE BEAMS
4 - CROSS MEMBERS. FUEL TANK SUPPORTS
5 - FRONT BULKHEAD, TILTED 15° REARWARD
6 - UPPER BULKHEAD, TILTED 7° FORWARD
7 - LONGITUDINAL BULKHEADS. THICK PLATES

Fig. 10-9 AStar body structure

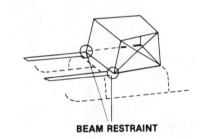

BEAM RESTRAINT

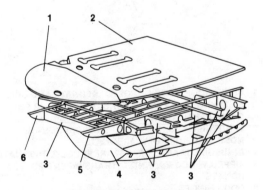

1 - CABIN FLOOR FORWARD PANEL
2 - FLOOR CENTER PANEL
3 - CROSS MEMBERS
4 - LOWER FAIRINGS
5 - BEAM, L.H.
6 - BEAM, R.H.

Fig. 10-10 Cabin floor assembly of the AStar.

and the lower skin panels. The cabin section attaches directly to the floor.

3. Cabin section

The canopy, or cabin section, is made almost exclusively from synthetic materials (Fig. 10-11). This portion is made of subassemblies which are the cabin roof, nose, and vertical members. All of the components are made of polycarbonate reinforced with glass fibers. They are heat molded and assembled by banding and ultrasonic spot welding. The canopy frame is then bolted to the cabin floor and the body bulkhead. Added to this frame are the upper windows, windshields, and lower window which are all made of polycarbonate. The transparent polycarbonate is known for its superior strength properties.

4. Rear section

The rear section of the fuselage connects to the body section (Fig. 10-12). The rear section is

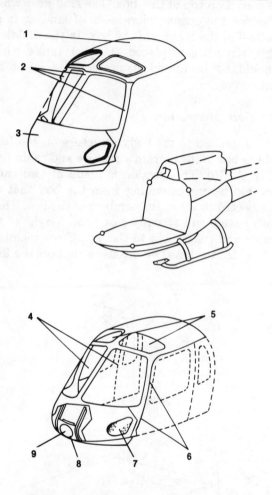

1 - CABIN ROOF MADE OF POLYCARBONATE AND CON-SISTING OF HALF SHELLS, INSIDE WHICH AIR FOR CABIN VENTILATION IS DUCTED.
2 - WINDSHIELD POST, MADE OF POLYCARBONATE
3 - NOSE, MADE OF POLYCARBONATE
4 - WINDSHIELD PANEL. TRANSPARENT POLYCARBONATE
5 - UPPER WINDOWS. TINTED TRANSPARENT POLYCAR-BONATE
6 - DOOR HINGES
7 - LOWER WINDOWS (R.H. AND L.H.) TRANSPARENT POLYCARBONATE
8 - INSPECTION PANEL
9 - LANDING LIGHT WINDOW. TRANSPARENT POLYCAR-BONATE

Fig. 10-11   AStar cabin enclosure

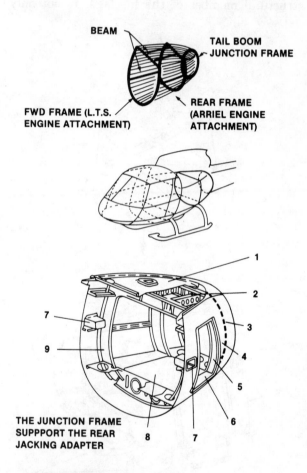

THE JUNCTION FRAME SUPPPORT THE REAR JACKING ADAPTER

1 - ENGINE DECK. STAINLESS STEEL PLATE
2 - BEAM UNDER ENGINE DECK
3 - JUNCTION FRAME
4 - SKIN
5 - REAR FRAME
6 - ACCESS TO BAGGAGE COMPARTMENT
7 - RECESS (FOOT STEP FOR ACCESS TO TRANSMISSION PLATFORM)
8 - BAGGAGE COMPARTMENT FLOOR
9 - FORWARD FRAME

Fig. 10-12   Rear section of the AStar

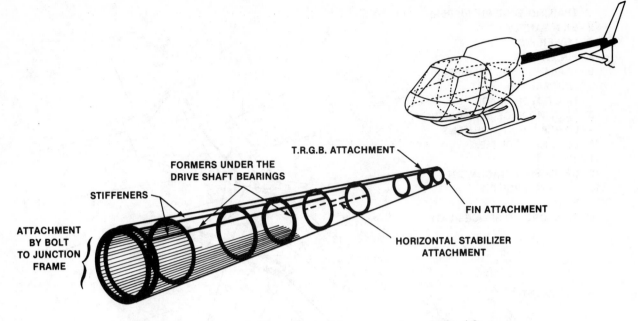

Fig. 10-13 Semi-monoque tail boom section of the AStar.

made up of three frames connected by beams to the body section. The frame acts as an attachment point for the engine, mounted on top of this section, with a stainless steel firewall. The inside of this section acts as a baggage area. The rear frame is the attachment point for the tail boom section. This section is attached by bolting the tail boom to the frame.

5. *Tail boom*

The tail boom (Fig. 10-13) is of conventional design with circular frames, stringers, and outer skin. The stringers or stiffeners give the boom assembly the required rigidity. The following items are attached to the tail boom: the tail rotor gearbox, the drive shafting, the vertical fins, and the horizontal stabilizer. In all of these areas additional stiffeners are attached to the structure.

6. *Lower vertical fin*

The lower vertical fin is a symmetrical airfoil. This fin is protected from damage in a nose-up landing by the tail rotor guard which is attached to the bottom of the fin. The fin is bolted to the tail boom at the leading edge and at the spar section of the fin.

The top fin is of similar construction except this is a dissymmetrical airfoil and is used in cruise flight to unload the tail rotor by exerting

force against the tail to correct for the torque of the main rotor. This attaches in much the same manner to the top of the tail boom and the rear (Fig. 10-14).

7. *Horizontal stabilizer*

The horizontal stabilizer is also a dissymmetrical airfoil located two degrees from the horizontal datum. This produces a downward force on the stabilizer, which tends to keep the helicopter level in forward flight. The stabilizer passes through a slot in the tail boom and is bolted on each side (Fig. 10-15).

8. *Skid gear*

The skid gear is attached to the body section of the helicopter. This supports the aircraft and dampens vibrations on the ground when the rotor is turning. The landing gear is made up of the following components: a forward cross tube, a rear cross tube, two skids, and two hydraulic dampeners. The rear cross tubes are clamped to the body structure with rubber bushings between the clamps for vibration dampening. The front cross tube is attached in much the same manner as the rear cross tube. The hydraulic dampeners are attached from the cross tubes to the front bulkhead of the body assembly to control the rate of leg distortion.

1 · TRAILING EDGE RIB (UPPER)
2 · SKIN PANELS
3 · LOWER RIB
4 · FIN FITTINGS
5 · TRAILING EDGE RIB (UPPER)
6 · SKIN PANELS
7 · TAIL ROTOR GUARD
8 · TRAILING EDGE RIB (LOWER)
9 · LOWER FIN ATTACHMENT
10 · LEADING EDGE RIB
11 · SPAR
12 · UPPER FIN ATTACHMENT
13 · LEADING EDGE RIB
14 · SPAR
15 · REINFORCING SPLICE PLATE

FINS ATTACHMENT

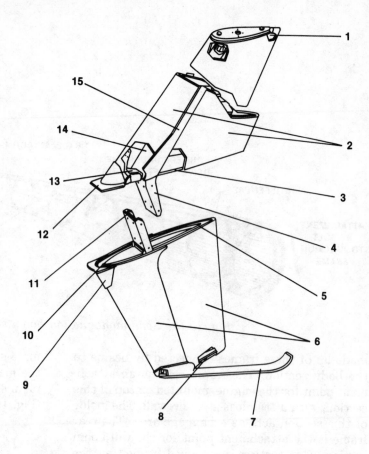
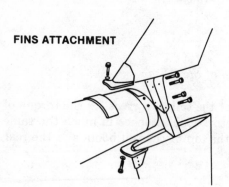

Fig. 10-14   AStar vertical stabilizer assembly.

1 · TRAILING EDGE SKIN
2 · TRAILING EDGE RIB
3 · CENTER SKIN
4 · END RIB
5 · SPAR
6 · REINFORCEMENT AND ATTACHMENT
     FITTINGS (CROSSED BY BOTH ATTACH-
     MENT BOLTS)
7 · LEADING EDGE RIB
8 · LEADING EDGE SKIN

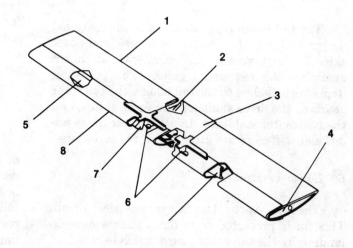
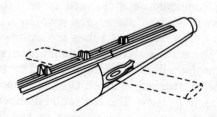

Fig. 10-15   Horizontal stabilizer used on the AStar.

436

The skids are equipped with skid shoes at both the front and the rear of the skid. In addition to the skid shoes, a long steel strip attached to the skids is bent downward. This is a vibration dampener and is used to eliminate the possibility of ground resonance of the helicopter (Fig. 10-16).

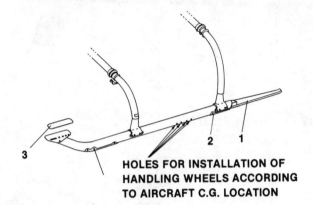

HOLES FOR INSTALLATION OF HANDLING WHEELS ACCORDING TO AIRCRAFT C.G. LOCATION

1 - FLEXIBLE STEEL STRIP

2 - WEAR PADS. STEEL

3 - ANTI-SKID PAD (CABIN FOOT STEP)

Fig. 10-16   Skid gear used on the AStar

9. Anti-vibration device

This is one of the few airframes that makes use of a fuselage anti-vibration device. This device is located under the pilot's seat and creates a node in vertical vibrations in the cabin section of the helicopter. This is accomplished by adding a steel blade which has a weight attached. This resonates with the vibrations of the airframe (Fig. 10-17).

This type of airframe is somewhat different from many in the use of materials. Basic structural concepts have been used by placing a strong center section in the fuselage and cantilevering the cabin and the tail boom from this portion.

F. Bell 206 Fuselage

The next fuselage is that of the Bell 206. In this airframe various materials will also be used, but most of the airframe is aluminum and honeycomb construction. It is made of three main sections joined together. The sections are the forward section, the intermediate section, and the tail boom (Fig. 10-18).

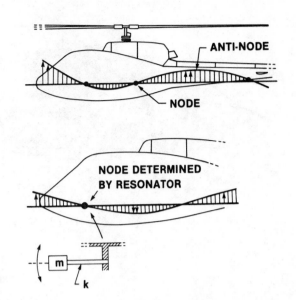

Fig. 10-17   Anti-vibration device used on the AStar.

1. Forward section

The forward section begins at the nose of the fuselage and extends aft to the rear cross tubes. This section consists of a tinted plastic enclosure and is constructed on one-thich thick honeycomb bonded to aluminum sheet formed to contour. This construction provides rigidity, strength and soundproofing.

This section of the fuselage is actually made of a top and bottom section of honeycomb joined by posts that connect the two units. The bottom unit is often referred to as the tub assembly. The curvature of this tub assembly gives great strength, like that of a beam, down each side of the floor and provides attachment points for seats and the roof structure. The roof structure is quite similar to that of the floor except that it is inverted. The forward section provides the primary strength for the lift and landing forces. Attached to the forward section is the intermediate section. This area is made of conventional semi-monocoque construction. The structure supports the engine mounts and forms the baggage area. It also serves as the attachment point for the tail boom.

2. Intermediate section

The forward and intermediate sections make up the cabin section which directly or indirectly

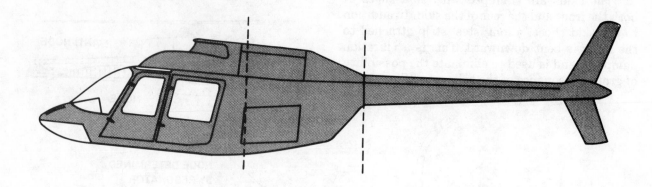

Fig. 10-18   Sections of the Bell 206 fuselage

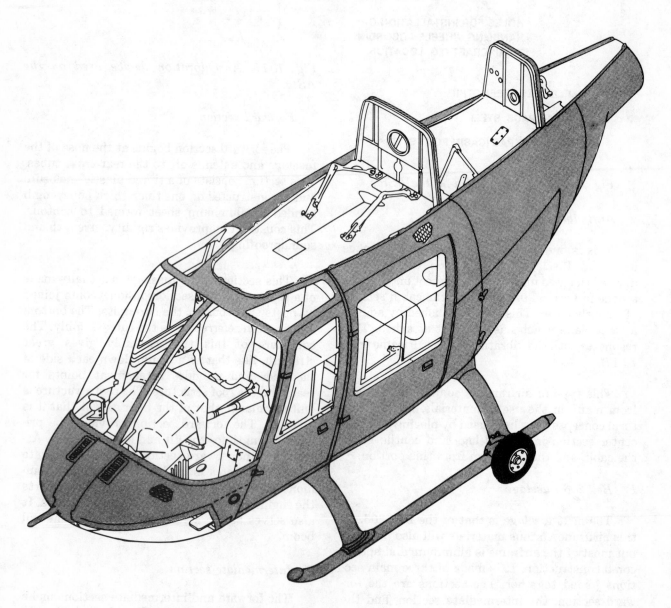

Fig. 10-19   Cabin and intermediate sections of the Bell 206.

supports all the systems and components of the helicopter as well as providing the seating area for the pilot and passengers (Fig. 10-19).

3. Tail boom

The tail boom is of monocoque construction and provides the supporting structure for the tail rotor shafting, 90° gearbox, horizontal stabilizer, and vertical fin. The tail boom is attached to the cabin section by four bolts (Fig. 10-20).

a. Vertical fin

The vertical fin is used to unload the tail rotor during forward flight. This is done by a slight offset. Its construction is of aluminum and aluminum honeycomb. It is attached to the right side of the tail boom by four bolts and has a tail skid mounted to the bottom.

b. Horizontal stabilizer

The horizontal stabilizer is of fixed position and standard construction with aluminum skin ribs and a tubular spar that passes through the tail boom. The horizontal stabilizer is an inverted airfoil which helps keep the fuselage level in forward flight.

4. Landing gear

The landing gear consists of two tubular aluminum alloy cross tubes, two skids, and removable skid shoes. These are attached to the cabin section by four strap assemblies.

G. Hughes 500 Fuselage

Another interesting type of construction is that of the Hughes 500. It uses conventional type

1. HORIZONTAL STABILIZER
2. TAIL BOOM
3. POSITION LIGHT

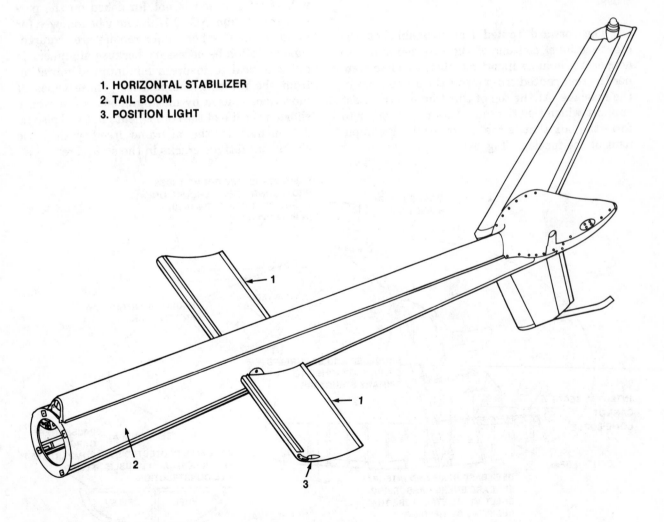

Fig. 10-20   Bell 206 tail section

439

materials but in a somewhat unconventional manner. The strength of this structure is the result of a beam and truss type of construction.

The main strength member is a center beam which extends longitudinally along the center line of the lower fuselage section. This center beam is made of aluminum panels, stiffeners, doublers, and forged landing gear fillings. Attached to this main beam assembly are a number of items used by the airframe and four major bulkheads. These bulkheads serve several purposes. At the most forward end of the center beam is the bulkhead that supports the pilot's floor. The pilot's seat structure bulkhead is at the forward end of the pilot's seat structure. The next bulkhead is attached to the forward canted frame which is the forward member of the basic airframe truss. The last bulkhead supports the rear canted frame which is the aft member of the basic airframe truss.

The forward canted frame establishes the cross-sectional contour of the fuselage and also acts as a primary support member. In a like manner the rear canted truss forms the aft contour of the fuselage. At the top of this frame is the mast support which ties the canted frames together to form the box that is the major strength component of the fuselage (Fig. 10-21).

Most of the other structure is quite conventional except for the construction of the fuselage concerning crash worthiness. It is designed with some thought regarding survivability of the occupants of the helicopter. This may be the result of the basic design of this helicopter being used by the military. These features include such items as seat belts attached to the primary structure, a deep fuselage structure, energy absorbing sheet metal seats and the truss construction in the cabin section.

H. Fuselage Maintenance

From time to time the helicopter fuselages require maintenance. This may include simple sheet metal repairs or may include major fuselage rebuilding. The manufacturers will usually furnish structural repair information either in the maintenance manual or a structural repair manual. If information is not furnished on the particular airframe, AC 43.13-1A may be followed for minor repairs. When major repairs are required, jigs will often be necessary because alignment is quite critical to insure a minimum of vibration from the rotating components. These types of vibrations caused by misalignment will not only shorten the life of the components but will also be detrimental to the airframe itself with loose rivets and fatigue cracks in the structure.

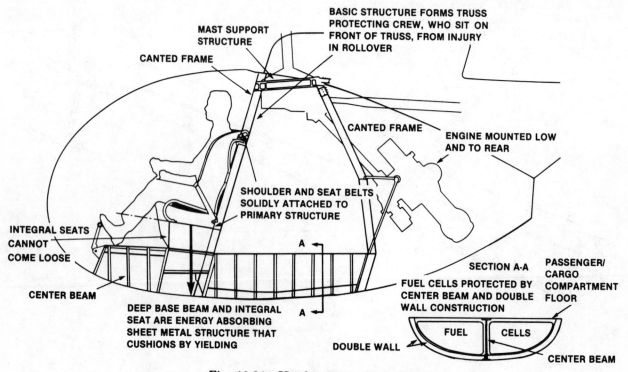

Fig. 10-21 Hughes 500 cabin section

1. Hard landings

Other detrimental items to the structure include hard landings. These often call for a special inspection of the airframe and will require attention to areas of attachment such as the tail boom, transmission, engine, and landing gear, due to the stresses placed on the components at the time.

Some of the rotating components may also be included in the special hard landing inspection such as transmission cases, gearbox cases and mast bearings which are all subject to these stresses.

Some hard landings may also result in other types of damage. These include nicking the tail boom with the main rotor blades or in severe cases, actually severing the tail boom with the main rotor. This may result in other damages to the rotating components such as the blades, rotor head, mast, and drive train. This is because impact forces can be transmitted from the point of impact through other portions of the helicopter and airframe.

Other special inspections that could be necessary because of a hard landing or other happenings include sudden stoppage of either the main rotor or tail rotor. Both of these situations can lead to both airframe and rotating component damage and often both. These inspections are usually classified as to with or without power.

2. Sudden stoppage

Sudden stoppage of the main rotor occurs when there is a sudden deceleration after contact with an object such as the ground, trees, etc. The force of this will be transmitted throughout the system, not only the point of impact. Damage to the blades is normally quite obvious at the point of impact but they may also have secondary damage in the root area of the blade meaning that bonds may be loosened and spars may have cracks, etc. In addition, this may be transmitted to the rotor head. The inspection could require complete disassembly of the rotor head and the normal overhaul inspection performed. On some rotor heads certain parts may be required to be replaced without inspection of the parts. On others, it may require replacement of the whole rotor head.

This could include the teardown and inspection of the mast bearings, transmission, transmission mounting, structural bolts and tail rotor drive assembly. The extent of this inspection may often be governed by the extent of the damage found in one or more areas such as bent drag braces, damaged mast bearings, etc.

Sudden stoppage of the tail rotor can also lead to this type of secondary damage and may include twisting of the tail boom structure, structural damage to the hanger bearing mounts and tail boom attachment points. This type of damage would be in addition to the damage to the rotor and drive train. On some helicopters, even though the blades were damaged, the hub portion may also have to be discarded. On others, the hub would be inspected by a teardown inspection. Other inspections of this type would be required throughout the whole drive system including the drive quill of the transmission.

Other special inspections that would affect the airframe slightly would be an overspeed or overtorque situation. In any such circumstance the maintenance manual will provide the inspection criteria for special inspections and the areas of the airframe to be inspected, including the method of inspection.

I. Airframe Systems

Other systems, in addition to the basic airframe and rotating components, must be incorporated into the airframe. These may be necessary for the operation of the helicopter, or may be special requirements for the type of work that is being done with the helicopter.

Necessary systems to be considered would be the fuel system, electrical system, a ventilating system, and possibly heating and air conditioning. For the most part these would be the same systems found in the fixed-wing aircraft.

1. Fuel system

The fuel system is usually made up of one or more tanks. These are usually force feed systems because there would be a few places that the fuel could be located for a gravity feed system. The Bell 47, however, is the exception to the rule because it does use a gravity feed system to deliver fuel to the engine. More typical, however, would be the fuel system found in the Bell 206 for a light turbine helicopter (Fig. 10-22).

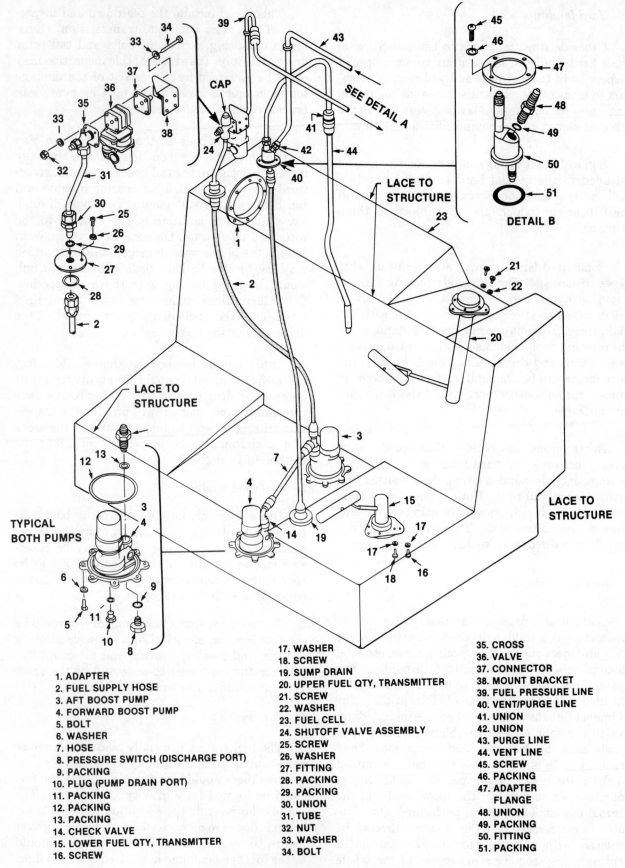

CAP

SEE DETAIL A

LACE TO STRUCTURE

DETAIL B

LACE TO STRUCTURE

LACE TO STRUCTURE

TYPICAL BOTH PUMPS

1. ADAPTER
2. FUEL SUPPLY HOSE
3. AFT BOOST PUMP
4. FORWARD BOOST PUMP
5. BOLT
6. WASHER
7. HOSE
8. PRESSURE SWITCH (DISCHARGE PORT)
9. PACKING
10. PLUG (PUMP DRAIN PORT)
11. PACKING
12. PACKING
13. PACKING
14. CHECK VALVE
15. LOWER FUEL QTY, TRANSMITTER
16. SCREW

17. WASHER
18. SCREW
19. SUMP DRAIN
20. UPPER FUEL QTY, TRANSMITTER
21. SCREW
22. WASHER
23. FUEL CELL
24. SHUTOFF VALVE ASSEMBLY
25. SCREW
26. WASHER
27. FITTING
28. PACKING
29. PACKING
30. UNION
31. TUBE
32. NUT
33. WASHER
34. BOLT

35. CROSS
36. VALVE
37. CONNECTOR
38. MOUNT BRACKET
39. FUEL PRESSURE LINE
40. VENT/PURGE LINE
41. UNION
42. UNION
43. PURGE LINE
44. VENT LINE
45. SCREW
46. PACKING
47. ADAPTER FLANGE
48. UNION
49. PACKING
50. FITTING
51. PACKING

Fig. 10-22   Fuel system of the Bell 206

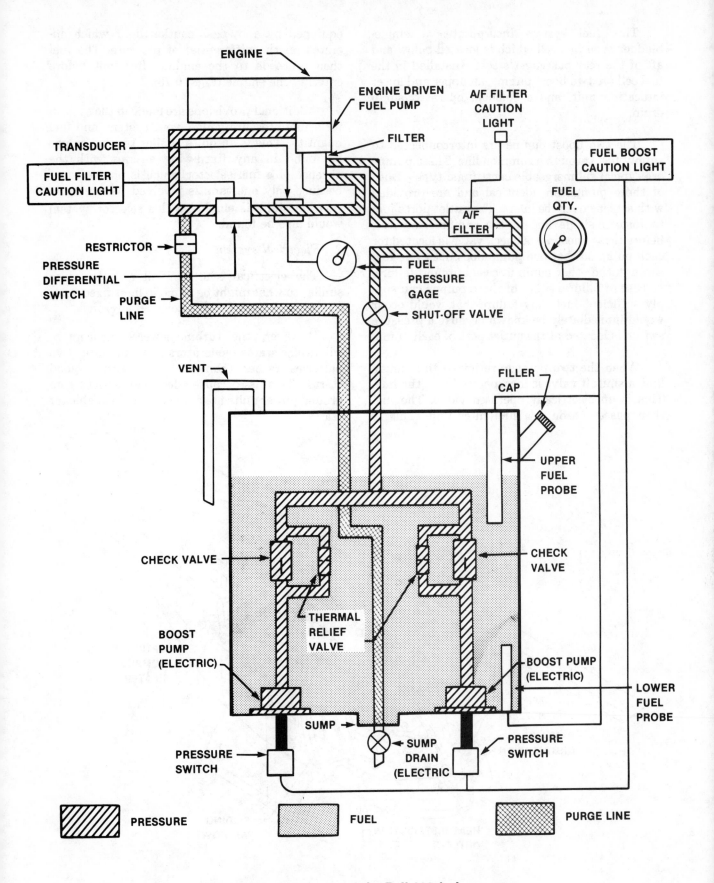

Fig. 10-23   Schematic of the Bell 206 fuel system.

443

This fuel system incorporates a single-bladder type fuel cell which is located below and aft of the rear passenger's seat. Installed in the fuel cell are two boost pumps, an upper and lower indicating unit, and a solenoid operated sump drain.

The two boost pumps are interconnected to supply fuel through a common line. These pumps are typical submergeable centrifugal types. Both of these pumps are identical and are provided with screens over the inlets. The outlet ports join to form a single line to the engine. However, before these lines join, a check valve is located for each pump so that one pump does not cycle fuel through the other pump in case of pump failure. In case of failure, either of these pumps can supply sufficient fuel. Any failure that would occur would immediately be known because a pressure switch is located at the outlet port of each pump.

When the two pumps are joined to a single line, a shutoff valve is incorporated into the line. This is an electrically operated valve. The fuel then passes through a fuel filter unit. This is equipped by a by-pass caution light which operates on the differential of pressure. The fuel then proceeds to the engine filter unit before entering the engine (Fig. 10-23).

Additional provisions are made in the system for a fuel pressure gauge, vent system, and fuel quantity. This is all quite similar to what might be found in any fixed-wing aircraft with the absence of a fuel selector which is not necessry because only one tank is involved. Where more than one tank is employed this selector system would also be found.

2. Electrical system

The electrical systems will also be quite similar to what might be found in light fixed-wing aircraft or a light turbine-powered aircraft.

However, the turbine-powered helicopters will utilize starter-generators and quite often two batteries rather than one for assuring good starts. This is because electrical assist from ground power units are almost never available for starts.

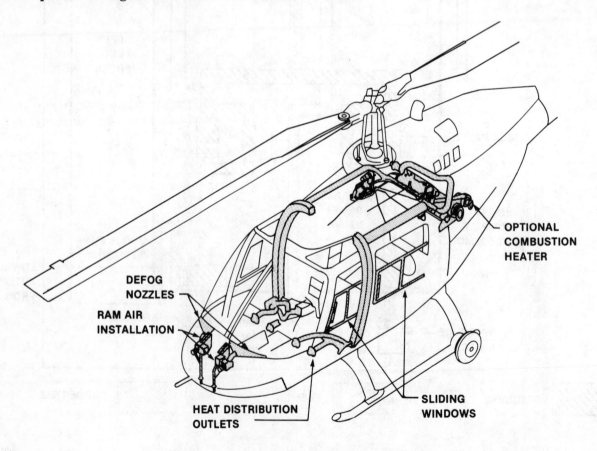

OPTIONAL COMBUSTION HEATER

DEFOG NOZZLES

RAM AIR INSTALLATION

HEAT DISTRIBUTION OUTLETS

SLIDING WINDOWS

Fig. 10-24 Combustion heat system for the Bell 206.

444

In addition to this the nickel-cadmium battery is used almost exclusively. As with all ni-cad batteries, special care and servicing is required.

3. Environmental systems

In recent years a few helicopters have started to use *environmental control units (ECU)*. These are air cycle machines which may furnish either hot or cool air, whichever is required, in the helicopter for the weather conditions. Fig. 10-24 shows a typical combustion heater and ventilating system.

J. Special Purpose Equipment

Since the helicopter is used for a variety of purposes, special equipment is often needed to perform these tasks. Some of these items will be available from the manufacturer as optional equipment while other items will be built by individuals or companies that will have the item certified by a Supplemental Type Certificate (STC) and sell the unit to the operator in usually a kit form for a particular type of helicopter. Such units may include high skid gear, pop-out floats, rescue hoists, ambulance configurations, cargo hooks, and spotlights.

1. High skid gear

One of these items which is quite commonly used is the high skid gear. This item may often be obtained from the manufacturer as optional equipment. The advantages of this type are many when the helicopter is to be used for landings in unimproved landing areas. Less tail rotor strikes are made by keeping the fuselage higher. In arctic regions the helicopter may also be fitted with additional plates, in addition to the high skid gear on the bottom of the skid preventing the skids from sinking into the tundra. These plates give more area for the helicopter to rest on. See Fig. 10-25 for a view of one type of high skid gear.

2. Floats

Some helicopters have such options as pop-out floats that may be installed with the high skid gear. These are used where over water flights are made. The advantage of this type of floatation device will require repacking and inspection periodically to insure their safe operation when required. On the system shown in Fig. 10-26 the air bottles are carried in the baggage area and may be activated by the pilot when necessary.

Still other helicopters may make use of such pop-out devices. They will be mounted on the bottom side of the circumference of the fuselage of the helicopter. Regardless of the location these are emergency type devices. If normal water landings are made routinely, floats of a permanent type are installed. These are normally filled with air compartments and made of material similar to that of fuel bladders. These may be patched and repaired. Often the use of this type of float limits the flight envelope of the helicopter.

A few helicopters have been built with provisions for amphibious landings. However, this is not a very common configuration for civilian helicopters.

3. Rescue hoists

The rescue hoists (Fig. 10-27) are most often used by civil agencies such as police departments and fire departments. These allow the helicopter to act as a hoist platform for rescue work and is capable of lifting comparatively light loads with only the capability of raising or lowering the load.

4. Cargo hooks

A cargo hook is used for heavy loads such as sling loads (Fig. 10-28). This type of lift work is usually very specialized with special FARs to cover this work. The hook itself normally has an electrical and a manual release as a safety device to insure that the load may be jettisoned at any time if difficulties exist with the load. Weight limitations are required with external loads. These may at times exceed the normal gross weight of the helicopter when operating in a restricted category. The normal location of the hook is as close to the center of gravity as possible.

5. Litter installations

Another modification that is sometimes used is a litter configuration. This may involve a rather extensive modification or it may be quite simple. Some of the more extensive modifications, such as the Bell 206, involve the cutting of the door post so the litters may be placed in the helicopter. This member is structural and must

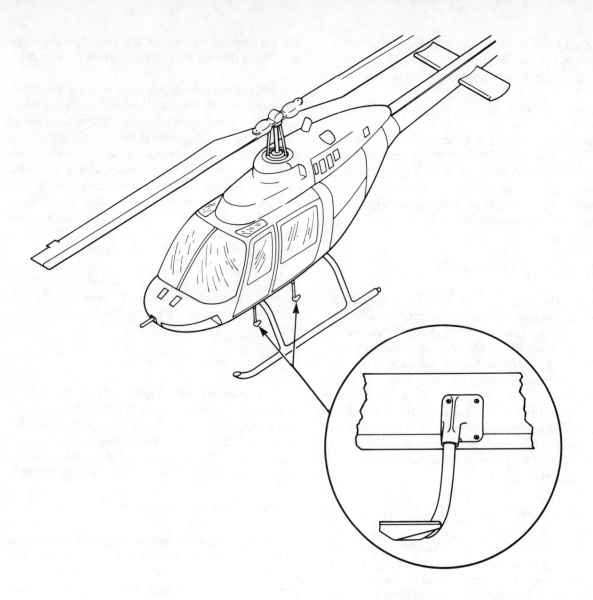

Fig. 10-25   A — High skid gear used on the Bell 206.   B — High and low skid gear used on the Hughes 500.

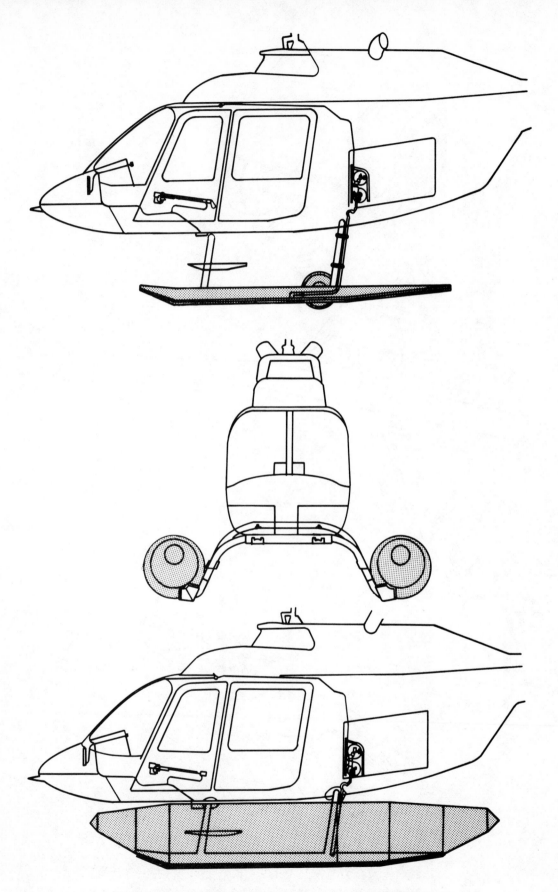

Fig. 10-26 Pop-out floats as found on the Bell 206.

447

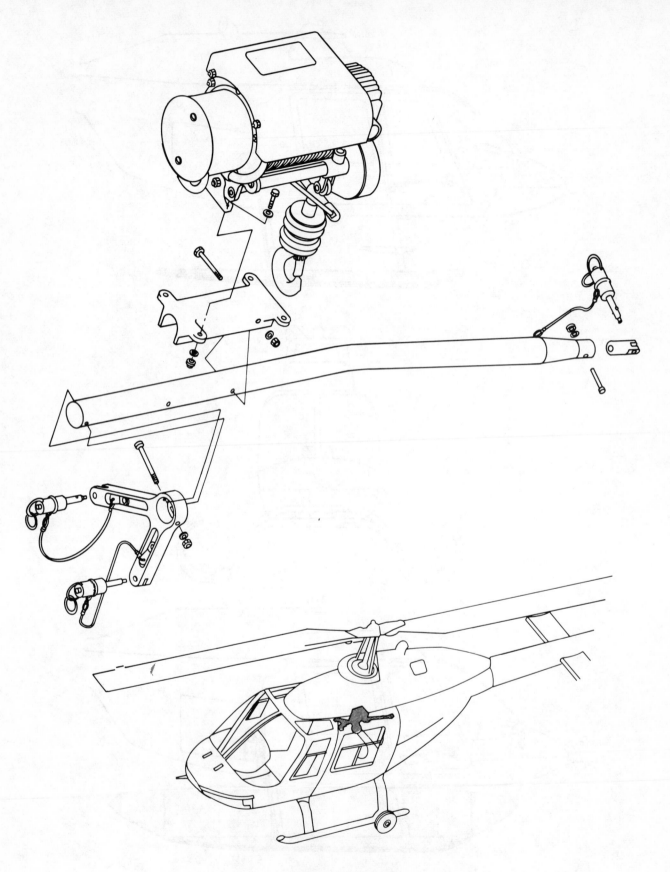

Fig. 10-27 Rescue hoist used on some helicopters.

448

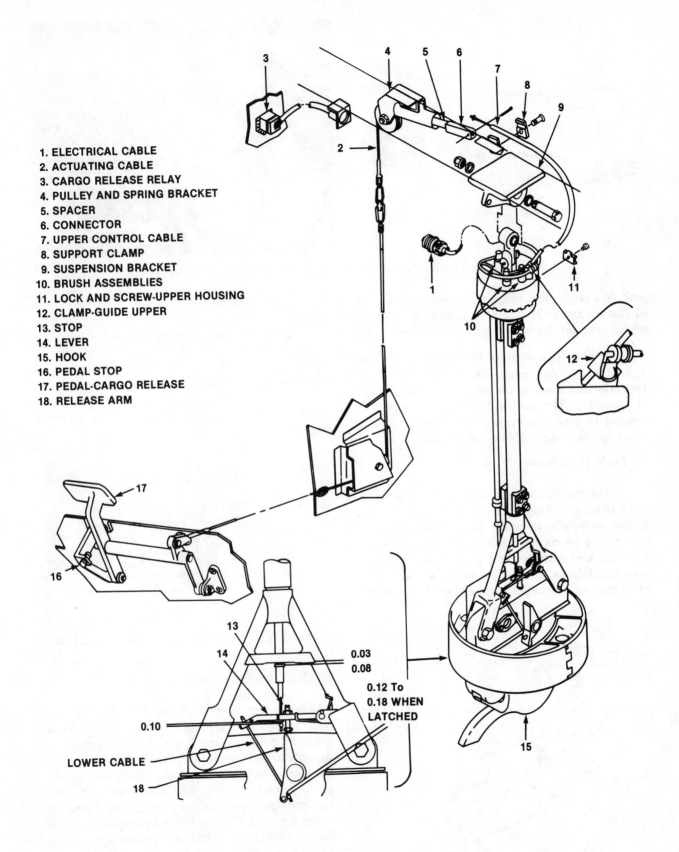

1. ELECTRICAL CABLE
2. ACTUATING CABLE
3. CARGO RELEASE RELAY
4. PULLEY AND SPRING BRACKET
5. SPACER
6. CONNECTOR
7. UPPER CONTROL CABLE
8. SUPPORT CLAMP
9. SUSPENSION BRACKET
10. BRUSH ASSEMBLIES
11. LOCK AND SCREW-UPPER HOUSING
12. CLAMP-GUIDE UPPER
13. STOP
14. LEVER
15. HOOK
16. PEDAL STOP
17. PEDAL-CARGO RELEASE
18. RELEASE ARM

0.03
0.08

0.12 To
0.18 WHEN
LATCHED

0.10

LOWER CABLE

Fig. 10-28   Cargo hook used for external loads.

449

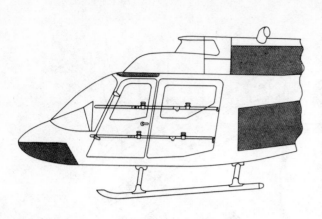

Fig. 10-29 *Litter configurations used on the Bell 206 and Hughes 500.*

include a latch mechanism to insure the integrity of the airframe. It will also include a latching mechanism for the litters themselves (Fig. 10-29).

Other configurations of this type may include special and wider doors. The wider door facilitates the movement of the stretchers in and out of the aircraft. The use of this type is generally limited to civil government and charter operations specializing in this type of work.

6. Light installations

A few helicopters may also be equipped as a light platform. There are many uses for Xenon lights, especially in police work. Some of these lights may be controlled from the cyclic control with tilt and rotation axis as well as flood and spot capabilities. Some of these lights are capable of producing 65 million candlepower (Fig. 10-30).

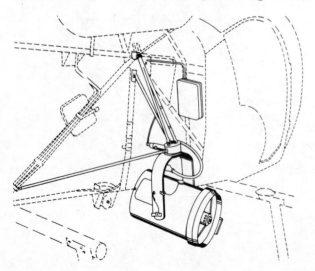

Fig. 10-30 *Xenon light installation on a Bell 47.*

7. Spray equipment

Equipment used in spraying is not built by the aircraft manufacturer. Spray equipment is constructed by specialized companies holding an STC for spray equipment. Some of this equipment is mounted on the aircraft while other units are self-contained and connect to the cargo hook (Fig. 10-31).

Fig. 10-31 *Typical spray boom installation.*

8. Stabilization devices

With the advent of the IFR helicopter, a number of different stabilization devices have appeared for helicopters. Some of these systems are manufactured in conjuction with the helicopter. At the present time, no helicopters are certified for IFR operations in this country without stabilization equipment. More aircraft are being certified for such flights. Some helicopters that are not certified for IFR have the equipment installed to ease the pilot's work load. Some of this equipment has been used by the military for a long time. As more and more tasks are performed by the helicopter and new helicopters are developed, more specialized equipment will be developed to perform these tasks.

Today the helicopter industry is the fastest growing facet of aviation. The size of the civil fleet has already exceeded the scheduled airline fleet by three times and it is expected to grow at a rapid rate for the next decade. Even at the present time, the production of some helicopters is exceeded by the demand for the equipment.

QUESTIONS:

151. The helicopter fuselage is stressed the same as the fixed-wing fuselage in flight.

    A. True

    B. False

152. Semi-monocoque construction is never used in helicopters.

    A. True

    B. False

153. Fiberglass and honeycomb material cannot be used for structural members.

    A. True

    B. False

154. The tail boom is normally cantilevered from the body section.

    A. True

    B. False

155. Lift and thrust forces are carried from the same point on a helicopter fuselage.

    A. True

    B. False

156. Skid gear absorbs landing forces through the cross tubes.

    A. True

    B. False

157. Vertical fins are often used to unload the tail rotor during cruise flight.

    A. True

    B. False

158. The horizontal stabilizer on some helicopters is an inverted airfoil.

    A. True

    B. False

159. The strongest section of the fuselage is the section that the transmission attaches to.

    A. True

    B. False

160. The only *special inspection* involving the fuselage is a sudden stoppage of the main rotor.

    A. True

    B. False

Glossary

This glossary of terms is provided to serve as a ready reference for the word with which you may not be familiar. These definitions may differ from those of standard dictionaries, but are in keeping with shop usage.

advancing blade Any blade located in a semi-circular part of the rotor disc where the blade direction is the same as the direction of flight.

airfoil Any surface designed to obtain a useful reaction of lift or negative lift as it moves through the air. Rotor blades and stabilizers are the most common airfoils on helicopters.

alignment pin A pin placed in the rotor blade at construction, for an index of the blade alignment procedure, used on semi-rigid rotor systems.

alpha hinge See lead-lag hinge.

angle of attack The acute angle between the direction of the relative wind and the chordline of an airfoil.

angle of incidence The acute angle between a fixed reference surface and the chordline of an airfoil.

angular velocity Velocity of a particle, moving around a center, at a given distance from the center, expressed in radians.

anti-torque pedals The pedals used to control the pitch of the tail rotor which are sometimes called the rudder pedals.

anti-torque rotor See tail rotor.

articulated rotor A rotor in which each blade is jointed at the root to flap, lead-lag individually or collectively. Sometimes called a fully articulated rotor.

ATA system Airline Transport Associations' standardized format for maintenance manuals.

autorotation The property of a rotor system to maintain its angular velocity without engine power, the relative force provided by the forward component of the lift forces, acting on the rotor blades.

back-to-back bearing See face-to-face bearing.

beep button A switch on the collective used to trim a turbine engine by increasing or decreasing the steady state RPM.

bifilar A system used for dampening rotor vibration, developed by Sikorsky.

BIM Blade Inspection Method — a system of using an indicator and inert gas to detect blade cracks, used by Sikorsky.

BIS Blade Inspection System — a method used by Bell to determine if blades have cracked.

blade alignment A procedure, used on semi-rigid rotor systems, to place the blades in proper positions on the lead-lag axis of the rotor system.

blade coning Acute angle between the blade's spanwise axis and the plane of rotation, result of lift vs. gravity.

blade cross over See climbing blade.

blade dampener A device installed on the vertical blade hinge to diminish or dampen blade movement on the lead-lag axis.

blade droop The angle of the spanwise axis of the rotor at rest, with only the forces of gravity acting on the rotor.

blade flap The ability of the rotor blade to move in a vertical direction. Blades may flap independently or in unison.

blade forks See blade grips.

blade grips The part of the hub assembly to which the rotor blades are attached. These are sometimes referred to as blade forks.

blade loading The ratio of the helicopter weight to the total area of the lifting area.

blade pins Pins or bolts used to hold the rotor blades to the hub.

blade pockets A term used by Sikorsky to describe sections of the rotor blade attached to the blade spar.

blade root The part of the blade which attaches to the blade grip.

blade span The length of the blade from the tip to the root.

blade spar The main structural member of the rotor blade running the length of the blade.

blade stall The condition of the rotor blade when it is operating at an angle of attack greater than the maximum angle of lift. This occurs at high forward speed to the retreating blade and all blades during "settling with power."

blade sweeping A maintenance procedure for adjusting dynamic chordwise balance in which one or both blades are moved aft of the alignment point.

blade tabs Fixed trim tabs on the trailing edge of a rotor blade for track adjustment.

blade tip The furthermost part of the blade from the hub of the rotor.

blade track The relationship of the blade tips in the plane of rotation. Blades in track will move through the same plane of rotation.

blade tracking The mechanical procedure used to bring the blades of the rotor in satisfactory relationship with each other under dynamic conditions so that all blades rotate on a common plane.

blade twist Variation in the angle of incidence of a blade between the root and the tip. This may be built into the blade or may be caused by aerodynamic forces.

blank blade Identification of one blade during electronic balancing. It is the blade with the single interrupter.

bleed air Air from the compressor section used for various purposes, including cabin heat and anti-icing. Sometimes called customer air.

bleed band See bleed valve.

bleed valve A device used to unload the compressor during acceleration by dumping air overboard from the compressor.

boosted control A control such as a cyclic, or collective, utilizing hydraulic power to assist the pilot in moving the control.

brush guard A device used to protect the tail rotor blades.

cam box See corrolation box.

center of pressure The imaginary point where the resultant of all aerodynamic forces of an airfoil is concentrated.

centrifugal clutch A clutch using centrifugal force to engage the clutch.

centrifugal force An outward force developed by rotation of a mass — such as a rotor.

Chadwick A term used to describe electronic balancing or tracking. It is actually the name of the manufacturer of the balancing and tracking equipment.

chord An imaginary line passing from the leading edge to the trailing edge of an airfoil.

chordwise axis A term used in reference to semi-rigid rotors describing the flapping or teetering axis of the rotor.

climbing blade A condition when one or more blades are not operating in the same plane of rotation during flight, which may not exist on ground operation.

co-axial rotor A rotor system utilizing two rotors turning in opposite directions on the same center line. This has been used to eliminate the need of a tail rotor.

cold section The compressor section of a turbine engine.

collective The control that changes the angle of incidence of all the blades simultaneously in order to control the thrust of the rotor.

compensating cam A cam used in conjunction with the collective to add the correct amount of power to the turbine for the pitch of the rotor.

composite blades Rotor blades constructed from more than one type of material, such as titanium and fiberglass.

coning angle See blade coning.

control shim A ground shim to set the lash and pattern of a gear set by the manufacturer.

corrolation box A cam used to corrolate engine controls, to add power to a reciprocating engine as the collective is raised.

corriolis force The force produced when a particle moves along a path in a plane while the plane itself is rotating.

counterweights Weights attached to some rotors that assist in raising the collective.

customer air See bleed air.

cyclic control The control which changes the angle of incidence of the rotor blades individually during a revolution of the rotor tilting the rotor disc.

delta hinge The hinge located at the root end of the rotor blade with its axis parallel to the plane of rotation of the rotor which allows the blade to flap equalizing lift between the upwind and the downwind sides of the rotor disc.

delta hinge bolt A bolt used on some tail rotor systems to provide the flapping hinge.

direct shaft turbine A shaft turbine engine in which the compressor and power section are mounted on a common driveshaft.

disc area The area of the projected outline of the rotor travel.

disc loading A ratio of the gross weight of the helicopter to the rotor disc area.

dissymetry of lift The unequal lift, across a rotor disc that occurs in forward flight due to the difference in airflow over the advancing and retreating blades.

downwash Air that has been accelerated downward by action of the rotor.

drag The force tending to resist an airfoil's passage through the air. Drag is always parallel to the relative wind and perpendicular to lift.

drag brace An adjustable brace used to position the main rotor in a fixed position, preventing movement of the blade at the attached point on semi-rigid rotors.

drag hinge See lead-lag hinge.

drive fork A device used on some helicopters to drive the tail rotor and provide the flapping hinge for the tail rotor.

droop The inability of the engine power to increase as the rotor pitch is increased causing the rotor RPM to slow down.

droop cam See compensating cam.

droop restraint A device used to limit the droop of the main rotor blades at low RPM.

droop stops See droop restraint.

dual actuator An actuator used for hydraulic boost, which is actually two units in one, utilizing two separate and independent hydraulic systems.

duplex bearing A matched pair of bearings with a surface ground on each bearing to make contact with the other matched surface. When three bearings are used, it is called a triplex bearing; when four are used, it is a quadplex, etc. They are usually ball bearings.

dynamic balance The balance of an object in motion.

dynamic stability The stability of the rotor system in flight to return to a position after a force is applied.

dynamic stop A device used to limit the vertical movement of the rotor while in operation.

ECU Environmental Control Unit. Air cycle and cooling unit.

EGT Exhaust gas temperature.

elastomeric bearing A metal and rubber composite bearing that carries oscillating loads.

elastomers Rubber or synthetic rubber materials used in the construction of elastomeric bearings.

ESHP Equivalent Shaft Horsepower.

face-to-face bearing The placement of two bearings, so thrust loads are carried by one bearing in one direction and the other bearing in the opposite direction. The same type of loading may be accomplished by back-to-back installation. The installation is governed by the mounting system.

feathering The changing of the angle of the rotor blades during a revolution equalizing lift on the advancing and retreating blades. This term is sometimes used in relation to pitch change through the collective.

feathering axis The axis of the mechanical movement of the rotor on the spanwise gimbal bearings to affect blade feathering.

fiberglass blades Rotor blades primarily constructed of fiberglass and glass rovings.

finite life The part has a definite time use limit.

flapping hinge The hinge used on fully articulated rotors which allows individual blade vertical movement.

flare A maneuver, accomplished prior to landing to slow the helicopter down.

flat rated An engine having a HP rating at higher than standard day temperatures.

flex coupling A device used with shafts to allow movement because of misalignment.

flexture assembly The flexible unit used in the Nodal System.

foot pedals See anti-torque pedals.

free shaft turbine A shaft turbine engine, in which there is no physical connection between the compressor and the power section.

free turbine A turboshaft engine with no physical connection between the compressor and power output shafts.

freewheeling unit A device which transmits torque in one direction only and disconnects in the other direction.

fully articulated rotor See articulated rotor.

gearlash The amount of movement of the teeth of one gear when the other gear is held stationary.

gauge pins Measuring devices used with a micrometer to determine gear tooth wear.

gear pattern The imprint of the tooth of one gear on another mating tooth. The prints may be a load or no load condition.

gimbal A device used to permit a body to incline freely in any direction.

gradient system A device used to give artificial feel to hydraulic boosted controls.

grip angle The angle set on the rotor head grip to place the rotor blades at the correct pitch angle.

ground cushion See ground effect.

ground effect Additional lift obtained when the helicopter is hovering within one rotor diameter of the ground due to increased air pressure below the rotor disc.

ground resonance Self-excited vibration occurring whenever the frequency of oscillation of the blades about the lead-lag axis of an articulated rotor becomes the same as the natural frequency of the fuselage.

gyroscopic precession A characteristic of gyroscopes that causes their axis to be displaced at 90° to the direction of application of any force tending to tilt its axis.

high frequency vibration A vibration with no distinguishing beat. It is felt as a buzz only.

high speed track The track of the rotor at normal operating speed.

hot section The combustor section of a turbine engine.

hover The ability of a helicopter to sustain flight with no movement in relation to the ground.

hub The center supporting member of the rotor system.

hunting Oscillatory motion of the blades of an articulated rotor about the alpha hinge caused by corriolic forces.

hunting hinge See lead-lag hinge.

inertia The property of matter by which it will remain at rest or in a state of uniform motion in the same direction unless acted upon by some external force.

interference fit See pinch fit.

IPS Inches Per Second — a vibration measurment used in electronic balancing.

irreversible valve A device used on hydraulic boosted controls to control fluid flow to the actuators when no movement is taking place.

isolation mount A rubber and metal composite mount used to prevent vibration transfer from one component to another.

ITT Inter Turbine Temperature

lash check A method of checking the amount of lash between gear teeth.

latch mechanism A device used on the Bell 206 to hold and adjust the main rotor blades. A replacement of the drag brace.

lateral vibration A vibration in which the movement is in a lateral direction, such as imbalance of the main rotor.

lead-lag hinge A hinge at the root of the blade with its axis perpendicular to the plane of rotation. This hinge is also known as the alpha hinge, drag hinge, and the hunting hinge.

lift That component of the total air force which is perpendicular to the relative wind and in the plane of symmetry.

linear actuator A device utilizing an electric motor to turn a jack screw making the actuator longer or shorter.

load lock valve See irreversible valve.

low frequency vibration A vibration in which a beat may be felt and distinguished.

low speed track Track of the rotor taken at speeds below normal operating RPM. This is done to determine the high blade with a "climbing blade" problem.

magnetic brake A device used to hold the cyclic controls in trim so that a minimum pressure will be required to fly the aircraft.

married needles A term when the two hands of an instrument are superimposed over each other, as on the engine-rotor tachometer.

Marvel The manufacturer of a commonly used universal balancer, used throughout the aviation industry.

mast The component that supports the main rotor. This unit normally drives the rotor head.

mast bump Action of the rotor head striking the mast, occurring on underslung rotors only.

matched gears Two gears used in a set and replaced only in a set.

mercury clutch A centrifugal clutch in which mercury is used to engage the clutch.

metal blades Rotor blades constructed primarily from metal, usually aluminum alloy and are bonded.

MGB Main gearbox. The transmission of the helicopter.

midspan weight A weight placed in the midspan of a rotor blade to add inertia to the blade.

mixed compressor A compressor used in a turbine engine utilizing both an axial and centrifugal compressor.

456

mixer A system of bellcranks preventing cyclic inputs from changing to collective inputs.

mixer box See mixer.

N_1 The compressor and turbine of a free turbine.

N_2 The power turbine of a free turbine engine.

N_2 **governor** A device used to maintain a constant speed of the N_2 system by limiting the fuel flow.

N_f See N_2.

N_g See N_1.

Nodal sytem A vibration dampening system used by Bell to reduce main rotor vibration.

offset hinge A hinge used in fully articulated rotors in order to increase stability.

overhaul schedule A record of the various components of a helicopter regarding time and recommended overhaul periods.

overspeed governor See N_2 governor.

particle separator Device used to remove foreign material from the air entering the engine.

pedal creep The tendency of the anti-torque pedals to move from the neutral position.

pinch fit The lack of clearance between two components — normally used to prevent bearing races from moving by the bearing cap.

pitch angle The acute angle between the chordline of the blades and a reference surface of the main rotor head.

pitch change link A rod with a spherical bearing attached at each end to move the pitch mechanism of the rotor.

pre-cone A built-in angle in a yoke assembly for the coning angle of the rotor in flight.

pre-track A method used by Sikorsky to preset the track of a rotor blade prior to installation.

relative wind Velocity of the air with reference to a body in it. Relative wind is always opposite of the flight path.

retirement schedule A list of parts and times of a limited life contained on helicopters. This list will contain the part, serial number, time installed, and the removal time.

retreating blade Any blade, located in a semi-circular part of the rotor disc, where the blade direction is opposite to the direction of flight.

reverse flow combustor An annular combustor in which the hot gases move through the combustor making a 180° turn.

rigid rotor A rotor capable of only changing pitch.

rotating star The portion of a swashplate that rotates on multi-bladed rotor systems. This received its name from its shape.

rotor A complete system of rotating airfoils creating lift for a helicopter.

rotor brake Device used to stop the rotor blades rotating during shutdown. It may be either hydraulic or mechanical.

SAS Stabilization Augmentation System.

seesaw rotor Term used for semi-rigid rotor.

semi-rigid rotor A rotor which may change pitch and flap as a unit.

service bulletin Recommended maintenance information from the manufacturer regarding flight safety which may be mandatory.

service letter Any informational letter from the manufacturer.

settling with power A state of rotorcraft flight during high rates of descent in powered flight during which the rotor is in a partial or complete state of cavitation because the rotor is operating in its own downwash.

SHP Shaft Horsepower

shaft turbine A turbine engine used to drive an output shaft commonly used in helicopters.

short shaft The main driveshaft between the engine and transmission.

skid shoes Plates attached to the bottom of skid landing gear protecting the skid.

sprag A figure 8 shaped item used in the sprag clutch.

sprag clutch Term used to identify a freewheeling unit.

sprag unit See sprag clutch.

sprag mount An adjustable bracing system used on the Bell 47.

spanwise See pitch change axis.

split needles Term used to describe the position of the two hands on the engine rotor tachometer, meaning that the two hands are not superimposed.

stabilizer bar A dynamic component used on some Bell helicopters to insure rotor stability.

standard day 59°F with a barometric pressure of 29.92 inches of mercury.

static balance The balance of an object at rest.

static stop A device used to limit the blade flap, or rotor flap, at low RPM or when the rotor is stopped.

strap pack A tension torsion system using sheet steel laminations to carry the loads of the rotor blades to the head, used by Hughes.

stringing See blade alignment.

strobe light A pulsed light used to make a rotating component appear as if it is motionless.

Strobex A brand name used by Chadwick Helmuth Corporation for an electronic tracking device.

swashplate Transfers motion to the rotating component.

symmetrical airfoil An airfoil having the same shape on the top and bottom.

syncro-rotor A rotor system utilizing two main rotors, side by side, so that the rotor blades mesh with each other.

tail rotor A rotor turning in a plane perpendicular to that of the main rotor and parallel to the longitudinal axis of the fuselage. Used to control the torque of the main rotor and to provide movement on the yaw axis of the helicopter.

tail rotor gearbox Changes the tail rotor drive 90° and either increase or decrease the speed of the tail rotor.

tandem bearings Placement of two ball bearings, so that the thrust load is shared by both bearings, only in one direction.

tandem rotor A rotor system utilizing two main rotors — one fore and one aft.

target blade The identification on one blade during electronic balancing. It is the blade with the double interrupter.

teetering axis See chordwise axis.

tension torsion bar A strap made of layers of sheet steel used to absorb tension of centrifugal loads between the blade and the hub, and also the torque of blade pitch change.

tension torsion strap A strap made of wire serves the same purpose as the tension torsion bar.

thrust The force applied to a body tending to motivate the body through the air, thus overcoming drag.

tip cap A removable tip on the rotor blade tip. This cap is often used to hold spanwise balance weights.

tip path plane See disc area.

tip pocket A place at the tip of the rotor blade to place weight for spanwise balance.

tip targets See tracking reflectors.

tip weight A weight placed in the tip of a rotor blade for spanwise balance.

tracking flag   A device used to check rotor track on the ground.

torque limited   A limitation placed on the drive train of the helicopter in regards to power input.

torquemeter   A device used to measure power output of an engine.

tracking reflectors   Reflectors placed on blade tips to determine track with a spotlight or a strobe light.

tracking stick   A stick with a wick on one end used to touch the rotor blades in operation and mark the blades determining track.

tracking targets   See tracking reflectors.

translational lift   The additional lift obtained when entering forward flight due to the increased efficiency of the rotor system.

trim switch   A switch button on the cyclic for the trimming of the helicopter laterally and longitudinally.

trunion   The part that splines to a mast or shaft to retain the rotor and provide the flapping hinge for a semi-rigid rotor.

turboshaft engine   A turbine engine transmitting power through a shaft as would be found in a turbine powered helicopter.

twist grip   The throttle control on the collective. It may also serve as the power lever control on turbine powered helicopters.

TCU   Torque Control Unit — used to automatically match the torques of twin engine helicopters and may also act as a torque limiter.

variable stators   A device used to vary the angle of attack of the compressor stators during acceleration.

vertical vibration   A vibration in which the movement is in the vertical or up and down direction, such as an out-of-track condition.

wet head   A term used to describe a rotor head that uses oil as the lubricant.

wooden blades   Rotor blades made primarily of wood laminates, although they are covered and may include some metal in the construction.

underslinging   Placing the rotor hub around and below the top of the mast as is done on semi-rigid rotor systems.

yoke   The main supporting member of a semi-rigid rotor.

90° gearbox   See tail rotor gearbox.

1:1 vibration   A low frequency vibration having one beat per revolution of the rotor. This could be either vertical or horizontal.